THE MEDITERRANEAN

THE
MEDITERRANEAN

and the Mediterranean World in
the Age of Philip II

FERNAND BRAUDEL

Translated by Siân Reynolds
Abridged by Richard Ollard

Quality Paperbacks Direct
London

This edition published 1992
by QPD by arrangement with
HarperCollins*Publishers*

Le Méditerranée et le Monde Méditerranéen à l'Époque de Philippe II
first published in France 1949, second revised edition 1966
© Librairie Armand Colin 1966

English translation of second revised edition
© HarperCollins*Publishers* 1972

This abridgement © Richard Ollard and HarperCollins*Publishers* 1992

The Author asserts the moral right to be identified
as the author of this work

Picture research by Georgina Bruckner and Josine Meijer

A catalogue record for this book is available from the British Library

CN 9401

Photoset in Linotron Sabon by
Rowland Phototypesetting Ltd,
Bury St Edmunds, Suffolk
Printed in Great Britain by
Butler and Tanner Ltd, Frome, Somerset

A Lucien Febvre,
toujours présent en témoignage
de reconnaissance et de filiale affection

Contents

Preface

To ABRIDGE a great book to well under half its length calls for some fortitude of mind – or shall we prefer Johnson's correction: 'No, sir. Stark insensibility'? That *The Mediterranean* is a great, a wonderful book, is an opinion in which I am fortified by the concurrence of historians far better qualified to judge than I, and confirmed by close and repeated re-reading. If particular conclusions have, as its author prophesied in every passage of summary, been overtaken by subsequent research it is hardly surprising. And it is not for particular conclusions that one reads Braudel, any more than one reads Gibbon or Macaulay. His book, as he once said to me, is a collection of images – the word he uses twice in the half-dozen pages with which he rounds off the work. It is this description which I have taken as my principle of abridgment.

Abridgment, I must emphasize, not editing. It is not only that I have no pretensions to the huge and various erudition such a task would demand. Braudel himself would not have undertaken it. His French publisher, Mme de Ayala, tells me that he would never emend. He preferred to write the whole passage *de novo*.

The qualities above all others that I have tried to preserve are those that are most his own: the tone of his prose – so admirably rendered into English by Siân Reynolds – and the marvellous evocation of scene and landscape and human activity that both in its tenderness and in its sharpness is reminiscent of the elder Breughel. To avoid adulteration I have kept interpolation to the bare minimum – perhaps a dozen brief passages in the whole book where the argument demanded a summary of what has been excised. Otherwise I have cut and omitted but have, I hope, in so doing preserved the intellectual structure as well as the original masonry.

Two omissions require special notice. The narrative part of the original Part III, *Events, Politics, People*, has been excised in its entirety. The author's misgivings as to this mode of the historian's art seemed reason enough.

The second decision, to cut all the footnotes (palliated by the occasional interpolation of some irresistible detail or authorial idiosyncrasy into the body of the text), springs from the nature and purpose of this edition. Here was a golden opportunity to bring new readers to Braudel by focusing on two of his greatest qualities, his visual sense and his power of delighting those who are not historians with the recognition that the past and the present are two sides of the same coin. Such readers, unlike the professed student of history, might be deterred by the magisterial citation of authorities which the notes contain, or by their learned and leisurely debate with other scholars, for the terms of which antecedent knowledge is often needed. In this connection the generosity with which Braudel acknowledges, sometimes invents, his debt to other writers is not at all adequately represented in this abridgment. This and all other losses are, however, easily supplied since the full edition has been kept continuously in print in both paperback and hard covers at a very modest price.

In conclusion I wish to thank Mme Braudel for encouraging me to accept her husband's invitation to make this abridgment. Self doubt was soon lost in the enjoyment of reading and re-reading the book and in the vivid awareness it brought of the author's personality.

RICHARD OLLARD

PREFACE TO THE FIRST EDITION

I HAVE LOVED the Mediterranean with passion, no doubt because I am a northerner like so many others in whose footsteps I have followed. I have joyfully dedicated long years of study to it – much more than all my youth. In return, I hope that a little of this joy and a great deal of Mediterranean sunlight will shine from the pages of this book. Ideally perhaps one should, like the novelist, have one's subject under control, never losing it from sight and constantly aware of its overpowering presence. Fortunately or unfortunately, the historian has not the novelist's freedom. The reader who approaches this book in the spirit I would wish will do well to bring with him his own memories, his own vision of the Mediterranean to add colour to the text and to help me conjure up this vast presence, as I have done my best to do. My feeling is that the sea itself, the one we see and love, is the greatest document of its past existence. If I have retained nothing else from the geographers who taught me at the Sorbonne, I have retained this lesson with an unwavering conviction that has guided me throughout my project.

It might be thought that the connections between history and geographical space would be better illustrated by a more straightforward example than the Mediterranean, particularly since in the sixteenth century the sea was such a vast expanse in relation to man. Its character is complex, awkward, and unique. It cannot be contained within our measurements and classifications. No simple biography beginning with date of birth can be written of this sea; no simple narrative of how things happened would be appropriate to its history. The Mediterranean is not even a *single* sea, it is a complex of seas; and these seas are broken up by islands, interrupted by peninsulas, ringed by intricate coastlines. Its life is linked to the land, its poetry more than half-rural, its sailors may turn peasant with the seasons; it is the sea of vineyards and olive trees just as much as the sea of the long-oared galleys and the roundships of merchants and its history can no more be separated from that of the lands surrounding it than the clay can be separated from the hands of the potter who shapes it. 'Lauso la mare e tente'n terro' ('Praise the sea and stay on land') says a Provençal proverb.

So it will be no easy task to discover exactly what the historical character of the Mediterranean has been. It will require much patience, many different approaches, and no doubt a few unavoidable errors. Nothing could be clearer than the Mediterranean defined by oceanographer, geologist, or even geographer. Its boundaries have been charted, classified, and labelled. But what of the Mediterranean of the historian? There is no lack of authoritative statements as to what it is not. It is not an autonomous world; nor is it the preserve of any one power. Woe betide the historian who thinks that this preliminary interrogation is unnecessary, that the Mediterranean as an entity needs no definition because it has long been clearly defined, is instantly recognizable and can be described by dividing general history along the lines of its geographical contours. What possible value could these contours have for our studies?

But how could one write any history of the sea, even over a period of only fifty years, if one stopped at one end with the Pillars of Hercules and at the other with the straits at whose entrance ancient Ilium once stood guard? The question of boundaries is the first to be encountered; from it all others flow. To draw a boundary around anything is to define, analyse, and reconstruct it, in this case select, indeed adopt, a philosophy of history.

To assist me I did indeed have at my disposal a prodigious body of articles, papers, books, publications, surveys, some purely historical, others no less interesting, written by specialists in neighbouring disciplines – anthropologists, geographers, botanists, geologists, technologists. There is surely no region on this earth as well documented and written about as the Mediterranean and the lands illumined by its glow. But, dare I say it, at the risk of seeming ungrateful to my predecessors, this mass of publications buries the researcher as it were under a rain of ash. So many of these studies speak a language of the past, outdated in more ways than one. Their concern is not the sea in all its complexity, but some minute piece of the mosaic, not the grand movement of Mediterranean life, but the actions of a few princes and rich men, a scattering of dust from the past, bearing little relation to the slow and powerful march of history which is our subject. So many of these works need to be revised, related to the whole, before they can come to life again.

And then, no history of the sea can be written without precise knowledge of the vast resources of its archives. Here the task would appear to be beyond the powers of an individual historian. There is not one sixteenth-century Mediterranean state that does not possess its charter-room, usually well furnished with those documents that have escaped the fires, sieges, and disasters of every kind known to the Mediterranean world. To prospect and catalogue this unsuspected store, these mines of the purest historical gold, would take not one lifetime but at least twenty, or the simultaneous dedication of twenty researchers. Perhaps the day will come when we shall no longer be working on the great sites of history with the methods of small craftsmen. Perhaps on that day it will become possible to write general history from original documents and not from more or less secondary works. Need I confess that I have not been able to examine all the documents available to me in the archives, no matter how hard I tried. This book is the result of a necessarily incomplete study. I know in advance that its conclusions will be examined, discussed, and replaced by others and I am glad of it. That is how history progresses and must progress.

Another point is that by its inauspicious chronological position, between the last flames of the Renaissance and Reformation and the harsh, inward-looking age of the seventeenth century, the Mediterranean in the second half of the sixteenth century might well be described, as it was by Lucien Febvre, as a 'faux beau sujet' (a deceptively ideal subject). Need I point out where its interest lies? It is of no small value to know what became of the Mediterranean at the threshold of modern times, when the world no longer revolved entirely around it, served it and responded to its rhythms. The rapid decline of the Mediterranean about which people have always talked does not seem at all clear to me; rather, all the evidence seems to point to the contrary. But even leaving this question aside, it is my belief that all the problems posed by the Mediterranean are of exceptional human richness, that they must therefore interest all historians and non-historians. I would go so far as to say that they serve to illumine our own century, that they are not lacking in that 'utility' in the strict sense which Nietzsche demanded of all history.

I do not intend to say much about the attraction and the temptations offered by such a subject. I have already mentioned the difficulties, deceptions, and lures it holds in store. I would add just this, that among existing historical works, I found none which could offer general guidance. A historical study centred on a stretch of water has all the charms but undoubtedly all the dangers of a new departure.

Since the scales were so heavily weighted on both sides, was I right in the end to come down on the side of the unknown, to cast prudence aside and decide that the adventure was worth while?

My excuse is the story of how this book was written. When I began it in 1923, it was in the classic and certainly more prudent form of a study of Philip II's Mediterranean policy. My teachers of those days strongly approved of it. For them it fitted into the pattern of that diplomatic history which was indifferent to the discoveries of geography, little concerned (as diplomacy itself so often is) with economic and social problems; slightly disdainful towards the achievements of civilization, religion, and also of literature and the arts, the great witnesses of all worthwhile history; shuttered up in its chosen area, this school regarded it beneath a historian's dignity to look beyond the diplomatic files, to real life, fertile and promising. An analysis of the policy of the Prudent King entailed above all establishing the respective roles played in the elaboration of that policy by the king and his counsellors, through changing circumstances; determining who played major roles and who minor, reconstructing a model of Spanish foreign policy in which the Mediterranean was only one sector and not always the most important.

For in the 1580s the might of Spain turned towards the Atlantic. It was out there, whether conscious or not of the dangers involved, that the empire of Philip II had to concentrate its forces and fight for its threatened existence. A powerful swing of the pendulum was carrying it towards its transatlantic destiny. When I became interested in this hidden balance of forces, the physics of Spanish policy, preferring research in this direction to labelling the responsibilities of a Philip II or a Don John of Austria, and when I came to think moreover that these statesmen were, despite their illusions, more acted upon than actors, I was already beginning to move outside the traditional bounds of diplomatic history; when I began to ask myself finally whether the Mediterranean did not possess, beyond the long-distance and irregular actions of Spain (a rather arid topic apart from the dramatic confrontation at Lepanto), a history and a destiny of its own, a powerful vitality, and whether this vitality did not in fact deserve something better than the role of a picturesque background, I was already succumbing to the temptation of the immense subject that was finally to hold my attention.

How could I fail to see it? How could I move from one set of archives to another in search of some revealing document without having my eyes opened to this rich and active life? Confronted with records of so many basic economic activities how could I do other than turn towards that economic and social history of a revolutionary kind that a small group of historians was trying to promote in France to the dignity that was no longer denied it in Germany, England, the United States, and indeed in Belgium, our neighbour, or Poland? To attempt to encompass the history of the Mediterranean in its complex totality was to follow their advice, be guided by their experience, go to their aid, and be active in the campaign for a new kind of history, re-thought, elaborated in France but worthy of being voiced beyond her frontiers; an imperialist history, yes, if one insists, aware of its own possibilities and of what it had to do, but also desirous since it had been obliged to break with them, of shattering traditional forms – not always entirely justifiably perhaps, but let that pass. The perfect opportunity was offered me of taking advantage of the very dimensions, demands, difficulties, and pitfalls of the unique historical character I had already chosen in order to create a history that could be different from the history our masters taught us.

To its author, every work seems revolutionary, the result of a struggle for mastery. If the Mediterranean has done no more than force us out of our old habits it will already have done us a service.

This book is divided into three parts, each of which is itself an essay in general explanation.

The first part is devoted to a history whose passage is almost imperceptible, that of man in his relationship to the environment, a history in which all change is slow, a history of constant repetition, ever-recurring cycles. I could not neglect this almost timeless history, the story of man's contact with the inanimate, neither could I be satisfied with the traditional geographical introduction to history that often figures to little purpose at the beginning of so many books, with its descriptions of the mineral deposits, types of agriculture, and typical flora, briefly listed and never mentioned again, as if the flowers did not come back every spring, the flocks of sheep migrate every year, or the ships sail on a real sea that changes with the seasons.

On a different level from the first there can be distinguished another history, this time with slow but perceptible rhythms. If the expression had not been diverted from its full meaning, one could call it *social history*, the history of groups and groupings. How did these swelling currents affect Mediterranean life in general – this was the question I asked myself in the second part of the book, studying in turn economic systems, states, societies, civilizations and finally, in order to convey more clearly my conception of history, attempting to show how all these deep-seated forces were at work in the complex arena of warfare. For war, as we know, is not an arena governed purely by individual responsibilities.

The final effect then is to dissect history into various planes, or, to put it another way, to divide historical time into geographical time, social time, and individual time. Or, alternatively, to divide man into a multitude of selves. This is perhaps what I shall be least forgiven, even if I say in my defence that traditional divisions also cut across living history which is fundamentally *one*, even if I argue, against Ranke or Karl Brandi, that the historical narrative is not a method, or even the objective method *par excellence*, but quite simply a philosophy of history like any other; even if I say, and demonstrate hereafter, that these levels I have distinguished are only means of exposition, that I have felt it quite in order in the course of the book to move from one level to another. But I do not intend to plead my case further. If I am criticized for the method in which the book has been assembled, I hope the component parts will be found workman-like by professional standards.

I hope too that I shall not be reproached for my excessive ambitions, for my desire and need to see on a grand scale. It will perhaps prove that history can do more than study walled gardens. If it were otherwise, it would surely be failing in one of its most immediate tasks which must be to relate to the painful problems of our times and to maintain contact with the youthful but imperialistic human sciences. Can there be any kind of humanism, in 1946, without historians who are ambitious, conscious of their duties and of their immense powers? 'It is the fear of great history which has killed great history,' wrote Edmond Faral, in 1942. May it live again!

MAY, 1946

PART ONE

The Role
of the Environment

THE FIRST PART of this book, as its title suggests, is concerned with geography: geography of a particular kind, with special emphasis on human factors. But it is more than this. It is also an attempt to discover a particular kind of history.

Even if there had been more properly dated information available, it would have been unsatisfactory to restrict our enquiries entirely to a study of human geography between the years 1550–1600 – even one undertaken in the doubtful pursuit of a determinist explanation. Since in fact we have only incomplete accounts of the period, and these have not been systematically classified by historians – material plentiful enough it is true, but insufficient for our purpose – the only possible course, in order to bring this brief moment of Mediterranean life, between 1550 and 1600, out of the shadows, was to make full use of evidence, images, and landscapes dating from other periods, earlier and later and even from the present day. The resulting picture is one in which all the evidence combines across time and space, to give us a history in slow motion from which permanent values can be detected. Geography in this context is no longer an end in itself but a means to an end. It helps us to rediscover the slow unfolding of structural realities, to see things in the perspective of the very long term. Geography, like history, can be asked many questions. Here it helps us to discover the almost imperceptible movement of history, if only we are prepared to follow its lessons and accept its categories and divisions.

The Mediterranean has at least two faces. In the first place, it is composed of a series of compact, mountainous peninsulas, interrupted by vital plains: Italy, the Balkan peninsula, Asia Minor, North

Africa, the Iberian peninsula. Second, between these miniature continents lie vast, complicated, and fragmented stretches of sea, for the Mediterranean is not so much a single expanse of water as a 'complex of seas'. Peninsulas and seas: these are the two kinds of environment we shall be considering first of all, to establish the general conditions of human life. But they will not tell the whole story.

On one side, to the south, the Mediterranean is a near neighbour of the great desert that runs uninterrupted from the Atlantic Sahara to the Gobi Desert and up to the gates of Peking. From southern Tunisia to southern Syria, the desert directly borders the sea. The relationship is not casual; it is intimate, sometimes difficult, and always demanding. So the desert is one of the faces of the Mediterranean.

On the other side, to the north, lies Europe, which if often shaken by Mediterranean influences has had an equally great and sometimes decisive influence on the Mediterranean. Northern Europe, beyond the olive trees, is one of the permanent realities of Mediterranean history. And it was the rise of that Europe with its Atlantic horizons, that was to decide the destiny of the inland sea as the sixteenth century drew to a close.

Chapters 1 to 3, then, describe the diversity of the sea and go far beyond its shores. After this we shall have to consider whether it is possible to speak of the physical unity of the sea (Chapter 4, *Climate and History*) or of its human and necessarily historical unity (Chapter 5, *Communications and Cities*). These are the divisions of a long introductory section whose aim is to describe the different faces, and the face, of the Mediterranean, so that we may be in a better position to view and if possible understand its multi-coloured destiny.

The Peninsulas: Mountains, Plateaux, and Plains

THE FIVE PENINSULAS of the inland sea are very similar. If one thinks of their relief they are regularly divided between mountains – the largest part – a few plains, occasional hills, and wide plateaux. This is not the only way in which the land masses can be dissected, but let us use simple categories. Each piece of these jigsaw puzzles belongs to a particular family and can be classified within a distinct typology. So, rather than consider each peninsula as an autonomous entity, let us look at the analogies between the materials that make them up. In other words let us shuffle the pieces of the jigsaw and compare the comparable. Even on the historical plane, this breakdown and reclassification will be illuminating.

1 Mountains come first

The Mediterranean is by definition a landlocked sea. But beyond this we must distinguish between the kinds of land that surround and confine it. It is, above all, a sea ringed round by mountains. This outstanding fact and its many consequences have received too little attention in the past from historians.

Physical and human characteristics. Geologists, however, are well aware of it and can explain it. The Mediterranean, they say, is entirely contained within the zone of tertiary folds and fractures covering the Ancient World from Gibraltar to the Indian Archipelago: in fact, it constitutes one section of the zone. Late foldings, some dating from the same time as the Pyrenees, others from the time of the Alps, raised and activated the sediments of a secondary Mediterranean much vaster than the one we know, chiefly enormous limestone deposits, sometimes over 1000 metres thick. With some regularity these violent foldings collided with ancient hard masses of rock, which were sometimes raised (like the Kabylias) or sometimes incorporated into great ranges, as is the case of the Mercantour and various axial ridges of the Alps or the Pyrenees. More often still, they collapsed – to the accompaniment of a greater or lesser degree of volcanic activity – and were covered by the waters of the sea.

Although interrupted by inlets of the sea, the mountains correspond on either side of the straits to form coherent systems. One range formerly linked Sicily and Tunisia; another, the Baetic range, existed between Spain and Morocco; an Aegean range used to stretch from Greece to Asia Minor (its disappearance is so recent in geological terms as to correspond to the Biblical flood) – not to mention land masses like the Tyrrhenides continent of which there remain only a few islands and fragments scattered along the coast to mark the spot, that is, if geological hypotheses have some foundation in reality – for these are all hypotheses. What we can be certain of is the architectural unity of which the mountains form the 'skeleton': a sprawling, overpowering, ever-present skeleton whose bones show through the skin.

All round the sea the mountains are present, except at a few points of trifling significance – the Straits of Gibraltar, the Naurouze Gap, the Rhône valley corridor and the straits leading from the Aegean to the Black Sea. There is only one stretch from which they are absent – but that is a very considerable one – from southern Tunisia to southern Syria, where the Saharan plateau undulates over several thousand kilometres, directly bordering the sea.

Let it be said too that these are high, wide, never-ending mountains: the Alps, the Pyrenees, the Apennines, the Dinaric Alps, the Caucasus, the Anatolian mountains, the mountains of Lebanon, the Atlas, and the Spanish Cordillera. They are impressive and demanding presences: some because of their height, others because of their density or their deep, enclosed, inaccessible valleys. They turn towards the sea impressive and forbidding countenances.

So the Mediterranean means more than landscapes of vines and olive trees and urbanized villages; these are merely the fringe. Close by, looming above them, are the dense highlands, the mountain world with its fastnesses, its isolated houses and hamlets, its 'vertical norths'. Here we are far from the Mediterranean where orange trees blossom.

The winters in the mountains are severe. Snow was falling thickly in the Moroccan Atlas when Leo Africanus, crossing in winter, had the misfortune to be robbed of clothes and baggage. But any traveller who knows the Mediterranean well will have seen for himself the winter avalanches, blocked roads and Siberian and Arctic landscapes only a few miles from the sunny coast, the Montenegrin houses buried in snow, or in Kabylia the Tirourdat col, the gathering point for tremendous blizzards, where up to four metres of snow can fall in a night. In an hour skiers from Chrea can reach Algiers where roses are in bloom, while 120 kilometres away in the Djurdjura, near the cedar forest of Tindjda, the local inhabitants plunge bare-legged up to their thighs in snow.

The traveller will have seen too the snows that linger until midsummer, 'cooling the eye', as a visitor once put it. The peak of the Mulhacen is streaked

1. *Opposite*: The Julian Alps where Yugoslavia borders Italy and Austria: view from the Vršič Pass.

with snow while down below, Granada swelters in the heat; snow clings to the slopes of the Taygetus overlooking the tropical plain of Sparta; it is preserved in the crevasses of the mountains of Lebanon, or in the 'ice boxes' of Chrea. These are the snows that explain the long Mediterranean history of 'snow water', offered by Saladin to Richard the Lionheart, and drunk to fatal excess by Don Carlos in the hot month of July 1568, when he was imprisoned in the Palace at Madrid. In Turkey in the sixteenth century it was not merely the privilege of the rich; in Constantinople, but elsewhere as well, Tripoli in Syria, for instance, travellers remarked on merchants selling snow water, pieces of ice, and water-ices which could be bought for a few small coins. Pierre Belon relates that snow from Bursa used to arrive at Istanbul in whole boatloads. It was to be found there all the year round according to Busbecq, who was astonished to see the janissaries drinking it every day at Amasia in Anatolia, in the Turkish army camp. The snow trade was so important that the pashas took an interest in the exploitation of the 'ice mines'. It was said in 1578 to have provided Muhammad Pasha with an income of up to 80,000 sequins a year.

Elsewhere, in Egypt, for example, where snow arrived from Syria by relays of fast horses; in Lisbon which imported it from great distances; in Oran, the Spanish *presidio*, where snow arrived from Spain in the brigantines of the Intendance; in Malta, where the Knights, if we are to believe them, would die if snow did not arrive from Naples, their illnesses apparently requiring 'this sovereign remedy', snow was, on the contrary, the height of luxury. In Italy as in Spain, however, snow water seems to have been used widely. It explains the early development of the art of ice cream and water-ice in Italy. Its sale was so profitable in Rome that it became the subject of a monopoly. In Spain snow was piled up in wells and kept until summer. Western pilgrims travelling to the Holy Land in 1494 were none the less astonished to see the owner of the boat presented, on the Syrian coast, with 'a sack full of snow, the sight of which in this country and in the month of July, filled all on board with the greatest amazement'. On the same Syrian coast, a Venetian noted with surprise in 1553 that the 'Mores', 'ut nos utimur saccharo, item spargunt nivem super cibos et sua edulia', 'sprinkle snow on their food and dishes as we would sugar'.

In the heart of the warm Mediterranean these snowy regions impress by their originality. Their massive bulk and their constantly moving population compel the attention of the plains, of the brilliant but narrow creations along the coastline, precisely to the extent, and we shall be coming back to this, that these 'favoured' regions require manpower and, since they depend on trade, means of communication. They compel the attention of the plain, but arouse its fear as well. The traveller tries to go round the obstacle, to move at ground level, from plain to plain, valley to valley. Sooner or later he is obliged to travel through certain gorges and mountain passes of sinister repute, but he resorts to them as little as possible. The traveller of yesterday was almost entirely confined to the plains, the gardens, the dazzling shores and teeming life of the sea.

2. Snow and snow water were important commodities in the hot summers of the Mediterranean. Woodcut of a Turkish water seller by Melchior Lorich, 1581.

To tell the truth, the historian is not unlike the traveller. He tends to linger over the plain, which is the setting for the leading actors of the day, and does not seem eager to approach the high mountains nearby. More than one historian who has never left the towns and their archives would be surprised to discover their existence. And yet how can one ignore these conspicuous actors, the half-wild mountains, where man has taken root like a hardy plant; always semi-deserted, for man is constantly leaving them? How can one ignore them when often their sheer slopes come right down to the sea's edge? The mountain dweller is a type familiar in all Mediterranean literature. According to Homer, the Cretans were even then suspicious of the wild men in their mountains and Telemachus, on his return to Ithaca, describes the Peloponnese as covered with forests where he lived among filthy villagers, 'eaters of acorns'.

Defining the mountains. What exactly is a mountain? To take some simple definition – all land in the Mediterranean region over 500 metres for instance – would be to draw a completely arbitrary line. What should be reckoned are the uncertain human boundaries which cannot easily be shown on a map.

Can we define the mountains as the poorest regions of the Mediterranean, its proletarian reserves? On the whole this is true. But in the sixteenth century there were plenty of other poor regions below the 500-metre level, the Aragon steppes and the Pontine marshes, for instance. Besides, many mountains are, if not rich, at any rate reasonably prosperous and comparatively well populated. Many mountains are also rich because of their high rainfall: according to Arthur Young, in the Mediterranean climate, 'the soil is the least object – the sun and water do the whole'. The Alps, the Pyrenees, the Rif, the Kabylias, all the mountains exposed to winds from the Atlantic, have green hillsides where grass and trees grow thickly. Other mountains are rich because of their mineral resources. Others, again, are unusually densely populated as a result of the lowland population having been driven up from the plain, an accident which we find frequently repeated.

For the mountains are a refuge from soldiers and pirates, as all the documents bear witness, as far back as the Bible. Sometimes the refuge becomes permanent. This is borne out by the example of the Kutzo-Vlachs, who were chased out from the plains by the Slav and Greek peasants, and from then on throughout the Middle Ages led a nomadic existence over the free spaces in the Balkans, from Galicia to Serbia and the Aegean Sea, continually being displaced but also displacing others. Nimble as mountain goats, 'they come down from the mountains to carry away some booty . . .', noted a twelfth-century traveller. Throughout the Peninsula, 'as far as Matapan and Crete, they travel with their

3. *Opposite*: Detail from *The Adoration of the Shepherds* by Andrea Mantegna, showing the poor mountain dwellers coming down to the rich plain.
Metropolitan Museum of Art, New York

4. Greek shepherds, mountain dwellers *par excellence*.

flocks of sheep and their black hoods, and the two highest ridges, the Haemus and the Pindus, afford them the best shelter. It is from these two mountains that they come down into Byzantine history at the beginning of the eleventh century.' And it is around these mountains that the nineteenth century finds them still, herdsmen, farmers, and above all drivers of the muletrains which are the chief means of transport in Albania and northern Greece.

Many mountains, then, form exceptions to the rule of poverty and emptiness, of which however there is so much evidence in the writings of travellers and other witnesses in the sixteenth century. The Venetian envoy, crossing the mountains of Upper Calabria on his way to join Don John of Austria at Messina in 1572, found them quite deserted; deserted too were the Sierra Morena in Castile and the Sierras of Espadan and Bernia, in the kingdom of Valencia, about which enquiries were made in 1564, when there were fears of unrest among the Moriscos and of a war that might be carried up into this difficult hill country, where the rebels of 1526 had resisted the German Landsknechte. Even more deserted, eternally deserted, are the wild bare mountains of the Sicilian interior, and so many other mountains scattered here and there, whose low rainfall makes them unable to support even pastoral life.

But these are extreme cases. According to the geographer J. Cvijić, the central Balkan mountains (we are free to extend his remarks or not as we choose) are a zone of dispersed habitat, where the predominant form of settlement is the hamlet; in the plains, on the contrary, it is the village. The distinction is valid for Wallachia and, almost absurdly so, for Hungary and the enormous villages of the Puzta.

But can this interpretation of a Balkan pattern be transposed as it stands to the rest of the Mediterranean world, to nearby Greece, or to the Western countries permeated with maritime culture, where for fear of pirate raids the people withdrew from the plains, which were frequently devastated and unhealthy as well? One thinks of the large hill villages of Corsica, Sardinia, Provence, the Kabylias, and the Rif. One thing at least is certain. Whether settled in tiny hamlets or in large villages, the mountain population is generally insignificant in comparison with the vast spaces surrounding it, where travel is difficult; life there is rather like life in the early settlements in the New World, which were also islands set in the middle of wide open spaces, for the most part uncultivable or hostile, and therefore deprived of the contacts and exchanges necessary to civilization. The mountains are forced to be self-sufficient for the essentials of life, to produce everything as best they can, to cultivate vines, wheat, and olives even if the soil and the climate are unsuitable. In the mountains, society, civilization, and economy all bear the mark of backwardness and poverty.

Mountains, civilizations, and religions. The mountains are as a rule a world apart from civilizations, which are an urban and lowland achievement. Their history is to have none, to remain almost always on the fringe of the great waves of civilization, even the longest and most persistent, which may spread over great distances in the horizontal plane but are powerless to move vertically when faced with an obstacle of a few hundred metres. To these hilltop worlds, out of touch with the towns, even Rome itself, in all its years of power, can have meant very little, except perhaps through the military camps that the empire established for security reasons in various places on the edges of unconquered mountain lands.

Later, when the Rome of the Emperors had become the Rome of Saint Peter, the same problem remained. It was only in places where its action could be persistently reinforced that the Church was able to tame and evangelize these herdsmen and independent peasants. Even so it took an incredibly long time. In the sixteenth century the task was far from complete, and this applies to Islam and Catholicism alike, for they both met the same obstacles: the Berbers of North Africa, protected by the mountain peaks, were still hardly at all, or very imperfectly, won over to Muhammad. The same is true of the Kurds in Asia; while in Aragon, in the Valencia region or around Granada, the mountains were, conversely, the zone of religious dissidence, a Moslem stronghold, just as the high, wild, 'suspicious' hills of the Lubéron protected the strongholds of the

Vaudois. Everywhere in the sixteenth century, the hilltop world was very little influenced by the religions dominant at sea level; mountain life persistently lagged behind the plain.

One proof of this is the great ease with which, when circumstances did permit, new religions were able to make massive, though unstable, conquests in these regions. In the Balkans in the fifteenth century, whole areas of the mountains went over to Islam, in Albania as in Herzegovina around Sarajevo. What this proves above all is that they had been only slightly influenced by Christianity. The same phenomenon was to recur during the war of Candia, in 1647. Large numbers of Cretan mountain dwellers, joining the Turkish cause, renounced their faith. Similarly, in the seventeenth century, when faced with the Russian advance, the Caucasus went over to Muhammad and produced in his honour one of the most virulent forms of Islam.

In the mountains then, civilization is never very stable. Witness the curious passage by Pedraça in his *Historia eclesiastica de Granada*, written in the time of Philip IV. 'It is not surprising,' he writes, 'that the inhabitants of the Alpujarras (the very high mountains in the Kingdom of Granada) should have abandoned their ancient faith. The people who live in these mountains are *cristianos viejos*; in their veins runs not one drop of heathen blood; they are the subjects of a Catholic king; and yet, for lack of instruction and following the oppression to which they are subjected, they are so ignorant of what they should know to obtain eternal salvation that they have retained only a few vestiges of the Christian religion. Can anyone believe that if the Infidel were to become master of their land tomorrow (which God forbid) these people would remain long without abandoning their religion and embracing the beliefs of their conquerors?'

A separate religious geography seems then to emerge for the mountain world, which had constantly to be taken, conquered and reconquered. Many minor facts encountered in traditional history take on a new meaning in this light.

The fact that Saint Teresa, who as a child dreamed of being martyred by the Moriscos of the Sierra de Guadarrama, should have established the first monastery of the reformed Carmelite order at Duruelo, although a detail, is worth remembering. The house was the property of a gentleman of Avila. 'Quite an adequate porch, a bedchamber with its attic and a small kitchen,' writes the saint, 'was the entire extent of this fine dwelling. After consideration, I thought the porch could be made into a chapel, the attic into a choir, and the bedchamber into a dormitory.' And it was in this 'perfect hovel' that Saint John of the Cross came to live, with a companion, Father Anthony of Heredia, who joined him there in the autumn, bringing a chorister, Brother Joseph. There they lived through the winter snow the most frugal monastic life, but not shut off from the world: 'often they would go barefoot, by the most terrible paths, to preach the gospel to the peasants as if to savages'.

A chapter of missionary history can be glimpsed too from the religious history of Corsica in the sixteenth century. The example is even more significant

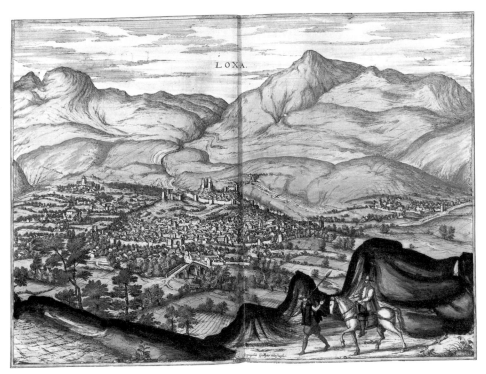

5. The mountain village of Loxa near Granada. Engraving from G. Braun and Hogenberg, *Civitates Orbis Terrarum*, Antwerp, 1575 and later.

if we remember that the Corsican people had been converted by the Franciscans several centuries earlier. What traces were left of the first Catholic conquest? Many documents show that by the time the Society of Jesus arrived at the island to impose upon it Jesuit law and the Roman order, the spiritual life of the population had reached an extraordinary state. They found that even those priests who could read knew no Latin or grammar, and, more seriously, were ignorant of the form of the sacrament to be taken at the altar. Often dressed like laymen, they were peasants who worked in the fields and woods and brought up their children in the sight and full knowledge of the whole community. The Christianity of their congregations was inevitably somewhat eccentric. They did not know the Creed or the Lord's Prayer; some did not even know how to make the sign of the cross. Superstitions fell on fertile ground. The island was idolatrous, barbaric, half-lost to Christianity and civilization. Man was cruel, unmerciful to man. Killings took place even in church and the priests were not the last to take up the lance, the dagger, or the blunderbuss, a new weapon that had reached the island towards the middle of the century and enlivened disputes. Meanwhile in the tumbledown churches, the rainwater poured in, grass grew, and lizards hid in the cracks. Let us allow a little for the natural exaggeration of even the best-intentioned missionaries. But the general picture was true. One stroke completes it. This half-savage people was capable of great religious outbursts, of spectacular devotion. When a foreign preacher passed through, the church was invaded by peasants from the mountains, late comers stood outside in the pouring rain, and penitents came to confession until late into the night.

Widespread, irresistible outbreaks of 'diabolism' swept through the old populations of Europe, holding them enthralled, and nowhere did these outbreaks occur more strongly than in the uplands whose primitive isolation maintained them in backwardness. Sorcerers, witchcraft, primitive magic, and black masses were the flowerings of an ancient cultural subconscious, from which Western civilization could not entirely separate itself. The mountains were the favoured refuge of these aberrant cults, which originated far back in time and persisted even after the Renaissance and Reformation. At the end of the sixteenth century, there were innumerable 'magic' mountains, stretching from Germany as far as the Milanese or Piedmontese Alps, from the Massif Central, seething with revolutionary and 'diabolical' ferment, to the healing soldiers of the Pyrenees, from the Franche-Comté to the Basque country. In the Rouergue, in 1595, 'sorcerers reign over the mass of the inhabitants and their ignorance'; because of the lack of local churches even the Bible was unknown. And everywhere the black sabbath seems to have been a social and cultural reaction, a mental revolution for lack of a coherent social revolution. The Devil seems to have been afoot in all the countries of Europe as the sixteenth century drew to a close, and even more in the first decades of the following century. He even seems to have crossed over into Spain by the high Pyrenean passes. In Navarre in 1611 the Inquisition severely punished a sect of over 12,000 adherents who 'worship the Devil, put up altars to him and deal with him familiarly on all occasions'. But we must leave this fascinating topic, as our chief interest for the moment is the problem of disparity between mountain and lowland, of the backwardness of mountain society.

Mountain freedom. There can be no doubt that the lowland, urban civilization penetrated to the highland world very imperfectly and at a very slow rate. This was as true of other things as it was of Christianity. The feudal system as a political, economic, and social system, and as an instrument of justice failed to catch in its toils most of the mountain regions and those it did reach it only partially influenced. The resistance of the Corsican and Sardinian mountains to lowland influence has often been noted and further evidence could be found in Lunigiana, regarded by Italian historians as a kind of mainland Corsica, between Tuscany and Liguria. The observation could be confirmed anywhere where the population was so inadequate, thinly distributed, and widely dispersed as to prevent the establishment of the state, dominant languages, and important civilizations.

A study of the vendetta would lead one towards a similar conclusion. The countries where the vendetta was in force – and they were all mountainous countries – were those that had not been moulded and penetrated by medieval concepts of feudal justice, the Berber countries, Corsica, and Albania, for example. Marc Bloch, writing about studies of Sardinia, points out that during the Middle Ages the island was an 'extensively manorialized, but not feudalized society' as a result of having been 'long isolated from the great currents which swept the continent'. This is putting the accent on the insularity of Sardinia, and

6. The Berber village of Erfoud in the Anti-Atlas Mountains, Morocco.
See page 17.

it is quite true that it has been a decisive factor in Sardinian history. But the mountains are an equally important factor, just as responsible for the isolation of the people of Sardinia as the sea, if not more so; even in our own time they have produced those cruel and romantic outlaws, at Orgosolo and elsewhere, in revolt against the establishment of the modern state and its *carabinieri*. This moving phenomenon has been portrayed by anthropologists and film directors. 'He who does not steal', says a character in a Sardinian novel, 'is not a man'. 'Law?' says another, 'I make my own laws and I take what I need.'

7. Where plain and mountain meet: the foothills of Mount Olympus.

In Sardinia, as in Lunigiana and Calabria, and everywhere where observation (when it is possible) reveals a hiatus between the society and the broad movements of history – if social archaisms (the vendetta among others) persisted, it was above all for the simple reason that mountains are mountains: that is, primarily an obstacle, and therefore also a refuge, a land of the free. For there men can live out of reach of the pressures and tyrannies of civilization: its social and political order, its monetary economy. Here there was no landed nobility with strong and powerful roots (the 'lords of the Atlas' created by the Maghzen were of recent origin); in the sixteenth century in Haute-Provence, the country nobleman, the '*cavaier salvatje*', lived alongside his peasants, cleared the land as they did, did not scorn to plough and till the ground, or to carry wood and dung on the back of his donkey. He was a constant irritation 'in the eyes of the Provençal nobility, who are essentially city-dwellers like the Italians'. Here there were no rich, well-fed clergy to be envied and mocked; the priest was as poor as his flock. There was no tight urban network so no administration, no towns in the proper sense of the word, and no gendarmes either we might add. It is only in the lowlands that one finds a close-knit, stifling society, a prebendal clergy, a haughty aristocracy, and an efficient system of justice. The hills were the refuge of liberty, democracy, and peasant 'republics'.

'The steepest places have been at all times the asylum of liberty', writes the learned Baron de Tott in his *Memoirs* (1784). 'In travelling along the coast of Syria, we see despotism extending itself over all the flat country and its progress stopt towards the mountains, at the first rock, at the first defile, that is easy of defence; whilst the Curdi, the Drusi, and the Mutuali, masters of the Lebanon and Anti-Lebanon, constantly preserve their independence'. A poor thing was Turkish despotism – ruler indeed of the roads, passes, towns, and plains, but what can it have meant in the Balkan highlands, or in Greece and Epirus, in the mountains of Crete where the Skafiotes defied, from their hilltops, all authority from the seventeenth century onwards, or in the Albanian hills, where, much later, lived 'Ali Pasha Tepedelenli? Did the Wali Bey, installed at Monastir by the Turkish conquest of the fifteenth century, ever really govern? In theory his authority extended to the Greek and Albanian hill-villages, but each one was a fortress, an independent enclave and on occasion could become a hornets' nest. It is hardly surprising, then, that the Abruzzi, the highest, widest, and wildest part of the Apennines, should have escaped Byzantine rule, the rule of the Exarchs of Ravenna, and finally the domination of Papal Rome, although the Abruzzi lie directly behind the city and the Papal State ran north through Umbria as far as the Po valley. Nor is it astonishing that in Morocco the *bled es siba*, lands unsubdued by the sultan, should be essentially mountain regions. Further examples: Napoleon was unable to control the mountains round Genoa, a refuge for deserters, in spite of the searches organized. In about 1828, the Turkish police were powerless to prevent outbreaks of brigandage by the peoples of Mt Ararat; they seem to be equally unsuccessful today in protecting the mountain's forest wealth from the ravages of the flocks.

Sometimes this freedom of the hills has survived into our own time and can be seen today in spite of the immense weight of modern administration. In the Moroccan High Atlas, notes Robert Montagne, 'the villages which are ranged along the sunlit banks of the mountain torrents, near immense walnut trees watered by the turbulent Atlas streams, have no *chikhs*' or *Khalifats*' houses. It is impossible to distinguish between a poor man's house and a rich man's. Each of these little mountain cantons forms a separate state, administered by a council. The village elders, all clad alike in brown wool garments, meet on a terrace and discuss for hours on end the interests of the village. No one raises his voice and it is impossible from watching them to discover which is their president.' All this is preserved, if the mountain canton is sufficiently high and sufficiently inaccessible, away from the main roads, which is a rare case today but was less so in former times before the expansion of road systems. This is why the Nurra, although connected to the rest of the island of Sardinia by an easily accessible plain, remained for a long time out of the reach of roads and traffic. The following legend was inscribed on an eighteenth century map by the Piedmontese engineers: 'Nurra, unconquered peoples, who pay no taxes'!

8. A survival of what is described on pages 23–24: the annual pilgrimage to
Moulay-Idriss, Morocco.

The mountains' resources: an assessment. As we have seen, the mountains resist
the march of history, with its blessings and its burdens, or they accept it only
with reluctance. And yet life sees to it that there is constant contact between the
hill population and the lowlands. None of the Mediterranean ranges resembles
the impenetrable mountains to be found in the Far East, in China, Japan, Indochina, India, and as far as the Malaya peninsula. Since they have no communication with sea-level civilization, the communities found there are autonomous.
The Mediterranean mountains, on the other hand, are accessible by roads. The
roads may be steep, winding, and full of potholes, but they are passable on foot.
They are a 'kind of extension of the plain' and its power through the hill
country. Along these roads the sultan of Morocco sent his *harkas*, Rome sent its
legionaries, the king of Spain his *tercios*, and the Church its missionaries and

travelling preachers (I am thinking in particular of the travels of Sixtus V, in his youth and middle age).

Indeed, Mediterranean life is such a powerful force that when compelled by necessity it can break through the obstacles imposed by hostile terrain. Out of the twenty-three passes in the Alps proper, seventeen were already in use at the time of the Romans. Similarly the Pyrenees have not always been the barrier one might imagine. Moreover, the mountains are frequently overpopulated – or at any rate overpopulated in relation to their resources. The optimum level of population is quickly reached and exceeded; periodically the overflow has to be sent down to the plains.

9. Detail from Nativity scene showing shepherds with their goats.
Byzantine mosaic, Church of the Saviour, Istanbul.

One of the advantages of the mountain region is that it offers a variety of resources, from the olive trees, orange trees, and mulberry trees of the lower slopes to the forests and pasturelands higher up. To the yield from crops can be added the produce of stockraising. Sheep and goats are raised, as well as cattle. In comparatively greater numbers than today, they used to be plentiful in the Balkans, and even in Italy and North Africa. As a result, the mountains were a source of milk, cheeses (Sardinian cheese was exported in boatloads all over the western Mediterranean in the sixteenth century), butter, fresh or rancid, and boiled or roasted meat. The typical mountain house was a shepherd's or herds-man's dwelling, built for animals rather than for human beings. In 1574, Pierre

Lescalopier, when crossing the Bulgarian mountains, preferred to sleep 'under some tree' than in the peasants' huts of beaten clay where beasts and humans lived 'under one roof, and in such filth that we could not bear the stench'.

10. Detail from *The Adoration of the Shepherds* by
Jacopo Bassano. *Museo Civico, Bassano*

The forests in those days, it should be pointed out, were thicker than they are today. They can be imagined as something like the National Park of the Val di Corte, in the Abruzzi, with its thick beechwoods climbing up to 1400 metres. The population of the forests included foxes, wolves, bears, and wildcats. The Monte Gargano's oak forests supported a whole population of woodcutters and timber merchants, for the most part in the service of the shipyards of Ragusa. Like the summer pastures, the forests were the subject of much dispute among mountain villages and against noble landowners. Even the scrubland, half forest, can be used for grazing, and sometimes for gardens and orchards; it also supports game and bees. Other advantages of the mountains are the profusion of springs, plentiful water, that is so precious in these southern countries, and, finally, mines and quarries. Almost all the mineral resources of the Mediterranean, in fact, are found in its mountain regions.

But these advantages are not all found in every region. There are chestnut tree mountains (the Cévennes, Corsica) with their precious 'tree bread', made from chestnuts, which can replace wheat bread if necessary. There are mulberry tree mountains like those Montaigne saw near Lucca in 1581, or the highlands of Granada. 'These people, the people of Granada, are not dangerous', explained the Spanish agent, Francisco Gasparo Corso, to Euldj'Ali, 'King' of Algiers in 1569. 'What could they do to injure the Catholic King? They are unused to arms. All their lives they have done nothing but dig the ground, watch their flocks, and raise silkworms . . .' There are also the walnut tree mountains: it is under the century-old walnut trees that even today, in the centre of the village, on moonlit nights, the Berbers of Morocco still celebrate their grand festivals of reconciliation.

All told, the resources of the mountains are not as meagre as one might suppose. Life there is possible, but not easy. On the slopes where farm animals can hardly be used at all, the work is difficult. The stony fields must be cleared by hand, the earth has to be prevented from slipping down hill, and, if necessary, must be carried up to the hilltop and banked up with dry stone walls. It is painful work and never-ending; as soon as it stops, the mountain reverts to a wilderness and man must start from the beginning again. In the eighteenth century when the Catalan people took possession of the high rocky regions of the coastal massif, the first settlers were astonished to find dry stone walls and enormous olive trees still growing in the middle of the undergrowth, proof that this was not the first time that the land had been claimed.

Mountain dwellers in the towns. It is this harsh life – life in Haute-Provence, for example, 'which endures long winters, fear of avalanches, and indoor life for months on end, behind the snowy window panes with prospects confined to winter rations, the cowshed, and fireside work' – as well as poverty, the hope of an easier existence, the attraction of good wages, that encourages the mountain people to go down to the plain: 'baixar sempre, mountar no', 'always go down, never go up', says a Catalan proverb. Although the mountain's resources are varied, they are always in short supply. When the hive becomes too full, there is not enough to go around and the bees must swarm, whether peacefully or not. For survival, any sacrifice is permitted. As in the Auvergne, and more especially as in the Cantal in the recent past, all the extra mouths, men, children, artisans, apprentices, and beggars are expelled.

The history of the mountains is chequered and difficult to trace. Not because of lack of documents; if anything there are too many. Coming down from the mountain regions, where history is lost in the mist, man enters in the plains and towns the domain of classified archives. Whether a new arrival or a seasoned visitor, the mountain dweller inevitably meets someone down below who will leave a description of him, a more or less mocking sketch. Stendhal saw the peasants from the Sabine hills at Rome on Ascension Day. 'They come down from their mountains to celebrate the feast day at St Peter's, and to attend *la funzione* (the mass). They wear ragged cloth cloaks, their legs are wrapped in strips of material held in place with string cross-gartered; their wild eyes peer

11. Mountain shepherds in Rome with their traditional musical instruments.
Italian popular print.

from behind disordered black hair; they hold to their chests hats made of felt,
which the sun and rain have left a reddish black colour; these peasants are
accompanied by their families, of equally wild aspect . . . The inhabitants of the
mountains between Rome, Lake Turano, Aquila, and Ascoli, represent fairly
well, to my way of thinking,' Stendhal adds, 'the moral condition of Italy in
about the year 1400.' In Macedonia, in 1890, Victor Bérard met the eternal
Albanian, in his picturesque cavalry soldier's costume. In Madrid, Théophile
Gautier came across water-sellers, 'young Galician *muchachos*, in tobacco-
coloured jackets, short breeches, black gaiters and pointed hats'. Were they
already wearing this dress when they were to be found, both men and women,
scattered all over sixteenth-century Spain in the *ventas* mentioned by Cervantes,
along with their Asturian neighbours? One of the latter, Diego Suárez, who was
to become a soldier and chronicler of the events of Oran at the end of the
sixteenth century, describes his own adventures, his escape, while still a child,
from his father's house, his arrival at the builders' yards of the Escorial where

he works for a while, finding the fare to his taste, *el plato bueno*. But some of his relatives, from the mountains of Oviedo, arrive in their turn, no doubt to find summer work on the farms of Old Castile, like so many others. And he has to move on so as not to be recognized. The whole region of Old Castile was continually being crossed by immigrants from the mountains of the North who sometimes returned there. The Montaña, the continuation of the Pyrenees from Biscay to Galicia, provided little sustenance for its inhabitants. Many of them were *arrieros*, muleteers, or the peasant-carriers from the *partido* of Reinosa, travelling south, their wagons laden with hoops and staves for casks, later returning to their northern towns and villages with wheat and wine.

In fact, no Mediterranean region is without large numbers of mountain dwellers who are indispensable to the life of towns and plains, striking people whose costume is often unusual and whose ways are always strange. Spoleto, whose high plain Montaigne passed through in 1581 on the way to Loreto, was the centre for a special kind of immigrant: pedlars and small traders who specialized in all the reselling and intermediary activities that call for middlemen, flair, and not too many scruples. Bandello describes them in one of his novellas as talkative, lively and self-assured, never short of arguments and persuasive whenever they want to be. There is nobody to beat the Spoletans, he says, for cheating a poor devil while calling the blessing of St Paul upon him, making money out of grass-snakes and adders with drawn fangs, begging and singing in marketplaces, and selling bean meal as a remedy for mange. They travel all over Italy, baskets slung around their necks, shouting their wares.

The people of the Bergamo Alps – in Milan commonly known as the people of the *Contado* – were equally familiar in sixteenth-century Italy. They were everywhere. They worked as dockers in the ports, at Genoa and elsewhere. After Marignano, they came back to work the smallholdings of the Milanese, left abandoned during the war. A few years later Cosimo de' Medici tried to attract them to Leghorn, the fever town where no one wanted to live. Rough men, clumsy, stocky, close-fisted, and willing for heavy labour, 'they go all over the world', says Bandello (there was even an architect to be found working at the Escorial, Giovan Battista Castello, known as *el Bergamasco*), 'but they will never spend more than four *quattrini* a day, and will not sleep on a bed but on straw'. When they made money they bought rich clothes and fed well, but were no more generous for it, nor any less vulgar and ridiculous. Real-life comedy characters, they were traditionally grotesque husbands whom their wives sent to *Corneto*: like the bumpkin in one of Bandello's novellas who has the excuse, if it is one, that he found his wife in Venice, among the women who sell love for a few coppers behind St Mark's.

The picture, as we see, quickly turns to caricature. The mountain dweller is apt to be the laughing stock of the superior inhabitants of the towns and plains. He is suspected, feared, and mocked. In the Ardèche, as late as 1850, the people from the *montagne* would come down to the plain for special occasions. They would arrive riding on harnessed mules, wearing grand ceremonial costumes, the women bedecked with jangling gold chains. The costumes themselves differed from those of the plain, although both were regional, and their archaic stiffness provoked the mirth of the village coquettes. The lowland peasant had nothing but sarcasm for the rude fellow from the highlands, and marriages between their families were rare.

Typical cases of mountain dispersion. Transhumance is by far the most important of these movements from the hill to the plain, but it is a return journey. We shall study it later in more detail.

The other forms of mountain expansion are neither as large-scale nor as regular. All the evidence is of particular cases; we shall have to present a series of examples, except perhaps in the case of 'military' migration, for all the mountain regions, or almost all, were 'Swiss cantons'. Apart from the vagabonds and adventurers who followed armies without pay, hoping only for battle and plunder, they provided regular soldiers, almost traditionally reserved for certain princes. The Corsicans fought in the service of the king of France, of Venice, or of Genoa. The soldiers of the Duchy of Urbino and those of the Romagna, whom their overlords sold by contract, were generally allotted to Venice. If their masters turned traitor, as they did at the battle of Agnadello in 1509, the peasants abandoned the cause of St Mark to follow them. There were always lords of Romagna to be found at Venice; having broken their ban and committed other crimes, they now sought absolution and restitution of their property from Rome, in return for which they went to the Low Countries to serve the cause of Spain and Catholicism. Or again there were the Albanians, the *pallikares* of Morea, and the 'Anatolian oxen' whom Algiers, and other similar cities drew from the barren mountains of Asia.

The story of the Albanians deserves a study in itself. Attracted by the 'sword, the gold trappings, and the honours', they left their mountains chiefly in order to become soldiers. In the sixteenth century they were to be found in Cyprus, in Venice, in Mantua, in Rome, Naples, and Sicily, and as far abroad as Madrid, where they went to present their projects and their grievances, to ask for barrels of gunpowder or years of pension, arrogant, imperious, always ready for a fight. In the end Italy gradually shut its doors to them. They moved on to the Low Countries, England, and France during the Wars of Religion, soldier-adventurers followed everywhere by their wives, children, and priests. The Regencies of Algiers and Tunis refused them, and the lands of the Moldavian and Wallachian boyars also denied them entry. So they hastened to the service of the Sublime Porte, as they had in the first place, and as they were to do on a massive scale from the nineteenth century on. 'Where the sword is, there is the faith'. They were for whoever would give them a living. And, if necessary, 'with', as the song goes, 'their gun for pasha and their sabre for vizir', they set up on their own account and became brigands. From the seventeenth century on, large numbers of Albanians, for the most part orthodox, spread over Greece where they camped as if in conquered territory. Chateaubriand could not fail to notice them in 1806.

The history of Corsica – outside the island – is no less rich in information. Famous Corsicans are claimed everywhere, with some reason let it be said. The inhabitants of the Milanese mountains have provided another longstanding source of immigrants. We mentioned the *Bergamaschi*, subjects of Venice. But every mountain valley in the Alps has its swarm always ready to leave. There is frequently a second homeland where the exiles can meet. The travelling tinkers of the Val Vigezzo traditionally went to France, sometimes settling there permanently, like the Mellerios who are today jewellers in the Rue de la Paix. The inhabitants of Tremezzo preferred the Rhineland; from their numbers came the Majnoni and Brentanos, the Frankfurt bankers. From the fifteenth century on, the emigrants from the Val Masino took the road to Rome. They can be found in the apothecaries' shops and bakeries of the Eternal City, and in Genoa too. From the three *pievi* of Lake Como – particularly those of Dongo and Gravedona – men left for Palermo as innkeepers. As a result there is a rather curious link, with visible traces, in the Val di Brenzio, in the costume and ornaments of the women. For these departures often ended in return journeys. We find a considerable number of typically Milanese surnames in sixteenth-century Naples; however, says the consul G. F. Osorio in 1543, 'these Lombards who come here in thousands to work, as soon as they have earned any money, go back to Milan with it'. Lombard masons – *muratori* – (doubtless from the Alps) built the castle of Aquileia in 1543; when winter came, they went back home. But if we were to follow these masons or stonecutters, the search would lead us all over Europe, and certainly throughout Italy. As early as 1486, *lapicide lombardi* were working on the construction of the Palace of the Doges at Venice.

Even a country as continental and enclosed as Armenia does not escape the inevitable fate of all mountain regions. We have plenty of evidence of the Armenian diaspora in the directions of Constantinople, Tiflis, Odessa, Paris, and the Americas. Armenia played a considerable part too in the rise of the great Persia of the Shah 'Abbās, at the beginning of the seventeenth century. It provided him with, among others, the indispensable travelling merchants who journeyed at that time to fairs in Germany, to the quaysides of Venice, and to the shops of Amsterdam. There exist trading manuals, in Armenian, specially written for the great northern city. Others before the Armenians had attempted this connection and had failed. If they succeeded, it is in small part because of their Christianity, and in large measure because they would take on hard work, had great fortitude and were very sober, that is real mountain people. It was with large fortunes in ready money that they returned home to Zolpha, the rich Armenian colony of Ispahan, where they led a life as ostentatious as the Persians, dressing their women sumptuously in Venetian brocades, and harnessing their horses with gold and silver trappings. True, they had two avenues of trade to choose from and not content with Europe, they dealt with the Indies, Tonkin, Java, the Philippines, 'and throughout the East except for China and Japan'. They might make the journey themselves: Tavernier travelled to Surat and Golconda with the son of a wealthy Armenian merchant of Zolpha. Some Armenians even owned ships on the Indian Ocean.

This emigration dating from the end of the sixteenth century and the early seventeenth, explains the Venetian caśt of the Armenian Renaissance. But was it not precisely because Armenia extended herself beyond her frontiers to such an extent, both to her advantage and her cost, that she ceased to be a state, if not a human reservoir of great potential, after the fourteenth century? Armenia was lost through her own success.

Mountain life: the earliest civilization of the Mediterranean? The mountains have always been a reservoir of men for other people's use. Mountain life, exported in generous quantities, has contributed to the overall history of the sea. It may even have shaped the origins of that history, for mountain life seems to have been the first kind of life in the Mediterranean whose civilization 'like that of the Middle East and Central Asia, cloaks and barely disguises its pastoral origins', a primitive world of hunters and herdsmen, of nomads and migrating flocks, with now and then a few crops hastily sown on burnt clearings. This is the life of the high places, brought under control by man in early times.

2 Plateaux, hills and foothills

This sketch of the mountain regions is necessarily incomplete. Life cannot be reduced to such a simple outline. The mountains are full of variety, in relief, history, customs, and even cooking. In particular, there is alongside the high mountains that half-mountainous region of plateaux, hills, and foothills that in no way resembles – indeed all its features clearly distinguish it from – the real mountains.

The high plains. Plateaux are large, high, open plains, where the soil, at least in the Mediterranean, is dry and therefore hard, occasionally interrupted by river gorges. Roads and tracks are comparatively easy to establish. The plateau of Emilia, for example, hardly a plateau at all – almost a plain – is criss-crossed with roads and has always been the seat of outstanding civilizations, of which Bologna is the prime symbol. Asia Minor, with its precious tertiary overthrusts (without which it would have been as wild as its neighbours, Kurdistan and Zagros), with its caravans, caravanserais, and stage-post towns, is the centre of an unrivalled history of communications. Even the high Algerian plateaux are like an uninterrupted chain of steppes, from Biskra and the Chott-el-Hodna

12. Plateau landscape: detail from *The Assumption of the Virgin*, ascribed to Francesco Botticini. *National Gallery, London*

basin to the Moulouya in Morocco. In the Middle Ages, a great east–west thoroughfare linked these markets and this main artery, before the rise of Bougie, before Algiers and Oran were founded, and the Saracen sea became important in the tenth century, embodied what was known as Africa Minor, between Ifriqiya and Morocco.

As for the two pre-Apennine plateaux that extended westward more or less over Umbria and Tuscany, and eastward over Apulia, should we follow Philippson and describe them as the vital theatres of the history and cultural development of the peninsula? Undoubtedly they played a significant role, simply because along these plateaux ran the all-important roads. To the west, on the tuff plateaux of southern Etruria, Rome lost no time in building the Via Flaminia, the Via Amerina, the Via Cassia, the Via Clodia and the Via Aurelia. In the sixteenth century their outlines were still there almost unchanged. Apulia, a vast limestone plateau, not too high, facing eastwards towards Albania, Greece, and the East, is equally accessible to traffic. It is crossed by two parallel strings of towns: one to the coast, from Barletta to Bari and Lecce; the other five miles inland, from Andria to Bitonto and Putignano. From antiquity Apulia has been a centre of habitation between the sea and the almost deserted interior of the Murge. And it was already a cultural centre. Its character as a communications region opened it to western influence – it was Latinized without difficulty – as well as to constant influences by sea from the east, from Greece and Albania; so much so that Apulia sometimes gave the impression of literally turning its back on the rest of the peninsula. It clearly bears the mark of man's continual intervention. I am thinking for example of the *trulli*, but even more of the irrigation system of the plateau-plain, the 'acquedotto pugliese'. In the sixteenth century, wealthy Apulia was a grain-store and an oil reservoir for the rest of Italy. People came

13. A plateau enjoying its prosperity: farmers at work on the land. Detail from the fresco *Good Government* by Ambrogio Lorenzetti in the Sala delle Pace, Palazzo Pubblico, Siena.

from all around in search of foodstuffs. They came in particular from Venice, which was always hoping to gain control of the region – and did twice, in 1495 and 1528 – but also from the other towns on the Adriatic, Ragusa, Ancona, Ferrara. Through the intermediary of the little archipelago of the Tremiti and the good offices of the Frati della Carità who lived there, the contraband passage of wheat persisted throughout the sixteenth century.

The finest example of these busy plateaux, however, is in the centre of the Spanish peninsula, the plateau of the two Castiles, Old and New, chequered with roads or rather tracks, which were none the less inundated with people on the move, swarming with caravans of *arrieros*. The carters, whose adventures Cervantes describes, only played a minor role by comparison. These unending processions of beasts of burden, mules and donkeys invisible under their loads, journeyed over the Castiles from north to south and from south to north. They transported anything that could be sold along the way, wheat and salt, wool and wood, earthenware and pottery from Talavera, as well as passengers.

This carrying trade enabled Castile to maintain the links between the peripheral regions of the peninsula which surround it and in places separate it from the sea. It was this, and not Castile unaided, as has been said, 'which made Spain'. This traffic determined and, it could be said, revealed the basic economy of the country. So it was that for a long period the movement of caravans was directed to the east coast, first to Barcelona, which therefore among its other functions was responsible for selling Spanish wool; then to Valencia, which reached the peak of its fortunes in the fifteenth century, especially in the reign of Alfonso the Magnanimous (1416–1458); and eventually to Málaga and Alicante, which were the great wool ports in the sixteenth century. In his work on the *Grosse Ravensburger Gesellschaft*, A. Schulte suggests that if Valencia declined at the end of the fifteenth century, it was because Castilian traffic, restored in all its vigour under the ordered regime of the Catholic Kings, turned to the North and its thriving towns, Medina del Campo, Burgos, Bilbao, through which Spain made links with powerful northern Europe. Ease of communication is one of the first conditions of effective government. Castile gradually became the heart, the centre of gravity of Spain.

A hillside civilization. Where mountain and plain meet, at the edge of the foothills – in Morocco known as the *Dir* – run narrow ribbons of flourishing, established ways of life. Perhaps it is because between 200 and 400 metres they have found the optimum conditions of the Mediterranean habitat, above the unhealthy vapours of the plain, but within the limits between which the *coltura mista* can prosper. The mountain's water resources also allow irrigation and the cultivation of the gardens which are the beauty of these narrow strips.

In Morocco, on leaving the Atlas for the *Dir*, which leads to the great plains of the west, one finds at the entrance of every valley irrigation channels and along with them the gardens and orchards admired by the Père de Foucauld.

Similarly the traveller from the North receives his first impression of Italy, that is of the real Mediterranean, only some time after crossing the Alps, when he reaches the first foothills of the Apennines whose gullied hillsides stretch from Genoa to Rimini dotted with delightful oases. Arriving in spring, he is greeted by a green landscape already bright with flowers, and cultivated fields where white villas stand among vines, ash, and olive trees, while in the Po valley, the leafless trees, poplar, willow, and mulberry, still seem to be in the grip of winter. For *coltura mista*, the combination of orchard, market garden and sometimes sown fields, is often localized at the level of the foothills.

The same kind of hillside landscape overlooks the Adriatic, along the edge of the Dinaric Alps, from around Istria up to Ragusa or Antivari. A narrow garland of Mediterranean life borders the mountains almost as far as the coast, running inland with the contours of the land, reaching as far as Postojna by the Carniola gate, as far as Livno by the Prolog col, or to Mostar in Herzegovina by the fever-ridden valley of the Narenta. In spite of these incursions, this is basically a ribbon phenomenon, quite unlike the vast expanse of Zagora, the *Karst* highland, which is as wide at the latitude of Ragusa as the Alps on a level with Munich, blocking the way to the Balkans.

It is difficult to imagine a more striking contrast. To the east, the vast mountain ranges, ravaged by the rigours of winter and the catastrophic droughts of summer, a land of herbs and unsettled existence, which ever since the Middle Ages, and perhaps before (particularly Herzegovina and Montenegro), has poured its men and animals down on the foothills, towards Moravian Serbia with its poorly drained fluvial beds, towards Sumadija whose forests were formerly impenetrable, towards Croatia-Slavonia to the north and as far abroad as Sirmia. One could hardly imagine a region more primitive, more patriarchal and, whatever the charms of its civilization, in fact more backward. In the sixteenth century this was a combat region, a frontier zone facing the Turks. The *Zagorci* were born soldiers, bandits or outlaws, *hajduk* or *uskok*, 'nimble as deer', their courage was legendary. The mountain terrain lent itself to their surprise attacks, and any number of folk songs, the *pesma*, glorify their exploits: the beys they trounced, the caravans they attacked, and the beautiful maidens they carried off. That these wild mountains should also spill over towards Dalmatia is not surprising. But this invasion showed none of the anarchy of the East and North. It was disciplined and carefully filtered by the lowlanders. The flocks of the *Zagorci* met a well-organized resistance: they might overrun Lower Albania, but not the narrow fields and gardens of the coast. They managed to penetrate in only a few places, in particular by way of the Narenta valley. As for the men, they were tamed by the new environment. The brigand became the gendarmes' auxiliary. A possible colonist, he might be directed towards the islands and, even more likely, through the efforts of Venice, towards Istria, where there were more empty fields than anywhere else.

For here, the invader had come face to face with an exceptionally stable and well-ordered civilization, unused to movement, or at any rate to the massive migration and wild flights of the mountain region, a closely knit rural civilization, patiently constructed by hacking out terraced gardens, orchards, vineyards, and fields where the hillside was not too steep. A series of urbanized villages and small towns with narrow streets and tall, closely packed houses was installed in the hollows, the *draga*, the promontories, the isthmuses of the coast.

14. View of Sibenik on the Dalmatian coast.
From *Civitates Orbis Terrarum.*

Here the people were hard-working and level-headed, comfortable, if not rich. For like anywhere else in the Mediterranean, only a modest living could be made. It was maintained by battling with nature, with the vast threatening Zagora, and with the Turks; in addition there was always the struggle against the sea. All this required coordinated activity, not people who were free to behave as they pleased. The peasant of Ragusa from the thirteenth century on was in the situation of a colonial settler, of a peasant in semi-slavery. In the fifteenth century a cadastral register reveals the similar situation of the peasants round Spalato. In the sixteenth century around the Venetian towns of the *altra sponda*, the fearful farmers had to have the protection of the soldiers. Work gangs of peasants would set off in the morning and return at night under the protection of the troops. This would hardly encourage individualism or peasant unrest, of which there is however some evidence.

The hills. We meet the same problem when we turn to the hills, particularly the hills of tuff or tertiary limestone which man occupied early and soon brought under control: the hills of Languedoc; the hills of Provence; the hills of Sicily; the hills of Montferrat, those 'islands' in northern Italy; the Greek hills whose classical names are famous; the hills of Tuscany, with their celebrated wines, their villas, and villages that are almost towns, set in the most heartbreaking landscape in the world; or the *Sahels* of North Africa, well-known in both Tunisia and Algeria.

Between the sea and the Mitidja, up against the miniature Massif Central of the Bouzareah, the Sahel of Algiers is the basic component of the *Fahs*, the Algiers countryside. It is an urbanized countryside, divided among the estates of the Turks of Algiers, and shares the dialect of the nearby city, a narrow 'oasis' among the 'nomadic' dialects that surround the urban centre. These hills, cultivated, equipped, and drained – the canals from the Turkish period have been rediscovered in our own day – are lush and green. The gardens, the pride of many Mediterranean towns, are magnificent here, surrounding the white houses with trees and running water. They won the admiration of a Portuguese captive, João Carvalho Mascarenhas, in 1627. His admiration was not feigned: Algiers, a corsair town that grew up American-style, was also a town of luxury and art in the Italian fashion at the beginning of the seventeenth century. With Leghorn, which grew up in the same way, it was one of the richest towns of the Mediterranean, and one of the most disposed to convert its wealth into luxury.

Viewed in detail, this fragile economy of terraced crops on a hillside is infinitely complex and variable with the passage of time. Between its low retaining walls the bank of earth, known in Provence as the *restanque*, or *oulière*, is broader or narrower depending on the slope of the hillside. 'Vines were planted on the edge of the *oulière*, trees more or less everywhere'; between vines and trees grew wheat, oats mingled with vetch (for the mules), and above all vegetables ('lentils, peas, *farouns*'). These crops were forced to compete with each other according to market prices; they also had to compete with the produce of neighbouring regions and be incorporated into the richness or poverty of a larger-scale economy than their own. Around Vicenza at the end of the sixteenth century the countryside was all of a piece, made up of 'uninterrupted gardens', although it covered plains, valleys, and *monti*. In the interior of Bas-Languedoc, on the other hand, there are innumerable barren hills that are not worth the trouble of making *rompudes* (clearings). A stony *pech* is often abandoned when times are hard. For the expenditure of human effort on terracing crops does not always pay.

In short, we should not exaggerate the importance of the hillside civilizations, relatively few in number. Sometimes they hold the longest-established human population of the Mediterranean, and the most stable landscapes. We should not be so led astray by the examples of the hills of Tuscany or Languedoc that their clear waters make us forget the other springs which have nourished the great Mediterranean body.

3 The plains

It is even more easy to be mistaken about the role of the plain in the Mediterranean. If we say mountains, it suggests austerity, harshness, backwardness, and a scattered population. If we say plain, it suggests abundance, ease, wealth, and good living. In the period we are studying, and with reference to Mediterranean countries, the suggestion is likely to be misleading.

There are certainly plenty of plains in the Mediterranean, large and small, installed between the Pyrenean and Alpine foldings, often resulting from a collapse followed by silting up: the age-long work of lakes, rivers, or seas. It is hardly necessary to stress that, whether they are great or small (and only about ten are of any significant size, regardless of their resources), whether they are near or far from the sea, the plains have a quite different aspect from the

15. A large, compact village such as is described on the next page. Detail from *The Madonna of the Meadow* by Giovanni Bellini. *National Gallery, London*

highlands surrounding them. They do not have the same light, the same colours, the same flowers, or even the same calendar. When winter lingers on in Haute-Provence or in 'Daufiné', it 'lasts no more than a month' in Lower Provence, 'so that even in that season, one may see roses, pinks and orange blossom'. The ambassador de Brèves who, on 26th June, 1605, went with his travelling companions to see the cedars of Lebanon, was astonished by the differences effected by the altitude: 'Here [on the mountains of Lebanon] the vines were only just beginning to flower, as were the olive trees, and the wheat was just turning yellow; and at Tripoli [on the coast] the grapes were growing, the olives were already big, the wheat had been harvested, and all the other fruits were well advanced.' A Flemish traveller, Peter Coeck of Alost, accompanies with illustrations his report in 1553 of the difficulties he encountered besides the 'rain, wind, snow, and hail', crossing the mountains of Slavonia. 'When one reaches the lowland countryside', everything improves: 'Greek women . . . bring to sell to travellers all sorts . . . of useful supplies and provisions such as horse shoes, barley, oats, wine, bread or round loaves baked in hot embers.' Similarly, Philippe de Canaye in 1573 was glad to reach the smiling plains of Thrace after the snow-covered mountains of Albania. Many others have like him rejoiced at the pleasant sight of the warm plains that are so hospitable to man.

Or so they appear. They must have been easy to bring under control when they were of small proportions. Man immediately took possession of the rising ground, the strategic hillocks, the fluvial terraces, and the foothills of the mountains; here he established his large, compact villages, sometimes even towns. But at the lowest point of the basin, always threatened by the waters, a dispersed habitat was often the rule. This was how Montaigne saw the plain of Lucca, and Pierre Belon the plain of Bursa; this is how we can still see the plain of Tlemcen, which was already being farmed in Roman times: in the centre, gardens and irrigated fields; on the outskirts, orchards and vineyards; further away the range of famous villages – the same spectacle that Leo Africanus had before his eyes in 1515. And as if by virtue of Thünen's law of circles, the largest estates of extensive cultivation were situated farthest from the centres of population. Rural space is organized as a function of and starting from the urban settlement, whether town or village.

When they were larger, the Mediterranean plains were far more difficult to conquer. For a long time they were only very imperfectly and temporarily taken over by man. Only recently, towards 1900, was the Mitidja, behind Algiers, finally claimed for cultivation. It was not until after 1922 that Greek colonization eventually triumphed over the marshes in the plain of Salonica. And it was on the eve of World War II that work was finished on the draining of the Ebro

16. *Opposite*: Palm orchard on the River Dra, Western Sahara. Under the variety of trees, lucerne, clover and mint are grown.

delta and the Pontine Marshes. In the sixteenth century, then, the big plains were not all rich, far from it. By an apparent paradox, they frequently presented a spectacle of misery and desolation.

Let us take them in turn. The Campagna Romana: a semi-desert, in spite of a further attempt at settlement begun in the fifteenth century. The Pontine Marshes: a roaming ground for a few hundred shepherds and a refuge for herds of wild buffalo; the only abundance here was of wildlife, all kinds of game including wild boars, a sure index of sporadic human habitation. The regions of the lower Rhône valley were equally deserted, hardly affected by the few riverside 'improvements' of the previous hundred years. The plain of Durazzo was completely empty; it still is today. Even the Nile delta was only very thinly populated. And the mouth of the Danube was as it has remained to this day, an incredible marshland, a tangled amphibious world, with floating islands of vegetation, muddy forests, fever-infested swamps and, living in this hostile environment where wildlife thrives, a few wretched fishermen. In 1554 Busbecq was passing through the plains beyond Nicaea in Anatolia where there were no villages or houses; it was here, he noted, that 'we saw also the famous goats from whose fleece or hair . . . is made the well-known cloth known as camlet', which tells us he was nearing Ankara. The inland plains of Corsica, Sardinia, and Cyprus at the same period were a scene of desolation. On Corfu, the *provveditore* Giustiniano travelled over an almost deserted plain in 1576. The marshes at Biguglia and Urbino in Corsica were a festering sore.

Water problems: malaria. But we need not complete the list of plains that had not reached prosperity in the sixteenth century. For a plain to become rich required prolonged effort and the solutions to two if not three problems. First, there was the problem of flooding. Mountain regions are sources of water: that water normally collects in the plains. In winter, which is the rainy season, plains tend to flood. To avert disaster their inhabitants must take precautions, build dams and dig channels. Even so, there is not a plain in the Mediterranean today, from Portugal to Lebanon, that is not threatened by the danger of flood waters. Even Mecca disappears under torrential rains in some winters.

In 1590 widespread floods submerged the Maremma in Tuscany devastating the sown fields. At that time the Maremma was, with the Arno valley, the chief grain supplier of Tuscany. The Grand Duke was obliged to go to Danzig (for the first time) in search of grain, without which it would not have been possible to bridge the gap. Sometimes violent summer storms alone can produce similar disasters, for water from the mountains rushes down very quickly, almost as soon as it has fallen. Any river bed dry in summer can become a foaming torrent in winter, within a few hours. In the Balkans the Turks built high hog-backed bridges without piles, to give as free a passage as possible to sudden rises in the water level.

When the waters reach the flats, they do not always run smoothly to the sea.

Waters from the Alban and Volscian hills form a stagnant stretch about 30 kilometres wide, the Pontine Marshes. The reasons for this are the flatness of the plain, the slow flow of water, and the high line of sand dunes barring the way to the sea. In the case of the Mitidja, the plain, which is bordered to the south by the Atlas, is literally blocked off on the north by the hills of the Sahel, only imperfectly breached by the Oued El Harrach and the Oued Mazafran, to the east and west of Algiers. In fact there is almost always stagnant water at these low levels. And the consequence is always the same: 'Acqua, ora vita, ora morte': here water is synonymous with death. Where it stands it creates vast stretches of reeds and rushes. At the very least, in summer it maintains the dangerous humidity of the marshes and river beds, from which come the terrible swamp fevers, the scourge of the plains in the hot season.

Before the use of quinine, malaria was often a fatal disease. Even in a mild form it led to a reduction in the vitality and output of its victims. It wore men out and led to frequent appeals for labour. It is a disease that directly results from the geographical environment. Plague, carried from India and China by long-distance travellers, although greatly to be feared, is only a passing visitor to the Mediterranean. Malaria is permanently installed there. It constitutes the 'background to Mediterranean pathology'. We now know that it is directly linked to the anopheles mosquito and to the haematozoa of the *plasmodium* species, the pathogenic agents of malaria of which the anopheles is only the carrier. Of the country round Aiguesmortes, in about 1596 Thomas Platter said, 'it is so infested with mosquitoes in summer that it is pitiful'. This is the malarial complex known to biologists and closely connected to the overall geography of the Mediterranean lowlands, the only region seriously and persistently infected, mountain fever being insignificant in comparison.

In order to conquer the plains, then, the unhealthy water had to be dealt with and malaria reduced. The next task was to bring in fresh water for the necessary irrigation.

Man has been the labourer of this long history. If he drains the marshes and puts the plain under the plough, if he manages to produce his food from it, malaria retreats. The best remedy against malaria, says an Etruscan proverb, is a well-filled pot. But if the drainage and irrigation channels are neglected, if the mountains are too quickly deforested, altering the conditions of the flow of the streams, or if the population of the plain falls and the peasant's hold on the land is relaxed, than malaria spreads again and paralyses everything. The plain will soon be reduced to its original marshy state: it is an automatic counter-improvement. This was apparently the case in ancient Greece. It has also been suggested that malaria was one of the causes of the decline of the Roman Empire. This theory is perhaps somewhat exaggerated and too categorical. Malaria progresses when man relaxes his efforts, and its dreaded return is as much a consequence as a cause.

It does seem, however, that there have been in the history of malaria, periods

of greater and lesser virulence. There may well have been an increase in marsh fevers at the end of the Roman Empire. That there was another increase towards the end of the fifteenth century is claimed by Philipp Hiltebrandt, who unfortunately does not give his sources. Fresh pathogenic elements made their appearance at this time. Along with the *treponema pallidum*, the recently discovered Americas contributed to the old Mediterranean world *malaria tropicalis* or *perniciosa*, which had hitherto been unknown. Pope Alexander VI himself was possibly one of its first victims in 1503. Leo X, who was fond of hunting, also seems to have succumbed to an attack of malaria. And did not Dante himself apparently die of malaria, as Guido Cavalcanti had twenty years before?

It is very difficult to pronounce with certainty. Antiquity and the Middle Ages must have witnessed a disease something like *malaria tropicalis*, but it was certainly less dangerous, since Horace crossed the Pontine Marshes without harm in spite of mosquito bites; and more particularly, since in September, 1494, the army of Charles VIII – 30,000 men at the lowest estimate – encamped safely around Ostia, in a particularly dangerous site. But these examples are hardly sufficient to formulate, let alone to solve the problem. We need far more precise documentation of the history of malaria than we possess at the moment. Was it malaria or dysentery that decimated Lautrec's troops in July, 1528, in the flooded countryside around Naples? We need precise knowledge of the regions that were seriously affected by it in the sixteenth century. We do know that Alexandretta, which served as a port for Aleppo from 1593, had to be abandoned later because of fever. We know that Baiae, on the gulf of Naples, which in Roman times was a resort for leisured high society, and which was described as a charming place by Petrarch in a letter to Cardinal Giovanni Colonna in 1343, was deserted by its population, fleeing from fever, in the sixteenth century. But we have only incomplete records of even these particular cases. Of Alexandretta we know that the town was later reoccupied by English and French consuls, and that it has survived; but how? and under what conditions? As for Baiae, is it not because it was already in decline, at least two generations before Tasso landed there in 1587, that fever was able to take such a firm grip? On the other hand we should note that about twenty years before Columbus, in 1473, the Venetian fleet, which was operating along the Albanian coast during the first siege of Scutari, was decimated by fever and had to put into Cattaro to recover. The *provveditore* Alvise Bembo died; Triadan Gritti came close to death. Pietro Mocenigo decided to go to Ragusa 'per farsi medicar'.

Nevertheless one cannot escape the impression that there was a fresh outbreak of malaria in the sixteenth century. Perhaps it was because at this time man was running ahead of the enemy. During the whole of the sixteenth century,

17. *Opposite*: Water-wheel, Fayum, Egypt. Some of the methods and perils of irrigation are discussed on the preceding pages.

18. Land reclamation started by the Dukes of Este near Ferrara in the fourteenth century.

as indeed of the fifteenth, he was in search of new land. Where was there a more promising prospect than in the shifting marshes of the plains? And precisely the greatest danger lies in the first disturbance of infested regions. To colonize a plain often means to die there: we know that the villages of the Mitidja had to be resettled many times at the beginning, before the plain was won over from fever in the painful struggle of the nineteenth century. The internal colonization which was carried out throughout the Mediterranean in the sixteenth century also took its toll. It was particularly marked in Italy. If Italy took no part in the great movement of colonization of distant territories the reason is perhaps partly to be sought in her preoccupation with reclaiming all available land within her own frontiers, from the flooded plains to the mountain peaks. 'Italy is cultivated right up to the mountain tops,' wrote Guicciardini proudly at the beginning of his *History of Italy*. The Italians took part in the great discoveries – Venezuela is, after all, little Venice – but the Italian population was not short of space at this period; the bourgeoisie was not interested in the world beyond the Mediterranean horizon; and finally, the Peninsula was not troubled by the religious disturbances which drove Englishmen and Dutchmen overseas.

The improvement of the plains. To conquer the plains had been a dream since the dawn of history. The vessel of the Danaides may be a folk-memory of the introduction of perpetual irrigation into the plain of Argos. The inhabitants of the shores of Lake Kopais began to encroach upon its marshy edges at a very early date. The network of underground canals covering the Roman Campagna, of which archaeologists have found traces, dates back to Neolithic times. We know too of the primitive works of the Etruscans in the narrow plains of Tuscany.

Throughout the sixteenth century, as indeed in the fifteenth, many improvement schemes were under way with the limited means available to the period: ditches, trenches, canals, low-powered pumps. In the following century Dutch engineers perfected more efficient techniques. Was the first of these 'Hollanders', these northerners, the engineer – or *dijkmeester* – whom the *nuncio* sent to Ferrara at the request of the Pope in 1598, and who seems to have been thinking of using windmills to drain the water? Otherwise the Dutch engineers had not yet made their appearance in the period under discussion. The inadequacy of means therefore limited the undertakings. The marsh was attacked sector by sector, which led to many failures. In Venetia, in the Adige Valley, Montaigne in 1581 came across 'an infinite expanse of muddy sterile country covered with reeds', formerly ponds that the Signoria had tried to drain, 'to put under the plough . . . ; they lost more than they gained by trying to alter its nature', he concluded. Similarly whatever the 'press' of the period – the official chroniclers – might say, the enterprises of Grand Duke Ferdinand in the Tuscan Maremma and the hollow of the Val di Chiana were not a success.

In the Maremma the grand dukes, from Cosimo on, tried to create a grain-producing region (the equivalent on a grander scale of what Genoa attempted in the eastern plain of Corsica). To this end measures to encourage population were taken, advances were offered on capital and yield, manpower was recruited and here and there drainage schemes were carried out. Grosseto on the Ombrona was then becoming a port for the export of grains to Leghorn. The reasons for the semi-failure of the scheme were spelled out long ago by Reumont in his *History of Tuscany*. The grand dukes were pursuing two contradictory ends. They were creating a grain-producing plain, which entails great outlay, and setting up a monopoly of the purchase of the grain for their own advantage, that is for selling at a low price. What they should have done was to throw the market open to the competition of all the Mediterranean buyers. For these improvement schemes were expensive and the return on them, the *utilità*, was not always worth the outlay. In 1534 the Orators of Brescia pointed out to the Venetian Senate that 'to divert and contain the waters requires infinite expense; so much so that several of our citizens have been ruined through wanting to further such enterprises. Besides the initial expense of bringing the water, there is the continual cost of maintenance, so that when it is all reckoned there is very little difference between expense and profit.' In this case evidently the people of Brescia were pleading poverty to avoid paying too many taxes, but it is nevertheless true that improvement schemes were large undertakings which required much financing. Ideally they were undertaken by governments.

In Tuscany it might be an 'enlightened' government that took charge of them, or as in 1572, a prince from the ducal family, the future Grand Duke Ferdinand who was interested in possible improvements in the marshy Val di Chiana. At Rome it was the pontifical government; at Naples, the viceroy who initiated an official project for draining the great marshes of Cherranola and Marellano near Capua. At Aquileia it was the Imperial government.

19. A celebration of civic water supply: marble tondo depicting the Fountain of Neptune, Piazza Signoria, Florence.

A series of improvements by individual capitalists in the sixteenth century established rice fields in the lowest parts of Lombardy which developed so quickly that they were certainly exporting their produce to Genoa by 1570, and perhaps even earlier. A former patrician of Venice – struck off the list of nobles, as the result of injustice, according to him, but still possessed of a good fortune – tried to lay sacrilegious hands on the Venetian lagoons. The authorities were alerted and became worried. Could anyone seriously be thinking of transforming the lagoons into cultivable land? Were not changes in the water level to be feared? The enterprise was classified as undesirable.

The capitalists led the way in lower Languedoc too, with the great drainage works beginning in 1592 and carried on with more or less energy and success until about 1660–1670. Identical works had been begun near Narbonne in 1558, in an attempt to drain the lagoons. But at the end of the century with the first embankments around Lake Launac, the movement gained speed. Provençal engineers, specialists in hydraulics and disciples of Adam de Craponne, lent their assistance. A 'group' (Bernard de Laval, Dumoulin, Ravel) directed this operation and the following ones, also in the Narbonne area. It was Laval, lord of Sault who provided the original sum of money, and later the 'supplements'. Adam de Craponne (1519–1559) built the canal named after him which irrigated the Crau in about 1558, between the Durance and the Rhône.

These improvement schemes arose in reply to the needs of the towns, whose population in the fifteenth and sixteenth centuries was steadily increasing. The urgent need for a food supply impelled the towns to develop crop cultivation all around them either by taking over fresh ground or by extending irrigation. This gave rise to many disputes but also to some fruitful agreements. 'We should achieve a good supply of water by diverting the Oglio,' say the Orators of Brescia in 1534, 'but it would lead us into endless litigation with the people of Cremona, not to mention the risk of assassination of which we have already had some experience.' In 1593 the Rectors of Verona, with the support of Venice, had the works of the Mantuans to retain the waters of the Tartaro demolished; this was followed by long-drawn-out wrangles. In Aragon in the eighteenth century the towns were still involved in disputes, each trying to seize the precious sources of irrigation from its neighbours. On the other hand, from the fifteenth century on, riverside communities cooperated with each other on the drainage works of the Lower Rhône valley, works which would in any case have been unthinkable without the capital provided by Italian immigrants and the labour force from the Alps.

Whether pursued in cooperation or in competition, the efforts made by the towns bore fruit. They created, within reach of the central markets, the vegetable gardens and wheatfields they needed. A Venetian ambassador passing through Castile concluded that it was cultivated only around the towns. The wide *paramos* where sheep grazed and the *secanos* reserved for wheat, yellow plains where even the houses built of earth can hardly be distinguished from their background, appeared to him to be stretches of barren countryside. Around the Castilian towns on the other hand he had seen the green patches of irrigated land. At Valladolid, orchards and gardens bordered the banks of the Pisuerga. In Madrid itself, Philip II could only extend the Prado by buying up vineyards, gardens and orchards: we have the deeds of sale to prove it. At Toledo, the Vega 'striped with trees and crops' is under the town walls. The same link between town and agricultural effort is found in Provence.

20. View of Valladolid, showing farming taking place outside the town walls. From *Civitates Orbis Terrarum*.

A large-scale transfer of urban investment to the countryside was therefore taking place. The search for new land for cultivation became of public concern from the end of the century. Olivier de Serres, in his *Théâtre d'Agriculture*, gives full instructions on converting marshy land. But the task was only tackled piecemeal. The striking fact about the history of the whole undertaking is the incredibly long time it took to bring the plains to life. Yet the work, hardly complete in the sixteenth century, had begun hundreds of years previously. This is true of all plains: of Murcia and of Valencia, of Lerida, Barcelona and Saragossa, of the Andalusian plain and the Po valley, the *campagna felice* of Naples and the Conca d'Oro of Palermo or the plain of Catania. Every generation contributed its strip of land rescued from the waters. One of the merits of the government of Pietro di Toledo at Naples was to have drained the marshy *Terra di Lavoro* near the city, between Nola, Aversa, and the sea, and to have made of it, according to one chronicler, 'la più sana terra del mondo', with its canals, its trenches, its fertile crops, and its drained fields.

The small plains were the first to be conquered. The plains of the coastal massif of Catalonia had been claimed by man for his precious crops as far back as the early Middle Ages. The digging of the *cequies* dates back traditionally to the reign of Hacam II. There is nothing to prove that they are not older still. It is quite certain however that Lerida, which was reconquered in 1148, had already been made fertile by the Clamor canals; that Tortosa had its irrigation channels from the time of the Arabs; that Camarasa, when it was reunited with the County of Barcelona in 1060, also had its water trenches. Following the example of the Moslems, the counts of Barcelona for their part set up the irrigation system of the territory covered by the town itself, and of the Llobregat plain. It is to one of them, Count Mir (945–966), that the famous *rech* of the

Barcelona county is attributed – the *rego mir* – as well as the construction of another canal, from the Llobregat to Cervello. The legacy was received, preserved and continually added to by later generations.

The example of Lombardy. But the best example of these progressive conquests – because it is the clearest to see – is that of Lombardy. Let us leave aside the higher regions: on one side the Alps, unproductive above 1500 metres, stony masses with terraced pastures and forests between 700 metres and 1500 metres; on the other, the Apennines, whose raging torrents rush down to the plains in winter, rolling stones and boulders in their swirling waters, but in summer dry up completely so that there is no water either for irrigation or consumption. As a result the Apennines above 1000 metres are as barren as the Alps above 2000 metres; in summer they afford only a few tufts of grass fit for goats and sheep.

Between these two ramparts, lower Lombardy is a complex of hills, plateaux, plains and river valleys. The hills are the region of vines and olives, and even citrus fruits grow near the great Alpine lakes. There are 'plateaux' in the true sense of the word only in the North. First a plateau without irrigation, a rectangular block defined to the south by a line joining Vicolungo and Vaprio, on

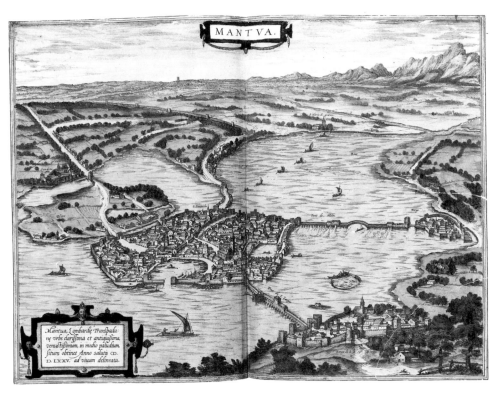

21. View of Mantua, surrounded by its flooded plain. From *Civitates Orbis Terrarum*.

the Adda, covered with barren stretches of scrubland and given over to growing mulberry trees; a low, irrigated plateau comes next, forming a triangle whose southern side runs from Magenta on the Ticino to Vaprio on the Adda, and where wheat, mulberry trees, and pastures are plentiful.

The most interesting feature of the Lombardy lowlands is the vast alluvial plain, between this plateau and the foothills of the Apennines, in other words the bottom of the bowl, the classic zone of rice fields, pasture lands, and equally important, of artificially created grasslands. The market price of hay has even been used as the basis of an attempt to show the general movement of prices in Milan in the sixteenth century.

Man has entirely transformed this plain. He has flattened the land, eliminated the swamps and made intelligent use of the water brought by the rivers from the Alpine glaciers. The regulation of the water began in at least 1138 with the works of the Benedictines and the Cistercians, at Chiaravalle Abbey. In 1179, work began on the *Naviglio Grande* which was finished in 1257 by the *podestà* Beno Gozzodini. The waters of the Ticino were now brought to Milan by an artificial river nearly 50 kilometres long which could be navigated and used for irrigation. Before 1300 the Basca *roggia* was diverted from the Sesia; later it would be tapped to feed the Biraga, Bolgara, and other *roggie* that irrigated the Novarese and Lomellina. In 1456 Francesco Sforza built the Martesana canal, over 30 kilometres long, bringing the waters of the Adda to Milan. It was widened in 1573 to make it navigable. Since Ludovic the Moor had already linked it with the *Naviglio Grande*, in 1573 the two great lakes of Lombardy, Lake Como and Lake Maggiore, were brought into communication at the very heart of the state. Milan now became an important waterways centre, which enabled it to receive wheat, iron, and in particular wood, at less expense, and to ship off to the Po and Ferrara the large artillery pieces made in its foundries – in fact to compensate for its major disadvantage of being a landlocked city.

Even this evidence, which only concerns waterways, shows how slow the process of land reclamation was. It was accomplished in states, each one corresponding to the arrival of different groups of people, so that the three Lombardies were encapsulated one within the other, each representing a different group of people. Upper Lombardy, the mountainous, pastoral region, which in the north comes close to the zone of the *brughiere*, is the country of small peasant proprietors, poor but free, devoting their lives to producing all their needs from their land, including the poor wine of their vineyards. Lower down on the well-watered plateau of the upper plain, the region of springs (*fontanili*) and grassy meadows, begins the ecclesiastical and noble property. At this level, a little higher than the plain itself are to be found the castles, the tenant farmers, and the monasteries shaded by their tall trees. Lower down again are the rice fields belonging to the capitalists. Their revolutionary initiative resolved the problem of cultivating the flooded fields. Economic progress was assured – but at the price of social misery.

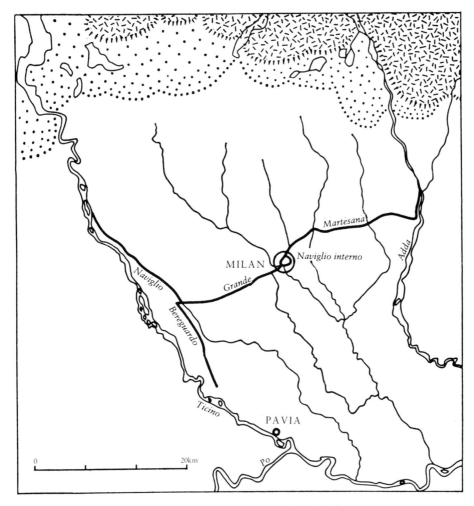

The great canals of the Lombardy plain

From Charles Singer, *History of Technology*, 1957, vol. III. The dotted area indicates morainic deposits and hills preceding the Alps.

Rice growing in Lombardy meant the enslavement under terrible conditions of workers who were unable to voice any effective protest since they were not organized. Rice fields do not require labour all the year round, but large numbers of casual workers for a few weeks, at the times of sowing, transplanting, and harvest. This kind of agriculture depends entirely on seasonal migration. It hardly requires the landowner to be present except for paying wages and over-seeing the gangs at work. Centuries later Cavour would go to his property in Leri in nearby lower Piedmont, personally settling wages and rising at dawn to supervise the labourers.

This is true of almost all the crops grown in the plain. Land which is easy

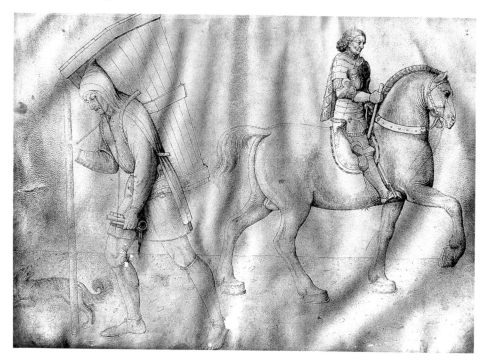

22. *Landlord and Peasant*, drawing by Jacopo Bellini. *Louvre, Paris*

to work, where the furrows can be drawn up with a line, lends itself to the regular employment of oxen or buffaloes, animal mechanization. It is only at the season of harvest and grape gathering that it calls for the massive recruitment of mountain labourers. After a few weeks of work these labourers return home. They are the true rural proletariat. But the peasant farmer who settles in the plain is often in very much the same situation.

The Spanish enquiry of 1547 on property in Lombardy indicates that the peasants possessed less than 3 per cent of the land in the fertile lower region, while the poor land on the hills was very largely in their hands. Nothing could indicate better than these figures the conditions of life in the plain. Here the peasant lived off very little, in deplorable conditions of health and hygiene. He had masters and what he produced went to them. Often a newcomer, a simple man from the mountains, he might be cheated by the landowner or his steward. In many ways he was a kind of colonial slave, whatever his precise position in law.

Big landowners and poor peasants. We were comparing the converted plains of the Mediterranean with the cleared forests of northern Europe. Like any other comparison this one has its limits. In the new towns in the forest clearings of the North there grew up a more free civilization on the American pattern. One of the problems of the Mediterranean, and one of the causes of its traditionalism and rigidity, was that (apart from a few regions where colonization encouraged agrarian individualism) newly-acquired land remained under the control of the wealthy. A pick and an axe might be enough in the North, as it was later to be in America, to make the soil productive. In the Mediterranean rich and powerful landowners had an essential role to play, increasingly so as small-scale improvements were abandoned in favour of extensive, long-term schemes. The goal could only be achieved by holding ranks under a discipline possible only through a rigid social order.

The plains were the property of the nobleman. One has to go down to the Portuguese *veigas* to find the houses of the *fidalgos*, the *solares* with their great coats of arms. The vast low-lying plain of the Sienese Maremma, a real fever trap, is, like its neighbour the Tuscan Maremma, dotted with noblemen's castles. Their anachronistic silhouettes of tower and keep conjure up a whole society, the crushing presence of the feudal landlords who dominated the country without even living there, for these residences were only their temporary abodes. Most of the year the masters lived in Siena, in the huge town houses still standing today, palaces into which Bandello's lovers find their way, with the ritual complicity of the servants, up staircases leading to the great attics where sacks of grain are stored, or along corridors leading to the rooms on the ground floor, always a little neglected. We can follow them into the houses of these old families to relive the comedies and tragedies whose dénouement would take place in secret in the old castle in the Maremma, far from town gossip and family control. Isolated from the world by fever and the sultry heat, what better place could there be for putting to death, according to the custom of Italy and the century, an unfaithful wife – or one suspected of being so? The climatic explanation would have delighted Barrès. But was there not also an element of social complicity, which allowed the murderer almost total impunity in the low lands where he was absolute master? Was the plain the rich man's fief to do as he liked with?

'In the plain,' writes Robert Montagne of the Moroccan Sous of today, 'the distance between rich and poor increases rapidly. The former own gardens, the latter work in them.' This seems to have been the rule in the Mediterranean plains. A considerable distance separates rich from poor; the rich are very rich and the poor very poor.

Large estates have remained the rule in the plains. Here, the seignorial system – which is often the façade for large estates – found natural conditions for survival. In Sicily, in Naples, in Andalusia, the entailed estates of the noble landowners have been handed down undiminished right down to the present day. Similarly, in the great eastern plains of the Balkans, in Bulgaria, Rumelia, and Thrace, in the grain and rice producing regions, the Turkish regime of large estates and serf-villages took strong root, whereas it more or less failed in the mountains of the West.

Short-term change in the plains: the Venetian Terraferma. We can attempt to
follow these short-term changes in one example at least: Venice.

The low-lying regions of the Venetian countryside, which are also the richest
and most populated, were the object of frequent improvements beginning before
the end of the fifteenth century. We can guess at their scale without unfortunately
knowing their geographical extent or their precise chronology. These costly
schemes that began so early do not usually seem to have brought any advantage
to peasant farmers or village communities.

At first sight there could be nothing more reasonable than the usual course
of these improvement schemes, kept to an unvarying programme over a period
of centuries, under the prudent procedures, generally governed by precedent, of
the Venetian administration, which after 1566 was in the hands of the *Provveditori ai beni inculti.* The *Provveditori* appear to have been introduced then with
the responsibility of supervising crops and drainage and promoting agricultural
activity by the setting up of land 'companies'. Every improvement, every *ritratto*,
established for a defined area of obviously marshy land a programme of various
hydraulic works: dykes built or to be built (*argile*), entry points of water (*presi*),
and canals and trenches for distributing irrigation streams (*scalladori*). Sometimes small craft used the canals that had already been constructed and a toll
was established, which partially recouped the expense. But in the short term,
the owners of the land had to pay for these costly installations, at the rate of
one or two ducats per *campo*, depending on whether the land was cultivated,
and whether it bore vineyards or only trees. If a landowner was unable to pay
his contribution when it fell due, half of his property was exacted in payment,
which indicates that the debt per *campo* was not insignificant. The *campo* varies
from one region to another but was generally reckoned at a little over one third
of a hectare.

The strength of the plains: Andalusia. Some plains, such as the Roman Campagna, have a long and chequered history. More commonly the fortunes of the
plains were less troubled. Or perhaps they seem so to us because we know less
about them. All the same there have been, between Roman times and our own,
considerable variations in the occupation and exploitation of land in lower
Tunisia, where there is abundant evidence of antique splendour. The same can
be said of lower Syria or Macedonia, deserted for centuries and only revived
since 1922, or the amazing Camargue, which continues to surprise us. These
great plains represent the essential agricultural history of the Mediterranean, the
last, the most difficult, and the most magnificent of its successes – that is if one
does not look too closely at the high cost in human terms of reclaiming them
from the marshes.

The most dazzling example of such success is that of the plains of lower
Andalusia. In the sixteenth century this was one of the richest regions of the
Mediterranean. Between the ancient Castilian shelf to the north and the forbid-

i. The Bay of Kotor, one of many magnificent anchorages on the Adriatic coast.

ii. *St. Blaize Presenting
a Maquette of the City of
Ragusa,* by Nicola
Bozidareviz. Like Genoa
and Venice, the prosperous
Adriatic port of Ragusa
was a self-governing
republic. Detail from the
altarpiece in the Dominican
church, Dubrovnik.

iii. *Following page:* Cultivated
fields on the lagoon
of Venice.

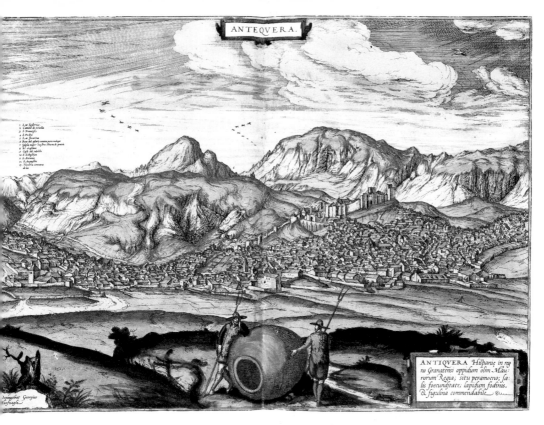

23. View of Antequera in Andalusia, the Cordillera behind the town.
From *Civitates Orbis Terrarum*.

ding mountains that form the Baetic Cordillera to the south, roll the gently undulating Andalusian plains with their meadows, sometimes, in the west, reminiscent of the fields of Flanders, their vineyards and vast olive orchards. Like all the other plains, they were conquered only gradually. In early Roman times, all the lower Guadalquivir was a marsh. But Andalusia, or Baetica, was fairly rapidly to become the heart of Roman Spain, a garden of towns that soon became too brilliant and overpopulated.

For the wealth of towns is the opposite of the wealth of plains. They specialize in a few products that bring profit, and depend in part on foreign goods for their daily bread. The Andalusian towns exported oil, grapes, wine, cloth, and manufactured goods and lived off North African wheat. Whoever owned the wheat had the towns more or less at his mercy. The Vandals, with their complicity, seized control of the wheat in the fifth century. When Byzantium chased them out in the next century, Andalusia fell under its power. Later it offered no resistance to the conquering Arabs.

Every time it was 'conquered', Andalusia became the jewel in the new crown. It was the centre of an expanding Moslem Spain, which did not reach much of the northern part of the Iberian peninsula, but spread over North Africa, with whose coastline, uncouth population, and turbulent history it was closely identified. In this garden of towns, there were two great metropolises: Córdoba and later Seville. Córdoba was the centre of learning for all Spain, and the entire Western world, whether Christian or Moslem, and both towns were capitals of art and centres of civilization.

Hundreds of years later, in the sixteenth century, this pre-eminence was still marked. And yet it has taken a long time to heal the scars caused by the Christian Reconquest in the thirteenth century. It had created in Andalusia, especially to the south, many desert regions which colonization, first military then pacific, had only gradually reclaimed. In the sixteenth century, the long labour of reclamation was still going on. But even so Andulasia was still a splendid land: 'granary, orchard, wine-cellar and cowshed of Spain', the object of the ritual praise of Venetian ambassadors in their *Relazioni*. To the blessings of its soil the sixteenth century added another gift: America was given to Seville in 1503 for almost two centuries. America, or rather the *Casa de la Contratación*, the fleets that sailed to the West Indies and those that brought back silver from Mexico or Peru, the trading colonies overseas, thriving and active. All this was given to Seville exclusively as a legal monopoly. Why? In the first place so that the profitable trade could be more jealously controlled – the rulers' chief consideration. Secondly because the route to America depended on the trade winds and Seville stood at the gateway of the trade winds. But behind this singular good fortune did there not also lie the weight of a town in a privileged position, so well served by the boats going down the Guadalquivir and by the famous carts pulled by four oxen? It was the great wine- and oil-producing plain that in part accounted for Seville's trade. It was for wine and oil from its slopes that the northern ships came from Brittany, England, Zeeland, and Holland, and not merely for salt from San Lucar – much prized for salting cod – and the produce of the Indies.

Andalusia's wealth encouraged – not to say forced – her to look outwards. In the sixteenth century, Seville and the Andalusian hinterland, still half-Moslem and hardly half-Christian, were engaged in sending their men to settle whole areas of Spanish America. These areas still bear the mark of their origins. Carlos Pereyra has described it perfectly. Spain sent all her sons down to this southern region opening onto the sea.

There is little room for doubt: the land improvement schemes of the plains could only be financed by an influx of big profits from trade, long-term and large-scale trade. And that, in concrete terms, meant the proximity of a big trading city with openings to the outside world and a stock of capital – one that could afford to carry the risks and responsibilities of the undertaking. And it is precisely in the regions near big cities – Venice, Milan, Florence – that all the sixteenth-century improvement schemes we have mentioned have been situated. Similarly, under the influence of Algiers, towards 1580, a thriving agriculture was set up in the Mitidja. It may have been short-lived, for the plain had not at

24. A route of transhumance: on the road from Roncesvalles to Pamplona in Navarre.

that stage totally eliminated the unhealthy swamps, but it began to produce for the expanding town and the luxurious houses of the Turkish and renegade corsairs – at a cost in human life we can only surmise – livestock, milk and butter, beans, chick peas, lentils, melons, cucumbers, poultry, and pigeons. It provided the boats in the port with wax, leather and large quantities of silk. It had fields of wheat and barley; and Haëdo, who perhaps had not been to see it for himself, came to the conclusion that it must be a garden of Eden.

4 Transhumance and nomadism: two Mediterranean ways of life

We have left to the last a description of the multiple problems of transhumance and nomadism, the regular movement of men and flocks which is one of the most distinctive characteristics of the Mediterranean world. We cannot attempt a total explanation of these continual migrations without looking eastwards and southwards beyond the Mediterranean peninsulas and without bringing into our discussion the pastoral life of the vast desert regions, which is why this topic – one not easily identified with any geographical region – has been postponed until now.

25. Below Mount Olympus. The sheep are leaving for the plain.

Transhumance. There are several kinds of transhumance: geographers distinguish between at least two, possibly three.

In the first place there is 'normal' transhumance: sheep-farmers and shepherds are in this case people from the lowlands; they live there but leave in summer, which is an unfavourable season for livestock in the plain. For these purposes, the mountains simply provide space. And even this space may often be the property of the lowlander although usually it is rented out to the mountain dweller. Arles in the sixteenth century, and possibly for four or five centuries previously, was the capital of large-scale summer transhumance, controlling the flocks of the Camargue and especially of the Crau, sending them every year along the drove roads of the Durance valley to the high pastures of the Oisans, the Dévoluy, the Vercors, and even to the Maurienne and Tarentaise. This was a real 'peasant capital': it was where the 'capitalists' lived – the top sheep-farmers were still known by that name in recent times – and it was where notaries drew up and registered contracts.

'Inverse' transhumance in the sixteenth century was, for example, the kind found in Spanish Navarre. Flocks and shepherds would come down from the highlands, the *euskari*. The lowlands served only for marketing purposes, that is when there was a market. This transhumance was a frantic rush down from the mountains in winter – cattle and men hurried to escape the cold of the mountains and flooded into lower Navarre like an invading army. All doors were padlocked against these unwelcome visitors, and every year saw a renewal of the eternal war between shepherd and peasant, first on the way down, until the flocks reached the open plains or the wide grazing lands of the Bardenas Reales, and then on the way back. The Bardenas Reales are a stony steppe on the borders of Aragon, where winter rains provide rather meagre grazing.

This inverse transhumance is also found in Calabria, where shepherds and flocks crowd into the narrow coastal strip during winter and spring. 'On the morning of Easter Day,' explains the Bishop of Catanzaro in June, 1549, 'some priests would go to the sea front, where there were many flocks, and were in the habit of celebrating mass on an altar made up of *formes* of cheese, afterwards blessing the cheese and the flocks and giving communion to the shepherds. The priest was then given all the cheese used to make the altar. I punished the priests who had held these services and . . . forbade any others under pain of terrible penalties to dare to hold them in the future'.

These are the two basic types of transhumance. There is also a third, less important, mixed type, which combines both summer and winter transhumance, where dwelling and starting point are halfway between summer and winter pastures. It is still practised in the Corsican Chataigneraie today.

But it is impossible to do justice to this complex phenomenon by rigid classification. Transhumance implies all sorts of conditions, physical, human, and historical. In the Mediterranean, in its simplest form, it is a vertical movement from the winter pastures of the plain to the summer pastures in the hills. It is a way of life combining the two levels, and at the same time a source of human migration.

Nomadism, an older way of life. Transhumance, so defined, is simply one form of the Mediterranean pastoral way of life, alternating between the grazing lands of the plains and the mountain pastures; it is a regulated and on the whole peaceful form, the result of a long period of evolution. Transhumance even in its most disruptive forms only concerns a specialized population: the shepherds. It implies a division of labour, a settled form of agriculture with crops to maintain, fixed dwellings, and villages. The villages may lose a part of their population according to the season, either to the plains or the mountains. Many documents of the sixteenth century mention these half-empty mountain villages, where only women, children, and old men remain.

Nomadism, on the contrary, involves the whole community and moves it long distances: people, animals, and even dwellings. But unlike transhumance, it has never been a way of dealing with enormous flocks of sheep. Even its largest flocks are scattered over a vast area, sometimes in very small groups. Today nomadism – which no longer exists around the Mediterranean in its residual state, it is true – consists of the knot of about ten people who might be seen round a fire at nightfall in one of the outer suburbs of Beirut; or at harvest time in Algeria, a few camels, sheep and donkeys, two or three horses, some women dressed in red, and a few black goat-skin tents amid the stubble; or in the plain of Antalaya, in Pamphylia to the south of Taurus, about twenty tents, sometimes, but not often arranged in a horse shoe, the relic of a tradition which is slowly disappearing.

Transhumance and nomadism seem to be activities dating from different ages. Is nomadism really an older way of life? Under our own eyes, throughout the desert and semi-desert zone that surrounds the south Mediterranean and continues into central Asia and beyond, the sedentarization policies of present-day governments have converted the old nomadism into a modified pastoral way of life (in the Sahara and Tripolitania, in Syria, in Turkey, and Iran), a way of life that is really transhumance, a division of labour. So the chronological order seems probable. One might add that in the context of the mountain regions of the Mediterranean, it looks as if inverse transhumance was practised earlier than what geographers call 'normal' transhumance.

This classification – nomadism, inverse transhumance, so-called normal transhumance – seems convincing. But things never happen as simply as an *a priori* model would suggest. The past has been richer in catastrophes and brutal revolutions than in slow evolution. Unfortunately catastrophes in these areas are less well-known than in the political arena.

In fact, when pastoral structures are studied in detail, inverse transhumance and normal transhumance often seem to operate simultaneously. In Haute-Provence in the fifteenth and sixteenth centuries farmers from the upper regions (the richest and most numerous) and from the lower used the same pastures. In these conditions it is the system of property owning alone that distinguishes the two kinds of transhumance. This leads us out of the geographical context into the social context of property owning and even into politics. For the movement of flocks offered fiscal resources which no state could ignore, which it would hasten to organize and always protect. Between the Abruzzi and the Apulian Tavoliere, inverse transhumance was established as early as Roman times and explains the textile industries of Taranto. It survived under a fairly liberal system until 1442−1447, when Alfonso I of Aragon organized it on authoritarian lines, with privileged and compulsory drove roads, the *tratturi*, connecting tracks (*tratturelli*), resting pastures (*riposi*), and winter pastures, and, in addition, rules stipulating that wool or beasts had to be sold at Foggia and nowhere else, with payment exacted all along the line, naturally. Once this system was in place it changed little and was to be protected from the obstinate and regular encroachment along the routes by peasants, planting vines, olives and, in particular, wheat.

The wheat yield from fields fertilized by the passage of the flocks reached record figures of 1 to 20 or 1 to 30. This led to exciting 'candlestick' auctions at Naples between would-be purchasers. Big interests were at stake: those of the taxation system for which the Apulian customs duties were an 'irreplaceable jewel', those of the wool and meat merchants, and those of the big sheep-farmers who were increasingly becoming distinct from the mass of small farmers.

The same duality is found in the Vicenza region – the *Vicentino*. The unpublished work of a sixteenth-century scholar, Francesco Caldagno, describes it as a *habitatissimo* region, with no land uncultivated, a continuous garden sprinkled with big villages, almost towns, with their markets, commerce, and 'fine palaces'. It has everything: wood, which arrives in waggons or by water, and charcoal; the farmyards are stocked even with peacocks and 'turkey-cocks'. On the rivers and streams there are countless mills, sawmills, etc. In the irrigated meadows, thousands and even 'hundreds of thousands' of animals graze. Calves, kids, and lambs are abundant, and in summer this entire animal population is sent 'alli paschi della montagna'. This was normal transhumance, which always stirred up trouble with the mountain dwellers about the letting and use of the high pastures; so there were quarrels with the Grisons about the 'Mandriole', a mountain rented by the *Vicentini*, which is hardly surprising. The men of Grisons had to drive their stock to the southern Alps and towards Venice, where they sometimes settled as butchers. But the Vicentino had its own mountain people, in the section of the Alps known as the *Sette Communi*, with their woodcutters, their trappers, and also their crops and their own flocks, notably at Galio which possessed between 50,000 and 60,000 sheep. In summer they stayed on the pastures of the *Sette Communi*, in autumn they went down and scattered over the countryside of the Vicentino, the Paduvano, the Polesino, the Trivigiano, the Veronese, and even the Mantovano. This is proof that the vigorous pastoral economy arising from the Vicentino plains did not have the monopoly of the area available for grazing. Everyone had his share.

26. Sheep farming in Ecija, near Seville. From *Civitates Orbis Terrarum*.

Transhumance in Castile. Castilian transhumance is a good example upon which to test all our definitions. It has been described a hundred times. We are familiar with its conditions, its constraints, and its complexities.

We should immediately distinguish between 'long-distance transhumance' which can lead to treks of 800 kilometres, and short or very short-distance transhumance. We shall only be concerned here with the long-distance variety, which depended on the illustrious sheep-farming 'syndicate' of the *Mesta*, whose letters of privilege went back to 1273. As an eighteenth-century naturalist wrote, Spain has 'two species of sheep: the first kind, whose wool is ordinary, spend their lives in one place, do not change pastures, and return every night to the sheepfold; the others, which have fine wool, travel every year, and after spending summer in the mountains go down to the warm meadows of the southern parts of the kingdom, such as La Mancha, Extremadura, and Andalusia. This second species is known as the "itinerant sheep".' Like all distinctions this is only approximate; the term 'itinerant sheep' should really be restricted to those that travelled, their precious fleeces smirched with red clay in the winter, to the 'utmost extremities' of Castile along the main roads, the *cañadas*, on which there were a dozen royal tolls.

Any transhumance presupposes complicated internal and external structures and weighty institutions. In the case of Castilian wool, it involved towns and markets like Segovia; Genoese businessmen who bought up wool in advance and, like the Florentines, possessed vats where the fleeces could be washed, not to mention the Castilian agents for these big merchants, the transporters of the bales of wool, the fleets that sailed from Bilbao for Flanders (controlled by the Consulate of Burgos), or the consignments sent off to Alicante or Málaga, destined for Italy; or even, to take an everyday detail, the indispensable salt which had to be bought and transported to the grazing lands for the flocks. It is impossible to explain Castilian transhumance outside this wide context, of which it was both product and prisoner.

Overall comparisons and cartography. The analysis of any example, whether important or not, seems to lead to similar conclusions.

1. All the cases studied in any detail show that transhumance is markedly institutionalized, protected by safeguards, rules, and privileges, and somewhat outside society, as is shown by the situation of the shepherds, who are always a race apart. Some studies, relating to southern Germany it is true, underline this 'untouchable', outcast aspect of the shepherd, and this in itself is revealing. And the admirable description by Marie Mauron of the lives of the migrating shepherds of present-day Provence takes the reader into a totally separate world and civilization.

Obviously precautions on behalf of or against transhumance may vary from region to region, but they are always there. Around Arles, in the Crau, some of the regulations were abused to the advantage of 'foreign flocks'; the municipal council deliberated the question in 1633 and authorized the captain of the watch to organize the necessary inspections and to levy a special tax to reimburse himself. Similarly in Aragon, pastoral life was governed by a Mesta with its privileges like that of Castile, but so far its archives have not tempted a historian.

2. Secondly, all transhumance is the result of a demanding agricultural situation which is unable either to support the total weight of a pastoral economy or to forgo the advantages it brings, and which therefore offloads its burdens according to local possibilities and the seasons, to either the lowland or the mountain pastures. It is this situation that determines the separation between the shepherds and peasants. In the case of Castilian transhumance we have noted the dominant role of the North and its entrenched peasant farmers. In the Vicentino we should think of the *paese habitatissimo* of the lowlands. And under our very eyes, in North Africa and Turkey or in Iran, we have the example of a rise in population and advances in agriculture breaking up a formerly pastoral way of life. What is happening today happened in the past too.

3. The only way to see beyond a series of particular instances is to project all known cases of transhumance on to a map of the whole Mediterranean region. This is possible for our own period, and was done in 1938 by Elli Müller. For the past, we would have to reconstruct such a map from successive fragments. The transhumance routes – about 15 metres wide – bear different names in different regions: *cañadas* in Castile, *camis ramaders* in the Eastern Pyrenees, *drayes* or *drailles* in Languedoc, *carraïres* in Provence, *tratturi* in Italy, *trazzere* in Sicily, *drumul oilor* in Romania. The remaining traces of this network indicate an overall geography whose message is clear. In the Mediterranean region in the sixteenth century, transhumance was confined above all to the Iberian peninsula, the South of France, and Italy. In the other peninsulas, the Balkans, Anatolia, North Africa, it was submerged by the predominance of nomadism or semi-nomadism. Only some parts of the Mediterranean possessed a sufficiently rich agriculture, large population, and vigorous economy to have been able to contain pastoral life within strict boundaries.

Outside this area everything becomes more complicated. But the skein of contradictions is not explained so much by geography, which is important of course, as by historical precedent.

Dromedaries and camels: the Arab and Turk invasions. History provides some far-reaching explanations. To the east and to the south the Mediterranean suffered two invasions, in fact two series of prolonged upheavals that altered everything: the Arab invasions which began in the seventh century and the Turkish invasions which began in the eleventh. The latter, coming from the 'cold deserts' of Central Asia, accompanied or reinforced the spread of the camel; the former, coming from the 'warm deserts' of Arabia, were aided, if not explained, by the spread of the dromedary.

27, 28. Camel and dromedary.
Above: Camel suckling her calf.
Eighth-century drawing from
Endere. *British Museum.*
Right: Sixteenth-century silver-gilt
table decoration of a dromedary.
Museum of Applied Arts, Budapest

The two beasts of burden differ from each other in spite of obvious similarities and possible confusion. The West persisted in confusing them, not without some excuse: Savary in his *Dictionnaire de Commerce* (1759) defined the dromedary as 'a double camel', which is certainly not the case. They are two quite different animals: the camel, originating in Bactria, is unaffected by cold or height; the dromedary, from Arabia, is an animal of the sandy deserts and warm zones. It is practically useless for climbing mountain paths or withstanding low temperatures. Even during the cool nights of the Sahara or Arabian deserts its master takes care to have its head sheltered under the canvas of the tent. Hybrids obtained by crossing camels and dromedaries in Turkestan towards the tenth century, played only a local role.

The ecology of the two animals is of special importance. A fairly large frontier zone separates their respective habitats, stretching between a line running along the southern edge of the Zagros and the Taurus (which is the decisive boundary) and a more hypothetical line running from the eastern tip of the Black Sea to the south of the Caspian Sea and the bend of the Indus. Very

29. *Opposite*: Camel market outside Cairo.

roughly, this zone is the Iranian plateau, cold during winter. The dromedary did penetrate into this zone, of course, and participated in the active caravans that in the sixteenth century centred around Ispahan. The dromedary even got as far as India and fetched prices there equal to or slightly higher than the horse, proof that it was something of a stranger there. In fact, neither in the plateaux of Anatolia nor the Iranian highlands was it really at home, and if the Arab conquest failed in Asia Minor, if it was never very assured in Persia, the reason is largely to be sought in the inferiority of the dromedary.

In any case, the two zones each have a separate history.

From Syria to the Maghreb the Arab invader disregarded the high lands. He left alone to their fate the old, dry mountains of the interior, facing the desert, which man had colonized early in time, such as the Aurès in North Africa; and he skirted the edge of the deserted mountains bordering the sea, where an abundant rainfall accounts for the thick forests of antiquity long respected by man. The forests, therefore, served as refuges for the native populations fleeing before the Arab conquerors. From the eighth to the eleventh century the Maronites and Druses settled in Lebanon; they cleared the ground and set up their states. In North Africa the Kabylias were settled from the tenth century, and particularly from the eleventh century, after the great push forward of the Hilalian nomads. 'Bedouinization' following the Arab conquest spread all over the land in between these mountains, whether early or lately settled, like a flood cutting off the mountain tops as islands. So an often archaic way of life was isolated in these high places, of which some characteristics (the ox as a pack animal, irrigated valley crops, grain stored in the attics, troglodyte dwellings where men and animals huddle together) have persisted almost to the present day.

In the mountains of Asia Minor, and to a lesser extent in the Balkans (where there were many exceptions), the invasion of the Turkish camel drovers meant violent upheavals, often without intermission, but of a completely different nature. An aggressive form of nomadism became established, wherever it was possible, up as far as the highest regions of the mountainous zones, above the upper limits of the forest. Perhaps it was because of 'what the term *yayla* – summer stay – means in the Turkish language and culture, where the notions of coolness, icy running water, and luxuriant pastures combine to form an image of Paradise'. As soon as spring arrives there is a great move to leave 'winter quarters, *pirelendi* . . . flea-ridden . . . and full of vermin', and above all to get away, to take to the road. A Turkish proverb, freely translated, says 'a *Yürük* [a nomad, walker] does not need to go anywhere, but needs to be moving', obeying traditional urges as much as, if not more than geographical necessities.

Nomadism in the Balkans, Anatolia, and North Africa as witnessed by western observers. It is, of course, an over-simplification, if a permissible and even necessary one, to explain everything in terms of invasions – the invasions of the seventh century and their consequences and those of the eleventh century and their consequences. The dromedary was already to be found in the Sahara and North Africa before the Arab invasions and the camel had reached Anatolia before the first Seldjuk advance. But the explanation is on the whole correct. The Mediterranean, where the hot and cold deserts cutting through the continental mass of the Ancient World come together, witnessed the surival – though attenuated and domesticated by the stubborn resistance of the peasantry – of the 'natural' nomadic way of life from Asia.

The survival of these ancient patterns of living completes the portrait of the Mediterranean peninsulas in the sixteenth century – the Balkans, Anatolia, North Africa – where transhumance, as defined by western sources, was pushed aside, driven to marginal areas, or considerably modified. This perspective is essential to the understanding of some of these 'mountain islands', independent but isolated, regarded with suspicion and having very little access to the outside world, such as the Jebel Druz, a self-governing enclave from which 'raids . . . on Moors, Turks and Arabs' were launched without warning, or Kabylia – the kingdom of Cuco as the Spanish texts call it – which had its independence but not freedom of movement. Its rulers sought in vain, notably at the little beach of Stora (near the present-day site of Philippeville), to make contact with the Spaniards. In North Africa the pattern was relatively simple. Every summer, the long-distance nomads would drive their flocks to the sea; at the approach of winter, they would return to the South and the Sahara. When the flocks returned to the lowlands they had left the previous autumn, these mountain people would pause for a while in their travels. There was nothing of the sort in Anatolia, as we have seen, nor in the Balkans, where transhumance and nomadism both intermingled and clashed. In the eastern part of the Peninsula, the Turkish government more or less deliberately installed colonies of nomads, the *Yürüks* of Asia Minor, in the hope of persuading them to adopt a sedentary way of life and thereby strengthen the Turkish military defences. And they were by no means the only nomads in the vast Balkan peninsula.

We might bear in mind that the learned word 'nomadism' does not appear in Littré's dictionary and that he only gives an example dated 1868 for 'transhumance'. The words 'transhumant' and 'transhumance' are of recent derivation: the Bloch-Wartburg dictionary (1960) gives the earliest use of the words as 1803. While the word 'trashumante' is found in the writing of Ignacio de Asso as early as 1780, it does not seem to be a very ancient word on the other side of the Pyrenees either, and *trashumancia* still does not exist. But this is straying from the argument.

Cycles spanning the centuries. Throughout the present chapter we have noted the extremely slow pattern of oscillation, whether from nomadism to transhumance or from mountain dwelling to settling in the plain. All these movements require hundreds of years to complete. While a plain is coming to life, overcoming its dangerous waters, organizing its roads and canals, one or two hundred years may pass by. Similarly from the time when a mountain region begins to lose its population until the moment when the economy of the plains has absorbed as many waves of immigration as it can use, another one or two centuries may have passed. These are processes which span the centuries and can only be grasped if the chronological field of study is extended as far as possible.

History usually only concerns itself with the crisis and high points of these slow movements. But these points are only reached after immense preparation and are followed by interminable consequences. It sometimes happens that in the course of their slow process these movements gradually change direction. One may find periods of construction and deterioration alternating indefinitely. A mountain region for instance may achieve everything it wants, only to lose it all or lose itself in its own success. When this history is not confined to mere accident or local particularity, these extremely slow-moving 'geographical' cycles, if one may use the term, tend to obey a very rough synchronism. So as the sixteenth century comes to an end, we find an explosion of liberation from the Mediterranean mountains which were in all cases overpopulated and subject to strain. The diffuse war which resulted was swallowed up in the interminable masked social warfare known as banditry – an ill-defined word if ever there was one. From the Alps to the Pyrenees, the Apennines or any other mountains, Moslem or Christian, a common destiny seems to emerge along these long mountain chains separated by the sea.

In this almost motionless framework, these slow-furling waves do not act in isolation; these variations of the general relations between man and his environment combine with other fluctuations, the sometimes lasting but usually short-term movements of the economy. All these movements are superimposed on one another. They all govern the life of man, which is never simple. And man cannot build without founding his actions, consciously or not, on their ebb and flow. In other words, geographical observation of long-term movements guides us towards history's slowest processes. Consciousness of this has directed our observation both in this and in following chapters.

2

The Heart of the Mediterranean: Seas and Coasts

LET US NOW leave the mainland and turn to the sea. Our journey will take us in turn to the different stretches of water within the Mediterranean, to the coastal strips, and to the islands. Our progress will be guided by these geographical units, but again our chief concern will be to select for analysis and comparison identical elements within them and by so doing to make the units themselves more intelligible.

1. The liquid plains of the sea

We shall of course have to measure these expanses of water in relation to human activity; their history would otherwise be incomprehensible if indeed it could be written at all.

Coastal navigation. The sea in the sixteenth century was an immensity of water: man's efforts had only conquered a few coastal margins, direct routes, and tiny ports of call. Great stretches of the sea were as empty as the Sahara. Shipping was active only along the coastline. Navigation in those days was a matter of following the shore line, just as in the earliest days of water transport, moving crab-wise from rock to rock, 'from promontories to islands and from islands to promontories'. This was *costeggiare*, avoiding the open sea – what Pierre Belon calls 'les campagnes de mer', 'the fields of the sea'. *Costeggiare*, to hug the shore, also means to go carefully. The Doge of Venice advises the Duke of Ferrara to go *costeggiando*. The opposite, to go straight ahead, is *s'engoulfer*, to plunge in, to go *a camin francese*. More precisely, according to the galley accounts of a Ragusan vessel, it was a matter of buying one's butter at Villefranche, vinegar at Nice, oil and bacon at Toulon. Or as a Portuguese chronicler puts it, travelling from one seaside inn to another, dining in one and supping in the next. Thomé Cano, the Sevilian, said of the Italians, 'They are not sailors of the high seas.' Sailing in the Adriatic, Pierre Lescalopier was 'amusing himself watching the mummers' on Mardi Gras in 1574 at Zara; two days later, on February 25th,

30. Detail from *The Rape of Helen by Paris*, by a follower of Fra Angelico. The roundship in the foreground has an after-castle but no forecastle.
National Gallery, London

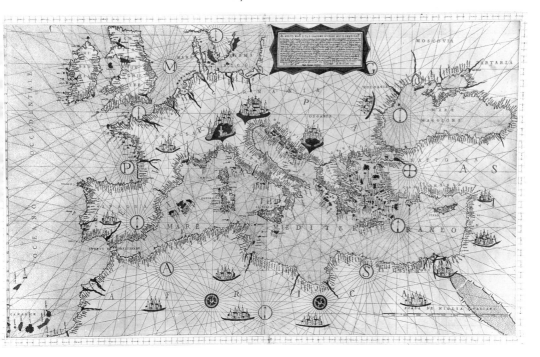

31. Sixteenth-century portulan of the Mediterranean by Paolo Forlani.
National Maritime Museum, Greenwich

he passed in front of St John of Malvasia and dined on the 26th at Spalato. This is how the princes and notables of this world would have travelled, from one coastal town to the next, taking time for festivities, visits, receptions, or rest while the crew was loading the boat or waiting for better weather. Marie de Medici took twenty-two days to get from Leghorn to Marseilles, (13th October – 3rd November, 1600). This is how even the fighting fleets travelled, doing battle only in sight of land. The word that springs to mind as one studies the itineraries or *arti di navigare* of the period, which are from beginning to end a description of the coastal route, is the humble word 'tramping'.

On exceptional occasions the ship might lose sight of the coast, if she was blown off course; or if she embarked on one of the three or four direct routes that had long been known and used. She might be going from Spain to Italy by the Balearics and the south of Sardinia, which was often called 'sailing by the islands'. Or from the straits of Messina or Malta, she might be aiming for Syria, by way of Cape Matapan and the coasts of Crete and Cyprus. Or she might take the direct route from Rhodes to Alexandria in Egypt, a swift crossing with a favourable wind and one which was undertaken in the Hellenic period. In 1550 Pierre Belon went 'straight through' from Rhodes to Alexandria. But these could hardly be called authentic high sea routes. Ships were not really taking to

32. Marble relief showing a man sailing a *corbita*, a small coastal vessel.
Carthage, Tunisia, A D 200. *British Museum*

the open sea when they sailed from one island to another, seeking shelter from the north wind on the east–west passage; or taking advantage on the north–south passage, on the Rhodes–Alexandria crossing which is after all quite short, of the wind which in one season blew from the north and in the other from the south. The venture might be repeated on shorter trips, crossing from one side of a bay to the other. But in January 1571, when a Venetian galleon, *Foscarini e Panighetto*, coming from Candia, ran into fog on the other side of Corfu and was obliged to advance blind with no land in sight, the crew was seized with despair.

The importance of the shore was such that the coastal route was scarcely different from a river. The owner of land on the coast might exact toll from all passing boats, which might be justified if the sum corresponded to a real service in the port. But this was not the case when the Dukes of Monaco and Savoy, both owners of an absurdly small portion of the coastline and most anxious therefore to have a share in the rich traffic passing under their noses, claimed the right to collect payment from all ships for the mere privilege of sailing past their land. Woe betide any sailing ship stopped by their galleys. The 2 per cent duty at Villefranche, as a result of French bad temper, almost turned into a diplomatic incident under Louis XIV. Nothing shows better than this the extent to which shipping was tied to the coast. The possession after the treaty of Cateau-Cambrésis of the *presidios* of Talamona, Orbetello, Porto-Ercole, and S. Stefano on the Tuscan coast, made it possible for Philip II to interrupt shipping between Genoa and Naples at will. The role played by La Goletta on the Barbary coast immediately becomes clear. A lookout post was sufficient to halt or impede the procession of coastbound ships.

If the practices of navigation on the high seas did not reach the Mediterranean, it was not for lack of technical competence. Mediterranean mariners knew how to handle the astrolabe and had used the lodestone for a long time; or could have if they had wanted to. Indeed the Italians had been the forerunners and instructors of the Iberians on the routes to the New World. Mediterranean – or 'Levantine' as they were known in Spain – ships yearly made the voyage from the inland sea to London or Antwerp. They were familiar with Atlantic waters. Ships from the Mediterranean even made direct crossings to the New World; the *Pèlerine* of Marseilles, for instance, which in 1531 sailed to Brazil and back only to be captured by Portuguese ships at Málaga at the end of the run. In November, 1586, the galleon of the Grand Duke of Tuscany on arriving at Alicante allowed herself to be chartered for the 'Indies'; she carried munitions for the fortress at Havana and brought back merchandise left behind by a vessel that had been unable to make the crossing. In 1610 two Tuscan vessels were unloading cargoes carried directly from the Indies. Ragusan ships may have rounded the Cape of Good Hope not long after Vasco da Gama; they certainly reached the New World.

If Mediterranean sailors persisted in using the old coastal routes, apart from the few direct crossings mentioned above, it was because the old ways fulfilled their needs and suited the complexities of its coastline; it was impossible to sail far in the Mediterranean without touching land. And a coastline always in sight is the navigator's best aid and surest compass. Even a low-lying coast is a protection against the sudden and violent Mediterranean winds, especially off-shore winds. When the *mistral* blows in the Gulf of Lions, the best course even today is to keep close to the coast and use the narrow strip of calmer water near the shore. So the lodestone was not essential to Mediterranean life. In 1538, unlike the Spanish galleys, the French galleys did not use it. Again they could have if they had wanted to.

Besides, sailing close to shore was more than a protection against the elements. A nearby port could also be a refuge from a pursuing corsair. In an emergency the ship could run aground and the crew escape by land. This was how Tavernier escaped a corsair in 1654 in the Gulf of Hyères; he even had the luck not to lose the ship in the incident.

'Tramping' also made it possible to take on cargo. It gave ample opportunity for bargaining, and for making the most of price differences. Every sailor, from captain to cabin-boy would have his bundle of merchandise on board, and merchants or their representatives would travel with their wares. The round trip, which could last several weeks or months, was a long succession of selling, buying, and exchanging, organized within a complicated itinerary. In the course of the voyage, the cargo would often have completely altered its nature. Amid

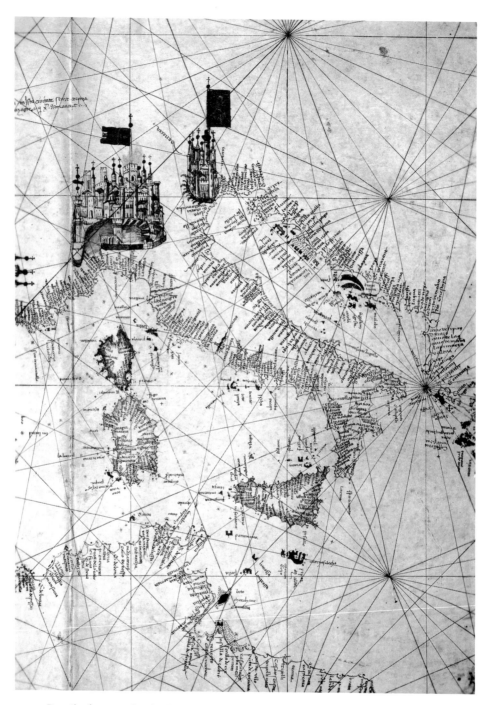

33. Detail of a portulan by Battista Beccari, 1613, showing the sovereign republics of Genoa and Venice. *Biblioteca Palatina, Parma*

34. Hispano-Moresque decoration (fifteenth century) of an
earthenware bowl showing the arms of Portugal on the mainsail of a
galleon running before the wind. *Victoria and Albert Museum*

the buying and selling, care was always taken to call at some port, such as
Leghorn, Genoa, or Venice, where it was possible to exchange spices, leather,
cotton, or coral for metal currency. Only the big specialized salt and grain ships
had any resemblance to the destination-conscious shipping of today. The others
were more like travelling bazaars. The calls at port were so many opportunities
for buying, selling, reselling, and exchanging goods, not to mention the other
pleasures of going ashore.

There was the further advantage of the almost daily renewal of supplies,
rations, water, and wood, which was the more necessary since the boats were of
small capacity and on board rations, even drinking water, quickly deteriorated.
Frequent stops were made to 'faire aiguade et lignade', 'to take on water and
wood', as Rabelais says.

The early days of Portuguese discovery. Finally, it is of some interest to watch
how the Portuguese, at the beginning of the fifteenth century, tackled the
immense problem of navigation on the high seas, in the Atlantic, which was

entirely new to them. At the time of the expedition against Ceuta in 1415, the inexperience of the Portuguese had been obvious. It was only with great difficulty that they had managed to master the currents of the Straits of Gibraltar. The chronicler de Barros says quite clearly that his compatriots were familiar with the declination and the astrolabe, but until 1415 'they had not been accustomed to venture far on the high seas'. One historian has even said of the early Portuguese discoverers, following the endless African coastline, that in the lifetime of Henry the Navigator they were still 'primarily timid and fearful coast-huggers, with no spirit of adventure' – Mediterranean sailors, in fact, despite their experience of the ocean. However, once the caravels had been perfected – the revolutionary ships developed in 1439–1440 to meet the difficulties encountered on the return voyage from Guinea of a head wind and contrary currents – they had to take to the open sea and make for the Azores in order to reach Lisbon, steering a vast, semi-circular course. After that they began to take to the sea in earnest and very quickly made up for lost time.

The narrow seas, home of history. The Mediterranean is not a single sea but a succession of small seas that communicate by means of wider or narrower entrances. In the two great east and west basins of the Mediterranean there is a series of highly individual narrow seas between the land masses, each with its own character, types of boat, customs and its own laws of history; and as a rule the narrowest seas are the richest in significance and historical value, as if man had found it easiest to impose himself on the Mediterranean in a small compass.

Even today, these seas still maintain their local life, with the picturesque survival of old sailing vessels and traditional fishing boats. At Sfax, in the Sea of the Syrtes, one can still see the *mahonnes* with their triangular sails, and the sponge fishers' boats, the *kamaki*, manned by men from the Kerkenna and Djerba islands who still fish with a trident, a vision from the past. Théophile Gautier had just passed Cape Malea and the Greek islands and calm waters were coming into sight when suddenly 'the horizon was filled with sails; schooners, brigs, caravels, argosies, crossing the blue water in all directions'. The narrow seas have kept their elusive enchantment to this day. The survival of these archaic forms of transport, of circuits that have been in existence for centuries, is in itself a subject for reflection. Their importance now as in the past lies in short trips, collecting small cargoes. Their security lies in the narrow and familiar compass in which they operate. Difficulties begin only when they embark on long voyages, if they have to leave their native sea and sail out past dangerous headlands. 'He who sails past Cape Malea,' says a Greek proverb, 'must forget his homeland.'

Linked by shipping routes which made large-scale trade possible, these narrow seas were far more important in the sixteenth century than the two great basins, the Ionian Sea to the east, and the western Mediterranean bounded by Sardinia, Corsica, Europe, and Africa. Both of these, particularly the former,

35. Different types of vessel to be met with in the Mediterranean in the sixteenth century. Note the emergence of the fully-rigged ship, top left and bottom right, the latter carrying the broadside that was to revolutionize naval warfare. From *Arte de Navegar* by Pedro de Medina, 1545.

were maritime Saharas; trading vessels would either skirt the edges of these expanses or cross as fast as they could.

The maritime activity of the Mediterranean was carried on at the edges of these two forbidding stretches, in the security of the narrow seas: to the east, the Black Sea, only partly Mediterranean; the Aegean or Archipelago Sea (in the sixteenth century even in French it was known by the Italian word *Arcipelago*); in the centre the Adriatic and the seas between Africa and Sicily which do not have a particular name; to the west the Tyrrhenian Sea, the true Sea of Italy, the 'Etruscan' sea between Sicily, Sardinia, Corsica and the west coast of Italy; and in the far west, between southern Spain and North Africa, another sea without a name, the 'Mediterranean Channel', which could have as its eastern boundary a line running from Cape Matifou near Algiers to Cape de la Nao, near Valencia, and which joins the Atlantic at the Straits of Gibraltar.

Even within these seas smaller areas can be distinguished, for there is hardly a bay in the Mediterranean that is not a miniature community, a complex world in itself.

The Black Sea, preserve of Constantinople. The far-off Black Sea, limit of Mediterranean shipping, was ringed round by wild lands, with a few exceptions, both uncivilized and de-civilized. Great mountains bordered it to the south and east, hostile mountains through which the roads made their difficult way from Persia, Armenia, and Mesopotamia to the great centre of Trebizond. To the north by contrast rolled the great Russian plains, a land of passage and nomadism, over which a jealous guard was still maintained by the Crimean Tartars in the sixteenth century. It was only in the following century that the Russian outlaws, the Cossacks, were to reach the shore of the sea and begin their piracy at the expense of the Turks. Already in the sixteenth century, the Muscovites were taking advantage of the winter to make 'courreries' towards its shores.

The Black Sea at this period, as indeed throughout its history, was an important economic region. In the first place there was the produce of its own shores: dried fish, the botargo and caviar of the 'Russian' rivers, the wood indispensable to the Turkish fleet, iron from Mingrelia, grain, and wool; the latter was collected at Varna and loaded along with hides on to the great Ragusan vessels; the grain was cornered by Constantinople. Secondly, there was the merchandise transported through the Black Sea; goods passing through to Central Asia and Persia and goods brought by caravan in transit to Constantinople and the West. Unfortunately we do not know a great deal about this two-way trade with the East in the sixteenth century. One has the impression that Constantinople monopolized the long-distance trade as well as the domestic trade of the Black Sea, acting as a screen between this Mediterranean extremity and the rest of the sea. Almost on its doorstep, the Black Sea was the supplying region without which the mighty capital could not survive, for it was only inadequately provided for by the tribute of the Balkans (mostly sheep) and the wheat, rice and beans

36. A typical merchantman of c.1400. Detail from *St. Nicholas Rebuking the Tempest* by Lorenzo di Bicci. *Ashmolean Museum, Oxford*

brought in by the fleets of Alexandria, along with spices and drugs. Pierre Belon mentions the butter that was carried from Mingrelia to Constantinople 'in the freshly flayed and undressed hides of oxen and cows', probably on board one of the innumerable Greek *caramusalis* that plied the Black Sea, although they were better suited to the short journeys in the Archipelago than to this dangerous sea, which was often rough and shrouded in fog. In October, 1575, a single storm sank a hundred of these little ships laden with grain.

In the sixteenth century the Black Sea was attached to Constantinople, just as in former times it had been the preserve of Miletus, of Athens, and after 1265 of the Italians and Genoese who installed themselves at Tana and Kaffa in the protected site in the south of the Crimea, sheltered by the mountains of the peninsula from the peoples of the northern steppe; they also settled in Constantinople (only leaving in 1453 and then not altogether), and were only dislodged from their Crimean ports by the Turks later on, in the last quarter of the fifteenth century. Kaffa was taken in 1479. There followed a major realignment of the land routes leading to the sea. They no longer went to the Crimea but to Constantinople instead. In the Moldavian lands the routes leading to Kilia and Cetatea Alba were replaced by the great trade route towards Galatz which thereafter tapped the trade of the Danube and, beyond it, that of Poland. From then on the Black Sea became the recognized granary of the enormous Turkish capital.

The Black Sea was the terminus not only of the roads that met at Trebizond or Sinope, but also of what is generally known as the silk route. Now it seems fairly clear that this route was interrupted from the fourteenth century on. The trade that had made it rich turned towards Persia. Turkestan certainly suffered from the change. Meanwhile, in the middle of the sixteenth century, the Russians advanced along the Volga. The khanate of Kazan, an eastern parallel to the kingdom of Granada, enriched by the caravan traffic and long coveted by the Russians, fell into their hands half-ruined as a result of troubles it is difficult to assess, which may or may not have followed the interruption of the Turkestan route. Ivan the Terrible took Astrakhan in 1556. This time the door was shut and bolted, in spite of the Turkish attempt of 1569–1570, the great unknown event of history.

The Archipelago, Venetian and Genoese. The Archipelago, 'the most hospitable sea of the globe', is a succession of barren islands and even poorer coasts. This too can only be understood in connection with a great town. In classical times it was the parade ground of Athens. Later it became the basis of Byzantine sea-power, which through its control of this sea was able to preserve the Aegean and then drive out Islam which had installed itself briefly in Crete in the ninth century. Through this sea too, communication with the West by the seas of Greece and Sicily and the routes of the Adriatic, was safeguarded, before Venice in turn rose to greatness.

Centuries passed, and the Archipelago became Venetian and Genoese. The two rival cities divided between them its principal islands. They installed upon them their patricians, guardians of the empire, landowners, planters, merchants too, in fact colonial aristocracies which remained separate from the Orthodox populations. These might become 'Latinized' in their habits, but would never be assimilated to the foreign invader. It was the usual story, and it ended with the mutual solidarity of the colonial settlers. When Venice supplanted Genoa in Cyprus in 1479, the planters of both colonial powers came to an agreement without too much difficulty: an obvious and inevitable case of class discipline.

In the Archipelago, the Latins defended their positions with greater ease and, above all, efficiency than they had in the Black Sea, with means that were for a long time superior to those of the attacker. However Negropont (Euboea) was captured in 1479; Rhodes fell in 1522; Chios was occupied in 1566 without a shot fired; Cyprus after an easy landing and two sieges, at Nicosia and Famagusta, in 1570–1572; and Crete in 1669, after a twenty-five-year war.

But the struggle for the Archipelago was by no means confined to a series of pitched battles. It also took the everyday form of a social war. More than once the Greek 'natives' betrayed their masters, at Cyprus and later at Crete. The Archipelago collaborated in the Turkish victory, and even before that victory Greek sailors had been tempted by employment in the fleet of the Grand Turk, whose crews often came from the Archipelago. The Cretans were perhaps the readiest to join the fleet of the Grand Signior at the beginning of each summer for the campaign that was about to begin. The recruiters would find them in the taverns of Pera, near the Arsenal; this was over a century before Crete fell into Turkish hands.

Constantinople could also offer the Greeks, besides employment in its armies, the profits of Black Sea and Egyptian voyages. In the gigantic task of supplying the capital, there was a place for the grain-bearing *caïques* and *caramusalis*, for the *gerbe* carrying horses and wood, indeed for all the Greek sailing vessels of the Archipelago. To all this could be added the attraction of religion: Constantinople was the Rome of the Orthodox Church.

And in the first decades of the sixteenth century there began a fresh phase of Greek expansion over the whole of the Mediterranean. The career of the Barbarossas, sailors from Lesbos converted to Islam, who settled first in Djerba then at Djidjelli, and provided transport for Spanish Moslems who wanted to leave the Peninsula, later becoming corsairs and, finally, after 1518, rulers of Algiers – this whole episode was not an accident. Neither was the career of Dragut, another Greek whom we find in the 1540s on the Tunisian coast and in 1556 installed at Tripoli in Barbary, in place of the Knights of Malta whom the Turks had expelled five years earlier.

Between Tunisia and Sicily. It will be difficult to denote with precision the role played by the ill-defined sea between Africa and Sicily, with its deep waters full of fish, its reefs of coral and sponges, and its islands, often uninhabited because they are so small. The essential axis of this sea is north–south, from Sicily to Africa. Ships travelling from east to west, from the Levant to the Atlantic, passed through, but this traffic was generally diverted to the north towards the main route passing through the Straits of Messina. Moreover, in the Sicily–Africa sector, this traffic did not have the frequency of the north–south currents.

These currents have dictated its history, making the whole complex shift sometimes to the south, sometimes to the north, with the tide of events. The whole region was Moslem with the Aghlabids, and so, from 827, when the conquest began, to 1071, when Palermo was recaptured, a citadel of Islam; then it was Norman, or on the way to being so from the eleventh century, for the Norman advance from Naples to Sicily did not stop at the reconquest of the island; it spread southwards by war, privateering, trade, and even emigration to the African territories. The Angevins and Aragonese were later to continue this policy dictated by proximity. Several times they attacked the African coast; levied tribute from the emirs of Tunis; held Djerba from 1284 to 1335. Meanwhile Christian merchants settled everywhere, particularly in the *souks* of Tunis and Tripoli, and obtained privilege upon privilege. Christian soldiers, and in particular the Catalan mercenary, later to be master of Sicily (the Sicilian Vespers took place in 1282), found adventures in Africa almost as profitable as in the East. As early as the twelfth century Catalan sailors were frequenting the coral reefs of Tabarka.

Political circles in Palermo and Messina were, even in the sixteenth century, continually suggesting projects of African conquest to the vanity and colonial ambitions of the viceroys of Spanish Sicily: first to Juan de la Vega, later to the Duke of Medina Celi, later again to Marcantonio Colonna. These projects translated the dimly felt necessity of uniting the shores and islands of this intermediary region, of bringing together Sicily's wheat, cheese, and barrels of tunny fish, and oil from Djerba, leather, wax, and wool from the southern lands, and the gold dust and black slaves of the Sahara trade; the need to control the whole maritime complex and ensure the policing of the coasts, the security of the tunny-boats and the safe fishing of the Barbary coral reefs by fishermen from Trapani, half-Catalans whose boats though poorly armed did not hesitate to attack the vessels of the Barbary corsairs in the sixteenth century; and finally the need to protect from the corsairs the *caricatori* of Sicilian wheat which were often threatened from the south, for piracy here as elsewhere often tended to re-establish a natural balance which had been disturbed by history.

It is customary when discussing Sicily to keep looking to the North, towards Naples, and to regard their two histories as fundamentally opposed, the rise of Naples leading to the decline of Palermo and vice versa. It is even more important to emphasize its links with North Africa, that is the value of this maritime world which our imperfect knowledge or lack of attention has left without a name.

The Mediterranean 'Channel'. The most westerly part of the Mediterranean Sea is an independent, narrow passage between the land masses, easily accessible to man, the Mediterranean 'Channel' as one geographer, René Lespès, has called it. It is a separate world, lying between the Straits of Gibraltar to the west and an eastern limit running from Cape Caxine to Cape de la Nao, or even from Valencia to Algiers. The east–west passage is never easy for shipping; to sail eastwards is to enter the great stretch of the western Mediterranean; to go westwards is to come to the even vaster expanse of the Atlantic, by way of the Straits which are themselves dangerous because of frequent fog, powerful currents, reefs, and sandbanks along the shores. All straits, like projecting headlands, cause an alteration in currents and winds. Here it is particularly marked and the passage is always a complicated operation.

By contrast the north–south journey is comparatively easy. The sea does not act as a barrier between the two great continental masses of Spain and North Africa; but rather as a river which unites more than it divides, making a single world of North and South, a 'bi-continent', as Gilberto Freyre has called it.

Like the corridor between Sicily and Africa, this channel was one of the conquests of Islam in the Middle Ages; a late conquest – in the tenth century – at the time when the caliphate of Córdoba was reaching the peak of its short-

Sicily and Tunisia cut the Mediterranean in two

lived glory. The success of the Ummayyads ensured that wheat, men, and mercenaries would be brought over from the Maghreb, and that the produce of the Andalusian cities would be exported in return. The free, or at any rate easy, access to this strip of water meant that the centre of Andalusian maritime life passed from Almeria, with its bustling shipyards, vessels, and silklooms, to Seville, where Mediterranean shipping concentrated in the eleventh century. It brought so much wealth that the port on the Guadalquivir soon began to rival in splendour the old continental capital, Córdoba.

Similarly, Moslem supremacy in the Mediterranean led to the rise or expansion of great sea-towns on the African coast: Bougie, Algiers, and Oran, the last two founded in the tenth century. And twice, the 'African Andalusia', under the Almoravids and then the Almohads, rescued the real Andalusia from Christian pressure, in the eleventh and twelfth centuries.

Right up to the end of Islam's hold on the Iberian Peninsula – until the thirteenth century at least and after – the 'Channel' remained in Saracen hands from the approaches of Algarve in Portugal to Valencia and even the Balearics. Islam held this channel even longer than the Sicilian Mediterranean, well after Las Navas de Tolosa in 1212, at least until the capture of Ceuta by Dom João of Portugal and his sons in 1415. From that day the passage to Africa was open and the Moslem community left in Granada was condemned; only the long Castilian disputes prolonged its existence. When the war of Granada began again for the last act of the *Reconquista* in 1487, Ferdinand and Isabella used ships from Biscay to blockade its coast.

After the conquest the Christian victors were drawn into taking the southern coast of the Ibero-African channel, but their efforts lacked the conviction and coherence that would have best served Spanish interests. It was a tragedy for Spanish history that after the occupation of Melilla in 1497, of Mers-el-Kebir in 1505, of the Peñon de Velez in 1508, of Oran in 1509, of Mostaganem, Tlemcen, Ténès and the Peñon of Algiers in 1510, this new war of Granada was not pursued with more determination, that this thankless but vital undertaking was sacrificed to the mirage of Italy and the comparatively easy gains in America. Spain's inability, or unwillingness, to develop her initial success, which was perhaps too easy ('It looks,' wrote the royal secretary, Hernando de Zafra, to their Catholic Majesties in 1492, 'as if God wishes to give Your Highnesses these African Kingdoms.'), her failure to pursue the war on the other side of the Mediterranean is one of the great missed opportunities of history. As an essayist wrote, Spain, half-European, half-African, failed to carry out her geographical mission and for the first time in history, the Straits of Gibraltar 'became a political frontier'.

Along this frontier there was constant warfare, a sign that the essential links had been severed here as well as between Sicily and Africa. Crossing the channel had become difficult. This is easy to see in the case of supplying Oran, which was a precarious undertaking throughout the sixteenth century. From the great

37. Detail from *Virgin of the Navigators* by Alejo Fernandez, 1535, showing *conquistadores'* ships. *Alcazar, Seville*

'central station' of Málaga, the *proveedores* organized convoys and chartered ships and boats to send to the *presidio*. They generally sent them in winter, taking advantage of breaks in the weather long enough for the short crossing. Even so the corsairs managed to capture supply ships, which they would then, in the normal process of bargaining, offer to sell back at Cape Caxine. In 1563, when the *presidio* was besieged by troops from Algiers, the ships that ran the blockade were *balancelles* and brigantines from Valencia and Andalusia. These small boats were like those that 'in the old days', as an enquiry in 1565 says, used to sail from Cartagena, Cadiz, or Málaga carrying caps from Córdoba and cloth from Toledo to the North African ports: or like the fishing-boats which on the other side of Gibraltar continued to sail the Atlantic, manned by a race of sailors from Seville, San Lucar de Barrameda, or Puerto de Santa Maria, who would fish as far away as Mauritania, and on Sundays go ashore to hear mass in one of the Portuguese *presidios* on the Moroccan coast; or the little boats from Valencia that carried to Algiers rice, Spanish perfumes, and, despite the prohibitions, contraband merchandise.

At the end of the century this now-quiescent part of the sea was aroused abruptly by a dramatic challenge, but not from Spain's traditional rivals: the sailors of Marseilles who had always frequented the Barbary ports, or the sailors of Leghorn, new arrivals after 1575, who were attracted by Tunis and lingered there but who sometimes voyaged as far as Larache and the Moroccan Sous. The new element was the massive invasion by northern ships, especially after the 1590s. These foreigners had to pass through the Straits twice, on the way in and out. On the way out they were expected and a watch was kept for them. Did the Hollanders, as has been claimed, discover a new way of passing through the Straits, which they afterwards taught their pupils, the corsairs of Algiers? It is possible if not altogether certain. In any event, the Spaniards put a great deal of effort into keeping watch and even preventing ships from passing through, using galleys in the calm summer days and galleons in the stormy winter months.

38, 39. Details from the remarkable tapestries depicting Charles V's expedition against Tunis (1535), after a drawing by the Flemish artist J. G. Vermeyen who accompanied the Emperor. *Below:* The *Mar de Berveria* and Spain. *Opposite:* The sea between Genoa and Tunis, *Mar de Affrica* and *Mar de Italia. Prado, Madrid.*

From Cape St Vincent on the Portuguese coast to Cartagena and Valencia, and even as far as Mers-el-Kebir, Ceuta, and Tangier, to Larache, which was occupied on 20th March, 1610, and La Mamora, occupied in August, 1614, we must imagine these lookout posts, alerts, patrols, and battles, often with no glory attached, which persisted until the eighteenth century. The rulers of Spain, her sailors, and advisers were always dreaming of a final solution: to install on Gibraltar itself reinforced cannons which would be sure to hit the ships; to fortify the little island of Perejil off Ceuta; or on the advice of the mad and brilliant adventurer in the service of Spain, the Englishman Anthony Sherley, to take Mogador and Agadir, and thereby hold Morocco, the Catholic King becoming 'absoluto señor de la Berberia' – and this in 1622!

But the struggle was never resolved. The enemy, English, Dutch, or Algerian, would pass through the Straits by stealth, taking advantage of a calm night in winter, or by force, seldom leaving a ship in the hands of the adversary, more often giving the patrol ships a battering with his superior vessels and artillery. An unspectacular or at any rate little-known war, this great Mediterranean drama was fought out at the very gateway to the sea, almost outside its waters. We shall have more to say about it.

The Tyrrhenian Sea. The vast Tyrrhenian Sea – the 'channels of Corsica and Sardinia', as it is called in the sixteenth-century documents – open to neighbouring civilizations and bordered by rich and populous lands, could not fail to have an eventful history.

Earliest times show an area divided among the Etruscans who ruled Tuscany, the cities of the Greek Empire and Sicily, the separate world of Marseilles and its empire, and finally the Carthaginians, who had settled in western Sicily and on the coasts of Sardinia and Corsica, where there were also Etruscan settlements. Roughly speaking the Etruscans controlled the central area; the others its extremities: the Greeks of the South held the route to the Levant; the Carthaginians the route which went from Panormos (Palermo) to Africa by way of Drepanon (Trapani); and lastly the Greeks of Marseilles the route linking the Etruscan sea to the West, just at the point where ships have to wait for favourable winds to cross the Gulf of Lions on the way to Spain.

This early situation already shows what were to be the permanent features of the Tyrrhenian: the value of the central 'lake' and the importance of the gateways to it. It gives some indication of the reasons why this sea, too vast and open, could never be under the control of one single power, economy, or civilization. Except under the levelling hegemony of Rome, no navy ever maintained a position of supremacy in the sea, neither the Vandals whom Byzantium brought to heel, nor the Saracen fleets since Italy eluded them in the end, neither the Normans nor the Angevins, the former meeting opposition from Byzantium, the latter from both Islam and the Catalans. And Pisa found herself up against the competition of Genoa.

In the sixteenth century, the first place belonged to Genoa, mistress of Corsica. But this position of supremacy had its weaknesses: Genoa was increasingly relying on foreign ships for transport, the first sign of decline. In addition she found herself faced with the Spaniards, who had captured several strong positions in the Tyrrhenian Sea. The trail had been blazed by the Aragonese, who had seized Sicily in 1282 and then in 1325, despite prolonged Genoese resistance, Sardinia, which they needed for communication with Sicily. Catalan expansion – and this was one of its original features – progressed due eastwards from the Balearics by way of Sardinia and Sicily. In these islands, the Catalans installed real maritime colonies, Alghero in Sardinia and Trapani in Sicily.

This expansion was victorious but exhausting. Coming late in time, it had to struggle to find a place for itself, combining piracy with shipping. Barcelona, where it had originated, gradually abdicated the leadership to Valencia, and it was the Valencians who led the successful conquest of the Kingdom of Naples under Alfonso the Magnanimous (1455). The Valencian act, however, was over almost as soon as it had begun, since the crown of Aragon was soon to fall under the control of Castile. At the time of the Italian wars, further change came to the Tyrrhenian: the Castilians replaced the Aragonese as soldiers and officials, both in Naples and in Sicily. From now on Spain with her galleys and *tercios* brought to bear on the Tyrrhenian the full weight of a maritime, military, continental power. It was not a merchant power, however. From the time of Charles V, and in spite of ancient commercial privileges, exports of Catalan cloth to Sicily and Sardinia actually declined. The Emperor, there as elsewhere neglectful of Spanish interests, let the Genoese merchants flood the market with their own textiles. Does this mean Genoa took her revenge and regained her supremacy?

The answer is not so simple. Towards 1550 Genoa forfeited some of her maritime activities, in the Tyrrhenian and elsewhere, to the Ragusans. With their merchantmen, the latter took over the transport of Sicilian wheat and salt and the long-distance voyages to Spain, the Atlantic, and the Levant. The Tyrrhenian Sea would almost have become a Ragusan lake if it had not been for the presence of Marseilles (at first modest, it was to become important after the 1570s), and the later rise of Leghorn, which was both a creation and a revival, for Leghorn represented both Pisa and Florence. It also represented the calculated policy of Cosimo de' Medici, who took an early interest in Genoese Corsica. Lastly through the wide passage between Sicily and Sardinia came the disturbing invasion of the Barbary corsairs, who often surprised the coastal areas, far to the north, of Savona, Genoa, Nice, and even Provence. The Tuscan barrage on Elba, at Portoferraio, gave warning of them more often than it stopped them.

This divided and composite sea, the Tyrrhenian, was too closely implicated in the general life of the Mediterranean to have a very distinct identity of its own. But by enabling it to live almost entirely off its own resources, its diversity gave it a certain autonomy. The grain that went to feed its towns and those

40. Detail from *The Harbour of Genoa* by Cristoforo Grassi, 1485.
Civico Museo Navale de Pegli, Genoa

regions that were either too densely populated or too pastoral to feed themselves, came from Sicily, and until 1550 from Provence – at least it was shipped from Provence, but often came from Burgundy or even further away. Salt came from Trapani; cheese from Sardinia; *vino greco* or *latino* from Naples; salted meat from Corsica; silk from Sicily or Calabria; fruits, almonds, and walnuts, as well as barrels of anchovy or tunny from Provence; iron from Elba; money and capital from either Florence or Genoa. The rest came from outside: leather, spices, dye-woods, wool, and before long salt from Ibiza.

Of these two sets of relationships, internal and external, the internal pattern was the richer. It explains the close intermingling of peoples, civilizations, languages, and arts. It also explains why this stretch of the sea, with its comparatively calm, sheltered waters should have been predominantly a region of small ships. In one year, from June, 1609 to June, 1610, the port of Leghorn alone received over 2500 barques and small vessels – an enormous figure. Only small ships could sail up the Tiber to Rome and its river port Ripa Grande, perhaps carrying the furniture and belongings of a bishop arriving at the Court of Rome, or the casks of *vino greco* that some church official had taken the care to have shipped from the Kingdom of Naples. At Genoa the customs registers divided incoming vessels into two classes, *venuta magna* and *venuta parva*, depending on whether the boats had a capacity of more or less than 150 *cantara* (about

30 tons). In a year the port of Genoa received a few dozen 'big' ships and one or two thousand 'small' ones: 47 big and 2283 small ships in 1586; 40 and 1921 in 1587; 107 and 1787 in 1605. (These figures, which underestimate the total number, relate only to ships paying entrance duty, from which the numerous ships carrying wheat, oil, and salt were exempt.)

However, small boats would not do for everything. If Carthage, in the 'Sea of Sicily', Marseilles at the extreme edge of the Tyrrhenian Sea, and, much later, Genoa were able to play such leading roles, it was because they had found a solution, as Vidal de La Blache has pointed out, to the great problem of sailing westward, exposed to the east wind, the dangerous *levante*, and the *mistral*. This required a different kind of ship. At the time of the Median wars both Carthage and Marseilles used for these voyages vessels that were rather heavier than those of other navies, hence their success. Centuries later, at the end of the Middle Ages, it was thanks to a technical innovation, the amplification of the lateen rig, that Genoa was able to find a more effective answer to the problem

41. The port of Leghorn. Marble inlay by C. Gaffuri after a design by J. Lipozzi. *Museo degli Argenti, Palazzo Pitti, Florence*

of long-distance shipping than her rivals. She gained so much from her discovery that from the end of the thirteenth century she was sending her sailors through the Straits of Gibraltar, as far as Flanders.

Genoa retained her preference for heavy ships. In the fifteenth century she was sending on the long run from Chios or Pera to Flanders ships and vessels of which some were over 1000 tons. On St Martin's day 1495, the two great 'Genoese ships', which arrived before the port of Baiae 'and there appeared and dropped anchor without entering the port', could have reversed the situation in favour of the French unaided according to Commynes, 'for these two ships alone would have sufficed to take Naples again; for the two ships were fine and tall, one being three thousand *botte* and the other two thousand five hundred *botte*; being called by name the Gallienne and the Espinole [a *botta* seems to have been about half a ton] . . .'. But neither of them intervened to the extent of moving from Baiae to the nearby city.

These details are more relevant to the central problem than they might seem. Power, supremacy and zones of influence in a maritime region may in the end be no more than technical superiority in details such as the sails, oars, helms, shape of hull, and tonnage of the ships.

The Adriatic. The Adriatic is perhaps the most unified of all the regions of the sea. It provides material by analogy for all the problems implied in a study of the Mediterranean as a whole.

Longer than it is wide, it is in effect a north–south passage. To the north it is bordered by the flat stretch of coastline from Pesaro and Rimini to the gulf of Trieste, where the plain of the Po meets the Mediterranean. To the west it is bounded by the Italian coast, often low and marshy, although only a short way inland, overlooking the *Sottovento*, runs the ridge of the Appenines from which a series of mountain buttes project towards the sea, one, the Monte Gargano, conspicuous by its oak forests. To the east it meets a string of rocky islands, the Dalmatian islands, immediately behind which rise the barren mountains of the Balkan land mass, the unending white wall of the Dinaric Alps, forming the edge of the great *karst* plateau behind the Dalmatian coast. Lastly, to the south, the Adriatic opens into the Ionian Sea through the Strait of Otranto between Cape Otranto on the Italian side and Cape Linguetta in Albania. The channel is narrow: the charts give its width as 72 kilometres. As early as the third century B.C. the *lemboi* could cross it in a day, under full sail with a favourable wind. So could the frigates that in the sixteenth century carried dispatches for the viceroy of Naples to the Italian coast from Corfu and Cephalonia and vice versa. A Spanish report indicates that 'dende Cabo de Otranto se veen las luces de la Velona'. From an aeroplane flying towards Athens, today's traveller can see simultaneously the Albanian coast and Corfu, Otranto, and the Gulf of Taranto; little apparently separates them.

This narrowing at the southern end is the essential characteristic of the basin:

it gives it unity. Control of that narrow passage amounted to control of the Adriatic. But the problem was to know which was the best vantage point for keeping watch over the straits. The key positions were not the active ports of Apulia, Brindisi, Otranto and Bari, which were occupied by Venice, twice but not for long, in 1495 and 1528, and which she thought of occupying again in 1580 for the sake of her trading interests. The Turks too held Otranto briefly, after the sack of 1480 which outraged Italian Christendom. But the gateway to the Adriatic could not be controlled from the Italian side.

In fact the key position was further south, on Corfu. And Venice had possessed the island since 1386. It was here that shipping concentrated, in the shelter of the east coast, poor but mountainous and therefore a protection. To enter or leave the Adriatic usually meant sailing past Corfu. This island, as a sententious text of the Senate (17th March, 1500) says, was the 'heart' of the Venetian State 'regarding shipping as much as any other aspect'. The Signoria therefore devoted much attention to it, sparing no expense in fortifying the island, spending such large sums of money, says a document of 1553, 'che chi potesse veder li conti si stupiria'. Fresne-Canaye, who was there in 1572, admired the huge fortress towering above the little Greek town that was the island's capital; its 700 pieces of artillery were said to have a firing range reaching to the Albanian coast. However, complaints flood from the pens of Venetian officials throughout the second half of the century: the impressive defences installed by the Signoria are out of date, incapable of preventing pirate raids; the mountains have no water, so cannot serve as a refuge, and the unfortunate population of Corfu has to take shelter as best it can in the fortress and even in the trenches, at risk of its life; the Turks are free to invade the deserted countryside and abandoned villages. The result was that Corfu, which had 40,000 inhabitants before the 'war of 1537', had only 19,000 in 1588. It is true that Venice relied principally for the island's defence on her galleons with their gilded prows that patrolled the Archipelago and the 'Gulf'.

In fact, with Corfu and her fleet, Venice controlled the entrance to the Adriatic and indeed the entire Adriatic. For the key position at the northern end of the sea was the city itself: the meeting point of sea routes and the continental land routes that in spite of the Alps linked central Europe with the Adriatic and the Levant. Venice's mission was to provide this link.

So she really was Queen of the Adriatic, of her 'gulf' as she called it. She would seize any ship when she pleased and police the sea with skill or brutality, depending on the circumstances. Trieste was an annoyance, so she demolished its saltworks in 1578. Ragusa was an annoyance, so she sent galleys into the waters of Ragusa Vecchia to pounce upon the grain ships supplying the city; she incited the allies of the Holy League against the city in 1571; in 1602 she gave support to the rebel Ragusan subjects on the island of Lagosta, famous for its fishing; she was still taking her rival's ships in 1629. Ancona was an annoyance, so she tried to wage a tariff war against her. Ferrara was an annoyance,

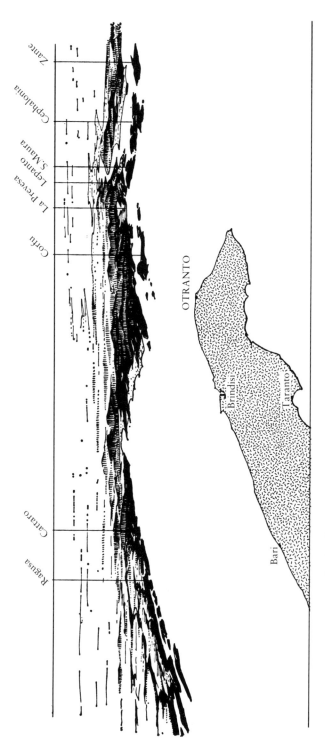

Corfu, lying opposite Otranto, commands the entrance to the Adriatic

Note the positions of the great naval encounters: La Prevesa, 1538; Lepanto, 1571. Sketch by J. Bertin.

42. View of Corfu. Woodcut by Reeuwic of Utrecht from *Peregrinationes*,
B. Breydenbach, Speyer, 1502.

so she contemplated seizing the port. The Turks were an annoyance; she did
not hesitate to attack them whenever she could do so without too much risk.

The golden rule, the 'ben noto principio', is quite explicit as laid down by
the *Cinque Savii alla Mercanzia*: 'ogni merce che entra nell' Adriatico o esce
dall' Adriatico deve toccar Venezia', all goods carried in the Adriatic must
pass through Venice, according to a typically urban policy of authoritarian
concentration of trade. This policy is quite clear regarding the saltworks of the
Adriatic which were almost all under Venice's thumb; or even salt imported
from further away. It was doubtless a necessary policy: in 1583–1585, for three
years, Venice's maritime export trade was worth 1,600,000 ducats 'dentro del
colfo fin a Corfu' and 600,000 outside it. Only the Signoria had the right to
grant exemptions if she saw fit, and she rarely saw fit. For her it was a way of
regulating traffic according to what she judged to be her interests, to defend her
fiscal system, her markets, her export outlets, her artisans, and her shipping.
Every action, even the apparently trivial seizure of two small boats from Trieste
carrying iron, was part of an overall calculated policy. In 1518, in order to
ensure her monopoly, Venice insisted that merchant vessels could not leave
Crete, Napoli di Romania, Corfu, or Dalmatia without leaving a deposit guaran-
teeing that their merchandise would be brought to Venice.

As for her more powerful neighbours, they raised their voices and invoked counter principles. The Spaniards had quarrels of precedence with the Republic and frequent disputes about captured vessels. 'For many years now this Signoria of Venice has claimed without any foundation that the gulf belongs to her', wrote Francisco de Vera, Philip II's ambassador at Venice, 'as if God had not created this part of the sea, like the rest, for the use of all'. The Venetians never tired of replying that they had bought the Adriatic not with their gold but with their blood, 'spilt so generously'.

The Signoria was of course unable to prevent her larger neighbours from opening doors and windows on to the Adriatic and using them. The Turks were at Valona in 1559, the Spanish in Naples; the Papacy at Ancona and later at Ferrara in 1598 and Urbino in 1631; the House of Austria was at Trieste. From 1570 Maximilian II was talking of asking Venice for 'negotium liberae navigationis'. This was an old demand previously formulated by the Papacy. In the turmoil preceding the battle of Agnadello, Julius II had proposed, in February, 1509, to absolve the Venetians if they would grant free shipping rights in

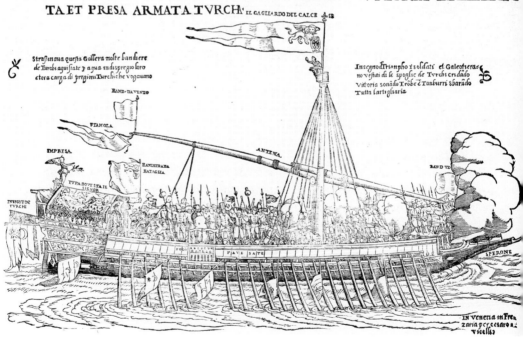

43. Venetian galley. Engraving by Cesare Vecellio. *National Maritime Museum, Greenwich*

44. Fort showing the Venetian lion, harbour of Heraklion, Crete.

the Adriatic to all subjects of the Church, and the same claims were untiringly advanced afterwards.

Finally there was Ragusa with her fleet of merchantmen. The tenacious republic of St Blaise played on its double status as protégée of the papacy and vassal of the Sultan. This neutral position was useful: in a hostile Mediterranean, Ragusan ships almost always passed unharmed. So Venice had Ancona and Ragusa for the present and Trieste for the distant future as enemies whom she could not afford to ignore. The two former took advantage of Venice's difficulties at the beginning of the century during the pepper and spice crisis. But Venice survived the crisis. And in any case her rivals were obliged to her for marine insurance, cash remittances, and transport. They often acted as her servants and could cause her little inconvenience except on short voyages from one side of the Adriatic to the other. This was minor traffic: iron from Trieste taken to be sold in Italy, western textiles, wool and wine from Apulia taken to Dalmatia without passing through Venice. The Venetian authorities tried to

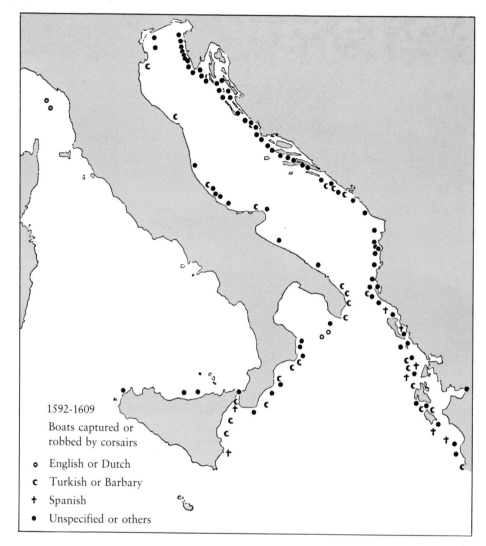

1592-1609

Boats captured or
robbed by corsairs

o   English or Dutch
c   Turkish or Barbary
+   Spanish
•   Unspecified or others

Origins of vessels captured or robbed in the Adriatic between 1592 and 1609

punish subjects of the Signoria who dealt in this 'black market'. But since they
frequently reiterated threats and punishments, it appears that these were neither
very effective nor dictated by extreme necessity.

After all these were only routine police actions. Venice was not only on the
lookout for smugglers and rivals; she was also on her guard against corsairs
attracted by the very abundance of trade in the Adriatic: wheat, fortified wines,
oil from Apulia and Romagna, meat, cheese from Dalmatia, not to mention the
ships carrying the rich long-distance exports and imports of the Signoria. Against

these pirates Venice waged a sporadic but never-ending war: driven from one area, the corsairs would reappear with monotonous and obstinate regularity in another. The fifteenth century had seen the last glorious years of Catalan privateering, based on Sicily. Venice had learned to arm a few big merchantmen against this if necessary, and to hunt down or at least neutralize the enemy. Retrospectively this privateering with big ships seems more spectacular than dangerous.

Turkish piracy was on the increase in the sixteenth century; it entered the Adriatic through the Albanian ports of Stapola, Valona, and Durazzo. It became a serious threat with the appearance of the Barbary corsairs and even more so with the arrival of Turkish armadas, preceded and followed by pirate ships. However we should not exaggerate this threat. On the whole, until the last quarter of the sixteenth century, Turks and Barbaresques made few incursions into the 'gulf' itself. It was not until after 1580 that there was a definite change in the Adriatic as elsewhere. A Venetian report of 1583 describes this change: for some time, and particularly since the Apulian coast has been fortified with watchtowers whose artillery is capable of protecting both the coast and boats seeking the shelter of their cannons, the corsairs have taken to carrying out their raids further north and have invaded the gulf. They have been making short and frequent forays and thus escaping the notice of the galleys.

To these hazards another, much worse, was gradually added. It had appeared before the middle of the century: this was the constant piracy of the Uskoks of Segna and Fiume. These towns, a rendezvous for Albanian and Slav adventurers, were only a stone's throw from Venice and her rich flow of traffic. These light-weight enemies were few in number it is true, about a thousand men, says the *provveditore* Bembo in 1598; 400 of them were in the pay of the Emperor and 600 'sono li venturieri che altro non fano che corseggiare et del bottino vivono'. A handful of men, but they were protected by the Emperor and were continually reinforced by the arrival of Balkan outlaws, 'per lo più del paese del Turco'. In any case there was little the Venetian ships could do against these tiny boats rowed at high speed, so light that they could use the shallowest channels between the islands where the galleys dared not follow them for fear of running aground. Such robbers were practically immune from any pursuer. It would be easier, says a Venetian senator, to stop the birds flying through the air with one's hands than to stop the Uskoks on the sea with galleys. If one of the latter should fall into a big ambush (600 men) it was lost; this was what happened on 17th May, 1587, at the mouth of the Narenta (Neretva). If a ship ran aground it fell a prey to them.

All these characteristics and the others from which one could easily compile a book on the Adriatic are a testimony and proof of the unity of the 'gulf', a unity that was as much cultural and economic as it was political, and whose predominant flavour was Italian. The gulf was Venetian, of course, but in the sixteenth century it was more than this, it was the sphere of a triumphant Italian

45. Uskoks attacking merchantmen around the island of Arbe near the Dalmatian coast.
Venetian print, 1598.

culture. The civilization of the peninsula wove a brilliant, concentrated web
along the east coast of the sea. This is not to suggest that Dalmatia was 'Italian'
in the sense that apologists of racial expansion would have understood it. The
entire sea-coast of the *Retroterra* is today inhabited by a Slav population. And
so it was in the sixteenth century in spite of superficial appearances. At Ragusa
at the time, Italianism was a commodity: Italian was the commercial language
of the entire Mediterranean. But fashion and snobbery entered into it as well.
Not only was it considered desirable that the sons of noble families should go
to study at Padua, and that the secretaries of the republic should be as fluent in
Italian as in Latin (the archives of Ragusa are almost all in Italian), but the
ruling families, who governed trade and politics, unhesitatingly invented Italian
genealogies for themselves. In fact, of course, these haughty *gentes* were
descended from some mountain Slav (the Italianized names betray their Slavonic
origins), and the coastal population continued to be drawn from the mountains.
Slavonic was the spoken language, the familiar tongue of the women and the
people, and even, after all, of the elite, since the registers of Ragusa frequently
record strict orders to speak only Italian at the assemblies of the Rectors; if an
order was necessary, clearly Slavonic was being spoken.
    On the basis of this knowledge it is certain that the Adriatic of the sixteenth

46. *Above:* Courtyard of the
Rector's Palace, Dubrovnik.

47. *Right:* The Sponza
Palace, Dubrovnik.

century was attracted by the sophisticated civilization of the nearby Peninsula, and drawn into its orbit. Ragusa was a town of Italian art; Michelozzo worked on the Palace of the Rectors. And yet of the towns of the *altra sponda*, it was the one least influenced by Venice, since except for a brief period it had always been independent. At Zara, Spalato, the island of Cherso and elsewhere, abundant documents record the names of schoolmasters, priests, notaries, businessmen, and even Jews who had come from the Peninsula, ambassadors and architects of the Italian civilization that was grafted on to this region.

But the Adriatic was not exclusively Italian. Strictly speaking it is not orientated north–south but north–west and south–east; it was the route to the Levant, with long-established trade and relations, open too as we shall see to the illnesses and epidemics of the East. Its civilization was profoundly complex. Here eastern influence could already be felt and Byzantium lived on; elements which combined to give the frontier zone its own originality. Its Catholicism was a fighting religion, faced with the threatening Orthodox world up in the mountains and with the immense Turkish peril. If, in spite of this mixed experience, Dalmatia remained loyal to Venice, as Lamansky noted long ago, it was because its loyalty lay basically beyond the Signoria, with Rome and the Catholic Church. Even a town like Ragusa, so awake to her own interests, firmly embedded in both the Orthodox and the Turkish world, surrounded that is by heretics and heathen, was remarkable for her fervent Catholicism. Her religious foundations would be as fascinating to investigate as her economic structure; interest played a part – and why not? – in some of her greatest religious outbursts. Her loyalty to Rome protected her on her threatened frontier, as was shown during the terrible crisis of 1571. And with the great economic withdrawal of the seventeenth century, after the splendours of a Renaissance which, like those of Venice and Bologna, developed late, her sons found magnificent careers in the Church, travelling all over the Christian world, even to France, merchants and bankers of the old days turned princes and servants of the Church.

Geography, politics, economics, civilization, and religion all combined to make the Adriatic a homogeneous world, extending beyond the coasts of the sea and into the Balkan continent to the final frontier between Latin and Greek worlds. On the other side, to the west, it was responsible for a subtle dividing line along the Italian peninsula. We are usually only conscious of the very marked opposition between northern and southern Italy. But the east–west division between Tyrrhenian and Levantine Italy, while less obvious, is no less real. Throughout the past it has acted as a hidden force. For a long time the east took the lead over the west of the peninsula; but it was the west, Florence and Rome, that produced the Renaissance, which would only reach Ferrara, Parma, Bologna, and Venice with the end of the sixteenth century. Economic advance followed a similar pendulum movement: when Venice was in decline, Genoa's fortunes rose; later Leghorn was to become the leading town of the peninsula. These swings from east to west, Adriatic to Tyrrhenian, were to determine the fate of Italy and of the whole Mediterranean on either side of the peninsula which acted as the beam of an enormous balance.

East and west of Sicily. The narrow seas are the active parts of the Mediterranean, teeming with ships and boats. But the vast empty stretches of water, the solitary wastes, are also part of the general structure of the sea.

In the sixteenth century the Mediterranean, which is so small by present-day standards of travel, contained enormous, dangerous and forbidden stretches, no-man's-lands separating different worlds. The Ionian Sea is the largest of these hostile areas, prolonging over the sea the desert of Libya and thus creating a double zone of emptiness, maritime and continental, separating East from West.

On the other side of the channel of Sicily another wide sea stretches from the Sicilian and Sardinian shores to the Balearics, Spain, and the Maghreb. This sea, which we might call the Sardinian Sea, is also difficult to cross with its inhospitable coasts and sudden blasts from the *noroît* and the *levante*. The east —west passage bristles with obstacles.

It is true that some of the earliest ships had overcome these obstacles and linked East with West; in the North, travelling from east to west and vice versa, they kept close to the Balkan coastline and the Neapolitan shore, using the Straits of Messina in preference to the Sicilian Channel, which was a more risky route. This was the Christian shipping route. The Islamic route, less convenient and less frequented, passed diagonally through the Sicilian Channel. This was the path taken by the Turkish armadas, from Valona to the shores of Naples and Sicily, and from Sicily to Bizerta or sometimes as far as Algiers. It was never as busy as the first.

To the south the obstacle was avoided by following the African coast, which, since there are reports of Christian privateers, must have been quite a busy area for shipping. The pirates' best course was to appear from the open sea and surprise ships coming from Egypt, Tripoli, Djerba, and sometimes from Algiers. At the beginning of the sixteenth century Venetian galleys were still operating the *muda* of the Barbary coast, which they reached by way of the coast of Sicily. At the end of the century, English and Dutch ships in their turn followed the coast of North Africa from Gibraltar to the Sicilian Channel, which they too crossed diagonally to reach the Sicilian coast and then the Greek coasts on the way to Crete, the Archipelago, and Syria. This was doubtless to avoid Spanish inspections at the Straits of Messina.

All these itineraries went the long way round the Ionian Sea and the Sea of Sardinia and avoided crossing them. They constituted the chief link between the eastern and western Mediterranean, or if one prefers between East and West, and are of capital importance to history. But the two halves of the sea, in spite of trading links and cultural exchanges, maintained their autonomy and their own spheres of influence. Genuine intermingling of populations was to be found only inside each region, and within these limits it defied all barriers of race, culture, or religion. All human links between different ends of the Mediterranean, by contrast, remained an adventure or at least a gamble.

For example, the Phoenicians long ago settled in Carthage and from there extended their influence westwards, triumphing over the long distances of the Mediterranean far west with their great ships. And the Ancient Greeks landed at Marseilles, which they too used as a base for expeditions. Similarly, the Byzantines for a while controlled Sicily, Italy, North Africa, and Baetica. The Arabs in the seventh, eighth, and ninth centuries seized North Africa, Spain, and Sicily. All these great victories were either short-lived or followed by the severing of connections between the advance parties and the country of origin: this was the fate of Marseilles, Carthage, and even of Moslem Spain which in the tenth and eleventh centuries received all its cultural nourishment from the East, its poets, doctors, professors, philosophers, magicians, and even its red-skirted dancers. Then it was cut off from the source and, thrown together with Berber Africa, began to evolve a western way of life. The men of the Maghreb who then travelled to the east, either as pilgrims or to study, were astonished to find themselves 'almost in a foreign world'. 'There is no Islam in the East,' exclaims one of them. This history was to repeat itself at the end of the sixteenth century, when the Africa of the Turkish Regencies freed itself from the Ottoman hand.

The double lesson of the Turkish and Spanish Empires. Every sea tends to live off itself, to organize the shipping circuits of its sailing vessels and small boats into an autonomous system. This was also true of the two great basins of the Mediterranean, east and west. They communicated and had links with each other but tended to organize themselves into closed circuits, notwithstanding a certain number of contacts, alliances, and relations of interdependence.

This is underlined only too clearly by sixteenth-century politics. What a marvellous geopolitical map one could draw of the western half of the Mediterranean between the middle of the fifteenth and the middle of the sixteenth century, with arrows showing the old and new directions of Spanish imperialism, the positions it seized and exploited in order to gain control of the western sea. For it did gain control. And after 1559, with the demobilization of the French fleet and the loosening of ties between the French king and the Sultan, the western sea became incontestably Spanish. The Moslems only held one coast, and that not the best, North Africa. They only held it by virtue of the corsairs, and their authority, kept in check by the defensive line of Spanish *presidios*, was constantly threatened from within and without. In 1535 Charles V was victorious against Tunis; in 1541 he was defeated, but only just, before Algiers; this setback could be rectified. At Madrid the *Consejo de Guerra* had permanently on its files a plan for attacking the city of the *re'īs*, which, one day, might be suddenly put into execution. It very nearly was in the time of Don John of Austria and again in 1601 with the surprise attempt by Gian Andrea Doria.

The Ionian Sea, the 'Sea of Crete', was by contrast the Ottoman sea. The Turks, masters of the coasts of the eastern Mediterranean after the occupation of Syria in 1516 and Egypt in 1517, found it necessary to gain control of the sea by creating a strong armed fleet.

These two different Mediterraneans were vehicles, one might almost say they were responsible for the twin empires. Zinkeisen has said as much of Turkey. Is it not also true of Spain? The two halves of the Mediterranean were in the sixteenth century two political zones under different banners. Is it therefore surprising that the great sea battles in the time of Ferdinand, Charles V, Sulaimān, and Philip II should repeatedly have taken place at the meeting point of the two seas, in the frontier zones? – Tripoli (1511, 1551), Djerba (1510, 1520, 1560), Tunis (1535, 1573, 1574), Bizerta (1573, 1574), Malta (1565), Lepanto (1571), Modon (1572), Coron (1534), Prevesa (1538).

Politics merely followed the outline of an underlying reality. These two Mediterraneans, commanded by warring rulers, were physically, economically, and culturally different from each other. Each was a separate historical zone. Physically the East had a more continental climate, with sharper extremes, worse droughts than the West, higher summer temperatures and therefore if that is possible more bare and desert lands. Could this be the reason for the advance that the Turkish fleet always seemed to have over its rivals? Should the swiftness of its attacks be attributed to the early fine weather in the Aegean? In a period when the rhythm of the seasons determined that of war, this could be important.

Beyond politics. The economic and cultural differences between the two zones became increasingly marked in the sixteenth century, while their respective positions were being reversed. Since the thirteenth century the East had gradually lost one by one her supremacy in various fields: the refinements of material civilization, technical advance, large industry, banking, and the supply of gold and silver. The sixteenth century saw her final defeat, in the course of an unprecedented economic upheaval when the opening up of the Atlantic destroyed the age-old privilege of the Levant, which for a time had been the sole repository of the riches of the 'Indies'. From that point on, every day saw a widening of the gap between the standard of living of the West, which was going through a revolution in technical and industrial progress, and the eastern world of low-cost living, where money coming from the West would automatically rise in value and acquire higher purchasing power.

But this difference in level in a way recreated the economic unity of the two seas, indeed it made it absolutely necessary, overcoming all barriers, including political ones, and using any means, including piracy. Differences in voltage determine electrical currents; the greater the difference, the greater the need for currents. For the easterners, it was essential to be associated with the superiority of the West, to share in its wealth whatever the price: from the West they wanted precious metals, in other words American silver, and they were obliged to follow the progress of European technical advance. In return, developing western industry had to find markets for its surplus production. These are big questions and we shall come back to them later. For it was the interaction of such pressing needs, such disturbances and restorations of economic balance, such necessary exchanges, which guided and indirectly determined the course of Mediterranean history.

48. Panel from a mosaic showing edible fish in the Mediterranean. Roman, AD 100.
British Museum

2 The mainland coastlines

The peoples of the sea. The Mediterranean waters are hardly more productive than the lands. The much vaunted *frutti di mare* are only moderately abundant; its fisheries provide only a modest yield, except in such rare spots as the lagoons of Comachio, the coasts of Tunis and of Andalusia (where there is tunny fishing). The Mediterranean, which is a deep sea, formed by geological collapse, has no shallow shelves, no continental platforms where submarine life could thrive

49. Red-figured fish plate. 350–330 BC. *British Museum*

down to a depth of 200 metres. Almost everywhere a narrow ridge of rocks or sand leads straight from the shore to the deep gulfs of the open sea. The water of the Mediterranean, which is geologically too old, is apparently, according to oceanographers, biologically exhausted. There are no long-distance fishing fleets except for coral, which is not for consumption. There is nothing here comparable to the long journeys of northern trawlers towards Newfoundland and Iceland or the North Sea fishing grounds. In February, 1605, when there was a shortage of fish, the Signoria of Genoa tried to limit consumption during Lent.

The scarcity of fish explains the scarcity of fishermen and consequently that

50. Octopus drying in the sun, Greece.

of sailors, which always acted as an unseen brake on the grand projects of Mediterranean powers. Between political dreams and reality there always lay this obstacle: the shortage of men capable of building, equipping, and handling the fleets. It is to this that we can attribute the difficult rise of Leghorn. It took a lifelong effort, that of Cosimo de' Medici, to provide the new port with the sailors she needed, and he had to search for them all over the Mediterranean.

A whole set of circumstances had to be united before the Turks could build their fleet, or the corsairs establish their base at Algiers. Equipping the galleys of all the armadas that were fighting in the Mediterranean was above all a problem of manpower. If it had not been for the slaves, prisoners of war, and convicts brought from their cells and chained to the oars, how could enough oarsmen have been found for the galleys? From the middle of the century on documents complain of the shortage of volunteers for the galleys, the *buonavoglia*; times are not hard enough for men to come forward and sell themselves as they used to, argues a Venetian admiral, Cristoforo da Canal in 1541. Venice even had to introduce a militia system of compulsory service in her Cretan galleys, and after 1542–1545 had to use *condannati* in her own galleys. There was not only a shortage of oarsmen; crews were equally hard to come by. The documents stress the incompetence and poor organization of Venice: if this or that was put right, if the pay was better, sailors from Venetian possessions would not leave to go and serve on foreign boats, on the Turkish armadas, or even those of the western sea. This may well be true. What is even more certain is that there were not enough sailors to man all the boats in the Mediterranean; and while they naturally went where conditions were best, no country in the sixteenth century could boast of having more men than it needed.

This is why at the end of the century the Mediterranean states and towns were enlisting or trying to enlist sailors from the North. In 1561 a Scottish Catholic brought a galley into the service of Spain. A document dating from after the Invincible Armada shows Philip II and his advisers actually trying to recruit sailors from England. At Leghorn it was a distinct feature of the policy of Ferdinand de' Medici to call on sailors not only from the Mediterranean but also from northern Europe. Algiers was to follow suit after the end of the sixteenth century.

From the better-equipped North the Mediterranean borrowed not only men but new techniques; for example the 'cog', or *Kogge*, a heavy cargo vessel, originally a single-masted square-rigged ship, which could brave the worst winter storms. It was the Basque pirates of Bayonne who first demonstrated its qualities to the Mediterraneans. It became the typical roundship both in the Baltic and the Mediterranean in the fourteenth and fifteenth centuries. In return, the voyage of the *Pierre de la Rochelle* to Danzig some hundred and fifty years later introduced the surprised Danzigers to a new type of ship, the carrack, incontestably a southern invention, derived from the cog but with an increased number of masts and multiple sails – a Mediterranean tradition – combining both square and lateen rig. It was a southern boat, but from the Atlantic regions, for it seems to have been the Biscay shipbuilders who developed it before it became the typical merchantman of the Atlantic and the Mediterranean in about 1485.

It looks as if the Atlantic led the way in developing technical progress in navigation. It was, however, the sailors of the Mediterranean who originally initiated direct and regular shipping between the inland sea and the Atlantic. They led the way in the fourteenth century, but were gradually overtaken as time went on. From the end of the fifteenth century until 1535, English ships in large numbers appeared in the Mediterranean and after an interruption, began to use the route again permanently in about 1572, preceding the Dutch convoys by a good fifteen years. After this it was inevitable that the Mediterraneans would finally lose, to the sailors from the North and the Atlantic, the struggle for world domination begun at the end of the fifteenth century.

Weaknesses of the maritime regions. If there were relatively few sailors in the Mediterranean it was because the coastal regions that traditionally produce sailors – and by their activity give the illusion of a Mediterranean whose warm waters breed a race of seafaring men – were few in number too: the Dalmatian coast; the Greek coasts and islands; the Syrian coast; the coast of Sicily (especially the west); some parts of the Neapolitan shore; the coast of Cape Corse; and finally the almost adjacent coastal regions of Genoa, Provence, Catalonia, Valencia, and Andalusia. In all a small portion of the Mediterranean coastline, and of these regions how many could boast the crowded streets and close-packed *campanili* of the Genoese Riviera?

Often the activity of a long seaboard can be accounted for by a few tiny but active ports some distance apart. The island of Mezzo, narrow and defenceless, off Ragusa, provided the port with most of the captains for her big merchant vessels. Perasto, at the end of the century, could only claim 4000 men *da fatti* (eligible to bear arms) but 50 ships both large and small. In fact, the *Perastani* were exempt from all taxes in return for policing the long gulf of Cattaro, whose entrance they guarded on behalf of Venice: thanks to them the *golfo* was *sicurissimo de mala gente.* In the Kingdom of Naples we may imagine the tireless but inconspicuous activity of a string of small ports, such as Salerno or Amalfi, whose names are famous, or on the Calabrian coast, S. Maffeo del Cilento, Amantea, Viestris, or Peschici. The last-named, a busy shipbuilding centre according to the Neopolitan documents of the *Sommaria*, was rarely idle, since it had the business of the Ragusan boatbuilders. Huge ships were launched from its beaches, one weighing 6000 *salme*, about 750 tons, in July, 1572.

Whether populous or not, these maritime provinces were overwhelmingly situated in the North, along the Mediterranean peninsulas; behind them there generally lay wooded mountains. The southern mountains because of the dry climate were poorly off for forests and therefore for shipyards. The woods near Bougie were an exception. But for them how could there have grown up in the thirteenth and fourteenth centuries a navy which was still very active in the time of Ibn Khaldūn? And cannot the decline of the maritime activities of the Syrian coast be attributed to the exhaustion of the forests of Lebanon? In Algiers not

51. *Opposite:* Detail from the main portal of San Marco, Venice, showing shipbuilding.

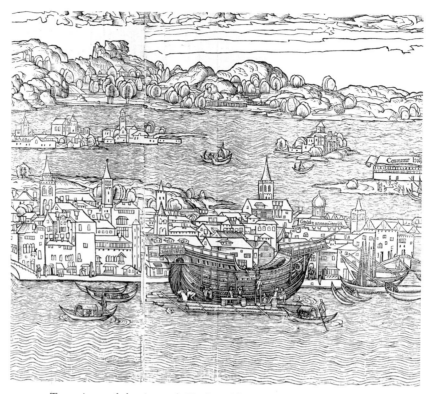

52, 53. Two views of the Arsenal, Venice. *Above:* Detail from a fifteenth-century view of Venice. Woodcut by Reeuwic of Utrecht from *Peregrinationes.* *Below:* View by Antonio di Natale. *Museo Correr, Venice*

only did the sailors come from overseas, so did, in spite of the use made of the forests behind Cherchel, the timber for building the boats; their oars were brought over from Marseilles.

In the case of all the prosperous seaports, we know either from documents (the arsenal accounts among others, when these have survived, as they have in Leghorn and Venice), from tradition, or from treatises on navigation, the source of the wood used for shipbuilding. Ragusa, which like Portugal specialized in the construction of merchantmen, took its timber from the oak forests of the Monte Gargano (also known as Sant'Angelo). This is in fact the reason, according to a treatise written in 1607, for the Ragusans' superiority over the Portuguese, who, if they had a Monte Sant'Angelo, would have the finest galleons in the world. The Turkish *caramusalis* were made out of great plane trees, an excellent wood which behaves particularly well in water. Galleys, which were expected to have a long life, required a range of different woods for the different parts of the boat: oak, pine, larch, ash, fir, beech, and walnut. The best oars were apparently made from the wood brought to Narbonne by way of the Aude and its canal. And one might quote the travelling diary of the Ragusan who crossed southern Italy between April and August, 1601, in search of timber to fell for the construction of a ship; or the documents concerning permission to fell trees in the forests of Tuscany, first given to and then withdrawn from the Spaniards; or the purchases made by Genoa, again in Tuscany, or by Barcelona at Naples, although Barcelona relied principally on the oaks and pines of the Catalan Pyrenees, which were renowned for galley-building.

But clearly what matters is the overall situation, not the exceptions. And that situation was one of scarcity of wood as can be deduced from a reading of the Venetian or Spanish documents, of marked deforestation in the western and central Mediterranean region, reported notably in Sicily and Naples (the very place where one of the great shipbuilding efforts for Philip II's navy was centred). Above all there was a shortage of oak, which was used to construct ships' hulls. After the end of the fifteenth century it was becoming rare and Venice passed a series of draconian measures to save what was left of her forests from destruction. The problem became even more pressing for the Signoria in the following century. Although Italy still possessed large reserves, there was a great deal of timber felling throughout the sixteenth century. We know that deforestation advanced quickly: the Monte Sant'Angelo for example was considered a precious exception. The Turks were better off, with the vast forests of the Black Sea and those of Marmara, in the gulf of Nicomedia (Izmit) almost opposite the arsenal of Constantinople. After Lepanto, Venice made strenuous representations to the Holy League that all the experienced seamen among the Turkish prisoners be put to death, in spite of the handsome sum of money they represented. For, she said, being short of neither timber nor money, the Turk would have no difficulty in building more ships as long as he could 'rihaver li homini'. Only men were indispensable. Venice's efforts do not seem to have been successful. Even if this policy had been adopted it is doubtful whether it would have had much effect.

Mediterranean sea powers gradually began to look elsewhere for what their own forests could not provide. In the sixteenth century northern timber was arriving in Seville in boatloads of planks and beams. For the building of the Invincible Armada, Philip II tried to buy, or at any rate had marked for felling, trees in Poland. Venice was finally obliged to countenance what regulations had previously strictly forbidden all her subjects to do: to buy abroad, not only timber, but ships' hulls which were then rigged at Venice, or even completed ships. Between 1590 and 1616, she received in this way eleven boats from Holland, seven from Patmos, four from the Black Sea, one from Constantinople, one from the Basque country, and one from the Straits of Gibraltar. There is no doubt that this timber crisis offers one major explanation for the development of techniques and maritime economies in the Mediterranean. It is not unconnected with the reduction in tonnages, the rising cost of construction, and the success of northern competitors. But other factors were also involved, such as price movements and the high cost of labour, for everything did not depend upon raw materials.

In any case, if maritime civilizations originally grew up near coastal mountains, it was not only because of their forests but also because they formed a natural barrier affording many sheltered places against the relentless north wind, the great enemy of Mediterranean shipping. 'Get under sail with a young south wind or an old north wind', says a proverb of the Aegean. A further explanation is that emigrants from the mountains would naturally go down to the sea, and the tempting waters might well be the best, or the only, way of reaching another part of the coast. So an association might grow up between a sea-going way of life and the mountain economy, which would then interact and complement each other, leading to the extraordinary economic combination of ploughed fields, market gardens, orchards, fishing, and sea-going. On the Dalmatian island of Mljet, a traveller reports that even today the men divide their time between farming and fishing, as they do in the other Dalmatian islands. The same is true of Pantelleria where in addition to the fishing, vines, and orchards, an excellent race of mules is bred. This is the traditional wisdom of the old Mediterranean way of life where the meagre resources of the land are added to the meagre resources of the sea. If it is disappearing today it rarely does so without provoking distress: the Greek fishermen of the Pelion region, 'increasingly drawn to the sea, have to give up their gardens and cottages and move their families to the harbour streets'. But once removed from the traditional balanced pattern of their former way of life, they swell the ranks of the sea poachers who fish with dynamite in spite of government prohibitions. For the sea alone is not rich enough to feed her fishermen.

Neither is the land, on these barren mountains, and this explains the considerable role played by the old rural villages in the economic development of the neighbouring coast. Overlooking the waters of Catalonia the white houses of the villages can be seen through the trees. It is the people of these villages who tend the terraced hillsides of the great massif and produce their horticultural miracles. There is often corresponding to the hill village a fishing village down by the sea, sometimes built out over the sea: Arénys de Mar below Arénys de Mount, Caldetes below Lievaneres, Cabrera below Cabrils. On the Genoese Riviera too the old villages up on the hill often have their fishing port, their *scala* down by the water, and throughout Italy, and not only Italy, there are hundreds of examples, with a continual coming and going of donkeys between the two levels. The seaside village is often more recent in date, an offshoot of the rural village with which it remains closely associated. Its existence is brought about by the economy of the coastal massifs, the terrifying poverty of their way of life, which even the combination of the two villages cannot transform into plenty. At Rosas, or at San Feliu de Guixols in Catalonia it was still possible quite recently (in 1938) to see food sold in the market in characteristically tiny quantities: a handful of vegetables, a quarter-chicken for example. In 1543, the inhabitants of Cassis, sailors and pirates if necessary, blamed poverty for forcing them 'to traffic on the sea and to catch fish, not without great risk and peril'. Hundreds of villages on the Mediterranean coast owe their existence to the poverty of the usually mountainous barren hinterland.

The big cities. Without Barcelona, and its craftsmen, Jewish merchants, even its soldier adventurers and the many resources of the Santa Maria del Mar quarter, the maritime expansion of the Catalan seaboard would have been incomprehensible. Such success required the intervention, discipline, and imperialism of the

54. Herd of cows by the sea, Gulf of Porto, Corsica.

55. Threshing floor by the sea, Sifnos, Greece.

big city. It was in the eleventh century that the Catalan seaboard first awoke to a *historically* visible maritime life. But its expansion only began two centuries later with the rise of Barcelona. Then for three hundred years the procession of ships from the little ports of the Catalan seaboard plied ceaselessly back and forth on the Barcelona 'beach', where sailing ships from the Balearics would also put in to harbour as well as boats from Valencia which was always something of a rival, Biscay whalers, and the constant flow of boats from Marseilles and Italy. But when Barcelona lost her independence, after the long struggle against John of Aragon, then twenty years later in 1502 suffered the equally grave loss of her Jewish community, her *juderia*, and finally when her capitalists gradually stopped putting their money into risky investments, preferring the regular income from the *Taula de Cambi* or investing in land near the city, then began the decline of the great merchant city and the Catalan seaboard dependent upon it. So great was its decline that Catalan trade practically disappeared from the Mediterranean and the shores of the county were left undefended when they were ravaged by French corsairs at the time of the wars between the Valois and the Habsburgs – and later by the equally dangerous Algerine corsairs, who all but settled in the wastes of the Ebro delta.

Marseilles, Genoa and Ragusa played similar predominant roles in the lives of the small ports surrounding them. There were even cases where the dependencies were not on the same coast as the metropolis, for example Venice's hold over the Istrian coast, the Dalmatian coast, and the distant Greek islands. The attraction of the big cities is the more understandable in that sailors in the Mediterranean have always been wanderers ready to migrate. In 1461, the Venetian Senate expressed anxiety at the shortage of crews and cabin boys and asked for details: the sailors 'go to Pisa . . . where they are well paid . . . to our loss and another's gain'. Many of these sailors left because they had debts to pay or heavy fines imposed by the *Cinque Savii* or the *Signor de nocte* – the night police of Venice.

As the result of a legal dispute in 1526, the accounts have survived of the ship *Santa Maria de Bogoña*, which sailed to the Atlantic, stayed for a while at Cadiz, and put in at Lisbon and the island of São Tomé before arriving at Santo Domingo with her cargo of Negro slaves. This takes us out of Mediterranean waters, but among the *marineros* and *grumetes* (cabin boys) on board her could be found sailors from Lipari, Sicily, Majorca, Genoa, Savona, some Greeks, and a seaman from Toulon – a boatload of adventurers.

The changing fortunes of maritime regions. This constant flow of migrations completes the picture of the maritime regions. Take once more the example of Catalonia. It was thanks to the teachings and techniques brought over by Italian immigrants from Genoa and Pisa after the eleventh century that Catalonia developed a thriving maritime economy, two hundred years before the glorious reign of Peter the Great, *Pere lo Gran*. History sooner or later takes back her gifts. By the sixteenth century the decline of Catalonia, already perceptible in the fifteenth, had become evident. Her shipping activity was reduced to sending a few boats to Marseilles or the Balearics. At the very end of the sixteenth century a few voyages began again between Barcelona and Alexandria. But until then activity was at such a standstill on the Catalan seaboard that when Philip II decided in the Grand Council of 1562 to build a great armed fleet, he was obliged to place orders in Italy. And in an effort to revive the arsenal of Barcelona he brought in experts from the boatyards of San Pier d'Arena, in Genoa.

3 The islands

The Mediterranean islands are more numerous and above all more important than is generally supposed. Some of the larger ones are miniature continents: Sardinia, Corsica, Sicily, Cyprus, Crete, and Rhodes. The smaller ones may combine with neighbouring archipelagos to form families of islands. Large or small, their significance lies in providing indispensable landfalls on the sea routes and affording stretches of comparatively calm water to which shipping is attracted, either between islands or between island and mainland coasts. To the east lies the Aegean archipelago, so scattered over the sea as to be inseparable from it; in the centre the group of islands between Sicily and Africa; in the north the Ionian and Dalmatian islands, which string out like a convoy of ships along the Balkan seaboard, in the sixteenth century flying the flag of St Mark. There are really two separate flotillas here: one in the Ionian Sea consisting of Zante, Cephalonia, Santa Maura, and Corfu; the other in the Adriatic, with the Dalmatian islands running from Meleda and Lagosta in the south to Quarnero, Veglia, and Cherso behind Istria in the north. Between the Ionian and Dalmatian convoys runs quite a long stretch of coastline including the inhospitable Albanian shore and the little territory of Ragusa. But taken all together, the islands provided a stopping route from Venice to Crete; from Crete a busy trade route linked Cyprus and Syria. These islands, running along the axis of her power, were Venice's stationary fleet.

The western groups of islands are equally important: near Sicily, Stromboli, the Egades, the Lipari islands; further north, the Tuscan archipelago where in the middle of the sixteenth century Cosimo de' Medici built the fortress of Portoferraio on the island of Elba; off the coast of Provence, the Iles d'Hyères and the Iles d'Or; further west, in the open stretch of the western Mediterranean, the Balearics, Majorca, Minorca, Ibiza – the salt island – and the scarcely accessible rock of Formentera. This group has always been of considerable importance: an entire shipping sector revolved around it.

Precarious lives. All islands have towns affected by the general life of the sea, and at the same time (if only because they handle imports and exports) looking inward to that world which the historian, preoccupied as he is with texts concerning political history, does not notice at first glance: the withdrawn and precarious way of life, the biology isolated as under a bell jar of which naturalists have long been aware. There is hardly an island that does not possess, alongside its human peculiarities, its animal and vegetable curiosities that are sooner or later revealed to the outside world. In his description of Cyprus which appeared in 1580, the Reverend Father Stefano (who claimed to be descended from the Royal House of Lusignan) describes 'the peculiar herbs' and 'perfumes' of the island: white *apium*, a sort of water-celery, which is eaten 'crystallized in sugar', *oldanum* which is used to make the liqueur of the same name, the tree known as the 'Cyprus tree' (black cypress), similar to the pomegranate tree, which flowers in clusters like the vine, and whose distilled leaves produce the orange dye that is used to colour the tails of gentlemen's horses, 'as is customarily seen there'. It is also surprising to find that cotton seeds were mixed with chopped straw as fodder for the animals. And what a wealth of medicinal herbs! Among the curious beasts there were 'wild cattle, donkeys, and boars', and the 'vine' birds, buntings, of which thousands of barrels were exported to Venice and Rome, pickled in vinegar.

But extraordinary fauna and flora can never be taken to indicate abundance. None of the islands was assured of the future. The great problem for all of them, never or only partly solved, was how to live off their own resources, off the soil, the orchards, the flocks, and if that was not possible, to look outwards. All the islands with a few exceptions (Sicily in particular) were lands of hunger. The extreme cases were the Venetian islands in the Levant, Corfu, Crete, or Cyprus, which were constantly threatened by famine in the second half of the century. It was a catastrophe when the *caramusalis* did not arrive on time, with their

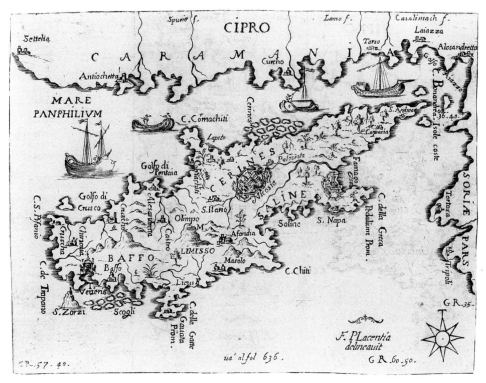

56. Seventeenth-century Venetian map of Cyprus.

providential cargoes of grain from Thrace, when the stocks of wheat and millet in the stores of the citadels had been exhausted. Indeed, a black market was organized around these Levantine islands, hence the endless prevarications of the officials reported in inquiries.

The situation was not as precarious as this everywhere. Particularly, and this may seem paradoxical, on the poorer and more backward islands, which had fewer inhabitants and above all were not exploited by crops grown for export. But the Balearics could hardly support their military or merchant towns, particularly since little progress had been made towards farming the land. The clearing of stones from the fields of Minorca in the plain behind Mahon, was not completed until the eighteenth century. They had to rely on cereal imports from Sicily and even North Africa. On Malta, too, food was short. In spite of the many privileges permitting the island to import wheat from both Sicily and France, Malta was always in difficulties, so much so that in the summer the galleys of the Knights would hold up grain ships coming from the Sicilian *caricatori*, exactly like the corsairs of Tripoli.

As well as the threat of famine there was also the risk from the sea, which in the mid-sixteenth century was more warlike than ever. The Balearics, Corsica, Sicily, and Sardinia, to take the islands we know best, were territories under

siege. They had constantly to be defended, watchtowers had to be built, fortifications erected, extended, and equipped with artillery, either pieces sent in from
outside or cast on the spot by the primitive methods of bell founders. And of
course garrisons and reinforcements had to be placed along the coast, as soon
as the fine weather arrived and with it the campaign season. It was not easy for
Spain to hold Sardinia, or even to be certain of an island as nearby as Minorca.
Charles V, after the sack of Mahon in 1535, envisaged, to forestall further
danger, nothing less than the evacuation of the entire population of Minorca to
the larger island, Majorca. The case of Elba, in the Tuscan archipelago, was
equally tragic. The island was brutally surprised in the sixteenth century by the
advance of the Barbary corsairs and became a maritime frontier under constant
enemy attack. Its coastal towns – the large villages along the sea front – fell into
abandon. The population had to flee to the mountains of the interior, until
Cosimo de' Medici undertook the fortification of Portoferraio in 1548.

On the paths of general history. A precarious, restricted, and threatened life,
such was the lot of the islands, their domestic life at any rate. But their external
life, the role they have played in the forefront of history, far exceeds what might
be expected from such poor territories. The events of history often lead to the
islands. Perhaps it would be more accurate to say that history has made use of
them. Take for example the role played by the islands as stages in the dissemination of crops: sugarcane, which was brought from India to Egypt, passed
from Egypt to Cyprus, becoming established there in the tenth century; from
Cyprus it soon reached Sicily in the eleventh century; from Sicily it was taken
west; Henry the Navigator had some brought from Sicily to send to Madeira,
which was the first 'sugar island' of the Atlantic; from Madeira, sugar growing
quickly moved to the Azores, the Canaries, the Cape Verde islands and beyond,
to America. The islands played a similar role in the dissemination of silkworms,
and generally in most cultural movements, some of which were extremely complicated. It was by way of Cyprus and the sumptuous court of the House of
Lusignan, that there came to the West, more slowly than the light of some stars
reaches the earth, the costumes of the ancient bygone China of the T'ang dynasty. The long pointed shoes and the hennins, which date a period of French
history so well that they immediately suggest the frivolous court of Charles VI
and the *Très Riches Heures* of the Duke of Berry, had been fashionable in China
in the fifth century. And this distant heritage was passed on to the West by the
kings of Cyprus.

We should not really be surprised. The islands lay on the paths of the
great sea routes and played a part in international relations. To their ordinary
day-to-day existence was added a chapter in the history of great events. Their
economies often suffered the impact of these events, since they could offer no
resistance to some demands. How many islands were invaded by foreign crops,
whose justification lay solely in their chance to reach Mediterranean or even

57. Genoese watchtower, Gulf of Porto, Corsica.

world markets? Grown for export only, these crops regularly threatened the equilibrium of the island's economy. Take the wheat-growing invasion of Sicily; until 1590 and even after, Sicily was the Canada or Argentina of the western countries of the Mediterranean. Chios produced mastic, both the resin and the drink; Cyprus, cotton, vines, and sugar; Crete and Corfu, wines; Djerba, olives. These single-crop economies were the result of foreign intervention, artificial and often harmful to what is expressed by the German term *Volkswirtschaft*.

At Cyprus this was to be proved in 1572 when the Turks captured the island from Venice. The wealth of the island under Venetian rule had been the vineyards, the cotton plantations, and the fields of sugarcane. But whose wealth? It had belonged to a Venetian and Genoese aristocracy whose sumptuous mansions can still be seen today in the old quarter of Nicosia; certainly not to the natives of the island, Orthodox Greeks. So the Turkish conquest unleashed a social revolution. We have a curious account of it from an English sailor in 1595. A Cypriot merchant had told him the history of the island, pointing out the ruined palaces of the former Genoese and Venetian noblemen, whom the Turks massacred as just retribution, according to our witness, for the extortionate demands they made on the peasants. Indeed, at the time of the invasion, the Venetians were abandoned by the Greeks both in the countryside and the towns. During the Turkish attack on Nicosia in 1570, 'the inhabitants, of all social conditions, . . . almost all remained sleeping in their houses'. It is true that the

58, 59. *Above:* View of Chios. From *Civitates Orbis Terrarum.*
Left: The mastic plant (see page 117). Dutch print, 1688.

departure of the Venetians was followed by a drop in exports of cotton, raw and spun alike, and by such a marked deterioration of the vineyards that Venice was able to arrange to buy back the precious leather flasks used for the manufacture of wine, as they were no longer of any use on the island. But this does not necessarily mean the decline of Cyprus. There is no evidence that Turkish rule led to a fall in living standards for the inhabitants of the island.

Crete and Corfu afford matter for similar reflections. Here, as in Cyprus, we must imagine a countryside converted by man for the cultivation of the vine, producing raisins and the wine known as malmsey. On Corfu, the vines spread from the hills and mountains to the plains, the *pianure*, which were easier to cultivate. They drove out the wheat, but in the exclusive production of one crop there is always the possibility of surplus production and a slump. On Crete vines were torn up on official orders in 1584, to cries of anger as may be imagined. The victims went so far as to declare that they would make 'no distinction between being subjects of Venice or of the Turks'. This 'colonial' economy evidently had its successes and failures. Many conditions had to be fulfilled before the system could work properly, bringing together vine growers, landowners, sailors, merchants, and distant customers. The wine and raisin trade had in fact long been established over a wide area. Even in England malmsey wine was known and appreciated as a luxury, the sixteenth-century equivalent of port today. 'He was so moved and dejected,' says Bandello of one of the characters in his *Novelle*, 'that she went to fetch him a glass of malmsey.'

A final example of monoculture is Djerba, off the southern coast of Tunisia. The Venetian islands were the wine islands; Djerba was the oil island. In circumstances far from clear, while mainland Tunisia was losing the groves of olive trees that were so plentiful in Roman times, Djerba succeeded in keeping hers. This preserved wealth meant that even in the sixteenth century the island was economically important. It had become an oasis of olive oil between Tunisia and Tripoli, which were in general, particularly in the South, rancid-butter countries. The island's oil was of excellent quality, cheap, and suitable for all uses, even the treatment of cloth and fabrics, an oil that was easy to export, as Leo Africanus remarked at the beginning of the century. After 1590 it was to Djerba that the English went for the oil that had previously been supplied to them by Spain.

As long as they did not impose too crippling a monoculture, however, these large-scale activities formed the vital wealth of the islands, if only because they ensured the returns necessary for their survival. They provided them with well-earned reputations. Ibiza was the salt island; the salt of Naxos was also famous, as was its wine 'both White and Claret'; Elba was the iron island. And there was Tabarka, the coral island, domain of the Lomellini, an island with several other resources: the exporting of grain and hides, and the ransoming of prisoners who took refuge there.

Emigration from the islands. But the commonest way in which the islands entered the life of the outside world was by emigration.

We need hardly dwell on the Greek migrations which affected the entire Archipelago, including the large island of Crete. But it is doubtful whether they were ever as important in the sixteenth century as the movements from the island of emigrants *par excellence*, Corsica. The population, too great for the island's resources, swarmed in all directions, and there can hardly have been an event in the Mediterranean in which a Corsican did not participate. There were even Corsicans at Genoa, the hated *Dominante*: one must take bread where one can find it. There were Corsicans at Venice. They were already to be found in the fifteenth century, working on the land of the Tuscan Maremma; in the sixteenth century the peasants of Niolo, who were being harassed by Genoa, went to colonize such fever-ridden lands in Italy and even Sardinia, where they often made their fortunes. Corsicans were numerous at Rome, where some of them were established as stock dealers and their boats frequented the Roman port on the Tiber, Civitavecchia and Leghorn. In Algiers there were hordes of Corsican immigrants, especially the *Capocorsini*.

Who were these Corsicans at Algiers? Some of them were prisoners. Others, sailors and merchants, did business in the port. More than one settled there among the richest renegades of the town: Hasan Corso was after all one of the 'kings' of Algiers. In about 1568, a Spanish report estimates that there were 6000 Corsican renegades out of a total renegade population of 10,000 in Algiers.

Other Corsicans were in Constantinople, Seville, and Valencia. But their favourite town, in the sixteenth century as today, was Marseilles, which must have been almost half-Corsican, at least round the docks, if the documents we have are anything to go by.

The Genoese rulers of the island cannot be either blamed for or absolved of this emigration. The obvious fact in the sixteenth century was that the Corsicans did not take kindly to Genoese rule. Whether or not this attitude was justified, it is quite unreasonable to attribute the exodus entirely to French intrigues and Valois gold. This is not to deny for a moment that there was a definite liaison between the island and France, or to doubt the overwhelming evidence of repeated journeys by French envoys and the dispatch of frigates, gunpowder and money to the island. France's policy towards Corsica was almost identical with that pursued more single-mindedly and with more resources, but less success, by Cosimo de' Medici. The point is – and it brings us back to our original subject – that if French policy succeeded, almost without trying, in stirring up the people of the Corsican mountains, it was less by virtue of any preconceived plans than because of the crucial link between a France that was rich in land and an island that was rich in men. France was open to Corsican emigration as the largest and most fruitful field for expansion, while Italy at the time was too populous itself and indeed regarded Corsica as a land to be colonized for its own use.

The peninsulas. The Mediterranean peninsulas are a set of independent land masses: the Iberian peninsula, Italy, the Balkan peninsula, Asia Minor, North Africa, the last apparently attached to the African continent, but in fact separated from it by the width of the Sahara. Between the peninsulas lie rather different intermediate regions: along the Gulf of Lions, Lower Languedoc and the lower Rhône valley; on the Adriatic, lower Emilia and the Venetias; further east, north of the Black Sea, the bare open lands that run from the Danube delta to the edge of the Caucasus; and lastly, in the south this time, the endless ribbon of blank coastline, where it is often difficult to land, stretching from southern Syria to Gabès and Djerba in Tunisia, the long barren front of a *foreign* world looking on to the Mediterranean.

Nonetheless, the peninsulas are the Mediterranean regions which are richest in men and in potential. They are key actors, who have always played leading roles, in turn gathering strength and then expending it. They are almost persons, to rephrase Michelet on France, but persons who may or may not be conscious of themselves. Their unity is obvious, but they do not have the coherence or self-confidence of say France under the Valois, nor the vehemence of its outbursts of political and national passion.

Nevertheless, there is strong evidence of Spanish nationalism. In 1559 it led to the debarring from high office of Philip II's non-Spanish advisers and inspired the much-repeated Spanish opinions of the Frenchmen of the day: unreliable, quarrelsome, argumentative, easily discouraged at the first setback, but impatient to wipe out a defeat or a concession. This Spanish nationalism was far from homogeneous or even widely expressed. It was only gradually, as the years of greatness piled up one after another, that it came into the open, found its themes, and was enticed by the mirage of the idea of empire. In this composite form nationalism became widespread, not in the reigns of Charles V and Philip II, who were its architects, but late in the seventeenth century, when the empire was already in decline, in the reign of the 'Planet' king, Philip IV, and his adviser, the Count Duke of Olivares, in the age of Velázquez, Lope de Vega, and Calderon.

There was no such coherence in Italy. And yet there too appeared an undeniable form of nationalism, or at any rate a pride in being Italian, in the sense that every Italian firmly believed that he belonged to the most civilized of societies with the most glorious of heritages. Was the present so unworthy either? 'From morning to night we hear that the New World was discovered by the Spanish and Portuguese, whereas it was we, the Italians, who showed them the way,' writes Bandello at the beginning of one of his *novelle*. And how can one ignore the many dreams of unity: the passionate appeals of Machiavelli; or Guicciardini's presentation of the years he had just lived through as a single pageant of Italian history? Rare as they are, these are unmistakable signs of feelings of national consciousness and unity.

Another and even more important sign (for national identity is not confined to politics) was the spread of the Tuscan language. Similarly the Castilian language spread over the whole Iberian peninsula in the sixteenth century, and became the language of literary expression used by Aragonese writers from the time of Charles V. It was in Castilian that an Aragonese nobleman, a contemporary of Philip II, kept his family record book.

The high barriers closing off the peninsulas have made each of them a marginal world with its own characteristics, flavours, and accents. Every time the political unity of a peninsula has been achieved, it has announced some momentous change. In ancient times the unification of Greece by the Macedonians and the unification of Italy round Rome had far-reaching consequences. At the beginning of the sixteenth century Ferdinand and Isabella set about forging the unity of Spain: it was to be an explosive force.

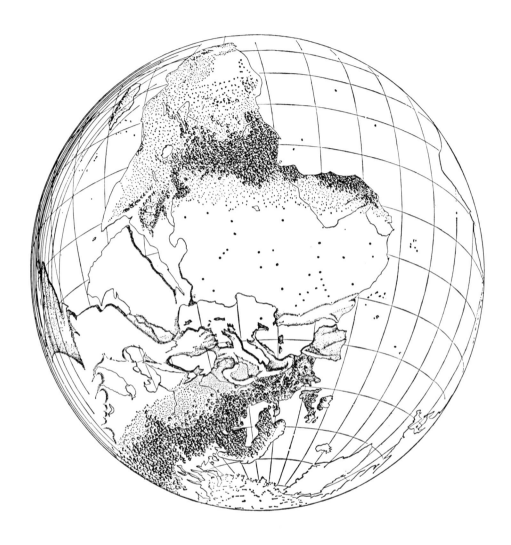

The Mediterranean and the rest of the world

Following the orientation of this map, rotating it as we go, we shall be looking in turn at each of the different world horizons of the Mediterranean: the Sahara, the Atlantic, the Indian Ocean, and Europe. The unusual orientation has been chosen to illustrate how the great Sahara desert dominates the sea, stretching from the shores of the Mediterranean to the tropical forests of Africa. The Mediterranean both acts as a frontier between these deserted lands and southern Europe (which reaches to the forests of the North) and, along with the Red Sea and the Persian Gulf punctuates them. The dotted area corresponds to the zones of early human settlement, emphasizing by contrast the emptiness of the mountainous peninsulas of the Mediterranean. Land and sea communications, whose routes and states leading in every direction the reader will imagine, created the movement in space which we have called the Greater Mediterranean. Map drawn by J. Bertin.

3

Boundaries: The Greater Mediterranean

THIS CHAPTER presents several difficulties. The reader however, may not immediately become aware of them. He is invited to undertake journeys that will lead him far away from the shores of the Mediterranean. He may be willing to make them. But this implies a willingness to accept what may seem to be an excessive extension of the field of study. To claim that there is a *global* Mediterranean which in the sixteenth century reached as far as the Azores and the New World, the Red Sea and the Persian Gulf, the Baltic and the loop of the Niger, may appear an unwarranted exaggeration of its boundaries.

It also disregards the conventional boundaries. Those drawn by a geographer are the most familiar and the most restrictive: for him the Mediterranean region stretches from the northern limit of the olive tree to the northern limit of the palm tree. The first olive tree on the way south marks the beginning of the Mediterranean region and the first compact palm grove the end. The geographical definition accords great importance to climate, which is undeniably a potent factor in the lives of men. But our Greater Mediterranean would disappear if we accepted these limits. Nor would we locate it by accepting the rather different boundaries allowed by the geologist and the biogeographer. They both consider the Mediterranean zone as a long ribbon, a mere linear feature on the earth's great crust; for the geologist it is the long belt stretching from the Atlantic to the Indian Ocean, a combination of tectonic fractures and recent foldings; for biogeographers, it is the narrow zone between certain parallels of latitude where certain plants and animals are typically found from the Azores to the distant Kashmir valley.

1. The Sahara, the second face of the Mediterranean

On three sides the Mediterranean touches the great chain of deserts stretching uninterrupted across the entire width of the Ancient World, from the Atlantic coast of the Sahara to northern China. On three sides: south of the Libyan coast lies the Sahara; east of the Anti-Lebanon lies the Syrian desert, close to 'one of the largest nomadic civilizations in the world'; north of the Black Sea stretch the south Russian steppes, the threshold of Central Asia. Along these vast fronts, an abundant caravan traffic entered into contact with Mediterranean trade, becoming both essential to it and in turn dependent on it. Contact was made not only at the important centres, like Egypt and Syria, through which all the fabulous trade of the Levant passed in the sixteenth century, but all along the desert frontiers. Oran, which the Spanish conquest of 1509 had virtually cut off from its hinterland, was still in mid-sixteenth century the centre of a trade in black slaves, small-scale but important enough to cause the local authorities some concern.

The Sahara: near and distant boundaries. The chain of deserts between the Atlantic and China is divided in two by the high Iranian plateaux: to the west lie the warm deserts; to the north and east the cold deserts. But there is a continuity between these barren spaces and their caravan traffic; in Anatolia and Iran, the camel simply replaces the dromedary of the central and western deserts.

Of these it is clearly the Sahara in the wide sense (the entire range of warm deserts as far as Iran and Arabia), that primarily concerns the Mediterranean. The route over the steppes of southern Russia leads to the great cold deserts of Central Asia, but reaches the Mediterranean as it were by the back door, only sporadically playing a leading role, for instance, in the thirteenth and fourteenth centuries, the period of the splendours of the 'Mongolian route'.

The Sahara, in the wide sense, African and Asian, is contained within two sets of boundaries, one close to, the other very far removed from the Mediterranean. A brief survey of these boundaries is the first step towards the characterization of our subject.

On the Mediterranean side, although the transition is rarely very sharply marked, the demarcation line is easily established as it coincides with the northern limit of the long zone throughout which the compact palm groves are scattered, running uninterrupted from east to west, from the Punjab – through Iraq, Syria, lower Egypt, Tripolitania, and the various southern slopes of the Atlas – to the Atlantic Ocean. As a rough limit, this line is as reliable as any that could be drawn from the indices of aridity. The map on page 126 shows it clearly. The whole of this region of palms and palm groves was slowly created by man.

But where is the southern and eastern limit of this great expanse? Thousands of miles from the Mediterranean, it is clear. To find it we must make an imaginary journey to the loop of the Niger, the Upper Nile, the mountainous land of Abyssinia, the Red Sea, Arabia, Iran, the Indus, Turkestan, India, and the Indian Ocean. The striking thing about this desert world is its colossal dimensions. The journey from one town to another, which in the Mediterranean would take a day or a week, would take weeks and months here. The Venetian Giacomo Soranzo, describing Persia in his report of 1576, suggests in one sentence its vast emptiness: 'one can travel through this land for four months without leaving it'.

A poor land, without water: here there are few springs, streams, plants, or

60. *Top:* Camel caravans
transporting goods to the
pastoral areas in the Inner
Mongolian grasslands.

61. *Above:* Camels resting on the
beach at Alanya, Turkey.

62. *Right:* Camel caravan in Italy.
Detail from *The Procession of the
Magi* by Benozzo Gozzoli in the
chapel of the Palazzo Riccardi,
Florence.

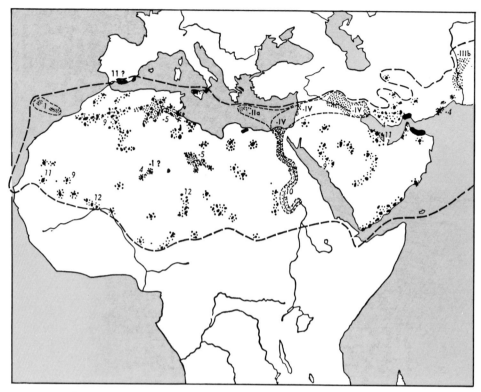

The implantation of palm groves from the Indus to the Atlantic

The Roman numerals indicate millennia, the Arabic numerals centuries. A minus sign preceding a
numeral means B.C. The Italic numerals indicate the date not of the first appearance of the palm
groves but their first recorded existence. The map is taken from the provisional *Atlas* of cultivated
plants by J. Hémardinquer, M. Keul, and W. Randles. It demonstrates the extremely slow progress
of man's effort of creation; palm groves and roads are clearly linked to each other throughout the
vast zone of the date-palm, from the Indus to the Atlantic.

trees. The sparse vegetation is graced with the name of 'pasture land'. Wood is
extremely scarce. So here in the arid zone begin the clay houses, the endless
string of towns that from India to tropical Africa are 'mud encampments'. Stone
buildings, when they exist, are masterpieces of an exceptional kind; built by a
technique of piling stone on stone without any timber joists. In the absence of
wood what must the precious cedar-wood caskets have been worth in Islam?
Think by contrast of the handsome furniture of Renaissance Italy, the chests
and writing desks decorated with gold and iron work wrought by the craftsmen
of Toledo. Here the problem was not, as in the Mediterranean, the building of
ships and galleys, but everyday cooking, the humble camp fire, lit between two
stones. Everything was fuel for it: a few sprigs of brushwood, dry plants, straw
or esparto-grass, the bark of palm trees, 'the dung of camel, horse or ox, which
is dried in the sun'. Even the privileged cities were not immune from this scarcity.

63. Nomad encampment at Biskra, Algeria.

For fuel the people of Cairo used dried dung, or the 'straw' from sugarcane, or the very rare and costly wood brought by ships and galleys from Asia Minor to Alexandria. The situation was always precarious. In November, 1512, even the officers' kitchens ceased to function for lack of fuel – for where could one find fuel near Cairo?

In this hostile territory, this 'ανοιϰουμευη', plants, animals, and men have in spite of everything survived, as if nature abhorred not only a physical but a biological vacuum, or so one geographer has said. In fact, in the course of the vast oscillations and climatic catastrophes of the quaternary period, man, like all other living things, was often surprised, trapped, and forced to adapt as best he could – residual populations are found among the Arabs of Arabia as well as alongside the Tuareg. In any case, apart from the oases, which rarely covered a large area, men have only been able to survive in small groups. Without the flocks of sheep even this would have been impossible. For thousands of years the deserts have been the homeland of the horse, the camel, and the dromedary. In the Sahara the dromedary is predominant. 'Man is a parasite of the camel,' as is often said. And the great history of the deserts begins with the beast of burden.

The nomads are tied to the grazing lands, obliged to move from one source of water to another. During the dry season no flock can wander more than 50 kilometres from a well. And of course conflicts arise over the possession of even the poorest grazing grounds. But it was even more profitable to attack settlers. Syria and Egypt in the sixteenth century could put up little resistance against these raids, these insect bites. Peter Martyr of Anghiera, the humanist whom Ferdinand and Isabella sent to the Sudan, and who reached Egypt in 1502, immediately recognized this. If the innumerable nomads, 'semper versans, semper in motu', had not been divided among themselves, they could easily have seized the lands of the Nile. For one successful punitive expedition against them, how many returned empty-handed or with the meagre bounty of a few prisoners, Bedouin women and children! Every day, or at least whenever they felt like it, the nomads would arrive at the gates of Aleppo, Alexandria, or Cairo. In November, 1518, a garrison had to be sent to Aqaba in order to protect the baggage of the pilgrims 'from the Bedouin raids, which are constantly increasing'.

Nomads who travel far. We should in any case distinguish between two types of nomad among the peoples of the desert. First there are the mountain nomads, who move within a short radius; they go down to pass the winter in the desert. This is even today the practice of the Oulad Sidi Cheikh south of Oran, the Tuareg of the Ajjers or the Hoggar, and the Regueibat, who go to 'the cliffs of Zemmur' in the Spanish Sahara. Secondly, there are the nomads who pass the summer away from the Sahara, on the neighbouring steppes; they often cover very large distances, like the Rwalla, who travel to the Mediterranean from the Syrian desert; or the Beni Larba who, following the rhythm of the seasons, pass to and fro on the 800-kilometre journey between Laghouat and the high plateaux of Tiaret which they reach in May and June; or, this time moving away from the Mediterranean, the Moors who journey to the banks of the river Senegal in the dry season.

We shall here be concerned only with these wide-ranging nomads, who regularly return with the seasons to the Mediterranean.

Every winter the Mediterranean is invaded by Atlantic depressions bringing rain. To the south and east these rains extend beyond the shores of the sea. In the region of Mecca, the winter rains from the Mediterranean are brief and sometimes violent. These downpours (one rain every two years, in some of the furthest regions every four years) create steppes providing pasture, immense grazing lands, but where the grass is widely scattered and soon disappears. Even in the wide depressions of the *oueds*, the tufts are often 20 to 40 metres apart. The grass, which grows in the winter, gradually dries up from the south to the north, from the end of spring. It vanishes before the advance of the flocks, leading them on to the shores of the Mediterranean, which they reach after harvest time. But the sheep are content to eat even stubble and dry grass. At the end of summer they return to the regions where the new grass will grow.

In the sixteenth century nomad shepherds were arriving in far larger numbers than today on the Mediterranean shores. The barrier that the coastal settlers had established and have consolidated since was still very fragile at that period. The nomads were quite at home in Asia Minor and Syria. Pierre Belon saw them in summer near Adana. Throughout the Maghreb the great nomad trails bisected the country from south to north, particularly across the Tunisian steppe, where they met no obstacle, or across the great, dry, exposed plateaux behind Oran to the west. Every year, towards the end of July, Diego Suárez saw the *Uled Abdala* arrive at Oran, where he was garrisoned for so long; they had sown some of the coastal fields in the preceding autumn and were trying to protect their harvest against raids from neighbouring tribes. The soldier-chronicler, who had seen the Arabs with their camels charging the Spanish arquebusiers, had also observed them in peacetime, closely enough to be familiar with their way of cooking, of preserving meat fried in its own fat, eating *alcuzcuzu* (couscous) and drinking the sour milk that they called *lebent*.

In Tunisia, there was a similar pattern. If Don John of Austria captured Tunis without a struggle in October, 1573, it was because the nomads had already left the shores of northern Tunisia. In August, 1574, on the other hand, the Turks took the town and fortress of La Goletta, because the nomads were on their side and served them as auxiliaries for earthworks and transport. History was repeated over the centuries. As early as 1270 the nomads serving in the Tunisian army threatened in the late season (just after the death of St Louis) 'to return as was their custom, to the southern pastures'.

Advance and infiltration from the steppe. These large-scale movements of nomads from the steppe to the coast, then from the sea back to the desert, inevitably acted as one of the pressures on Mediterranean history, or perhaps one should say, one of its rhythms. All would be well if the migrations had the regularity of the tides of the sea. But there were a hundred causes, apart from intermittent droughts, for the machinery to go wrong and for the nomad to be dissatisfied with the land he was allotted; hence a hundred opportunities for disputes with permanent settlers. Basically nomadic life requires grazing lands; but it may also possibly seek land to grow crops on, even towns that will act as victualling centres and form the basis of its political structures.

In practice, the Bedouin is often called into the house he covets. Agriculture in the Mediterranean as it has been and is practised, leads to the rapid exhaustion of the soil, wearing it out more thoroughly than the often-blamed depredations of the sheep and goats of the nomads. The handing over of these lands to the flocks for grazing may then be a way of meeting the need to rest them.

The conflict between the Mediterranean and the neighbouring desert is something more than plough versus flock. It is the clash between two economies, civilizations, societies, and arts of living. Russian historians see all invasions from the steppe as preceded by a change in the structure of its civilizations, their transition from primitive to 'feudalized' societies. The part played by certain explosions of religious mysticism in the victorious expeditions of Islam is well known, as is that played by demographic explosions. The nomad takes advantage of all the failures and weaknesses of the settler, in agriculture certainly, but also in other ways. Without the intentional or unintentional complicity of the settled civilizations these dramatic oscillations would be incomprehensible.

Gautier thought that North Africa in the sixteenth century was more than usually overrun with nomads. (I am drawing here on an impression gained not so much from his books, as from personal conversations with him in Algiers.) One of the great events of history was the withdrawal of the Marabout centres to the south, which was so marked from the fifteenth to the eighteenth century. There followed the improbable spectacle of order being restored in Morocco by the Sharifs of the Sous, by the desert in fact. In the regencies of Algiers, Tunis, and Tripoli, the troubles at the end of the sixteenth century were linked with the unrest among the *Alarabes* as the Spanish texts call them, that is Arab nomads, often allied with the *moros* of the towns against the Turkish invader. This explains the extent of the unrest that was endemic during the last ten years of the sixteenth century all along the south shore of the Mediterranean, from Gibraltar to Egypt. So the nomad seems to have played a role of increasing importance in North Africa, but perhaps it would be more true to say that the whole region was caught up in the movement of the times, nomadic life as much as the rest. In the end, though, the nomad was to prove no match for the Turkish arquebuses and artillery or the cannon of the Moroccan Sharifs. He might still here and there carry off a local victory, make successful surprise attacks, and rally whole areas to the dissident cause. But he no longer had the last word. Militarily, the rules had changed. The nomad, until then always victorious, unrivalled in horsemanship, was defeated by gunpowder. This was as true of the nomads of Kazan on the Volga or the Mongols of northern China, as of the tribes of Africa and the Middle East.

64. Camels carrying jars containing wine and olive oil. Mosaic from Deir el-Adas, Syria.

The gold and spice caravans. We must distinguish between the everyday history of nomadism and the great caravan trails, long-distance voyages from one side of the desert to the other, linking the Mediterranean on one side to the Far East, and on the other to the *Bled es Soudan* and Black Africa. They were as different from the first as long-distance shipping from coastal trade. The caravans served

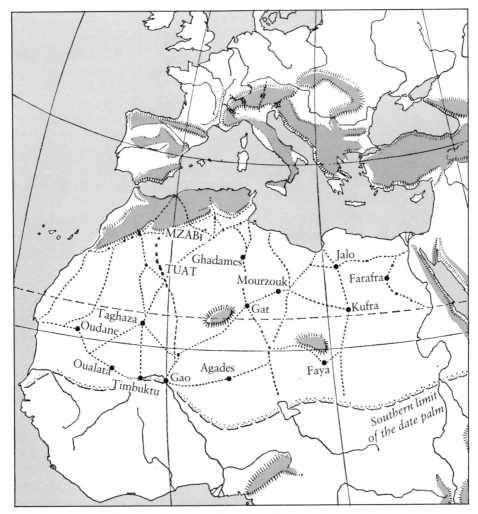

Saharan caravans, fifteenth and sixteenth centuries

Map taken from Vitorino Magalhães Godinho, *Os descobrimientos e a economia mundial*, 1963, which has more particular reference to the fifteenth century. The routes across North Africa towards Oran and Tunis are barely outlined. The rise of Algiers only occurred in the last decades of the sixteenth century. Naturally the routes from the Maghreb to Black Africa were subject to change and variation in activity. Towards Abyssinia, the Nile was the principal route.

merchants, and therefore towns and active economies in a world context; they were a luxury, an adventure, a complicated achievement.

The sixteenth century inherited them; it used an instrument which it had not created, preserved it intact, and passed it on to later generations who did not appreciably modify it. The descriptions of later writers agree, *mutatis mutandis*, with the account of the anonymous Englishman who in 1586 followed the sumptuous caravan of pilgrims to Mecca. It formed at 'Birca', three leagues

65. Arab miniature showing a camel caravan making its
way through the desert. Illustration by al-Wasiti from
Maqamat by al-Hariri. *Bibliothèque Nationale, Paris*

from Cairo, twenty days after Ramadan, and consisted of up to 40,000 mules
and camels and 50,000 people, the merchants anxious to protect their goods
walking at the head, sometimes selling along the wayside the silk, coral, tin,
grain, or rice that they would for the most part exchange at Mecca, and the
pilgrims, free of possessions, looking only after their own persons, coming
behind. This procession of rich and poor had its military commander, the 'captain' of the caravan, and some guides; at night, the latter would carry dry-wood
torches to light the way, for they preferred to journey between two o'clock in
the morning and sunrise, to avoid the heat of the day. An escort was provided
against Arab raids on the Red Sea coast: 200 spahis and 400 soldiers, plus field
artillery, some six pieces drawn by twelve camels, which served to terrify the
Bedouin and make a noise at the triumphal entry into Mecca, 'to make triumph',
as the narrator calls it.

It was clearly an enormous caravan, half-religious, half-commercial, and
moving quickly: this one covered the difficult journey from Cairo to Mecca in
forty days. On every occasion we must imagine vast numbers of pack animals
(the victualling of the Turkish army sometimes required the requisitioning of
30,000 to 40,000 camels) and large numbers of travellers, bound by the strict
discipline of the convoy, living by their own means, asking little from the country
they journeyed through apart from the water and fuel necessary for cooking and

caring for the animals. The mounting of these costly and powerful operations therefore required profitable commercial dealings: in the Sahara there was traffic in salt, slaves, fabrics, and gold; in Syria a luxury trade in spices, drugs, and silk. And these were all regular trades.

It is probable that the overall volume of the Sahara trade increased in the fifteenth and sixteenth centuries even after the great Portuguese discoveries and in spite of them. Certainly after the 1460s Portuguese settlement on the coast of Guinea diverted some of the Sahara trade in that direction, hence the evident gold crisis to which we shall return later. Nevertheless, the great Sahara trails continued to transport the precious metal in the sixteenth century towards North Africa and Egypt and consequently to draw a compensating flow of goods and men towards the south.

In the Middle East there were two basic caravan zones: one corresponding to the Mecca routes, setting out either from Syria or Cairo; the other running from Aleppo to the Tigris. The Euphrates, according to Tavernier, was not considered for shipping because of its mills, at least until 1638, when the Turkish army was to use it as a communications route. The Tigris was only navigable below Baghdad.

Both sets of routes led towards the Indian Ocean, one in the direction of the Persian Gulf, the other to the Red Sea, ending at the Egyptian ports of Tor and Suez, and further on at Jiddah, the pilgrim port and the terminus of shipping routes linking the Red Sea with India and the East Indies. These links had been in existence for centuries, and their prosperity, dating from the twelfth and thirteenth centuries, was still buoyant in the sixteenth. They provided the link between shipping and the caravan traffic and although from time to time there were delays, missed connections, and threats of competition, the system always righted itself somehow and continued to run efficiently.

2 Europe and the Mediterranean

From the Black Sea to the Straits of Gibraltar, the Mediterranean's northern waters wash the shores of Europe. Here again, if he wants to establish boundaries, the historian will have more hesitation than the geographer. 'Europe, a confused concept,' wrote Henri Hauser. It is a twofold or even threefold world, composed of peoples and territories with which history has dealt very differently. The Mediterranean, by its profound influence over southern Europe, has contributed in no small measure to prevent the unity of that Europe, which it has attracted towards its shores and then divided to its own advantage.

The isthmuses and their north–south passages. The land mass of Europe, lying between the blue waters of the Mediterranean and the other, northern Mediterraneans, the Baltic, the North Sea, and the English Channel, narrows

66, 67. *Above:* Wheeled traffic by the River Nyeman outside the town of Grodno, Lithuania. Engraving by Matthias Zundt, Nuremberg, 1568. *National Museum, Cracow. Left:* Wheeled traffic by the town of Deventer in the Netherlands. From *Civitates Orbis Terrarum.*

progressively to the west. It is intersected by a series of north–south routes, natural isthmuses that are still decisive influences on exchanges today: the Russian isthmus, the Polish isthmus, the German isthmus, and the French isthmus.

To the west the Iberian peninsula is also intersected by routes, but this time running from west to east, from the sea to the ocean: the routes from Barcelona to Navarre and the Basque provinces by way of the Ebro; the important passage from Valencia to Medina del Campo and Portugal; or the short cuts overland from Alicante and Málaga to Seville by which one can avoid the Straits of Gibraltar. These Spanish routes are not our present concern. Their orientation puts them in a very different category, and the perennial question raises itself: is Spain wholly European? So let us come back to the geologists' line from the Bay of Biscay to the Caucasus. We shall consider only the routes to the north of this line as presenting the real problem of Europe's relationship to the Mediterranean, or rather, the series of real problems.

For this northern half of Europe was far from a homogeneous territory although it contrasted violently with the Mediterranean landscape. Compared with the orchards and vineyards of the South, it was the land of thick forests, open plains, meadows, and wide navigable rivers, only rarely producing the food-bearing trees and plants that were the safeguard of Mediterranean life. It was, over vast expanses, the land of wheeled traffic, so that Dantiscus, the Polish ambassador, travelling from Antwerp to Bruges and Calais in the autumn of 1522, naturally writes: 'ex Antwerpia per currus ut hic fieri solet', 'from Antwerp by wagon as is the custom here'. The South by contrast was the land of mule-trains. The future queen of Spain, Elizabeth of Valois, and her suite, arriving at the Spanish frontier in January, 1560, with their carriages and belongings were transferred to pack animals that carried them to the interior of the Peninsula. The same thing had happened in 1502, half a century earlier, on the occasion of the first visit to Spain of Philip the Fair.

The North was the land of beer and drinks made from fermented grain, as Germany already was in Tacitus' time. In the sixteenth century the first breweries were set up in Konstanz; the Dominicans introduced beer to Lorraine; it was soon to reach England, as the popular song said, along with hops, as one might expect, and the Reformation. Marco Ottobon, the secretary sent from Venice to Danzig during the winter of 1590–1591 to purchase grain, was astonished, the following summer, by the arrival of two hundred Dutch ships, all in poor condition and inadequately equipped, calling to pick up second-rate grain, 'gli grani per birra'.

For a man from the Mediterranean these were strange countries (not only Poland), where wine was a luxury, to be had only at unbelievable prices. When he was briefly imprisoned in the Low Countries, Bayard, although without fortune, kept a good table, but 'he might in a day spend twenty crowns on wine'. A foreigner in these parts, if he came from a Mediterranean country, would consider the people coarse and unrefined barbarians. Often good 'barbarians', showing great religious devotion (whether Germany before Luther or Normandy in the time of François I), and honest too (the same Ottobon said of Poland that one could travel there 'l'oro in mano senza pericolo di essere offeso'). And then there was the great advantage that living was much cheaper there than in Italy. In Danzig our Venetian observed, 'for two *thaler* per person per week, I may say that I have a banquet morning and evening'.

But we should beware of generalizations. The Mediterranean was not the exclusive domain of the pack animal, nor northern Europe the undisputed zone of beer and wheeled traffic. And the Mediterranean had its own backward regions, of primitive religion and cheap living.

Europe was indeed diversity itself. Civilization reached it at varying times, along different roads. So within Europe the Mediterranean was confronted by

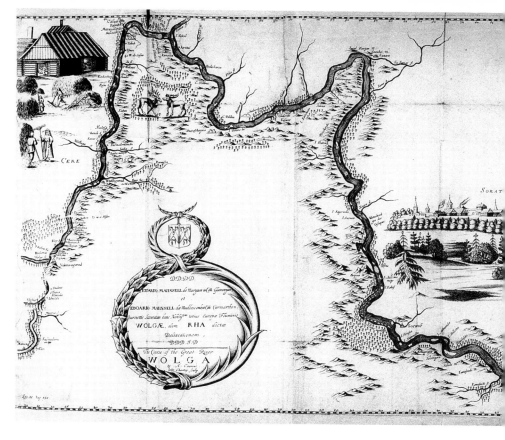

68. The Volga as a trade route. From A. Olearius, *Voyages*, 1662.

a series of different regions, societies, and civilizations resembling each other neither in origin nor in cultural and economic status. They were of different complexions, different ages, and have felt the pull of Mediterranean attraction in varying ways.

By and large, we should distinguish between *at least* four European groups, corresponding to the routes running north and south through the isthmuses, four skeins of history, each tied more or less securely to the warm sea, the source of prosperity, but also linked to each other, which does not simplify the observer's task.

The Russian isthmus: leading to the Black and Caspian Seas. It would be easy to say, and almost to prove, that in the sixteenth century there was no Russian isthmus, no isthmus, that is, playing a connecting role and bringing large exchange movements to the Mediterranean. The whole of southern Russia was a deserted land, crossed only by the bands of Tartar nomads, whose swift horses carried them to the northern edge of the Caucasus or to the shores of the Caspian Sea, as well as towards Moscow – which they burnt in 1571, massacring 150,000 people including Flemish, English, German, and Italian merchants living there – or into the lands of the Danube, which they ravaged unmercifully. At the end

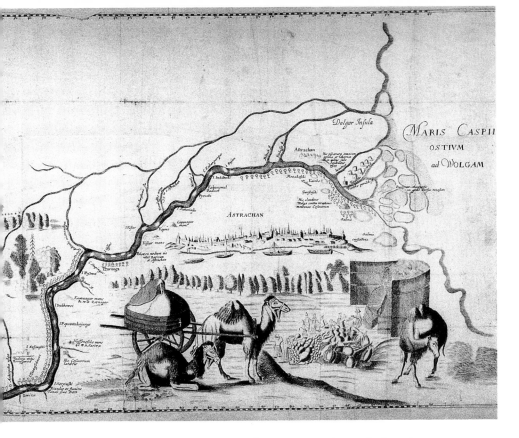

of the eighteenth century Russian settlers were again to find an immense waste land, empty except for a few nomadic brigands raising their camels and horses.

The raids of the brigands did not people the vast steppes (where there was not a single town) any more than the ships of the corsairs peopled the sea. But they made it dangerous country. Based in the Crimea, which its relief protected on the mainland side, and supported by the Turks who had several strongholds on the peninsula including Kaffa, these southern Tartars proved impossible for the 'Grand Duke' to subdue as he had those of Kazan and Astrakhan. For the Turks had armed them with arquebuses and artillery, thus neutralizing the only advantage that the Russians could have had over them. In return, the Tartars after their raids would provide all the Turkish houses and villages with Slav servants and workers. Large numbers of Russian and sometimes Polish slaves arrived by their good offices in Constantinople, where they fetched high prices. These dealings in human cattle were on such a scale that in 1591 Giovanni Botero spoke of them as one of the reasons for the low population of Russia. The shortage of men possibly explains why the Russians did not attempt to take the shores of the Black Sea in the sixteenth century; they contented themselves with a few counterraids in winter into these empty lands, when the frozen rivers allowed troop movements. At the beginning of the seventeenth century the Russian outlaws, the Cossacks, like the Uskoks or Haiduks, were to arm light vessels and disturb Turkish shipping on the Black Sea. As early as 1602 some 'Polish' Cossacks brushed with a galley at the mouth of the Danube.

If the Russians had as yet only slight connections with the South, it was partly because they had not made any serious efforts in that direction; because they were attracted, through the primitive northern lands, by the economic expansion of the Baltic and by the European countries facing them on the western front, Poland and Germany. Lastly, it was because they tended to focus on the Caspian Sea, which led them towards Persia: they faced south-east, rather than due south.

Russia was not yet Europe, but it was becoming Europeanized. Along the western routes, over the Alps and the lands of Bohemia and Poland, there came to Moscow the Italian architect-masons, builders of the onion-shaped domes. From the West came the precious secrets of gunpowder. The Poles were always protesting the danger of such exchanges. When the Tsar seized Narva, and held it from 1558 to 1581, thus acquiring a window on to the Baltic, the king of Poland was alarmed at the fresh possibilities this opened up to the Muscovites. The only way to keep them in check would be to leave them 'in their barbarism and ignorance'. So the Danzigers did well, wrote King Sigismund to Queen Elizabeth, on 6th December, 1559, to stop English ships going to 'the Narve'. The quarrel dragged on and extended to others besides the English. In June, 1570, a French ship from Dieppe, the *Espérance*, was seized on its way to Narva by Danziger pseudo-corsairs. In 1571 the Duke of Alva warned the German Reichstag against exporting cannon and munitions which would be used to arm the enemies of Germany, and perhaps of all Christendom. These and other details show that the centre of gravity of the Russian economy was gradually moving north, but the south, in the wide sense, and in particular the south-east continued to be important to it.

In Moscow there were Greek, Tartar, Wallachian, Armenian, Persian, and Turkish merchants. Above all there was the flow of traffic along the Volga. Downstream went soldiers, artillery, and grain; upstream in return came salt and dried sturgeon. After the Russian occupation of Kazan and Astrakhan in 1551 and 1556, the entire waterway was seized and regular trade was disturbed only at long intervals by raids from Cossacks or Nogais Tartars. So when the Turks, supported by the Tartars, tried to advance into Astrakhan (with the intention of digging a canal from the Don to the Volga so as to be able to supply their troops, who were engaged against Persia, by way of the Caspian Sea), their expedition ended in the rout of 1569–1570 in the face of stiff Russian resistance. For this southern feeler was Moscow's means of contact with the nomads of the south-east, with Persia and with her old monetary economy. It was from these southern provinces that the Tsar would exact tribute in money; the northern provinces enriched his treasury often only with furs and hides. These furs, incidentally, led to substantial Russian trade with the Balkans, Constantinople, and Persia, Turko-Russian relations having improved after 1570, with the Novosiltsov diplomatic mission.

69. Detail from *Loading Timber in a Northern Port* by Aart van Antum, c.1625. *National Maritime Museum, Greenwich*

More interesting for general history was the English attempt between 1556 and 1581 to establish a connection not with the Black Sea (there was little point in aiming at a Turkish lake and a well-guarded one) but with the Caspian Sea. This was an effective attempt to get round the Mediterranean, not by a sea passage, as the Portuguese had succeeded in doing in 1498, but by a mixed route, over land and sea.

English ships, in fact, disappeared from the Mediterranean towards the middle of the century, and with them went the advantages that Oriental trade had brought English merchants, who became all the more anxious to participate in the profitable commerce of the Indies, the monopoly of the Mediterraneans and Iberians. The association of Merchant Adventurers in London began sending explorers and ships towards the Arctic regions in the hope of finding a new northern passage as Magellan had a southern. It was one of these boats, Chancellor's, which in 1553 landed by chance in St Nicholas Bay, not far from Archangel. This chance was soon turned to profit and the resources of the region – whale blubber, wax, furs, flax, hemp, seal's teeth, timber, and cod – were soon on the way to England, in return for textiles and money.

The Muscovy Company quickly realized that the original project could be achieved by going overland through Russia, and that by way of the Caspian Sea they could reach the spices, pepper, and silk. In 1561 an English agent arrived in Persia with his merchandise and regular voyages were soon established. For a few years all the marvels of the East travelled up the Volga, to be loaded on

70. The timber market at Danzig. German print, seventeenth century.

to London vessels in St Nicholas Bay. For a few years only, it is true. The project eventually collapsed for political reasons and because after 1575, the English again had access to the direct Mediterranean route. The long trips to the Caspian Sea and Persia lost their attraction. But they did continue: the Russians did not give up Persia, their chief eastern ally; when later they were driven out of Narva in 1581, they became interested in Archangel, the last window left to them in the far north, and soon the Dutch were sending ships there.

To return to the English venture: the volume of goods concerned was not large (enough though to bring good profits to English merchants and some anxiety to Spaniards in London), but it provides us with information about Mediterranean life in general, the difficulty of shipping between the Atlantic and the inland sea, and then the reopening of the Mediterranean to the northerners. It was through Russia that for a few years Anglo-Mediterranean trade tried to open a passage for itself. In the minds of its originators, the scheme was to have been even more ambitious. It was to capture by the back door Portuguese trade on one side and Syrian on the other. As late as 1582, there was talk in London of an Anglo-Turkish agreement that would have resulted in diverting the spice trade to the Caspian Sea by way of the Black Sea, by concentrating it on Constantinople. This was a grandiose scheme for a monopoly that would in this case have been shared by England, a scheme that could not be realized, however, for more than one reason. Curiously enough, Père Joseph was later, in 1630, to think of using the Russian detour – certainly not by agreement with the Turks, but on the contrary using this route to bypass their positions and commercial privileges. This scheme like the previous one underlines the usefulness of the

Russian isthmus as a route to the Levant, and the relevance to Mediterranean history of the continental interior.

From the Balkans to Danzig: the Polish isthmus. What we have called the Polish isthmus did not lead, or no longer led, in the sixteenth century, to the Black Sea but to the Balkan Peninsula; it firmly turned to the west and led from the Baltic to the Danube, and in a roundabout way to Constantinople (perhaps beyond). Does this mean that the Black Sea when it passed from Genoese into Turkish hands, lost its attraction for Poland? Yes and no. While the Turkish occupation of Kaffa in 1475, Kilia in 1484, and Bialograd in 1484, interrupted a previously thriving commerce, we should also take account of the crises of Middle Eastern trade. The insecurity of the southern roads, because of the Tartars, also played a part. So there was a decline in the long-distance overland trade which since the thirteenth century had brought to Poland from the Black Sea, particularly from Kaffa, the produce of the Levant, chiefly spices and pepper.

But Poland was, like Muscovy, caught up above all in the dominant Baltic economy behind which lay the demands of the markets of the Low Countries, which bought wheat, rye, and forest products. Amsterdam, from a distance, dictated prices and their fluctuations. In these circumstances the role of Danzig was both enlarged and limited. 'This side of the Denmark straits' it was the best situated and most prosperous commercial centre. One should buy there, noted a Venetian in 1591, and not in the neighbouring smaller centres of Königsberg or Elbing, 'because of the greater reliability of the persons with whom one deals, who are richer and less barbaric than elsewhere'. It was also relatively easy to reach Danzig for settling bills at the St Dominic's Fair, which was held in the town itself, or the St Bartholomew's fair at Gniezno, or the St Michael's Fair at Poznán (Posen). Besides, there were the financial facilities of Nuremberg which were effective in Vienna, Breslau, Cracow, and Danzig itself.

But between, on one hand, the underdeveloped economy of Poland and the neighbouring regions which Danzig exploited in the name of the sacrosanct principle of 'freie Handel und Commercien', and, on the other, Amsterdam, which dominated it, the town played a limited role, that of an intermediary in a system that continually dwarfed it. Its role was to buy grain (and other products but chiefly grain) at the winter fairs that were held at Torun (Thorn) and Lublin. It was there that nobles would sell their harvests (threshed during the winter and transported after the thaw, in April–May). At Danzig they were bonded, the quality was supervised, and all speed was made to sell them, for at best this was last year's grain, and it was impossible to keep it in store any longer. Exports to the Mediterranean, except during the crisis years at the end of the century, bore no comparison with the massive shipments to the Iberian peninsula. At all events, Poland's economy was trained on this key port. Danzig was the window through which she saw the world, not always to her advantage obviously.

To the south, beyond Cracow, Lwow, and Galatz, avoiding Hungary with its frequent wars, a long trade route ran to the Balkans and beyond, to Constantinople. In 1530 and 1531 we find Armenian merchants from Kamieniec bringing saffron and rice of Turkish origin to the fair of Lublin. In 1548 Lublin obtained the privilege of testing various *res aromaticae* imported from Greece and Turkey. The little town then entered a period of prosperity of which its fairs provided the evidence. It was a convenient halt on the way to Danzig, between Lwow to the south, and Warsaw, and had the advantage of being a town without the rights of a 'staple', a *Sklad*, unlike Lwow, which had its privileges and defended them. Goods could come in and out of Lublin as merchants pleased. At Lwow they had to stop and be put on sale.

To the latter town, where Jewish, Levantine, and Italian merchants concentrated, came the southern trade too. In 1571 an agent of the firm of Hureau, merchants originally from Valenciennes and established at Antwerp, went from Danzig to Lwow and then on to Constantinople. In 1575 an Italian in the service of one of his compatriots established at Cracow was buying malmsey wine and muscatel at Lwow. These precious beverages like the sweet Greek wine that was drunk in the town must have come from the shores of the eastern Mediterranean. And fairly regularly there passed through Lwow what was called the 'Polish caravan', on its way to Constantinople, a collection of merchants and carriers, stopping at the *hans* of the towns, sometimes benefiting from the protection of the authorities, sometimes not, sometimes halting in the open countryside around campfires. But we do not always know what was being transported to the Bosphorus in those heavy wagons drawn by oxen or horses.

Along these difficult roads travelled the Bologna merchant Tommaso Alberti, who has left an all too brief account of his journeys. He reached Constantinople by sea; he left there on 26th November, 1612, passed through Adrianople and crossed the Dobrudja. Since the carters were Turkish, they deserted him on the day of *Beïram*, which they went to celebrate in a nearby village. The interminable Romanian plains left the traveller with the impression of a 'sea on dry land'. It was easy to lose oneself if the tracks of preceding vehicles were not there to show the way. He arrived with the snow at Jassy. Six days later he was at Lwow, sold his goods there, bought others and in the spring set off back to Constantinople with sixty wagons each drawn by six horses. On 23rd May, 1613, a wagon overturned during the weary crossing of the Balkans. 'Inside it there were thirty sacks of Spanish *reales*, each sack containing 500 *reales*, sables, and other goods.' Everything was recovered and on 1st June the convoy entered Constantinople, which our merchant left again on the 21st. He reached Lwow again on 27th July, then went on to Cracow and Prague, Nuremberg and Milan, arriving back in Bologna on 25th October.

In spite of these picturesque details and the obvious deficit of the Polish balance of trade towards the south, the volume of this traffic was not in any way comparable to the lateral trade links between Poland and her neighbour

Germany, with Frankfurt-am-Oder, Nuremberg which bought furs, or Silesia, with its tariff disputes caused by the ambition, sometimes thwarted, of the merchants of Wroclaw (Breslau). Nor can it be compared to the diagonal trade links leading via Breslau, Leipzig, Nuremberg, Augsburg, and southern Germany towards Italy and Venice and back again. In June, 1564, the Signoria of Venice granted a whole consignment of arms to an agent of the Polish Crown, including 100 corselets, 500 arquebuses, and 30 halberds. From Italy came an endless flow of artists, merchants, and artisans, three of whom set up a brickworks in Cracow in 1533. Then there were luxury or pseudo-luxury fabrics. There was manufactured at Venice and Naples a kind of loosely woven silk which was given body by soaking it in a preparation. It was known as 'robba per Polonia'! Towards 1565 there were between fifteen and twenty 'botteghe d'Italiani' for the whole of Poland, including that of the Soderini, an extremely rich merchant family. But as the century advanced, men and merchandise from Italy became more plentiful – a movement analogous to that which we shall find in southern Germany, as if at the end of the century, the invasion of central and eastern Europe by Italian men and goods was compensating for the northerners' invasion of the Mediterranean. Italian merchants were everywhere in Poland and they were there to stay, at Cracow, Lwow, Warsaw, Lublin and Sandomir. The great period of Italian presence was from the end of the sixteenth to the middle of the seventeenth century. The ledger belonging to one of these merchants, dated 1645, reveals his activities at the Polish fairs, notably Lublin. He lists the moneys handled, the prices, quantities, carriage and a bewildering list of fabrics of every origin sold at Lublin: a taffeta, 'verdegaio a onde', from London, a velvet, 'verde piano', from Florence, a 'caravaccia nera' from Naples, a 'raso azuro piano' from Venice, a 'rosa seccha' material and a 'raso nero' from Lucca. The names are not easy to identify and the stated origins are not necessarily genuine. But they are evidence, like the memoirs of Tommaso Alberti, of the Italian presence well after the sixteenth century. The same remarks could be made of neighbouring Transylvania, where merchants, workmen, architects, masons, stone cutters, and soldiers from Italy were all clearly active.

The preceding outline helps to explain the overall situation of Poland. What it lacked, in the sixteenth century, was not dynamism, of which there is plenty of evidence, but an active and far-reaching monetary economy. If the Polish state was so fundamentally fragile, and the king 'more to represent than to wield power', the reason is to be sought in the social and political order of the 'republic', and the impossibility of centralizing sufficient reserves of money, and therefore of having a modern army. On the Turkish and Tartar borders frontier defence was left to Cossacks, groups of bandits from all nations as a Spanish text says, adding: 'a warlike people, always moving and unsettled, cruel, capable of the greatest endurance but also the most rascally in the world'. At any rate, they were a people free to act as they pleased, not a modern army. In January, 1591, the payment of the soldiers stationed on the Muscovy borders raised

71. View of the town of Komarom on the Danube, after a drawing by G. Hoefnagel, 1595. Note the Dutch flag flown by the three vessels in the foreground. The artist no doubt took pride in his country's preeminence in the carrying trade.

difficult problems for the Diet meeting at Warsaw. The soldiers meanwhile were living off the land and devastating it, regardless of which side of the frontier it lay, as has also been the case in some of the richest countries of the West.

Economic considerations explain why, predominantly concerned with the North, Poland pursued a pacific policy towards the South. The Turks and the Poles were in no hurry to come to blows. The allies of the League in 1572 were wasting their time trying to persuade Poland to advance against the Grand Turk. The Turks for their part furthered the election of the Duke of Anjou as king of Poland. In 1590, on the eve of the Turko-Hungarian War, the English intervened to arrange an amicable settlement between Turkey and Poland.

So there was peace in the south, which is not sufficient to explain the curious spread through Poland of fashions in costume and sumptuous tents from Turkey, of which one can still see examples in museums. It is possible that commercial exchanges with the South have been underestimated.

The German isthmus: an overall view. By the German isthmus we mean all of central Europe in the widest sense, between France on the west side and Hungary and Poland on the east; between the North Sea and the Baltic to the north and the Adriatic and Tyrrhenian to the south. The whole forms a remarkable complex of countries, exchanges, and trade routes as is shown by the map on page 146.

We can limit this area by drawing two lines, one from Genoa (or even Marseilles) to London, the other from Venice to Danzig; these are somewhat arbitrary lines, of course, but we are looking for a general picture. This great block of central Europe is bounded to the north and south by its seacoasts: the North Sea, the Baltic, and the Mediterranean. To be more accurate, these crucial seas are an extension of it. We should certainly prolong it beyond the northern seas to take in Sweden (which was investigated with some curiosity by Venetian traders at the end of the sixteenth and the beginning of the seventeenth century), Norway, and above all England, which although caught up in the great Atlantic adventure, was nevertheless firmly moored to Europe. One of the most important of England's trading activities was in cloth, which was exported depending on circumstances by way of Emden, Hamburg, Bremen or Antwerp (and on occasion Rouen). So England – and cloth is merely the best example – was for the time being associated to the continent, and to the particular zone we are concerned with here. It was certainly an active zone, the outstanding example perhaps of an economy based on land transport, the equivalent of what the fairs of Champagne must have been in the twelfth and thirteenth centuries – an early and potentially explosive form of north–south contact.

Taken as a whole this area is curiously proportioned: narrow towards the south in northern Italy, it widens out to become an immense continental expanse on the other side of the Alps. A letter sent by the king of Poland, on 25th July, 1522, to Antwerp, where Dantiscus, his ambassador to Charles V, was impatiently waiting for it, did not arrive until 12th September, taking almost fifty days. Or to take another dimension: Marco Ottobon, travelling from Venice to Danzig, in winter it is true (1590), was on the road for thirty-nine days including halts. There was certainly no common measure between the linked plains of Piedmont, Lombardy, and Venezia, with easy access to their seaports, and the vast continental countries north of the Alps. In the South the roads converge; in the North they fan out over a wide area. The Alps thus divide central Europe 'by a long and wide barrier' and the two fragments on either side are both geographically and historically of very unequal importance.

The 'German isthmus' then consists in succession of Italy, particularly northern Italy, the Alps, then the immense plains and plateaux of central Europe, between the Meuse or the Rhine on one side, and the Oder and the Vistula on the other. Italy needs no introduction. This book will have much occasion to come back to her cities and landscapes so decisive in Mediterranean history. But we should devote some space here to the Alps, the magic mountains where nothing ever seems impossible. Their mountain walls presented an obstacle to central Europe: they were very soon breached. Travelling was difficult: spontaneous solutions appeared. The Alpine societies and villages seem to have existed for the express purpose of organizing the crossing of the mountains and furthering the progress of this profitable traffic in both directions, south and north.

The Alps. This is because the Alps are contained within a three-dimensional geometry relating together societies and economies from different levels: hamlets and villages at the upper limit of arable land; compact villages in the deep valleys; small towns on the banks of the rivers, with perhaps a firm of 'Lombards' and a few artisans' workshops. Finally, on the outer edges, near the plains and waterways, where traffic begins to move quickly again, are to be found the cities

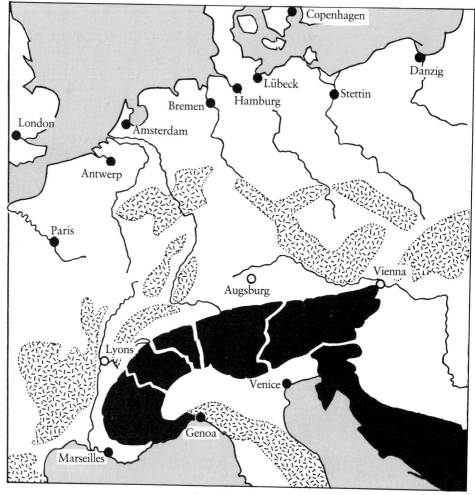

The Alpine barrier

This deliberately schematic map shows the narrow area of northern Italy compared with the lands beyond the Alps. Northern Italy is ringed around with mountains to the west, north, and east (the Dinaric Alps). The great Alpine routes (Mont-Cenis, Simplon, St. Gotthard, Brenner, Tarvis, and a few others) break through the barrier. The map indicates major rivers only below the point at which they become generally navigable.

of the *piedmont*: Geneva, Basel, and Zurich; Salzburg, Villach, and Klagenfurt; Susa, Vercelli, Asti, Como, Bergamo, Brescia, and Verona; often towns that held fairs (Zurzach, Hall, Linz, Bolzano), frequently the centres of transport firms (Chur, Chiavenna, Plurs), and always 'halfway' towns between south and north, where the mountain dweller would find necessary, everyday goods, 'ordinary fabrics for clothing, metal for tools and above all salt, which plays an essential role in stock farming'.

So there was a flow of traffic proper to the Alpine regions along which men, beasts, flocks, and goods daily moved. A different kind of traffic was

72. View of Arco in the Italian Alps between Trento and Lake Garda. Drawing by Albrecht Dürer. *Louvre, Paris*

73. Portrait of a Swiss linen merchant. Anonymous painting. *St. Gallen Historical Museum, Switzerland*

superimposed onto these everyday movements, using the same men and the same means of transport, and penetrating the whole network through and through. These crossings would have been impossible without the waggoners' and carriers' villages, each jealously guarding the profits it derived from the trade route. Primolano in the Brenta valley, in the Vicenza Alps, was in 1598 a *viletta* numbering barely fifty hearths, whose 'inhabitants almost all live off the wages they get by transporting goods in their carts'. Hundreds of other villages were in the same situation. Convention ruled that all the villages along a route, either when it was being set up or when it was already established, should cooperate, dividing the labour among them, settling the stages, undertaking to ensure the safe passage of travellers and goods and sometimes, on payment of a supplementary sum, providing them with continuous transport, day and night.

Thereafter, these coordinated movements seem to have run very smoothly. Even winter did not interrupt them: it offered the relative ease of sledges. On 16th December, 1537, a transporter-entrepreneur of Vercelli took charge of 132 bales of merchandise at Geneva, promising to deliver 42 at Ivrea on the following 4th of January, 'saulve le temps'. Marco Dandolo, who was travelling to France to represent the Signoria of Venice, crossed the Mont-Cenis in a litter in December, 1540. True, he retained an unpleasant memory of it, as did Girolamo Lippomano, who crossed it in April, 1577: 'The horses and mules plunged up to their bellies in snow and were only able to extract themselves with great

74. *The Arnolfini Marriage* by Jan van Eyck. Arnolfini was a Lucchese merchant who lived in Bruges much of the time. *National Gallery, London*

difficulty', but, he adds, 'a countless throng of travellers passed through there, on their way to Italy, France, England, and many also bound for Spain'. The village of Novalesa, which had no crops or vines, provided unofficial guides who were never short of work. A strange land was this miserable mountainous Savoy, he thought, 'which sees the sun only three months of the year, gets a yield from its wheatfields of only two to one', and that as far as Lanslebourg, where downhill trips were made by sledge, or even as far as St Jean de Maurienne.

From these familiar accounts and so many others, and from Aloys Schulte's patiently collected evidence about the Middle Ages, what conclusions should we draw? That the twenty-one Alpine passes were all usable – given favourable circumstances. Scores of successes, of semi-successes, attempts, and failures are recorded: there is a whole comparative history and an immense range of archives to explore. Naturally the towns and the merchants played their part. It was the merchants of Milan who, in the thirteenth century, constructed the then revolutionary St Gotthard route; they were later, in order to reach the upper Rhine valley, to use the Splügen, Maloja, and Septimer passes, which political history was to make famous in the seventeenth century at the time of the occupation of the Valtellina. These routes, too close together for comfort, competed with or replaced each other according to political and financial circumstances and even as a result of route disturbances far from the Alps. When in 1464, Lyons obtained royal authorization to receive pepper and spices directly, Aigues-mortes and the Rhône route lost their privileged position to the Mont Genèvre, the Mont-Cenis, and the Little and Great St Bernard passes. Any quarrel, large or small, repays close study. In 1603 when Venice had concluded a political alliance with the Grisons, the route from Morbegno to Chiavenna was completed, enabling it to capture, to Bergamo's advantage, part of the trade going towards Milan; a small detail that again reveals Venice's vigilance over Alpine traffic.

These changes did not happen overnight. Geography distributed both obstacles and permanent advantages that were difficult to bypass. There was, for example, the need to connect with the waterways, lakes, and rivers, the Isère, the Lac du Bourget, Lake Geneva, Lake Constance, the Rhône, the Rhine, the Inn, or to the south, the Italian lakes which had their role to play, and particularly a river like the Adige, where the chains put in place by successive administrations could not prevent floating logs or transport in small boats. These were permanent advantages, but they operated against each other. Statistics for transport from Antwerp to Italy show the clear superiority in 1534–1545 of the St Gotthard pass, which benefited from its central situation; it was a gateway either to Genoa or Venice. The Brenner in the east was the other great crossing point. It was the lowest of all the Alpine passes (1374 metres) and had the advantage of using two divergent waterways, the Inn and the Adige, and of leading to Venice. It was also a route accessible to the heavy German wagons –

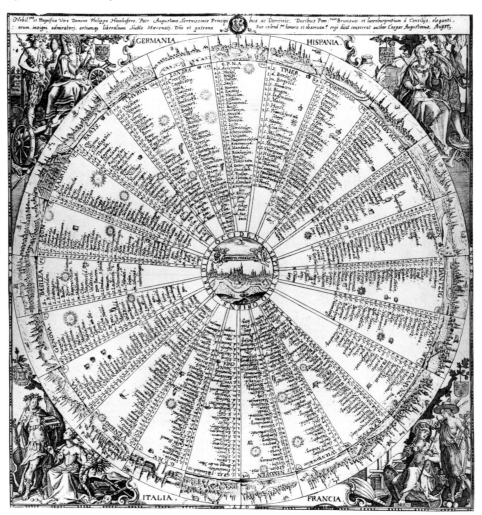

75. The *Meilenscheibe*, with Augsburg at its centre and the main trade routes radiating out from the town. *Stadtsbibliothek, Augsburg*

carretoni, as they were known south of the Alps – which would travel down after the grape harvest for the new wine from Venezia, and even from Istria, an enormous trading operation repeated every year unless Venice forbade it (as in 1597) which was, however, rarely. Usually she permitted it, preferring for her own consumption the full-bodied wines of the Marches or the islands. With the aid of the wine trade, the Brenner was from the beginning of the sixteenth century, and even more at the end, one of the most active Alpine routes, but its preeminence was not unchallenged. From 1530 the Archbishop of Salzburg had transformed the Tauern route, previously merely a *Saumweg*, or mule-track, into a passable road for wheeled traffic; the Provincial States of the Tyrol, who

76. Seventeenth-century view of the Fondaco dei Tedeschi, Venice. *Museo Correr, Venice*

defended the Brenner, and for good reason, opposed this competition, trying, in vain as it happened, to draw Ferdinand, King of the Romans, into outright opposition. This example is sufficient to indicate the flexibility of the Alpine routes: man constructed them, maintained them and if the need arose, he could divert them.

The third character: the many faces of Germany. Beyond the Alps lay the green expanses of Europe, with its forests, its wide and busy waterways, and its carriage roads; so cold in winter! In 1491 there was so much snow that the merchants of Nuremberg could travel from their hometown to Geneva by sledge.

The view looking northward from Italy brings into prominence south Germany, which for our purposes stretches as far as Cologne, Frankfurt, and Nuremberg. Thoroughly Italianized, a customer for the wines of the southern Alps, it had for centuries been in contact with the cities of the Peninsula, Genoa, Milan, Florence, Venice above all, but also Rome, Naples, and Aquila, the saffron town, as well as all the towns along the road. All roads from this Germany led south-east to the *Fontego dei Todeschi* (*Fontego* is a Venetian form of *Fondaco*, as is *Todeschi* for *Tedeschi*), a sort of miniature Germany, with both controls and privileges, an enormous building on the Grand Canal, facing the Square and Bridge of the Rialto, which was to be rebuilt in great magnificence after the fire of 1505. German merchants were allotted their own offices and could store their goods there. Sometimes the *Fontego* would be piled to the roof with fustians (the revolutionary fabrics made with linen warp and cotton woof).

77. Portrait of Jacob Fugger by Albrecht Dürer. *Bayerische Staatsgemäldesammlung, Munich*

In the *Fontego* too were to be found copper, tin, silver, and ironware. Spices, pepper, drugs, cotton, the *Südfrüchte*, were redispatched to the North.

Venice was also full of German travellers, famous and not so famous: pilgrims about to leave for the Holy Land, merchants learning the trade like Jacob Fugger, artists like Albrecht Dürer, students, or the servants of students on their way to the University of Padua. There were soldiers too, although after the Treaty of Cateau-Cambrésis in 1559, the great days were over (on this side of the Alps) for the Swiss mercenaries and the *Landsknechte* of Würtemberg. Often they were humbler folk: bakers' men, servants, artisans in the wool industry, waiters at inns and taverns, who competed in the profession with natives of Florence or Ferrara. Venice naturally had her German inns, the *White Lion* and the *Black Eagle*, as did other Italian towns: there was *Il Falcone* at Ferrara in 1583, or the *Tre Rei* at Milan. Southern Germany grew up and matured in the shadow of the greatness of northern Italy, but also not uncommonly derived advantage from its limitations. Within the partnership, Germany was entrusted with secondary tasks: manufacturing cotton, the ersatz textile of the fourteenth century, cheap fabrics, working iron, copper, and leather. Without Germany's constant support, neither the trade of Genoa and Venice, nor the economic activity of Milan would have been conceivable. 'Germans and Venetians,' wrote

78. View of the main square of Augsburg with the Italian 'Augustus Fountain' in the centre. Painting by Elias Schemel. *Städtische Kunstsammlungen, Augsburg*

Girolamo Priuli in 1509, 'we are all one, because of our ancient trading partnership.' 'Germans and *Italians*' would have been more accurate.

This shared life lies behind the extraordinary spread of Italian civilization towards the north, recognizable today simply from the façades of the houses. It also resulted in an obvious exploitation of the North by the South. But there were times when south Germany stood to gain from crises in Italy. It was Protestants, fleeing from Italy, who brought the brocade and silk velvet industry north to Nuremberg. In the fourteenth century bankruptcies in Florence had brought some profit to German merchants. German civilization too advanced, spread southwards and very quickly invaded the upper Adige valley, extending beyond Trent, the episcopal seat, as the Venetian who was received there by the bishop in 1492 could not fail to observe. The three tables were 'quadre, more germanico'; the meal began with salad, according to German custom, meats and fish were offered on the same dish, with whole-meal wheaten bread in the Bavarian style.

To a traveller starting from the Rhine, the further east he went the more Germany would appear to be a new country, still undeveloped. In the fifteenth century and during the first decades of the sixteenth, the swift rise of the mining industry created a string of new but short-lived towns, springing up quickly but soon falling into decline in the face of competition from American silver, after 1530, or rather 1550, unless the mid-century recession alone was responsible. During the subsequent recovery which was to last until the end of the century and beyond, Germany, and more generally central Europe, was to see an industrial revival on all fronts, of which the linen cloth industry of Bohemia, Saxony, and Silesia was the most important item but not the only one. So it is not true that Germany (any more than her neighbours) went into decline in the years after Luther's death in 1546. The Peace of Augsburg (1555), which was long-lasting, brought substantial benefits. And even very far to the east, the health and vigour of the towns tell their own story. Pierre Lescalopier in 1574 admired the German towns of Transylvania and the first one he came to, Brasov, 'which the Saxons call Coronestat', gave him the illusion of 'arriving at Mantua so fair is the town, the walls of the houses shining with paint'.

These two views have shown us two Germanies. There is yet another bordering the Low Countries on the shores of the North Sea, at Emden, Bremen, and Hamburg. These towns derived profit from the Atlantic trade which reached them, from their proximity to the Low Countries (first to Antwerp and then to Amsterdam), from their high economic voltage and also from the discord that was to result from it. Hamburg, the most vigorous of them, was just embarking on her long career which even the Thirty Years War did not interrupt.

From Genoa to Antwerp, and from Venice to Hamburg: the conditions of circulation. As we have seen, Mediterranean life was caught up and prolonged northwards by an overland traffic exceptional for the period. That is not to say that the zone north of the Alps between Lyons and Vienna was a scene of bustling activity and modernity, but certainly it was animated by a flow of energy more marked perhaps than in France, particularly if we include Lyons, the city serving the Alps, and the Rhône valley in the central rather than the French part of Europe. Clearly it was a zone with many modern features. Numerous firms grew up, with their roots in the Italian towns, the Low Countries, and the Iberian peninsula. The big family firms, inclined to be inward-looking and often of monstrous size (Fugger, Hochstetter, Welser, Affaitati) gave way to firms that were smaller, but more numerous, and above all, more active than the general histories of the period would suggest: the della Faille in the Netherlands, on whom a book has recently appeared, the Torrigiani, Bartolomeo Viatis (and his associate Fürst) at Nuremberg and Breslau, the Pestalozzi, Bartolomeo Castello at Vienna, the Montelupi at Cracow, to name only a few Italian firms in foreign countries towards the end of the century. Many more names could be added to the list.

A new practice appeared. Firms would work on a commission basis, relying on other merchants who agreed to represent them and act as their agents. It

79. Merchant's goods being packaged. Seventeenth-century
German print.

reduced operating costs. At the same time, some firms began to specialize in transport, which became a separate activity. We have records of big transport firms at Hamburg and Antwerp: Lederer, Cleinhaus, Annoni, and many others, often of Alpine origin. At Lyons and Venice too, similar developments occurred. An undated Venetian document of the seventeenth century says, 'The merchandise which is transported from Venice to Lombardy and Germany is entrusted to the transporters [*conduttori*] who undertake on payment of an agreed sum to deliver it to the stated destination in good condition and within a specified period agreed by both parties.' These *conduttori* themselves relied on the services of the *spazzadori* who conveyed the loads by boat, wagon, or pack animal from inn to inn, the inn-keeper providing them with the necessary animals and vehicles.

Long-distance trade was inevitably confined to goods whose value was sufficient to defray the cost of transport: copper, silver, hardware, pepper, spices, cotton from the Levant (of which Venice continued to be the chief importer, re-exporting it to the north), silk, the *Südfrüchte*, and finally and above all, fabrics, which were always of primary importance. In one direction traffic was in English kerseys ('one of the most important foundations of trade in the world', as a Venetian document was already saying in 1513), linen, serges (from Hondschoote then from Leyden), grosgrain (from Lille), 'mixed' fabrics (fustians, burats, bombazines) and linens from the German and Swiss towns. In the other direction, from Italy, came velvets, taffetas, high-quality woollen cloth, silken cloth woven with threads of silver or gold, and luxury fabrics. The Antwerp firm della Faille was to set up a branch at Venice and another at Verona, which bought raw silk and spun it on the spot with such care that the quality of their products was unequalled. The firm's accounts certainly do not give the impression of a falling-off in trade, quite the reverse.

The movement of goods led to movements of money, from north to south and south to north. The great event of 1585, the promotion of Frankfurt-am-Main, previously known for its trade fairs, to the rank of currency-exchange fair, was well-timed. This event was followed by others, the founding of the Bank of Amsterdam in 1609 (to be of world importance), the Bank of Hamburg in 1619, and the Bank of Nuremberg in 1621. By then these lines of communications were beyond the pioneer stage and routes, means of transport, and stopping places were all but settled.

Emigration and balance of trade. Can any positive conclusions be drawn from all these transactions, whether political or not, and from these developments at which we can only guess? We can, I think, offer two general observations: first, there was a definite balance of trade in favour of the South. Second, there was the breakthrough by Italian merchants into German trading centres, Venetians in the forefront after 1558. Until then, the German merchants of the *Fondaco* had had the monopoly, north of the Alps, of purchases destined for Venice, except for horses, arms, and victuals. During the second half of the sixteenth century, the old ruling fell into disregard, and Venetian merchants were increasingly to be found in German marketplaces. These were more likely to be Venetians from the mainland than from Venice itself, a new generation of traders. Such was the case of Bartolomeo Viatis, from Bergamo, who went to live in Nuremberg at the age of twelve, in 1550, and fought his way to the top place, alongside the Kochs. He dealt on a large scale in linens, products from the Levant, ostrich feathers and chamois hides; he owned several offices at the *Fondego dei Todeschi* and, on the occasion of Marco Ottobon's mission to Danzig, he disregarded his own interests and put his credit, which was great, at the disposal of the Signoria of Venice. When he died in 1644, rich in years and descendants, he left a fortune valued at over a million florins. Not all Italian merchants achieved this spectacular success, but their assets often represented large sums, whether in Cologne (in spite of many bankruptcies) or Nuremberg, Prague or Augsburg, and the two towns which were on the rise, Frankfurt and Leipzig.

Clearly these immigrant merchants helped their native cities to adapt to a

80. A Nuremberg merchant's establishment. Anonymous sketch for a mural.
Stadtgeschichtliche Museen, Nuremberg

Germany which in the seventeenth century was gradually finding 'its new cardinal points', based roughly on the new Frankfurt–Leipzig line, midway between north and south, and the Hamburg–Venice axis. The battle waged by Italian merchants against local merchants, and even more against Dutch dealers – the Calvinists against whom the Leipzig riots of May, 1593, were directed – was to last a long time. In Frankfurt in 1585 when the exchange fairs were set up, out of eighty-two firms who applied for this change in the town's status, twenty-two were Italian. This was a phenomenon of the end of the century and of the beginning of the next. A Dutch report of 1626, to the States General of Holland, pointed out that the Venetians provided, not only their neighbours, 'but even Germany, at far less cost than the Dutch, with all the goods of the Levant'. At Cologne, Frankfurt, Nuremberg, and Leipzig, the presence of the Italian merchants which was already more noticeable after 1580, was maintained well after 1600. In 1633 when the Swedes took Nuremberg, the Venetians ran up the banner of St Mark to protect their shops, proving at any rate that they were still there. And in 1604, Venice, which had preserved almost intact the monopoly of supplying the German fustian industry with cotton, still required five times as much transport for the journey to Germany as for the return trip.

So Italy, and through her the Mediterranean, kept the door open for a long time on the wide spaces of northern Europe, and remained firmly entrenched at Antwerp, a financial centre that maintained its role uninterrupted, in spite of (or possibly because of) the festering war of the Netherlands. In 1603 the mission of B. C. Scaramelli restored good relations with England. Soon, in 1610, friendly relations were established between Venice and Amsterdam. In 1616 the proconsuls and senators of Hamburg asked Venice to send a consul to the city.

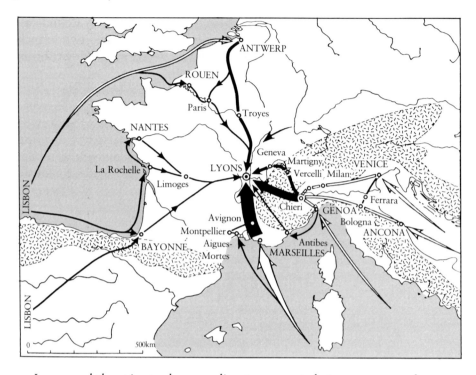

Lyons and the spice trade, according to accounts between 1525 and 1534

From R. Gascon, 'Le siècle du commerce des épices à Lyon, fin XVe–fin XVIe siècle', in *Annales E.S.C.*, July–August, 1960. Note the predominance of the routes from Marseilles and from Chieri, over the Alps, in the concentration of traffic at Lyons.

As early as 1599, Sebastian Koch, the Hamburg consul at Genoa, offered to represent at the same time the interests of the Danziger captains. In short, although an overall description can sometimes be deceptive, it seems probable that this central trade area kept doors open on both sides, well after the beginning of the seventeenth century.

The French isthmus, from Rouen to Marseilles. The French isthmus can be visualized as based on the roads leading from Marseilles to Lyons, then through Burgundy to Paris, and beyond it to Rouen. But a detailed examination will reveal the inadequacies of this over-simple outline.

There were four routes one could take from Lyons to Marseilles: the Rhône itself, which at Beaucaire met the main road to Spain via Montpellier and Narbonne; the main road, chiefly used by mule-trains, running along the left bank; a second road forking east and passing through Carpentras to Aix; and lastly a road leading over the Alps, by the Croix-Haute pass and Sisteron, again to Aix-en-Provence.

Between Lyons and Paris there were three routes: one going by Roanne used the Loire, at least as far as Briare, then went on to Orléans; and two branches separating at Chalon, one passing through Dijon and Troyes, the other through Auxerre and Sens.

In addition, this network was linked, in the east and north, to the roads of central Europe. Two roads led from Lyons to Italy via Grenoble or Chambéry; they met up again at the Mont-Cenis and beyond at the 'pass of Susa' which was the gateway to Italy for both merchants and soldiers. Susa was one of the busiest roadposts of the Alps, with a constant procession of mule-trains or 'great wagons' arriving and leaving. From Lyons too, one or two roads led towards the Rhine, over the Jura, and two roads led to Antwerp, one via Lorraine and the other via Champagne.

That the road network of the French isthmus should have been drawn towards the East, attracted by its busy flow of traffic, is an important observation in support of which at least two examples can be cited. First, it can be calculated that Lyons was still receiving a large proportion of its pepper and spices by way of the Mont-Cenis, at least between 1525 and 1535, while Marseilles was still a modest port. And second, the importance of the Antwerp connection is strikingly revealed by the very large quantities of goods belonging to French merchants, which were brought to the Scheldt port for distribution or redistribution by land and sea, or bonded there, and were sometimes of other than French origin, of course. But the connection is clearly established.

The French network was also drawn towards the south-west and Spain. We have already mentioned the Beaucaire route. An active route also ran from Lyons to Bayonne, crossing the Massif Central by Limoges where it met the main road from Paris to Spain. This great road, starting in the capital in the Rue St-Jacques, was not only the ancient pilgrim route to Santiago de Compostela, but the most active thoroughfare of France in the second half of the sixteenth century. The whole of the Atlantic west coast was caught in the toils of Spanish silver, for which Bayonne, because it was a frontier station, was one of the principal entry points, though not the only one. The other was Rennes, because of the voyages made by Breton boats carrying the grain that fed Lisbon and Seville. There was no comparison between a western France rich in silver coins, and poor Burgundy reduced to copper pieces.

This Spanish silver route was for many years a source of profit to Lyons. Like Geneva the creation of Italian capitalism – not merely the brainchild of Louis XI – Lyons, the city of fairs among the silk looms, amassed the metal currency that was to swell the assets of the Italian merchants in France. It was a door that long stood wide open for this flight of currency. This role was the culmination of a wide range of activities. One of the great turning points in French economic history was to be when the financial centre of the country was transferred from Lyons to Paris. This was a change as important and as difficult to explain as the transfer of Antwerp's supremacy to Amsterdam. In short, any reference to the French isthmus is bound to lead eventually to discussing the whole of France, as we have already hinted.

After this brief summary, we can return to the Rhône corridor which particularly concerns the Mediterranean. There was a large volume of trade going down the river. Orange, built some distance from the Rhône, was thinking in 1562 of constructing a canal as far as Camaret in order to reach the river traffic. The chief cargo was grain, pargicularly grain from Burgundy, which was transported in casks (as in Tuscany, another wine-growing region) and directed towards Arles. For this reason, Provence was for a long time a leading grain exporter to the Mediterranean countries. Grain from Provence often enabled the king of France to put pressure on Genoa. After 1559, by contrast, there is no sign of export on this scale, with a few exceptions, such as the small boats that sailed from Avignon to Rome with their loads of grain. Does this mean that after that date the grain from the Rhône valley and Provence was all for home consumption? These river boats also carried, alongside the casks of grain, *brocz* of mineral coal (probably from the Alès basin), which gave Marseilles the privilege of being possibly the only Mediterranean town to use coal for fuel in the sixteenth century.

The river traffic was paralleled by overland traffic also going towards the sea. This time the load was books, for the most part from the presses of Lyons, which were exported in packs to Italy and Spain; and cloth of every origin, English and Flemish, woollen cloth from Paris and Rouen. These were old, established currents of trade, which increased in the sixteenth century, to the advantage of the textile production of western and northern France which drove everything before it, Catalan as well as Italian goods. Crowds of pedlars and country merchants would flock to the towns and fairs of the South. At Pézenas and Montagnac in Languedoc, fabrics from the North alone would fill pages: 'cloth from Paris and Rouen, scarlet, black, yellow, violet, or ash-grey' . . . linens from Auvergne, Berry, Burgundy, and especially from Brittany 'to clothe the poor, line cloaks and make sheets and mattresses for the hospitals'.

River traffic and mule-trains cooperated on the journey up river. The small boats of the Rhône carried great quantities of salt for the northern countries. From the time of Louis XI the capitalists of Montpellier had been interested in this lucrative trade, which later even the Wars of Religion did not disrupt. By water, too, went raw wool from Languedoc or Provence, or verdigris from Montpellier. Along the land routes, which were often in poor condition and full of potholes, went everything Marseilles had to send to the interior: spices, pepper, drugs, wool and leather from the Barbary coast, cheeses from Sardinia, barrels of fish, sometimes cases of dates, oranges from Hyères, Turkish carpets, silks, rice from the Levant, steel from Piedmont, alum from Civitavecchia, and malmsey wine. It is possible to compile this list from the chance survival of a Marseilles register dated 1543. It also indicates the towns which as direct customers for this trade made up the economic zone of Marseilles, centred on the

81. View of the Rhône at Valence. Engraving by Née after Le May.

axis of the Rhône as far as Lyons. Some goods were dispatched to Toulouse, but this was rare. And very few went as far as Paris; on the whole the Marseilles trade was appropriated by a series of intermediate inland towns. Its volume decreased the further north one went – at Arles, Beaucaire and Pézenas – to disappear altogether when it was swallowed up in the activity of Lyons. This was probably true of all other Mediterranean towns: none of them was in a position at that time to control to the end of the journey the goods it sent inland.

There can be little doubt of the modest scale of Marseilles trade, as it appears from the 1543 register. Yet at this period the city was the unchallenged mistress of the Provençal coast. The neighbouring ports were at her service, some bringing grain from Arles, others ferrying the indispensable casks from Fréjus just before the fishing season. From this time on, it exercised a strong attraction over Cape Corse. But the rise of Marseilles cannot have preceded the capitulations of 1569, or more decisive still, the 1570–1573 war, which immobilized Venice, and greatly disrupted its relations with the Levant. This crisis made Marseilles' fortune, increasing the voyages of her merchant fleet and at the same time swelling the volume of traffic along the Rhône corridor, since some of the German trade, for instance, was diverted via Lyons and Marseilles. Towards 1580 the barques and galleons of the Phocaean city were sailing over the entire Mediterranean.

Clearly the fortunes of Marseilles were not entirely sustained by the roads of the isthmus. They also prospered from sea traffic: the Marseilles barques were at the service of Genoa, Leghorn, Venice, and the ports of Spain and Africa. Like

Ragusan ships they made a living from the sea and its commercial exchanges, the more so since there was no Colbert in the sixteenth century, no strong French industry behind Marseilles. But there was already France, France and her markets. And there was a main road right down through the middle of France making Marseilles one of the gateways through which English cloth and Flemish serges reached the Mediterranean.

But a great continental road is not only a trade route. The French axis was not only the channel along which salt travelled northwards or textiles south-wards, but also the route taken by the victorious advance after the 1450s of the French language, which spread south, overlaying the language and civilization of the *Langue d'Oc*, eventually reaching the shores of the Mediterranean itself. In the other direction, it was also the route used by the throngs of Italian immigrants of all conditions: merchants, artists, workmen, artisans, labourers, hundreds, thousands of Italians, brilliant and quarrelsome. We can imagine them sitting down to eat at the French inns, whose abundant fare threw into ecstasies even Girolamo Lippomanio himself, the ambassador of opulent Venice. At Paris, he said, 'there are innkeepers who can give you meals at all prices: for one teston, for two, for a crown, for four, ten or even twenty per person, if you wish!' These Italians were responsible for whole chapters of French history: the draining of the lower Rhône valley; the growth of the bank and bourse of Lyons; and in general for the Renaissance and the art of the Counter-Reformation, powerful advance-posts of Mediterranean civilization.

French influence was in the first place that of a great political power: but it was quickly followed by a fresh flowering of French culture, still modest in the century of the Renaissance and the Baroque but discernible in many small details that foreshadowed what was to become an overwhelming influence – in, for instance, the raptures of the ladies of the Spanish court when the 'Queen of Peace', little Elizabeth of Valois, whom Philip II had just married, unpacked her trunks; or in the way French fashions took hold of even Venice, which was the capital of masculine and feminine elegance until the seventeenth century; or in the pains taken by the Marquise de Gast, at Naples, to win over the Grand Prieur who visited her in 1559: 'Madame la Marquise', wrote Brantôme, who was present, 'greeted him in the French fashion, then the visit commenced. She asked her daughters to keep him company in the French manner, and to laugh, dance, play and talk, freely, modestly, and correctly as you do at the French court.' The French song began to have its champions in the South; early enough not to compete with Italian opera which was to become popular everywhere at the end of the century. These are small signs, apparently superficial. But is it so unimportant that in sixteenth-century Italy, it should already be the Frenchman, as we may imagine him with his gesticulations, his extravagant manners, and his hectic social life, exhausting and wearing out his lackeys, who served as a model for polite society?

Europe and the Mediterranean. The European isthmuses, as we have seen, pro-vided the essential lines along which Mediterrean influence was transmitted. But the north–south routes, although important, by no means totally conditioned the mass of countries and peoples they passed through. The barriers lying between the Mediterranean and northern Europe played their negative role. So southern influence did not spread through the North in waves, although that night be the image that first comes to mind. When it penetrated deeply into a region, it was along narrow channels running northwards with the great trade routes and reaching with them the most distant lands. It is sometimes to these distant lands that we must go to explain the history of the sea.

But these channels, often running into lands that were completely foreign – Russia, for example – were only linear extensions of the Mediterranean into a Europe where the influence of the sea was felt in very varying degrees. Strong Mediterranean influence was felt, through the many ramifications of these vital arteries, only at a relatively short distance from its shores. This is where we shall find the zone which can properly be said to be impregnated with Mediterranean culture: a privileged but imprecise zone; for its boundaries may vary depending on whether one is thinking of religious, cultural, or economic factors.

3 The Atlantic Ocean

It may seem paradoxical to end a chapter on the boundaries of the Mediter-ranean region with the Atlantic itself, as if it were merely an annexe of the inland sea. But in the sixteenth century the ocean did not yet have a fully independent existence. Man was only just beginning to take its measure and to construct an identity for it with what could be found in Europe, as Robinson Crusoe built his cabin from what he could salvage from his ship.

Several Atlantics. The Atlantic in the sixteenth century was the association and more or less literal coexistence of several partly autonomous areas. There was the transversal ocean of the English and French, of which the Gulf Stream with its storm-shaken routes was the usual axis, and Newfoundland the first landfall. The Spanish Atlantic was an ellipse whose outline was marked by Seville, the Canaries, the West Indies, and the Azores: its port of call and its driving forces. The Portuguese Atlantic was the great triangle of the central and southern part of the ocean, one side running from Lisbon to Brazil, the second from Brazil to the Cape of Good Hope, and the third, the route followed by sailing ships returning from the Indies, from St Helena along the African coast.

These different Atlantics, linked to national histories, have had no difficulty in finding historians. There is another Atlantic which has been neglected, poss-ibly because it links together these particular sectors, and whose full significance will only become apparent in the comprehensive history of the Atlantic that has

82. *A Storm at Sea* by Joos de Momper. *Kunsthistorisches Museum, Vienna*

yet to be written. Yet it is the most ancient of all, the Atlantic of the medieval and even classical navigators from the Pillars of Hercules to the Cassiterides, that narrow sea with its frequent wild storms, which lies between the coasts of Portugal, Spain, France, Ireland, and England, in fact the simple north–south route rivalling the land routes of the European isthmuses. From this one followed all the other Atlantic oceans of the fifteenth and sixteenth centuries. It was the nursery of Atlantic exploration.

It was a treacherous sea indeed and one where voyages were difficult. The Bay of Biscay, with its long swells and furious waters, enjoys a bad reputation which is as justified as that of the Gulf of Lions in the Mediterranean. No ship could be sure, on leaving the Mediterranean, of safely negotiating the entry to the English Channel to the northeast, although it is so wide. Charles V's younger brother Ferdinand found himself in 1518 quite unintentionally lying off the wild coast of Ireland, with the fleet that had brought him from Laredo. Coming from the North, like Philip II in August, 1559, one was by no means sure of a straight passage to the ports of the Cantabrian coast. The ambassador Dantiscus, who was for so long Poland's representative at the court of Charles V, experienced this voyage, from England to the Peninsula, in December, 1522. He declared that nothing in the Mediterranean or the Baltic could be compared with the horrible violence of the 'Sea of Spain'. 'If I were to gain the empire of the world for the price of that voyage, I should never enter upon such a perilous venture,' he said.

It was indeed through the perils of the nearby Atlantic and the Bay of Biscay that the 'empire of the world' was purchased. On these rough seas Europe underwent her hardest-won apprenticeship of the sea, and prepared to conquer the world.

The Atlantic learns from the Mediterranean. How did these 'Atlantics' influence the Mediterranean, and how did the inland sea affect these great expanses?

In the sixteenth century the Mediterranean had clear prerogatives in the western Atlantic. The prosperous trade of the ocean was beneficial to the inland sea; at all events it took part in it. Barrels of cod from Newfoundland; sugar from the islands (Madeira, São Tomé); sugar and dye-woods from Brazil; gold and silver from Spanish America; pepper, spices, pearls, and silks from the Indian Ocean, shipped round the Cape of Good Hope – the Mediterranean had a share in all these foreign riches and new trades. During the sixteenth century it was very far from being the neglected and impoverished world that the voyages of Columbus and Vasco da Gama are supposed to have ruined. On the contrary, the Mediterranean shaped the Atlantic and impressed its own image on the Spanish New World. One historian reviewing the first edition of this book, regretted that the donkey, the symbol of everyday life in the Mediterranean, was not given more space. To see peasants riding past on burros in Mexico, he said, is to be irresistibly reminded of a Mediterranean landscape. If so, there are plenty of other occasions! The cereals sown as soon as possible, the vines quickly planted in Peru and Chile, the mule-trains of the *arrieros*, the churches, the Plaza Mayor of the Spanish towns, the flocks brought over from the Peninsula, which soon propagated themselves in the wild state, the astonishing flowering of the colonial Baroque: this whole new civilization had roots in the Mediterranean.

But the benefits worked both ways: at the end of the century the rise of Naples, for instance, as a centre for the purchasing of northern products and for the export of Mediterranean goods, was entirely due to the arrival of Atlantic vessels; and the Dutch ships that transported Spanish wool directly to Venice were partly responsible for the spectacular boom at the end of the sixteenth century in the city's cloth industry. In short, it is not easy to draw up a balance sheet of the credits and debits of both sides.

The Atlantic destiny in the sixteenth century. For our purposes it would be more useful to outline a history of the Atlantic from the point of view of its relations with the Mediterranean.

From the beginning of the century until 1580, the Iberians, that is men of

83. View of Lisbon. From *Civitates Orbis Terrarum*, 1572.

the Mediterranean, controlled the part of the ocean between Seville and the West Indies – 'Seville's Atlantic', as Pierre Chauna has called it. They also controlled the great Portuguese ocean from Lisbon. Apart from a few French privateers practically no other ship ventured into these well-guarded waters. No other power interrupted or diverted their economic growth. Beyond the isthmus of Panama, the Sevilian Atlantic joined up with the sea route to Peru, as far as Arica, the port for the Potosi mines. After 1564 the Manila galleon regularly crossed the Pacific from Acapulco to the Philippines and effectively linked up with the Chinese economy. The Portuguese had from the start sent their ships to India, then beyond to the East Indies, China, and Japan. They also organized the great slave trade between Africa and America, not to mention the clandestine export of silver from Potosi by way of the overland routes of Brazil and, even more, by Buenos Aires and the little boats of the Rio de la Plata.

It all added up to an immense and complicated system, drawing on the economy of the whole world. There were a few mishaps, a few difficult patches, but on the whole this Iberian-dominated economy maintained itself until 1580 and even longer. Proof of this is to be found in the rise in consignments of silver arriving at Seville as well as of the various goods returning from the 'Indies': leather, Brazil-wood, cochineal – the last figuring among 'royal merchandise', the profits from which were fought over by merchants. Another proof is the vast series of examples of marine insurance at the Consulate of Burgos, where for a considerable period the premium rate was lower for the Atlantic than the Mediterranean. And Lisbon kept her position in the spice trade well after 1600. Finally, when the skies darkened with the first signs of Protestant privateering, the two giants, Spain and Portugal, joined forces. Who would have suspected in 1580 that this was the association of two monumental weaknesses?

But there were shadows, and serious ones, on this optimistic scene: the near Atlantic, the north–south Atlantic, was very soon lost. This route had been pioneered by Mediterranean sailors several centuries earlier. In 1297 Genoese galleys had made the first direct voyage to Bruges, and they were followed about twenty years later by the Venetian *galere da mercato* (some time between 1310 and 1320, probably in 1317) and many other ships. This move coincided (without necessarily being its consequence or cause) with the end of the prosperity of the fairs of Champagne. It brought many Italian merchants to the Netherlands and England; they settled there as if in conquered lands. This maritime triumph immediately brought supremacy to Italy; with her colonies in the Levant and her counting houses in the North, she was able to detach herself from the backward economies surrounding her, now becoming the most advanced and richest of all. Another unexpected consequence was the bringing to life of the European Atlantic seaboard, particularly Andalusia and Portugal, which was to prepare the way for the Age of Discovery.

When the slow but powerful economic advance of the mid-fifteenth century began, it was again the Italian system, both continental and maritime, which drew most profit from it. Venice and Genoa dominated the English and Flemish markets. It was not until the sixteenth century that this system began to decline. In about 1550 trade between the North Sea, Portugal, and Andalusia was taken over by northern ships. Twenty years later at the time of the Anglo-Spanish crisis of 1568–1569, the Iberians had virtually to abandon the northern route. Once launched on their career, the northern sailing vessels were soon to take the road to Gibraltar and to achieve the conquest of the Mediterranean which they had only partially accomplished before 1550. But their progress was slow. An old Spaniard (he was 87), relating his memoirs in 1629, remembered a time when the English were hard put to maintain fifteen men-of-war.

Overall, these years meant a series of direct or indirect losses for the Mediterranean, but they were not necessarily disastrous for the Mediterranean countries. Spain and Portugal were marshalling their strength to maintain their great Atlantic routes as chief priority. The case of Viscaya is revealing. It provided the best ships of the *Carrera de Indias*, its galleons set off for the Indies, but its *zabras*, by contrast, which before 1569 had carried wool and silver from Spain to Antwerp, became increasingly rare on the northern routes. But the vital link between Seville and the North was maintained despite these fluctuations. For the northerners bringing grain, fish, wood, iron, copper, tin, gunpowder, woollen cloth, linen, hardware, and ready-made ships, the Spanish trip was worth it for the salt, wine, and silver they could bring back. The Peninsula was well able to pay for their services.

So there were overall losses, but they were compensated within a world system that was wide open to Italian merchants, who had been in Lisbon and Seville from the very start. It was the Genoese who launched Seville on her career and set up the indispensable and slow circulation of capital, without which nothing could have been accomplished anywhere on either side of the Atlantic. The Spanish economy provided a basis for their activities as well as for the more discreet but still important contribution of the Florentines. The Italian capitalists, Venetians and Milanese, joined in and held the key routes to the Low Countries. Italian merchants of every origin were to be found at Antwerp, Nuremberg, and even at the other end of the world, at Hormuz or Goa. In short the Mediterranean was not out of the picture at all. Or rather it was never out of any picture. Through the Genoese it even controlled the imperial finances of Spain, and through the so-called Besançon fairs, the entire movement, at the summit, of European capital.

The system was to prove long-lived. There was to be no major disaster for the Mediterranean, before the Dutch ships of Cornelius Houtmann rounded the Cape of Good Hope, in 1596 on the outward trip and 1598 on the return journey. Only then was the system touched in its vitals at the moment when, give or take a few years, the secular trend was being reversed. In such reversals the most spectacular achievements are usually the first to suffer. But in this case there was no sudden change. The most indicative dates are perhaps 1620–1630, when the Portuguese *marranos*, those only semi-converted *novos christãos* who were often the straw men of northern capitalism, became installed at the centre of Spain's finances. They took up a decisive position alongside the Genoese *hombres de negocios*. On 8th August, 1628, off Matanzas, near Havana, the *armada y flota* of New Spain was surrounded and captured by the Dutch vessels of Piet Heyn.

These late dates reduce, to my mind, the importance conventionally attached to the year 1588, the year of the Invincible Armada. There are several good reasons why this should be so. First, Spain was still capable, after the failure of 1588 – occasioned by winds and storms and the absence of skilled pilots along the sandbanks of the North Sea quite as much as by the enemy – of launching two more expeditions against England, in 1597 and in 1601, as well as fostering a diversionary war in Ireland which was a drain on Elizabeth's financial resources. Second, the failure occurred during a period of general prosperity when it was still possible for a wound to heal over. Third, English privateering slowed down of its own accord; it had clearly dealt the enemy some very nasty blows (the sack of Cadiz in 1596 affected Spain's prestige even more than her wealth), but gradually the islands and the Spanish coast took up arms. Fourth, while England may have prepared the way for Spain's collapse, she did not immediately gain from it. An important detail to be noted is that she signed a peace treaty with the Catholic King in 1604, six years after France, and five years before the United Provinces.

This corresponds to the impression given by the Spanish documents of the end of the century. The struggle against England was often waged in an empty ocean. The English, who controlled the Channel, would leave it before the squadrons of the Adelantado of Castile were ready for them at Lisbon or Cadiz;

they could easily sail to the Canaries or the Azores, even up to the Straits of Gibraltar with its guard of galleys, galleons, and Spanish troops. It was not until after the return of the English ships, at the very end of the summer, that the Spanish ships would sail up from Gibraltar to El Ferrol. It is true that the Straits of Gibralter were passed by force by English and Dutch ships. But they did not find it easy. The English ships, according to representatives of the Levant Company, would go through in winter for more security, 'when the water in the straits is very rough and when they are unlikely to meet the Spanish patrol galleons, which are at their moorings'. Meanwhile every year the Spanish fleets from the New World would return with more and more riches, as if 'the hand of God was guiding them'. This was what really mattered to Spain and her Mediterranean associates.

A late decline. So this final voyage in search of a Greater Mediterranean complements the others. The narrow sea set between the great land masses was until 1600 the scene of a thriving, flexible, and powerful economy. It was not abandoned by history, suddenly, bag and baggage, at the end of the century. The retreat was not sounded until later. The general outline of our subject has now been sketched. It is time to block in the main lines and look more carefully at the detail.

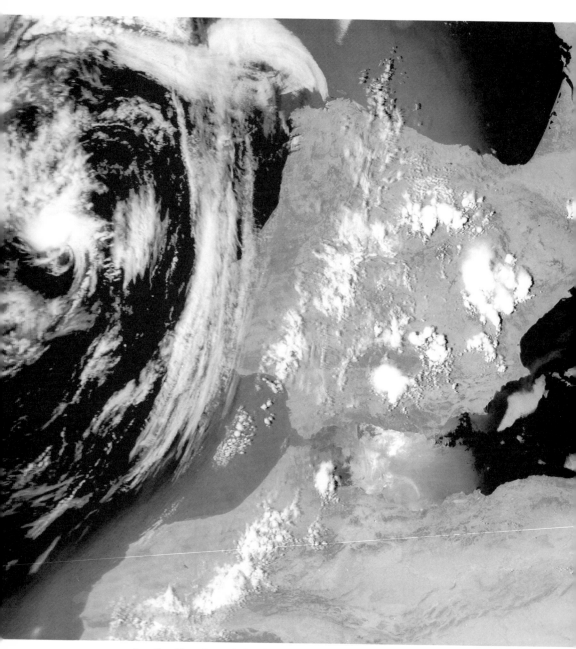

84. Satellite view of cloud coming in from the Atlantic towards Spain.

4

The Mediterranean as a Physical Unit: Climate and History

. . . the wanderings of Ulysses, ever under the same climate.
J. de Barros, *Asia*, I. IV, p. 160.

IT WOULD BE DIFFICULT to recognize any unity in this dense, composite, and ill-defined world we have described at such length other than that of being the meeting place of many peoples, and the melting-pot of many histories. Nevertheless it is significant that at the heart of this human unit, occupying an area smaller than the whole, there should be a source of physical unity, a climate, which has imposed its uniformity on both landscape and ways of life. Its significance appears by contrast with the Atlantic. The ocean too is a human unit and one of the most vigorous of the present day world; it too has been a meeting place and a melting-pot of history. But the Atlantic complex lacks a

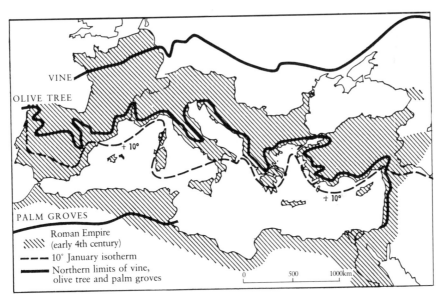

VINE

OLIVE TREE

+ 10°

+ 10°

PALM GROVES

Roman Empire
(early 4th century)
- - - 10° January isotherm
—— Northern limits of vine,
olive tree and palm groves

0   500   1000km

The 'true' Mediterranean, from the olive tree to the great palm groves
The limit of the palm groves refers only to *large*, compact groves. The limit for the date-palm growing isolated or in small clumps is much further north.

homogeneous centre comparable to the source of that even light which shines at the heart of the Mediterranean. The Atlantic, stretching from pole to pole, reflects the colours of all the earth's climates.

The Mediterranean of the vines and olive trees consists, as we know, only of a few narrow coastal strips, ribbons of land bordering the sea. This falls very short of the historical Mediterranean, but it is of great importance that the Mediterranean complex should have taken its rhythm from the uniform band of climate and culture at its centre, so distinctive that it is to this that the adjective 'Mediterranean' is usually applied. Such a force operating at the centre could not fail to have far-reaching repercussions, since it affects all movements into and out of the Mediterranean. Nor is this climate merely confined to the coastal strips, for since they surround the whole sea, it is also the climate of the waters in between. It is a great deal more than a beautiful setting.

1 The unity of the climate

Above the Mediterranean of land and water stretches the Mediterranean of the sky, having little or no connection with the landscapes below and, in fact, independent of local physical conditions. It is created by the breath of two external forces: the Atlantic Ocean, its neighbour to the west, and the Sahara, its neighbour to the south. The Mediterranean itself is not responsible for the sky that lights it.

The Atlantic and the Sahara. Within this not entirely closed vessel, two forces are at work, turn by turn: the Sahara brings dry air, clear light, the vast blue sky; the Atlantic, when it is not spreading clouds and rain, sends in abundance that grey mist and moist air which is more widespread than one would think in the Mediterranean atmosphere during the 'winter semester'. The early Orientalist painters created an enduring false impression with their glowing palettes. In October, 1869, Fromentin, leaving Messina by boat, noted, 'grey skies, cold wind, a few drops of rain on the awning. It is sad, it could be the Baltic.'

The rains have always been a fact of life throughout the region. In Florence, notes a diarist for the entry 24th January, 1651, the inclement weather has lasted five months. The previous year, Capua had been swamped by torrential rains. In fact there was hardly a winter when the rivers did not burst their banks and the towns were not subjected to the terrors and destruction of flooding. Venice suffered more than most, of course. In November, 1443, her losses were enormous, 'quasi mezo million di ducati'; on 18th December, 1600, there was an identical disaster, the *lidi*, the canals, the houses, the private stores at street level, the public stores of salt, grain, and spices all suffering great damage, 'con dano di un million d'oro', which is also evidence that prices had risen in the meantime.

85. *View of Toledo* by El Greco. The correspondence with the satellite photograph on page 170 is striking. *Metropolitan Museum of Art, New York*

In winter, or more precisely between the September equinox and the March equinox, the Atlantic influence is predominant. The anticyclone over the Azores lets in the Atlantic depressions that move one after another into the warm waters of the Mediterranean; they come in either from the Bay of Biscay, moving quickly over Aquitaine; or, like ships, they enter the Mediterranean by the Straits of Gibraltar and the Spanish coasts. Wherever they enter they cross the Mediterranean from west to east, travelling quickly. They make the winter weather most unsettled, bringing rain, causing sudden winds to spring up, and constantly agitating the sea, which when whipped by the *mistral*, the *noroît* or the *bora*, is often so white with foam, that it looks like a plain covered with snow, or 'strewn with ashes' as a sixteenth-century traveller described it. Above Toledo, the Atlantic humidity contributes in winter to bring those turbulent and dramatic skies of storm and light painted by El Greco.

So every year, and often violently, the Atlantic banishes the desert far away to the south and east. In winter rain falls over the Algerian provinces and sometimes in the heart of the Sahara. Rain falls even on the mountains of western Arabia.

Around the spring equinox, everything changes again, rather suddenly, at about the time when, as the calendar of the Maghreb says, the season for grafting trees arrives, and the first notes of the nightingale are heard. Of real springtime there is little or none; perhaps a short week that suddenly brings out leaves and flowers. As soon as the winter rains are over, the desert begins to move back and invade the sea, including the surrounding mountains, right up to their peaks. It moves westwards, and above all northwards, passing beyond the furthest limits of the Mediterranean world. In France, the burning air from the south every summer warms the southern Alps, invades most of the Rhône valley, crosses the basin of Aquitaine diagonally as a warm current, and often carries the searing drought through the Garonne region to the distant coasts of southern Brittany.

Torrid summer then reigns uncontested in the centre of the Mediterranean zone. The sea is astonishingly calm: in July and August it is like a millpond; little boats sail far out and low-lying galleys could venture without fear from port to port. The summr semester was the best time for shipping, piracy, and war.

The physical causes of this dry, torrid summer are clear. As the sun moves further north, the anticyclone of the Azores increases in size again. When their passage is blocked, the long chain of Atlantic depressions is halted. The obstacle is removed only when autumn approaches; then the Atlantic invasion begins again.

A homogeneous climate. The *extreme* limits of such a climate could be said to lie far from the shores of the Mediterranean, if they are extended on one side, over Europe, to the regions touched by the Saharan drought in summer, and in the other direction to the regions in Asia and Africa, even in the middle of the vast steppes, which are affected by the rain of the Atlantic depressions. But to set such wide limits is clearly misleading. In general, the geographer's well-known observation must be accepted without question: the Mediterranean climate lies between the northern limit of the olive tree and the northern limit of the palm grove. Between these frontiers we may count the Italian (or rather Apennine) peninsula, Greece, Cyrenaica, Tunisia, and, elsewhere, a few narrow coastal strips rarely more than 200 kilometres wide. For the mountain barriers soon

86, 87, 88. *Above:* Ashurbanipal in his garden surrounded
by date palms and vines. Relief from Nineveh, seventh century
BC. *British Museum. Right:* Detail from a Neo-Punic votive
relief from Carthage showing the goddess of fertility
holding a bunch of grapes and a pomegranate, c. AD 200.
British Museum. Below: Detail from a Greek black-figure vase
showing olive gathering, c.520 BC. *British Museum*

loom up. The Mediterranean climate is often the climate only of a coastal fringe, the riviera, bordering the sea, a ribbon as narrow as the coastal strip in the Crimea where figs, olives, oranges, and pomegranates all grow freely, though only in the southern part of the peninsula.

But this narrow framework, by reason of its very narrowness, provides undeniable homogeneity, both from north to south and from east to west.

From north to south the entire coastal riviera forms only a thin lengthwise band on the globe. Its widest point from north to south is the distance of 1100 kilometres from the northern end of the Adriatic to the coast of Tripolitania, and that is an exception. In fact the greatest widths vary on an average between 600 and 800 kilometres for the eastern basin and 740 kilometres between Algiers and Marseilles. The entire area, both land and sea, forms a long belt straddling the 37th and 38th parallels. The differences in latitude are not great. They are sufficient to explain the contrasts between the northern shores and the southern, the latter being the warmer. This mean difference in temperature between Marseilles and Algiers is 4°C. The 10°C January isotherm on the whole follows the general shape of the sea, cutting off southern Spain and southern Italy, regions that have more in common with Africa than with Europe. In general, all parts of the Mediterranean experience what is perceptibly the same 'geometrical' climate.

It is a matter of some importance to the historian to find almost everywhere within his field of study the same climate, the same seasonal rhythm, the same vegetation, the same colours and, when the geological architecture recurs, the same landscapes, identical to the point of obsession; in short, the same ways of life. To Michelet, the 'stony' Languedoc interior recalled Palestine. For hundreds of writers, Provence has been more Greek than Greece, unless, that is, the true Greece is not to be found on some Sicilian shore. The Iles d'Hyères would not be out of place among the Cyclades, except that they are greener. The lagoon of Tunis recalls the Lagoon of Chioggia. Morocco is another, more sun-baked Italy.

Everywhere can be found the same eternal trinity: wheat, olives, and vines, born of the climate and history; in other words an identical agricultural civilization, identical ways of dominating the environment. The different regions of the sea are not, therefore, complementary. They have the same granaries, wine-cellars and oil presses, the same tools, flocks, and often the same agrarian traditions and daily preoccupations. What prospers in one region will do equally well in the next. In the sixteenth century all the coastal regions produced wax, wool, and skins, *montonini* or *vacchini*; they all grew (or could have grown) mulberry trees and raised silkworms. They are all without exception lands of wine and vineyards, even the Moslem countries. Who has praised wine more highly than the poet of Islam? At Tor on the Red Sea there were vines, and they even grew in far-off Persia, where the wine of Shīrāz was highly prized.

The Mediterranean countries, then, were in competition with each other; at

89. *Still Life with Lemons* by L. E. Melendez, with olive oil in the jar
and wine in the bottle. *Private collection*

least they should have been. They had more goods for exchange outside their climatic environment than within it. But the sixteenth century was a time when the total volume of exchange was small, the prices modest and the distances travelled short. Arrangements had somehow to be reached between neighbours, between regions that were rich or poor in manpower, and the chief problem was the supply of food for the towns, constantly on the lookout for all kinds of foodstuffs and in particular those that could be transported without too much spoilage: sacks of almonds from the Provençal coast, barrels of salted tunny or meat, sacks of beans from Egypt, not to mention casks of oil and grain, for which, of course, demand was greatest. So identical production did not restrict exchanges within the Mediterranean as much as one might expect, at least during the sixteenth century.

In human terms the unity of the climate has had many consequences. This basic uniformity was established far back in time, nature and man working to the same end. As a result, in the sixteenth century, a native of the Mediterranean, wherever he might come from, would never feel out of place in any part of the sea. In former times, it is true, in the heroic age of the first Phoenician and Greek voyages of antiquity, colonization was a dramatic upheaval, but not in later years. To later colonial settlers their journey simply meant finding in a new place the same trees and plants, the same food on the table that they had known in their homeland; it meant living under the same sky, watching the same familiar seasons.

On the other hand when a native of the Mediterranean had to leave the shores of the sea, he was uneasy and homesick; like the soldiers of Alexander the Great when he left Syria and advanced towards the Euphrates; or the six-teenth-century Spaniards in the Low Countries, miserable among the 'fogs of the North'. For Alonso Vázquez and the Spaniards of his time (and probably of all time) Flanders was 'the land where there grows neither thyme, nor lavender, figs, olives, melons, or almonds; where parsley, onions, and lettuces have neither juice nor taste; where dishes are prepared, strange to relate, with butter from cows instead of oil . . .'. The Cardinal of Aragon, who reached the Netherlands in 1517 with his cook and his own supplies, shared this opinion. 'Because of the butter and dairy produce which is so widely used in Flanders and Germany', he concluded, 'these countries are overrun with lepers.' A strange land indeed! An Italian cleric stranded at Bayeux in Normandy in the summer of 1529 thought himself 'for del mondo'.

This explains the facility with which the Mediterranean dweller travelled from port to port. In striking contrast was the exhausting process of colonizing the New World carried out by the Iberians. Traditional history has preserved, with more or less accuracy, the names of those men and women who were the first to grow wheat, vines, and olives in Peru or in New Spain. Not without courage, battling against the hostile nature of the climate and soil, these Mediter-ranean expatriates tried to build a new Mediterranean culture in the tropics.

iv. The personification of autumn, carrying hoe and spade together with the newly harvested grapes. Wine, like olive oil and bread, was a staple of Mediterranean diet in Christian countries. Ferrarese painting, c.1450. *Gemäldegalerie, Berlin*

SENZA PAVRA OGN'VOM FRANCO CAMINI
E LAVORANDO SEMINI CIASCVNO ·
MENTRE CHE TAL COMVDO
MANTERRA QVESTA DONNA T SIGNORIA
CHEL ALEVATA AREI OGNI BALIA

...ELLA CITTA OVE SERVATA · QVESTA VIRTV KEPIV 'DALTRA RISPREDE · ELLA GVARDE DIFEDE · CHI LEI ONORA 7 L...

PASCIE · DA LA SVO LVCIE NASCIE · EL MERITAR COLOR COPERA BENE · 7 AGLINIOVI DAR DEBITE PENE

v. *Preceding pages:* Hill farming in Tuscany. The gentry go hunting while the merchants, bargaining as they go, take their goods to market in the town towards which the peasant is driving his pig. In the background the corn is being threshed with flails. The vines have been well pruned and the woods are properly kept. *Good Government* by Ambrogio Lorenzetti, *Sala delle Pace, Palazzo Pubblico, Siena.*

vi. Lateen-rigged Turkish ship. Mid-seventeenth century, probably Nicaean. *Benaki Museum, Athens*

The attempt failed. Although there were occasional successes the rural and alimentary civilization of their native lands could not be transplanted to the soil of Spanish and Portuguese America, a zone of maize, manioc, pulque, and before long of rum. One of the great trans-Atlantic supply operations from Spain and Portugal was devoted to maintaining artificially in the New World the alimentary civilization of the Mediterranean: ships laden with flour, wine, and oil left Seville and Lisbon for the other side of the ocean.

Yet it was Mediterranean man who almost alone of Europeans survived the transplantation to a new land. Perhaps it was because he was already accustomed to the harsh conditions of one climate, that of the Mediterranean, which is not always kind to the human organism, and was hardened by his struggle against endemic malaria and the regular scourge of plague. Perhaps too it was because he had always been schooled in sobriety and frugality in his native land. The deceptively welcoming climate of the Mediterranean can sometimes be cruel and murderous. It is the filter that has prevented men from distant lands from settling on the shores of the warm sea. They might arrive as conquerors, yesterday's barbarians, today's men of property: but how long could they resist the 'scorching heat of summer and . . . the malaria'?

Drought: the scourge of the Mediterranean. The disadvantage of this climate for human life lies in the annual distribution of rainfall. It rains a good deal: in some places there is exceedingly high precipitation, 4 metres a year in the Gulf of Cattaro. But the rains fall in autumn, winter, and spring, chiefly in autumn and spring. It is broadly the opposite of a monsoon climate. The monsoon climate fruitfully combines warmth and water. The Mediterranean climate separates these two important factors of life, with predictable consequences. It is not only a garden, but, providentially, a land of fruit-bearing trees.

On the other hand the climate does not favour the growth of ordinary trees and forest coverings. Very early the primeval forests of the Mediterranean were attacked by man and much, too much, reduced. Hence the large area covered by scrub and underbrush, the debased forms of the forest. Almost everywhere, wood became expensive, often very expensive indeed. At Medina del Campo 'richer in fairs than in *montes* [i.e., wooded mountains]', the humanist Antonio de Guevara, reflecting on his budget, concluded, 'all told, the wood cost us as much as what was cooking in the pot'.

Another consequence is the scarcity in the Mediterranean zone of true pastures. As a result there are few of the cattle so useful to the rich farming, necessarily based on the use of manure, practised in the northern countries where the soil is so washed by the rain that it loses its fertile elements – of which the Mediterranean drought is, it is true, a better guardian. Cattle are only found in really large numbers in Egypt and in the rainy Balkans, on the northern margins of the Mediterranean, or on high lands where more rain falls than elsewhere. Sheep and goats (the former raised for their wool more than for their flesh) could not compensate for the deficiency in meat rations. Apropos of the Mediterranean a geographer once wrote jokingly to me, 'Not enough meat and too many bones.'

To the northerner, even in the sixteenth century, the livestock of the Mediterranean seemed deficient. At Valladolid, for 11,312 sheep slaughtered between 23rd June and 5th December, 1586, an average yield of 11·960 kilogrammes of meat per beast has been calculated. Similarly for 2302 cattle slaughtered during the same period, the meat per beast was 148·12 kilogrammes. So the weight of the stock was low; the same was true of horses. There were some very fine horses in the Mediterranean, Turks, jennets from Naples, Andalusian chargers, and Barbary horses from North Africa, but they were all saddle horses, fast and nimble, and went out of fashion during the following century which was to see the popularity of the heavy horses, asses, and mules of the North. Increasingly, for the mails, for the carriages then coming into fashion, for the artillery's gun-carriages and limbers, the strength of the horses was becoming a decisive factor. Besides what fodder was there for horses in the south? Oats had only just made their appearance in certain regions, such as Languedoc, and human mouths competed with the horses for barley. Pity the French horses, who once over the Spanish border began to whinny with dismay, according to Barthélemy Joly, for now they would be on a diet of 'short and unappetizing straw'.

Without suggesting that it explains everything, we might note that if the swing-plough, which did little more than scratch the surface of the earth, survived in the Mediterranean countryside, it was not only because of the fragility of the thin layer of loose topsoil, but also because the teams of oxen or mules were not strong enough. Shallow ploughing, the *raies*, were done as often as seven or eight times a year. It would have been better, as time was to prove, to plough more deeply, as in the North, where the wheeled plough with swivelling fore-carriage was a great instrument of progress.

The truth is that the Mediterranean has struggled against an underlying poverty, aggravated but not entirely accounted for by circumstances. It affords only a precarious living, in spite of its apparent or real advantages. It is easy to be deceived by its famous charm and beauty. Even as experienced a geographer as Philippson was dazzled, like all visitors from the North, by the sun, the colours, the warmth, the winter roses, the early fruits. Goethe at Vicenza was captivated by the popular street life with its open stalls and dreamed of taking back home with him a little of the magic air of the South. Even when one is aware of the reality it is difficult to associate these scenes of brilliance and gaiety with images of misery and physical hardship. In fact, Mediterranean man gains his daily bread by painful effort. Great tracts of land remain uncultivated and of little use. The land that does yield food is almost everywhere subject to biennial crop rotation that rules out any great productivity. Michelet again was the historian who best understood the basic harshness of all these lands, starting with France's own Provence.

There is one visible sign of this poverty: the frugality that has never failed to impress the northerner. The Fleming Busbecq, when in Anatolia, wrote in 1555, 'I dare say that a man of our country spends more on food in one day than a Turk in twelve ... The Turks are so frugal and think so little of the pleasures of eating that if they have bread, salt, and some garlic or an onion and a kind of sour milk which they call *yoghoort*, they ask nothing more. They dilute this milk with very cold water and crumble bread into it and take it when they are hot and thirsty ... it is not only palatable and digestible, but also possesses an extraordinary power of quenching the thirst.' This sobriety has often been noted as one of the great strengths of the Turkish soldier on campaign. He would be content with a little rice, ground meat dried in the sun, and bread coarsely cooked in the ashes of the camp fire. The western soldier was more particular, perhaps because of the example of the many Germans and Swiss.

The peasants and even the city-dwellers of Greece, Italy, and Spain were hardly more demanding than these Turks, whose frugal habits were noted only a century ago by Théophile Gautier. Commines on the other hand went into raptures over the abundant fare of Venice. He had the excuse of being a foreigner. And Venice was Venice, a town privileged for food. In fact this luxurious market in a rich and well-situated town created, as we know, great problems of supply, and cost the Signoria much anxiety and vigilance.

Has the very small part played in Mediterranean literature by feasts and banquets ever been remarked? Descriptions of meals – except of course princely tables – never suggest plenty. In Bandello's novels, a good meal means a few vegetables, a little Bologna sausage, some tripe, and a cup of wine. In the Spanish literature of the Golden Age an empty stomach is a familiar character. Witness the ultra-classical Lazarillo de Tormes or his brother in *picardia*, Guzmán de Alfarache, eating a crust of hard bread without leaving a crumb for the ants. 'May God save you from the plague coming down from Castille,' the same Guzmán is told, 'and from the famine coming up from Andalusia.' And we may remember Don Quixote's bills of fare, or the proverb: 'If the lark flies over Castille, she must take her grain of corn with her.'

Crops in the Mediterranean, more than elsewhere, are at the mercy of unstable elements. Drought, floods, frost – one can never be certain of the harvest until the last moment. The violent winds from the south that are dreaded in the Archipelago often ruined ripe harvests on Corfu and are still feared today throughout the cereal growing area of North Africa; this is the *sirocco*, against which there is no remedy and which in three days can destroy a whole year's work. One other item can be added to the list of dangers to the fields of the Mediterranean: the plague of locusts, a greater threat in the past than it is today.

A few changes in temperature and a shortage of rainfall were enough to endanger human life. Everything was affected accordingly, even politics. If there was no likelihood of a good barley crop on the borders of Hungary (for, in the Mediterranean, barley was the equivalent of oats in the North), it could be

90. Gastronomy is the more keenly appreciated when famine is just round the corner.
The Sense of Taste by Jusepe Ribera. *Wadsworth Atheneum, Hartford, Connecticut*

assumed that the Grand Turk would not go to war there that year; for how
would the horses of the *spahis* be fed? If wheat was also short – as sometimes
happened – in the three or four main sources of supply for the sea, whatever
the plans of war drawn up during winter or spring, there would be no major

war at harvest time, which was also the season of calm seas and great naval campaigns. Accordingly brigandage on land and piracy on sea would at once redouble in vigour. Is it any wonder then, that the only detail of daily life that regularly finds its way into diplomatic correspondence concerns the harvests? It has rained, it has not rained, the wheat has not sprouted; Sicily promises well, but the Turkish harvest was poor, the Grand Turk will certainly not let any wheat out. Will this year be a year of scarcity, of *carestia*, of dearth?

That Philip II should be kept minutely informed of the variations in the weather from seedtime onwards; that the price of bread should rise and fall depending on the rainfall; that these details should be found in a series of letters where one searches in vain for any other precise details of economic history: all this is very revealing of the state of the Mediterranean food supply in the sixteenth century. It was no mere 'economic' problem, but a matter of life and death.

For famine, true famine when people died in the streets, was a reality. In 1521, relates the Venetian Navagero, 'there was such famine in Andalusia that countless animals died and the countryside was deserted; many people died also. There was such drought that the wheat was lost and not a blade of grass could any longer be found in the fields; that year the breeds of Andalusian horses for the most part died out and they have not been restored to this day [1525].' This was an extreme case. But we constantly find *carestia* recorded as the years go past.

A double constraint has always been at the heart of Mediterranean history: poverty and uncertainty of the morrow. This is perhaps the cause of the carefulness, frugality, and industry of the people, the motives that have been behind certain, almost instinctive, forms of imperialism, which are sometimes nothing more than the search for daily bread. To compensate for its weaknesses, the Mediterranean has had to act, to look further afield and take tribute from distant lands, associating itself with their economies: in so doing it has considerably enriched its own history.

2 The seasons

The sea's climate, with its two clearly defined seasons, regulates Mediterranean life into two phases, year in, year out, sending the Mediterranean people by turns to their summer then to their winter quarters. The countless records we have of the quality and nature of the weather can be classified without reference to the year: only the months matter here, and almost invariably we find the same story. The 'gates of the year' open and shut at the appointed time. Gates of the year: this is the name by which solstices and equinoxes are known in Kabylia. 'Every time a new season arrives for men, bringing its chances with it: barley bread or famine.'

The winter standstill. Winter begins early and finishes late: its arrival is dreaded and its departure viewed with disbelief. It is expected ahead of the calendar, as wisdom counsels. What lies behind such concern? In Venice a desire not to be surprised by winter, to lay up in good time the *galee grosse*, the *navi* and the light galleys, and to dismiss all unnecessary troops. Now was the time when everyone looked to his personal health, which might be affected during the slightest indisposition by the 'malignità de la stagione'. The roll begins of disasters, trials, restrictions, and abandoned activities, for this was the 'stagione horrida', hard on men and things alike: the season of continual rain, floods sparing neither countryside nor town, heavy falls of snow, storms, tempests at sea, and the cold, cruel to all and particularly to the poor. The hospitals would be filled with poor folk. And one never knew what might happen, even when the trees were in blossom again, or the plains around Montpellier were blue with wild hyacinths. On 15th April, 1594, at Bologna, five days after Easter, 'there fell heavy snow, after the beginning of a fine spring, with all the trees in bloom. God protect us!' On 23rd May, 1633, at Florence, after rain on the 21st, it suddenly grew so cold that fires had to be lit, 'come per li gran freddi di gennaio', and the mountains were covered in snow.

Most affected by this enforced retirement was country life. The peasant perforce must rest, said Aristophanes, while Zeus waters the earth. During clear spells he sows barley (unless he has already done so in October), wheat in December, and at the beginning of spring, maize. In the sixteenth century maize had only just been introduced from America. And these are light duties, which do not call for the mass labour of summer, or the help of one's neighbours, work *por favor*, as they say in Portugal. Even if one adds sowing vegetables and a little ploughing, winter is still a time of leisure and festivities. In Christian countries there is the killing of the pig in December, mentioned in Boccaccio's tales. In January in the mountains of Kabylia, at the winter solstice the feast of the *Ennayer* is celebrated, marking the separation of the sun's cycles, when copious meals lasting long into the night use up precious reserves. This extravagant feasting is to propitiate the coming year.

Cut off by snow, most of the mountain ranges are abandoned for the lowlands by flocks and shepherds. The mountain dwellers who stay at home will have sold at the autumn fairs the young animals they can no longer feed. This is still so today in the foothills of the Pyrenees and it was no doubt for the same reason that calves and lambs were being sold cheaply at Lucca, when Montaigne passed through in 1581. The mountains deserted by the shepherds were usually avoided by the traveller. In the snowy highlands one might risk losing life and possessions: 'Sire,' writes the French ambassador from Constantinople, 12th

Opposite: 91, 92. Terracotta reliefs showing personifications of the seasons. *Above:* Spring and summer. *Below:* Autumn and winter. Roman, made in Italy, 20 BC–AD 50. *British Museum*

February, 1578, 'the snows here have been so continuous and so heavy for fifty days that they have held me besieged and kept me from leaving last week as I had resolved.' Gédoyn 'the Turk', French consul at Aleppo in 1624 describes the hazards of his journey through the Balkan mountains in winter: he narrowly avoided freezing to death or falling prey to bears and wolves. In the Moroccan Atlas, explains Leo Africanus, the merchants bringing dates from the South after October are often caught in extraordinary mountain blizzards. No one escapes them. Even the trees are buried under a great snowy shroud.

Winter journeys were difficult in the lowlands too; with the constant rain, the rivers might overflow their banks, carrying away the bridges 'to such a degree', relates Bandello at the beginning of one of his tales, 'that our Mantuans who have estates on that side of the Po cannot make use of the supplies or goods of their lands'. In October, 1595, the river rose so high that 'the Ferrarans up in arms were preparing to open a breach in the dykes on our side', writes a Venetian. Another time it was the Tiber that overflowed. In 1598 it carried away half the 'Aemilius' bridge, which had already been repaired in 1575. In 1594 it was the Arno. That year in Tuscany once again the waterways were all frozen over and the fruit trees damaged by frost. During some particularly cold winters the canals froze in Venice. At best, sixteenth-century travellers had to face waterlogged roads full of potholes, impassable during the continuous snow and rain.

Shipping at a halt. The sea also becomes hostile in the winter, so much so that in the past it brought shipping to a standstill. In Roman times ships were laid up by order between October and April, a step counselled by prudent seamen. From the sea voyages of the Apostle Paul, we learn that the *Boniportus* of Crete was not suitable *ad hiemandum*, and that the Alexandrian ship that was to carry Paul had wintered at Malta. Centuries later similar stipulations are found in the maritime codes of medieval towns, in the *Constitutum Usus* of Pisa of 1160, when inactivity was compulsory between St Andrew's Day and the Kalends of March in the maritime statute of 1284 at Venice, in the maritime statute of Ancona of 1387. Legislators maintained for centuries the precautions and prohibitions dictated by experience. Until the end of the eighteenth century sailors of the Levant put to sea only between the feasts of St George (5th May) and St Dmitri (26th October).

But after 1450, shipping gradually began to triumph over the obstacles of winter weather. Even so these were only partial victories still involving great risk. Spectacular wrecks occurred every year to remind men of winter's powers. So much so that Venice in 1569 brought back the old prohibitions, in a milder form it is true, since now they forbade sea voyages only between 15th November and 20th January. It was clearly impossible to turn the clock back in such matters. The new laws were so little observed that the Signoria had to repeat them in 1598. All the same, the measure is symptomatic, indicating the yearly toll that winter took of shipping even at this period. On 1st December, 1521, a 'Greek' wind sank many ships in the Adriatic, one laden with grain in the very port of Ragusa; on 11th November, 1538, a single storm drove thirty-eight of Barbarossa's galleys on to the coast, where they were broken up by the raging seas, after which the survivors were killed and the cargoes looted by the Albanians; on 9th November, 1544, seven Ragusan ships fell victim to a storm; in January, 1545, the *greco tramontana* sank fifty vessels in the Adriatic, including three Venetian ships on their way to Syria with over 100,000 ducats on board; on 29th December, 1570, during the 'greatest misfortune' of the Adriatic, two ships laden with grain sank right inside Ragusa harbour. There are countless similar episodes, for example, the entire fleet of Spanish galleys lost in the bay of La Herradura in October, 1562; a hundred ships and twelve galleys driven on to the coast by the raging sea before Constantinople in October, 1575.

On clear days small boats might venture out over short distances, of course, on voyages lasting a few hours. Bigger ships, offering greater resistance to the winter, could accomplish even in bad weather voyages that were the more profitable because of the season. But there was clearly an overall reduction in shipping. As for the galleys, they remained completely inactive in port, under the *volte* of the arsenals, well-sheltered and drawn up out of the water, while the oarsmen languished with little work to do.

As for the naval squadrons, the Spanish government was only too eager to use them in the off-season, when it could be sure that the Turkish armadas would be in port. The corsairs did the same, whenever they thought it worth the risk; the perils of the seas were after all no more formidable than an encounter with a large armada in summer. But the sailors in the service of Spain were continually protesting against these winter voyages. 'My zeal in the service of Your Majesty obliges me to say,' the Prince of Melfi wrote in August, 1561, 'that to have the galleys sail in winter is to risk losing them, in particular along the Spanish coastline, which has so few ports. Even if the ships escape, the gangs will be lost ... and will be in no condition to serve at the proper time [next season].' He was then Philip II's naval commander, and was taking his precautions.

Galley warfare was indeed impossible during winter, a fact that the professionals had to keep explaining to their political masters who remained deaf to their advice. Don Garcia of Toledo, who was also 'general de la mar' to Philip II explained his reasons for not sending his fleet against the Corsican uprising in 1564 as Genoa had requested. 'It is a fact, clearly established,' he wrote to the Spanish ambassador at Genoa, Figueroa, 'that all sea expeditions during winter are a complete waste of money ... We shall squander money without the least return as has already happened on many occasions and will happen again until the end of time if anything is undertaken at this time of year.' In addition (the troops on board had come from the engagement of the Peñon de Velez and were tired), there was a risk of compromising the spring operations

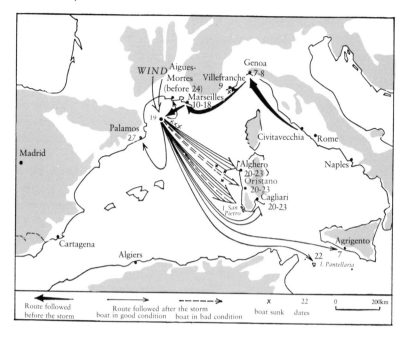

Effects of the mistral, *19th April, 1569, and days following*

The squadron of galleys of the Grand Commander of Castile, Don Luis de Requesens, was making for the coast of Spain. Its intention was to reach the shore of the kingdom of Granada, whose frontier lay south-west of Cartagena, and where the Moriscos had risen on Christmas night of the previous year. The galleys were to intercept the Barbary raids that provided the insurgents with men and arms. The *mistral* surprised the squadron in the Gulf of Lions and drove most of the galleys towards the coast of Sardinia. Note the voyage made against the wind by one galley which reached Aiguesmortes; the arrival on the 27th of Don Luis de Requesens' galley at Palamos, where he was preceded by soldiers who had left the squadron at Marseilles and were on their way to Spain on foot; the two courses that led one galley to Pantelleria and the other to Agrigento, where she arrived on 7th May. This map is based on the many documents that I have examined and summarized at Simancas, from which J. Gentil da Silva and Jacques Bertin have drawn up the geographical projection reproduced here. It would also have been possible to provide a map of the discovery and communication of the event. In fact, Genoa seems to have been Spain's chief source of information about the accident.

for the sake of chasing after a shadow, or as he put it 'of catching the pigeon by the tail when we might catch it by the head'. Even if this was to be a mere display of force it would be dangerous. Crossing the channel of Piombino 'is a terribly long, uncertain and perilous undertaking'.

Galleys that failed to observe the rule were courting disaster. They lay too low in the water to resist the heavy swell and winter storms. It is easy to guess why Charles V tried to take Algiers by surprise in October, 1541. But he fell a victim to the season he had chosen, the time of year 'which the Moors call *Cassem*, which means section and marks the passage from the fair season to the foul'.

Winter: season of peace and plans. Bad weather thus forced a truce in the great maritime wars. There was an equally regular truce on land, for campaigning was impossible 'with winter on one's back'. Hostilities might not officially come to a halt, but they clearly lost much of their impetus. This was so of the dramatic Persian War from 1578 to 1590, and of any war in the Mediterranean or para-Mediterranean regions. 'The approach of the day of Kasim (St Demetrius' day, 26th October) ordinarily marks the end of the Turkish campaigns on land and sea,' notes Hammer in his invaluable book on the Ottoman Empire. For war had to live off the land. It had to bide its time – and this was the crucial factor – until the harvest was either over or about to start. Still in Turkish territory, the historian Zinkeisen writes apropos of the siege of Belgrade by the Turks in 1456, 'During the month of June, just as the wheat was beginning to ripen, the Ottoman army set out to besiege Belgrade.' The calendar was commander-in-chief.

In short, the 'winter semester' was a calm and peaceful period. National wars were halted, and so were minor wars, except for a few sudden alarms, for, both on land and sea, bad weather made surprise attacks particularly worthwhile. It was during the winter that Protestant bands came up close to the frontier of Roussillon in 1562; in September, 1540, that corsairs from Algiers tried to take Gibraltar by surprise, with the result that their retreat was harassed by the *mistral*; it was often at the end of winter that the *ponentini* with galleons or reinforced galleys went privateering on the stormy seas of the Levant.

For the governments themselves it was a time for making plans and holding great councils. Staff work increased out of all proportion. Winter was the time of bulging files. One might almost call them winter files, to be used with caution by historians. For there was all the time in the world to discuss, predict, and finally to draw up plans in black and white. 'This is what we should do if such and such happens; but if the Turk or the king of France . . .' and so on and so on, filling pages and pages. These grandiose schemes and brilliant plans which historians analyse with so much respect and conviction were often dreamed up by the side of a blazing log fire or brazier, in a cosy room, while outside, in Madrid (or wherever it was) the *cierzo*, the snowy wind from the mountains, was howling. Nothing seemed too difficult or dangerous. Plans to blockade the Netherlands, to deprive them of salt, to buy up all the Hanseatic grain they lived on, to close the Spanish ports to them, were all winter plans. In 1565–1566, after the great failure of the Turks at Malta, the feeling of insecurity that persisted into the early autumn led to a suggestion that 12,000 men, Italians and Spaniards, should be sent to La Goletta. How would they be lodged in the tiny *presidio*, even with the enlargements made in the 1560s? Well, they would be lodged under the walls, on the Cape Bon side, which on the map looked a reasonable suggestion. It was all arranged, and as so often, never put into execution. Summer, from this point of view, was not necessarily a more reasonable but it was a more realistic time of year; to be more accurate, in summer events took their own course without always responding to the control of governments.

But there was one positive activity in winter, the only one: negotiations, diplomatic talks, and pacific resolutions. From this point of view winter provided a salutary breathing-space. In any case, it is a fact that all the peace treaties studied in this book date from the winter months, that they were signed before the upheavals and irreparable events of summer. The Treary of Cateau-Cambrésis was the result of discussions during the winter of 1558–1559, and was signed on 2nd and 3rd April, 1559. The Turko-Spanish truces were all in midwinter: that of 1581 was signed on 7th February, the peace of Vervins on 2nd May, 1598. The Twelve Years' Truce was signed at the Hague on 9th April, 1609. Only the Anglo-Spanish peace treaty signed on 28th August, 1604, is an exception to the rule. But this one was virtually a certainty from the time of Elizabeth's death in March, 1603, before the voyage to England by Don Juan de Tassis, Count of Villamediana (June, 1603).

The hardships of winter. The Mediterranean winter, then, was a time of peace and rest. Pleasant enough indeed, one might suppose, remembering the traditional images: the January sunshine claimed in advertisements for the Côte d'Azur; or the flocks of migrating birds, alighting exhausted on the lands of the South to which they appeared as manna from heaven, especially in Egypt, whose fields Pierre Belon saw 'quite white' with birds, in the days no doubt when one could pick up quails in the fields like fruit.

In fact, winter in the Mediterranean, as in Europe, is not so gentle. In the towns particularly it was a time of great hardship for the poor. On 6th November, 1572, Gian Andrea Doria wrote to Don John of Austria, 'Your Highness must know that as there is no grain harvested on the territory of Genoa, and very little of any other kind of food, there is in consequence great poverty, not only in the mountains but in the city itself. It is so great that the poor find it difficult to survive, especially in winter when the need for clothing is added to the lack of bread, and there is no possibility of work.' 'So,' concludes the letter, 'it will be possible to collect at Genoa for next spring, voluntary prisoners for the manning of ten galleys.' A revealing document both about the Genoa of the bankers and about the Mediterranean winter.

I would not go so far as to claim that the Mediterranean winter is bitterly cold. But it is less warm than is commonly supposed and often wet. Above all it is an intruder, arriving suddenly after six months of sunshine, and the inhabitants are always ill-prepared for its coming. Every year it is as if the cold airstreams take the sea by surprise. It is a fact that Mediterranean houses, built to an open design, with tiled instead of wooden floors, not always well heated, or indeed heatable, are not built for keeping out the cold; they only offer protection against the heat. Ferdinand of Aragon used to say that contrary to the generally held opinion, one should spend summer in Seville and winter at Burgos: it might be colder there, but at least there was some protection.

The accelerated rhythm of summer life. With the coming of the luxuriant spring, often wet, with 'impetuous' winds ... 'which bring the trees out in bud', the short-lived spring (almond and olive trees are in flower within a few days), life takes on a new rhythm. On the sea, in spite of the dangers, April is one of the most active months of the year. In the fields, the last ploughing is being done. Then follows the rapid succession of harvests, reaping in June, figs in August, grapes in September, and olives in autumn. Ploughing begins again with the first autumn rains. The peasants of Old Castile had to have their wheat sown towards mid-October, so that the young plants would have time to grow the three or four leaves that would help them withstand the winter frosts. In the space of a few months some of the busiest pages of the farmer's calendar are turned. Every year he has to make haste, take advantage of the last rains of spring or the first of autumn, of the first fine days or the last. All agricultural life, the best part of Mediterranean life, is commanded by the need for haste. Over all looms fear of the winter: it is vital to fill cellars and granaries. Even in town houses, provisions are put by in a safe place, wine, grain, and the essential firewood for heating and cooking. Before the approach of winter, towards September, in order to pay for desperately needed pastures and the year's expenses, Spanish shepherds in Medinaceli and elsewhere would sell their fleeces in advance to the merchants. In May they would have to hasten to deliver them to their pressing creditors. But the half-million ducats advanced meant security for the winter. The buried silos of the Arabs of the Oran region, and the 'trenches' of the Apulian and Sicilian peasants were another way of providing for the future.

With summer's coming, war sprang to life in all its forms: land warfare, galley warfare, pirate attacks at sea, and brigand raids in the countryside.

The roads grew busy with traffic. On land the traveller's chief enemy was now the heat. But he could travel by night or in the early morning. At sea the warm air from the Sahara brought fine weather, and, equally important, stable atmospheric conditions. In the Aegean Sea the Etesian winds blow regularly from north to south between May and October until the early autumn storms. Crossings throughout the summer months were relatively calm and reliable. The old Prince Doria used to say, 'In the Mediterranean, there are three ports: Cartagena, June, and July.'

Shipping was more active in these calm summers since harvest time increased trading. The peak periods were at reaping, threshing, fruit picking, and the grape harvest. The appearance of the new wines was a great trading occasion. At Seville at least, *la vendeja* was a kind of wine fair set at a fixed date, 'from the 7th to the 19th October ... the season known as *la vendeja*', wrote the Duke of Medina Sidonia in 1597. It was for the wines of Andalusia as much as for salt, oil, and overseas goods that the northern boats came to Spain. Cervantes, in the *Coloquio de los Perros*, describes the tricks of a woman of easy virtue whose accomplice was an *alguazil* (of course). She specialized in exploiting 'Bretons' (i.e., Bretons, Englishmen, and northerners in general). With one of

93–98. *Above and opposite:*
Roundels showing the Labours of
the Months. Luca della Robbia, made for the
Medici Palace, Florence, 1450–1456.
Victoria and Albert Museum

her friends she would go 'in search of foreigners, and when *la vendeja* came to Seville and Cadiz, their prey arrived too; no Breton escaped their clutches'.

Throughout the Mediterranean the grape harvest was an occasion for merry-making and licence, a time of madness. At Naples the grape harvesters challenged anyone they met, man or woman, monk or priest. This led to various abuses. Pedro de Toledo, viceroy of Naples, champion of *onestità* and enemy of these pagan customs, even issued an edict against such troublesome habits. We are not told whether the measure was successful. Is there any way of fighting the combination of summer and new wine, of preventing collective revelry, at the fig harvest in one place, or the gathering of the mulberry leaves at another, the plain of Murcia, for instance?

Summer was also the season for good catches for the fishermen. Tunny in particular depends on seasonal variations. It was in summer that the *madragues*, the tunny nets, were set to work, and that the Duke of Medina Sidonia, who had the monopoly of the Andalusian *madragues* in the time of Philip II, had

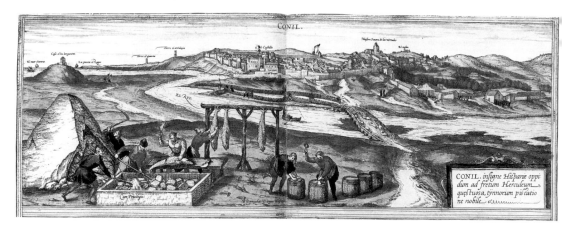

99. Tunny fishing at Conil, near Gibraltar. From *Civitates Orbis Terrarum*, 1575.

recruiters drum up the labour he needed. He levied them like a private army. It was at the turn of the season (just before and just after winter) that the fabled fisheries of the Bosporus took place. It was at the end of winter, too, in April, 1543, that there arrived at Marseilles just before the fishing season boatloads of empty barrels sent from Fréjus ready for salt fish: 1800 on the 17th, in three boats; 200 on the 21st; 600 on the 26th; 1000 on 30th April.

The summer epidemics. But the hot weather also caused fresh outbreaks of the endemic diseases that only temporarily subsided in winter. Baron de Tott notes that the plague 'begins its ravages in the spring and usually lasts until the beginning of winter'. The same could be said of all the Mediterranean epidemics, except exanthematous typhus, which was endemic in North Africa, but which regularly abated at the approach of summer. As usual the towns were the most threatened. Every summer Rome was a graveyard of fever. So the cardinals took refuge in their country houses, their *vigne*, which were not merely an ostentatious luxury, despite Scarron's opinion of them.

Everywhere, in Rome, Avignon, Milan, and Seville, the rich, whether nobles or bourgeois, laity or clerics, abandoned the hot cities. Philip II, in the Escorial, sought not only solitude, but coolness and relief from the pitiless Castilian summer. Who is better qualified to describe this summer migration of all men of means than Bandello, their table companion, entertainer, and chronicler? How sweet it is in the heat of summer to be in a garden at Milan, near the Porta Beatrice; to eat mellow fruits and drink 'un generoso e preziosissimo vino bianco'. 'Last summer,' he relates, 'to escape the heat which is excessive in Milan, I went . . . with Lord Alessandro Bentivoglio and his wife, Lady Ippolyta Sforza, to their residence, on the other side of the Adda, to the Palace, as they call it, and I stayed there for three months.' Another time, he was on the other side of Brescia, at San Gottardo. Another time, the little society in which one of the novels is set picnics near Pinaruolo, in a meadow of sweet-smelling grasses, while cool and clear water runs nearby in the canal. Elsewhere the little court is held beneath some olive trees, but still near springs of running water. In just such a setting three hundred years earlier the tales of the Decameron had been told.

The Mediterranean climate and the East. The seasonal rhythm of the desert is the reverse of that of the Mediterranean. For there the slowing down or ceasing of activity occurs in summer rather than in winter. The overwhelming heat of summer brings everything to a standstill. After October–November, after the date harvest, life and commerce start afresh.

So the desert begins to wake up just as everything is going into hibernation further north and west. The flocks that left the steppe in summer return to the renewed pastures and, like the caravans, take to the desert roads again. The time of uncertainty is over, life becomes easier, more prosperous, and more industrious at the same time. The archaeologist Sachau was astonished to see people at work at Kut al 'Almara in winter, repairing the canals and growing vegetables. In fact this was perfectly normal, the accustomed rhythm of life on the steppes.

Seasonal rhythms and statistics. We should look a little more closely at these great problems which have for the most part escaped the attention of historians. Can we use statistics? They are very incomplete and inadequate for the sixteenth century, but it is worth looking at them.

The record of marine insurance policies taken out at Ragusa for the year 1560 on the following page reveals the importance of the months of April and

100, 101. Roundels showing the Labours of the Months: grafting fruit trees and pruning vines. Luca della Robbia. *Victoria and Albert Museum*

Number of marine insurance policies in Ragusa in 1560

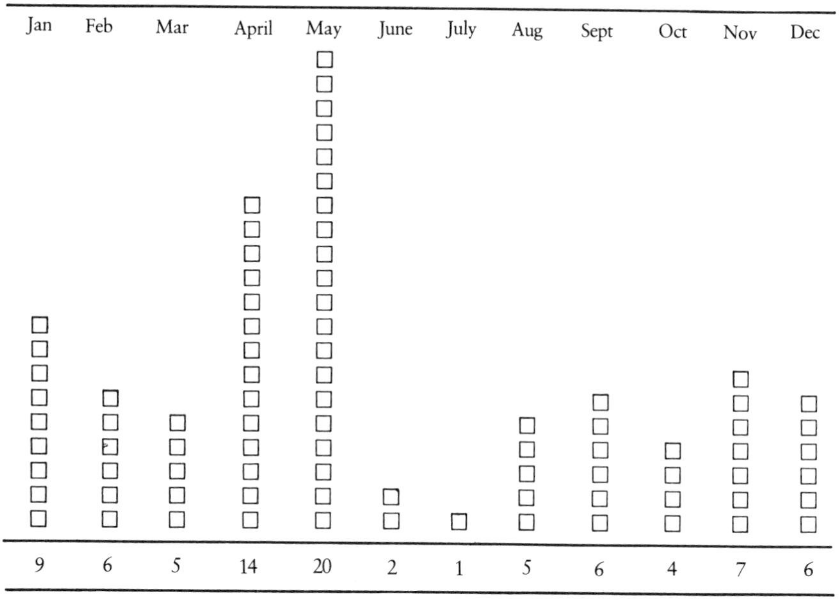

Jan	Feb	Mar	April	May	June	July	Aug	Sept	Oct	Nov	Dec
9	6	5	14	20	2	1	5	6	4	7	6

Recorded by month □ = one policy (from Ragusa Archives)

May. Boats were insured – as of course one would expect – just before the long voyages began. The records of the *portate* of Leghorn (i.e. the harbour records of the arrival of ships and goods) give details of the cargoes landed at the port with the name of the boat and her port of origin. These files enable us to locate the arrivals of silk between July and October; the arrivals of pepper from Alexandria between January and July or August; and cheeses from Sardinia after October. These are small seasonal movements that would all repay study. The Leghorn calendar is not absolutely identical with that of other ports, not even with that of Genoa, its nearest neighbour.

But I do not think it is possible to use these documents to establish once and for all economic variations according to the season. The Leghorn statistics do not offer such a simple answer because they are sixteenth-century statistics, incomplete and with no standardization of measures. It is impossible, for example, to calculate the gross tonnage of goods unloaded there in any single month, which would be the most valuable information they could give. The *portate* of Leghorn record the arrival of boats of very different capacities.

Simply to count every ship named as a single unit would lead to very unrealistic figures: one might as well add up kilos and tons. To classify them by category would not mean very much either, except for *navi* and galleons (the largest cargo ships), and that is what we shall try to do here. If this method is adopted, the following figures will be obtained:

Arrivals at Leghorn in 1578, 1581, 1582, 1583, 1584, and 1585

Year	Ships of every description* arriving between 1st April and 30th September (summer semester)	Ships of every description* arriving between 1st October and 31st March (winter semester)	Total
1578	171	126	297
1581	84	107	191
1582	199	177	376
1583	171	171	342
1584	286	182	468
1585	147	160	307
TOTAL	1058	923	1981

*Excluding galleys.

Monthly record of the shipping traffic* at Leghorn for the same dates

Year	Jan.	Feb.	Mar.	Apr.	May	June	July	Aug.	Sept.	Oct.	Nov.	Dec.
1578	27	40	40	49	24	27	30	26	15	6	7	6
1581	13	4	5	9	7	15	20	23	10	29	27	29
1582	27	27	33	38	29	44	52	19	17	17	37	36
1583	22	18	21	37	22	28	27	33	24	39	38	33
1584	57	36	31	36	46	55	46	72	31	21	30	7
1585	34	27	17	20	33	17	25	28	23	18	37	28
TOTAL	180	152	147	189	161	186	200	201	120	130	176	139

*Excluding galleys.

Navi and galleons entering Leghorn for the same dates

Year	Jan.	Feb.	Mar.	Apr.	May	June	July	Aug.	Sept.	Oct.	Nov.	Dec.	Total
1578	9	7	3	3	4	2	1	3	—	4	3	4	43
1581	11	4	3	4	6	3	—	4	2	8	4	3	52
1582	5	1	4	6	—	3	1	1	4	2	4	6	37
1583	—	2	5	1	1	3	—	3	—	2	1	3	21
1584	8	2	6	3	6	2	2	1	2	5	2	2	41
1585	1	7	9	2	—	2	3	—	—	2	2	3	31
Total by month	34	23	30	19	17	15	7	12	8	23	16	21	
Total of other ships	146	129	117	170	144	171	193	189	112	107	160	118	

These figures are clearly incomplete and imperfect. It is not easy to work from the information they provide. According to the monthly statistics three months appear to have been more active than the others: April, at the end of winter, the time for necessary stock clearance; July and August, after the grain harvest. The two least active months were September and October. On our table, April totals 189 arrivals; July 200; August 201, but September 120; October 130; there is a perceptible drop.

The records of *navi* and galleons refer to large cargo ships and long distance voyages. The activity of these ships is to be distinguished from that of boats of smaller tonnage. The latter worked in April, July, and August, the *navi* and galleons reached their lowest figures in July and their highest in January: 34; March: 30; February and October: 23. The massive arrival of northern ships was to accentuate this discrepancy in the Leghorn shipping. Over short distances grain could be carried in small boats in July and August, as the *portate* indicate, while the long-distance voyages were undertaken by the big ships, in which all merchandise from far countries was carried.

We shall hardly fare better with records of the voyages made by German pilgrims from Venice to the Holy Land between 1507 and 1608, a total of about thirty trips, described in the valuable and erudite collection of records by Röhricht. But these are voyages which are at least comparable with each other, and they provide examples from the whole of the century.

The pilgrims would set off in June or July, in the middle of the fine season. Of twenty-four known cases there was one departure in May (20th May); ten in June; eleven in July; one in August, and one in September. They would arrive at Jaffa or Tripoli in Syria in July, August, or September. Of the twenty-three known arrivals, one was in June; seven in July; eleven in August; ten in September; one in October; none in November; and one in December. From the coast to Jerusalem and back, including two or three days in Jerusalem, the pilgrimage was extremely rapid, taking from three weeks to a month. The pilgrims would then re-embark, generally on the same ship that had brought them. Departures from Jaffa, Beirut, or Tripoli in Syria were usually in August (out of twelve cases, there was one in June; six in August; two in September; three in October). It was usually in December that the pilgrims set foot in Venice once more (of thirteen arrivals, four were in November; seven in December; one in January; and one in February).

From these few figures useful information can be sought about the comparative length of the journey in summer and winter, on the outward and return voyage.

The return journey took almost double the time of the outward trip. Was this simply due to the season? Or was there some difficulty connected with the prevailing wind in following the route in the opposite direction?

Determinism and economic life. It is only too clear that these calculations, which appeared in the first edition of this book, are not adequate to solve the problems we are dealing with. Since then I have analysed the statistics of the Leghorn *port-ate*, but they do not add anything to this debate. There are in existence other harbour records: at Barcelona, where access to the archives is difficult; at Ragusa-Dubrovnik where the figures are in order and easily accessible only after 1563, and at Genoa, where the overwhelming mass of documents has discouraged researchers; but in any case I doubt whether a systematic study of these records would take us very far. The impression one has, whether rightly or wrongly, but I suspect rightly, is that the seasonal determinism that so clearly affects rural life has continually been thwarted by the will of man, particularly in the towns. Winter on the sea was an obstacle, but small boats could conquer it over short distances, and large merchantmen on long voyages, even if they had to throw overboard bales of wool or barrels of grain during a storm; and sometimes they sped over the waves, for a while at least 'a sembianza di veloci delfini'. Winter in the mountains was certainly an obstacle, particularly in the Alps, but we have seen that there were regular crossings nevertheless.

Winter was clearly a quiet season, as plenty of unmistakable evidence shows. Perhaps the most unexpected is that of the banks of Naples, which regularly in winter invested their clients' money in government bonds whereas in summer they used it to buy up the many agricultural products of the kingdom, a profitable avenue for speculation. But winter was also the season of domestic crafts, when looms were busy. As the *provveditore* of the *Arte de Lana* said in Florence in October, 1604, the artisans must be helped at all costs 'now that the cold weather and long nights are here and they need light and clothing, besides food . . .'.

So there were many exceptions: human life responds to the commands of the environment, but also seeks to evade and overcome them, only to be caught in other toils, which as historians, we can reconstruct more or less accurately.

102. Pilgrims travelling to Jerusalem by land and sea. Drawing from the fifteenth-century manuscript *The Travels of Sir John Mandeville*. *British Museum*

5

The Mediterranean as a Human Unit: Communications and Cities

TO PASS FROM the true Mediterranean, as defined by its climate, to that greater Mediterranean where its influence is felt, is to pass from a physical unit to that human unit with which this book is concerned. This human unit is not merely the result of nature, or more particularly of the waters of the Mediterranean. The sea is everything it is said to be: it provides unity, transport, the means of exchange and intercourse, if man is prepared to make an effort and pay a price. But it has also been the great divider, the obstacle that had to be overcome. The art of navigation may perhaps have been born far back in time, in the stretches of calm water between the Aegean islands and the coast of Asia Minor, or in the nearby Red Sea; we shall never know for certain. It is at any rate accepted that at the dawn of history long ages elapsed before man learned to master the sea. Gradually the small boats overcame it, creating their own links and building by degrees the coherent entity that was to be the Mediterranean of man and history, for built it was and by the hand of man. Even today, when the Inland Sea is by modern standards of travel little more than a river, easily bridged by airways, the human Mediterranean only exists in so far as human ingenuity, work, and effort continually re-create it. The different regions of the Mediterranean are connected not by the water, but by the peoples of the sea. This may seem obvious, but it is worth saying in an area that has attracted so many bewildering formulas and descriptions.

1 Land routes and sea routes

The Mediterranean has no unity but that created by the movements of men, the relationships they imply, and the routes they follow. Lucien Febvre wrote, 'The Mediterranean is the sum of its routes,' land routes and sea routes, routes along the rivers and routes along the coasts, an immense network of regular and casual connections, the life-giving bloodstream of the Mediterranean region. We may be tempted to linger over its picturesque aspects, to accompany Cervantes along the Spanish cart tracks from *venta* to *venta*, to follow the voyages of merchant

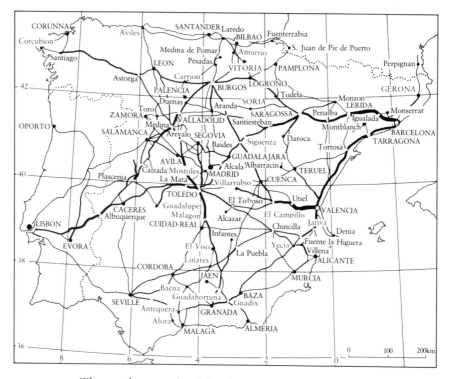

The road network of the Iberian peninsula in 1546

From Gonzalo Menéndez Pidal, *Los caminos en la historia de España*, 1951. The roads are marked with lighter or heavier lines according to the number of times they are mentioned in the Guide by the Valencian Juan Villuga (Medina, 1546). This 'weighting' reveals that Toledo was the traffic centre and therefore the most diversified city of the Peninsula. Other large crossroads were Barcelona, Valencia, Saragossa, Medina del Campo. Madrid's hour of greatness (it was to be the capital after 1556) had not yet struck.

or pirate vessels as we read their log books, to go down the Adige aboard the *burchieri*, the heavy cargo boats working below Verona, or to embark 'upon the water to go to Venice' at Fusina on the edge of the lagoon, with Montaigne's belongings. But the essential task before us is to measure the relationships this network implies, the coherence of its history, the extent to which the movement of boats, pack animals, vehicles and people themselves makes the Mediterranean a unit and gives it a certain uniformity in spite of local resistance. The whole Mediterranean consists of movement in space. Anything entering it – wars, threats of war, fashions, techniques, epidemics, merchandise light or heavy, precious or commonplace – may be caught up in the flow of its life blood, ferried over great distances, washed ashore to be taken up again and passed on endlessly, maybe even carried beyond its boundaries.

The routes are of course the channels of this movement. But they are more than mere ribbons over the land, lines across the sea, caravans on the road to

Aleppo, the long processions of horses, mules, and camels on the Stambulyol (the road to Istanbul along the Maritsa) or the wagons Busbecq saw in 1555, carrying to Constantinople men, women, and children captured by the Turks in Hungary. There would be no routes if there were no stopping-places: a harbour; an open roadstead; a caravenserai or a *Han*; in western Europe it might be an lonely inn, or in the old days a fortified castle. For the most part, these halts, the resting places without which no route could survive, were the towns, the busy centres towards which the traveller hastened his steps and where he arrived with joy, perhaps with a feeling of thankfulness, like Guzmán de Alfarache entering Saragossa, staring in amazement at the grand monuments, the efficient police force, and, perhaps more than anything else, the abundance of good things. He had all the more reason to hasten since in many cases Mediterranean roads did not run from village to village, for these were more likely to be removed some distance from the road for safety. The traveller in Bulgaria and Anatolia, even today, passes through countryside that appears much more deserted and depopulated than it actually is. We should imagine the great trade route to the East as something like today's *autostrada*, a great crosscountry highway linking towns but very rarely passing through villages.

The Mediterranean region in the sixteenth century (and it must be extended to its maximum when we are talking of towns) was unique in its immensity. In the sixteenth century no other region in the world had such a developed urban network. Paris and London were just on the threshold of their modern careers. The towns of the Low Countries and southern Germany (the latter bathing in the reflected glory of the Mediterranean, the former stimulated economically by merchants and sailors from the South), further north the industrious but small towns of the Hanseatic League, all these towns, thriving and beautiful though they might be, did not make up a network as closely knit and complex as that of the Mediterranean, where town followed town in endless strings, punctuated by great cities: Venice, Genoa, Florence, Milan, Barcelona, Seville, Algiers, Naples, Constantinople, Cairo. The last three were over-populated: Constantinople was said to have a population of 700,000, that is double the size of Paris and four times the size of Venice. And to this list should be added the large number of minor towns that nevertheless took part in international exchanges, playing a role more important than the size of their population would suggest.

The prevailing human order in the Mediterranean has been one dictated primarily by towns and communications, subordinating everything else to their needs. Agriculture, even on a very modest scale, is dictated by and directed towards the town; all the more so when it is on a large scale. It is because of the towns that man's life has taken on a faster rhythm than it would under natural conditions. It was thanks to the towns that trading activities came to predominate over all others. The history and the civilization of the sea have been shaped by its towns.

Vital communications. Mediterranean communications consisted, in the first place, of shipping routes and, as we have seen, for the most part in the sixteenth century these were coastal routes. Then there were the many land routes: some running along the coast from port to port, like the endless succession of roads, tracks, narrow and hazardous paths, running uninterrupted from Naples to Rome, Florence, Genoa, Marseilles, then through Languedoc and Roussillon, to the Spanish littoral, Barcelona, Valencia, Málaga. Others run at right angles to the coast, for instance the natural routes of the Nile or the Rhône valley, the roads leading to the Alps or the caravan trails from Aleppo to the Euphrates, or from North Africa, to the Sudan. To these could be added the many 'isthmus roads' as Bérard called them, such as the south–north road that ran from Syria through the Cilician Gates, passing over the Taurus and through Anatolia before arriving at Constantinople, either directly by Eskisehir or via the detour to Ankara; or the roads crossing the Balkans, roughly from east to west, from Salonica to Durazzo, Valona or Cattaro, from Üskub to Ragusa, from Constantinople to Spalato (whose sudden economic rise at the end of the sixteenth century is discussed below); or the series of roads crossing Italy, from the Adriatic to the Tyrrhenian: the road from Barletta to Naples and Benevento, the most important of these southern highways (by the Ariano Pass); further north is what one might call the commercial axis of Tuscany – from Ancona to Florence and Leghorn – and the Genoese axis, from Ferrara to Genoa; finally, in the west, the roads crossing Spain from Barcelona to the Bay of Biscay, from Valencia to Portugal, from Alicante to Seville. Crossing an isthmus from one side to the other could mean taking one of several roads. So between Lombardy and the Romagna on one side, and Tuscany on the other, sixteenth-century travellers had the choice of eight routes, all difficult since they crossed the Apennines: the most convenient one, and the only one accessible to artillery, was the furthest south, running from Rimini, through the valley of the Marecchia, to Arezzo and Sansepolcro.

To complete the list we should add the river routes, often on the outskirts of the Mediterranean world: for instance the active waterways of the northern Italian plains, the Adige, the Po and its tributaries the Adda, the Oglio and the Mincio; the 'Russian' rivers; all the Portuguese waterways; the Guadalquivir as far as Seville, and above Seville as far as Córdoba; the Nile, only half-Mediterranean, whose enormous quantities of fresh water spill out beyond its delta 'all clouded and yellow' into the sea; or the true Mediterranean waterways, such as the Ebro with its flat-bottomed boats carrying passengers and Aragonese grain to Tortosa, the lower reaches of some of the rivers in Valencia and Granada, and in Italy the lower Arno, the lower Tiber, which was open to sea-going boats as far as Rome and was the home of the curious river boats with lateral rudder and two raised ends that served as steps for disembarking on the steep banks of the river.

All these routes differed very little in the sixteenth century from the roads

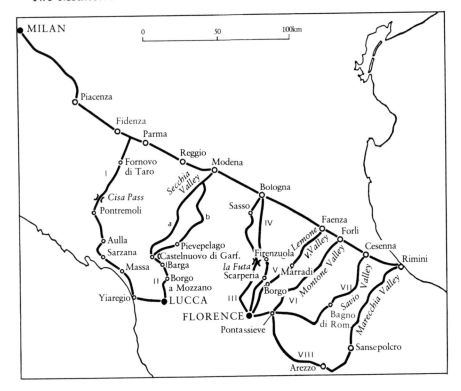

Roads over the Tuscan Apennines

The highway from Rimini to Milan, the old Via Aemilia, bounds the eastern edge of the Apennines. The many roads running at right angles to it leading to Lucca and Florence give some idea of the number of transversal roads throughout the peninsula. The road from Bologna to Florence via La Futa corresponds to the great *autostrada* of the twentieth century. The document on which this map is based lists only the trans-Apennine roads from Florence and Lucca.

along which the Roman Empire advanced or from those of the Middle Ages. But whatever their pattern, whether varying or not over the centuries, they have always both reflected the range of Mediterranean economic systems and civilizations and governed their fate. I am even more convinced now than when I wrote the first edition of this book of the importance of these communications. They are the infrastructure of all coherent history. But it will be no easy task to estimate the precise role they played.

Archaic means of transport. Between 1550 and 1600 there was some improvement in roads and navigation, in the speed and regularity of the mails, the cost of transport fell, but these changes were never of revolutionary proportions. Proof of this is provided by the way the small towns, that is the secondary halts, survived the political and economic transformations of the century. It was because they defended themselves, and, above all, because the cities could not do without them, any more than the traveller along a road could do without somewhere to change his horses or lay his head. The life of these intermediary places was linked to the arithmetic of distances, the average speed of travel along the roads, the normal length of voyages, all measures that did not substantially change during a century which was not outstanding for its technical progress, which still used the old roads (Rome's ancient splendour survived into the sixteenth century with her roads) and boats of small tonnage (the giants of the Mediterranean were rarely over a thousand tons); which still called on the pack animal more often than the wheeled vehicle. The latter was not unknown in the century of Philip II, but its progress was slow, almost negligible, if indeed it progressed at all in the years between 1550 and 1600. It is worth remembering that in 1881 the wheeled vehicle was still unknown in Morocco; that it only appeared in the Peloponnesus in the twentieth century; and that its appearance has always led to the adaptation of old roads and the creation of new, amounting almost to a revolution, as Cvijić has said of nineteenth-century Turkey.

So we should not anticipate: in the sixteenth century, Spain was not yet the country of mule-drawn carriages jingling with bells; nor was Italy the country of the famous *vetturini* of the Romantic period. Here and there vehicles were to be seen (some more or less sophisticated, others still primitive), drawn by horses, mules, oxen, or buffaloes. There were wheeled carts along the Stambulyol, in the countryside around Bursa, in the Constantine region (where they were seen by Leo Africanus) on the Brenner route, throughout almost all of Italy. Casks of wine were conveyed by cart round Florence; Cervantes ridiculed the carters of Valladolid, and when the Duke of Alva invaded Portugal in 1580 he commandeered many *carros* for his army's use. The removal of the court of Philip II from Valladolid to Madrid in 1606 was accomplished by ox-cart.

Wheeled traffic was certainly used then near the big cities, and in the rear of armies which required massive transport. But was it frequent elsewhere? The wheeled cart was not yet in general use in southern Italy; it was considered a German fashion there, even if by the end of the century it seems to have conquered the road from Barletta to Naples, described in official reports of 1598 and 1603, however, as imperfect and unfinished. Even in France at the end of the century carriage roads were not very frequent. Over large areas the pack animal was still the chief means of transport. In the seventeenth and eighteenth centuries the road network of the Ottoman Empire, object of much admiration in Europe, consisted of narrow paved tracks, one metre wide, for horsemen, on either side of which flocks and pedestrians had beaten out footpaths ten times the width. On such roads there was little or no wheeled traffic.

Did land routes increase in importance towards 1600? And yet traffic continued to flow along these poor roads and even increased in volume towards the end of the century. Both cause and consequence of this increase was the rise in the numbers of mules, at any rate in the European peninsulas: in Spain an

Above: 103. The Via Appia near Terracina, showing an inn and travellers. From *Civitates Orbis Terrarum.*
Right: 104. A mule train. From *Civitates Orbis Terrarum.*

agriculturalist contemporary of Charles V, Alonso de Herrera, considered this phenomenon a terrible calamity; in Italy, especially in Naples, in order to save horse-breeding, rich Neapolitans were forbidden, under pain of severe penalties, to use mules to pull their carriages; in Cyprus after 1550 the breeding of mules of both sexes led to a disastrous drop in the number of horses; in Andalusia draconian measures were introduced to save the horse; in the Balkans during the Turko-Hungarian War of 1593–1606 mules were among other spoils of war seized by the Christians. Haëdo also mentions a Moor travelling from Algiers to Cherchel astride a mule. In 1592 she-mules were sent from Sicily for the works at La Goletta.

The triumph of the mule in the sixteenth century is undeniable although it was bitterly opposed by governments in the name of wartime requirements. The mule was more than an agricultural implement, as Herrera explains at length in his writing on Spain. It was a marvellous pack animal, strong and docile.

Rabelais, who took an interest in everything, refers to this in the *Quart Livre*: 'mules are more powerful, more robust and more hard-working than other animals'. As against 600,000 mules used for ploughing, Herrera estimated that 400,000 were used in Spain for 'cavalry', that is for transport. With a little imagination, this increase in mule traffic can be compared to what was to happen in the eighteenth century in Spanish and Portuguese America, where man conquered the empty interior by means of endless processions of mules.

News and letters were mainly carried overland. Waterways were only rarely used for dispatches. The same was true of precious goods, for land transport (undoubtedly a luxury) was a possibility open to them. So at the end of the sixteenth century raw silk from Naples came to Leghorn *by land*, and from there, *still by land*, travelled to Germany and the Low Countries. It was by land too that serges from Hondschoote travelled in the other direction, to Naples, where over sixty specialized firms handled their redistribution between 1540 and 1580.

Finally, at the very end of the century there was a new and important increase in land traffic in the eastern Mediterranean. Ragusa, which had previously made her living from a variety of different shipping trades, some local, others long-distance (among them the Black Sea trade), now abandoned these activities and withdrew into the Adriatic. It was not that the hides and wool of the Balkans had stopped coming into the city, but now they came from the great centre at Novi-Pazar, by overland routes, which had replaced the sea routes. Similarly, the striking fortune in the seventeenth century of Smyrna, perched at the very end of the Asia Minor peninsula, can be interpreted as a victory for the overland route. For Smyrna captured part of the rich traffic of Aleppo (notably the Persian trade) possibly because it provided a point of departure further to the west for the sea voyage to the western Mediterranean.

The same movement explains the Spalato venture. Because of the threat from Uskok piracy and later from the competition of Ragusa and Ancona which regularly stole trade from Venice, attention began to be paid, after 1577 and particularly after 1580, to a suggestion made by Michael Rodriguez, a Jew living in Venice who was said to be of extraordinary intelligence. He suggested that the port of Spalato should be developed – at the time the little town had fallen into decay but still possessed an excellent harbour and had links with the Balkan interior – and that a system of protected convoys be set up between Spalato and Venice. The plan was not realized until after 1591 because of opposition from an influential senator, Leonardo Donato, who was hostile to any risky enterprise: at least that is what Nicolò Contarini says and it may well be true. It could also be that until 1591 Venice did not feel any pressing need to take such a step.

But once this solution had been adopted, it soon had considerable consequences. The Venetians built a completely new town at Spalato: custom houses, warehouses, and hospitals in which merchandise was disinfected and persons quarantined 'for epidemics are rife amongst the Turks'. They repaired the city

105, 106. *Above:* Mule trains in
Andalusia. *Right:* A peasant going to
market. Engraving by M. Mittelli after
A. Carracci.

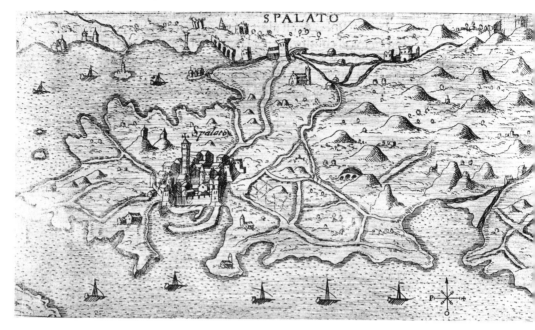

107. View of the roads leading to Spalato (Split). Venice, 1598.

walls and fortifications. The Turks for their part put the roads leading to Spalato in good order and fixed certain dates for journeys so that merchants could travel in large bands 'known there as caravans', Contarini thinks it necessary to add. Immediately riches and abundance poured into the Dalmatian port. Since piracy was increasing on the sea, the new overland route attracted merchandise from very distant places. Goods that had previously been carried by sea from Syria, Persia, and India were now, after an extraordinary overland journey, arriving at Spalato. Great merchant galleys (shorter and lower in the water than those which used to make the voyage from Venice to Southampton, but well protected against the small boats of the Uskoks) were used for the brief journey from Spalato to Venice.

Venice's rivals and enemies knew from then on that to hurt Venice they would have to strike Spalato. The venture was no mere temporary success, but a permanent link. Spalato became the headquarters for trade between Dalmatia and Venice, trade for which there are some statistics: an average of 11,000 *colli* of merchandise were dispatched annually between 1586 and 1591; 16,460 *colli* from 1592 to 1596; 14,700 from 1614 to 1616; 15,300 from 1634 to 1645. Of course *colli* (which simply means large bundles) cannot be accepted as a regular unit of measurement; neither has the Spalato traffic been properly distinguished from the total volume of Dalmatian trade with Venice (although the *Cinque Savii* mention in July, 1607, 12,000 *balle* (*balla = collo*) of merchandise from Spalato alone, 'besides sums of money in cash'). The documents reckon the horses of the caravans in hundreds and soon a throng of merchants was arriving at Venice, coming even from Bursa: Armenians, Jews, Greeks, Persians, Wallachians, people of 'Bogdiana' and Bosnia. The care with which Venice defended these close connections, for instance during the plague that struck Spalato during the summer of 1607, and the strengthening of a commercial link with Morea, are signs that the Balkan connection had become stable, and was no longer an expedient but a permanent solution.

In any case there is no lack of evidence, at the end of the century and the beginning of the next, of the increase in road traffic in the Balkans. To take Ragusa, commercial papers for 1590–1591, on the eve of Spalato's rise to fortune, reveal the extent of her traffic with the interior; as does the construction of a new bazaar near the town for Turkish merchants. In 1628 a more spacious quarantine building was set up at the end of the port. This detail, insignificant in itself, suggests, when taken together with others, that these overland communications must have eliminated or at least reduced the halts in Syria and Egypt and the long sea voyages from the East to Italy; they furthered the movement westwards of merchants and merchandise from the Levant. The *Fontico dei Turchi* in Venice at San Giovanni Decollato dated from 1621. Ragusa also witnessed the arrival of large numbers of Jewish and Turkish merchants. So if the seventeenth century saw a recurrence of outbreaks of plague, particularly in Italy, and also in the Balkans, according to Jorjo Tadić, there was perhaps a connection of cause and effect between these outbreaks and the revival of overland transport. ·

The intrinsic problem of the overland route. Competition between different means of transport is common to all ages. But we historians of the early modern period have often mistakenly assumed that a sea or river route automatically took precedence over a land route. A road challenged by a waterway we have at once dismissed as doomed to decline. In fact, wheeled vehicles and pack animals offered more resistance to competition than we have credited them with and were not ousted so easily.

It is undeniable, for instance, that the prosperity of the German isthmus was due, among other things, after the fifteenth century, to the increased speed and modernization of wheeled vehicles. The rise of Antwerp thanks to overland traffic forms a contrast with the 'seaward' fortune of Bruges in the previous centuries, Bruges having merely been as a port on the way north for the triumphant advance of the Mediterranean ships. Indeed, between northern Europe and the Mediterranean, sea routes and overland routes clearly coexisted and competed with each other, the cargoes often, if not always, being divided into the heavy and cheap on one hand and the light and costly on the other, the whole system operating over an immense area, both more extensive and easier to assess than the Balkans. I do not now think, as I did when I wrote the first edition, that the Atlantic route and the 'invasion' by northern ships which will be discussed later, immediately and permanently eclipsed the great German and French roads running down to the Mediterranean at the end of the sixteenth century. Some evidence on this point has been produced by Wilfrid Brulez in his book on the Antwerp firm of the della Faille. When trading with Italy between 1574 and 1594 the della Faille firm preferred the Alps to the sea nine times out of ten. It is of no small importance that they should have chosen the former rather than the latter. A close look at the figures shows that they were simply guided by their own interests. The overland route was not without its disadvantages, but it was relatively reliable and the average profits it procured (16·7 per cent) were greater than those yielded by the long sea passage (12·5 per cent) where there were wild fluctuations from 0 (or rather a minus figure) to 200 per cent. The overland route was much steadier (maximum profit 30 per cent).

This particular example concerns luxury goods, of course. There is no evidence that an overall comparison between the Atlantic shipping route and the roads crossing Europe from north to south would show that the former carried (or did not carry) more merchandise than the latter (it certainly did in weight, but whether it did in value is more doubtful). At all events traffic continued to flow along the roads from Istanbul to Spalato, Hamburg to Venice, or Lyons to Marseilles. It was perhaps only in the seventeenth century that the sea passage was to become more important with the advance of the northern ships, the generalization of marine insurance and the establishment, again in the North, of powerful commercial firms.

These general observations are made with a purpose. They will not in themselves solve our Mediterranean problems, but they may shed some light upon them.

Two sets of evidence from Venice. From the preceding paragraphs we can certainly conclude that during the second half of the sixteenth century there was an increase in land traffic and that some abandoned roads were even revived and brought back into use. What about traffic by sea during the same period? There does not seem to have been any corresponding drop in shipping to offset the increased volume of trade on the roads, quite the contrary. The general upward trend seems to have maintained a certain balance between the two.

This can be illustrated by the case of Venice. At the same time as the Spalato venture, and even earlier, there was clearly a large reduction in the Venetian fleet. But the volume of traffic in the port remained the same until at least 1625, according to the figures given by Sella himself: 1607–1610, an average of 94,973 *colli* of which about 15,000 came from the Dalmatian ports and the routes over the Balkans; in 1625, 99,361; in 1675, 68,019; in 1680, 83,590; in 1725, 109,497. Foreign ships must have compensated for the deficiencies of the Venetian fleet. We can certainly talk of Venice's decline *as a sea-power*, but not of a decline in the traffic entering and leaving the port, which is our present concern. A small and unexpected detail is that the insurance rates did not budge during these difficult years, at least until 1607, for Venetian ships. Let us suppose, and it is not a totally unreasonable supposition, that the average insurance rate was 5 per cent. For the underwriter to balance out gains and losses, he would need to set twenty voyages without incident against one total disaster. For the sake of argument, all ships are assumed to be equivalent to each other, and the disaster befalling the twenty-first as total. Obviously this is an oversimplification: in the first place because disaster was never total for the underwriter since he was re-insured; second, he would have a legal claim to any goods salvaged; third, if he reimbursed the victim, he would usually secure a reduction on the total insurance payment; and fourth, if gain and loss balanced, he would meanwhile have been collecting the interest on the sums received for as long as the insurance had been held. These points complicate the problem, but not impossibly so. In short, and this is my point, it is not absurd to suppose that wrecks were compensated by many safe and successful voyages. For 37 boats lost, there were perhaps 740 voyages a year. In fact, the port of Venice was busier than has been supposed; shipping there was far from sluggish in those latter years of the sixteenth century which are supposed to have been disastrous. In 1605, it is true, Venice possessed only 27 big ships, but if the ratio of small to big ships was the same as elsewhere, she should have possessed over 200 small ships (10 to 1).

There was no outright victor in the competition between sea and land communications, at least in the sixteenth century: general prosperity brought benefit to both. And the respective positions held by each remained fairly constant; at any rate the relative value of goods carried did.

Venice offers a little more evidence on the subject of rivalry between shipping and overland routes through the chance survival of a register of bales of wool arriving from 'the west', i.e., Spain, from 1508 to 1606. The bales that came all the way by sea are listed separately from those that came overland using the roads crossing Italy. The choice of the first route was encouraged by the virtually free entry granted in 1598 to wool arriving by sea. These direct shipments were carried in Dutch vessels. And yet, in spite of these advantages and these superior ships, the overland route, via Genoa and particularly via Leghorn, held its own and even had the advantage over its rival. Why was this? The reason is not hard to guess. In the first place there was the force of habit, and of established interests. We know that the Genoese and Florentines had the monopoly of purchases in Spain; that there was a line of payments (in fact of a sort of credit by remote control) running all the way from Medina del Campo to Florence, and back, as the correspondence of Simón Ruiz bears witness; that Venetian merchants bought wool on a commission basis, that is, on credit on Florence, and that the first choice of wool stayed in Florence, the second choice going to Venice for processing. The role played by Florence as a go-between explains the frequent use made of the land route.

2 Shipping: tonnage and economic change

We have records of thousands of Mediterranean ships; we know their names, their approximate tonnage, cargoes, and itineraries. But it is not easy to introduce order and meaning into this mass of detail. The reader will, I hope, forgive me for tackling the problem from various angles, in the first place for widely extending the chronological field of observation, making frequent reference to the fifteenth and seventeenth centuries; secondly, for treating the Atlantic as one with the Mediterranean. The reasons for taking these unexpected steps should emerge from the following discussion, and three or four general rules which must be stated at the outset should help to clarify the problem.

1. Mediterranean shipping was not fundamentally different from Atlantic shipping. Techniques, insurance rates, intervals between voyages might differ, but the basic instrument, the wooden ship propelled by the wind, had the same technical limitations. It could not exceed a certain size, number of crew, surface of sail, or speed. Another unifying feature was that no new type of ship appeared in the ocean without examples appearing fairly soon in the Mediterranean. Even at Venice, a city that had her own types of boat and did not readily change them, there were caravels when Marino Sanudo was a young man, at the end of the fifteenth century, and galleons and *bertoni* before the end of the sixteenth. Even the Turks were by then using the ocean-going galleon, 'navis gravis, navis oneraria', the heaviest of all merchant vessels, explains Schweigger, a German traveller who saw them at Constantinople and elsewhere in 1581.

2. In the Atlantic as well as in the Mediterranean, boats of small tonnage were in an overwhelming majority. They loaded quickly, were off at the first puff of wind; proletarians of the sea, they often sold their services cheaply. Two Capuchin friars were returning, in June, 1633, from Lisbon to England: the master of a *naviguela* from Honfleur (35 tons) carrying salt and lemons, offered to take them to Calais for 8 *livres* per passenger. In April, 1616, the Venetian ambassador Piero Gritti, travelling to Spain, chose to board a Provençal felucca, a small two-masted boat, at Genoa; he wanted a fast crossing, and reserved places for his family on a big ship sailing to Alicante. The felucca, wrote Père Binet in 1632, 'is the smallest of all oarships'.

The small ships then were in a majority, their names varying according to port, region, or period: *grippi* or *marani* or *marciliane*, in the Adriatic, feluccas or tartans in Provence, barques as port statistics sometimes call them with no further detail. These little boats, mostly under 100 and even under 50 tons, plied in the Atlantic as well as in the Mediterranean. There were ten of them for every large merchantman, according to Valencia statistics for 1598 to 1618. When we find that there were thirty-one *navi* (i.e., large merchant ships) at Venice in 1599 we must imagine several hundred small boats surrounding them.

3. It must be accepted once and for all that we shall never have complete

108. *View of the Port of Naples* by Pieter Breughel. *Galleria Doria, Rome*

knowledge of tonnages in the sixteenth century, let alone the average tonnage that would enable us, where we know the number of ships entering or leaving a port, to calculate their total tonnage. I have suggested the figure of 75 tons, based on statistics from the Andalusian ports. This figure is probably much too high. The recorded tonnages are in any case never very precise. Experts calculated them from the ship's measurements (height, breadth, and length). When a boat was being hired out to another state, the figure was of course exaggerated, quite openly when the customer was Spain. Even if we assume honesty all round, we still have to translate *salme, stara, botte, cantara, carra*, into our own measures. This is an area full of pitfalls: if anything it is even worse than trying to convert nominal prices into grammes of silver. The 'nominal' tonnages of the sixteenth century dropped suddenly at Seville, a source of several problems for Huguette and Pierre Chaunu. I once worked briefly on some French consular documents (A.N. series B III) that recorded the arrivals of boats with their cargoes at a series of foreign ports in the eighteenth century. Several times the same boat – same master, same name, identical details of route followed and cargo carried – was described in these official papers as being of different tonnage from one port and one consulate to another. In short, all our calculations must be approximate, with the disadvantages that implies.

4. The bulk of the evidence undoubtedly relates to big and very big ships. This takes us not to the borderline between medium and large tonnages, but to

the upper limit, around 1000 or even 2000 tons. The Spanish *proveedores* were not usually likely to put an embargo on some Breton fishing smack of about 30 tons, or a caravel that would hold a maximum of only ten horses, as they did in 1541, for instance, before the Algiers expedition. It was the larger ships they were after and in fact the latter accepted the situation with more equanimity than they expressed, for the Spanish state reserved bounties for them, allowed them good freight rates and generous supplies.

At this period a ship of 1000 tons was a giant and a rarity. On 13th February, 1597, Thomas Platter, the medical student from Basel who had just completed his studies at Montpellier, was in Marseilles. In the port he had eyes only for an enormous Genoese ship that had just been seized by the Marseillais, 'It was one of the largest ships ever launched in the Mediterranean; it was like a great house of five stories rising from the middle of the sea. I estimated that its capacity must be at least fifteen thousand quintals [about 750 modern tons]. It had eight or ten sails on two masts of prodigious height, one of which I climbed by means of rope ladders. From that height I could see far and wide including the Château d'If, which has a windmill similar to those in the town.' This example is one of hundreds of similar descriptions.

5. The problem facing us if we wish to establish even an approximate average tonnage, in order to build up a general picture, is the relation of these very large tonnages to the rest. Big ships were linked to long distances: they monopolized these interminable voyages for a long time. In addition, behind them there were always states with their requirements and resources, cities, and invariably rich shipowners; these large merchantmen usually carried heavy, bulky cargoes whose price per unit was low and which logically required water transport. So they offered cheap freighting facilities. Before the revolution brought about, quite late, by naval artillery, these floating fortresses spelt security. They might be exposed to the hazards of bad weather like any frail barque, but they could resist an enemy attack. What pirate would seek an encounter with the large crews, soldiers, slingers, and archers they had on board? The big ship was the rich man's best policeman. There were certainly times when the big ships appropriated all transport. The early fifteenth century was a time of monopolies, whether legal or actual, and the sixteenth century was to reintroduce them on the passage to Spanish America and the Portuguese Indies. But if for one reason or another these monopolies were thrown open, there was a host of small and medium-sized ships waiting to rush in. *This comeback by boats of small tonnage almost always seems to have occurred during a period of trade expansion.* If we find big ships alone, business is probably bad; if we find big ships accompanied by little ships, business is certain to be good. This indicator shows every sign of being reliable, but it will be discussed further. The reader is asked to accept it provisionally.

Big ships and little ships in the fifteenth century. The prosperous career of the big ships in the Mediterranean had begun in the fifteenth century. Mediterranean vessels were already sailing from one end of the Mediterranean to the other and pressing on to London or Bruges, the longest voyages as a rule being undertaken by the Genoese. This gave Genoa a head start in the race for big ships, the more so since she virtually specialized in the transport of bulky goods, notably alum from Phocaea in Asia Minor and wines from the islands of the Levant – which she shipped direct to Bruges and England. The Genoese carrack, which approached 1000 tons, often more, was for a long time the rational solution to a difficult technical problem.

Venice followed suit but much later. In the first place she was nearer than Genoa to the Levant, where much of her activity was centred; second, her system of *galere da mercato*, efficiently organized by the state, regulated traffic into particular voyages; there were galleys to Tana, Trebizond, Romania, Beirut, Alexandria, Aiguesmortes, Flanders, Barbary, and the *trafego* (both the Barbary and Egyptian coast). This system meant that difficulties and risks were shared and direct voyages from the Levant to Bruges, in the Genoese manner, were forbidden; all goods had to pass through Venice, providing the Signoria with the dues on which she lived. The *galere da mercato* hardly reached 200 to 250 tons at the end of the century. Moreover they only carried luxury commodities, such as pepper, spices, expensive fabrics, silks, malmsey wines. This being so, it was wisest to spread the risks between several loads. Only the Flemish galleys, returning from the North would load, besides the kerseys and amber, bales of wool, lead and tin from England, otherwise they would have returned empty. However, it was the experience of long voyages to the Black Sea on one hand, and to England on the other, that led to the increased tonnage of the galleys (in the fourteenth century they were only about 100 tons burden) and then to their increased numbers.

Besides the *galere da mercato*, a private or only partly controlled shipping sector existed at Venice. These were the roundships, 'cogs', which handled in particular the transport of the bulky bales of cotton from Cyprus or Syria. Cotton had become an important textile as early as the thirteenth century, compensating for insufficient woollen production, and was to be much in demand with the development of fustians (linen and cotton mixture). The cotton was transported annually in two *mude*: one, the larger, in February (about half a dozen ships); the other, in September, might consist of only two ships. The large bales required roomy carriers. A document from the *Notatorio di collegio* dated 1st December, 1449, lists the names and tonnages of six roundships that were to make up the *muda* of the following February: 1100, 762, 732, 566, 550 and 495 *botte*, or between 250 and 550 tons. These were very respectable tonnages even for the fifteenth century.

Another advantage of the big ships was that they could defend themselves against pirates. A Catalan roundship of 2800 *botte* (about 1400 tons) in August,

1490, gave chase to the Barbary galleys, which took refuge in the port of Syracuse. In 1497 Sanudo mentions a Venetian *nave* of 3000 *botte*, a French 'barque' of 3500, a Genoese *nave* the *Negrona*, of 4000. Two years later, in 1499, he gives some measurements of the Venetian ships that were to join the French fleet. The average tonnage of the thirty ships (including seven foreign ones) was 675 *botte*, or about 338 tons, an average that will seem abnormally high to any historian of the sixteenth century. By way of comparison, in July, 1541, 52 ships listed at Cadiz and Seville, just before Charles V's expedition against Algiers, amounted to a total of just over 10,000 tons, or an average of 200 tons per ship. So it must be accepted that the fifteenth century had tonnages as high as anything in the eighteenth century; some of the Indiamen which then carried the 'China trade' were only in the region of 2000 tons.

The first victories of the small ships. At some point during the fifteenth and sixteenth centuries, there was a reduction in the number of big ships and a rapid extension of boats of smaller tonnage. This movement can be traced to the middle of the fifteenth century and indeed to Venice, where in 1451 there is already mention in a Senate debate of the demand for small boats for the voyages to Syria and Catalonia. Small ships from the Atlantic became numerous in the Mediterranean after this, Basque, Portuguese and Spanish invaders 'che prima non solevano passar il stretto de Zibilterra', according to a curious Senate debate dated 21st October, 1502; something one does not expect to hear at that date. Venice, if we are to believe her, was on the brink of unspeakable disaster. Her fleet of big ships which had previously numbered 300 (an exaggeration) 'dal 1420 sino al 1450', had dwindled to 16, each with a capacity of at least 400 *botte* and for the most part indeed fit only for scrap; besides these big ships there were few small ships, even including the Dalmatian caravels and the *marani*.

There was no lack of explanation for this crisis: the heavy dues placed on shipping; the absurdly low freight rates; the prohibition placed on loading salt from Languedoc in the *mar de Lion*; the authorization granted to foreign ships to load wines directly at Crete; and then there were those intruders, who had crossed the Straits of Gibraltar and 'are enriching themselves at the expense not only of the *cittadini* but also of the State which they now imperil, of the *mude* of the galleys and of our roundships'. These intruders were the small ships.

Similar developments occurred in the Atlantic, the English Channel, and the North Sea, as Aloys Schulte reported in his marvellous book on the *Grosse Ravensburger Gesellschaft* where one can find information about everything if one is prepared to look for it. The great roundships or *naus* of Genoa and other Mediterranean cities were overtaken by the light and elegant caravels, the new young hope of the world. The difference between the two categories was enormous. In 1498 four roundships loaded 9000 quintals of merchandise at Antwerp; 28 caravels between them could only take 1150.

The victory of the light sailing vessel over the great ships of the Mediter-

109. A merchant's roundship. Relief from the tomb of Alessandro Contarini, Cathedral of St. Anthony, Padua.

ranean, of the swifter, cheaper boats over the great giants that took an age to load and worked with the monopolists' privileges, marked the beginning of a great transformation both in the Atlantic and the Mediterranean. It was to last until about the 1530s, slowed down towards 1550 (at least in the Mediterranean), started again after the 1570s, and lasted until after the end of the century.

In the Atlantic in the sixteenth century. To set the problem of Atlantic shipping in the sixteenth century in perspective, we should consider separately from the rest the two great Iberian monopolies: the *Carrera de Indias*, based in Seville, and the long shipping route between Lisbon and the East Indies.

On these favoured routes the little ships of the explorers soon disappeared. Of Columbus' three ships, the *Santa Maria* was a vessel of 280 tons, the *Pinta* 140, and the *Nina* only 100. Fifty years later, the 1552 regulations would not accept any ships below 100 tons, with a minimum crew of thirty-two men, on the American convoys; a decision by Philip II on 11th March, 1587, raised the minimum to 300 tons. But at the end of the sixteenth century there were few ships over 500 tons on the West Indies route, for 400-ton sailing ships had difficulty crossing the bar at San Lucar de Barrameda, on the Guadalquivir below Seville. It was only in the second half of the seventeenth century that galleons between 700 and 1000 tons were to become common, and the acute problem arose of transferring the *Casa de la Contratación* and the monopoly of the West Indies trade from Seville, which the ships could no longer reach, to Cadiz.

At Lisbon, where there was unimpeded access to the harbour, vessels of large tonnage were not uncommon in the sixteenth century. The *Garça*, which in 1558 carried the viceroy Constantino de Bragança to the Portuguese Indies, was a vessel of 1000 tons; in fact at the time she was the largest ship ever seen on the Indies route. In 1579, according to a Venetian ambassador, the *navi grandissime* at Lisbon were of over 2200 *botte* (over 1100 tons). This figure was often exceeded at the end of the century. The carrack *Madre de Dios*, which Clifford seized in 1592 and brought back to Dartmouth, could not apparently be taken to London because of her draught. She was over 1800 tons, could carry 900 tons of merchandise plus 32 pieces of ordnance, and 700 passengers. From stem to stern, she measured 166 feet, and her breadth at the widest point, on the second of her three decks, was 46 feet 10 inches; she drew 31 feet of water; her keel was 100 feet long, her mainmast 120 feet high and ten feet round. The admiration of the English was not lessened by the publication on 15th September of the lengthy list of goods she carried, which were to be put up for auction. Forty years later the Portuguese were still building ships as big as this. A traveller in 1604 admired a carrack of 1500 *toneladas* under construction in the port of Lisbon. 'The Portuguese used to make many more of them. The amount of wood which goes to make one is quite incredible: a forest of many leagues would not suffice for two. Three hundred men working on a single ship can hardly finish it in a year. The iron to provide nails and other necessary metalwork weighs 500 tons. These carracks were formerly of 2000–2500 tons. For the mast they choose eight of the greatest and tallest pine trunks and bind them together with hoops of iron; it requires a crew of nine hundred men.' As late as 1664, Varenius in his *Geographia Generalis*, recognized that the Iberians built the biggest ships. But long before that date the heavy vessels had already lost the battle against the light Dutch ships.

The decline of the giants and the spread of small sailing vessels had begun in the sixteenth century. The latter especially calls for our attention. The ships used in the great English naval exploits of the sixteenth century, whether for voyages of discovery or privateering, were often under 100 tons. In 1572, Drake was aboard the *Pasca*, a vessel of only 70 tons; the *Primrose* of London in 1585 was of only 150 tons burden. In 1586 Cavendish's three ships were respectively 140, 60, and 40 tons. In 1587, Spain was given information about fourteen ships standing in the river at London. They were all between 80 and 100 tons. Even in 1664 France possessed in all a few thousand ships over 30 tons, of which scarcely 400 were more than 100 tons and only 60 over 300 tons. Most of her shipping links with the Baltic, for example, were worked by ships of

110. Stained-glass window, King's
College Chapel, Cambridge.

between 30 and 50 tons. In the sixteenth century as in the seventeenth, seas and
oceans were populated by small sailing ships. Between 1560 and 1600 the
arsenals of Lübeck built two thousand four hundred ships, according to Baasch's
research and calculations; their average tonnage was 60 *Lasten*, or 120 tons.
And yet we have records of some big ships from Lübeck: the *Grande Barque*,
600 tons, master 'Roqueresbart', was in the bay of Cadiz in spring 1595; the
Joshua of 300 tons was at the same time at anchor at San Lucar. The Hanseatic
towns sent down to Spain large ships that were either hired or bought by the
Sevillians for the trips to the New World, and by the Portuguese for Brazil and
the Indian Ocean.

In 1575, 1578, and 1579 a record of foreign vessels arriving in Andalusia
gives the total figure for 800 ships as 60,000 tons, i.e., a modest average per
vessel of 75 tons. The figures are naturally higher when they include the big
foreign ships requisitioned for troop transport, such as those listed in 1595 in
three registers drawn up in the ports of San Lucar and Cadiz. The average
tonnage of the first group, twenty-eight ships, listed on 29th March, 1595, was
about 200 tons; for the second group, thirty-seven ships entered in the inventory
on 3rd August and including some or all the ships from the first group, the total
tonnage was 7940 tons, the artillery consisted of 396 cannons, and the crews
of 665 men in all; on average then each ship had a capacity of 214 tons, carried
ten pieces of artillery and about twenty men (eighteen to be precise). To simplify,
we may say that a piece of artillery corresponds to about 20 tons, a seaman to
about 10.

The English and Dutch vessels, banned from the Peninsula after 1586, took
to privateering, scouring the Atlantic, looting poorly guarded coasts and attacking the great unwieldy ships on the Indies route. In these encounters the little
ships often came off best because of their greater speed and manoeuvrability,
and also because of their artillery, for as a contemporary of Richelieu was to

explain much later, in 1626, unlike the old days, a vessel of 200 tons can today 'carry as much cannon as a vessel of 800 tons . . .'

Similar developments appeared in merchant shipping; the small ships were driving out the large, peacefully or with violence. Small boats could load and unload where big ships could not even attempt to go. Big ships might be held up waiting for a complete load, since their great holds had to be filled. Small ships sailed more frequently, spreading the risk. Marco Ottobon, the Venetian secretary who was chartering ships in Danzig in the summer of 1591, to carry grain to Venice, gave preference to ships of 120 to 150 *lastri* (240 to 300 tons) 'of which there are many; they do not hold a great quantity, but as a result the grain is not so likely to perish on the way, . . . and, since we are not insured, the potential loss will be smaller'. And above all they 'expedite' their trips more quickly than the big ships. Another significant point was that grain could be loaded straight into the holds, *a rifuso*, which eliminated the need for sacks or barrels. Small ships offered every advantage.

In the Mediterranean. The galley, which had faced strong competition in the fifteenth century, was to be practically eliminated during the first thirty years of the sixteenth century by the roundship (*nave*): the large merchantman replaced the long powerful oarship, although the latter did not disappear for some time, for reasons that are not altogether clear. in Bandello's time the Beirut galleys were still a typical feature of Venetian life. Galleys worked the route to the Barbary coast until 1532, the Egypt route at least until 1569 when two galleys made the voyage to Alexandria and Syria. At the end of the century the galley was still in service on the Venice–Spalato run, since this short trip required a ship which could choose her own course and which would have the means on board – cannon and men – to meet the threat from pirates.

The galley's immediate successors were larger ships, which then held the front rank for some time, maintaining an average size of about 600 tons, carrying wines to England, grain and salt within the Mediterranean, and taking over the voyages to Syria.

The fortune of Marseilles after the 1570s had many causes: the flow of French, English, and German goods along the Rhône route, the lack of competition from Venice during the years 1570–1573 when she was at war with the Turks, the privileges that, for better or worse, the *entente* between the French king and the Turks and Barbary nations brought her. It was also the result of the design of the vessels of Marseilles and of Provence, *navi*, galleons, tartans, saëtes, or simply barques, as they are called in the Leghorn shiplists. We should not be misled by these names. They were in no way comparable to the splendid galleons of the Duke of Provence in the old days. In 1612 a Venetian consul in Syria mentions boats from Marseilles of 60 *botte*. Often, as the master of one Marseilles ship said, this would only be a *galeonetto*, carrying beans, hides, and cheeses between Cagliari and Leghorn. Marseilles saëtes at the end of the century

III, II2. A Venetian galleon
(*above*) and a galley (*right*).
Reliefs from the tomb of
Alessandro Contarini, Cathedral
of St. Anthony, Padua.

were between 30 and 90 tons. A *nave* of 3000 *salme* (450 tons) was built at Antibes during the summer of 1593, but we should note that she was partly owned by a Genoese, Giovanni Battista Vivaldo.

The barques, tartans, saëtes, galleons, and *galionetti, navires* and *navi* of Marseilles, gradually invaded the sea in the sixteenth century. There was not a port in Spain, Italy, or North Africa where they were not to be found unloading their goods on to the quayside. From the 1560s Venice was obliged to use their services. Throughout the Mediterranean they would sail in fleets, attracting the fury of the big ships. If in 1574 a Ragusan merchantman seized a *nave* from Marseilles, looted and sank her, drowning her entire crew down to the cabin boy, was it not perhaps from vindictiveness as much as search for gain? For the business of the great Ragusan carrying ships was suffering from the transport crisis. They were still sailing the sea, from the Levant to the West, from Sicily to Spain. In the wake of Philip's armadas, they were even to venture into and perish in the Atlantic at the end of the century. But after ten or twenty years, Ragusa, like Venice, indeed more than Venice, withdrew into the quiet waters of the Adriatic.

There was nothing mysterious about these changes. They were dictated in every case by time and circumstance. Marseilles at the end of the century had many ships, but they were all of only moderate size, whereas in a petition to François I in 1526 she had declared that her port was equipped with 'grosses nefz, navires, galions' for trading with Syria, Egypt, and Barbary. So in the course of the century the port had changed. When Ragusa, which according to an eyewitness, in 1574 still owned the biggest ships in the Adriatic, re-entered the shipping world after a long period of eclipse during the eighteenth century, it was with a fleet consisting of dozens and dozens of small boats which from 1734–1744 appeared on the routes both within and outside the Adriatic: *navi*, polaccas, frigates, *marciliane*, feluccas, pataches, *vacchette, tartanelle, trabaccoli.* As one might expect, names, forms, fittings, and ships had changed.

In fact, in the sixteenth century small boats sprang from everywhere responding to the expansion of trade. But the true dimensions of the problem only emerged gradually. Everything played its part: rising prices, rising living standards, return freights, and changed circumstances. So argued an anonymous Venetian in a document which is not dated but is certainly from the beginning of the seventeenth century. Without stirring from his native city he could appreciate the loss in long distance trades and monopolies that the Mediterranean had suffered; appreciate also the general price rise that persisted uninterrupted for so long.

But in fact Venice's economy did not decline at the same time as her navy. The throng of little boats that invaded the Mediterranean in the sixteenth century were, on the contrary, a sign of the sea's prosperity, of its ability to enlist and pay for the services of the proletarians of the Atlantic. We shall have more to say about this important problem.

3 Urban functions

Towns and roads. Without markets and roads there would be no towns: movement is vital to them. The heart of Constantinople was its 'bazestan' with its four gates, its great brick arches, its everyday foods and its precious merchandise, its slave market, where men stood to be handled like animals at a fair, the buyers spitting on their faces and rubbing to see whether the merchants had powdered them or not. It did not matter whether the bazaar was at the centre of the city – and then it was always situated in the lowest part, as if everything should naturally flow down into it – or outside the city, as was the case in the Dinaric zone of Turkish colonization, where all the towns, Mostar, Sarajevo, etc. had 'exobazaars', as Tangier did in the quite recent past. Whatever its site or form, a bazaar, a market, or a town is the meeting place of a number of movements. To Algiers came the donkeys hidden under their enormous loads of wood from the nearby Atlas Mountains, entering the city at Babel-Oued, the northern gate; camels from the Mitidja or the distant south were lodged in front of Bab-Azoun, the southern gate; the harbour was teeming with pirate and merchant vessels, laden with rancid butter from Bône, linens, woollen cloths, and wood from Marseilles, oil from Djerba, perfumes from Spain, not to mention Christian merchandise stolen from ships all over the sea, or ransom money paid by Valencia, Genoa, and other places. On all this the city of Algiers was built and nourished. Every town is founded on movements which it absorbs, uses for its own purposes, and then retransmits. The evocative images of economic life are images of movement, routes, and voyages, even to the bills of exchange, which sixteenth-century authors compare to ships, or ships' cargoes setting out on hazardous journeys, whence the *agio*, a form of marine insurance which is, as they say, proportionate to the risk.

Interruption in its communications might lead to a town's stagnation or death. This was the case of Florence in 1528. Her links with the South had been severed since the sack of Rome in 1527, so she was losing every week the 8000 ducats her Roman clientele had brought her, as well as the 3000 she earned from sales to Naples. There was trouble in the north too, where all communications with France were blocked by Genoa and all the roads to Germany blocked by Venice. Florence was therefore obliged to cut down her production of *panni garbi* (best quality cloth) *o fini o d'oro* and to make use of roundabout smugglers' routes in order to survive and to continue exporting goods, by sea to France and Lyons, Asola, Mantua and even Trieste; by land to Germany. The advantage of territorial states with control over a wide area lay in being able to interrupt at will the communications of the city-states, thus upsetting from a distance the delicate balance of their economies. Genoa accused France of aiding the Corsican rebels, but, wrote Fourquevaux indignantly in February, 1567, if France wanted to harm Genoa, she need not use such indirect methods. She

Above: 113. Detail from *The View of Ankara*, Turkish school. Ankara commanded the important Anatolian caravan route from Syria and the Near East to Constantinople. A caravan can be seen setting out across the bridge. *Rijksmuseum, Amsterdam*

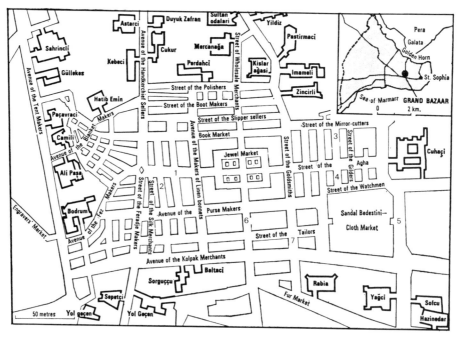

1 Street of the sellers of ladies' garments   2 Street of the cloth designers and printers
3 Street of the honey-sellers   4 Street of the agate merchants   5 Street of the han of the cloth merchants
6 Street of the ribbon-makers   7 Passage of the chief tailor

could simply prohibit the use of silks and other Genoese goods at home and forbid the merchants of Provence to trade with Genoa and her riviera which they furnished with grain and wine. In 1575, at the time of the Genoese troubles, one of the first actions of Spain, fearing the worst, was to cut off supplies of Sicilian grain.

A meeting place for different transport routes. Large towns, which all stand at crossroads, did not necessarily grow up because of them (although Piacenza, for instance, was certainly born of the meeting of the Po and the Via Aemilia). But it is to them that they owe their survival. 'They derive their importance from their geographical situation', as the textbooks say. The place where two routes meet may imply a change of transport, a compulsory halt. At Arles the flotillas of the Rhône met the coasters of Martigues, Bouc, and the Provençal coast which carried all traffic to Marseilles. At Verona the Adige became navigable, taking over from the mule-trains and wagons that had come over the Brenner pass. The caravans reached the sea at Tripoli in Barbary, Tunis, or Algiers. Aleppo owed its existence less to the resources of its site than to the need for an intermediate stage between the Mediterranean and the Persian Gulf, where as Jacques Gassot said, the merchandise of the Indies could meet the 'cloth, kerseys, and others coming from the West'. It was here that the caravans from Baghdad would stop, in front of the mountains of Lebanon, and other caravans of mules, horses, and little donkeys would take over, the same ones that carried western pilgrims to and fro on the neighbouring route from Jerusalem to Jaffa.

From roads to banking. Roads and the exchanges they permitted led to the gradual division of labour by which the towns grew up, painfully distinguishing themselves from the surrounding countryside, though only at the price of an unremitting struggle. This struggle in turn had its effect inside the towns, organizing their different tasks, transforming them internally, according to patterns that were regular only in the very broadest sense.

The starting point of this process, with its many variants, was naturally commercial activity, ever-present, all-important and the source of all economic organization. This was obviously the case of Venice, Seville, Genoa, Milan, and

The Great Bazaar at Constantinople, sixteenth–seventeenth centuries

The great bazaar was the heart of the commercial activity of Constantinople. It consisted principally of two *Bedesten-s* (the word is a corruption of *Bezzazistan*, hence the frequent use of *Bazestan* and a variety of different spellings: the root of the word is *bez*: linen, and it originally meant the bazaar of the linen merchants). The old *Bedesten* was built by Muhammad the Conqueror after the fall of Constantinople. This was the central building with its four gates and two main streets, marked Jewel Market. The new one was the *Sandal Bedesteni* (from sandal: a mixed silk fabric). Around these two great buildings ran a series of streets of shops and artisans. The names printed in heavy type mark the courtyards of the *han-s*. These were the strictly controlled warehouses where supplies of food for the Seray and the city were kept. Wholesalers would sell their merchandise there.

POPULATION IN 1586
Each dot represents 10 inhabitants

SHOPS IN 1661
Each dot represents 1 shop

Marseilles, quite indisputably so in the case of the last-named, whose industry consisted only of some textiles and soap manufacturing. It was clearly true of Venice, too, which exported her own woollen cloth and silks to the East, but alongside them the woollens and velvets of Florence, Flemish cloths and English kerseys, fustians from Milan and Germany, and from Germany also linens, hardware, and copper. As for Genoa, the medieval proverb said: *Genuensis ergo mercator*, a Genoese, therefore a trader. So our systems of classification use the term 'commercial capitalism' to describe the agile, already modern and indisputably effective form taken by economic life in the sixteenth century. All activity did not necessarily contribute to its advance but much depended on its dynamism and magnetism. The imperatives of large-scale, long-distance commerce, its accumulation of capital, acted as driving forces. It was in the space defined by a commercial economy that industrial activity was kindled at Genoa, Florence, Venice, and Milan, particularly in the new and revolutionary textile industries, cotton and silk. The classic theory of Paul Mantoux was already true of the sixteenth century: industry is created and fostered by commerce. Perhaps this was truest of all of the Mediterranean where exchange, transport, and reselling were activities central to life.

The industrial centre of southern France was Montpellier, a town behind which lay a rich past, a mass of acquired wealth, capital available for investment, and invigorating contacts with the outside world. Colbert's dream for seventeenth-century France – a native textile industry to supply the French trade with the Levant – had already been realized elsewhere through force of circumstance. Venetian industry first developed in the thirteenth century; but as her commercial activity increased at a much faster rate during the same period, this medieval industry came to appear insignificant beside the volume of external trade. The real industrial growth of Venice came much later in the fifteenth and especially in the sixteenth centuries, as there was a gradual shift from counting house to

The heart of Venice

The two maps taken from D. Beltrami, *Storia della popolazione di Venezia*, 1954, pp. 39 and 53, raise the same problem: the organization of an urban area. The reader should take his bearings from the Grand Canal, through the centre of which runs a line separating the various quarters of Venice; then the tiny square representing the bridge of the Rialto, the only one which crosses the Grand Canal; St. Mark's Square; to the north-east the white patch representing the Arsenal; to the south the island of San Giorgio and the Giudecca separated from the rest of the city by the wide channel of the Zattere; the point between the Grand Canal and the Zattere corresponds to the Customs House. The six quarters of the city are San Marco; San Polo, on the right bank of the Grand Canal, to the left of the Rialto; Castello (the Arsenal); S. Croce (the third quarter on the right bank); Cannaregio on the northern side, containing the ghetto; Dorsoduro. The centre of the city lies between the Rialto and St. Mark's. Beyond the bridge, in the middle of the black patch of shops in the second diagram, the Rialto square (white) was the daily meeting place of the merchants. The ghetto, to the north-west of the city, has an abnormal density of population because of the measures of segregation. The quarters are divided into parishes whose boundaries are more visible on one diagram than the other, varying from place to place.

workshop, a shift not consciously intended but urged and dictated by the secular trend. Venice was tending to become an industrial port, and it was possibly only the outstanding successes of France and northern Europe in the following century that prevented the transformation from running its full course.

If large-scale industry is the second stage of a town's economic life cycle, banking is perhaps the third. From a town's earliest beginnings all forms of economic activity are undoubtedly under way, finance like any other. But it is not usually until a later stage that money-dealing becomes established as an activity in its own right. Economic functions remain confused during the early period. The Florentine firm Giucciardini Corsi, who advanced money to Galileo, also had interests in Sicilian grain and in the cloth and pepper trade; the Capponi, whose great ledgers have survived, not only issued and received bills of exchange but also transported wine and handled shipping insurance; the Medici, more than half of whose interests lay in banking, owned silk workshops in the fifteenth century.

This many-sidedness was a long-established rule; to engage in several activities was a sensible way of spreading risks. Dealings in money, in other words private loans (more or less disguised since the Church forbade usury), money openly advanced to cities and princes, investments (*accomandite* as they were known in Florence), marine insurance, all purely financial transactions, are difficult to separate from other forms of commerce. It is only in Amsterdam towards the end of the eighteenth century that we see them emerging in their most sophisticated form.

Even in the sixteenth century, financial transactions had already reached a high level, producing in ever larger numbers the quasi-specialist bankers known in Spain as *hombres de negocios*. In eighteenth-century France they would have been called 'financiers' in the service of the state. This phenomenon was only to be found however in a few established merchant cities that had reached full maturity: Venice, where banks and bankers dated back to the fourteenth and even the thirteenth century; Florence, whose great merchant firms had held sway in Europe and the Mediterranean, from England to the Black Sea, since the thirteenth century; and most of all, Genoa, which, in spite of what Michelet said was not 'a bank before it was a town', but where the *Casa di San Giorgio* operated the most sophisticated credit machinery of the Middle Ages. A detailed study has shown that the city was already modern, ahead of its time, in the fifteenth century, daily handling endorsements of bills of exchange. Genoa's early role as intermediary between Seville and the New World, her official alliance with Spain in 1528 did the rest: she became the leading financial city of the world, in the period of rising inflation and prosperity that characterized the second half of the sixteenth century – the century of Genoa, the city where commerce was beginning to appear a rather inferior activity. The *Nobili Vecchi* might occasionally speculate, on a grand scale, in alum, or woollens or in Spanish salt; but on the whole they left trading very much to the *Nobili Nuovi*, them-

114. Interior of a Florentine bank. Italian woodcut, Florence, 1490.

selves devoting their energies to speculation in gold and silver, government bonds, and loans to the king of Spain.

However, in apparent contradiction with this simple picture, many financial centres, *piazze*, sprang up in Europe in towns that were of recent origin. But if we look more closely at these sudden, and quite considerable developments, we shall find that they were in fact ramifications of Italian banking which had by then established its own traditions. In the days of the fairs of Champagne it was already the bankers from Siena, Lucca, Florence, or Genoa who held the moneychanger's scales; it was they who made the fortune of Geneva in the fifteenth century and later those of Antwerp, Lyons, and Medina del Campo. They were on the scene again in 1585, when Frankfurt-am-Main created the exchange fairs. To the uninitiated their dealings were clearly suspect, if not downright diabolical. A Frenchman in 1550 was amazed by these 'foreign [i.e. Italian] merchants and bankers', who would arrive empty-handed 'without bringing from the said countries anything beside their persons, with a little credit, a pen, ink and paper, and skill in handling, turning and diverting the said exchanges from one country to another, according to the information they have of the places where money is dearest'.

In short, throughout Europe a small group of well-informed men, kept in touch by an active correspondence, controlled the entire network of exchanges in bills or specie, thus dominating the field of commercial speculation. In 1580, when Portugal was united with Spain, Spanish businessmen were astonished by the technical backwardness of the Lisbon exchange, which was entirely commodity-based. Investments in Marseilles were still coming from Lyons, Montpellier, and Genoa at the beginning of the seventeenth century. Ragusa, which was commercially so prosperous, was financially dependent on the Italian cities: in the seventeenth century her entire fortune lay in government stocks either in Naples, Rome, or Venice. The case of Venice is even more revealing. A long report by the *Cinque Savii*, in January, 1607, indicates that all 'capitalist' activity, as we should call it, was in the hands of the Florentines, who owned houses in the city, and the Genoese, who provided silver; between them they controlled all exchanges. By 'drawing' on Venice, Genoese and Florentines speculated 'on the exchanges' (chiefly at the so-called Besançon fairs, in fact held at Piacenza) with the plentiful money of Venetian investors. They thus 'captured' the available currency in the city. The Piedmontese, Giovanni Botero, grasped the situation when in 1589 he compared Genoa to Venice, giving his preference to the latter. At Genoa the fortunes of the money-dealers were extremely far advanced, but it was to the detriment of the city's other gainful activities. Her industry (textiles and shipbuilding) was sluggish; the *arti* of course meant life or death to the ordinary people of Genoa, whose level of income was low. Alongside her great rival, Venice remained a less developed town, where all the economic functions were still carried on. Her people were therefore less wretched than those of Genoa and the difference between rich and poor was less marked.

Urban cycle and decline. If urban life advances by stages, it also deteriorates by stages. Towns rise, thrive and decline according to the pulses of economic life. In their decline, they are forced to abandon, sector by sector, the sources of their strength. Was it a coincidence that at Genoa the first warning sign (the presence of Ragusan cargo ships) concerned transport, the primary source of a city's wealth, while at the other end of the scale, it was her banking activities, the latest in time to develop, which held out the longest? At the lowest ebb of their fortunes, in the eighteenth century, Genoa and Venice were still banking centres. Was Barcelona's misfortune, in the sixteenth century at any rate, not a consequence of her past, the price she had to pay for a fortune acquired too quickly and not consolidated on the banking level? It was lack of liquid currency, exchange facilities, *giro*, wrote Capmany, that paralysed the town in the sixteenth century.

By stretching this argument to its limits might it not be possible to say that the development of the industrial phase in a city's life often indicates some difficulty in its trading functions, that industry is in a sense a response to a decline in trade? Whether or not this is a permissible assumption, it may be regarded as symptomatic that industry flourished most in cities far from the sea, cities that were prevented by their position from fulfilling all the functions of communication centres, Lucca, for instance, the home of silk weaving, Milan, Como, or even Florence. Industry also flourished in towns whose communications or merchandise were threatened in the sixteenth century, such as Florence or Venice. Is it possible to go even further and say that banking increases in importance when commerce and industry are in difficulty; that one type of activity can only develop to the detriment of others and not necessarily in harmony with them? My intention in raising these questions is not to attempt an overall interpretation, but to indicate, very briefly, the full complex of problems posed by urban dynamism.

A very incomplete typology. The typology of towns outlined above is necessarily incomplete. They led complicated lives. Every town was contained within a certain economic framework. At local level this implied a system of relationships with the surrounding countryside and the neighbouring towns, within which the town might play a dominant or subordinate role. At national or international levels, it implied systems of relationships, depending on distances within the Mediterranean or even the Greater Mediterranean region. Finally there was political change. In the sixteenth century political change destroyed the old independence of the city-state, undermined the foundations of its traditional economy, creating and imposing new structures.

Felipè Ruiz Martin, in a work on the typology of the towns of Castile in the sixteenth century, has established the following distinctions: bureaucratic towns, such as Granada and Madrid – the latter growing so fast that the machinery for supplying food for its unproductive population was always breaking down and one might see, according to some correspondence in 1615 'bread lacking for days on end, and the people in the streets, money in hand, searching and begging for it "per l'amor di Dio"'; commercial towns, such as Toledo, Burgos, and Seville; industrial towns (in the sense that modern industry grew up there with the capitalist forms of the *Verlagssystem*, by no means peculiar to Germany) such as Córdoba and Segovia; towns whose industrial production was largely in the hands of artisans, such as Cuenca; agricultural towns, dependent on the surrounding countryside, if not invaded by it, such as Salamanca or Jerez de la Frontera; clerical towns like Guadalajara; a sheep-farming town like Soria. There were also several military towns, which in the sixteenth century were as difficult to distinguish from other towns as warships from ordinary merchantmen. This classification gives some idea of the complexity of the problem.

There is the additional problem that no sooner does a town appear to fit into a classification than it changes its nature. Seville, which was late to develop

115. Olive oil transported from the country to the town.
From the fourteenth-century Italian manuscript
Tacuinum Sanitatis. Austrian National Library

financially (although the city did possess banks), could be described equally as
a city of bureaucrats, rentiers, and artisans; it was a luxury city, providing a
living for a proletariat whom we can imagine herded together in houses shared
by several poor families, as in the Triana quarter where lye and soap were
manufactured.

Salamanca was a rural town, but it was also, of course, a great intellectual
centre. Padua, another renowned university town, was also deep in the countryside. Bayard and his companions in 1509 saw the city engaged upon agricultural
tasks: 'every day much hay was harvested', relates the *Loyal Serviteur*, 'and in
that quarter the loads were so great that they almost had to be forced through
a gateway'. A similar situation, if not an identical sight could have been found
at Lucera, a small Apulian town that held active fairs. These scenes from agricul-

tural life, frequently in conflict with the arts of military defence or the honesty of those in power, show how open sixteenth-century towns were, whatever the cost, to their surrounding countryside. How else could they have survived?

4 Towns, witnesses to the century

We should now turn our attention to the points of resemblance between these widely-differing towns, each of which had its own particular balance of activities, to see what features they had *in common*, in so far as they were subject to the changing economic climate applying equally or almost equally well to all parts of the Mediterranean during the second half of the sixteenth century. For those we know most about the evidence concurs: the urban population was rising: despite the crises in their daily life, of which there was no shortage, *in the long term*, they were healthy, since they were still expanding; at any rate they overcame crises and difficulties; however all towns without exception saw their liberties being whittled away by the extension of the territorial states, which were growing even more rapidly than the towns, surrounding them, subjugating them, or even chasing them from acquired positions. A new political and economic age was beginning. From this point of view the Mediterranean was ahead of its time.

The rise in population. We only know a thousandth part – if that – of the evidence that historians might be able to unearth concerning the movement of urban populations in the sixteenth century. However it is possible to give a fairly reliable picture of the overall situation. For example, a graph showing the shift in the urban population of the cities of Castile would give a clear message: all the curves – with a few exceptions that merely prove the rule – would show a steady rise until the final years of the sixteenth century.

A very similar graph could be produced from the figures for Italy and both European and Asian Turkey. It is fairly safe to assume that the situation was broadly the same throughout the Mediterranean, both Moslem and Christian. The increase in population was a fundamental characteristic of the 'long sixteenth century' both in Europe and the Mediterranean, the basis on which everything or almost everything else depended.

All categories of towns shared in this increase, from very small and modest communities to important towns and great cities, whether characterized by industrial or artisan production, by bureaucracy or commerce. When the population declined in the seventeenth century, as in Venezia where figures are available, the towns declined more rapidly than the surrounding countryside. Had the picture changed by the eighteenth century? M. Moheau claimed that rural France was then growing faster than urban France. These rapid comparisons may help us to understand the decisive yet fragile fortunes of the towns in the sixteenth century.

Hardships old and new: famine and the wheat problem. The sixteenth century was not always kind to urban communities. Famine and epidemics waged a continuous onslaught on the towns. Because of the slowness and prohibitive price of transport and the unreliability of the harvests, any urban centre could be exposed to famine at any time of year. The slightest pressure could tip the balance. When the Council of Trent met for the third and last time in 1561 (and although the town was on the great Brenner–Adige route, the route taken by the Bavarian grain which sometimes served Verona), the first problem facing the delegates to the Council and their staff was the difficult question of supplies, about which Rome was justifiably anxious. Both in the Mediterranean regions and outside famine was a commonplace hazard. The famine in Castile in 1521

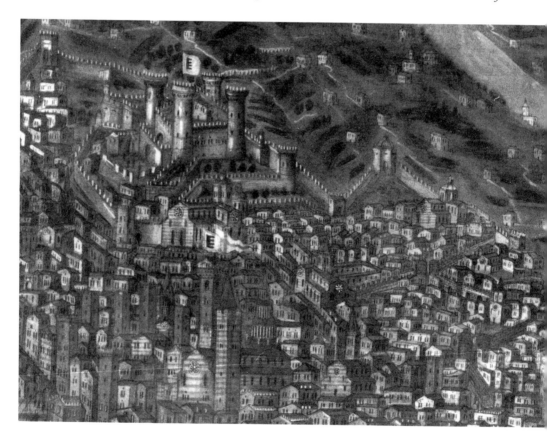

116. Detail from *The Harbour of Genoa* by Cristoforo Grassi, 1485. Cramped between the sea and the mountains, the city expanded upwards. *Civico Museo Navale de Pegli, Genoa*

VERO ADOBO PER OGNI CASA

BELISSIMA CREATVRA

FIOR AMATISSIM.   TVLIPAN ODORIFER.

CARISSIM SGNOR.

MOLT MAGNIFICH

ASIG. GVSTOSISSIM

TVLIPAN

MSIER PAN CRACI

in Bologna 1696. MInl. E.Fi

117. The starving populace. Italian popular print, Bologna, 1696.

coincided with the beginning of the war against France and the rising of the *Comuneros* at home. Nobles and commoners alike were panic-striken by the lack of bread during that year which was known in Portugal as the year of the Great Hunger. In 1525 Andalusia was devastated by a terrible drought. In 1528 famine brought terror to Tuscany: Florence had to close her gates to the starving peasants from surrounding districts. In 1540 the same thing happened. Again Florence was about to close her gates and abandon the countryside to its fate, when the region was saved by the arrival of ships at Leghorn carrying grain from the Levant; but that was something of a miracle. In 1575, in the Romanian countryside, which was normally rich in cereals, the flocks died by the hundreds; the birds were surprised in March by snowdrifts five feet deep and could be caught in the hand. As for the human inhabitants, they would kill their neighbours for a piece of bread. In 1583 the scourge swept through Italy, particularly in the Papal States where people starved to death.

More often, however, famine did not attack entire regions, but struck only the towns. The striking feature of the famine in Tuscany in 1528 was that it extended to the entire countryside surrounding Florence, and as we have remarked, the peasants flocking to the city found the gates closed against them. Similarly at Perugia in 1529 there was no grain at all for a radius of fifty miles.

These were still rare catastrophes. In normal times the peasants would obtain from their own land almost all the frugal fare on which they survived. Urban famine on the contrary, within the city walls was an extremely frequent occurrence in the sixteenth century. Florence, although it certainly does not lie in a particularly poor region, experienced 111 famines between 1375 and 1791, as against sixteen very good harvests over the same period. Even the wheat ports, such as Messina and Genoa, suffered terrible famines. Every year, even at the beginning of the sixteenth century, Venice had to part with millions in gold to secure the city's food supply.

Because of their requirements and their resources, the towns were the great customers for grain. A whole book could be written on the grain policy of Venice or Genoa. The latter was always quick to seize any opportunities of obtaining supplies, and in the fifteenth century turned towards France, Sicily, and North Africa: the former engaged in the grain trade of the Levant and negotiated with the Turks, from 1390 on, which did not prevent her from applying to other sources, such as Apulia and Sicily. Venice also had permanent regulations: notably, in 1408, 1539, 1607, and 1628 she prohibited the export of any grain outside her 'gulf'.

In the sixteenth century there was hardly a town of any importance which did not possess what was in Venice known by the strangely modern-sounding name of the Grain Office (the files of which for the years we are interested in have been lost). This was a remarkable institution. The Office controlled not only grain and flour entering the city, but also sales in the city markets: flour could only be sold in two 'public places', one near St Mark's, the other at the 'Rivoalto'. The doge was to be kept daily informed of the stocks in the warehouses. As soon as he discovered that the city had reserves only for a year or eight months, the College was duly informed, provision was made by the Office, on the one hand and on the other by the merchants to whom sums of money were immediately advanced. The bakers were also supervised: they had to provide the public with loaves made from 'good grain', white, whose weight might vary according to the abundance or otherwise of supplies, but whose price per unit remained constant, as was the rule in almost every town in Europe.

Such a Grain Office was not necessarily to be found in every town – there was only one Venice – but under different names and different organizations there were grain and flour offices almost everywhere. When there was no separate institution, grain policy was in the hands of officials either of the town's government or the administration. At Ragusa, whose poor location made her well acquainted with food shortage, the Rectors of the republic themselves handled it. At Naples it was the viceroy in person who controlled it.

When famine threatened, the measures taken were everywhere identical. To the sound of trumpets it was forbidden to take grain out of the town, the guard was doubled, searches were conducted and available supplies were inventoried. If the danger increased sterner measures were taken: the number of mouths to

118. A baker. Engraving after
A. Carracci.

feed was reduced, the city gates were closed, or else foreigners were expelled,
the normal course at Venice, unless they had brought enough grain into the city
to feed their staff or household. The Protestants were expelled from Marseilles
in 1562, a double gain for the city, which was opposed to the Huguenots. At
Naples during the famine of 1591 the University bore the brunt of the disaster.
It was closed and the students were sent back home. After that, rationing was
generally introduced, as in Marseilles in August, 1583.

If all else failed, the last great resource was to turn to the sea, to watch out
for grain ships, seize them, then to pay the party concerned for the cargo later,

not without some discussion. Marseilles one day seized two Genoese barques which had imprudently strayed into her port; on 8th November, 1562, she ordered a frigate to board all ships carrying grain that it found off the coast of the town. In October, 1557, the local authorities made ships carrying wheat from Apulia and the Levant unload at Messina. The Knights of Malta, who were not well off for supplies, regularly watched the Sicilian coast. Their behaviour there was hardly different from that of the Tripoli corsairs. They paid up, it is true, but they boarded ships in the same manner as pirates. And nobody was more skilled at this unpopular practice than Venice. As soon as her food supply was endangered, no ship loaded with wheat was safe in the Adriatic. She had no compunction in posting one or two galleys off Ragusa Vecchia, which would then under the very noses of the Ragusans seize ships carrying grain loaded by the *sectors* at Vólos, Salonica, or in the neighbouring ports of Albania. Or she would seek out grain ships along the Apulian coast and make them unload at Corfu, Spalato, or directly at Venice. It is true that she had been unable to maintain the foothold she had twice obtained in Apulia and had lost this providential granary and oil and wine cellar. That did not inhibit her from returning to help herself whenever necessary, either peacefully or by using force. Her behaviour was the source of persistent, quite justified, and completely ineffective protest from Naples, backed up by Spain: the ships seized by Venice were usually those that Naples had chartered for her own supplies. Venice's captures were likely to provoke riots in a city swarming with poor people.

All this proved a great financial burden. But no town could escape its crushing weight. At Venice, enormous losses had to be registered at the Grain Office, which on the one hand gave large bonuses to merchants and on the other often sold the grain and flour it had acquired at lower than normal prices. It was even worse at Naples, where fear made the authorities not merely liberal, but prodigal. At Florence the Grand Duke made up the difference. In Corsica, Ajaccio borrowed from Genoa. Marseilles, which kept a tight hold on the purse strings, also borrowed, but always looking ahead, would forbid grain to enter the town just before the harvest, and would exhaust the remaining stocks when there were any. This was the practice of many towns.

These policies were difficult to enforce and never reliable. The result was suffering and disorder: suffering for the poor, sometimes for a whole town; disorder for the institutions and the very foundations of urban life. Were these small units and medieval economies adequate for the pressures of the new age?

Hardships old and new: epidemics. One could draw an incomplete but eloquent map showing the incidence of plague, the dreaded visitor to the Mediterranean. If the plague years were marked alongside every town they touched, no city would escape even this brief survey and fail to score. Plague would appear for what it was: a 'structure' of the century. The cities of the East suffered its impact more often than the others. At Constantinople, the dangerous gateway to Asia,

119. Detail from *The Plague at Naples* by D. Gargiullo. *Museo Nazionale, Naples*

plague was permanently installed, for this was a breeding-ground for epidemics which then spread to the West.

The visitations of epidemics, combined with famine, led to the perpetual renewal of the urban population. Venice was stricken by an outbreak of plague in 1575–1577 so terrible that 50,000 people died, a quarter or a third of the population. Between 1575 and 1578 there were 40,000 deaths at Messina. The figures given by contemporaries often indicate by their exaggeration the terror these sufferings inspired. Bandello talks of 230,000 victims at Milan, in the time of Ludovico Sforza! In 1525, if we are to believe another source, nine-tenths of the population of Rome and Naples perished; in 1550 half the population of Milan again fell victim; in 1581 the plague was said to have left only 5000 people alive in Marseilles, and to have killed 60,000 in Rome. The figures are not accurate, but they undoubtedly show that a quarter or a third of the inhabitants of a town could suddenly vanish at a time when imperfect knowledge of hygiene and medicine afforded little protection against infection. And they concur with the familiar accounts of streets littered with corpses, the death cart passing every day carrying so many bodies that they could not be buried. Such visitations could completely destroy and transform a town. When the plague finally left Venice in 1577, quite a different city with a new set of rulers emerged. There had been a complete changeover. A *frate di San Domenico* preaching in Naples in March, 1584 – was it purely a coincidence? – maintained that 'for some time, Venice had been acting imprudently for the young men had taken over from the old' ('poiche i giovanni havevano tolto il governo a vecchi').

The wounds healed sooner or later. If Venice never entirely recovered after 1576 it was because the secular trend was to turn against her in the seventeenth century. Plague and other epidemics were only serious, in fact, during periods of food shortage and material difficulty. Famine and epidemics went hand in hand, an old truth with which the West had long been familiar. Every town had long tried to protect itself against disease, using disinfectants based on aromatic herbs, destroying by fire the belongings of plague victims, enforcing quarantine on persons and goods (Venice was a pioneer in this respect), recruiting doctors, introducing health certificates, the *cartas de salud* in Spain, *fedi di sanità* in Italy. The rich had always sought their salvation in flight. At the first signs of disease they would flee to neighbouring towns, or, more often, to their precious country houses. The poor always remained inside the diseased town, besieged, regarded with suspicion, and liberally provided with food from outside in order to keep them quiet. This was an old conflict, as René Baehrel has noted, a source of lasting class hatred. In June, 1478, Venice was hit by plague; as usual, looting immediately began in the town. In 1656 at Genoa, according to the *Capuchin Charitable*, the situation was word for word the same.

However, the great epidemics of the early seventeenth century at Milan and Verona in 1630, Florence in 1630–1631, Venice in 1631, Genoa in 1656, and even London in 1664, seem to have been of a much more serious order than those of the previous century. During the latter half of the sixteenth century the towns seem to have suffered comparatively mildly. Plague was not the only disease that attacked them. They were also afflicted by venereal diseases, sweating sickness, measles, dysentery, and typhus. Illness did not spare the armies either, towns as it were, on the move, which were even more vulnerable. During the Hungarian War (1593–1607) a kind of typhus, known as the *ungarische Krankheit* decimated the German army but spared the Turks and Hungarians; it spread through Europe as far as England.

This prevalence of epidemics made a significant contribution to the insecurity of life in the towns, to the 'social massacres' of the poor which did not end until the eighteenth century, if then.

The indispensable immigrant. Another regular feature of Mediterranean towns is that the urban proletariat could not maintain itself, let alone increase without the help of continuous immigration. The town had the capacity, and the obligation, to attract, besides the eternal mountain immigrants who provided labour of all kinds, a throng of proletarians or adventurers of every origin, a source of supply to meet its demand.

In Marseilles the typical immigrant was the Corsican, and particularly the *Capocorsino*. In Seville the standard immigrants (not counting those attracted by voyages to the Indies, who came from everywhere), the permanent proletariat were the Moriscos. They came from Andalusia and became so numerous in the city that by the end of the century the authorities feared uprisings no longer in the mountains but in the city itself, in conjunction with English landings. At Algiers the new arrivals were Christians, who swelled the ranks of the corsairs and the prisoners; Andalusian or Aragonese fugitives (arriving at the end of the fifteenth and the beginning of the sixteenth century), artisans and shopkeepers, whose names can still be found in the present day quarter of the Tagarins; even more were Berbers from the nearby mountains of Kabylia who had already provided the original ethnic base of the city. Haëdo describes them as wretched folk, digging the gardens of the rich, their ambition to get if possible a place in the militia as a soldier: only then will they have enough to eat. Throughout the Ottoman Empire, there was not a single town, in spite of state controls and suspicious corporations that did not receive a continuous stream of immigrants from the poor or overpopulated countryside. 'This clandestine and desperate labour force was a bonus for the rich, who obtained cheap servants for their gardens, stables, and houses . . .'. These wretched people even competed with slave labour.

At Lisbon, where there was a constant flow of immigrants, those worst off were the black slaves. In 1633 they numbered over 15,000 out of a total population of 100,000, and would all walk through the streets of the city on the festival of *Nuestra Señora de las Nieves*, Our Lady of the Snows, an occasion upon which they dressed in loin cloths and colourful fabrics. 'Their bodies are well made and more beautiful than white men's,' remarked a Capuchin friar 'and a naked Negro is more handsome than a clothed white man.'

The immigrants to Venice came from neighbouring towns, and from the nearby mountains and countryside (Titian came from Cadore). If the people of Friuli – the *Furlani* – were good recruits for domestic and heavy labour, and agricultural work outside the town, the criminal elements, and there were some, all or almost all came from the Romagna and the Marches. Undesirable and usually clandestine visitors, they would enter the city at night by regular passages, using the services of some *barcaruol* who could not refuse his boat to men often armed with firelocks, *de roda*, and who forced him gently or otherwise to carry them to the Giudecca, Murano, or some other island. To forbid entry to these visitors would have kept down crime, but it would have required constant vigilance and local spies.

The Venetian empire and the surrounding regions also provided a crop of immigrants: Albanians, quick to quarrel, dangerously jealous; Greeks, honourable merchants of the 'Greek nation' or poor devils who prostituted wives and daughters to overcome the initial difficulties of settling in the town, and who developed a taste for this easy living; *Morlachi* from the Dinaric mountains. The Riva degli Schiavoni was not only a point of departure. Towards the end of the century Venice became even more oriental with the arrival of Persians and Armenians, of Turks too, who from the middle of the sixteenth century had been quartered in an annexe of the palace of Marco Antonio Barbaro until the *fontico dei Turchi* was established in the seventeenth century. Venice also became a halfway house, which might be more or less temporary, for Jewish families of Portuguese origin who were travelling from northern Europe (Flanders or Hamburg) towards the East. Venice was also the refuge of exiles and their descendants. The descendants of the great Scanderbeg still lived there in 1574: 'the race survives . . . in respectable circumstances'.

These indispensable immigrants were not always unskilled labourers or men of little aptitude. They often brought with them new techniques that were as indispensable as their persons to urban life. The Jews, driven out by their religious beliefs not their poverty, played an exceptional role in these transfers of technology. Jews expelled from Spain, at first retail merchants in Salonica and Constantinople, gradually built up their businesses until they were competing successfully with Ragusans, Armenians, and Venetians. To these two great eastern cities they brought the art of printing, the woollen and silk industry, and, if some statements are to be believed, the secret of manufacturing gun-carriages. These were useful gifts! It was also a handful of Jews expelled from Ancona by Paul IV, who made the admittedly modest fortune of the Turkish port of Valona.

There were other valuable immigrants, itinerant artists for instance attracted by expanding towns which were improving their public buildings; or merchants, particularly the Italian merchants and bankers, who activated and indeed created such cities as Lisbon, Seville, Medina del Campo, Lyons and Antwerp. An urban community needs all sorts and conditions of men, not least rich men. Towns attracted the wealthy just as they attracted the proletariat, though for very different reasons. In the complex process, much discussed by historians, of *inurbamento* it is not only the poor *contadini* who flock to the nearby town, but also the noblemen, the rich, landed proprietors. A lord of Siena would have his country seat in the Maremma and his *palazzo* in Siena, as Bandello has described it for us, with its seldom-used ground floor and its state rooms where silk was making its triumphant first appearance.

These palaces are the visible evidence of a chapter of history which preceded a new exodus from the towns by the rich, the return to the fields, orchards, and vineyards, the 'bourgeois' search for fresh air, which was so evident in Venice, Ragusa, Florence, Seville, and generally in the sixteenth century. This was a seasonal emigration: even if he frequently visited his country house, the lord who had built his palace in the city was now a city-dweller. The country house was merely another luxury, and often a question of fashion.

In the seventeenth and even more in the eighteenth century, what happened in Venice was a reconversion of rich city-dwellers to the virtues of real estate. Venice in the time of Goldoni let her most beautiful urban palaces fall into decay while all expense was concentrated in the villas on the banks of the Brenta. Only the poor remained in the city in summer; the rich were on their estates. Fashions and fancies, here as always when the rich are concerned, are only part of the story. Villas, country houses, where the landlord lived side by side with his

120. *The Medici Villa at Poggio a Caiano* by Justus Utens. *Museo Topografico, Florence*

farmhands, *bastides* as they were called in Provence, were so many steps towards a social takeover of the countryside by the money of the towns.

So there was an alternating ebb and flow between town and countryside. In the sixteenth and seventeenth centuries the flow was from country to town, even where the rich were concerned. Milan, becoming a city of nobles, changed its character. At the same time, the Turkish landowners of the *čiftliks* abandoned their villages and their serfs for the neighbouring cities. At the end of the six-teenth century, many Spanish noblemen left their estates to go and live in the cities of Castile, particularly Madrid. The change in climate between the reign of Philip II and Philip III, attributable to so many variations, was not unconnec-ted with the arrival of the Spanish nobility in the urban centres where until then they had only temporarily taken up residence. Does it explain the so-called feudal reaction under the successor of the Prudent King?

Urban political crises. Chronicles and political histories recount an interminable catalogue of urban catastrophes. Their casualties were not merely institutions, habits, local vanity; but economies, the creative skills, the happiness even of urban communities. But what collapsed was not always very solid in the first place; conflicts were often resolved without recourse to violence, without appar-ent drama, and the new and sometimes bitter fruit was a long time ripening.

For the first signs we have to go back to the beginning of the fifteenth century, at least in Italy, which here again was remarkably ahead of the times. Within the space of a few years Verona fell to the Venetians in April, 1404; in 1405 Pisa surrendered to Florence; in November, 1406, Padua was taken by

Venice, which then captured Brescia in 1426 and Bergamo in 1427, on the borders of the Milanese; these cities now became the western outposts, constantly on the alert, of the Venetian *Terraferma*.

Years passed: internal crises, undying quarrels, the economic difficulties that preceded and followed them caused even Genoa to totter. In forty years, from 1413 to 1453, fourteen revolutions broke out in the city. The prize was tempting: the king of France seized it in 1458; then the Sforza in 1464; Genoa liberated herself from her masters, then recalled them, first the Sforza then the kings of France. Meanwhile her empire in the Black Sea was slipping away. Nearer home she lost Leghorn. Miraculously she recovered in spite of these blows, almost selling herself to France and François I, then under Andrea Doria going over to Spain in 1528 and adopting an oligarchic constitution. But even before that date, she was strong enough to defend her possessions and seize those of others. In 1523 the Genoese militia took Savona; from 1525 to 1526 the conqueror relentlessly attacked her prey, demolishing the breakwater, filling up the harbour, then after an abortive revolt by the town, which would willingly have delivered itself up to the Turks, knocking down its towers in 1528, with the intention of building fortresses. But by then much greater catastrophes had taken place.

The year 1453 saw the fall of Constantinople, symbolic in more ways than one; in 1472 Barcelona capitulated to the troops of John II of Aragon; in 1480 the king of France peacefully gained control of Provence and Marseilles; Granada fell in 1492. These were the years of the collapse of the city-states, too narrowly based to resist the onslaught of the territorial states who were henceforth to play the leading roles. At the beginning of the century cities had captured other cities, enlarging their territory: Venice was building up the *Terraferma*, Milan the Milanese, Florence was becoming Tuscany. But from now on the conquerors were the Turks, the Aragonese, the king of France, the joint monarchs of Aragon and Castile.

What disappeared in the course of this prolonged crisis? The medieval town, the city-state, mistress of her own fate, set among her surrounding gardens, orchards, vineyards, wheatfields, and nearby coasts and roads. And it vanished as historical landscapes and realities do, leaving behind extraordinary survivals. The Venetian *Terraferma* remained a federation of towns with their liberties, tolls, and semi-independence. The same was true of Lucca, which we can see through the eyes of Montaigne, without smiling too much at the military vigilance of the tiny republic. Better still, let us stop at Ragusa. At the height of the sixteenth century, Ragusa was the living image of Venice in the thirteenth century, one of the city-states of which there had once been so many along the trading shores of Italy. The old urban institutions were in place, intact, and the precious documents which correspond to them are still today in perfect order. When as historians we complain that sixteenth-century documents are never in the right place, we may blame negligence, fires, destruction, and pillage, for they

121. *Angelo Correr Receives the Tribute of Vicenza* by A. Maganaza.
Museo Correr, Venice

have all played their part. But we should also blame, far more, the transition from the city-state to the territorial state, with all the institutional upheavals it brought. At this moment in history the city-state with its meticulous discipline was no longer in control and the territorial state had not yet replaced it – except perhaps in Tuscany where the 'enlightened despotism' of the Medici hastened the transition. But at Ragusa, the unchanging city, everything is in remarkable order in the Palace of the Rectors: judicial papers, registers of certificates, property deeds, diplomatic correspondence, marine insurance, copies of bills of exchange. If there is any chance of understanding the Mediterranean in the sixteenth century it is in this unique city, which has the added advantage that Ragusan merchantmen sailed the whole sea, from Islam to Christendom, from the Black Sea to the Pillars of Hercules and beyond.

But was what is so perfectly preserved at Ragusa reality or illusion? Ragusa agreed to pay tribute to the Turk. This was the condition on which she saved her trading posts scattered throughout the Balkans, her riches, and the precise mechanism of her institutions. She was neutral, and therefore in a good position during the troubled years of the century. She was heroically and skilfully neutral let it be said: she could stick to her guns, plead her case, and offer prayers for Rome and Christendom, for was she not a fervently Catholic city? To the Turks she spoke firmly. The master of a Ragusan ship which was quite unjustifiably captured by the corsairs of Algiers complained, shouted, and argued so much that one day his captors threw him into the sea with a stone around his neck. Even neutrals cannot always have everything their own way.

There can be no doubt of the illusion in the case of Lucca, a thinly disguised Spanish protectorate in the Milanese. It was the only town in Italy, said Cervantes with candour, where the Spaniards were loved.

But those exceptions merely prove the rule. The cities were unable to survive intact the prolonged political crisis of the fifteenth and sixteenth centuries. They had suffered major upheavals and had to adapt themselves. They might, like Genoa, in turn surrender, betray, negotiate, lose their identity only to recover it, give or sell themselves to another power; or they might struggle, as Florence did, with more passion than lucidity; or, as Venice with a superhuman effort managed to do, they might struggle and what was more stand firm. But they all had to adapt; it was the price of survival.

The privileged banking towns. The victorious states could not take control of and responsibility for everything. They were cumbersome machines inadequate to handle their new superhuman tasks. The so-called *territorial economy* of textbook classification could not easily stifle the so-called *urban economy*. The cities remained the driving forces. States that included these cities had to come to terms with them and tolerate them. The relationship was accepted the more naturally since even the most independent cities needed the use of the space belonging to territorial states.

Even the whole of Tuscany could not support unaided the super-rich Florence of the Medici. It did not produce even a third of the city's annual consumption of wheat. The apprentices in the shops of the *Arte della Lana* came from the Tuscan hills, but also from Genoa, Bologna, Perugia, Ferrara, Faenza, Mantua. Until about 1581–1585 investments of Florentine capital (the *accomandite*) flowed all over Europe, even as far as the East; colonies of Florentine merchants were present on almost all the important exchanges, much more influential in Spain than has usually been assumed, predominant at Lyons, in a commanding position even at Venice at the beginning of the seventeenth century. After the accession of the Grand Duke Ferdinand in 1576 there was a more explicit search for new outlets, not the least amazing of which were the cruises of the San Stefano galleys or the agreements with the Dutch to exploit Brazil or the Indies.

The great cities of the sixteenth century with their agile and dangerous capitalism were in a position to control and exploit the whole world. Venice cannot be explained simply by her *Terraferma* or her empire of shores and islands, although she exploited them with tenacity. She lived in fact off the great Turkish Empire, as the ivy draws its nourishment from the tree to which it clings.

Nor did Genoa rely upon her poor rivieras, east and west, to feed her rich appetite, or upon Corsica, a precious but awkward possession. The real drama of the fifteenth and sixteenth century did not lie in the political fortunes of the city, which were merely a consequence and frequently a façade. The real drama was that Genoa lost one empire only to gain another. And the second in no way resembled the first.

Genoa's first empire was essentially composed of trading colonies. She had sent settlers beyond Constantinople, to the edge of the Byzantine empire, to Kaffa, Tana, Soldaia, and Trebizond. These were her overseas trading stations. Tabarka, on the North African coast, built up by the Lomellini, was to be another, draining away to Genoa the fabulous rewards of coral fishing, and still thriving in the sixteenth century, a strange citadel of trade.

Genoa's second empire looked westwards and was based on very ancient bases, old and powerful merchant colonies which merely had to be maintained – in Milan, Venice, Naples. At Messina in 1561 the Genoese colony received a large share of profits from the wheat, silk, and spice trades. Officially, according to a consular document, this amounted to 240,000 crowns a year. Ten, twenty, or thirty of these colonies were scattered all around the Mediterranean.

But the empire that compensated Genoa for her losses in the east at the end of the fifteenth century was built up in Spanish territory, in Seville, Lisbon, Medina del Campo, Valladolid, Antwerp, and America. Its founding charter at Seville was the 1493 convention signed between Genoa and the Catholic Kings; it recognized the right of Genoese colonies to elect a consul of their own nation, *consulem subditorum suorum*, and to change him when they wished. These western colonies that were to affect so profoundly and penetratingly the financial and fiscal affairs of Spain on the eve of her American greatness, were quite separate from the others; in fact they were colonies of bankers. Genoa compensated for her commercial defeat in the east by a financial victory in the west.

It was through the art of *cambios* that the Genoese were to set up Sevilian trade with America; that they were very early to seize control of the great monopolies of salt and wool; that they were to have a stranglehold on the government of Philip II himself from mid-century on. Was this a triumph for Genoa? One cannot entirely say so. This financial empire, whose net spread over the whole of the western world with the setting up of the Piacenza fairs in 1579, like the London Stock Exchange in the nineteenth century, was the creation of the great patrician families, the *Nobili Vecchi*, rather than of the city of Genoa. This extraordinary financial aristocracy devouring the known world was the greatest enterprise undertaken by any city in the sixteenth century. Genoa seemed to lead a charmed life. She had no fleet of her own, at least no adequate fleet, but benefited from the timely arrival of Ragusan cargo vessels and the barques of Marseilles. She lost her Black Sea colonies, then in 1566 Chios, which had been the centre of her trading operations in the Levant. But the register of the *caratti del mare* from 1550 to 1650 indicates that she was still receiving silk from central Asia and white wax from Russia and the 'Khazaria' just as she had in the thirteenth and fourteenth centuries. The Turks no longer negotiated 'wheat treaties' with her, but she still consumed Turkish grain on occasion. The seventeenth century saw an economic recession, but Genoa remained powerful and aggressive, declaring herself a free port in 1608. These miracles were all brought about by money, no simple miracle itself. Everything flowed into this city of the rich. A few *carati* of a Ragusan ship were bought, and it was at the service of the *Dominante*. A little money was invested at Marseilles and the barques of the whole Provençal coast were offering their services. Why should silk not come to Genoa from the depths of Asia? The price was only a little precious metal.

And Genoa, after about 1570–1580, was the centre for the redistribution of American silver, controlled by the financial barons, the Grimaldi, the Lomellini, Spinola, and so many others. The money they did not invest in their tall and splendid palaces in Genoa, they placed in land or fiefs at Milan, Naples, in the *Montferrato inferiore* (the poor mountains around Genoa did not offer very safe investments) or in government bonds in Spain, Rome, or Venice. In Spain where the people instinctively disliked these haughty merchants, and where Philip II on occasion treated them as subordinates and had them arrested – the list of their misdeeds remains to be compiled.

So while the territorial states and empires acquired lands in plenty, they were unable to exploit unaided the resultant huge economic units. This incapacity again opened the door to the cities and the merchants. It was they who behind the fanfares of conquest were making their fortunes.

Royal and imperial cities. Naples had no equivalent in Christendom. Her population – 280,000 in 1595 – was twice that of Venice, three times that of Rome, four times that of Florence, and nine times that of Marseilles. The whole of southern Italy flocked to the city, both the rich, often very rich, and the hopelessly wretched poor. The size of the population was one reason why so many luxury goods were produced there. Neapolitan goods in the sixteenth century were what would be called fancy goods today: lace, braids, frills, trimmings, silks, light fabrics (taffetas), silken knots and cockades of all colours, and fine linens. These goods travelled as far as Cologne in large quantities. The Venetians claimed that four-fifths of the workers of Naples lived off the silk industry, and we know that the *Arte di Santa Lucia* enjoyed a great reputation over a wide area. Pieces of so-called Santa Lucia silk were even resold at Florence. In 1642 the proposal of sumptuary laws in Spain, which would have threatened Neopolitan

122. *Tribuna della Vicaria* by Luciano Asciano, showing the piazza outside the judicial tribunal in Naples. *Museo di Capodimonte, Naples*

exports of silk and silken goods, endangered the annual fiscal income of 335,220 ducats. But there were many other industries either already established in the city or which the vast labour force could have attracted there.

Peasants from throughout the provinces of the vast, mountainous, and pastoral kingdom flocked into the city. They were attracted by the *arti* of wool and silk; by the city's public works begun in the time of Pietro di Toledo and carried on long after him (some buildings were still unfinished in 1594); by domestic employment in the households of nobles, for it was becoming the fashion for aristocrats to live in the city and display their wealth; if all else failed, they could always rely upon the countless religious establishments with their throngs of servants and hangers-on. By seeking employment in the city, which was to be had 'in all seasons', the peasants automatically released themselves from heavy feudal obligations to an overlord who might have inherited or bought, as Genoese merchants frequently did, his title and estates, which were always on the market. As the proverb says, 'the city air brings freedom' – but not necessarily happiness or a full stomach. So the city continued to grow.

Inevitably the outstanding problem in a conurbation of this size was its food supply. Through the Prefect of the *Annona* (provisions) whom he appointed after the 1550s (and who was in fact a minister of supply, in charge of purchases, storage, resale to bakers and to the itinerant oil merchants), the viceroy personally controlled this strictly municipal service. Unaided, the city could not have subsidized such an operation, which always ran at a loss. A document dated 1607, which seems reliable, indicates that the city spent at least 45,000 ducats a month, while her income was under 25,000. Grain and oil were often retailed at a loss. Loans made up the difference, but unfortunately we do not know under what conditions. Her daily life was always beset by problems, even the supply of drinking water (brought from the springs of Formale in 1560), the upkeep of the streets, or the traffic in the harbour. The breakwater which protected moored ships was by the end of the century so encumbered by refuse, by residue from sewers, and earth unloaded there by the builders of houses and public monuments, that in 1597 serious consideration had to be given not to cleaning it, but to replacing it with a new breakwater. Naples was excessive in every respect. She consumed 40,000 *salme* of Apulian wheat a year, besides her other supplies, and in 1625 she imported the unbelievable quantity of 30,000 cantars of sugar (1500 tons) and 10,000 cantars of honey, re-exporting a large amount in the form of *siropate, paste*, and *altre cose di zucaro*, but needless to say it did not go into the mouths of the poor.

Order could never be maintained and at night the only law was that of the strong and cunning. Certainly, even if one allows for the bragging of Spanish soldiers who were always ready to let their pens run away with them, it was the most astonishing, most fantastically picaresque city in the world. It was a more hard-working city than its very bad reputation gives it credit for, but that reputation was not undeserved. On one occasion action had to be taken against the vagabonds who were overrunning the town and on another against the many organized bands which were already the training-grounds of the *lazzaroni*.

Naples corresponded to the dimensions of southern Italy and the *Reame*; Istanbul was cast in the image of the immense Turkish empire which was so rapidly created. The city as a whole developed at the same rate as the empire. It numbered perhaps 80,000 inhabitants after the conquest in 1478; 400,000 between 1520 and 1535; 700,000 according to westerners at the end of the century; it foreshadowed the development of London and Paris in the seventeenth and eighteenth centuries, as privileged cities whose political preeminence permitted every kind of economic paradox, chief among which was the ability to live well above their income and the level that their internal production permitted. And indeed, like London and Paris and for the same reasons, Constantinople did not decline. The reverse occurred, in fact, during the seventeenth and eighteenth centuries.

Constantinople was not a town; it was an urban monster, a composite metropolis. Its site made it a divided city and this was the source both of its greatness and its difficulties, certainly of its greatness. Without the Golden Horn – the only safe harbour between the Sea of Marmara, which was exposed to bad weather and often rough, and the Black Sea which had a well deserved reputation as a 'punishing sea' – without the Bosporus, neither Constantinople nor its successor Istanbul would have been conceivable. But it also meant that the urban area was interrupted by successive stretches of water, and extensive sea fronts. A population of boatmen and ferrymen manned the thousands of barques, *caïques, perames, mahonnes*, lighters, and 'door-ships' (for the transport of animals from Scutari to the European side).

Of the three cities, Constantinople, or Stambul, or Istanbul, was the largest. It was the triangular city between the Golden Horn and the Sea of Marmara, shut off on the landward side by a double wall 'not in very good condition either' where 'round about, there are ruins in quantity'. It had a circumference of 13 to 15 miles while Venice had only 8. But this urban enclosure was full of trees, gardens, squares with fountains, 'meadows', and promenades, and counted over 400 mosques with lead roofs. Around each one was an open space. The Mosque of Sulaimān the Magnificent, the Sulaimānīye with 'its esplanade, its *medreses*, its library, its hospital, its *imaret*, its schools and gardens, constitutes a whole quarter in itself'. Finally the houses were clustered together, low-lying, built, 'in the Turkish fashion', of wood, 'earthen walls', and half-baked bricks, their façades 'daubed in pastel colours, pale blue, pink and yellow'. The streets 'are narrow, twisting and uneven', not always paved and frequently sloping. People travelled along them on foot, on horseback, but barely on wheels. Fires were frequent and did not spare even the Seray. In autumn, 1564, a single outbreak destroyed 7500 wooden shops. Inside this great city lay another, the Bedesten ('bazestan'), 'like the St Germain Fair', as Lescalopier put it, admiring the 'great staircases of fine stone and the beautiful shops selling haberdashery

123, 124. Sixteenth-century Turkish manuscript illuminations showing a butcher's shop, a tailor and a pottery shop. *Bibliothèque Nationale, Paris*

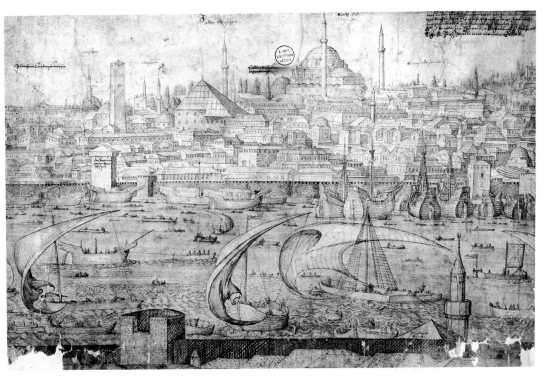

125. Detail from a view of Constantinople by Melchior Lorich, c.1580.

and cotton fabrics embroidered with gold and silk . . . and all manner of beautiful and charming things'. Another was the 'Atbazar', the horse market. Finally, the most sumptuous of all, the Seray, at the southern end of the city; a succession of palaces, kiosks, and gardens. Istanbul was predominantly a city of Turks, their white turbans outnumbered the others: 58 per cent of the population, in the sixteenth as in the seventeenth century. But there were also a number of Greeks with blue turbans, Jews with yellow turbans, as well as Armenians and Tziganes.

On the other side of the Golden Horn, Galata occupied the ribbon running along the southern shore between the Arsenal of Kasim Pasa with 'about a hundred vaulted stone arches each long enough for a galley to be built there under cover . . .', and further to the south the second Arsenal of Top Hane 'where they make powder and artillery'. Galata was the port frequented exclusively by western ships; here were the Jewish commission agents, the shops, and warehouses, the famous cabarets where wine and *arak* were served; behind on the hills were the Vines of Pera, where, first among the western envoys, the French ambassador had his residence. It was the city of the rich, 'quite big, populous, built in the French style', inhabited by merchants, Latin and Greek, the latter often very rich, dressing in the Turkish style, living in grand houses, adorning their women with silk and jewels. These women, rather too given to coquetry, 'appear more beautiful than they are, for they paint their faces as much as possible and spend all their wealth on clothes, many rings on their fingers, and jewels for their head-dresses, most of which are false'. Galata and Pera together, which travellers took for the same place, 'form a town comparable to Orléans'. The Greeks and Latins were not masters there, far from it, but they were free to live and worship there as they pleased. Notably 'the Catholic religion is practised in this city in all freedom, including the Italian processions of flagellants and at Corpus Christi, the streets are decorated under the surveillance of two or three janissaries, to whom a few aspers are given'.

On the Asian side, Scutari (Üsküdar) was almost a third city, different from the other two. It was the caravan terminus of Constantinople, the point of arrival and departure for the great routes across Asia. The number of caravanserais and *hans* alone was a sign of this, as was the horse market. On the sea front there was no sheltered harbour. Goods had to pass by quickly and trust to luck. A Turkish town, Scutari was full of gardens and princely residences. The sultan had a palace there, and it was a great spectacle when he left the Seray and took a frigate to the Asian side 'to enjoy himself'.

A description of the whole would not be complete without mentioning the most important suburb, Eyüp, lying at the point where the Sweet Waters of Europe meet the Golden Horn, together with the long strings of Greek, Jewish, and Turkish villages on both sides of the Bosporus, villages of gardeners, fishermen, sailors, where the summer residences of the rich soon appeared, the *yali-s* with their stone basements and two storeys made of wood; their 'many unlatticed windows' opened on to the Bosporus where there was no indiscreet neighbour. These 'houses for leisure and gardens' can, not unreasonably, be compared with the villas in the countryside around Florence.

The whole formed a vast conurbation. In March, 1581, eight ships from Egypt laden with wheat only provided food for a single day. Records dated 1660–1661 and 1672–1673 give us some idea of the city's appetite which was much the same as in the previous century. Its inhabitants daily consumed 300 to 500 tons of grain, which provided work for its 133 bakers (in Constantinople itself, out of 84 bakers, 12 made white bread); in one year almost 200,000 cattle, of which 35,000 went to make the salt or smoked meat, *pastirma*; and (one has to read the figures two or three times before one can believe them) almost 4 million sheep and 3 million lambs (the precise figures are 3,965,760 and 2,877,400); plus the barrels of honey, sugar, rice, sacks and skins of cheese, caviar, and 12,904 cantars of melted butter, brought by sea, i.e., about 7000 tons.

These figures, too precise to be accurate, too official to be entirely false, give some idea of the order of the operation. Without doubt, Constantinople drew continually on the inexhaustible riches of the empire, under a system organized by a meticulous, authoritarian and *dirigiste* government. The supply zones were chosen to suit the convenience of methods of transport, prices were fixed, and if necessary requisitioning was enforced.

So Constantinople consumed the thousand products of the empire as well as the fabrics and luxury goods of the West; in return the city gave nothing or virtually nothing, except for the bales of wool and hides of sheep, oxen, and buffalo that passed through the port. It would bear no comparison with the great export centres at Alexandria, Tripoli in Syria, and later Smyrna. This capital enjoyed the privilege of the rich. Others worked on her behalf.

In favour of capitals. The Spanish peninsula lacked a forceful capital. The historian J. Gounon-Loubens claimed long ago that Philip II's greatest mistake was not to have made his capital city Lisbon, where the Prudent King stayed from 1580 to 1583, before leaving it for good. He might have made it a city comparable to Naples or London. This argument has always impressed me. Philip II's court at Madrid is a foretaste of those governments that were later to set up their capitals in 'artificial towns'. Philip II in the Escorial foreshadows Louis XIV at Versailles. But although it is rather a temptation to rewrite history, it is after all only a game, a method of argument by which we attempt to familiarize ourselves with an immense subject that sometimes evades our grasp.

PART TWO

Collective Destinies and General Trends

MY INTENTION in the first part of this book was to explore, using the concept of geographical space, all the permanent, slow-moving, or recurrent features of Mediterranean life.

In the pursuit of a history that changes little or not at all with the passing of time, I have not hesitated to step outside the chronological limits of a study devoted in theory to the latter half of the sixteenth century. I have taken evidence from witnesses of every period, up to and including the present day. Victor Bérard discovered the landscapes of the *Odyssey* in the Mediterranean under his own eyes. But often, as well as Corfu, the island of the Phaeacians, or Djerba, the island of the Lotus-Eaters, one can find Ulysses himself, man unchanged after the passing of many centuries.

From this long-term perspective the second part takes us to a history closer to the individual: the history of groups, collective destinies, and general trends. This is a *social history*, whose subject is man, human beings, and not 'things' as Maurice Halbwachs would say, or to put it another way, what man has constructed from things.

This second part has, in fact, to meet two contradictory purposes. It is concerned with social structures, that is with mechanisms that withstand the march of time; it is also concerned with the development of those structures. It combines, therefore, what have come to be known as *structure* and *conjoncture*, the permanent and the ephemeral, the slow-moving and the fast. These two aspects of reality, as economists are well aware – indeed it is to them that we owe the original distinction – are always present in everyday life, which is a constant blend of what changes and what endures.

But it will not be easy to convey this complex spectacle in a single attempt. The chapters that follow share the task among them, tackling in turn the problems relating to economic systems, states, societies, civilizations, the indispensable instruments of exchange, and lastly the different forms of war. But the reader should not be misled. They are all contributions towards a unique, comprehensive view of the subject, impossible to achieve from any one vantage point.

126. A camel caravan in Italy. Detail from *The Procession of the Magi* by Benozzo Gozzoli in the chapel of the Palazzo Riccardi, Florence.

Economies:
The Measure of the Century

OUR FIRST TASK is to discover the measure, the economic dimensions of the sixteenth century. The aim of this chapter can be compared with Lucien Febvre's aim in the last section of his *Rabelais*: to take stock of the intellectual apparatus of sixteenth-century man, to take its measure so as to eliminate those false and distorting solutions to the problems facing the historian which so flagrantly ignore the possibilities and the intellectual level of the age. We shall find it equally valuable to discover, very broadly, what the economic apparatus of the sixteenth century was, what limits it imposed upon man's achievement, before studying what man actually constructed – or tried to construct – from these beginnings in the Mediterranean.

1 Distance, the first enemy

Today we have too little space, the world is shrinking around us. In the sixteenth century there was too much and it could be both an advantage and an obstacle. Of all the commonplaces about the Mediterranean in which literature abounds, that it is a 'sea within the measure of man' is one of the most deceptive – as if the measure of man could be taken once and for all. The Mediterranean was certainly not within the measure of sixteenth-century man; it was only at the cost of much effort that he mastered its immense area, much as twentieth-century man has found it difficult to master the Pacific.

For letter-writers: the time lost in coming and going. To have an idea of the problem, we have only to listen to the complaints of men tackling the details of their own lives. Letter writers have bitter words to say about delays in the mails. If a letter arrives quickly, its recipient is astonished. 'To come from as far as Valencia to Granada,' writes the humanist Antonio de Guevara to a friend, 'your letter must have had swift carriers for it was sent on the Saturday and arrived here on the Monday.' A letter from the Constable of Castile reached him at Valladolid, again in record time: 'If it had been a trout it would still have been fresh.' The image was one that pursued him, for several years later he wrote to the Marquis de los Velez, 'your letter arrived here very quickly, fresher than the salmon which they brought us from Bayonne'. These are the exceptions which as always prove the rule.

Statesmen and ambassadors, whom we usually imagine with weighty matters on their minds, are often preoccupied by the arrival or delays of the mail. On 24th February, 1575, Don Luis de Requesens writes from Antwerp to Don Diego de Zuñiga, Philip II's ambassador at Paris: 'I do not know how your Lordship fares for letters from Spain; for myself, I have heard nothing from the king concerning the affairs of the Netherlands since 20th November last . . . His Majesty's service has suffered greatly by it.'

The arrival or imminent arrival of the mails could become an obsession. Even the ordinary post did not have a fixed hour, sometimes not even a fixed day. 'I am waiting for the regular Flanders mail to go past at any hour,' notes Chantonnay in December, 1561. This obsession was not of course peculiar to the ambassadors of the Catholic King. It is a waste of time, writes the Cardinal de Rambouillet to Charles IX, to hasten to send us letters, 'because of the knavery and negligence of the postmasters in carrying Your Majesty's dispatches . . . which is such and so great . . . that the said dispatches often spend a month or six weeks on the road between the Court and Lyons. So that when I receive them, the time when I could have availed myself of them and had occasion to execute the orders contained in them is often, to my very great sorrow, past . . .'. We find similar complaints from Fourquevaux. 'Five or six couriers, bearing the king's arms,' he writes from Madrid in January, 1567, 'natives of the said Lyons, who sometimes carry the regular mail for Rome, say that they are in the service of Monsieur de Nemours when they are on the road. This is in order to get better treatment from the postmasters.' But they would carry money and dispatches for bankers of any nationality. One of them for example, 'came with all speed these last days to the "gennevois" attached to this [the Spanish] court, to bring them letters from other "gennevois" bankers living in the said Lyons'. Meanwhile the letters of the king of France stayed on the road. Another time, the correspondence suffers because of the 'masters of the Landes' and uncommon delays always result. Longlée, Henri III's agent in Spain, indicates in February, 1584, that he has been without news of his government for two weeks but 'that many [letters] have remained at Burgos coming from the direction of Valladolid'. All kinds of accidents and incidents were possible. It might be that two ordinary mails failed to make the connection; or that the normal routes had been interrupted; or that the couriers, forewarned of brigands, refused to travel at night. Every time, this would mean unexpected delays in distant places. The viceroy of Naples is without instructions, the government of the Prudent King does not know what is happening in the Netherlands; and the Venetian ambassador at Madrid remains sixty days without news from Italy.

These were no doubt exceptional cases, resulting from human error, local circumstances, or bad weather, but it was an 'exception' frequently repeated, which aggravated an already tense situation. The struggle against distance might remain a matter of constant vigilance, but it was also one of chance and luck. At sea a favourable wind and a spell of fine weather might make the difference between taking six months for a voyage or completing it in a week or two. Pierre Belon sailed from the Sea of Marmara to Venice in thirteen days, a journey which frequently took half a year. Similarly on land, where the differences are less remarkable, a war, a state of alert, roads flooded by heavy rain, or passes blocked by a snowfall could mean that even the most liberal estimates would be exceeded. Distances were not invariable, fixed once and for all. There might be ten or a hundred different distances, and one could never be sure in advance, before setting out or making decisions, what timetable fate would impose.

In fact, men of the sixteenth century were resigned to every kind of delay. A letter travelling from Spain to Italy was as likely to go by Bordeaux and Lyons as by Montpellier and Nice. A letter sent to Henri IV by Monsieur de Villiers, his ambassador in Venice in April 1601, arrived at Fontainebleau by way of Brussels. During the 1550s the king of Portugal's ambassadors at Rome often sent their letters by way of Antwerp. This was because the length of the journey depended less on the distance travelled than on the quality and frequency of the mails. And after all everyone was used to it. Three or four days' delay was neither here nor there. At the end of 1587, when the 'Prince of Béarn's' Protestants were occupying the Limousin, regular communications between Bernardino de Mendoza in Paris and Philip II's government were interrupted. Dispatches had to be sent by new routes, along which unfortunately there was no organized postal service, 'por donde no hay postas'. In the margin of the letter informing him of these circumstances, Philip II wrote, 'it is more important that the letters should travel by a safe route than that four or five days be gained, except on occasions when speed is essential'.

The dimensions of the sea: some record crossings. The available figures vary a great deal. What is more they only rarely form coherent series. The best one can say is that some notion of 'pure' distance can be obtained by noting exceptional crossings which give, as it were, the minimum dimensions of the sea.

The fastest speeds, 200 kilometres or more per day, were hardly ever attained except by sea, in fair weather and preferably in well-manned galleys, such as the one Don John of Austria sent from Messina in June, 1572, which reached the Catalan coast (Palamos) in six days. The galley sailed alone and was well armed: according to a Tuscan correspondent she sailed without putting in to land. The feat was not unique. Two years earlier, and in winter, Gian Andrea Doria had crossed from Genoa to Palamos in five days; the distance and the speed were less but the obstacles overcome were comparable. And sixty years earlier Cardinal Cisneros had made the 200-kilometre crossing from Oran to

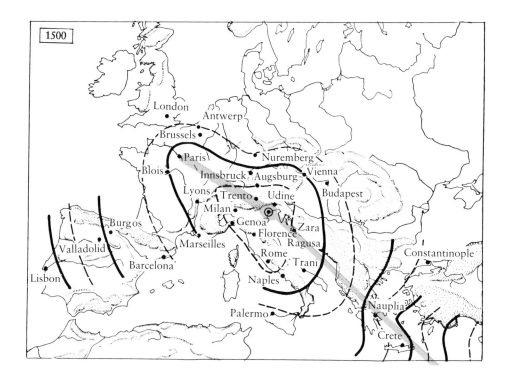

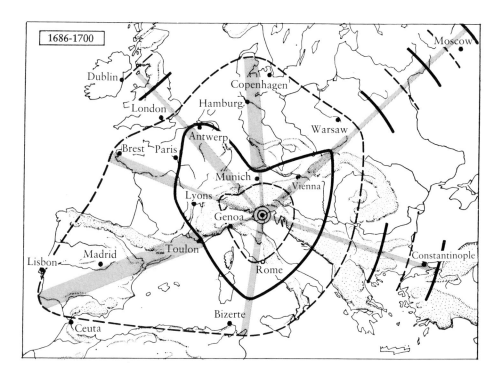

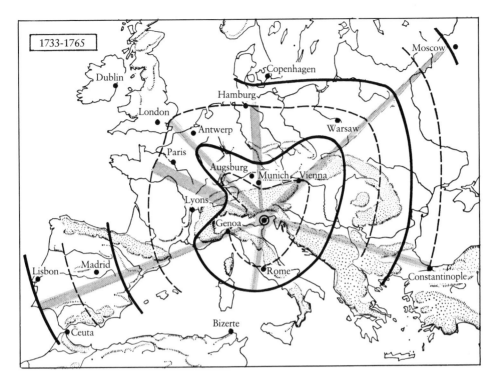

News travelling to Venice

The isochronic lines representing intervals of *one week*, give a broad indication of the time required for the dispatch of letters which in all three diagrams are travelling *towards* Venice.

The first map is based on the research of Pierre Sardella about 1500, to be precise 1496–1534. The second and third maps are based on the evidence of Venetian *avvisi* in the Public Record Office at London where they were analyzed for me by Frank Spooner.

The width of the shaded lines increases with the average speed of communications.

The differences from one map to another may seem very marked in certain directions. They are a result of the varying frequency of communications, depending on the urgency of the circumstances. Generally speaking communication seems to be as slow on the third map as on the first while the second shows noticeably shorter delays. But it cannot be regarded as definite proof. Theoretically speeds should be compared over distances defined by comparable isochronic lines. But such distances cannot be ascertained with sufficient accuracy. However if one imagines the maps as being superimposed on each other, they are very roughly equivalent, an extension in one direction being compensated by a reduction in another. Needless to say, the step from areas expressed in square kilometres to daily speeds should only be taken with extreme caution.

Cartagena in a single day, Wednesday 23rd May, 1509. This was a miraculous voyage, 'as if he had had the winds at his command'.

On land, with some exceptions, record speeds fell short of those achieved by sea (except for the incredible relay races between Rome and Venice, a distance of over 400 kilometres, of which there were three between 1496 and 1530, according to Pierre Sardella: time taken one and a half days, an hourly speed of 10 to 15 kilometres. The average time for the journey was four days. See the tables in Pierre Sardella). For postal communications the overland route,

127. Merchants awaiting the arrival of a ship. Miniature from a sixteenth-century silver repoussé icon cover from the Pontos. *Byzantine Museum, Athens*

although more expensive, was preferred to the sea route because the time taken was more predictable. The fastest speeds in Europe were probably reached by the couriers working for the postal service organized by Gabriel de Tassis on the Italy–Brussels route, via the Tyrol; this was a route that had been carefully planned, halts were kept to a minimum, and, particularly in the Eifel, well-known shortcuts were regularly used. The itinerary in itself was a record. And its 764 kilometres were covered in five and a half days, that is at about 139 kilometres a day. This falls short of the exceptional speeds reached by sea, but exceeds by far the usual speed for the overland route. By way of comparison, the sensational news of the St Bartholomew Massacre (24th August, 1572) travelled from Paris to Madrid at rather less than 100 kilometres per day: it reached Barcelona on 3rd September and was only known in the Spanish capital on the evening of the 7th.

On the other hand, the rate at which important news travelled can be a good indication of record speeds, for it often travelled on wings.

The capture of Nicosia, 9th September, 1570, was known in Constantinople on 24th September; in Venice, via Ragusa, on 26th October and in Madrid on 19th December.

News of Lepanto, 7th October, 1571, reached Venice on 18th October, Naples on the 24th, Lyons on the 25th, Paris and Madrid on the 31st.

The Turco-Venetian peace treaty, agreed secretly on March 7th, 1573, and announced at Venice on 4th April was known at Rome on 6th April, Naples on the 8th, and Palermo and Madrid on the 17th.

News of the capture of La Goletta and Tunis, 25th August, 1574, reached Vienna on 1st October, just as Pierre Lescalopier was arriving there, having left Istanbul on a diplomatic mission and crossed Bulgaria, Wallachia, and Transylvania before arriving exhausted in the Habsburg capital. The news gave him reason to reflect. He had seen this victorious Turkish armada leaving Constantinople on the previous 15th May, only two weeks before his own departure. How much it had accomplished while he had been on the road!

The length of these journeys as measured in waves of communication around Nicosia, Lepanto, Venice, and Tunis provides at best only approximate measurements. From our first example it would appear that the Mediterranean was ninety-nine days long – but this is surely too much. In fact, the news took some time to reach the outside world from Nicosia on the besieged island, and we may be sure that Venice was in no hurry to pass word on to the West. Any measurements must in fact be treated with caution and cannot be regarded as accurate when confined to a single figure. We must remember what we are measuring. The speed of news and the passage of letters is only one aspect of the battle against distance.

Average speeds. Our task becomes very much harder when we leave the question of record speeds for averages. Even when supported by documents, how can average speeds mean very much when we know that the length of any one voyage could vary from twice to three, four, even seven or ten times the shortest time recorded? The essential point to note here is this very variety, the wide range of times taken to travel the same journey: it is a *structural* feature of the century. The modern transport revolution has not only increased the speed of travel to an extraordinary degree; it has eliminated (and this is also important) the uncertainty imposed in the past by the elements. A Venetian ambassador on his way to England in January, 1610 waited for fourteen days at Calais facing a sea so rough that no ship dared put out. In June, 1609, a Venetian ship bound for Constantinople had to stand for eighteen days off the open beach of Santa Anastasia in the shelter of Chios, waiting for the bad weather to abate.

The sea-crossing from Constantinople to Alexandria took about a fortnight including calls at port, a week not counting stops. It was only two days' sail from the castles of the Hellespont to the island of Chios. In October or November, 1560, a Ragusan roundship left Messina and reached Alexandria 'fra novi giorni', and this time is not presented as a record.

The sea-crossing in the central zone varied according to the season, the ship, and the route. The same boat that sailed from Malta to Tripoli in Barbary in nine days, took seventeen days to return from Tripoli to Messina. In April, 1562, a *nave* made the trip from Tripoli to Sciacca on the south coast of Sicily in six days. A series of voyages from Tunis to Leghorn (one in 1600, two in 1608, eight in 1609, two in 1610) took the following times: six, seven, eight, nine, nine, nine, ten, eleven, twelve, thirteen, fourteen, fourteen, and twenty days, i.e., an average of about eleven days. The two fastest crossings – six days and seven days – as if to confound expectations were accomplished by a *nave* in January, 1600, and by a barque in July, 1609.

We have little information about the length of crossings from Marseilles to Spain on the one hand and North Africa on the other. They were often undertaken in secret. Using the royal galleys, the French king's ambassador d'Aramon took a week to sail from the Balearics to Algiers, in fair weather (at least after the second day). Two voyages in 1609 and one in 1610 on the Algiers–Leghorn route lasted respectively thirteen, fifteen, and five days: five to fifteen – so one voyage was three times as long as the other.

The difference could be very great over long distances. A Venetian roundship sailed in October–November, 1570, from Crete to Otranto in twelve days; another, in May–June, 1561, sailed almost the entire length of the Mediterranean from Crete to Cadiz in a month. But in July, 1569, two galleys from Algiers reached Constantinople only after seventy-two days at sea. A roundship that left Alexandria on 7th January, 1564, arrived at Messina on 5th April; her voyage had lasted eighty-eight days. The 'normal' figure in the fifteenth century for the Venice–Jaffa voyage was of the order of forty to fifty days, according to one historian. But the average time for the voyage from Venice to the Holy Land that emerges from Röhricht's figures, discussed on page 198, was very much longer.

The *portate* of Leghorn have some information to give us. For five voyages from Alexandria to Leghorn (two in 1609, one in 1610, two in 1611) they give the following figures: twenty-three, twenty-six, twenty-nine, thirty-two, and fifty-six days, i.e., an average of thirty-three days. For eight voyages (five in 1609, three in 1610) from Cartagena or Alicante to Leghorn we have the

I	II	III	IV	V	VI	VII	VIII
Alexandria	266	19	89	65	55	17	323
Antwerp	83	13	36	20	16	8	200
Augsburg	110	19	21	11	12	5	240
Barcelona	171	16	77	22	19	8	237
Blois	345	53	27	14	10	4½	222
Brussels	138	24	35	16	10	9	111
Budapest	317	39	35	18	19	7	271
Burgos	79	13	42	27	27	11	245
Calais	62	15	32	18	14	12	116
Candia	56	16	81	38	33	19	163
Cairo	41	13	99	72	63	20	315
Constantinople	365	46	81	37	34	15	226
Corfu	316	39	45	19	15	7	214
Damascus	56	17	102	80	76	28	271
Florence	387	103	13	4	3	1	300
Genoa	215	58	15	6	6	2	300
Innsbruck	163	41	16	7	6	4	150
Lisbon	35	9	69	46	43	27	159
London	672	78	52	27	24	9	266
Lyons	812	225	25	12	13	4	325
Marseilles	26	7	21	14	12	8	150
Milan	871	329	8	3	3	1	300
Naples	682	180	20	9	8	4	200
Nauplia	295	56	60	36	34	18	188
Nuremberg	39	11	32	20	21	8	262
Palermo	118	23	48	22	25	8	312
Paris	473	62	34	12	12	7	171
Ragusa	95	18	26	13	14	5	280
Rome	1053	406	9	4	4	1½	266
Trano	94	14	30	12	12	4	300
Trento	205	82	7	3	3	1	300
Udine	552	214	6	2	2	1½	133
Valladolid	124	15	63	29	23	12	191
Vienna	145	32	32	14	13	8	162
Zara	153	28	25	8	6	1	600

Column i shows the places in communication with Venice; Column ii the number of cases observed; Column iii the number of normal cases; Column iv the maximum time (in days); v the weighted arithmetical average (in days); vi the normal time in days; vii the minimum time in days; viii the normal time as an expression of the minimum time (min. = 100), in other words, the relation between the minimum time and the normal time.

following figures: seven, nine, nine, ten, fifteen, twenty-five, thirty, and forty-nine days, i.e., an average of nineteen days. One might therefore say, *with a modicum of truth*, that the voyage from Spain to Leghorn to Alexandria could take about fifty-two days, but we cannot call this figure an average.

Talking in averages then, we may draw the general conclusion that the Mediterranean crossing from north to south could be expected to take one or two weeks; and that it was likely to be a matter of two or three months if one were sailing from east to west or vice versa. We might add moreover that these were to remain the dimensions of the sea throughout the seventeenth century and even later.

Letters: a special case. It would clearly be more useful to have a homogeneous series of measurements than these rather unsatisfactory approximations. And we have a very ample one in the letters (yet again) sent by governments, ambassadors, merchants, and private citizens. Between 1497 and 1532, Marino Sanudo, who was always well informed of the actions of the Signoria of Venice,

128, 129. *Left:* Engraving of a letter carrier, after A. Carracci. Rome, 1646.
Right: A letter carrier from Ragusa. Sixteenth-century woodcut.

kept a faithful record of the arrival of letters and news, which provides us with a total of 10,000 usable figures. This huge mass of material has been subjected to statistical analysis by Pierre Sardella and the results are summarized in the table on p. 269 and the map on p. 264. Even so, one has to be a little careful in interpreting information that relates only to news *arriving* at Venice and beware of reading too much into it.

Quite clearly, the area measured is heterogeneous, and far from *isotropic*. If one took the distance from Venice to Paris as a radius and described a circle with Venice as its centre, one would be in theory defining an *isotropic* circular area within which news (like light, but slower) would travel at an identical speed from all points on the circumference to the centre. But of course what we have is nothing of the sort. News was held up by natural obstacles, such as the Alps, the Straits of Dover, the sea. Fast speeds depended on the goodwill, calculation, and needs of men. During the period 1497 to 1532, Venice hung on the decisions of the French king, on any rumours and news from France, and from Paris these precious packets raced towards her.

Our maps and averages impose an artificial regularity on the journeys travelled by these dispatches. In fact, their movements were extremely unpredictable: the very wide range of times taken (see column VIII, relation of normal to minimum times) would be even wider if one compared minimum times with maximum times. A surprising detail is that the coefficient of irregularity seems to be in inverse proportion to the distance travelled. It also increases, but that is to be expected, when a sea-crossing is involved. So it is not astonishing that Zara should hold the record (a ratio of 1 to 6), since it falls into both categories: it was near Venice, but separated from her by the unpredictable Adriatic crossing.

In short, this table provides us with a basic framework for comparison and verification. Its only disadvantage (or advantage, depending on which way one looks at it) is that all the times it establishes are relatively fast ones. They testify to the vigilance and indeed the means available to a city as rich as Venice. They correspond to an alert system of communications. For Venice, the news from Paris, Valladolid, or Constantinople was not a matter of curiosity but of essential information.

If we look to other records we nowhere find the same briskness. Letters from every city in Europe piled up on the desks of Philip II. It was customary to record on the back of the last page (*la carpeta*) the dates of dispatch and of arrival, as well as the equally interesting but infrequently noted date of sending the reply. Hundreds of thousands of examples are therefore available for statistical analysis. Philip II, apart from his few well-known voyages to Córdoba, Lisbon, Saragossa, Barcelona, or Valencia, hardly stirred from the centre of Castile after his return from the Netherlands in 1559. If there is sometimes uncertainty as to the whereabouts of his correspondents or the route followed by the letters, these are points that can usually be cleared up.

I was tempted to use these data to compile a set of measurements comparable to Pierre Sardella's, again with Venice as the centre of the co-ordinates. From a sample of forty cases at the end of the century, the correspondence of Spain's representatives at Venice, the shortest time taken on the Madrid–Venice route (which can be assumed roughly equal to the Valladolid–Venice route of Sanudo's day) is twenty-two days (as against twelve days recorded by Sanudo) and the longest time eighty-five days (omitting one aberrant case of 145 days). The arithmetical average (unweighted) is forty days (as against Sardella's weighted average of twenty-nine days). Over the distance Constantinople–Venice, sixteen recorded cases during the same years give a minimum length of twenty-nine days, a maximum of seventy-three and an average time of about forty-one-and-a-half days. These figures are nearer, but still higher than Sardella's (which were of course obtained from a much larger number of examples). Should we conclude that at the end of the sixteenth century communications along the length of the Mediterranean were still as difficult and hazardous as they had been at the beginning? More evidence is needed before we can say so with certainty.

What we can say is that in both sets of calculations, mine and Sardella's, Venice figures as very roughly a halfway point between Madrid (or Valladolid) and Constantinople. The sum of the average time taken over each half – forty and forty-one-and-a-half days according to the Spanish figures, twenty-nine and thirty-seven days, according to Sanudo's – gives us a Mediterranean world either eighty or sixty-six days long, a figure certainly greater than the arbitrary time of fifty-two days obtained by adding the Alexandria–Leghorn time to the Leghorn–Cartagena time. Of course they are not strictly comparable since the distance from Alexandria to Cartagena is not the same as the distance, also reconstructed, from Constantinople to Venice to Madrid. But we shall have to accept that we cannot measure the sea with any great degree of accuracy even with the valuable aid of the correspondence of statesmen and merchants.

News, a luxury commodity. News, a luxury commodity, was worth more than its weight in gold. 'No courier', wrote his agent at Venice to the Duke of Ferrara, 'will accept less than a ducat per letter' and this was between two neighbouring cities, Venice and Ferrara. At the beginning of the sixteenth century the tariff between Venice and Nuremberg varied according to the time taken: four days, 58 florins; four days and six hours, 50; five days, 48; six days, 25 (we might note in passing that the fastest speed recorded for this trip by Sardella is two days longer than the last). These were evidently ultra-fast communications available only to rich merchants, in that early part of the sixteenth century when it is probably true to say that price differences between one market and another were greater than ever. It was worth paying even large sums of money to be able to send an order off at top speed. Later on the situation became more settled. The correspondence of Simón Ruiz during the second half of the sixteenth century gives the impression that the rapid dispatch of orders and information was no longer as important as it had been in the past. Only rich bankers or governments could afford such luxuries, the price of which continued to rise throughout the century. On July 14th, 1560, Chantonnay, who was then Philip II's ambassador at the French Court, sent a courier from Chartres to Toledo and back; in all he covered 179 stages and was paid a total of 358 ducats (2 ducats a stage). This was an enormous sum of money, much more than the annual salary of a professor at the University of Padua or Salamanca! The stages must have been about 10 or 12 kilometres each and if the courier covered them

130. A postman. German print, 1698.

at a rate of 18 leagues a day it is clear that we have briefly glimpsed a journey accomplished in record time. Rich men could buy superhuman achievements.

Letters depended both on regular and irregular mails, and the former were the more important statistically. Any survey of correspondence would sooner or later lead us to the regular postal services, whose official times we already know. The Tassis firm undertook to transport letters from Rome to Madrid in twenty-four days, between 1st April and the end of September; in twenty-six days during the winter season.

The conclusion is therefore plain to see. Distance was a constant. However man tackled the obstacle of distance, splintering the oars of close-manned galleys, driving the post-horses to death, or apparently flying over the waves under a fair wind, he always met with passive resistance and distance took a daily revenge for his most strenuous exploits. We may still be curious, as contemporaries were, to hear of record speeds: the news of Charles IX's death travelled from Paris to Cracow in thirteen days, as Sully himself tells us and the 'king of Poland' forsook his subjects the next day . . . ; news of the birth of a grandson for François I took only two days to reach Lyons from Fontainebleau (420 kilometres) and a Turkish *estafette* on one occasion covered the distance between Istanbul and Erzurum in eighteen days, exhausting many of its horses en route. But the essential point to bear in mind is that both average and record speeds remained perceptibly the same before and after the sixteenth century. Goods, boats, and people travelled as fast, or as slowly, in the days of the Avignon Popes or to Venice during the first half of the fifteenth century, as they did in the age of Louis XIV. Major change and advance did not occur before the end of the eighteenth century.

Present-day comparisons. The Mediterranean in the sixteenth century was comparable, *mutatis mutandis*, to the entire globe in 1939. It was vast, immeasurable, and its reputation as a 'human' area was earned only by contrast with those other monsters which sixteenth-century man was just beginning to tackle – the Atlantic Ocean, not to mention the Pacific. These were truly monsters, alongside which the Mediterranean was more like a domestic animal, but certainly not the 'lake' it has become in the twentieth century, the sunny resort of tourists and yachts where one can always reach land within a few hours and along whose length the traveller might be transported in the Orient Express. To understand what it was like in the sixteenth century, one must mentally magnify its area to a maximum and draw on remembered images from travellers' tales of the days when months, years, even a whole lifetime, could be spent on a voyage.

Will the reader suspect me of a facile paradox if I say that I was curiously reminded of France during the Wars of Religion by the spectacle of China in the first decades of this century, with its monstrous civil wars, foreign invasions, massacres, and famines, and its towns set in the midst of a vast countryside, defensive towns, surrounded by walls whose gates were closed at night? A band of partisans could, by slipping between the towns, make its way unchallenged from upper Szechwan right down to Shantung. It was in a similar setting that France under the last of the Valois saw her strength ebb away, as she was overrun by bands of adventurers, French or foreign. Such inroads consume a nation's wealth in the end, and yet if any nation was wealthy in the sixteenth century it was France – a land flowing with plenty!

This may seem an odd digression. But it is one way of conveying the notion of almost unlimited space, a rather difficult concept for the modern imagination to apply to the Mediterranean.

Empires and distance. An understanding of the importance of distance leads one to view in a fresh light the problems of administration in sixteenth-century empires.

And, in the first place, there was the enormous Spanish Empire, which depended on what was for the period an unprecedented combination of land and sea transport. It required not only continual troop movements but the daily dispatch of hundreds of orders and reports. The policy of Philip II necessitated these troop movements, transfers of bullion and bills of exchange, all fundamental concerns that in turn help to explain a great many of Philip's actions and in particular why France was of key importance to him. It has always been customary to say of France that she was surrounded by Habsburg possessions. But if their empire could threaten her from without she could threaten it from within, and who shall say which was the greater peril? France under François I and Henri II had been hostile and closed to Spain; except for his swift passage through in 1540, Charles V all his life gave France a wide berth. Between 1559 and 1589, on the other hand, for thirty years, the road through France was more than half-open to the services of Philip II's diplomatic and financial staff. And if the Prudent King did not himself set foot outside Spain, sitting at the centre of his web, it was for many reasons, the financial and economic predominance of Castile and the vital link with America, for example, but it was also because the French frontier was no longer completely closed to his envoys.

So to look over Philip II's shoulder as he deals with his papers, means constantly being aware of the dimensions of France, for him an intermediary zone; it means becoming familiar with the postal services, knowing which routes have regular stages and which have not; noting the delays in the mails caused here and there by the civil wars; measuring their extent, duration, and relative importance; and also learning the detours taken by money, particularly bills of exchange on their way to banking centres.

A state had indeed to wage not one but many struggles against distance. The Spanish Empire, which was poorly situated from the point of view of its European and world possessions, expended the better part of its energy in these struggles. And yet it was better adapted than any other to these necessary tasks and better organized to deal with them. Although much criticized, the Spanish Empire was equal or indeed superior to other leading states for transport, transfer, and communications. It is curious, to say the least, that from the 1560s on, it employed a sort of specialist in troop and goods transport, in the person of Francisco de Ibarra, about whom and his emulators it would be interesting to know more.

Historians have paid too little attention to the gigantic tasks demanded of the Spanish administrative machine. They have noticed only the 'delays' of *el rey papelero*, the bureaucratic king 'with feet of lead', 'himself both master and secretary, which is a great virtue . . .' as the bishop of Limoges wrote of him in 1560, and 'wholly devoted to his affairs, never losing an hour for he is all day among his papers', the overworked king who even a quarter of a century later was still unwilling to abandon his superhuman task in spite of the protests of Cardinal Granvelle who wished in vain for innovations.

So we must distinguish between the different kinds of 'delays' in Spain. There were delays resulting from the mail: reports were delayed on the way in and replies and instructions were delayed on the way out. No government could escape these delays and Spain was particularly vulnerable. But over equal distances Spanish communications were on the whole a match for anyone's. If they had weaknesses they were shared. The Turkish Empire, for instance, was also a sum of delays laid end to end. It took sixteen or seventeen days to travel from Constantinople to the Adriatic, to Cattaro or Spalato, at full speed. In the Black Sea, the *Mar Maggiore*, both itinerary and the length of voyage were extremely unpredictable. In the Aegean, or the White Sea, as the Turks called it, the fastest times recorded seem ridiculously slow. Even in 1686 it was considered worthy of note (in December, it is true) that a Turkish galley should have sailed from Constantinople to Negropont in eight days. Sulaimān Pasha's fleet took two months to cross the Red Sea in 1538. Some of these distances remained invariable, requiring the same time for centuries. Pegolotti in the *Pratica della Mercatura* (1348) says that it takes twelve to thirteen days to travel from Trebizond to Tauris on horseback, thirty to thirty-two days by caravan. In 1850, Goedel, the Austrian consul at Trebizond, claims that the same route takes twenty-seven to thirty days by caravan 'when the road is in good repair'.

A second source of delay was the deliberation and discussion preceding the dispatch of orders. Here all the contemporary evidence is in agreement: Frenchmen and Italians felt temperamentally alien when they set foot in this land of phlegmatic Spaniards who were as long in making up their minds as they were skilful at dissembling. That does not mean to say that the image, though familiar, is necessarily correct. The view of a nation that a foreigner may form and express is frequently as unshakeable as it is misleading. But it does seem that the dilatoriness of the Spanish government, or as the bishop of Limoges called it, 'the lengthiness of this country' was beyond question. When news of Drake's exploit at Cadiz was brought to Rome in 1587, the Pope exclaimed 'that his

Majesty was a man of little vision who never made up his mind until the occasion had passed'. At Paris, 'this remark has not only been much repeated, but it has also been published along with the added jibe that the queen of England's spinning wheel is worth more than the king of Spain's sword'.

This was malicious talk no doubt. However, if we turn once more to diplomatic correspondence, it seems that the French government, for example, was more prompt in the execution of its affairs. But was this necessarily the fault of the king in Madrid who insisted on reading everything? Spain lay at the centre of an empire whose boundaries stretched much further than those of France (or England). Philip II had to wait for reports to arrive from very distant places before taking decisions. At this point both kinds of delay came together. The Spanish bureaucratic machinery turned over at its own deliberate pace, but also suffered from the delays of shipping in the Atlantic, the Indian, and even the Pacific Oceans; it had to respond to the workings of the first economic and political system that spanned the known world. This was one reason why the pulses of Spain beat at a slower pace than others. After 1580 and the annexation of Portugal, these pulses beat even slower. Let us pause to reflect with Sassetti, the Florentine who travelled to the East Indies in 1585 and has left us his valuable correspondence: if people had any idea, he wrote from Cochin on 27th January, 1585, to his friend Piero Vettori at home in Florence, what the seven-month voyage is like, 'living off ships' biscuit and brackish water, confined in a small space with 800 or 900 other people, all suffering from hunger, thirst, sea-sickness and discomfort', few would be eager to sail to the Indies. But there it is, when one sees a boat one is filled with the urge to sail in it. And the king of Spain's orders had to endure the seven months of this voyage and many more besides.

So there can be no doubt: Spain waged an unremitting struggle against the obstacle of distance, one that tells us more than any other source about the 'measure of the sixteenth century'.

Distance and the economy. Every activity had to overcome the obstacle of physical distance.

Even bills of exchange, which were privileged goods, did not escape the general rule of passive resistance. The time taken to reach other exchanges was regularly added to the usance specified on the bill itself. At the beginning of the century the times allowed from Genoa were five days for Pisa, six for Milan, ten for Gaeta, Avignon, and Rome; fifteen for Ancona, twenty for Barcelona, thirty for Valencia and Montpellier; two months for Bruges; three for London. Sums in specie travelled even more slowly. When, during the latter half of the century the arrival of the fleet at Seville becomes the predominant factor in the European, Mediterranean, and world economy, it is retrospectively possible to trace the route taken by each annual consignment of silver swelling the stock of currency and circulating from one western financial centre to another according

131. Merchants loading camels in Smyrna. Engraving from Thevet, *Cosmographie*, Paris, 1575.

to a very long-drawn-out timetable. Merchandise encountered similar difficulties: it took time to process, spent more time in warehouses and changed hands with varying degrees of slowness. Wool from Spain was imported by Florence: many months passed between the purchase of the fleeces and the finishing of the cloth, and it might even be years before it reached customers in Egypt, Nuremberg, or elsewhere in its finished form. We have already mentioned as typical the case of the wheat and rye of Poland, which was sold a full year after being harvested and consumed up to six or twelve months later, sometimes later still if it was sent to the Mediterranean.

Moreover, merchandise sometimes had to wait for the arrival of other goods from distant places. At Aquila in the Abruzzi the thriving saffron trade attracted a large concourse of merchants every year. But saffron was not the only merchandise which had to be at the rendezvous; it had to be packed in linen bags (eight bags to a load), and the bags were in turn wrapped four by four in a leather pouch. In addition payment was effected in copper bars used by the Aquila mint which struck small coins, *cavali* and *cavaluzzi*. So the transfer of saffron depended on the arrival of linen cloth and copper plate from Germany, bales of leather from Hungary, and vice versa. The two streams had to meet. Similarly in the Levant, spices, pepper, drugs, silk, and cotton had a rendezvous with silver coins and woollen cloth from the West. Along the route that led from Ragusa to Venice and from Venice on to Antwerp and London we have intermittent records of the exchange of goods which was the livelihood of the Gondola family, merchants of Ragusan origin, with branches in Ragusa itself, Ancona, Venice (later apparently at Messina), and finally in London, which was the centre of operations. They handled the exchange of raisins, *uve passe*, or *curanti*, as they were called in anglicized Italian, imported from the Levant, and rosaries (*paternosters*), not a very successful line, for the kerseys manufactured in the English countryside. Both shipping and overland routes were used, via Ancona or Venice, but the transactions took so long that in 1545 in order to settle outstanding payments the firm had to resort to the Lyons exchange through the good offices of the Salviati. There can be no doubt that the collapse of private banks in the sixteenth century was the result of their being too ready to place their clients' money in commercial circuits that moved too slowly. If there was a panic or an emergency, payments could not be made within a few days, for the money was still on the road, a prisoner of the mortal delays of distance.

Time was money, as every merchant, 'with ink-stained fingers' – from the endless number of letters he wrote – well knew. The expression was already in the air. If a merchant of Venice in the fifteenth century prefers to deal in Syrian cotton, it is because the whole business can be concluded within six or seven months, a much shorter interval than that allowed by the long voyages of the England or Flanders galleys. Only the really large-scale capitalists of the period, the most skilful and the most fortunate – the Genoese – were able to arrange for payments to be made across the Atlantic from Seville. This was an immense operation – but for the even more extraordinary establishment of regular commercial links between Lisbon and the Indian Ocean, the Portuguese state with all its credit had to intervene, and the king turn pepper merchant, and even then it soon proved unequal to the task. Inevitably the longer the distance over which trade was carried out, the more money had to be invested and the longer it would spend en route. Merchant shipping from Seville to America or from Lisbon to Asia would have been impossible if it had not been for the previous concentration of capital, in the fifteenth century, in southern Germany and Italy.

These long-distance links called for great feats. Feats of endurance by the participants: in July, 1602, a great ship from the Indies put in a few miles from Lisbon, with the equivalent of more than 2 'millions in gold' on board, but of her crew there survived only thirty men. It was this exhausted ship that the

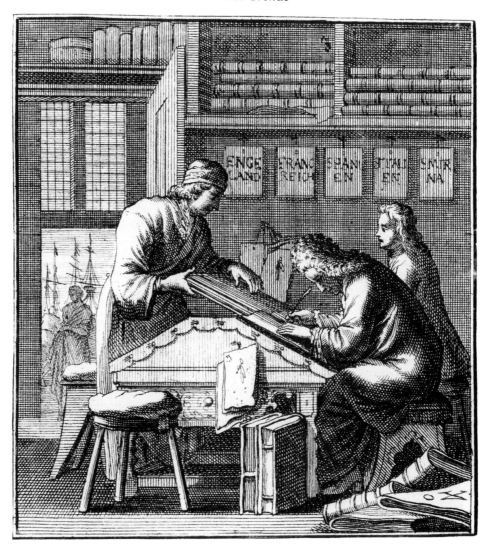

132. German merchant in a port, dealing with his correspondence. Engraving from Christoph Weigel, *Abbildung der Hauptstände*, Regensburg, 1698.

English privateers seized without difficulty under the noses of the defending galleys. In September, 1614, there was a similar occasion (without the final blow of total loss this time), when a ship from 'the Indies' arrived off Lisbon, carrying 'a million' on board, and sixteen survivors left of the original 300 men who had embarked on her. The extreme case is of the return of a Manila galleon to Acapulco, on the Pacific, without a single living soul on board, but still carrying all her treasure; the ghost ship sailed into port on her own.

They also required great feats of money raising, as we shall see later. Immense resources had to be made available, as the wild fluctuations of the commercial centres regularly reveal. The 'Indies' fleet had not even left (it crossed the bar at San Lucar between 24th and 29th March, 1563) before Simón Ruiz' correspondent was writing to him from Seville on 15th February: 'for several days now, it has been impossible to borrow a single *real* at any price on the market'. All the available money had gone on last-minute purchases of merchandise to send abroad; the mercantile community at Seville would have to wait for the return of the fleets before it again had an 'abundance' (*largezza*) of metal currency.

Fairs, the supplementary network of economic life. The fairs of Champagne died out in the fourteenth century, to be resurrected by Chalon-sur-Saône, Geneva, and later at Lyons. In northern Italy and the Netherlands, countries where there was intense *urban* activity, fairs although still glittering occasions in the sixteenth century, began to decline. When they survived, as at Venice, it was largely as a façade. At Ascensiontide the spectacular fair held in St Mark's Square and known as *La Sensa* (from the religious festival), was the scene of much festivity including the celebrated marriage of the doge to the sea. But this was no longer the heart of Venice, which now beat on the *piazza* and bridge of the Rialto.

In this constant dialogue between the towns (or commercial centres) and the fairs, the former since they operated without interruption (at Florence the exchange rates were quoted every week on Saturdays) were bound in the long run to count for more than the fairs, which were exceptional gatherings. Or so one would assume, but evolution is never a simple affair. Surprises and about-turns were still possible. The establishment in 1579 of the exchange fairs (known as the Besançon fairs) at Piacenza in northern Italy was the event of the century from the point of view of the history of capitalism. For many years the relentless 'heart' of the Mediterranean and entire western economy beat here at Piacenza. We shall have more to say about this crucial event. It was not, in fact, the city of Genoa, but the discreet quarterly meeting of a few businessmen at Piacenza that dictated the rhythm of the material life of the West. Only paper changed hands, and not a penny of currency, reports a Venetian observer with only a little exaggeration. And yet everything – new arrivals and returns, arterial blood and veinous blood – culminated at this vital 'pole', from which flowed drafts and remittances, debts and letters of credit, settlements and returns, gold and silver, the symmetrical or asymmetrical transactions upon which all trade depended.

But at a more humble level local fairs had a part to play: a similar one in kind to that played by the more illustrious fairs, Lyons, Medina del Campo, Frankfurt, and later Leipzig, not to mention the fairs authorized by Venice at Bergamo or Brescia, the Bolzano fairs in the Tyrol that became so prosperous in the seventeenth century, or in Syria the seaside fair at Jeble and the caravan fair of Mzerib (El Muzeirib) held inland, 100 kilometres south of Damascus, in the middle of the desert. And then there were the tiny fairs, hardly more than

SERENISSIMO COSMO

Nundinas Imprunetanas, quæ in Diui Lucæ Festo quotannis innumerabili populi frequentia, atqꝫ affluenti
solo extructum, fundatumasꝫ, vbi eiparæ Virginis Imago, miraculorum fœcunda, ab eodem Diuo Luca, vt fertur, depicta
Iacobus Callot Nobilis Lotharingius delineatas æreqꝫ incisas dedi

MAGNO DVCI ETRVRIÆ
ariarum mercium copia celebrantur, iuxta Templum insigne a Nobilissima Bondelmontium Familia olim in proprio
ui e spineis eruta, religione summa asseruatur, & colitur
uit conserauitque, grati animi sui perpetuum testimonium. An. Sal. M.D.CXX

133. *The Fair at Imprunete, Near Florence* by Jacques Callot. *Albertina, Vienna*

134. A local market. Detail from *The Life of St. Barbara*, fresco in the chapel, Villa Suardi, by Lorenzo Lotto, 1524.

weekly markets, dynamic points scattered throughout western Europe and the Balkans. In New Castile alone, in about 1575–1580, twenty-two fairs were still regularly held and there were dozens in Portugal. All, even the humblest, were like hastily assembled towns where previously there had only been, as there was at Medina del Campo, a street – *La Rua* – and a market place; or a vacant lot outside the town as at Lanciano. The fairs would mean a fortnight, three weeks, or at most, a month of feverish activity. At Darroca in Aragon the principal fair began on the feast of Corpus Christi; on this occasion the Brothers of the Trinity would bring out of their church the miraculous wafers that had once been transformed into flesh and blood ('et ciò si vede chiarissimamente', said some young Venetian travellers with conviction in May, 1581). The fair, which lasted a week, attracted a large number of mule dealers, selling beasts for ploughing, saddle or draft, the latter capable of pulling 'those carts which in Spain always have only two wheels' – a detail we may note in passing.

After the fair everything returned to normal. The stands were dismantled and moved on somewhere else like Count Potemkin's villages. Merchants, merchandise, and pack animals would travel on from one town to the next. One fair would end and another would begin. The seven or eight Flemish merchants who left the 'August' fair at Lanciano in September, 1567, were still in time, as they had hoped, for the second Sorrento fair which began on the 21st of the month.

The fairs were always a rendezvous for the wealthy merchants who were familiar with bills of exchange and credit machinery (whose bundles of bills of exchange have been found at Lanciano), and imported spices, drugs, and rich fabrics. But even at Lyons, in March, 1578, according to the innkeepers, 'for every merchant who comes to the fair on horseback and who can afford a good lodging and has money to spend, there are ten more on foot who are grateful for a room at the humblest inn'. The fairs also drew modest pedlars, genuine representatives of country life offering its products for sale: livestock, bacon, barrels of salt meat, leather, skins, cheeses, new casks, almonds, dried figs, apples, modest local wines and celebrated vintages such as the *mangiaguerra*, barrels of anchovy or sardines, and raw silk. The vital function of such fairs in the broad kingdom of Naples, whose picturesque side we have just glimpsed was to bring into contact the great trade routes and the country paths, muletracks, and 'capillaries' of trade that wound down from the mountains behind Lanciano 'following the beds of the streams'. Fairs clearly gave a tremendous fillip to exchange and circulation, and in fact to a whole series of transactions whether in money or kind, a vast movement that benefited by the absence of tolls, for one of the obstacles posed by distance was the number of customs posts, city tolls, and barriers. So the fairs were a way of breaking into the ordinarily closed and inward-looking regional economies and made possible the establishment, or at least the beginnings, of a 'national market'.

135. Market in Marrakesh, Morocco.

Local economies. The Mediterranean region was sprinkled with half-enclosed local economies, both large and small, with their own internal organization, their innumerable local measures, costumes, and dialects. Their number is impressive. The islands of Sardinia and Corsica, for example, were virtually outside the main flow of Mediterranean trade. The Sardinian peasant was never offered any incentive to increase his production, to experiment with new crops or change his methods; he was used to burning off the stubble (*narboni*) and did not leave fields fallow. Some parts of the island, even in 1860, Orosei and Posada on the east coast and Gallura to the north, had no wheeled vehicles and all trade 'is conducted on horseback'. In this island which was more pastoral than agricultural in the sixteenth century, money was often unknown. The Jesuit fathers who had been settled at Cagliari since 1557 were overwhelmed with gifts in kind: poultry, bread, kids, perhaps a capon or a sucking pig, good wines, and calves. 'But', says one of their letters, 'the alms we receive in money never amount to 10 crowns.'

Sicily, although a rich island, was equally poorly served in the regions of the interior. The islanders paid taxes for the building of road links, but the government used the money for other things, so the Sicilian interior had no properly maintained roads until the eighteenth century.

The more inward-looking these archaic economies were, the more likely it was that gold and silver, on their rare appearances there, would be over-estimated. The cost of living in Sardinia, noted a Venetian in 1558, is about a quarter or a fifth that of Italy, that is for those with well-filled purses. Similarly, when a Venetian ship was obliged by unforeseen circumstances to put in, on Ascension Day, 1609, to Fasana, a little port near Pola on the Istrian coast, her passengers and crew went ashore and found provisions in abundant supply: veal at 3 *soldi* a pound, a kid for 40 *soldi*, oil at 3 *soldi*, bread and wine at very low prices, 'insomma', says one traveller, 'buonissimo vivere'. Mediterranean countries, like other European countries, were checkered with low-cost regions, which in every case were separate worlds by-passed by the general economy.

The quadrilateral: Genoa, Milan, Venice, and Florence. We have looked at the advantages and the disadvantages, the factors that both encourage and at the same time restrict the economic organization of an area where distance is an obstacle: in other words, the geographical division of labour. This division can be seen quite clearly within the Mediterranean as a whole.

This world, sixty days long, was, indeed, broadly speaking a *Weltwirtschaft*, a world-economy, a self-contained universe. No strict and authoritarian order was established, but the outlines of a coherent pattern can be discerned. All world-economies for instance recognize a centre, some focal point that acts as a stimulus to other regions and is essential to the existence of the economic unit as a whole. Quite clearly in the Mediterranean in the fifteenth and sixteenth centuries that centre was a narrow urban quadrilateral: Venice, Milan, Genoa, Florence, a zone of conflicts and inter-city rivalries as the relative weight of each

136. Boats with local produce landing in front of the Zecca, the mint. Detail from *Venice from the Salute* by Jacopo Bassano. *Prado, Madrid*

city changed. The centre of gravity can gradually be seen to shift from Venice, where it still lay at the beginning of the century, to Genoa, where it was so brilliantly established between 1550 and 1575.

In the fifteenth century Venice was unquestionably the vigorous heart of the Mediterranean. She was less concerned with matters of diplomatic policy than with money, bills of exchange, fabrics, spices, and shipping – in her usual, that is, almost incredible manner. In May, 1472, the Council of Ten at Venice held discussions every day without intermission, with 'the *zonta* of the 35', as it had not done 'gran tempo fa'. The subject of debate was not the Turkish war, which had broken out again in 1470, but the depreciation and finally the proscribing of silver coins, *grossetti* and *grossoni*, in the first place those which had not been struck by the Zecca at Venice. A stop had to be put to the invasions by bad money, of which Venice suffered so many and with which she always dealt ruthlessly. Long before Thomas Gresham, Venetians already knew very well that 'bad money will drive out good', 'che la cativa cazarà via la bona', as the agent for Gonzaga writes in June, 1472. The same source adds that 'there is nothing new to report here, except that no one seems to care any longer about the Turks. No steps are being taken against them.' So Venice, which had lost Salonica in 1430 and had just sacrificed to the Turks the wheat-growing island

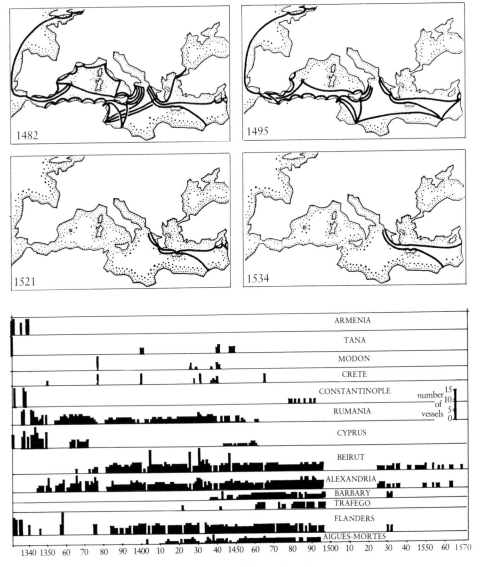

Venice: the voyages of the galere da mercato

The four sketch maps above are taken from the long narrative by Alberto Tenenti and Corrado Vivanti in *Annales E.S.C.*, 1961, and summarize the stages by which the old system of convoys of *galere da mercato* declined (they had sailed to Flanders, Aiguesmortes, Barbary, the 'Trafegi', Alexandria, Beirut, and Constantinople). All these lines were working in 1482. By 1521 and 1534 only the profitable links with the Levant survived. To simplify the map, all routes are shown from the entrance to the Adriatic only, not from Venice.

of Negropont in 1470, was entirely self-preoccupied, for her confidence in herself, her wealth, and her superiority was complete. The Turkish fleet was modelled after her own; her strongholds, armed with artillery and regularly maintained and supplied by the Arsenal, were unequalled. And business was good. Throughout the Mediterranean, and outside it as far as Flanders, the distributive system of the *galere da mercato* was functioning for the greater profit of the patricians who chartered these state-owned vessels.

The Signoria had lost, it is true, some vital positions: Salonica (1430), Constantinople (1453), 'truly our city', as a Senate text says; Negropont (1470), and we might add the Tana on the Sea of Azov (1475) from which galleys and roundships sailed to Venice, one of them according to a late document 'carga de schiave et salumi', carrying slave women and salt meat. All these blows struck home, but the Republic's adaptable shipping system could always transfer its bases to other places, to Crete or Cyprus, where Venice was undisputed ruler after 1479. In 1489 Alexandria represented possibly 3 million ducats in returns for Venice. In 1497 the Signoria sent to Syria and Egypt, along with her precious wares, over 360,000 ducats in specie. Immediately the silver mark (for silver was already the metal used) rose more than 5 *grossi* in price. Venice was sacrificing all her metal currency in order to bring back, as usual, pepper, spices, drugs, cotton, linens, and silks. This was a regular and established trade (who would yet have suspected the voyage Vasco da Gama was about to make?) and, as it were, politically guaranteed. Syria and Egypt were united under the Mameluke state with its old commercial traditions. How could anyone have foreseen the victories of the Turks against the sultans of Cairo in 1516 and 1517? So Venice slept the sleep of the rich. She protested indeed against excessive luxury in women's dress, against the scandalous expenses incurred in festivities, and against embroidered coats for men. But who did not, like Sanudo, secretly admire the sumptuous dowries that were becoming the rule at patrician marriages, never less than 3000 ducats, sometimes over 10,000? A few shouts in front of the Palace of the Doges from galley crews demanding their wages, a few complaints from the poor men of the *Arte della Seta* or *della Lana*, and a pessimistic senatorial decree on the crisis in large shipbuilding cast the only shadows on an otherwise dazzling picture.

But the new century was to declare war on rich cities. Venice escaped by a miracle the storm of Agnadello in 1509. In turn, Genoa, Milan, and Florence suffered irreparable disasters. If the sack of Rome in 1527 had not surpassed all previous horrors, the sack of Genoa in 1522 would have the hideous reputation it deserves. Nothing was spared in the captured city, except – a significant detail – the bills of exchange of the merchants, which the soldiers respected on orders from above. Finally in 1528 Genoa went over to Charles V, sealing her fate. As for the Milanese, they shouted by turns, as they had to, 'Long live France', or 'Long live the Emperor', then learned to live under the Spanish as they had learned to live under the Sforza and before them the Visconti. In any case, under the control of the Spanish authorities a local administrative aristocracy remained in charge of Milan and Lombardy. All around might change, but their positions were safe.

In short the cities were not to be so easily eliminated from the land of the living and the powerful. The omens remained favourable at least until 1530. In the new constellation, in which Seville and Lisbon were in the ascendant, a chain of cities from Antwerp to Venice ruled the world, with Venice still maintaining her supremacy in the eastern Mediterranean, though not without difficulty. Her merchants were dispersed all over the world from Nuremberg to Hormuz. In 1569 a Neapolitan document gives us the names of *five hundred* Venetian merchants who bought wine and wheat in Apulia, principally at Bari. Towards 1600 the coffers of the Venetian state treasury were overflowing with money; seven or eight hundred ships went in and out of her port every year if our calculations are correct. And, above all, on the Rialto there was always an abundant supply of specie, perhaps the best stock in Christendom.

But this brilliant façade cannot entirely hide the truth. Venice, although she was perhaps even richer than during the fifteenth century, had declined in *relative* importance. She was no longer the centre of the Mediterranean. The commercial activity of the sea, concentrating more and more in the West, tipped the balance, spelling the inexorable decline of the eastern basin which had for so long been

137. Detail from *The Market in Genoa* by Alessandro Magnasco. *Museo Civico d'Arte Antica, Milan*

the source of wealth. The shift brought little joy to Milan, but brought Genoa and Florence to prominence. Genoa for her share, and a lion's share it was, acquired the Spanish and American trade; Florence promoted Lyons and took over France, without losing her position in Germany; she also had many representatives in Spain. These two cities were now the dominant forces in the quadrilateral, particularly since they did not confine their activity to commerce in the humble sense but became financial centres on a grand scale. In the second half of the century, Genoa moved into the lead.

With the establishment of the great exchange fairs at Piacenza in 1579, the Genoese bankers became the masters of international payments, of the fortune both of Europe and of the world, the not unchallenged but well-entrenched masters of the political silver of Spain, from 1579 or perhaps 1577 on. They could reach out and take anything they pleased. It looked for a moment in 1590 as if they were going to pounce on the Portuguese pepper privileges which were up for sale. 'Indeed', wrote a Spanish merchant living in Florence on hearing this (he disliked the Genoese), 'they are a kind of people who would think the world itself but a small thing to take on.' The 'age of the Fuggers', such a short one, was truly over and the age of the Genoese was belatedly beginning, not to end until the 1620s when the rise of the 'new Christians' of Portugal announced the hybrid capitalism of Amsterdam.

Thanks to fresh research, these broad historical perspectives are now more clearly visible. It was during the decisive years 1575–1579, after a spectacular trial of strength against Philip II and his advisers, that Genoese capitalism won the day. The fall of Antwerp, sacked by the army in 1576, the difficulties and failure of the fairs of Medina del Campo, the increased weakness of Lyons after 1583, were all signs accompanying the triumph of Genoa and the Piacenza fairs. From then on there could be no question of equality between Venice and Genoa, Florence and Genoa and *a fortiori* between Milan and Genoa. All doors were open to Genoa, all her neighbours dominated by her. They were only to take their revenge, if indeed at all, in the following century.

2 How many people?

Most important of all and the clearest indication both of the measure and the trend of the century is the number of people. First, how big was the population – a difficult question. Second, was it increasing as all the evidence seems to suggest – no less difficult to answer, particularly if one sets out to distinguish different stages and percentages of growth and to compare one population with another.

A world of 60 or 70 million people. There are no definite figures. Only approximate numbers can be given, reasonably reliable ones for Italy and Portugal, and not too unrealistic for France, Spain, and the Ottoman Empire. As for the other Mediterranean countries the lack of demographic data is total.

In the West the probable figures *at the end of the century* are the following: Spain, 8 million; Portugal, 1 million; France, 16 million; Italy, 13 million: a total population of 38 million. Then there are the Islamic countries. Konrad Olbricht (writing in 1939) accepted 8 million as an estimate of the population of the European part of Turkey in about 1600. Since the two parts of the Turkish empire, the Asian and the European, usually seem to have been equivalent (the latter if anything slightly superior), a figure of 8 million for the Asian part of Turkey is a reasonable assumption. We are now left with the whole of North Africa. Can we attribute 2 or 3 million to Egypt and about the same to North Africa? This would give us a maximum of 22 million for Islam and its dependent peoples on the shores of the Mediterranean. And the total population of the Mediterranean would be in the region of 60 million.

Of these figures, the first total, 38 million, is comparatively reliable, the second much less so. But the overall estimate is well within the bounds of probability. In this world of 60 million people, the density per square kilometre was about 17, if the desert is not included in the Mediterranean region. This is an incredibly low figure. Of course there were large differences from region to region. In 1595 the average population density of the Kingdom of Naples was 57 to the square kilometre; it was as high as 160 in Campania, around Mount Vesuvius. In about 1600 the population density in the area between the Ticino and the Mincio, the centre of gravity of the Italian population, was 100 to the square kilometre and sometimes even higher (117 in Cremona and the surrounding region; 110 in Milan and its rural districts and Lodi; 108 in the plain of Bergamo; 103 in the plain of Brescia); density decreased to the east and to the west (49 in Piedmont; 80 even in the rich region of Padua). The average density for the whole of Italy was 44, a very high figure; in France there was an average of only 34 inhabitants to the square kilometre, and in Spain and Portugal the figure was only 17.

Mediterranean waste lands. In fact population density was even lower than our figures suggest, since geographical space was so much vaster in relation to human settlement than it is now. We must imagine a population only about a third or a quarter the size of today's, scattered over a far more unmanageable area.

And there were waste lands. 'In Aragon, near the Pyrenean mountains', says a French account of 1617, 'one can walk for days on end without meeting a single inhabitant'. Similarly in Portugal, the population dwindled towards the south in the regions of Algarve, Alemtejo, and Beira. There were deserts even around Lisbon, fragrant with the perfumes of wild herbs. But every region in the Mediterranean had its wilderness, rang hollow. In Provence man has a 'quarter of the land, the low-lying basins which are oases with harvests, olive trees, vines, and ornamental cypresses. Nature has three quarters of the land, layered rocks, reddish-brown or silver grey'. And from these rocks man had to wrest the narrow belt along the foothills, the terraced hillsides where he practised a kind of farming requiring agility and mobility; little enough, but here as elsewhere, the peasant survived by working narrow strips of land.

138. *Peasants Hunting Rabbits with Ferrets*. Franco-Burgundian tapestry, 1460.
Burrell Collection, Glasgow

These depopulated lands yawned like gaping wounds to the south and east. Busbecq travelled through deserts in Asia Minor. Leo Africanus on his way from Morocco to Tlemcen had to cross the Moulouya desert where herds of gazelles fled away before the traveller.

No villages, no human dwellings. These territories were a haven of animal life. It is no surprise to find that the mountains were literally over-run with wild creatures. In Bayard's native Dauphiné, bears abounded. In Corsica in the sixteenth century huge boar-, stag-, and wolf-hunts had to be organized to protect the flocks, and the island exported wild beasts for the menageries of mainland princes. Hares, rabbits, and partridges were plentiful in Spain and this game was carefully guarded by royal keepers around the woods of Aranjuez. But the most plentiful game was foxes, wolves, and bears, even around Toledo, and Philip II in the very last days of his life went on a wolf hunt in the Sierra de Guadarrama.

A similar but even more exotic sight could be seen in North Africa. In October, 1573, Don John of Austria went to hunt lions and wild bulls on the very site of Carthage. A Spanish deserter trying to re-enter the *presidio* of La Goletta related that his travelling companion had been eaten by lions.

Even Italy, the image of prosperity in the sixteenth century, still had her wildernesses: forests, brigands, and wild beasts were plentiful in Boccaccio's time, and the body of one of Bandello's characters is abandoned without burial near Mantua to the wolves and wild dogs.

The wide, uninhabited areas of Islam help to explain its reputation for horse-breeding and consequently its military strength, for the Balkans and North Africa were protected from Christian Europe in the first place by their immensity and in the second place by their abundant supply of horses and camels. Following the advance of the Turks, the camel successfully conquered the great flat spaces of the Balkan peninsula, as far as the foothills of the Dinaric Alps to the west and to the north as far as Hungary. Sulaimān's army, encamped before Vienna in 1529, was brought supplies by camel. 'Door-ships', with doors for the embarkation of animals, continually ferried camels and horses over from Asia and Europe. Their comings and goings were part of the daily sights of the port at Constantinople. And we know that caravans of camels accomplished immense journeys in North Africa. Horses, donkeys, and mules took over in the mountains of the Balkans, Syria, Palestine, or on the routes from Cairo to Jerusalem.

The cavalry of any other country looked slow and clumsy in action against the Turks, of whom Botero wrote: 'if they beat you, you cannot escape from them by flight, if they scatter under your attack, you cannot follow them, for they are like hawks, they can either pounce upon you, or fly from you at great speed . . .'.

Quality and quantity: this double wealth was well-known. When Don John's advisers were discussing a landing in Morea and Albania, in December, 1571,

139. Horse fair in Constantinople. Sixteenth-century Venetian traveller's drawing.
Museo Correr, Venice

the prince was of the opinion that horses need not be shipped. It would be sufficient to take on board the requisite number of saddles and harnesses and enough money to buy the animals on landing. In Christendom, by contrast, even in the famous horse-breeding regions, such as Naples and Andalusia, horses were treasures jealously guarded and notoriously the subject of smuggling. Philip II would delegate to no one the duty of dealing with applications for export licences for Andalusian horses, personally examining every request.

In short, on one side there were too many people and not enough horses; on the other too many horses and not enough people. This imbalance may have been a reason for the tolerance exercised by Islam, only too eager indeed to receive men, of any origin, whenever they came within reach.

A population increase of 100 per cent? Everywhere in the sixteenth century mankind was on the increase, suggesting once again that Ernst Wagemann was right to insist that any large population increase must occur simultaneously throughout entire humanity. Stepping beyond the limit of prudence, for in this instance it is a bad counsellor, let us say that the population of the Mediterranean may by and large have doubled between 1500 and 1600. It rose from 30 or 35 million to 60 or 70 million, i.e., an *average* annual rate of increase of 7 per 1000. The very striking, and indeed revolutionary advance of the first sixteenth century (1450–1550) on the whole slowed down during the second (1550–1650) (approximate dates). This is the very general proposition I would make, without any guarantee of its soundness. This biological revolution was the major factor in all the other revolutions with which we are concerned, more important than the Turkish conquest, the discovery and colonization of America, or the imperial vocation of Spain. Had it not been for the increase in the population would any of these glorious chapters ever have been written? This revolution is more important too than the 'price revolution', of which it may have been a contributory factor even before the massive arrivals of bullion from America. This increase lay behind all the triumphs and catastrophes of a century during which man was first a useful worker and then, as the century wore on, a growing burden. By 1550 the turning-point had been reached. There were too many people for comfort. Towards 1600 this overload halted expansion in new directions and together with the rise of banditry, the latent social crisis whose effects were felt everywhere or almost everywhere, prepared the way for the bitter awakenings of the seventeenth century.

Another indicator: migration. If the Mediterranean had not been open on every side and particularly to the Atlantic in the west, it would have had to resolve the problem of a surplus population without recourse to the outside world, to absorb the extra mouths, by redistributing them throughout the area. And indeed this was partly what happened.

Proof of the overpopulation of Mediterranean Europe after the end of the fifteenth century appears in the frequent expulsions of the Jews, who were driven out of Castile and Portugal in 1492, from Sicily in 1493, from Naples in 1540 and 1541, from Tuscany in 1571, and finally from Milan in 1597. The largest group of these involuntary exiles, the Iberian Jews, were to go as far as Turkey, to Salonica, and Constantinople, and North Africa, where they settled. In countries whose population was too great for their resources, as the Iberian peninsula under Ferdinand and Isabella may already have been, religion was as much the pretext as the cause of this persecution. The law of numbers was later to operate against the Moriscos in Spain under Philip III and later again, as George Pariset long ago noted, against the Protestants in Louis XIV's France.

Further evidence is provided by the massive emigration from mountain regions to the plains and cities, already discussed at some length. Another pointer is the flow of men from Christendom to Islam which seems to have obeyed some law of equilibrium. Algiers, the city that sprang up on the 'American' pattern, was peopled almost entirely by immigrants. Emigration from Italy was responsible for the spread into northern Europe, the countries of Islam, and even the

Indies, of a skilled labour force of artisans, artists, merchants, and artillerymen. Venice, at the end of the century claims that 4000 or 5000 Venetian families were living in the Middle East. Here and there we find traces of these emigrations, such as the workers from Como who at the end of the sixteenth century left for Germany and Moravia; or the agricultural day-labourers who left Liguria in about 1587 for the plains of Corsica; or the 'technicians' whom one finds almost everywhere, particularly in France, bringing with them the manufacturing skills of the Italian peninsula, the weaving of gold and silk brocade, the secrets of glass-making from Murano or of majolica from Albissola. Italian inventors, artists, masons, and merchants travelled along every road in Europe. But how does one begin to draw up a list of all these individual adventurers or estimate the size of the persistent immigration, in the opposite direction, from Germany into Italy? Historians have been inclined to assume that in both cases only small numbers of people were involved. But small numbers can add up to a large total in the end, at least in sixteenth-century terms. A hundred thousand Spaniards are said to have left the Peninsula for America during this period; a hundred thousand spread over a century, about a thousand a year: not many by modern standards. But Vivero has strong words to say about it in 1632: 'The way things are going', he writes, 'Spain will soon be depopulated', and the Indies are in danger of being lost by these lazy newcomers (Vivero was born in New Spain and prejudiced). As soon as they arrive, 'Those who were cobblers want to be gentlemen of leisure and the labourers are unwilling to take up a pick . . .'. Clearly the problem was exaggerated by contemporaries and by all those who having seen Seville have reflected on the destiny of Spain in their own times.

On the other hand, there has been almost total silence on the subject of the stream of French immigrants into Spain, the scale of which in the sixteenth century has been revealed in recent studies. A typically overpopulated country, France continually dispatched artisans, itinerant merchants, water-carriers, and farm-workers to the neighbouring Peninsula. They came principally but not exclusively from the south of France. Catalonia received large contingents of these workers, who often settled there permanently; as early as August, 1536, a Spanish report notes that more than half the population of Perpignan was French, as was the majority of the Catalan population at the beginning of the seventeenth century. 'I have heard that there are a third as many Frenchmen again as natives of the place,' as a traveller says in 1602. The same writer, Joly, also remarks that there were arriving 'every day' in Catalonia people from 'Rouergue, Auvergne, Gévaudan, and Gascony'. The newcomers also went to Aragon, artisans attracted by the high wages 'because manufactured goods in Spain are dear', unskilled men, taken on as pages and then 'clad in livery, for these gentlemen [their masters] take great pleasure in such vanity', or peasants, who were even better received 'because of the indolence of the natives' – as our French informer tells us, adding 'they marry if they can their masters' widows'. All were in any case fleeing from the crippling French *tailles* – and all much

140. *Conquistadore.* Anonymous painting, early sixteenth century. *Prado, Madrid*

taken with the Spanish prostitutes, 'beautiful ladies, scented with musk, painted, and dressed like French princesses'.

It was not only to Catalonia and Aragon that they came. In Valencia, there were to be found among the shepherds and farmhands of the villages of the Old Christians, Frenchmen, arrived there who knows how. In Castile the Inquisition has plenty to tell us about the French artisans with their imprudent talk, the psalms they sing, their movements and the inns that are their regular rendezvous. If imprisoned, they will denounce each other. In this connection we find mention of every trade: weavers, cloth-croppers, tinkers, shovelmakers, blacksmiths, goldsmiths, locksmiths, cooks, roast-meat sellers, surgeons, gardeners, peasants, sailors, seacaptains, merchants or rather pedlars of books, professional beggars; often young men under twenty or twenty-five. One learns with astonishment of the journeys made right across France by these immigrants, like the group of printers of playing cards who left Rouen to meet a tragic fate at Toledo.

If this flow of immigrants dried up in about the 1620s, as has been suggested, it certainly started again later. From Béarn, says a text written in 1640, 'there passes every year a great quantity of haymakers, reapers, cattle gelders, and other workers who relieve their households of the burden of feeding them and bring back some profit to their families . . .'. It was not only from the Auvergne, as was still thought only recently, that these immigrants, whether temporary or permanent, set out for the employment and high wages in Spain. I think we may take it that these arrivals amply compensated the Peninsula for its losses to Italy and the Indies.

3 Is it possible to construct a model of the Mediterranean economy?

Have we enough material to measure the Mediterranean, to construct a comprehensive, quantitative 'model' of its economy? As a unit it could then be compared to other 'world-economies' either bordering on the Mediterranean or prolonging it geographically.

A model on this scale will provide at best some indication of orders of magnitude, the faintest of guide lines. It is simply one way of presenting the material. Such a model, if we can construct it, must aim to represent not any particular year or period but the century in its entirety, looking beyond times of crisis or of plenty. What it should convey, if at all possible, is the mean, the water-line, so to speak, of the successive phases of the century. We shall fall far short of our aim, but the attempt is worth making, despite the obstacles ahead.

Can it be said for a start that the Mediterranean is an internally coherent zone? On the whole the answer is yes, in spite of the indefinite and above all changeable boundaries both on its continental and on its seaward sides: the Black Sea, the Red Sea, the Persian Gulf, the Straits of Gibraltar, and the Atlantic

Ocean. These problems we have already discussed without reaching any hard and fast conclusion.

It was my original idea, in the first edition of this book, that the many dimensions of the Mediterranean in the sixteenth century could be suggested through a series of examples, by selecting certain important and indicative details: a city of 700,000 inhabitants, Constantinople; a grain fleet which every year, good or bad, ferried a million quintals of wheat or other cereals; the 3000 or so tons of wool which in 1580 lay on the quaysides of Leghorn; the estimated 100,000 combatants, both Turks and Christians, assembled in the gulf of Lepanto on 7th October, 1571; the 600 vessels (totalling perhaps 45,000 tons) that participated in Charles V's expedition against Tunis in 1535; the highest recorded level of shipping at Leghorn, 150,000 tons entering the port in 1592–1593, probably an exaggerated figure; or two rather different annual totals at Naples: 1,300,000 ducats of business transacted on the exchanges, against 60,000 or 70,000 in insurance. But this would mean leaving enormous blank spaces between the specks of colour; at best, it would only give an impressionistic notion of the distance that separates our world from that of the sixteenth century.

Today, on the other hand, I am more attracted towards the language of what economists call 'national accounting'. I should like to try to draw up a tentative balance sheet of the Mediterranean in the sixteenth century, not in order to judge its relative backwardness or modernity but to determine the relative proportions and relationships between the different sectors of its activity, in short, to form a picture of the major structures of its material life: a difficult and hazardous project. The risks involved will be apparent to any economist who has studied the economies of underdeveloped countries which have never been fully penetrated by the monetary economy. The same was true everywhere in the sixteenth century. And the variety of currencies, real and artificial, complicate any calculations, even when precise data is available, which of course it usually is not. We also have to bear in mind the casual way in which contemporary records refer to ducats or crowns in Spain, ducats, crowns, or florins in France.

There were of course many kinds of ducats, Venetian, Genoese, Florentine, Neapolitan, and Spanish . . . Each had its own particular and by no means fixed value. These ducats were *all*, sooner or later to become moneys of account. It would be logical, rather than to speak simply of ducats unspecified, to calculate the equivalent in gold or silver. Contemporary writers when estimating sums of money simply refer to 'millions of gold', that is millions of ducats. In the documents of the financial authorities of Spain, the abbreviation for the ducat is a triangle, the letter delta $\triangle$; for the gold *escudo*, real money, a triangle upside down $\triangledown$. The relation of the ducat to the *escudo* in Spain was for a long time 350 *maravedis* (ducat) to 400 (*escudo*). Businessmen were of course well aware of the relative values of ducats (of different kinds) and crowns, especially since the exchange rates on the money market varied according to supply and demand.

However, all this having been said, we can still accept the ducat for the purposes of our extremely approximate calculations as a valid unit without reference either to its local value or the exchange rate. Any errors this may contain will be absorbed by the highly approximate nature of all our figures.

Agriculture, the major industry. It is generally admitted that the annual per capita consumption of wheat (and other cereals) was of the order of two (present day) quintals. (The modern quintal is equivalent to 100kg (220·5 lbs).) This figure obviously conceals wide variations in actual consumption. But as an average it will do on the whole for the Mediterranean in the sixteenth century. If the population was 60 million, the total annual consumption of wheat or other *bread crops* must have been about 120 million quintals. Other foodstuffs, meat, fish, olive oil, and wine were merely complementary to the staple diet. If we take the average price of the quintal in about 1600 to be 5 or 4 Venetian ducats, Mediterranean consumption (assumed equal to production) must have reached 480 or 600 million ducats every year, in other words a level out of all proportion to the odd 'six millions in gold' that arrived every year at Seville. Grain alone establishes the overwhelming superiority of agricultural production over all others. Agriculture was the leading industry of the Mediterranean, and of course cereals accounted for only part of agricultural revenue.

The preceding estimate is no more than a lower limit. The figures one encoun-

141. The produce of the land and its flocks offered by the shepherds. Detail from *The Adoration of the Shepherds*, ascribed to Murillo. *National Gallery, London*

ters in the course of research are often higher. Venice, for instance, in about 1600 was consuming, both in good years and bad, about 500,000 *staia* of wheat (as well as rice, millet, and rye). The population of the city then stood at about 140,000, plus another 50,000 in adjoining territories (the *Dogado*), i.e., a total population of 200,000 inhabitants and an individual rate of consumption of 4 quintals if the figures refer only to the city and 3·1 quintals if the whole area is included. At 2 quintals per person, the supply would have fed 300,000 inhabitants. Perhaps the actual number of consumers was indeed higher than our figures suggest. Or perhaps Venice, a city with high wages, consumed more than others. Figures, here omitted, are adduced from Spain and the Spanish possessions in Italy during the sixteenth, seventeenth and eighteenth centuries to support the general argument: but the author emphasizes that they fall short of proof. There may have been local variations then, but since we are reasonably certain of the overall total, let us turn to some of its consequences:

1. Wheat shipped by sea totalled at most 1 million quintals, or 8 per cent of consumption – which is a large volume of trade for the period (a million people might depend on it), but insignificant as a proportion of total consumption. So Gino Luzzatto is justified in minimizing it while I was justified in giving it prominence in the first edition of this book. The dramatic crisis of 1591, of which we shall have more to say, resulted in the arrival in Spain and Italy, even Venice, of between 100,000 and 200,000 quintals of northern wheat, a large quantity in terms of transport, very little in relation to everyday consumption. However it was enough to save whole towns from starvation.

But both before and after this crisis, the Mediterranean was able to live largely off its own agricultural produce. No pattern was to emerge here comparable to that developing in the Low Countries, in the case of Amsterdam, or which was much later to be wholeheartedly adopted by England under free trade. Urban centres did not rely on outside sources of food. 'Wheat from overseas' remained a last resort, to rescue the poor, rich consumers preferring the good grain of the nearby countryside: in Lisbon the reputed wheat of the Alemtejo; in Marseilles the grain of the Provençal plains; in Venice the grain they called *nostrale*. 'We are now being given', say the Venetian bakers in 1601, 'grain from outside that does not produce such good results as ours', by which they meant Paduan, Trevisan, Po Valley and Friuli grain. Even grains accounted *forestieri* (foreign) were most often produced in the Mediterranean.

2. Agriculture not only assured the Mediterranean of its everyday livelihood, but also provided a range of costly goods for export, sometimes in limited quantities, such as saffron and cumin, but sometimes amounting to a large volume, such as the so-called Corinth raisins, the *uve passe*, choice wines like malmsey that continued to be highly prized until the appearance of port, Malaga and Madeira; or the wines from the islands and ordinary table wines which a thirsty German market imported every year, after the grape harvest, from the southern side of the Alps. Soon there were to be spirits – which make their first

appearance on the customs registers of Venice during the final years of the sixteenth century – not to mention olive oil, the fruits of the south, oranges, lemons, raw silk. This surplus combined with manufactured exports to pay for the purchases of grain, dried fish, or sugar from the Atlantic (as well as the lead, copper, and tin of the North) and as late as 1607 the balance of payments between Venice and Holland was still favourable to Venice, according to the *Cinque Savii.*

142, 143. Italian peasants by G. Boetto, 1634.

3. So the Mediterranean remained a world of peasants and landlords, a world of rigid structures. Methods of farming, the balance maintained between different crops, or between crops in general and the meagre pasturelands or the vines and olives that were both making rapid progress (in Andalusia, Portugal, and Castile for instance, even more on the Venetian islands), changed very little unless there was persistent pressure from outside. It was the demand from the colonies that led to increased oil and wine production in Andalusia. And there was to be no 'internal' revolution until the introduction of maize, which arrived

first it seems in the Basque provinces and in Morocco and took longer to reach other places. It did not appear in the Venetian countryside before 1600 or in the northern Tyrol before 1615. The revolution of the more easily assimilated mulberry tree occurred earlier.

4. Land continued to be the most coveted of possessions. The whole country-side both inside and outside the Mediterranean region was a bewildering tangle of rents, *censos*, mortgages, tenancies, ground-rents, with numerous entailed properties, and a continual coming and going of money loans and repayments between town and countryside. Everywhere it was the same monotonous story. In the countryside around Geneva, about which evidence has recently become available, it is possible to detect a very short-term circulation of money from the fifteenth century on, a decisive factor 'in a closed-circuit economy that was permanently out of breath', where the usury practised by townsfolk did not (in a Protestant country) have to be disguised under cover of rent and quit-rent. A sixteenth-century Spanish *arbitrista*, Miguel Caxa de Leruela, refers to the natural tendency to invest money in land or vineyards near the town. 'As every man could see that a capital of 2000 ducats brought in 200 a year in return, and that the capital was repaid at the end of ten years, it seemed to them a good investment.' Commerce or government loans rarely offered lenders such good returns. So land competed with them for capital, land which was such a solid and visible guarantee (if the peasant could not pay the interest or did not repay the capital the land was repossessed). And the investor could always see with his own eyes how his money was bearing fruit on vine or in farmhouse. Such security was worth a great deal. And since agriculture was the greatest single source of revenue in the Mediterranean, an immense amount of wealth was tied up in this sector. So there is no reason to doubt Valle de la Cerda's statement in 1618 that there were in Spain over a hundred million ducats lent in *ducados a censos*.

5. The enormous cereal bill of 400 or 600 million ducats may seem either too much or too little, depending on the angle from which it is viewed. Cereals can have represented only half of the agricultural 'product' if one accepts the proportions recently established for France (in the eighteenth century it is true), and for Spain in 1799. So it is possible to talk in very general terms of a total agricultural production of 800,000 to 1,200 million ducats. It must be stressed that this is a very tentative estimate. The prices on the Venetian market from which we started are high, representative only of the economy of a rich city. Second, and most important, not all the grain that was consumed went on to the market. So our estimate remains extremely theoretical and could hardly be otherwise. Certain Castilian villages in 1576 are calculated to have consumed 26,000 quintals of the 60,000 they produced, that is about 50 per cent; but the other half did not necessarily go on to the market: some of it went straight into the tithe barns or granaries of urban landlords. So 60 per cent or perhaps 70 per cent of the overall production of the Mediterranean never entered the money economy to which our methods of accounting mistakenly seek to assimilate it.

6. The fact that a large percentage of the agricultural product remained outside the monetary economy with its comparative flexibility, increased the inelasticity of what was, in the Mediterranean and elsewhere the predominant economic activity. Techniques and yields, moreover, were undistinguished. Even in the eighteenth century in Provence, the seed sown was still giving a yield of only 5 to 1, and this can probably be assumed as the average yield in the sixteenth century. To obtain an annual product of 120 million quintals – assuming one quintal of seed-corn to the hectare – at least 24 million hectares of Mediterranean land must have been under the plough: an enormous area when one remembers that 24 million hectares in any one year meant, under a two-field system, an available area of 48 million hectares (one field lying fallow for every one under crops), and when one is told that in 1600 the *total* arable surface in France was 32 million hectares.

These calculations must be very tentative and the suggested figures are probably too low, for wheat (and other cereals) were not always in biennial rotation. Some land was only cultivated every three, four, or even ten years. And it is true that yields higher than 5 to 1 have been recorded.

In Cyprus, where 1/20th of the land was cultivated, the wheat yield was 6 to 1, barley 8 to 1. In Apulia, on the new lands taken over from time to time from sheep-farming, grain could give yields of 15 to 20 to 1. But these were exceptional. And there were bad harvests and catastrophes. Climatic conditions continued to be the principal factor and man's unaided efforts, however determined, could not always bring him fortune. So there was inelasticity in agriculture. The figures we have for agricultural exports, which bear a certain relation to production when they compose fairly long series, generally show a constant level, whether of wool exported from Spain to Italy or wheat and silk sent to outside markets by Sicily, graphically represented by a set of lines roughly parallel to the x-axis.

Progress was sometimes possible. Technically, the replacement of oxen by mules in Castile meant that ploughing could be done faster and the wheat yield depended on the number of ploughings. But this replacement was by no means general. The northern plough made its appearance in the sixteenth century in Languedoc, where its role remained modest, and probably in northern Italy, but the swing-plough, which neither adequately turned nor aired the soil, continued in general use.

We have already discussed the improvements brought about by land reclamation schemes. There is no doubt that during the fifteenth century, when the population was small, new land became available to the peasants of the Mediterranean. It was a time of expansion, or rather of recovery of a former prosperity, that of the thirteenth century. An agricultural revolution undoubtedly preceded and supported all the expansionist movements of the sixteenth century as Ruggiero Romano has rightly argued. But in the end this forward movement was brought to a halt by the very inelasticity of agriculture, under the same conditions as in the thirteenth century. The reclaimed land often gave an inferior yield. The number of mouths to feed was increasing more quickly than the resources and the logic of later Malthusian arguments was already visible.

The entire secular trend reversed direction perhaps as early as 1550, more certainly towards 1580. The foundations of a crisis were being laid, just as the improved circulation of silver (let us avoid for the moment calling it the silver revolution) was gathering speed. Historians of Spain are inclined to think that sooner or later agricultural investment ran into difficulties, peasants found it less easy to obtain credit, unpaid creditors seized the property, and even the big landowners themselves were affected by the financial crisis of the years 1575–1579, when the Genoese let their own creditors bear the brunt of their losses, as we shall see. These and other explanations (in the case of Languedoc, for instance) are both credible and valid. But the basic explanation must lie in the inelasticity of agricultural production. It had reached its ceiling and the result of this impasse was to be the 'refeudalization' of the seventeenth century, an agricultural revolution in reverse.

An industrial balance sheet. John U. Nef, writing of Europe at the beginning of the seventeenth century, reckoned that out of a total population of 70 million there must have been two or three million artisans. A similar figure could therefore in theory be advanced for the Mediterranean world with its 60 to 70 million inhabitants. But if the towns represent roughly 10 per cent of the population, that is about 6 or 7 million people, it is unlikely that two or three million of these, between a third and a half of the total, were actually artisans. In one particular example, Venice, it is not difficult to reach this kind of proportion: 3000 workers at the Arsenal, 5000 *lanaioli* (of whom 3300 were weavers, with a ratio of one master weaver to two men), 5000 *setaioli* (apparently equal in number to the *lanaioli*, which must be an exaggeration), that is, 13,000 artisans, with their families 50,000 people, out of the total Venetian population of 140,000. And of course there were all the artisans in the many private shipyards whose names and occupations we know, as well as the army of masons, the *muratori*, for the city was continually being built and rebuilt, wood was being replaced with stone and brick, and the *rii*, which were prone to silt up, had to be dredged. And we should include the fullers of cloth near Venice at Mestre for example. A little further outside were the millworkers who ground the grain, tore up rags for paper, or sawed up planks and beams for the great city. One should also include the coppersmiths, blacksmiths, goldsmiths, workers in the sugar refineries, the glassmakers of Murano, stonecutters, and leather-workers, the latter on the Giudecca. And there were many more. Not to mention the printers, for Venice in the sixteenth century produced a large proportion of Europe's printed books.

Then there was the countryside. The possibility must be envisaged that in

144. A stonemason. Detail from *The Tower of Babel*
by Leonardo Bassano. *National Gallery, London.*

the sixteenth century rural industry, *in terms of the number of people involved,*
if not of quality or total revenue, was the equal of urban industry. This can
neither be confirmed nor contradicted. The entire manufacturing community
serving the Mediterranean market economy may have consisted of at most three
million country people and three million of the less well-off townsfolk. Of these
perhaps 1,500,000 were active workers. Let us suppose that their average wages
were equivalent to those received by the mine workers in the copper mines that
Venice possessed at Agordo, that is, 15 *soldi* a day or 20 ducats a year (feast-days
were holidays but paid). The total wage-bill would be something like 30 million
ducats. This is probably too low, for urban rates were much higher (and it was
indeed from excessively high wages that urban industry sometimes collapsed).
At Venice a worker in the *Arte della Lana* at the end of the century was earning
144 ducats a year and asking for more. So our figures should or could be raised
to 40 or 50 million. Finally, and this time it is practically a leap in the dark, if
we reckon the value of industrial *production* as three or four times the total sum
paid out in wages, we would get a maximum total of 200 million ducats. Even
if this figure were multiplied further, it would still remain far below the 860 or
1200 million at which we have *hypothetically* estimated agricultural production.

145. *The Woollen Factory* by Mirabello Cavalori. Studiolo of Francesco de' Medici.
Palazzo Vecchio, Florence

The putting-out or 'Verlag' system and the rise of urban industry. From about 1520–1540 there began a decisive period of expansion of urban industry in the Mediterranean, as capitalism gained its second wind both in the Mediterranean and Europe. Commercial capitalism, its heyday past, was being succeeded by an industrial capitalism that was to realize its full potential only with the latter, 'metallic' phase of the century. Industry compensated for recession elsewhere.

Almost everywhere (where it can be observed) this industry was of a capitalist nature, conforming to the familiar pattern of the *Verlagssystem* (the domestic or putting-out system): the merchant, the entrepreneur, or *Verleger*, puts out to the artisan the material to be worked on for a salary. This system was not new in the sixteenth century, but during the period it spread to places where it had previously been unknown (such as Castile apparently) or where it had been little practised (such as Venice). Wherever it was introduced it struck a blow against the guilds, the Italian *arti*, the Spanish *gremios*. Wherever it was introduced it benefited the merchant class which financed the slow production process and kept the profits from sales and exports. The role of these merchants 'qui faciunt laborare' was even more crucial in the relatively new process of silk manufacture than in the longer established production of woollens. Concentrations of looms were of course quite visible in the vast workshops, at Genoa for instance where no effort was apparently made to stop this concentration; or even at Venice, where it was already provoking protests and government intervention. The law of 12th December, 1497, had forbidden any silk-manufacturer to employ more than six *tellari*. The question was raised again in 1559, when attention was drawn to 'the greed of certain persons who since they have twenty or twenty-five looms working are causing evident inequalities'.

The merchant then would advance the raw materials and money for wages, and handle sales of the finished product himself. The whole system can be reconstructed from the slightest significant detail. We are in Venice in the winter of 1530: Charles V's ambassador, Rodrigo Nino, has been charged by his master to order silk fabrics, green, blue, red, and crimson damask, and crimson velvet. He will send some samples he says and negotiate about the price, but in any case once the order is placed 1000 ducats must be advanced and the balance will be paid when the work is finished. For the weaver must buy the silk from the merchant, who has is brought from Turkey in skeins and then made up at his expense. In this case, the purchaser is taking the merchant's place, so it is he who must advance the raw material, in the form of money. A minor incident at Cattaro in August, 1559, is even more revealing. In this lonely corner of the sea the *filatogi* had taken to working raw silk which they bought directly, contravening the law of 1547 that forbade spinners to work *per conto suo*. Order must be reintroduced, decided the Senate: the *filatogi* must from now on spin only silk belonging to the merchants so that the latter will not have to buy spun thread at prices decided by these over-independent *filatogi* – a crystal-clear example.

An itinerant labour force. The artisan community in the sixteenth century was made up of many races, rarely native to the area. Florentine crafts employed workmen from Flanders and Brabant in the fourteenth century. In the sixteenth century the apprentices of the *Arte della Lana* at Florence were recruited over a large area extending well beyond the borders of Tuscany as we have already noted. At Verona, which had obtained from the Signoria of Venice the right to manufacture *velluti neri* there were twenty-five master craftsmen in 1561: not one of them was Venetian (something the Signoria would never have tolerated); fourteen came from Genoa, three from Mantua, two from Verona, two from Brescia, one from Vicenza, and one from Ferrara. As for the merchants 'che li fanno lavorare', there were only four of them: two from Verona and two from Genoa. This affords a glimpse of the mobility of both artisan and merchant classes.

For industry followed the merchants, or rather their capital: Tommaso Contarini, who was travelling in the spring of 1610 to England as Venetian ambassador, stopped first at Verona, then on his way to Trent passed through Rovereto. He found to his astonishment in this little place an active *negocio delle sede* with a good number of *filatogi* and over 300 'telleri che lavorano ormesini': these workers had left Verona. Four years later, in May, 1614, the Signoria of Venice accepted the following extraordinary proposition. In return for the services of the anonymous person who had advanced it, in reporting to the authorities any workers or master craftsmen in important sectors of the city's industry, and in particular in the *Arte delle Seta*, 'che intendono partire', he would be granted the release of a *bandito*, an outlaw or a brigand who was, of course, in prison. Similarly, during the same period, Venice threatened reprisals on the persons or the possessions of any workers or master craftsmen in her sugar refineries ('practico o professore di raffinare zuccari') who left the city to exercise their trade elsewhere.

The volume of commercial transactions. Commerce is a many sided activity. It will not fit easily into our calculations. 'Commerce' can mean the fruit that a peasant woman takes to market or the glass of wine which a poor man drinks at the door of the rich man's cellar (for the wealthy often indulged in this kind of retail trade) or it can mean the goods handled by the Venetian *galere da mercato* or the *Casa de la Contratación* at Seville. The range of activities it may embrace is immense. Besides, in the sixteenth century all goods were not commercially handled, far from it. The market economy covered only a fraction of economic life. More primitive forms – barter and autarky – rivalled it everywhere. If one accepts the view that commerce is the final stage of the production process, in other words, that it adds surplus value to the goods it transports, one must recognize that this plus-value, and especially profits, are difficult to estimate, even in an example on which we are apparently well-informed. In the 1560s something like 20,000 quintals of pepper were annually transported to

RVSTICA MVLIER GALLICA.

146. French peasant woman going to
market. Woodcut from Hans Weigel,
Trachtenbuch, Nuremberg, 1577.

Europe from India and the East Indies. It was bought in Calicut for 5 *cruzados* per light quintal, and sold at Lisbon for 64, that is at twelve times the price. It was clearly more than a simple matter of the same individual buying and selling: the cost of transport, taxation, and risks involved were both very great and variable and we do not know how much of the 1,300,000 *cruzados* selling price went into the merchant's pocket.

Handling merchandise was moreover only one of the occupations of the sixteenth century 'merchant', as is clear from his books, clearer still from the countless bankruptcy records. Every kind of operation and speculation appears there higgledy-piggledy: purchases of land or houses, industrial investment, banking, marine insurance, lotteries, urban rents, peasants' quit-rents, stock-farming, advances from the loan banks (*Monti de Pietà*), speculation on the foreign exchanges.

Gambling held an important place not only in the life of the nobility (particularly towards the end of the century), but also in the lives of merchants. Any subject was a pretext for a wager, the number of cardinals to be promoted, the death or survival of famous men, the sex of unborn children. At Venice, when it was odds on that the French had captured Pavia, a Spaniard, Calzeran, insisted on wagering on the opposite. He was no doubt in touch with Lannoy or Pescara, in any case he won a fortune.

Actual transactions involving merchandise and artificial transactions on the money market figure side by side. The importance of purely financial transactions, with all their sophisticated ramifications, increases the further one goes up the scale of merchants and with the passing of the relatively prosperous years of the late sixteenth century. It was becoming widely known that commercial operations could be settled at the fairs almost *miraculously*. In 1550 de Rubis talks of the Lyons fairs where 'a million pounds can be paid sometimes in a morning without a single sou changing hands'. Fifty years later, Giovan Battista Pereti, who kept the *giornale* of exchanges at the Banco di Rialto, explains in a report to the Signoria of Venice, that 3 or 4 million crowns' worth of business is transacted at every Piacenza fair, and that most of the time 'non vi è un quatrino de contanti'.

The significance and limitations of long distance trade. The *raison d'être* of long distance trade is that it connects, sometimes with difficulty, regions where goods can be bought cheaply with others where they can be sold for high prices: buying kerseys or having them made in the Cotswolds, for example, and selling them in Aleppo or Persia; or buying linen cloth in Bohemia and selling it in Lisbon, Venice, or Lübeck. To make them worthwhile, these long journeys presupposed wide differences in ecomonic levels, indeed enormous differences at the beginning of the sixteenth century, particularly at Lisbon, where commercial profits sprouted like tropical plants. As Porchnev said of Baltic trade in the seventeenth century, what counted was not so much the volume of trade as the ultimate rate of profit. Capitalism in its agile youth (for it was now the most modern and wideawake economic force) was attracted by these high profits and their rapid rate of accumulation. In the long run of course all differences in price levels tend to be eliminated, particularly when business is good. Long distance trade then has to change its options. So there were periods when it was more or less profitable: very profitable was the first half of the sixteenth century; profits levelled off in the second half; and there was renewed prosperity in the seventeenth century. It was the relative slump in trade that no doubt encouraged so many businessmen to invest their money in government loans and on foreign exchanges, culminating in a kind of financial capitalism in the second half of the sixteenth century. Let it be understood that there is no question of a drop in the volume of trade, which indeed continued to increase during this period. Our remarks apply exclusively to the *profits* obtained by the larger merchants.

The historian Jacques Heers has protested against the exaggerated importance usually attributed to the spice and drug trades, which are sometimes spoken of as if they far outweighed any other traffic in the sixteenth century. 'When the history comes to be written not only of the alum trade but of the trade in wine and grain, salt, cotton and even sugar and silk', he writes, 'we shall see a very different economic history of the Mediterranean world emerge, in which pepper and drugs will only play a very minor role, particularly after the fourteenth century . . .' It all depends which way one looks at it. From the point of view of economic geography, Heers is right. From the point of view of the history of the rise of capitalism and of profits he is wrong. We should remember Porchnev's observation. In the area with which we are concerned the only thing that matters is the rate and facility of gain, the accumulation of capital. There is no doubt at all that in turnover the grain trade far outweighed pepper. But Simón Ruiz was unwilling to commit himself to buying grain, because it was riskier for the merchant. Grain was not like pepper or cochineal, a 'royal merchandise' and a relatively safe risk. When dealing in grain one had to reckon with the demands of transporters, and the vigilance of states and cities. Except when large sums of money were involved, as in 1521 or 1583 or on the occasion of the massive purchases of 1590–1591, large scale capitalism did not participate in any regular way in the grain trade, at least during the second half of the century; nor always in the closely supervised salt trade.

So at the top commercial capitalism consisted of a series of careful choices; or one might describe it as a system of supervision and control, intervening only when large profits were assured. An entire 'strategy' can be glimpsed, sometimes even emerging into broad daylight, intervening in one place then another according to variations in the price of commodities and also to the degree of risk involved. One often stood to gain more but also to lose more by handling merchandise than by playing the money markets. Giovanni Domenico Peri, who is a reliable informant, tells us that 'there is often more profit to be made with 1000 crowns in merchandise than with 10,000 crowns on the exchanges'. But we know that on the exchanges businessmen were more likely to risk other people's money than their own and that the transfer of huge sums of money was concentrated in a few hands. No doubt greater overall gains could be made on the 5 million ducats that the sea-borne grain trade represented in the Mediterranean at the end of the century than on the million ducats that pepper from Asia may have been worth on its arrival in Europe. But in the one case literally thousands of parties were involved, in the other a few powerful combines dominated the market. It was in their favour that the accumulation of capital operated. In 1627 the Portuguese *Marranos* who ousted the Genoese bankers were after all originally spice and pepper merchants.

The total tonnage of Mediterranean shipping. We have little in the way of reliable figures to help us estimate the total tonnage of shipping in the Mediterranean. England, France, the rebel provinces of the Netherlands, and Spain each possessed in about the 1580s about 200,000 tons of shipping, the Netherlands probably more (an estimated 225,000 tons in 1570), the three others certainly less, Spain something in the region of 175,000 (estimates in 1588), France and England considerably less, but we do not know exactly how much. If we accept

147. Grain export. Detail from *The Life of St. Nicola da Bari* by Ambrogio Lorenzetti. *Uffizi, Florence*

the total of 4000 ships given by Saint-Gouard (he says between 4000 and 5000 ships) for the whole of the French fleet, and if we accept an average tonnage per vessel of 40 or 50 tons, the minimum estimate would be 160,000 tons. If we accept that in 1588 the English fleet consisted of 2000 ships, the highest possible figure would be 100,000 tons. It is true that according to the same source the figure in 1629 was 200,000 tons, following the expansion of English shipbuilding. So in the Atlantic there were perhaps 600,000 or 700,000 tons, not counting other northern navies or the ships in Mediterranean ports in France and Spain. But we need go into no further detail since the tonnage of Atlantic shipping is only marginal to the central issue.

If we now try to calculate the tonnage of Mediterranean shipping during the last thirty years of the century, we can first of all include a third at most of the Spanish fleet, 60,000 tons. The Venetian shipping fleet in 1605 according to fairly reliable figures consisted of 19,000 tons in big ships only, and a total of 30,000 or 40,000 tons for all classes of ship. The same figure of 40,000 tons can be accredited to Ragusa, Genoa, and Marseilles, to the fleet of Naples and Sicily and double that for the Turkish empire, i.e., a maximum of 280,000 tons which, added to Spain's 60,000, gives a total figure for the Mediterranean of rather under 350,000 tons. Even so the disproportion between the sea and the ocean is not too ludicrous: 300,000 or 350,000 on one side and 600,000 or 700,000 on the other, that is a ratio of 1 to 2. On one side the not insignificant Mediterranean, and on the other the Atlantic and the Seven Seas. And voyages within the Mediterranean were of course more frequent than those on the oceanic routes. A Ragusan vessel could easily make two or three voyages a year.

Should we include as 'Mediterranean' shipping the northern vessels that appeared there after the 1570s, possibly a hundred in number, that is at about 100 or 200 tons per ship, a total of 10,000 or 20,000 tons? It does not greatly signify: this tonnage is to the Mediterranean tonnage as 1 to 15 or 1 to 35; not much at most. Nor have we counted the hundred or so roundships of the Barbary corsairs, which may have totalled 10,000 tons at the beginning of the seventeenth century.

The figure of 300,000 or 350,000 thus reached is far from certain, but this calculation does establish: 1) that the Mediterranean was predominantly the province of Mediterranean vessels and their crews; 2) that the northerners were an anomaly; their presence did not drastically alter the structure of Mediterranean shipping, which as we have seen was solidly based; 3) that at least half of these northern ships were in any case in the service of Mediterranean cities and economies, sailing round the sea from port to port, picking up cargoes, leaving through the Straits of Gibraltar now and then, to return later the same way. So let us neither exaggerate nor minimize the role of these intruders which were in fact serving cities too rich to be self-sufficient.

The state: the principal entrepreneur of the century. The state in the sixteenth century was increasingly emerging as the great collector and redistributor of revenue; it derived income from taxation, the sale of offices, government bonds, and confiscation, an enormous share of the various 'national products'. This multiple seizure of funds was effective because state budgets on the whole fluctuated with short-term economic change and followed the rising tide of prices. So the rise of the state is in the mainstream of economic development, neither an accident, nor an untimely force, as Joseph A. Schumpeter was perhaps a little too ready to believe. Whether intentionally or not the state became the principal entrepreneur of the century. It was on the state that modern warfare depended, with its constantly increasing requirements in manpower and money; as did the biggest economic enterprises: the Seville-based *Carrera de Indias*, the shipping route between Lisbon and the East Indies, for which the *Casa da India*, in other words the king of Portugal, was responsible.

The *Carrera de Indias* worked, *mutatis mutandis*, on the same principle as the Venetian *galere da mercato*, proof that this form of state capitalism was beyond its initial stages. In the Mediterranean state capitalism was indeed to remain very active: the Arsenal at Venice and its copy, the double arsenal at Galata, were the greatest centres of manufacture in the known world. Also dependent on the state were all the mints that were at work both in Christendom and Islam, in Christendom often under direct state control. They were farmed out but strictly supervised in the Turkish Empire or the Regency of Algiers. Dependent on the state too were the public banks whose hour of glory came at the end of the century, as we shall see. Here it was the city-states, or at any rate states of a predominantly urban character that led the way. The territorial states had some time to wait, and the first of their banks was in fact to be the Bank of England in 1694. Philip II paid no heed to the advice of the Fleming Peter van Oudegherste, who first tried to persuade him to create a state bank in 1576.

This gap does not prevent the list of 'public' works from being very long. As a historian has pointed out, the huge installations set up by the Papal government at Tolfa and Alumiere for the extraction of alum were in fact an 'industrial complex'. The Turkish government itself, outstandingly *dirigiste*, was responsible for many works; the rapid construction of the Sulaimāniye mosque (and we now have an excellent recent study of work on the huge building site) is a good example. If we extended the label state capitalism in the west to such mixed enterprises, part public, part private, as the building of the Escorial, with its remarkable constructional techniques, the list would be even longer. Through all these activities the state put back into circulation the money that arrived in its coffers, and in order to meet the demands of wars even overspent its income. War, public works, and state enterprises were therefore more of an economic stimulus than might be supposed. What was disastrous for the economy was when money piled up in the state coffers, in the treasury that Sixtus V amassed in the Castel Sant' Angelo, in the coffers of the Zecca at Venice or in those of Sully at the Arsenal.

All this having been said, it will not be too difficult to calculate the wealth of the states. We already know a good deal about their budgets and we can fairly easily find out more. If we accept the following figures for the end of the century: 9 million gold ducats for Castile, 5 million for France under Henry IV, 3·9 million for Venice and her Empire, 6 million for the Turkish Empire, that is 24 million for a population of about 30 million, and if we multiply this figure by two to correspond to the 60 million inhabitants of the Mediterranean as a whole, we arrive at the no doubt artificial total of 48 million. On this showing, a man contributed rather less than a ducat a year to his ruler (and a ducat to his landlord too, no doubt).

I am sure that this figure, after the huge sums we have been conjuring with, will appear very low. Was the mighty state, striding across the stage of history, no more than this? And yet these figures are probably the most reliable of any yet mentioned. But it must be borne in mind that all the states, even the Turkish Empire, had moved beyond the primitive economy. Their yearly tribute was exacted from the 'fast-flowing blood' of the circulation of metal currencies, whereas all the other estimates we have so far given are a translation into monetary terms of transactions which for a very large part escaped the market economy. So these states had the flexibility of the modern economy. The modern state had just been born, both fully armed and unarmed, for it was not yet sufficient to its task. In order to make war, collect taxes, administer its own affairs, and conduct justice, it was dependent on businessmen and the bourgeoisie hungry for social advancement. But even this is a sign of its new energy. In Castile (which is a particularly clear example) everyone participated in state enterprise: merchants, noblemen, and *letrados*. The competition for honours and profits had begun. And a competition for hard work too. From even the humblest secretaries of the *Consejo de Hacienda y Junta de Hacienda* we have reports, letters, proof of their devotion to the king and the public good, alongside requests and denunciations dictated by self-interest.

Whether the rise of the state was beneficial remains an open question. It was in any case inevitable, just as the sharp-eyed capitalism of the merchants was inevitable. An unprecedented concentration of resources operated to the advantage of the prince. Forty or fifty million ducats (an actual figure this time, not a tentative estimate) was an extraordinary lever to have at one's command.

Precious metals and the monetary economy. In history as in other scientific disciplines, classic explanations lose their force after a time. We no longer regard the sixteenth century as a period characterized by the tumult of precious metals and prices, the view of François Simiand. Frank Spooner and I put forward a tentative estimate of the total amount of metal money in circulation in Europe and the Mediterranean *before the discovery of America*. The figure we obtained, based on simple but unverifiable equations, was an approximate total of 5000 tons of gold and 60,000 of silver. The arrivals of bullion from America during the century and a half between 1500 and 1650 according to Hamilton amount to 16,000 tons of silver and 180 of gold.

Simiand thought American minerals were the decisive factor. The stock of bullion according to him doubled between 1500 and 1520, doubled again between 1520 and 1550, and more than doubled between 1550 and 1600. 'Over the whole sixteenth century,' he wrote, 'this stock therefore increased more than five-fold. In the seventeenth century by contrast, as well as the eighteenth and the first half of the nineteenth, stocks barely doubled over any hundred year period.' We can no longer accept this interpretation. The sixteenth century did not loose unprecedented riches on the world. The rising population, currency devaluations, a relative economic expansion, and certainly the accelerated circulation of coined money and the means of payment are other explanations for the high levels and revolutions (or *pseudo-revolutions*) of the sixteenth century. We shall have more to say about this.

In any case, the Mediterranean, despite the expansion of credit, in the sixteenth century possessed neither the specie nor the paper equivalents sufficient to effect the annual balance of the exchanges and wages of a population of 60 million inhabitants. This shortage was endemic. In Venice, in 1603, although the city's coffers were well filled, there were not enough silver coins to pay the wages of the workers. How much greater was the shortage in backward regions, where payments in kind had constantly to fill the gap in order to get anything done. Not that payment in kind was altogether lacking in flexibility: it prepared the way for the monetary economy, but only payments in cash would make it work and prosper.

But the important and unsurprising conclusion is the following. The circulation of money (here understood to mean every type of currency, even the lowest) only penetrated certain areas of human life. The natural flow of rivers is drawn by gravity towards low-lying regions. The flow of money on the other hand seems to have been restricted to the upper reaches of economic life. It thus created a series of perpetual inequalities: inequality between the most dynamic regions – the towns – and those where little or no money circulated – the countryside; inequality between advanced zones and backward zones, developed countries and under-developed countries (for this distinction already existed, the former constantly moving ahead, the latter even when making progress, like Turkey for example, never catching up with the lenders); inequality between forms of human activity, for only transport, industry, and above all commerce and government taxation had access to the flow of money; inequality between the very few rich (perhaps 5 per cent) and the great mass of poor and very poor, with the gap between the small minority and this huge majority continually widening. I believe that if the observable attempts at social revolution failed, were not even clearly formulated, it was because of the intense, relative pauperization of large numbers of the population.

Was one fifth of the population in great poverty? An estimate made with the help of parish priests in 1559 at Málaga, which we shall take as an example (a fairly well-off one), gave a total of 3096 households (*vecinos*), that is, at four persons to a household, a little over 12,000 inhabitants. Three classes were distinguished according to income: the *razonables*, the *pequeños*, and finally the *pobres*. Of the latter there were over 700 widows and 300 workers (widows counted for a half-*vecino*, workers for a whole one), that is, about 2600 very poor people, over 20 per cent of the whole. The 'reasonably well-off' (and this does not mean rich) numbered 300 *vecinos*, that is about 1200 people (10 per cent). The *pequeños* formed the immense majority, 70 per cent, about 8500 people. These proportions may well be representative. Twenty per cent of the population living in extreme poverty constitutes a large but quite credible percentage both inside and outside the Mediterranean region. Contemporary observers, moreover, noted abject poverty at the heart of the most prosperous cities: in Genoa, where it was aggravated every winter, at Ragusa, so rich and yet socially so unbalanced, where in 1595, according to one report, 'there is also much misery'. We have no proof, of course, that the findings of Málaga are relevant to larger or less-favoured towns or above all that the same scale of measurement can be applied to peasant communities, whose income measured in money would be very small, but whose way of life though less sophisticated

148. *The Poor Man.* Fifteenth-century
Florentine engraving from a series
illustrating the *Ranks and Conditions of
Men. British Museum*

might be better balanced. If this percentage is accepted it would mean that 12 to 14 million Mediterranean inhabitants were living near the starvation level: it is a possibility that cannot be ruled out.

For we are never dealing with full-employment economics. An ever-present pressure on the labour market was the mass of underemployed workers, vagrants, or semi-vagrants that had been a constant, indeed one might say a *structural*, feature of European and Mediterranean life since at least the twelfth century. As for the standard of living of the peasantry, we know next to nothing about it, so we shall be obliged to make the most of a few surveys which cannot of course be considered universally representative.

A village in the Brescia region was destroyed by fire on 8th May, 1555. A dependency of the Alpine commune of Collio de Valnopia, the small settlement at Tizzo nevertheless measured half a mile around. It had consisted of 260 houses, all burned, of which the investigator found only the walls standing. The village had paid 200 ducats annually in taxes to the Signoria of Venice. In these 260 houses, 274 families between them accounted for 2000 people, which means if the figures are accurate (and we have every reason to think they are) that each *household* contained seven people. Not counting the price of the houses, the total damage was valued at 60,000 ducats, or 30 ducats per person. A fire in July of the same year, 1555, destroyed two peasants' houses in Trevisano, in the plains; one was valued at 250 ducats, the other at 150. In the first, furniture, hay and grain amounted to 200 ducats, in the second, hay and grain amounted to about 90, without furniture (perhaps it had been saved). The two victims of the fire described themselves as *poveri* in their application for help, and said that they were now *nudi*, natural expressions no doubt from people asking for money, but which cannot have been in contradiction with the official estimate of their worldly goods. Now let us suppose that these individual figures can be used as a unit of measurement. Returning to Tizzo, let us complete the record of damage. Each house can be valued at 200 ducats, adding another 52,000 ducats to the bill, bringing the total damage to 112,000 and therefore the accumulated capital to 56 ducats, instead of 30, per head of the population. If we suppose that each family received a harvest similar to that of the poorer of the Trevisano fire victims, about 100 ducats, the total annual income of the village would have been about 27,400 ducats, or 13·7 ducats per head. This series of calculations brings us to the borderline of extreme poverty, perhaps it would be more correct to say of destitution. But we are never quite sure where this borderline lies.

I discovered too late to make full use of their extraordinary resources the documents of the *Sommaria*, the accounts office of Naples. Through these fiscal records we are led along a multitude of paths into areas of extreme poverty and hardship. Pescara on the Adriatic was a humble little town of 200 or 250 households, about 1000 inhabitants in all, and all foreigners, *romagnuoli, ferraresi, comachiesi, mantovani, milanesi,* and *slavoni.* Of these thousand immigrants, 'fifty families [200 people] own their own houses, vines, and ply a craft; the others have absolutely nothing but their huts or rather their piles of straw; they live from day to day, working at the salt-pans or digging the ground'. If only, the text goes on, the better-off peasants could afford to buy oxen to plough with, proof that they had none. This is utter poverty one would think. And yet the town had its port, its shops, and even its fair *della Annunziata* in March.

The *Sommaria* also gives details of the villages it sells and resells, according to the accidents of succession, to purchasers of seignorial revenues. Usually each inhabitant pays one ducat to the owner of the land, in one form or another. This rule of a ducat per head, a rough and ready calculation, is given for what it is worth. Another rule of thumb is that the per capita income of the peasant was approximately 10 ducats. But to take a particular case: Supertino in the territory of Otranto was a village of 395 households, in May, 1549, a large village then, almost a small town. It had a higher population than Pescara. Its wealth lay principally in olive trees. The rule of a ducat per head rent to the landlord does not seem to work very well here. There were about 1600 inhabitants, and the landlord received 900 ducats. But this time we have a record of tithes paid to him in kind and therefore an opportunity to calculate the village's production and income in money (3000 kegs of wine, 11,000 *tomola* of wheat, 4000 *tomola* of barley, 1000 *tomola* of oats, 1250 *tomola* of beans, 50 *tomola* of chick peas and lentils, 550 *galatri* of flax, 2500 *staia* of olive oil – money value 8400 ducats). The income, if the list of incomes is complete and if the tithe was indeed one-tenth, must have been a little over 5 ducats per head of the population.

But the villages of Castile, according to the *Relaciones topográficas* of the 1576 and 1578 enquiries, provide higher figures. The income level calculated from a selected sample is 15,522 *maravedis* or 44 ducats per family; per capita income, supposing a family to consist of four people, is 11 ducats.

I did at one time think these problems could be solved by taking as a minimum level the price of slaves or galley men, or the wages of volunteers for the galleys, or even of soldiers, or the pay of domestic servants. But I am not convinced that these prices put on men were really *marginal*. A slave in Sicily or Naples could be sold for perhaps 30 ducats in the first half of the century; after 1550 the price doubled. One cannot conclude anything from this, for the slave market was very restricted; if there was a temporary influx of slaves, prices dropped sharply: in June, 1587, on his return from a pirate expedition with his galleys, Pietro di Toledo (the son of the famous viceroy of Naples) sold the slaves he had captured for a mere 30 ducats each. I have come to the conclusion that oarsmen in the galleys, even slaves, and certainly soldiers and domestic servants (at Ragusa for instance) did not always come off worst in the division of men into those who were looked after by their society, and assured of their keep however meagre – and the others. This dividing line runs below even these miserable classes and if anything moves downwards.

A provisional classification. Whatever the accuracy of the preceding calculations and others yet to be made, we shall not go far wrong in the scale of retrospective values if we fix the following rates for the active members of the population: an income below 20 ducats a year was at subsistence level; between 20 and 40 ducats 'small'; and between 40 and 150 'reasonable'. This scale does not allow either for local variations in the cost of living, or for variation over the years, which might be considerable during periods of inflation. It will do only as a very rough classification.

So we know at once, when we learn that a professor at the University of Padua received a salary of 600 florins a year, that he was *ipso facto* a member of the privileged class, without needing to know that he held the first chair in civil law, and we need not take account of the generally high wage level in that summer of 1506. It will be of some value to place any of the many wages mentioned in the documents against this elementary grid: to note that at the Zecca at Venice the wage pyramid began at the bottom with the beggarly sums paid to the boys who kept watch (20 ducats a year in 1554) and went up to 60 ducats for the salary of a *partidor* (1557), the official in charge of separating gold and silver, and only became really rewarding for an accountant at 180 ducats (in 1590, it is true, after the known rise in wages); to note that a workman in the Arsenal received only a modest wage in 1534, earning 24 *soldi* a day, from 1st March to 31st August, and 20 *soldi* from 1st September to the last day of February; the caulker, who was a skilled worker, was in the same year paid 40 *soldi* in summer and 30 in winter. So Venice's two great centres of power, the Arsenal and the Zecca, depended on a poorly paid labour force. Even the secretaries appointed by the Council of Ten only drew an average of 100 ducats a year. By contrast the 'inzegner' in the service of the Signoria, Zuan Hieronimo de San Michel, who was asking in March, 1556, for his salary to be increased from 20 to 25 ducats *a month*, seems to have been very comfortably off, earning in a month as much as a worker earned in a year.

In short, large sections of the community were either poor or very poor. They formed a huge proletariat whose existence historians are gradually beginning to recognize from the fragmentary evidence available, a proletariat whose presence was felt in every sector of the century's activity, increasingly so as years went by. It bred persistent outbreaks of brigandage, an endless, fruitless form of social revolution. The general impoverishment settled differences, relentlessly driving poor and possessionless alike towards the very bottom of the social ladder. In Spain the survival of ancient inherited wealth and a marked demographic decline contributed in the seventeenth century to produce a strange social category, a proletariat comparable to the plebeians of ancient Rome. Whether genuinely poor, rascals from the towns whom the picaresque novel made famous, highway-men, false or authentic beggars, all this *gente de hampa*, these *hampones* or tramps, had done with work maybe, but work and employment had done with them first. They had become entrenched, like the poor in Moscow under the last

Tsars, in their poverty-stricken idleness. Without the soup that was distributed at the doors of monasteries, how would these *sopistas*, eaters of *sopa boba*, have survived? Ragged folk playing cards or dice at street corners, they also provided the enormous numbers of domestic servants in rich houses. The young Count Olivares, when a student at Salamanca, had a tutor, twenty-one servants, and a mule to carry his books from his lodgings to the university.

This was as typical of Spain as it was of France during the wars of religion, of Italy under Sixtus V, or even of Turkey at the end of the century. The growing burden of the poor was sufficient in itself to announce the impending violent economic downturn, from which the poor, on whatever shore of the Mediterranean, were to gain nothing.

Food, a poor guide: officially rations were always adequate. There is no shortage of documents for an enquiry into sixteenth-century diets. They are only too easily found. But they offer what seems very suspect evidence on the lower standards of living. According to them everything was for the best in the best of all possible worlds. That the Spinola family should have an abundant and varied diet is not surprising. Nor will it astonish us to find that the diet of the poor should consist very largely of cheap foodstuffs such as bread and biscuit. Cheese, meat and fish were also eaten. The gradual decline in meat consumption throughout Europe, and no doubt in the Mediterranean too, had begun, but was not yet far advanced. The unexpected element in these past diets is that when the rations allotted to soldiers, seamen, galley-slaves, and poor-house inmates are measured for calorie content, they yield something like 4000 calories a day.

All would indeed be for the best if we did not know that official menus were always and without exception *officially* good. Everything on the menus posted up or sent to the authorities looks satisfactory, even very satisfactory. But we hardly need the evidence of a few disputes about the distribution of food on board the galleys to sow doubt in our minds. And yet there are the figures, or the comments for example of the *veedor* of the Naples galleys, who had been in charge of supplies for years and who spoke freely before the investigators from the *Sommaria*. Even on board the Turkish galleys, ordinary rations included generous distributions of biscuit. So we shall have to resign ourselves to accept what we find, that is, the balanced diet that is described and confirmed by so many documents, and which may simply mean that galley-slaves and soldiers were servants precious enough to have their health cared for. And let us say at once and quite emphatically, for nothing that has gone before would suggest it: these menus were those of privileged people. Any man who had a regular ration of soup, *vaca salada*, *bizcocho*, wine, and vinegar was sure of his keep. Diego Suárez as a very young man worked on the building site of the Escorial, where he found that the rations were good: *el plato bueno*. The true poor were those who found no official provider, whether military or charitable. And they were legion. They form the dramatic background of the century of

149. Soup distribution. *Refreshing the Thirsty* by Michael Sweerts, c.1650.
Rijksmuseum, Amsterdam

which we occasionally catch a violent glimpse; on 27th May, 1597, at Aix-en-Provence, according to a chronicle, 'the rectors and bursars of the Church of the Holy Spirit were giving out bread to the poor, and in the crush of the said poor, six or seven persons died, children, girls and a woman, having been pushed

to the ground, trampled and suffocated, for there were more than 1200 poor people there'.

Can our calculations be checked? If we add together all the different sources of income (although they are both indeterminate and partly overlapping) the gross annual produce of the Mediterranean lies between 1200 million and 1500 million ducats, giving a per capita share of 20 or 35 ducats. These figures are by no means reliable and are probably too high. The average income could hardly have reached this level. The error arises from the misleading process of estimating everything in terms of money, and it is impossible to proceed otherwise. This *would be* the average level if everything had passed through the market economy, which is not of course the case. But that need not cause us to dismiss all our hypothetical figures as meaningless, still less as irrelevant. Our object has been to make the necessary initial survey, to situate, as it were, the huge inaccessible regions of the Mediterranean landscape in relation to each other. Let us now turn the page and leave an area where as yet quantitative history is unrewarding, where all the valid statistics are hidden from our gaze.

Lisboa

+

A su M.G.

1563

De don Alonso de Touar a xxv. de Mayo. 1563.

recibida a. 29. del mismo.

N.177

E 38ɪ

150. *Left:* The annual fishing for tuna at Cadiz. Detail from engraving by Hoefnagel. From *Civitates Orbis Terrarum,* 1572. 151. *Above:* Facsimile of the *carpeta* of a letter from Philip II's ambassador in Lisbon, with dates of dispatch and arrival.

152. The Monstrance of Belem, fashioned from the first gold brought back by Columbus.
National Museum, Lisbon

2

Economies: Precious Metals, Money, and Prices

THE ROLE of precious metals has never seemed more important than in the sixteenth century. Contemporary writers unhesitatingly accord them pride of place and economists of the seventeenth century are even more emphatic. For one, they are 'the substance of the people'; another considers 'that we draw our living less from traffic in commodities than from gold and silver'. And a Venetian speaker goes so far as to say that precious metal, whether gold or silver is 'the sinews of all government, it gives it its pulse, its movement, its mind, soul, and it is its essence and its very life ["l'esser et la vita"]... It overcomes all impossibilities, for it is the master, the *patron* of all: it carries with it the necessity of all things; without it all is weak and without movement.'

Patron del tutto: now we are not so sure. Money was not the universal driving force it was so readily assumed to be. The role played by precious metals was determined not only by the stocks inherited from previous centuries, and therefore by accidents in the past, but equally by the velocity of circulation, by international relations, economic competition, the deliberate policies of states and mercantile communities, even by 'vulgar opinion'. And often money acted merely as a screen, as an economist would say, masking the realities of goods, services, and exchanges. Finally, gold and silver (and even copper) did not simply add up to form a homogeneous stock of bullion. The metals used for currency were in constant collision and competition.

So every time the value of gold coinage was raised (in relation to silver) it led to a run on gold, which immediately took on the role of *bad money*, arbitrarily in favour and chasing out the good, in this case silver coins. Such an event was never entirely fortuitous. If it occurred with obstinate regularity at Venice, might this not be because it facilitated the massive export of silver that was one of the mainstays of the republic's trade with the Levant? This was a deliberate attempt to force the market with all its consequences and limitations: if gold went up, so did prices on all the exchanges, and the cost of living rose with them. Further consequences were, for example, the unprecedented return of 250,000 sequins from the Turkish Empire in 1603; or, at about the same time, currency specu-lation by the Grand Duke of Tuscany who, under an assumed name, sold

200,000 gold crowns to the Venetian Zecca, making a safe profit of 12,000 crowns 'as a result of our ignorance', says a Venetian who wanted gold to be put once and for all at a fixed ratio to silver, as the price of flour was related to that of wheat. The rest of the story is easy to guess. The relative scarcity of silver coin opened the door wider than usual to clipped, lightweight silver pieces of low metallic content, which Venice was then obliged, not without some difficulty, to eliminate from circulation. Did these troubles stem, in part at least, from the need to export silver to the Levant?

This explanation, which was not one suggested by contemporaries, might nevertheless account for the curious situation in Sicily, where, since at least 1531, gold had systematically been overvalued in relation to silver (1 to 15). Because of this 'disproportion', Sicily was constantly short of silver coin, which it was profitable to buy up in exchange for gold and then melt down, as the Naples mint frequently did to its advantage. But some mystery still persists about this scandal, those whom it profited, and why it was allowed to continue.

Elsewhere, the relationship between gold and silver was more varied in its effects, but did not go unobserved once men had become aware of the nature and reciprocal action of different currencies, strong against weak, good against bad, gold against silver or even 'black' money (vellon and before long pure copper coinage), later still metal against paper. 'Money' in the sense of wealth or fortune has never been of one single nature.

153. Detail of money bags from a majolica plate of *Doge and Senators*. *Fitzwilliam Museum, Cambridge*

154, 155, 156. *Above and opposite:* Hungarian, Venetian and Ancona ducats. *British Museum*

1 The Mediterranean and the gold of the Sudan

The flow of precious metal towards the East. And yet at first sight there could be nothing simpler than the circulation of precious metals in the Mediterranean. Centuries passed and nothing changed. Whatever their source – the silver mines of Old Serbia; the Alps; Sardinia; the gold-washing of the Sudan and Ethiopia, or even Sofala by way of North Africa and Egypt; the silver mines of Schwaz in the Inn valley; of Neusohl in Hungary, Mansfeld in Saxony, Kuttenberg near Prague or the mines of the Erz-Gebirge; the mines in the New World after the first years of the sixteenth century – whatever their origin, precious metals once absorbed into Mediterranean life were fed into the stream that continually flowed eastward. In the Black Sea, Syria, and Egypt the Mediterranean trade balance was always in deficit. Trade with the Far East was only possible thanks to exports of gold and silver, which depleted Mediterranean bullion reserves. It has even been suggested, not unconvincingly, that the vitality of the Roman Empire was sapped by the haemorrhage of precious metals. It is a fact that coins from the Julio-Claudian era have been found as far away as Ceylon.

The Mediterranean did, however, constantly try to stem this ruinous flow. Alexandria, in the time of the Roman Empire, paid for some of her purchases from the Far East with glassware. In the Middle Ages western Europe exported slaves instead of gold and silver. Byzantium, by introducing the breeding of silkworms in the time of Justinian, succeeded in limiting her exports of money to the East. These attempts merely underline the necessity, exhausting in the

long run, of making repeated payments to the Far East, which exported a great deal to the Mediterranean and imported comparatively little in exchange.

So during the sixteenth and seventeenth centuries there circulated throughout the vast Asian continent, source of spices, drugs, and silk, the precious gold and above all silver coins minted at Venice, Genoa, or Florence, and later the famous Spanish silver pieces of eight. Away to the east flowed these currencies, out of the Mediterranean circuit into which it had often required so much patience to introduce them. The Mediterranean as a whole operated as a machine for accumulating precious metals, of which, be it said, it could never have enough. It hoarded them only to lose them all to India, China, and the East Indies. The great discoveries may have revolutionized routes and prices, but they did not alter this fundamental situation, no doubt because it was still a major advantage to westerners to have access to the precious merchandise of the East, in particular pepper, which according to one Venetian 'brings with it all the other spices . . .'; no doubt also because in the sixteenth century, as in the past, the purchasing power of precious metals rose above that of Christian countries as soon as one crossed the border into the Orient. In about 1613, according to Antonio Serra, Venice was still annually exporting over 5 million ducats in specie to the Levant, although, in an effort to save her bullion reserves, she also sent cloth, glass trinkets, mirrors, hardware, and copper. The role of the *fattori* and resident agents whom the Venetian merchants employed 'on the quaysides' of the Levant from Syria to the Persian Gulf was to keep informed, 'be advised', and to keep an eye open for good business, but they were also daily engaged in bartering goods for other goods, *dar a baratto* or *barattare*, in other words buying and selling without using money.

The bill of exchange, which moved freely throughout Christendom, made only exceptional appearances in Islam, so exceptional indeed as to suggest that it was unknown in the East. The Christian merchant, always pressed to find payment, could hardly ever borrow money in the Levant except at usurers' rates that might run to 40 per cent and more. Some Ragusan papers in 1573 refer to loans offered at this rate by Portuguese Jews in Egypt.

It was through Seville and Spain, rich first in gold then in silver, in theory hoarding her treasure but in practice letting it escape, that the trade of the Mediterranean and indeed the known world was stimulated. But this influx of precious metals was a new and revolutionary feature, of more recent origin than the chronology of the great discoveries would suggest.

Sudanese gold: early history. Audacious historians used to date the beginning of the Sahara gold traffic from the tenth century. But there is every reason to think that it began very much earlier, even preceding the arrival of the camel in the desert in the second century AD, for before that date, 'the horses and oxen of the Garamantes pulled carts in the Libyan desert'. It is probable that gold dust from the Sudan reached North Africa before the tenth century and led, after the year 1000, to the emergence in the South of coherent and spectacular states in the loop of the Niger and in the North, in the Maghreb, to the founding of new towns like Algiers and Oran. Moorish Spain, whose masters in the tenth century held the key position of Ceuta, found the gold to make its *dirhems* in North Africa.

But Sudanese gold provided more than a basis for the prosperity of North Africa and Moslem Spain, the Western Islamic bloc which its isolation from the chief trade routes in the twelfth century obliged to be self-sufficient. This gold played its part in the history of the Mediterranean as a whole, entering general circulation from the fourteenth century, perhaps after the spectacular pilgrimage to Mecca of Mansa Musa, King of Mali, in 1324. North Africa with its supply of gold gradually became the driving force of the entire Mediterranean. In the fifteenth century it was invaded by Christian merchants who settled without difficulty in Ceuta, Tangier, Fez, Oran, Tiemcen, Bougie, Constantine, and Tunis.

With the help of the gold and slave trade, commercial penetration of the continent was far-reaching, extending south as far as the Tuat and the Niger. All the merchandise of Christendom on sale in the commercial quarters of North Africa (textiles, kerseys, hardware, and trinkets) crossed the Sahara, the Maghreb lending itself the more easily to this invasion since it lacked political cohesion.

Five commodities dominated the trade routes: gold dust (*tibar*), black slaves, copper, salt, and textiles. The black Africans possessed the first two. Goods were exchanged at the point where the camel caravans from the North met the processions of bearers or the canoes of the South. On the whole the North, that is Islam, and behind Islam the western merchant, gained most from this trade. It was said that in Mali salt was exchanged for its weight in gold in 1450. Certainly by 1515, according to Leo Africanus, Venetian cloth was being sold at exorbitant rates at Timbuktu and the local aristocracy was deep in debt to merchants from the Levant or the Maghreb. This then was the wider economic context, but local economic conditions had a part to play as well. The gold supply ultimately depended upon elasticity of production in the three zones where gold-washing was carried out, about which there is no mystery and which are still known today: Upper Senegal, Upper Niger, and the Guinea Coast.

The Portuguese in Guinea: gold continues to arrive in the Mediterranean. The advance of the Portuguese along the Atlantic coast of Africa was an event of major importance. At Cape Blanc there was a first contact between the explorers and the *Mouros brancos* of Barbary and a little gold dust found its way to the ocean. The Gulf of Guinea was reached in about 1440 and the *resgate* of slaves, gold, and ivory took place at the mouths of the rivers, at local fairs, in exchange for brightly coloured fabrics, usually of poor quality, rings, copper bracelets or bowls, coarse woollen cloth, as well as wheat and horses. In 1444 the first convoy of black slaves was landed at Lagos in Portugal. In 1447 the *cruzado*, Portugal's first national gold currency, was created. By the time of Henry the Navigator's death in 1460, commercial colonization of the coast of Guinea was virtually accomplished. The conquest was completed in January, 1482, by the unexpected construction, within the space of a few weeks, of the castle of São Jorge da Mina, built with materials brought from Portugal, notably blocks of ready-cut stone.

The immediate prosperity of these trades (in gold, slaves, ivory, and malaguetta and other pepper substitutes) is beyond dispute. In the case of gold, transactions were conducted in the name both of the king and of private citizens. During the period 1500–1520 about 700 kilos of gold were probably exported annually. But after 1520 there was a perceptible decline and in 1550 there opened a long period of crisis, lasting until at least 1580 and more likely until 1600; the Dutch made their appearance after 1605. So three phases can be distinguished in the African gold trade: a period of conspicuous activity from 1440 to 1520–1550, followed by a long recession between 1550 and 1600 and a fresh impetus in the new century.

It is the long recession between roughly 1520 and 1600 which is the most difficult to explain. There are three possible causes: competition from England, France, and Spain during these years of decline (and of this there is plentiful evidence); the rising costs experienced by the Portuguese armadas and garrisons, so that gold became too costly (and this is quite plausible); and finally competition from American gold: the New World's earliest export to Europe was gold; 43 tons *officially* landed at Seville between 1551 and 1560, that is over 4 tons a year compared to 700 kilos at most from the Atlantic coast of Africa.

But the important point to note is that the Atlantic gold route did not, between 1440 and 1520, inhibit the passage of gold across the Sahara to North Africa, from where it passed into the Mediterranean. Proof of this is provided by coins minted in Sicily and the re-export of gold in both coins and ingots from the island. In 1489, as in 1455, massive shipments of Sicilian wheat to Africa (75,000 quintals) brought in return half a ton of gold to the island.

The gold trade and the economic cycle. Prosperity and crisis within the gold trade were linked. When gold from Guinea reached Lisbon it was immediately launched on to the principal trade routes. At Antwerp it encountered silver from the German mines, and in the Mediterranean it solved balance-of-payments problems. The gold from the first shipments arriving at Seville was also drawn into the inevitable channels and the Mediterranean received its share. Before the discovery of the New World, Seville had provided the Genoese merchants with their supplies of African gold; afterwards it provided them with American gold. It seems probable that the collapse of the Sudanese gold trade in the 1520s observable on both coasts, the Atlantic and the Mediterranean, was a consequence of imports from America. The gold of Bambuk then lost some of its foreign customers, and found a market only in North Africa (in the widest sense) where its presence is recorded throughout the century.

2 American silver

America, having succeeded Africa as a source of gold for the Mediterranean, to an even greater extent displaced the German mines as a source of silver.

American and Spanish treasure. Everything the official figures and documents have to tell us about imports of American treasure to Spain has been made available by the studies of Earl J. Hamilton. The first quite modest shipments arrived in the early sixteenth century. Until 1550 they included both gold and silver. It was not until the second half of the century that imports of gold became comparatively insignificant. From now on the galleons brought nothing but silver to Seville, though in huge quantities it is true. For in America the revolutionary amalgamation process in which silver ore was treated with mercury had been introduced in 1557 by the Spaniard Bartolomeo de Medina in the mines of New Spain; it was applied at Potosí from 1571 on, increased exports ten-fold, and they reached their peak between 1580 and 1620, thus coinciding with the great age of Spanish imperialism. In January, 1580, Don Juan de Idiáquez wrote to Cardinal Granvelle. 'The King is right to say that the Emperor . . . never amassed as much money as himself for his enterprises . . .' The Indies, in the words of Montchrestien, were beginning to 'disgorge' their riches.

This flow of silver poured into a country traditionally protectionist, fenced around with customs barriers. Nothing could enter or leave Spain without the consent of a suspicious government, jealously guarding the arrival and departure of precious metals. So, in principle, the huge American treasure was being drawn into a sealed vessel. But Spain's insulation was not complete. If it had been, the Cortes would not have complained so frequently, in 1527, 1548, 1552, 1559, and again in 1563 of the drain of precious metals, which according to them, was impoverishing the nation. Nor would it have been so commonly remarked that the kingdoms of Spain are 'the Indies of other foreign kingdoms'.

In fact, precious metals were all the time escaping from Spanish coffers and travelling all over the world. In 1556, a Venetian, Soranzo, claimed that every year there entered France up to five and a half million gold crowns. Foreign merchants resident in Spain were always sending home minted coins. In 1554 the Portuguese ambassador reported that on the at first undisclosed orders of Prince Philip, Don Juan de Mendoza searched the passengers travelling on his galleys from Catalonia to Italy. The result was the confiscation of 70,000 ducats, most of it from Genoese merchants. So the treasure of Spain was not always too

157. Silver mining in Peru. Eighteenth-century Peruvian
manuscript, *Trujillo del Peru. Royal Library, Copenhagen*

well guarded. And official checks (which are often the only evidence available
to historians) do not tell us everything we want to know.

Silver could leave Spain legally as well as illegally. Every shipment of cereals
to Spain entitled the supplier to the explicit right to payment in coin, which he
was then allowed to export. But for the greatest drain on silver reserves, the
king himself and Spanish foreign policy in general were responsible. Instead of
using their silver at home to set up new and profitable enterprises, as the Fuggers
used the silver from their Schwaz mines at Augsburg, the Spanish Habsburgs let
themselves be drawn into foreign expense, already considerable in the time of
Charles V and quite extraordinary under Philip II – a thoughtless policy, it has

Tota pulchra es, Maria, Et macula, originalis non est inte. Tu gloria Ierusalem: Tu laetitia israel: Tu honorificencia populi nostri. Tu aduocata pecatorum. O. Maria i Virgo Prudentissima. Mater Clementis.ª ora pronost.

158. *The Virgin of Potosí, Bolivia*, with views of the silver mining towns of Potosí in the background. *Museum of the Casa Real de Moneda Potosí, Bolivia*

often been said. But it may be that this was the price of empire, that its mere existence and often its mere defence required sacrifices on this scale. The historian Carlos Pereyra has called the Netherlands Spain's folly, swallowing up if not all then a very large proportion of her American treasure. But Spain could hardly abandon the Netherlands. It would have meant bringing the war nearer home.

Be that as it may, the Peninsula, heavy with treasure, willingly or unwillingly acted as a reservoir of precious metals to be tapped. The problem for the historian, now that we know how the precious metals arrived in Spain from the New World, is to see how they were redistributed.

American treasure takes the road to Antwerp. During the first half of the sixteenth century, treasure was exported from Spain to Antwerp, a city as much (if not more) the true capital of the Atlantic as Seville or Lisbon. Documents at Antwerp refer to links between the port on the Scheldt and the farthest regions of the ocean, West Africa and the early settlements in Brazil. The Schetz family, for instance, owned an *engheno* (sugar-mill) near São Vicente. In 1531 the Antwerp bourse was created. From this time on Spanish silver was sent to Antwerp and Bruges in the capacious *zabras* of Biscay. In 1544 it was still being carried in Biscayan ships, which in that year also transported Spanish infantry, and the same happened in 1546–1548 and in 1550–1552.

This traffic was common knowledge. The Venetian ambassadors informed the Signoria in the spring of 1551 that 800,000 ducats' worth of silver from Peru were to be minted in the Netherlands at a profit of 15 per cent. In exchange the Netherlands was to provide Spain with artillery and powder. In 1552, the year of Innsbruck, Charles V's desperate situation opened the flood gates that caution usually kept closed. So while the export of coin by individuals was reduced, exports from the public treasury were greatly increased. That did not prevent foreign firms established in Spain, for whom consignments of bullion were a matter of life and death, from continuing to dispatch them, taking advantage of the fact that they were often the agents for the government's own exports. In 1553 silver arrived by official channels at Antwerp, for the Fuggers.

Fortuitous circumstances brought a share even to England. The voyage of the future Philip II in 1554 brought large sums of money to the island. They helped restore the fortunes of an ailing English currency which, in 1550, had reached its lowest level yet. Between the year 1554 and his return to Spain in 1559, Philip, during his stay in England and the Netherlands, received a constant supply of silver by the Atlantic route. During the difficult war years of 1557–1558 the arrival of the ships carrying bullion were the great events of the port of Antwerp. Today, 20th March, 1558, says one report, there arrived in Antwerp four vessels from Spain, after a voyage of ten days. They are carrying 200,000 crowns in coin and 300,000 in bills of exchange. 'The last load of silver from Spain,' wrote Eraso to Charles V on June 13th, 'aboard the *zabras* of Pero

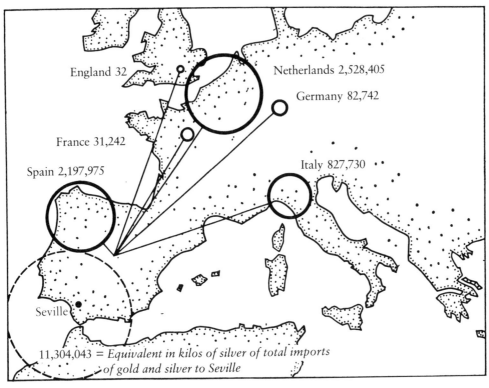

England 32

Netherlands 2,528,405

Germany 82,742

France 31,242

Spain 2,197,975

Italy 827,730

Seville

11,304,043 = *Equivalent in kilos of silver of total imports of gold and silver to Seville*

Spanish 'political' silver in Europe 1580–1626

The money referred to is that spent by his Catholic Majesty through the *asientos* concluded with merchants. From this diagram it can be seen that the greatest expenditure was, predictably, in the Netherlands. Less well known, in order of importance are: expenditure on the Court and the defence of Spain (1580 saw the beginning of the war in the Atlantic; the Peninsula had to be defended along its threatened coastline); the relatively small sum spent in Italy; and the virtually nonexistent expenditure in France. France did not sell herself to Spain, but was occupied with her own internal strife. These payments were of course on behalf of the Spanish government and do not represent the total volume of precious metals leaving Spain for Europe. Map by F. C. Spooner, from the figures and calculations of Alvaro Castillo Pintado.

159. *Overleaf:* Anonymous sixteenth-century *View of the Roadstead of Antwerp and the City from the Flemish Bank. Nationaal Scheepvaartmuseum, Antwerp*

Menéndez, arrived just in time to enable us to pay the German infantry and cavalry we are recruiting . . .'

Any number of documents testify to the circulation of Spanish silver. The most instructive beyond question are the *asientos*, or '*partis*', as sixteenth-century Frenchmen called them, which Charles V and Philip II concluded with their moneylenders. After the Innsbruck crisis, first the Fuggers and then the Genoese bankers insisted that their contracts should be accompanied by *licencias de saca*, that is, permission to export from Spain the equivalent in specie of the sums they had advanced. For example the two *asientos* concluded in May, 1558,

with the Genoese bankers Nicolo Grimaldi and Gentile, stipulate among other conditions the transfer of silver from Laredo to Flanders.

This flow of coin and ingots overseas, steering well clear of the enemy nation France, is not only of great interest to the historian of the final struggles of the sixteenth century between the Valois and the House of Austria. It makes it plain that the Netherlands was not merely a parade ground for Charles V's Empire, but also a distribution centre from which American silver was passed to Germany, Northern Europe, and the British Isles. This distribution was crucial to European economic activity, which was after all not totally spontaneous. A system of exchange, circulation, and banking came into being, centred on the Scheldt port and extending as far as Germany, England, and even Lyons, which for years worked in liaison with the great financial turntable in the North.

Possibly already disrupted after 1566, with the outbreak of the revolt of the Netherlands, the traffic in bullion between Spain and the North was practically brought to a standstill between 1568 and 1569. That does not mean that none at all went north along the old route. But the transport of money was no longer effected on its former scale, nor was it as easy. It travelled now almost exclusively in specially assembled fleets like that commanded by the Duke of Medina Celi in 1572, and virtually had to run a blockade. The shipping route had become dangerous. Lazaro Spinola, the Genoese consul at Antwerp, and his advisers Gregorio di Franchi and Nicolò Lomellino wrote to this effect to the Republic of Genoa in July, 1572: the nation has debts and knows not how to pay them.

Medina Celi's fleet in 1572 had been fairly small. It was decided to assemble a larger one in Biscay in 1573–1574. It is hardly an exaggeration to call it the first Invincible Armada. It was placed under the command of a distinguished commander, Pero Menéndez, but he died in 1574; then funds ran short, epidemics broke out, and the fleet was left rotting away in the harbour. That year, 1574, struck a decisive blow at the vitality of Spain, from the Bay of Biscay to the distant Netherlands. There were a few subsequent shipments from the Peninsula to the Scheldt. In 1575 a small fleet under Recalde sailed from Santander to Dunkirk, where it arrived on 26th November, putting in on the way at the Isle of Wight, which suggests that relations with England had not yet reached breaking point. On the other hand there is no evidence that Recalde's fleet was carrying silver.

In any case it would probably have been incapable of doing so. It is easy to ascertain how abnormal it had become to transport silver using the Atlantic route. Just after the state bankruptcy of 1575, declared to his advantage, Philip II found himself with several million crowns in liquid assets. Nothing could apparently be simpler, since they were needed in the Netherlands, than to convey the money to Laredo or Santander and ship it north. But no merchant would touch it. Instead, he had to beg the Fuggers to consent to convey 70,000 crowns (delivered to them in chests sealed with the royal seal to avoid trouble with the customs) to Lisbon, where they obtained in exchange good bills of exchange on Antwerp from local *marranos* who needed the silver coins for their trade with the Portuguese Indies. Even for such relatively small sums, Thomas Müller, the Fuggers' agent in Spain, preferred to operate through Portugal because of the semi-neutrality of Portuguese merchants in the northern troubles. Thanks to this subterfuge, the money was transferred without leaving the Peninsula.

The French detour. Since the route from Laredo and Santander was no longer usable, an alternative had to be found. Philip II resorted to the roads across France. Although shorter, they might at any time be interrupted by France's internal troubles, and transport required long convoys and a heavy escort. The transport of a mere 100,000 crowns, for example, from Florence to Paris at the end of the century required seventeen wagons, escorted by five companies of cavalry and 200 foot soldiers. To reduce the weight, gold alone might be sent. This was tried several times in about 1576, using reliable carriers, men in the service of Spain, who carried up to 5000 gold crowns each, sewn into their garments, from Genoa to the Netherlands. But such an expedient was only for exceptional, desperate, and dangerous occasions. In 1590 six couriers coming from Italy were robbed near Basle of 50,000 crowns intended for Ambrogio Spinola at Antwerp. Each courier could carry 10,000 crowns in gold pieces.

It was at the end of 1572, after the St Bartholomew Massacre, that the first large consignment of bullion from the Spanish crown passed through France. The Duke of Alva, who had been short of money since his arrival in the Netherlands, was in desperate straits. It was rumoured at the beginning of 1569 that he had already spent 5 million ducats. Two years later in 1571 the documents repeatedly insist on 'the tightness of money', 'la estrecheza del dinero', in which he found himself. Merchants were no longer willing to do business with him. With no liquid currency, his credit diminished, the Duke saw that the possibility of using bills of exchange was receding, just as a bank never needs reserves so badly as when its customers suspect it has none. By 1572 the situation was so serious that in April the Duke decided to appeal to the credit of the Grand Duke of Tuscany. His approaches were successful, but the Spanish government was on poor terms with the Grand Duke, suspecting him of intriguing both inside and outside France against Spanish interests; Alva's request was disowned and the credit that had been granted was never used.

Meanwhile, Philip II had sent through France 500,000 ducats in cash. 'We wish,' he wrote to his ambassador, Diego de Zuñiga, 'to send to the Duke of Alva, from the Kingdom of Spain, a sum of 500,000 ducats in both gold and silver. Since they cannot now be transported by sea without great danger, for the route is closely guarded, it seems to us that the best and most convenient solution would be to send them through the kingdom of France, if my brother, the Most Christian King, would be good enough to give his permission and to issue orders that they may pass with the desired security . . .' Permission was granted and the money was transported in several loads. On 15 December, 1572, Zayas gave notice to the French ambassador, Saint-Gouard, that in accordance with the authorized passage of 500,000 crowns, Grimaldi was sending 70,000 in reals (that is in silver) and Lorenza Spinola 40,000 in Castilian crowns (that is in gold). These were not the only consignments. In March, 1574, Mondoucet wrote from the Netherlands: 'If I am to believe what is publicly voiced here . . .: ducats from Castile are trotting through France to disturb all good plans.' *Political* money was not moreover the only Spanish money travelling along the roads of France. There was that sent by the merchants, not to mention smuggled silver (often one and the same thing).

In 1576 Philip II and his advisers examined the possibilities of the route from Nantes, where the solid credit of the Spanish merchant Andres Ruiz could be used as a pivot for transfers through 'Normandy and France'. It provided an opportunity for Zuñiga, who had made the suggestion, to point out French claims, notably their intention of 'freezing', as we should say, a third of the money in transit. It was also an opportunity for the Spanish ambassador to deplore the poor organization of *credito, trato*, and *comercio* in France, about which he was certainly right.

In July, 1578, Henri III gave permission for Spanish troops and silver (150,000 ducats) to pass through France. But, a sign of the changed times, the ambassador, Vargas, wondered whether it was prudent to continue to send them, when thieves in the pay of the Duke of Alençon were on the watch for it. It would be better, he added, to use 'the surveillance system of the merchants'.

Spanish coins continued to circulate in France well after the year 1578, if only those sent directly by the king of Spain to Frenchmen, payments to the Guises, and others. In 1582 one document refers to the dispatch by Philip Adorno of 100,000 crowns each to Lyons and Paris, there to be made available to Alexander Farnese. In 1585 a remittance of 200,000 crowns to Lyons by Bartolomeo Calvo and Battista Lomellini is recorded. But there is no proof that this money was sent in specie or that it travelled beyond Lyons to Flanders. Until there is more evidence, let us conclude that the Spanish only resorted to the routes across France until about 1578, and that this was never more than an emergency expedient. Perhaps it would have been abandoned even earlier had it not been for the difficulties that arose between 1575 and 1577 between Philip II and his Genoese creditors. The agreement they signed in 1577 – the *medio general* – was to lead to the predominance of the shipping route from Barcelona to Genoa.

The great route from Barcelona to Genoa and the second cycle of American treasure. It is not known exactly when this route assumed importance – perhaps during the 1570s, which marked the beginning of the great war against the Turk in the Mediterranean. As a result, Spanish capital was diverted towards Italy.

This was certainly not an entirely new development. Well before 1570, American gold and silver had already been reaching the central Mediterranean, although never in quantities comparable to the steady stream that flowed to Antwerp. In October, 1532, Spanish galleys arrived at Monaco carrying 400,000 crowns bound for Genoa. In 1546, Charles V borrowed 150,000 ducats from the Genoese and this loan probably resulted in the export of bullion to the *Dominante* in compensation. A Portuguese correspondent unequivocally refers to the remittance to Genoa of a sum of specie intended for the Pope in 1551. Ehrenberg says that in 1552 large quantities of silver were arriving in Genoa as well as in Antwerp. In January, 1564, a letter from Baltazar Lomellini to Eraso refers to a payment made on the orders of Philip II, in November of the previous year, of 18,000 ducats on the Milan market into the account of Lomellini's father-in-law, Nicolò Grimaldi. In 1565 some Florentine merchants agreed to a loan of 400,000 ducats, payable in Flanders. Did they demand in return that bullion should be sent to Florence? In 1566, Fourquevaux, the French ambassador in Spain, mentions two Genoese loans, one of 150,000, the other of 450,000 crowns, and the Tuscan ambassador Nobili refers, in May, to the dispatch of 100,000 crowns, this time to Genoa. The Duke of Alva, travelling from Spain to Genoa in 1567, took with him both troops and silver. And from time to time the need arose to supply Sicily and Naples with money, often indeed by means of *cambios* agreed on the Genoese or Florentine exchanges, naturally drawing some American treasure to these cities in return. 'In the last few days, eighteen loads of silver have been brought to Barcelona for Italy,' writes Fourquevaux in December, 1566. During the summer of 1567 Nobili succeeded in sending some of the silver intended for the pay of the Tuscan galleys in the service of the Catholic King; not without some difficulty, however, for the assignment that had been promised to him out of church revenues was dispersed throughout the whole of Spain. Of what he had assembled by May Nobili proposed to send off 25,000 'escudi'; in June he announced that eight chests containing 280,000 'reali' would be on their way; finally in September, not having heard any certain news, he was hoping that it had all been safely loaded aboard the galleys.

All these examples laid end to end still do not give the impression of a regular flow: as long as *dinero de contado*, coined money, travelled to Flanders (and this was where Genoese loans usually went), the Mediterranean only attracted a modest quantity. We have plenty of negative evidence.

Specie was in fact scarce in the Mediterranean. In 1561, when Philip II wrote to the viceroy of Catalonia, Don Garcia de Toledo, at Barcelona asking him to obtain 100,000 ducats for the October and May fairs, the viceroy replied on 5th May that it was quite impossible: 'Credit is so tight here and the merchants are very short of money! . . . I pray your Majesty will believe me that, when I have sometimes obtained 8 or 10,000 ducats here to aid our troops, I have had to name local merchants as guarantors and, what was more, pawn my silver plate. Even then I was charged 9 or 10 per cent interest.'

160. Detail from *The Covetous Man* by David Teniers II. *National Gallery, London*

Something can be deduced too from the *partido* of 100,000 ducats *de oro di Italia* concluded in Genoa in April, 1566, and under scrutiny in Naples later that year. This was an ordinary *asiento*, that is to say, it came under the heading of the contracts with many clauses that the monarchy often made with the bankers. Philip II, in return for the 100,000 ducats paid to him on the Genoa exchange, gave an assignment on the *donativo* of Naples, or if that should be insufficient, on a tax in the kingdom, to be paid back the following year. Since Naples was acting as the centre for reimbursement, the *partido* concluded at Genoa through the offices of the Spanish ambassador, Figueron, was sent for the signature of the viceroy of Naples. The latter had his treasurer and an expert examine the clauses and terms of repayment; when everything had been checked, the money was lent at the enormous rate of $21^3/_5$ per cent interest. This is surely further proof of the 'tightness' of money at Genoa. The situation in Naples at the same period was even worse.

But the 1570s brought a new situation. The Spanish state machine was obliged, in order to pay for its arms requirements in the Mediterranean, to find new routes for sending money whether in bills of exchange or specie. Gian Andrea Doria, in April, 1572, notified the republic of Genoa that he was going to fetch from Cartagena the money which the Genoese merchants preferred to ship from there rather than take it by land to Barcelona, since the roads were unsafe. These shipments were not interrupted even by the second bankruptcy of the Spanish state in 1575, which shook Genoa to its foundations, but also contributed to demolish what was left of the Antwerp connection. In April, 1576, Philip II had 650,000 ducats *de contado* sent to Genoa. In the same year he offered to transport for the Fuggers 10,000 crowns 'of gold in gold' in his galleys to Italy. It was along this same route that between 1575 and 1578 the Fuggers' agent was to send up to 2 million *couronnes* intended for the Netherlands. When Philip II in July, 1577, ordered Gian Andrea Doria to go to Barcelona, it was to load silver for Italy. Once his vessel was loaded, the captain was to weigh anchor quickly, with or without the Admiral of Castile, who was supposed to be joining the ship, for the money was urgently required in Italy, and it was important that 'the corsairs should not discover that the money is being carried in a single galley'. The new route did not of course end in Italy; Genoa had become the clearing-house for money and bills of exchange travelling north. But that did not prevent Italy from receiving her share of Spanish treasure, on the contrary; and one of the first to benefit was the Grand Duke of Tuscany, who by 1576 was back in favour in Spain and from whom Philip II was in 1582 to request a loan of 400,000 ducats for Flanders.

With the increase in imports of silver to Seville after 1580, this traffic also increased. For an indication of its proportions during the years 1584–1586, rather than embark upon a confusing journey through the mass of known documents, we could not do better than read the well-informed letters of the French *chargé d'affaires* in Spain, the secretary, Longlée. His dated reports detail shipments of more than 8 million ducats between January and August 1584, besides various unspecified, but obviously large, sums. In 1585 between April and September 4½ million crowns, and in 1586, on 25th March alone, 1,200,000 crowns were sent to Italy.

In subsequent years, the flow of bullion swelled to even greater proportions, as can be seen simply from the level reached by the *asientos* during the last twelve years of the reign of Philip II. In 1586 the Fuggers must have lent him 1,500,000 gold crowns payable in Italy and Germany; in 1587 Agostino Spinola gave him an advance of 1,000,000 *scudi*; in 1589 the Florentines lent him 600,000 crowns; in the same year the Genoese merchants arranged a *cambio* of 2,000,000 for the Netherlands. The following year Ambrosio Spinola paid out 2,500,000 in the Netherlands. In 1602 Ottavio Centurione advanced 9 million and even more – the large sum has been questioned by prudent historians but without justification. I have also found evidence of an agreement with Agostino Spinola in 1587, for 930,521 *escudos*, and contrary to what Ehrenberg says, it was made out not for Italy but in the form of a bill of exchange on the Netherlands to the Duke of Parma.

These are mere details; the important point is the vastly increased traffic in specie and credit throughout the western Mediterranean, which had now been promoted to imperial silver route. No one would contest the historical importance of these repeated voyages by galleys laden with chests or barrels of money. When talking of American gold and silver we should remember not only the famous galleons of the Indies fleets, but also the Biscayan *zabras* and 'naves' and those galleys, which once peace had returned to the Mediterranean, were occupied in conveying to Italy no longer troops but passengers and mounds of silver pieces and on such an amazing scale. There were accidents of course. In April, 1582, a galley sailing from Barcelona to Genoa was surprised by bad weather and had to throw some of her precious cargo overboard; fifty-six cases of *reales* were thrown into the sea, as well as a whole case of *escudos* and other gold pieces. But such accidents were rare, as the insurance premium of 1·5 per cent clearly demonstrates. Accidents on land were equally if not more frequent. In January, 1614, 140,000 crowns belonging to Genoese bankers were carried off, only six leagues from Barcelona, by about a hundred thieves.

161. Medal by Giampaolo Poggini showing the West
Indies fleet, 1559. *British Museum*

The Mediterranean invaded by Spanish coins. This fortune of the Mediterranean exactly coincided with a drop in Atlantic traffic and the decline of Antwerp, along with all the other money markets and economic activities which had depended on the regular functioning of the Antwerp bourse. I am inclined to date the decline of Antwerp and the Netherlands before the great turning-point of the years 1584–1585, which was undeniably important, before even the sack of the town in 1576 and before the second Spanish state bankruptcy of 1575. I think it can be detected as early as 1567, as A. Goris suggested, or even better in 1569. There were even total stoppages in that year, for example in the woollen centre of Hondschoote, although it was still extremely prosperous and of world importance. On the arrival of the Duke of Alva, such was the recession in the textile industry that he was unable to obtain locally enough blue cloth for the servants in his palace. The sack of Antwerp in November, 1576, certainly did not destroy a city at the height of its career. A Portuguese report of 1573 indicates that since at least 1572 all trade with Flanders had been at a standstill. As early as 1571 a Spanish merchant returning to Antwerp felt he was in a different town. Even the Exchange 'no es . . . lo que solia', is not what it used to be.

The decline of Lyons dates from roughly the same time. What remained of its important financial functions were transferred to Paris between 1570 and 1580. In 1577, on the Place aux Changes, once more a village square, the grass had begun to grow again.

It was at about the same time that the great exchange fairs of Medina del Campo came to an end, an event conventionally dated by historians as contemporary with the second Spanish state bankruptcy in 1575. Less attention has been drawn to the more or less simultaneous decline of both Burgos and Bilbao to the north of Medina. To all intents and purposes, the large registers of marine insurance at the consulate of Burgos were now closed. This signified

162. Bronze plaque by J. Jongheling c.1580, showing
the sack of Antwerp. *Victoria and Albert Museum*

the collapse of the long axis from Medina to Bilbao and through to Flanders which, at the beginning of Philip's reign, had been one of the main routes of the Spanish Empire.

So the Mediterranean was attracting away from the North a large share of the world's currency. A sign of the times was the renaissance of Barcelona, whose exchange fairs were re-opened in 1592, and whose ships by the end of the century were sailing out beyond Sardinia, Naples, and Sicily, which had previously marked the boundaries of her commercial zone, to Ragusa and Alexandria in Egypt. In addition, the whole of Italy was now flooded with precious metals. The ambassador du Ferrier, who for so long represented France in Venice and was well acquainted with both Italian and Levantine affairs, was disturbed in 1575 by rumours of war threatening the Peninsula. Would Spain take advantage of the internal troubles of Genoa to seize the city and along with it the rest of Italy? This Italy 'which has never been so wealthy', as he says in a letter to the king of France. What then would he have said of Italy in the subsequent decades? A man as well informed as the Duke of Feria could write in a long report in about 1595 that England's best course would still be to come to terms with Spanish authority 'following the example of Naples, Sicily, and Milan, which under their present regime flourish as they have never done before . . .'. This quotation should perhaps be dedicated to those who have hastened to speak of the decline of the Mediterranean from the beginning of the sixteenth century.

In fact by degrees Spanish money invaded every part of the sea. It soon became a part of everyday life. Towards 1580 the coins in most common use on the Algiers markets were the Spanish gold *escudo*, silver *reales*, pieces of eight, six, and four, particularly pieces *de a ocho reales*. All these coins were at a premium on the market and were a commodity figuring largely in exports to Turkey, where *reales* were shipped by the chestful. The registers of the French Consulate at Algiers, which go back to 1579 and of the French Consulate at Tunis which begin in 1574 make frequent reference to the predominance of Spanish currencies. It was in Spanish coin that ransom prices were usually stated. In February, 1577, when the prisoners aboard an Algerian ship mutinied at Tetouan, the Turks hastily jumped overboard, unfortunately for them. Laden with *reales* and gold coins many sank straight to the bottom.

Besides the large official shipments, small boats coming straight from Genoa or Spain to Leghorn carried among the bales of merchandise cases of 'reali'. In May, 1604, a Frenchman from Marseilles recognized at Ragusa that he owed a Florentine 'duo centum sexaginta tres peggias regaliorum de 8 regaliis pro qualumque pezzia'. So Ragusa was by now affected by the invasion of Spanish money. What city or country indeed was not? Reals were arriving in Turkey as we have already seen, from as far away as Poland in the heavy carts on the roads from Lwow to Constantinople.

After 1580 the true centre of distribution of Spanish silver, at least as much if not more than Spain herself, was Italy and her city-states. From this position Italy derived much benefit, her responsibility being to export to the Levant (and this was both easy and profitable) some of her surplus Spanish silver, and also to supply the rather more elusive gold coins, as well as silver and bills of exchange, to the tight corner in the Netherlands where Spain was fighting for her empire and for the future of the Catholic faith, and where the flow of coins pouring into the country sustained Protestant rebels as well as Spanish troops and loyal subjects. Italy then lay at the centre of a system that created its own liaisons, synchronizations, and glaring imbalances.

Italy, the victim of 'la moneda larga'. It was not of course simply because it lay on the imperial route of Spanish silver that Italy was thus privileged. It was a useful coincidence, but a greater factor was the active Italian economy which has been persistently underestimated by historians, but which was healthy enough in these final years of the century to maintain a positive trade balance with Germany, Eastern Europe, the Netherlands, France, and Spain (apart from Florence's deficit arising from her purchase of Castilian wool). These positive balances helped Italy to accumulate wealth and to pay off the deficit owed in the Levant and Turkey, of which we have spoken at such length, and the profitable returns from which stimulated the entire commercial and industrial activity of the Peninsula. Italy then found herself at the centre of a traffic in precious metals and bills of exchange, in effect mistress of an interdependent circuit. In a period of silver inflation gold became the safe investment, the metal that was hoarded and the one used for international payments. Unless specifying the contrary, bills of exchange were payable in gold. It was in gold coin too that the Flanders army demanded to be paid, if not in full then at least in part. And finally, gold was the only metal that could be carried by courier as we have seen. So if Italy depended on Spain, Spain depended on Italy for payments in the North, which frequently had to be made in gold at the Flanders end, through the good offices of Genoa. The Italian money markets alone were able to provide the gold coin and bills of exchange that were to end up in Antwerp in the hands of the paymasters of the Flanders army.

So Italy stood at the crossroads where the south–north axis maintained by Spanish policy and the Genoese *asientos* met the east–west axis running to the Levant and the Far East, or to put it another way where the golden road from Genoa to Antwerp met the silver road to distant China.

The age of the Genoese. These preliminary observations will help us to situate the great age of Genoese finance, which takes its place in the history of capitalism between 1557 and 1627, following the brief age of the Fuggers and preceding the rise of the hybrid capitalism of Amsterdam. I confess that I would prefer to say 1640 or 1650 rather than 1627 but that is not crucial. Obviously the fortune of the Genoese was not created by the wave of a magic wand in 1557, after the

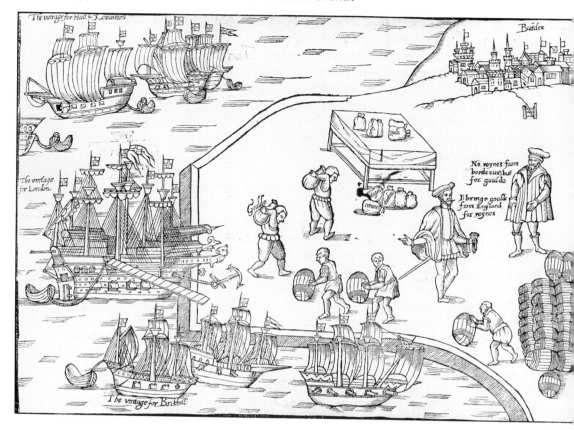

The vintage for Hull & Newcastell

Burdex

The vintage for London.

Goulde

Realls

Crownes

No. roynes from bordeaux but for goulde

I bringe goulde from England for roynes

The vintage for Bristoll

163. A Bordeaux merchant receiving bags of English gold in return for the hogsheads of claret that are being rolled along the quay to the ships waiting to sail for Bristol and London. Note how well-armed they are. Sixteenth-century woodcut.

extraordinary bankruptcy of the Spanish state, nor did it end abruptly in 1627, the date of the fifth or sixth suspension of payments in Castile, when the Count Duke Olivares promoted the Portuguese *marranos* to the rank of principal moneylenders to the Castilian crown. Genoa was for many years afterwards to remain a fulcrum of international finance.

Their great opportunity was provided by the exhaustion and depleted resources of the Fuggers and their acolytes, who had been hard hit by the mid-century recession and who were to withdraw (apart from brief reappearances in 1575 and 1595) from the dangerous business of the *asientos*.

The *asientos* were contracts with multiple clauses drawn up between the government of Castile and the *hombres de negocios*. They consisted of short-term loans, repaid principally out of imports of treasure to Seville. Since the Indies fleets could not be relied upon to be punctual, the king required an alternative regular source of funds, in particular for the monthly payment *usually in gold* of the wages and other expenses of the Spanish army in Flanders. The astuteness of the Genoese in the period after 1557 lay in drawing not only on the various resources of the Catholic King inside and outside Castile, but also, in order to assemble and guarantee their enormous loans, on public savings, Spanish and even Italian. For the king (between 1561 and 1575) conceded to them *juros de resguardo*, in theory state bonds handed over as a guarantee for the agreed loan, but which the *asentistas* were free to use as they pleased. They sold these bonds to their friends and acquaintances as well as to subscribers who flocked to buy them. Of course the Genoese would then have to buy back these *juros* to return them to the king, but only when he had reimbursed the loan. Second, *sacas* of specie were forbidden, between 1559 and 1566, years during which the finances of Castile were reorganized, all outstanding debts being referred to the *Casa de la Contratación*, which became a sort of *Casa di San Giorgio* using its resources to ensure the payment of *juros* 'situated' on the *Casa*. This was the object of the important Toledo ruling of November, 1560, which is regarded by historians as a supplementary bankruptcy, decided, like the first in 1557, with the tacit consent of the business community, who received in *juros* the equivalent of most of the payments due to them, but were able to pay their own creditors in the same currency. In settlements of this nature the Genoese suffered less than the Fuggers. If they could no longer export their profits in the form of specie, they could easily invest them in Spanish commodities, alum, wool, olive oil, silk, etc., which could then be exported to Italy and the Netherlands, providing them with the liquid assets they required in these distant places. It was of course much more convenient when after 1566, because of the troubles in Flanders, they were once again authorized to export silver coins and ingots more or less as they pleased.

But the crucial problem continued to be the transfer and payment of gold to the Low Countries. In order to solve it Philip II was obliged to apply to the international capitalists, the bankers of south Germany before the middle of the century, the Genoese after 1557. Philip was obliged to follow this course even more than Charles V had been. On the international market he controlled silver, but not copper, bills of exchange, and gold. Copper was really only a subsidiary. But this humble metal was unknown in the Iberian Peninsula, being obtained first from Germany and later, in the seventeenth century, from Sweden and Japan. Spain could easily obtain it on payment and the situation was only difficult in Portugal, where copper fetched unprecedented prices until 1550 because of the demand from the East Indies. It was still said in 1640 that in the time of King Manuel copper was more expensive than gold in Portugal. As for bills of exchange, a distinction should be made between those which were an instrument of credit, sometimes going beyond the bounds of reason, and those which went to compensate for surpluses in the balance of trade. Spain, staggering under the weight of her American treasure, had a trade balance in deficit all around; the countries with surpluses were (or had been) the Netherlands and Italy (which continued in surplus). The latter countries' bills were therefore the ones to buy. For in theory payable in gold, bills of exchange governed the complicated movements of gold coins. Since Europe's gold supply was only meagrely replenished from the New World, these payments often depended on existing reserves.

In all these directions, Genoese capitalism was quickly to establish its superiority, but such an achievement would never have been possible, it should be stressed, without the cooperation of all Italy. This cooperation made success a certainty. The Genoese, when selling silver, found in their native city and to an even greater degree in the rest of Italy, the gold coins and bills they required. The soldiers in Flanders always demanded that part of their pay should be in gold coin, which was both profitable and convenient. Gold pieces were much sought after and they were easily transported in small quantities. So there was a continual exchange of silver pieces for gold. The merchants did, it is true, attempt to shake off this onerous obligation by trying to impose silver coins, or even better, pieces of cloth, as part of the soldier's pay. In this respect progress was slow. In February, 1569, for instance, the Duke of Alva was about to send an expeditionary force under Mansfeldt to the aid of the Catholics in France. In order to provide the gold pieces carried in the three-horse carriage of the detachment's paymaster, Diego de Gueines, it was necessary first to apply to the merchants of Rouen, Paris, and Lyons, and then, at some cost, to change for gold crowns the silver currency received from the merchants. This trivial incident enables us to put our finger on something that was an everyday reality and to glimpse something of the wider context. The general system of the Genoese bankers, which received its finishing touch in 1579 with the creation of the Piacenza fairs and was to last until after the end of the century, viewed from the Netherlands, represented a vast gold-draining operation dependent upon the existence of a series of circuits in commodities, silver, bills of exchange, in a word all the wealth of the West. It was a winning game but it meant respecting certain imperative rules.

The Piacenza fairs. The triumph of the Genoese did not become apparent until after 21st November, 1579, when the so-called Besançon fairs were moved by them to Piacenza, where they remained, except for a few brief interruptions until 1621 under continuous Genoese control. The Besançon fairs may have originated as far back as 1534. The Genoese merchants had encountered such opposition first at Lyons from the king of France who had not forgiven them for their treachery in 1528, and then, when they retreated to Chambéry, from the Duke of Savoy, who, under pressure from the French king, expelled them from his states, that they had to find another rendezvous for the financiers and their correspondents, first at Lons-le-Saunier, in January, 1535, at the Epiphany Fair, then at Besançon for the next Easter fair, the first of a long series. It was not Charles V but the Republic of Genoa itself that arranged this move, and favoured the new rendezvous all the more since the French occupied Savoy and Piedmont in 1536, and Besançon could be reached by way of Lombardy, the Swiss Cantons, and the Franche-Comté; since this distant meeting-place, 'inconvenient and tiresome' though it was, nevertheless had the advantage of being within striking distance of Lyons and the money and merchandise attracted there by its fairs, whose timetable was for a long time exactly mirrored at Besançon. Lyons was still the true capital of world wealth, halfway between the Mediterranean and Antwerp, which explains why, when they encountered at Besançon difficulties about which we know very little, the Genoese transferred their fairs to Poligny, probably in 1568, then to Chambéry, moving south all the time, but remaining within the orbit of Lyons. This proximity was vital, as is proved by the large number of payments recorded at Montluel, the first village of any size on the road from Lyons to Savoy.

The transfer of the fairs to Piacenza, on the territory of the Duke of Parma, represented then a decisive step, the final break with Lyons, which was now separated from the new rendezvous by the width of the Alps. The establishment of the fairs at Piacenza was also the last act of the long crisis spread over the four previous years, whose true causes historians are only now beginning to discover. This was the major episode in the fortunes of the Genoese bankers.

The system of *asientos* associated with *juros de resguardo* had developed into a major activity as a result of the troubles in Flanders since 1566 and the growing numbers of *licencias de saca* and in spite of the Channel blockade. The insolent success of the Genoese, now openly installed in the new capital, Madrid, where all the important contracts were signed, and where they had introduced an exchange linked with Alcalá de Henares, did not fail to arouse violent feelings of jealousy in Spanish public opinion, and, what was more serious, among Philip II's entourage. The Cortes, between 1573 and 1575, had reacted strongly against these foreigners. But attacking them was one thing, replacing them another. Philip II's advisers and the king himself assumed rather too readily that it would be possible to apply instead to merchants in Spain and elsewhere. The decree of 1st September, 1575, then, was a blow struck at the entire fortunes of the Genoese. All *asientos* agreed since 14th November, 1560, were annulled, and considered 'illegal' and fraudulent. All accounts were to be settled according to the terms laid down unilaterally in the Pragmatic that appeared in December, 1575 (although bearing the date 1st September). To the Genoese this brought massive losses. They protested, applied for legal redress to the jurisdiction of the *Camara* of Castile, but above all they effectively blocked payments of gold to Flanders. It is even probable that they supported the Protestant rebels in the Netherlands. But in December of this dramatic year, the city of Genoa was convulsed by a political and social revolution of an extremely violent character (the underlying causes of which are unfortunately little known) with on one side the *Nobili Vecchi*, who dealt exclusively in finance, and on the other the *Nobili*

164. View of Lyons. Engraving by Israël Silvestre. *Bibliothèque Nationale, Paris*

Nuovi (di San Pietro), ordinary merchants supported by the *arti*, the craft guilds. The rebels won, seized the levers of command, and raised wages. But the victorious party proved unequal to the administration of the city, still less to the restoration of the vast financial machine dislocated by Philip II's September decree. So everything still seemed very much in the balance at the end of 1575. The struggle in Genoa, the struggle in Spain, the competition between Genoese and non-Genoese merchants in every commercial centre in Europe were all part of a single campaign.

Total victory for the Genoese bankers did not come until two years later with what was for them the compromise agreement, the *medio general* signed with the king of Spain on 5th December, 1577, abrogating the draconian measures of 1575. It was a victory owed entirely to the incompetence and inexperience of the Castilian merchants and of anyone else, including the Fuggers, 'unconditional servants' of the Habsburgs, who joined in. The capital they advanced was insufficient, it was recalled too soon and yet it moved too slowly. Moreover, the Genoese embargo on bills of exchange and gold was effective. They held all the best cards, leaving their would-be competitors little room for manoeuvre. Whether it was sent through Florence, Lisbon, Lyons, or even Paris and the French roads, their rivals' money did not travel quickly enough. As a

165. Italian money changers and bankers. Fourteenth-century Italian manuscript, Genoa.
British Library

result, the unpaid Spanish troops mutinied and, after a series of disturbances, captured and violently sacked the city of Antwerp in November, 1576. These dramatic events – in which it would be as naïve to assume that the Genoese had no hand as it would be to assume that Spain had nothing to do with the December uprising in Genoa – forced the king into a reconciliation. Agreement was reached only on 5th December, 1577, when the *hombres de negocios* immediately made available to the Spanish king five million 'golden crowns in gold', payable at Genoa, Milan, and if necessary Naples or Sicily.

Meanwhile order was being restored in Genoa, and with the support of the merchant bankers of the Milanese and Tuscany, a new solution was envisaged: that the fairs should be held at Piacenza, on the territory of the Duke of Parma. Here, apart from a few interruptions (at Easter, 1580, they were held at Montluel, near Lyons, in Savoy), they were to remain along with the system they incarnated, and under Genoese control, until 1621. Through Genoa the Mediterranean long held the key to the control of world wealth.

At Piacenza the spectacle resulting from this victory was an apparently modest one. These fairs in no way resembled either the tumultuous gatherings of Lyons or the popular fairs of Frankfurt and Leipzig. The watchword at Piacenza was discretion.

Four times a year – at the fairs of the Annunciation (1st February); Easter (2nd May); August (1st August) and All Saints (2nd November) – about sixty bankers would meet together. These were the *banchieri di conto*, a few Genoese, Milanese, Florentines, all members of a kind of club, to enter which one had to have the vote of the present members and a large sum of caution money (4000 crowns). These were the men who on the third day of the fairs would fix the *conto*, or official exchange rate, the importance of which need not be stressed. Alongside these *banchieri di conto* were the exchange-merchants or *cambiatori*, as they were often called, who were entitled on payment of caution (2000 crowns) to follow the fairs and present their payments (or *bilanci*). Into the third category came the *heroldi* (or *trattanti*), firms' representatives or brokers. In all then a maximum of two hundred people, bound by strict discipline, the final decision in cases of dispute lying with the all-powerful Senate of Genoa.

The fairs functioned as a clearing-house. Every merchant presented a bound volume, the *scartafaccio*, or market book, containing records of all the bills due to or from him, in other words his payments and withdrawals. The first step was to order all these accounts, to obtain recognition of the sums involved; then all the transactions to be settled at the fair were brought together in a series of cancellations or compensatory payments. The final result was a set of assets and liabilities bearing no relation to the fantastic sums originally quoted, which had all melted like snow in the sun. The regulations of the fair stipulated that all differences were to be paid in gold, but for this only a small quantity of specie was required and the creditor would often accept an extension of credit to another fair or exchange. So credit machinery was set up for the benefit of debtors. The details of these transactions were of course much more complicated; if one turns to the classic book by the Genoese Domenico Peri, *Il Negociante*, which was published in Genoa in 1638, one sees that in practice there were often serious problems, in spite of the fact that exchange rates were fixed in advance. There were many disputes. For participants unacquainted with the rules, the organizers of the fairs would circulate on the fifth day model bills of exchange where the merchant had only to fill in the blank spaces.

Huge sums of money changed hands at these expeditious fairs. From about 1588, according to Davanzati, over 37,000,000 *écus de marc* were handled and some years later, according to Domenico Peri, the figure reached 48,000,000. The exchange rate quotations can be reconstructed from surviving commercial correspondence. But unless at least the accounts and correspondence of one of the Genoese bankers come to light, we shall never have more than an outsider's view of the fairs. The entire fortune of the Genoese depended upon a subtle mechanism, subtly operated. Their reign was the reign of paper, as the Fuggers' agent in Spain ill-temperedly said, accusing them in 1577 'of having more paper than hard cash', 'mehr Papier als Baargeld'.

The reign of paper. The age of negotiable paper money did not begin in 1579 with the first Piacenza fairs. The whole century had prepared the way for it. But after 1566, or rather 1579, it assumed an importance that no one who came into the slightest contact with business could fail to observe. As different functions began to emerge, the occupation of banker began to be distinguished from other commercial activities: banker, or rather 'financier', since from the first, banking operations concerned the money of princes. It is essential to grasp how strange and new a profession it seemed at the time, if we are to understand the astonishment of contemporaries. Wise and honest men had always assumed that money followed trade in commodities; by 'real exchange' they meant what resulted from such straightforward dealing, but that money should lead an existence apart from commodities was difficult for them to accept; or that at Piacenza everything could apparently be settled by juggling with a set of figures. Philip II himself confessed that he understood nothing about exchange and it may have been a contributory factor in his dislike of the Genoese.

In Venice, still half-immersed in the past, paper for some time remained only a discreet visitor. But Venetians could be severe judges, like the ambassador at Madrid, who wrote to the Signoria in 1573 that the Genoese *asentistas* neglected the true and honest trade in commodities, concerning themselves only with the *negoziatione dei cambi* and even declaring commodity trading 'cosa da bezarioto et da gente più bassa', an occupation fit only for paupers and men of low condition. In 1573 such sentiments were still comprehensible. But thirty years later in a Venice that was experiencing an all too brief 'age of enlightenment', where so many thinkers were interested in economic questions, Leonardo Dona, for instance, when one finds excellent 'discourses', a little florid perhaps but clearly argued, on trade, politics, and money, it is less easy to understand the persistent astonishment of such men at the proliferation of paper, at the novelty of payments being made through the exchange, instead of being made in cash.

And yet this financial world was really the 'reasonable' world because it held the key to the future and because its operations were intelligent operations, notwithstanding the criticisms of those who did not understand them. The coming of the age of paper, its extension if not its first appearance, in fact marked the beginning of a new economic structure, an extra dimension that had now to be reckoned with. The Genoese were pioneers in this respect and derived from it the usual advantages brought by progressive techniques. Their mistake was to stake everything on their superiority in this field and by devoting themselves to financial affairs to withdraw from the Atlantic trade where they were still very well placed in 1566. The Atlantic economy, more or less left to itself was to develop and mature, producing its own merchants and before long its

166. *The Money Changer* by Rembrandt. *Gemäldegalerie, Berlin*

own financiers. The defeat of the Genoese did not, as it is often rather hastily assumed, represent the failure of pure finance and paper money and the triumph of the merchant who had remained faithful to traditional commerce; it signified rather the rise of a new capitalism with a different geographical centre of gravity, which had been in the making since the discovery of America, but which took over a century to reach completion. Ultimately it marked the victory of new financiers, the Portuguese moneylenders who were to intervene at Madrid in 1627 and, behind them, the heavy hand of the capitalists of the North. It was in fact one of the stages in the development of Dutch capitalism, the superstructures of which, including the most modern form of credit machinery, were in place by at least 1609: the force that was to replace Mediterranean capitalism.

But the old model, patiently assembled over time, was in every respect a pattern for the new.

From the last state bankruptcy under Philip II to the first under Philip III. The last suspension of payments by Philip II in 1596 and the first by Philip III in 1607 bring us face to face with these problems of forbidding magnitude. Our aim must be not so much to describe the eventful history of these changes as to discover their underlying mechanisms, the permanent factors at work, in order to test the explanatory schemas that have been so strikingly improved by recent research.

In our search for the right perspective, we must avoid being dazzled by the dramatic history of events which has regularly been viewed from too close up. We must constantly remind ourselves that any supremacy, whether political, economic, social, or cultural, has its beginnings, its apogee, and its decline, and that the stages in the rise of capitalism, that is, the points at which its course has been interrupted or altered, have parallels elsewhere. Like the age of the Fuggers, the age of the Genoese, and the later age of Amsterdam was to last barely the space of three generations.

Having said this, in order to go to the heart of the subject, it would be as well to note at once:

1. That the conflicts between the Castilian state and the bankers always contained two stages: first, the quarrel, then the reconciliation; in winter the quarrel might be prolonged (there was no urgency), as in 1596–1597, then with the coming of summer and the urgent needs of state, all parties hastened to reach agreement: the resulting compromise was known as the *medio general*. There was one *medio general* in 1577, one in 1597, two in 1607, one in 1627. The quarrel, or rather suspension of payments, was always known as the *decreto*.

2. That if the Castilian state lost every time, it was because it was no match for the *hombres de negocios*, who were centuries ahead of it. Philip II's raging against the Genoese was a sign of his obstinacy, his thwarted will, but not of his common sense. Had he been clear-sighted he would have set up a state bank, as was suggested to him in 1582, or a number of *Monti*, on the Italian pattern, as was suggested to him in 1596; he would have embarked upon a deliberately inflationist policy (but could he have controlled it?). In fact Philip II seems to me to have been constantly placed in the position of a nineteenth-century South American state, rich in the product of its mines or its plantations, but hopelessly out of its depth in the world of international finance. Such a government might show its displeasure, even move to action, but in the end it would be forced to submit, to yield up its resources and its commanding posts, and show itself to be 'accommodating'.

3. That every time the state declared itself bankrupt, bringing contracts to a violent end, there were always some actors who lost, fell through a trap-door, or tiptoed away towards the wings: in 1557 it was the merchants of South

167–170. *Top:* A Spanish gold piece of 8 reales (a 'piece of eight')
of Philip II. *Bottom:* A piece of eight of 1604. The metal has
been debased to copper ('*vellon*'). *British Museum*

Germany; in 1575, the Italian merchants apart from the Genoese; in 1596 and
1607 the Spanish merchants; in 1627 the Genoese merchants themselves, though
they, like the Fuggers in 1577, did not leave the stage for good. The rule however
still holds.

4. That in each case the brunt of the losses was borne by the taxpayers of
Castile, already overburdened with a heavy fiscal load, and by small savers and
investors in Spain and Italy. As long as there are bankers, there will always be
people 'left holding Russian stocks'.

By about 1590 and even more clearly in 1593 and 1595 everything pointed
towards another bankruptcy by the Crown of Castile. Its expenditure continued
to rise above all reasonable limits while its income was declining, with a visible
drop in fiscal revenues. The general economic depression was the cause of many
bankruptcies and imprisonments for debts. Amid these difficulties only the
imports of silver from America were on the increase, so that the circulation of
precious metals at Seville and Barcelona, Genoa and Venice, or along the Rhine,
which was used for transport to the Low Countries, was unaffected and functioning normally. The abundance of money at lower levels could and did create

illusions, a false sense of security even in hard-headed businessmen, despite the immense war in which Spain was engaged with much of the rest of Europe, despite their habitual prudence and despite the restraints brought once again by the suspension of the *sacas de plata* after 1589. The most alarming sign was undoubtedly fiscal tension in Castile which was becoming excessive; all tax-payers were being harried: the grandees, the nobility, the clergy, the towns, and even the merchants if not the *hombres de negocios*, and enormous sums in *juros* were launched on a market that was still comparatively willing to buy. It was a situation that appears more explosive to historians with the benefit of hindsight than it did to the financiers of the day. They were surprised by the royal *decreto* of mid-November by which Philip II suspended all payments and thereby recovered all the income and capital in the hands of the moneylenders.

In the early stages of this trial of strength, Philip II's government, while unable to avoid contacts, pressures, and conversations, refused to make any promises. It seems clear that the king and his advisers were not out to 'metter per terra la contratatione', to bring to the ground the system of *asientos* and the group of powerful businessmen known as the *contratación*. Their aim, and this was known before the decree, was to curb the demands of the financiers, to limit the profits of the *asentistas*, to obtain substantial long-term loans valid over a period of at least three years even if the 'Indies fleets did not arrive'. Relations would soon have been established once more on a mutually suspicious footing no doubt (indeed how could it be otherwise between the king and his creditors?) if the Fuggers had not intervened. The German firm came to the rescue in early December, or rather one of their three agents in Spain, Thomas Carg, did. Without consulting the other two he reached an agreement with the Spanish king to advance twelve monthly payments of 300,000 crowns, payable 'through the local branch' in the Netherlands, against an advance of half the total in cash, plus corresponding assignments, plus the promise that a monumental backlog of debts would be paid. The Genoese did not at first take this manoeuvre seriously. It was a trick, an 'artifice', an *asiento 'aereo'*, in the air. Moreover they were themselves proposing to the king better terms spread over a longer period, or so they said with apparent sincerity. By February the Genoese realized that the manoeuvre was serious, that all it now required to become reality was the consent of the Fuggers in Augsburg. The subsequent disputes and dissension within this great banking family, divided against itself, would provide a fascinating excursion into biographical history, as would the eventful journey of Anton Fugger to Madrid in April, 1597. In the present context, the Fuggers' intervention gave Philip II a year's breathing-space. But by the end of 1597 the Fugger interlude was over and agreement was to be reached fairly quickly. The Castilian government could no longer afford the luxury of putting it off.

Concluded between two of Philip II's 'ministers' and four representatives of the financiers, the agreement of 13th November, 1597, was to become the *medio*

171. The Spanish tax collector. Detail from *The Calling of St. Matthew* by Juan de Pareja.
Prado, Madrid

general of the 29th of the same month. The victims of the decree of 1596, the *decretados*, were to advance to the king, in eighteen monthly payments, 4,500,000 crowns in Flanders and 2,500,000 in Spain, between the end of January, 1598, and the end of June, 1599. For his part, the king agreed to grant them a series of substantial benefits, and in particular granted them an enormous sum in *juros*, over 7 million ducats.

About ten years later the whole process began again, as if the system contained within it the structural necessity for bankruptcy at more or less regular intervals. I do not think I need describe in detail the decree of 9th November, 1607, the *medio general* of 14th May, 1608, to show how Spain entered upon a new crisis only ten years after the last suspension of payments by Philip II, in spite of the pacific policy of the Duke of Lerma, but because of the extravagance of the new reign, the plundering of public funds and the general recession of the economy after 1595. The 1608 ruling created, to the sole advantage of the Genoese, a complicated but reliable system for paying off the floating debt,

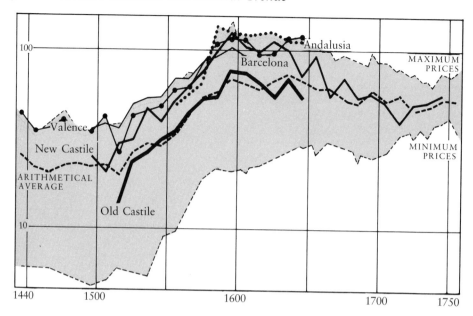

Wheat prices in the Mediterranean and Europe

From F. Braudel and F. C. Spooner, Vol. IV of the *Cambridge Economic History* (p. 470). From about fifty series of wheat prices, calculated in grams of silver per hectolitre, it has been possible to construct the range of cereal quotations (the shaded zone represents the range between maximum and minimum prices) for the whole of Europe and the arithmetical average (dotted line) of all these prices. Prices rose universally of course throughout the sixteenth century. On this 'envelope' I have superimposed, in two separate diagrams for the sake of clarity, various Mediterranean price-curves. It will be noted that the curve for Old Castile coincides almost exactly with the arithmetical

bonds for which were in the hands of their business associates. So the Genoese held the field alone and were correspondingly detested and despised. And it was alone that in 1627 they were to meet the onslaught, engineered by the Count Duke Olivares, of the Portuguese financiers who had already been sounded out in 1596, applied to in 1607, and thrown into the fray in 1627, by which time they already occupied in the various cities of Castile (above all at Seville) a series of strong commercial positions. This triumph crowned their previous achievements and marked a turning-point in the history of international capitalism, as well as the immediate prelude to their endless difficulties with the frowning and implacable Inquisition.

3 The rise in prices

The general price rise of the sixteenth century was felt with force in the Mediterranean countries, especially after the 1570s, and was accompanied by its many familiar consequences. The violent character and the length of this 'revolution'

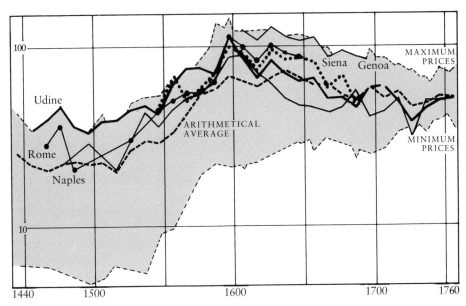

average. All the other Mediterranean curves are well above average, at least until 1620 and in some cases even later. The Mediterranean, or at least the Christian Mediterranean, since there are no price series available for the eastern part of the sea where prices were certainly lower, was a zone where bread was expensive, reaching almost the maximum price for the period. After the middle of the seventeenth century Mediterranean prices are much nearer the average, but it should be noted that during this period European prices in general were tending to converge as is clearly shown by the pronounced narrowing of the shaded zone. The distance between maximum and minimum was to decrease even further during the eighteenth century.

– which in fact extended into the seventeenth century – could not fail to be noted by contemporary observers. For them it was an occasion to reflect on the complex problem of currency, the new and revolutionary power of money, and the general fortunes of men and states. Historians in their turn have looked for the culprit or culprits, and sometimes thought they have found the answer, but the truth appears more and more complex as fresh facts daily come to light.

Although it has come under much attack I shall continue to use the term 'price revolution'. Opinions may differ as to its causes, its true dynamics and its extent, but not about its brutally novel character. The quantity theory has come down to us more or less intact. It was restated in its modern form in the monumental work of Earl J. Hamilton, which accepts its basic validity.

Wages. Inflation, which was felt everywhere, brought its usual consequences.

Wages followed in the wake of the price rise but more slowly, sometimes failing to move at all. That life was hard for the poor we have already seen. Nominal wages rose more or less rapidly along with prices and remained high temporarily at times of recession; but translated into real wages, these figures

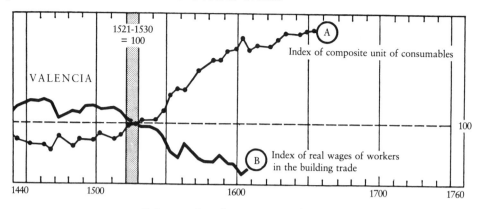

Prices and real wages at Valencia

After E. H. Phelps Brown and Sheila Hopkins: the cost of living to the consumer went up and real wages fell correspondingly.

tell the same story and testify to the extreme poverty of the lower-paid workers. In Spain, taking the years 1571–1580 as 100, real wages which in 1510 had been at an index of 127·84, fell in 1530 to 91·35; after fluctuating for a while they reached 97·61 in 1550; 110·75 in 1560; 105·66 in 1570; 102·86 in 1580; 105·85 in 1590; 91·31 in 1600. It was not until after the crisis of 1600 and the widespread epidemics that reduced the population of the Peninsula, that wages, following *vellon* inflation, shot up to 125·49 in 1610, 130·56 in 1611. The price

172. Weighing gold. Woodcut, Florence, 1493.

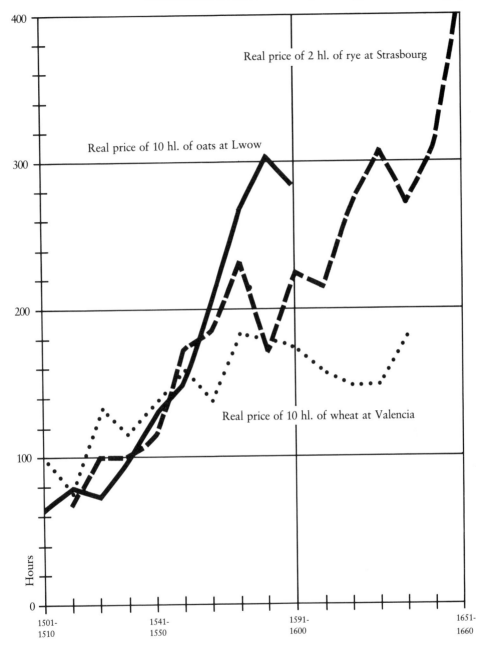

400

Real price of 2 hl. of rye at Strasbourg

Real price of 10 hl. of oats at Lwow

300

200

Real price of 10 hl. of wheat at Valencia

100

Hours

0

1501-
1510

1541-
1550

1591-
1600

1651-
1660

Real prices of cereals at Strasbourg, Lwow and Valencia

After René Grandamy in J. Fourastié, *Prix de vente et prix de revient*, 13th series, p. 31. The prices are calculated in hourly rates for bricklayers' labourers. The drop in the standard of living is less marked at Valencia than in the two other continental towns.

revolution brought little prosperity to Spanish wage-earners, although it treated them better than it did the artisans of France, England, Germany, or Poland. The situation was equally depressing in Florence where real wages tumbled during the price increase.

In fact one should really speak of a tri-metallic rather than a bi-metallic ratio. In order to bring copper and *vellon* currencies into line, they were continually being recalled to the mints, where they were reminted as even lighter coins and put back into circulation. This constant devaluation of copper was out of all proportion to the necessary harmony of currencies. On each occasion the state profited, not the public, and least of all the poor. Such manipulation began early in Spain and Sicily, where the *piccioli* were being melted down and reminted as early as 1563 and 1568.

Income from land. Inflation struck both rich and poor, but it affected some rich men more than others. It hit the 'industrialists', merchants, financiers (I should apologize for using these convenient but slightly anachronistic terms). It hit all those who were directly or indirectly caught up in the dangerous currents of money. It had much less effect upon landed proprietors. This is apparent from the detailed study by Carlo M. Cipolla ('Finanze dei Borghi e Castelli sotto il dominio spagnuolo') of the *castello* of Tegiole near Alessandria, the ancient fief of the bishop of Pavia, during the late sixteenth and early seventeenth century. In this particular instance, it appears that dues in kind and feudal labour had not all become money payments (and where money payments were customary, the lord or his representatives always had the right to re-estimate the amount): so alongside feudal revenues worth comparatively little, the *castello* had other, as it were more modern sources of income, corresponding to rent from its tenants, which meant that it received from the *contadini* sacks of wheat, oats, and beans, casks of wine and cartloads of hay – a revenue providing the basis of the *castello*'s budget.

If, bearing this in mind, one thinks of the Spanish ambassador Bernardino de Mendoza, whose sister administered his estates in his absence, selling his wheat every summer; of the Duke of Alcalá, viceroy of Naples, who in 1559 acquired 1500 vassals of the royal domains; if one remembers those Aragonese nobles, landlords of small estates, or the grandees of Castile, owners of land, flocks, and wheatfields, or the Sicilian lords who sold cereals, wine, or silk, one is everywhere impressed by the fact that for these noblemen, so very different from one another, land was a constant standby: during the insecure age of rising prices, it protected them from the abyss of inflation. If this seignorial class dominated Europe at the beginning of the seventeenth century, it was because it had lost much less ground than is commonly assumed. So it was no folly on the part of merchants and *nouveaux riches* to buy up estates and property in the countryside. The relentless pursuit of land and titles in Naples by rich Florentines and super-rich Genoese may have been a form of vanity but it was also a

vii. Detail from the Fra Angelico altarpiece of St. Nicholas of Bari, a port that derived
much of its wealth from the export of grain as depicted here.
Pinacoteca, Vatican, Rome

viii. *Following pages:* The Market in Genoa by Alessandro Magnasco.
Museo Civico d'Arte Antica, Milan

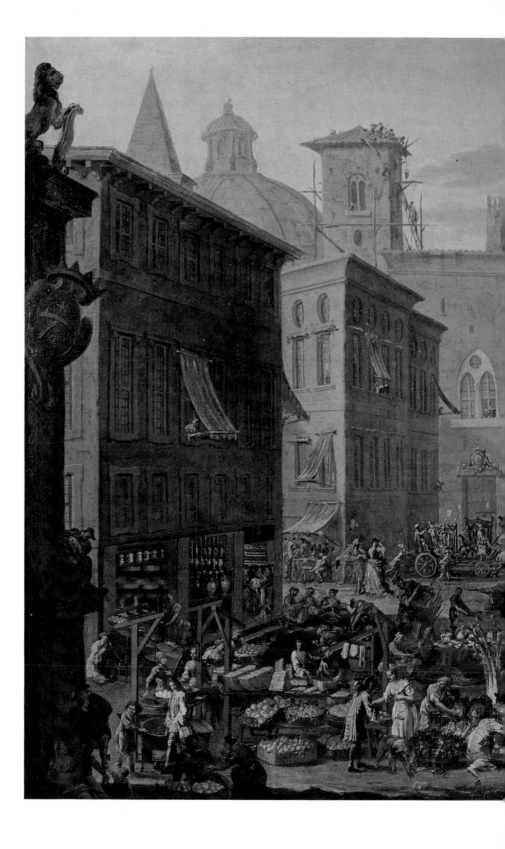

ix. The export of bullion from Venice, the Doge in the foreground directing operations.
The majolica dish is itself probably Venetian, c.1495.
Fitzwilliam Museum, Cambridge

173. Venetian silver ducat. *British Museum*

far-seeing policy, a prudent and responsible course of action from their point of view.

Even the less well off were attracted by such safe investments. Towards the end of his life (he died in 1570) Benvenuto Cellini became the proprietor of a small estate near Florence which he bought in March, 1560, as a lifetime investment from some peasants whose honesty he suspected. Whether they really tried to poison him or not we shall never know, for Cellini had a vivid imagination and tended to exaggerate. But the interesting point is that he chose to provide security for his old age by investing in land.

Banks and inflation. Except for land, every 'business' sector was affected, and in particular the banks. All banking operations were conducted in moneys of account, not in real moneys and were therefore exposed to the perils of inflation. For these fictional moneys, Venetian and Genoese *lire*, Sicilian *oncie* and *tari*, Spanish *maravedis* and ducats, French *livres tournois*, were constantly losing their intrinsic value. The Sicilian ounce, which in 1546 still corresponded to 91·09 Italian *lire* of 1866, was worth only 20·40 in 1572–1573. Similarly the *livre tournois*, expressed in *francs Germinal*, fell from 4 in 1515 to 3·65 in 1521 (this devaluation was a method of attracting foreign currency, in particular Castilian gold, into France); to 3·19 in 1561; to 2·94 in 1573; to 2·64 in 1575; to 2·46 in 1602. So the relationship of real money to money of account was continually being adjusted, and of the two the former was consistently better placed. Who bore the loss? If, after an interval of several years, a bank deposit registered in a money of account was repaid in the same terms as the original deposit, the depositor lost. If a banker's advance was repaid in the same terms, the banker lost. Time operated against money registered in units of account if it lay idle.

For whatever reason the number of bank failures increased after 1550–1570, a trend aggravated by the 'royal cycle of money' which was also the royal cycle of inflation. The disease had such a hold that the only remedy was to come from the state banks which began to appear one by one at precisely this juncture. The only public foundation to receive its charter before this time had been the Bank of Palermo, organized under the protection and guarantee of the city's Senate, in 1551, with headquarters in the premises known as *La Loggia*. Its origins unquestionably lay in the *Tavola Communale o della Prefetia* of Trepani, which went back as far as the end of the fifteenth century.

The great age of the creation of public banks was not to begin until thirty years after the foundation of the Palermo bank. In 1586 the *Casa di San Giorgio* resumed the banking functions it had abdicated over a century earlier in 1444 at the time of the gold crisis. On 23rd September, 1587, there was established the *Tavola della città di Messina*, whose statutes were not approved by Philip II until 1st July, 1596. Through this bank it was hoped – not unreasonably – that an end could be put both to the series of bank failures and to fraud on the part of the *collettori* of public revenue. This new bank naturally had the privilege of holding public funds in deposit. It was placed under the guarantee and control of the city of Messina. In 1587 appeared the famous *Banco della Piazza di Rialto* at Venice, which was taken over in 1619 by the no less famous *Banco Giro*. In 1593, the *Banco di S. Ambrogio* was founded at Milan with an independent governing body as a *banco giro*. The same period saw the founding at Naples of the bank annexed to the *Monte di Pietà* and the Hospital of the *Santa Casa dell' Annunziata*, and at Rome the bank annexed to the Hospital of the Holy Ghost. The creation of so many banks, within a definite period of time and over a fairly widespread area, can be considered evidence in itself.

But it is far from simple evidence. Particularly in the north, the functions of

174. Venetian silver ducat. *British Museum*

the state banks were soon to extend beyond the strict limits of public finance. The *Banco della Piazza di Rialto*, for instance, in spite of prohibitions, from the start allowed overdrafts, using its customers' money. It had in fact widely issued 'bank money' which was in greater demand than metal currency. In so doing the banks were not innovating, merely imitating the practices of the old private banks. Their originality lay in the unprecedented scale of the loans they made. But it was clearly the failure, imperfection, and insecurity of the private banks that led to this sudden outcrop of public banks. One has only to think of the long series of bank failures, from the bankruptcy of Priuli in 1552 to that of the second Pisani bank in 1584 or the long series of financial crashes at Naples, from that of the Genoese Ravasquez (a partial bankruptcy to be more accurate) to the reduction (from eleven to four banks) so long discussed, if not realized, in 1580.

Undoubtedly in both Naples and Venice these crashes were often caused by the untimely intervention of the public authorities. At Naples in 1552, for example, the viceroy seized Ravasquez' gold reserves, exchanging them for newly minted coins of lesser value. At Venice the Signoria had always compelled the banks to make loans on patriotic terms. But in both cases the secret evil was probably inflation. Everywhere it made state intervention necessary. A detail of the new banking organization of the *Casa di San Giorgio* gives food for thought: is it a vital clue or is that reading too much into it? In 1586, the bank opened to depositors its *cartulario-oro*, its gold-account; in 1606, its *cartulario-argento*; and in 1625, perhaps the most curious of all, an account for Spanish pieces of eight. What does this mean? That the depositor was credited in the currency which he had deposited and repaid in the same coin, if necessary, and therefore assured of a solid gold or silver guarantee against devaluation? The bank was protecting itself as well as its customers from the risks of money of account, preferring the solid values of metal currency.

States and the price rise. The states did better out of it. State finance comprised three sectors: receipts, expenditure, and debts. The third and by no means the least important was automatically alleviated by the rising tide of prices. Meanwhile, expenditure and receipts both increased at the same rate. The states all succeeded in increasing their revenues and floating with the current of inflation. They continued to spend on an impossible scale, of course, but they could draw on what were for the period extraordinary – and growing – resources.

Ehrenberg long ago warned historians – who ignored the warning – against trusting the budget estimates so frequently given by ambassadors (or indeed any others, I would be inclined to add). The word budget, with all its present day associations, is not strictly appropriate to the realities of the sixteenth century. But even inaccurate figures can provide an order of magnitude. They show that state budgets were steadily increasing. Take two Sicilian budgets a quarter of a century apart: in 1546, receipts: 340,000 *scudi*, expenditure: 166,000 *scudi*, which would leave a positive balance, but there were old debts to be paid off; in 1573 receipts were 750,194, expenditure, 211,032. But from this positive balance such a series of extraordinary expenses had to be deducted that the Spanish ministers of Sicily were obliged to borrow at 14 per cent and 16 per cent in order to balance expenditure and receipts. There were similar increases at Naples. In Spain, Charles V's revenues tripled during his reign, those of Philip II doubled between 1566 and 1573. In 1566 they totalled 10,943,000 ducats, in 1577, 13,048,000 ducats. Jumping fifty years, we find that in 1619, Philip III's revenues totalled 26,000,000.

Descriptive studies of budgets however fail to tackle the true problems, which all require some measurement of the price increase. Broadly speaking, the states grew progressively more defenceless against the rising cost of living, hence their determination to create their own resources, to swim against the tide of rising prices. The clearest element of the history of the state in the sixteenth century is the fiscal struggle; the war of the Netherlands was not only a fight for freedom of conscience, for the defence of cherished liberties, it also represented an unsuccessful attempt to bring the Spanish state into a fruitful association with the economic fortune of the great commercial crossroads.

It is a fact that Philip II's empire saw its European possessions one by one cease to be positive sources of income. In the Netherlands, Milan, Naples and Sicily, the 'revenants bons', as they were called in France, were progressively absorbed by local needs. There remained Spain, or rather Castile. The presence of Philip II in the Peninsula meant, with the help of internal peace, until 1569, that taxpayers, including the grandees, could be brought to heel. 'His Catholic Majesty,' writes the bishop of Limoges in 1561, 'is making more and more economies, desiring to provide for the future, giving orders concerning his finances and his domains; his vigilance is such that I would say any more might cause him to be accused of parsimony . . .' In other words the king did not cease to consult his experts. He was never short of advice from them throughout his long reign, the financial aspects of which were so dramatic. I have already referred to the great assembly of Toledo and its decision of 14th November, 1560. From then on the catalogue of taxes levied in Castile was constantly being lengthened and altered, by the addition of new items and the internal modification of existing taxes. The *alcabalas*, taxes on consumption for which towns contracted for fixed payments, in theory represented one-tenth of all sales. They were raised on four occasions by a hundredth, so the percentage rose to 14 per cent. Total revenue from the *alcabalas*, which was 1,200,000 ducats in 1561, had reached 3,700,000 by 1574. In 1577 it even had to be reduced by a million.

Naturally, the taxpayers complained. Cadiz in 1563 declared that all the taxes levied on commerce in the city since 1560 had ruined its trade. There were repeated protests from the Cortes, to whom however it never occurred to blame

175. Men being paid to join the Indies fleet. Detail from a view of Cadiz. From *Civitates Orbis Terrarum*.

imports of American treasure for the disquieting price increases, rather seeing the cause in what was before their eyes, namely the growing monstrous burden of taxation imposed by the royal government. 'There have resulted from this,' say the Cortes of 1571, 'so many charges, and the necessities of life have become so dear, that few men now can live without difficulty . . .'

A complete study of the budgets of the sixteenth century, comparable to what is known of English receipts and expenditure during the period would provide the answer to one important question. Under the assault of prices, did Mediterranean or near-Mediterranean states suffer more than others? It seems probable, at least in the case of Spain, especially when one remembers the enormous sums of money that war cost this too-vast empire. 'War,' writes a French pamphleteer, 'is extremely costly to him [Philip II], much more so than to any other prince, for example in his naval forces: he must take the greater part [of the crews] from foreign lands far away, which consumes a great quantity of his finances. And as for his wars on land, in the Low Countries for example, which is the principal, it costs him six times as much as his enemies to wage them, for by the time he has levied a soldier in Spain and taken him to the frontier of Artois ready to fight a Frenchman, that man has already cost him 100 ducats, while the French soldier has cost his king only ten . . .'

And from the point of view of naval equipment, which had to meet the requirements both of Atlantic warfare and Mediterranean battles, Spain was again at a disadvantage. Here too, prices were rising all the time. Tomé Cano, in his *Arte de Navegar*, explains that a vessel of 500 tons which in the time of Charles V would have cost 4000 ducats is now worth 15,000; a quintal of sailcloth from Flanders which was formerly worth 2½ ducats now costs 8 ducats. I have carried merchandise, he says, from Cartagena to the Indies, at 14 ducats a ton: the asking price is 52 today, 'and even so ships do not earn as much now as they earned in the past'. With prices rising, wages, but also profits, were often much reduced, a factor that must have been partly responsible for the difficulties of Spain's Atlantic navy at the end of the sixteenth century. What was true of the great ships on the Atlantic was equally true of the narrow galleys in the Mediterranean. In 1538 it cost Spain 2253 ducats to fit a single galley without artillery (the hull of the galley costing about 1000 ducats). In 1582 there was some talk of Gian Andrea Doria selling his galleys at 15,000 crowns each – a figure merely plucked out of the air. We do not know if it refers to galleys complete with oarsmen and artillery, but in any case the price difference is staggering.

The dwindling of American treasure. Imports of American treasure slowed down after the first and even more after the second decade of the seventeenth century. Whether symptom, consequence, or cause, this cessation marked a turning-point in world history. On the whole it would be wrong to attribute this 'event' to purely American causes as if America was the prime mover in this instance. It is said, for instance, that mining costs had risen, according to the law of diminishing returns; and that larger amounts of bullion were now being kept in America, both through fraud and in order to meet local currency requirements. Some of it may have been diverted by spectators from New Spain to the Far East and China on the Manila galleon. And again in America the decimation of the indigenous population may have hindered and slowed down recruitment of the Indian labour necessary for silver extraction.

There is some truth in all these explanations, but they have been advanced without the possible benefit of research still to be carried out not only in the archives at Seville but at Simancas and above all in American archives. There is no *a priori* reason to assume that a declining population cannot maintain a particular, privileged sector such as the mines; the active smuggling via the Rio de la Plata seems to have ended with the general mining recession of about 1623; exports of bullion on the Manila galleon also stopped after about 1635. But the basic shortcoming of these explanations is obvious: they essentially concentrate on America, as if fraud, for example, was not equally commonplace on both sides of the Atlantic. Above all, such arguments neglect the economic ties which, through the Spanish Empire, associated the New World with the dynamic forces of Europe. In other words they make no reference to the changing economic circumstances, to the widespread recession observable in Europe after 1580, 1595, 1619–1622, before the great divide of the 1640s, and Spain's subsequent troubles in Catalonia and Portugal, later in 1647 with Naples, and

176. *The Copper Mine* by Enrico de Bless, late sixteenth century. *Uffizi, Florence*

the suppression in the same year of the Barlovento fleet, the former protection of the West Indies.

Devalued currency and false currency. In any case, by the middle of the seventeenth century the great age of American silver had come to an end. It was then that counterfeit money began to appear in large quantities. It had not been unknown in the sixteenth century. But by the seventeenth century, lightweight coins were entering the general circulation of the Mediterranean and were carried as far as the Levant, whereas during the previous fifty years they had been unknown in these waters.

Debased money had previously only been common in northern Europe and in Islam, that is, on the outskirts of the Mediterranean world, and even here had not appeared until fairly late. In the north, while English currency, once it had been put on a sound footing by Elizabeth, did not budge thereafter, the currency of the rebel provinces of the Netherlands underwent a series of fluctuations until the devaluation of November, 1585. Even before this measure, since at least 1574, counterfeiters had been at work, particularly at Liège, and in that year their coins reached the gates of Spain itself. To exchange this money by fraud for good money was as effective a way as any of opening a breach in the Spanish monopoly and of obtaining a share in American treasure. This traffic which was carried on in the very ports of Spain swelled to enormous proportions after the signature of the Twelve Years Truce in 1609. The Dutch then began to ship in vast quantities of small coin, a traffic previously only possible on ships from Lübeck or Hamburg, through the good offices of the English (England having made peace with Spain in 1604), or even the French. This small coin, of low metallic content, arrived by the chest or barrelful. On the return journey, gold and silver coins would be concealed under salt or other merchandise. In 1607, in and around Bordeaux, four 'mints' were engaged in melting down Spanish coins obtained by every kind of subterfuge: they had only to be put in the melting-pot to bring an immediately profit of over 18 per cent.

And for the time being, this was almost fair dealing. The age of relative honesty was short-lived however. From 1613 on, false *vellon* began to appear, in imitation of Spanish coins. Over two million *pesos* of this kind were manufactured a year and production increased later. According to experts this counterfeit coin could bring profits of over 500 per cent. Outside the Low Countries, similar false money was coined in Denmark, England, and Italy. *Quartillos falsos* would arrive by the boatload on the Cantabrian coast or at San Lucar de Barrameda.

During the period that concerns us, if Mediterranean internal trade was little affected by these extraordinary upheavals, a serious crisis was stirring in the Turkish empire, from Algiers to Egypt and Constantinople. Much has been written of the magnificent and unalterable Turkish finances. They may have been so during the long reign of Sulaimān the Magnificent (1522–1566). But in the very last year of this glorious reign, just after the unsuccessful siege of Malta, if the information contained in Hammer's book is correct, in Cairo, the only Turkish 'mint' where gold coins were struck, these coins were devalued by 30 per cent. It is possible that this was an adjustment rendered necessary by the depreciation of silver. It would be interesting to know what it signified, and whether or not a devaluation in 1566, after the prolonged strain of the siege of Malta, marked the first sign of exhaustion of the Turkish empire.

By 1584 there is no room for doubt. There was a serious currency crisis. The usual currency in Turkey was a small silver coin, more square than round in shape, the asper (in Turkish *akce*, pronounced ak-che), made of pure silver 'not alloyed but purified', according to Pierre Belon. They were assayed, says a traveller, by throwing them into a red-hot pan. In weight they represented a quarter of a silver drachm. At the beginning of the century, the asper represented the 135th part of a sequin or *sultanin*, which was made of fine gold, hardly inferior *di bontà* to the Venetian sequin, but equal and often superior to the best *ongari* of Germany. On the accession of Selim I, the *sultanin* was worth 60 aspers, the official rate which does not appear to have been modified until 1584. So if there was a devaluation in 1566, it did not affect the equivalence in silver of the new style sequin. The Turkish *thaler*, a silver coin slightly inferior to the Austrian *Kronenthaler* or the Italian *escudo*, was worth 40 aspers, while the *Kronenthaler* and *escudo* were worth 50. These values are confirmed by the documents: in 1547, 300 aspers were worth 6 crowns. The Venetian *bailo* in 1564 indicates that his everyday expenses over three months amounted to 34,487 aspers, or 574 ducats and 47 aspers: which means the exchange rate was 60 to a ducat. He then made out a bill of exchange for 9,170 *scudi* and obtained an exchange rate of 50 aspers per *scudo*. . . . In 1561, another *bailo* was only able to obtain 47 aspers to the *scudo* because of the shortage of specie; in 1580 the rate was back at 50 aspers.

To complete the list of Ottoman coins we should include one more, Arabic this time, which was current in Egypt and Syria and the area between the Mediterranean, the Persian Gulf, and the Red Sea: the *maidin*, similar to the asper but containing one and a half times as much fine silver. So about 40 of these *maidins* were equivalent to a sequin, and 35 to a crown or a *Kronenthaler*. As the English traveller Newberie said in 1583, '40 medins maketh a duckat'.

The substantial devaluation of 1584 followed a similar devaluation in Persia, the consequence of the enormous cost, made necessary by the war, of maintaining increased numbers of paid troops. The sultan, to whom Egypt in 1584 was supplying gold sequins at the rate of 43 *maidins*, forced the rate up to 85 in order to make his payments. So the sequin went up from 60 to 120 aspers. Since of course the sequin did not change, the aspers were made lighter and part of the refined silver was replaced by copper. By 1597, 10 or 12 aspers instead of 4 were now being coined from one drachm of silver. After the troubles of 1590, the sequin went from 120 to 220 aspers. With the debasement of the currency, Turkey was now to experience an exact parallel of the *vellon* inflation in Castile, the mechanics of which and the havoc it caused between 1600 and 1650 have been described by Hamilton. But the crisis, which was to last until the middle of the seventeenth century, had begun twenty years earlier. It was difficult to bring under control. Towards 1625–1630, further inflation occurred: the sequin reached 240 aspers, the *thaler* 120; an authoritarian devaluation of 50 per cent brought the sequin down in 1642 to 151–157 aspers (not 120), but inflation began again after 1651 and the long war of Candia against Venice brought chaos. If in 1660 the sequin was still worth 240 aspers in Serbia, it was quoted at 310 aspers at Sofia in 1663.

These devaluations had a prodigious effect on the economic health of the empire, where the asper did duty both as a real money and a money of account. Such were the most obvious aspects of Turkish currency upheavals.

Three ages of metal. The reader will forgive me for stopping at this point. We shall have further cause to return to the difficult problems of the *conjoncture*, the economic cycle. A fairly clear outline has nevertheless already emerged. Historians are now aware of three metallic ages following one upon the other: the age of Sudanese gold; the age of silver and gold from America; and the age of *vellon* or counterfeit currency, whether officially sanctioned or not, making its first timid appearance at the end of the sixteenth century, then swamping circulation in the first decades of the seventeenth. An over-simplified schema certainly; for these ages did not succeed one another in an orderly procession – there were overlaps, discrepancies, and periods of confusion which have yet of course to be charted and explained.

The age of gold: all payments were preferably made in gold coin. In 1503, Bayard seized a paymaster of the Spanish army near Barletta. 'When they arrived,' relates the Loyal Servant, 'their purses were opened and fine ducats found' – yet another piece of confirmation. Then we find the king of France paying his soldiers (in 1524) 'with gold from Spain'. Every battle in the early days of the conflict between Habsburgs and Valois was fought with pieces of gold. A single messenger could carry enough money to make crucial payments. In May, 1526, Charles V's ambassador was anxious: 'four horsemen carrying the Pope's money' had passed through Mirandola; he had good cause for alarm.

Later, during the long reign of silver (from perhaps 1550 to 1650 or 1680) the transport of money became more obvious, for silver was a conspicuous traveller, requiring carts, ships, pack animals, not to mention the escort – at least fifty arquebusiers for the transport of silver from Genoa to Flanders in 1551. The movement of large sums in gold was usually easily concealed and, apart from the parties involved, no one need be aware of them. But when it was learned in September, 1586, that Philip II had sent 100,000 gold crowns to Italy, there was much speculation as to the internal necessity that had obliged him to take this unusual step. For as a rule gold did not leave the Peninsula. Being rare, it was highly valued and every time it was involved in a transaction, it dictated its own lordly terms. The masters of the mints and other experts covered many sheets of paper explaining to anyone who would pay attention that all would be well if only the gold mark were worth 12 marks of silver, as traditional wisdom decreed, but at Venice where gold was always being revalued, precise calculations show that the old ratio was out of date; as was registered without enthusiasm by the officials of the Venetian Zecca in November 1593. A mark of gold, they explained, is worth 674 *lire*, 9 *soldi*, 12 marks of silver 633 *lire*, 16 *soldi*, in other words an advantage of gold over silver of 40 *lire*, 13 *soldi*, a slight but indisputable lead.

Years passed and European currency entered the age of copper. Its heyday coincided with the development of the copper mines in Hungary, Saxony, Germany, Sweden, and Japan. Portugal might have been flooded with copper coin through her proximity to Spain where the tide of inflation was rising, but Portugal could always pass it on to the Indies. Even during these disastrous years Portugal was always short of copper: indeed the third metal was so highly valued there that in 1622, not 12 but 13 reals had to be given for a ducat paid in small copper coins.

But gold was soon to show its face again. Dispatched from Brazil, it reappeared at the end of the seventeenth century in Lisbon, England, Europe. The Mediterranean too had its share, but was not to be the centre of this new gold inflation, as it had for so long been the centre of silver inflation.

177. The triumphal entry of the Portuguese Viceroy João de Castro into Goa. Brussels tapestry, 1558. *Kunsthistorisches Museum, Vienna*

3

Economies: Trade and Transport

My INTENTION in this chapter is not to describe Mediterranean trade in all its complexity, but to discover a general pattern. I have therefore selected three different problems: the pepper crisis, the wheat crisis, and the invasion of the Mediterranean by ships from the Atlantic. Between them these problems cover every dimension of the economic life of the sea: taken together they give some idea of its vast compass: stretching on one side to the Indian Ocean, and on the other to the Atlantic and the Mediterraneans of the north – the Channel, the North Sea, and the Baltic.

1 The pepper trade

The circumnavigation of the Cape of Good Hope did not strike an immediate death-blow to the Mediterranean spice trade, as German historians were the first to point out; it could not escape their attention that Germany continued to receive spices and pepper from Venice, and therefore that the Portuguese could not have established a permanent monopoly in this precious traffic.

But there is no doubt that news of the Portuguese achievement led to a serious crisis in Venice, and a wave of gloomy prophecies. The consequences of the Portuguese discoveries were envisaged with alarm; disaster appeared irremediable. To the city of St Mark, the loss of the spice trade 'would be like the loss of milk to a new-born babe', wrote Girolamo Priuli in his journal in July, 1501. Prices at once began to fluctuate wildly and countless difficulties arose, particularly after the king of Portugal, Dom Manuel, had fixed an official price for pepper in 1504 and two years later turned the 'spicery' concentrated at Lisbon into a Crown monopoly. In 1504 the Venetian galleys found no spices at Alexandria or Beirut.

It was not long before the new spice-dealers had captured part of the European market. They had little difficulty in promoting their products on the Atlantic coast of the continent. They reached the Netherlands in 1501 and England in January, 1504 when five Portuguese vessels docked at Falmouth, carrying

178. Venetian merchants exchanging cloth for spices in Asia. Miniature from Marco Polo,
The Book of Marvels, early fifteenth-century manuscript. *Bibliothèque Nationale, Paris*

380 tons of pepper and spices from Calicut. They also found markets in northern
and southern Germany, where the old firm of Anton Welser and Konrad Völin
of Augsburg turned in 1503 towards the rising sun of Lisbon; where the *Magna
Societas* of Ravensburg decided in 1507 to buy pepper and spices henceforward
at Antwerp, the northern centre of the Portuguese trade; where Viennese merchants in 1512–1513 were complaining that supplies of pepper and spices from
Venice were inadequate and asking the Emperor to authorize foreign merchants
to bring spices from Antwerp, Frankfurt, or Nuremberg. The new suppliers were
successful too in western France and in Castile, where in 1524, according to an
eyewitness, Portuguese pepper was on sale at Medina del Campo. Nor can there
be any doubt that this same pepper very soon penetrated the Mediterranean,
where Portuguese sailing vessels played an important role, perhaps reaching
Genoa as early as 1503: Venice closed her mainland frontiers in June of that
year to products coming from Genoa (and special mention was made of cloth
of gold or silver, wool, *spices*, and sugar) or any other foreign place. She obliged
the towns of the Terraferma to come to Venice for all their purchases. In order
to increase imports of pepper and spices from the Levant, she granted permission
in May, 1514 for spices to be transported in any vessel, instead of, as in the past,
exclusively in the *galere da mercato* which now had to face stiff competition; she
also waived customs duties on their entry to Venice. Despite these measures, the

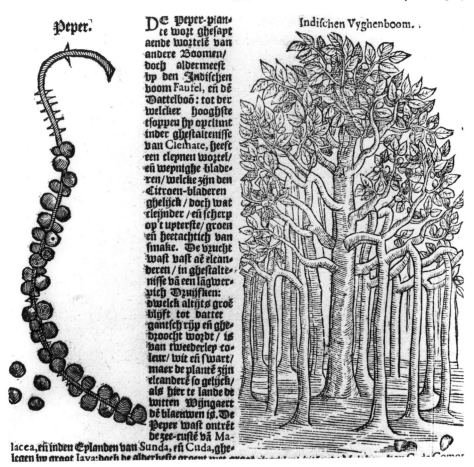

Peper.

De peper-plante wozt ghesapt aende wozrelē van andere Boomen/ doch aldermeeft by den Indischen boom Faufel, en dē Dattelboō: tot der welcker hooghfte tsoppen sy opclimt inder ghestaltenisse van Clematie, heeft een cleynen woztel/ en wepnighe bladeren/welcke zijn den Citroen-bladeren ghelijck/ doch wat cleijnder/en scherp op't upterste/groen en heetachtich van smake. De vzucht waft vast aē elcanderen/in ghestaltenisse vā een lāgwerpich Dzuijfken: dwelck altijts groē blijft tot datter gantsch rijp en ghedzoocht wozdt/ is van tweederley coleur/ wit en swart/ maer de plantē zijn elcanderē so gelijck/ als hier te lande de witten Wijngaert dē blaeuwen is. De Peper waft ontrēt de zee-custē vā Malacea, en inden Eplanden van Sunda, en Cuda, ghelegen by groot Iava: doch de alberbefte groeut

Indischen Vyghenboom.

179. Pepper tree. Woodcut from J. H. Linschoten, *Itinerarium*, Amsterdam, 1604.

Signoria was obliged in the following year, 1515, to send to Lisbon to replenish her own stocks. In 1527 the Venetian Senate proposed to the king of Portugal, John III, that the sales contract for all pepper imported to Lisbon be farmed out to Venice, after allowing for Portuguese home consumption. The project never came to anything. It is an indication of Venice's position in 1527 and proof of the great headway made by the Lisbon market.

Mediterranean revenge: the prosperity of the Red Sea after 1550. At what point did the tide turn – for there is no doubt that turn it did – in favour of Venice and the Mediterranean? It is hard to say. One factor was no doubt the fall in prices after the 1540s, which may be presumed to have disturbed the prosperous trade of Lisbon; and another the reputedly inferior quality of Portuguese commodities, whose aroma, according to connoisseurs, was diminished by the long sea voyage. The rumour, spread by Venice, was not without foundation; the

180. Harvesting pepper in the Indies. Woodcut from Thevet, *Cosmographie*, Paris, 1575.

same allegation appears in a Spanish document of 1574 otherwise hostile to Venice. Mediterranean trade, with its intermediary Arab connections, was probably able, by paying higher prices, to reserve superior products for itself. The Portuguese may have been going too far when they insisted on offering extremely low purchasing prices in Asia. True, they had to meet the expenses of the long voyage, frequent loss of ships and deficits on the cargoes themselves, which were often damaged en route. The Mediterranean circuit, on the contrary, with its many intermediary stations along routes that were both shorter and more familiar, held less risk. For the Venetians the chief hazard was the sea voyage from Egypt and this was compensated by a high rate of return, the result of astonishing price differences between East and West. 'They make a profit,' noted Thénaud in 1512, 'of a hundred per cent or more, on merchandise which is of little value here.' Even when pepper (the only commodity that gave rise to a massive trade and the one the Portuguese were the most anxious to control) was in short supply, it was still possible to trade in luxury spices, drugs, and other produce of the East. For their part, eastern merchants urgently needed precious metals: gold from Egypt or silver from the West, which only reached the Indian Ocean in return for the spices and other goods travelling along the routes to the Mediterranean. India and the Far East welcomed coral and saffron from the Mediterranean, opium from Egypt, woollen cloth from the West, quick silver, madder from the Red Sea. These established trades were maintained by a series of powerful, organized companies all round the Indian Ocean, which the Portuguese arrival had disturbed but not eliminated; they were able to react fairly quickly.

Since Mediterranean trade with the East had not lost any of its attractions for intermediaries, the only way to stop it would have been by force, in other words, a close guard over the sources of supply. The Portuguese succeeded in doing so several times, indeed whenever they tried, in the early days of their presence, for instance when they dealt a blow to the privileged Red Sea route, and even later. During the winter of 1545–1546, off the Malabar coast, 'the Portuguese squadron patrolled so effectively that all clandestine exports of pepper were prevented', or at any rate smuggling was considerably reduced. But this close guard was maintained only for a while and Portuguese vigilance lapsed of its own accord. Portugal was not rich enough to maintain this vast complex with its costly apparatus of fortresses, squadrons, and officials. The empire had to be self-supporting.

It took time for the Portuguese Empire to become firmly established, time too for the Turkish Empire to take the measure of its weaknesses, limitations and what could be termed reasonable interests in the Indian Ocean, to abandon its original project of concentrating all the trade of the Levant at Constantinople, then to contemplate a serious advance southwards and eastwards, a project afterwards to all practical purposes abandoned, the Portuguese meanwhile doing everything within their means to avoid being the target of such a formidable enemy. The Turks were to wait another ten years before launching another offensive from occupied Egypt. It was not until 1529 that work began on a canal between the Nile and the Red Sea, but the preparations were interrupted by the need to face the enemy in the Mediterranean: 1532 was the year of Coron. A further interval of six years elapsed before Sulaimān Pasha led a naval expedition that captured Aden in 1538 but failed to take Diu in the same year. In 1542, the Portuguese only just managed to hold Christian Ethiopia; in 1546,

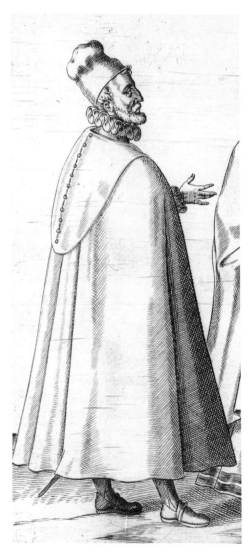

181. Portuguese merchant. Engraving,
Antwerp, sixteenth century.

Diu, their fortress on the Gujarat peninsula, was once more besieged and only saved by a miracle. From every eastern horizon, even distant Sumatra, a constant stream of ambassadors arrived at Constantinople to solicit the sultan's aid against the Portuguese, bringing him the rarest gifts: brightly coloured parrots, spices, perfumes, balms, black slaves, and eunuchs. But in 1551, at the mouth of the Red Sea, there was a fresh defeat – this time of the galleys commanded by Pīrī Re'īs; in 1553, Sidi 'Alī, the poet of the *Mirror of Lands*, was defeated at the entrance to the Persian Gulf. However, the following years saw a détente in relations between Turkey and Portugal and this détente favoured Mediterranean trade.

The old spice route was indeed once again busy and prosperous by the middle of the century. From then on Mediterranean pepper began to make inroads in the western half of the sea, pushing the pepper sold by the merchant-king of Lisbon further towards the Atlantic, but without there being any clear demarcation line. Mediterranean pepper had been arriving regularly at Antwerp, for instance, during the first half of the sixteenth century, perhaps even later. In 1510 a ship sailed directly from Alexandria to Antwerp. In 1540 Mediterranean pepper was influencing prices on the Scheldt market. In the same year, by trying to operate a pepper blockade against France, the Iberians assisted the rival trade of Marseilles, which François I seemed anxious to protect, since he refused Portuguese proposals and promises of spices in May, 1541, wishing to give satisfaction, says a Venetian, *al Signor Turco*, and not wishing to aid Flanders, 'where Antwerp would, it seems, have become the first city of the world'. In any case, a register of exports from Marseilles in 1543 indicates that pepper was being sent to Lyons – and probably beyond – as well as towards Toulouse. By 1565 it had reached Rouen and Toulouse where it competed with pepper from Lisbon, re-sold at Bordeaux. Towards mid-century, French and English merchants were exchanging pepper, notably at Rouen, La Rochelle, and Bordeaux. These must have been different products obtained from both sources. Circumstances favoured first one then the other. In 1559, for instance, the introduction of an *ad valorem* customs duty of 10 per cent discriminated against Portuguese pepper on the Castile market but, no doubt because of its proximity, this pepper does not seem to have vanished from the Peninsula. Imports to Leghorn at the end of the century leave the same impression as the Anglo-French exchanges, that is that the two kinds of pepper were different commodities which competed with but did not exclude each other. In fact there was a single European pepper market until the end of the sixteenth century and even later. Take for instance the chance remark of a Spanish merchant in Florence (29th November, 1591): at the news that the *naos de Yndias* are not coming to Lisbon that year, spices have gone up in price. 'Only pepper has remained the same,' he notes, 'since large supplies have arrived at Venice from the Levant.'

What is quite clear is that the Mediterranean had recaptured a large portion of the pepper trade, indeed the lion's share. Trade with the Levant was

GOA *fortiſsima Indiæ vrbs in Chriſtianorum*

Benes ferry

182. 'Golden Goa'. From *Civitates Orbis Terrarum*.

flourishing, supplied by numerous caravans, some from the Persian Gulf, others from the Red Sea. And at the end of these routes, looking on to the Mediterranean, two double cities owed their prosperity to this trade: to the north, Aleppo and the active quays of Tripoli, to the south, Cairo and its port Alexandria, the latter as if drained of its substance by the over-sized capital. In the west the revival of the spice trade brought most benefit to the Venetians, the grand masters of trade, alongside whom the merchants of Marseilles and Ragusa cut a very modest figure. The arrival of the Venetian merchants in Cairo and Aleppo signified the prosperity of these inland markets, of their capitalists, their caravan traffic and, at the other end of the caravan routes, efficient buying by Arab merchants in India and the East Indies. The Mediterranean was recapturing the treasures of the Indian Ocean.

Routes taken by the Levant trade. Any number of documents will testify to this revival. But since the opposite view has generally been accepted, let me warn that some details can be misleading. To avoid confusion it must be realized that the two routes leading to Cairo and Aleppo had always been in competition. When one was closed, the other opened. Aleppo, during these years when trade was picking up again, had the disadvantage of being both on the road to Persia – particularly during the war of 1548–1555 – and on the route to Hormuz, the route to the Portuguese war. During the war between Turkey and Portugal

no Salutis 1509. deuenit

Nuradoyro.

(1560–1563) the caravans from Basra were very small. It is not surprising then that Aleppo should be thriving one day, and the next suffering from extraordinary price increases. In July, 1557, Christofano Allegretti, a Ragusan factor, declared himself discouraged and decided to leave for Egypt: 'I do not believe this land of Aleppo has ever been as empty of merchandise, for there is nothing to be found but soap and ashes [*cenere*]. Gall-nuts cost about 13 to 14 ducats and since four French ships have arrived [at Tripoli], I do not doubt that the prices will reach the sky. For there are more than eight French ships here at the moment, ruining everyone by buying goods at any price.' Two years earlier, in 1555, perhaps following the end of the Turco-Persian wars, many Moorish and Venetian merchants of Aleppo 'son passati in le Indie', went to the Indies. Of course not all merchants followed the example of our Ragusan or these travellers and moved right away. In 1560, when Lorenzo Tiepolo arrived at Aleppo, he was met by 250 merchants on horseback. In November, 1563 the Venetian *bailo* at Pera announced that the *galee grosse* had left Syria for Venice. A Venetian report of the previous year indicates that Aleppo employed 5000 workers in the weaving industry. Throughout the crises, the city remained a great industrial and commercial centre. And Aleppo's difficulties were special. They did not always concern the whole of the eastern Mediterranean.

In particular they did not concern the Red Sea, which was often the only route – but what an important one – taken by the Far East trades. 'This Red Sea,' wrote Pierre Belon, who saw its shores towards the middle of the century, 'is, if not a narrow channel, certainly no wider than the Seine between Harfleur and Honfleur, where one can navigate only with difficulty and much danger, for the rocks are very frequent.' A flotilla of little sailing vessels operated there, curious ships whose 'planks were held together, not with nails, but with cords made of cocoa-nut fibre, while the hull was caulked with the fibres of date-palms, soaked in fish oil'. There were also great *houlques* and galleys, the latter trans- ported in pieces from Cairo to Suez, a bad and 'discommodious' port, set among sandbanks and poorly protected from the winds. Big ships and small, sailing by Aden or by the Abyssinian coast carried north the treasures of the Indies, of Sumatra and the Moluccas as well as pilgrims from all over Asiatic Islam. The need to take shelter during the sometimes catastrophic storms had multiplied the number of ports along these difficult coasts: Suakin, Aden, Jiddah – the port for Mecca – Tor, the rival of Suez. It was at Jiddah, 'Juda' or even 'Ziden' as the texts call it, that the greatest number of long-distance ships called. And this brought to the port near Mecca enormous concourses of caravans, of up to 20,000 people and 300,000 animals at a time. Meat was never scarce in the holy city though wheat was often hard to come by. From Jiddah ships and boats sailed to Tor, the starting-point for the caravans that took nine or ten days to reach Cairo. Depending on the point of departure of the great shipping convoys of the Indian Ocean – Sumatra, Cambay (at the mouth of the Indus region), the Malabar coast, Calicut, Bul, Cannanore, and other leeward ports – spices reached the Red Sea in May or November every year.

So the difficult gateway to the Red Sea stood wide open, and a huge volume of trade flowed through. The presence of costly porcelain, surely from China, although Belon refuses to believe that it really came from the far-off 'Indies', is proof enough of this, for fragile porcelain would only be shipped along with a stream of other merchandise. As for spices, of which pepper was by far the most important, there was an annual flow of 20,000 to 40,000 light quintals (about 50 kg) between 1554 and 1564. In 1554, the Venetians alone took 600 *colli* of spices, about 6000 quintals, from Alexandria. Now the Venetians controlled only a part, half at most, of the Alexandrian trade, and to western trade must be added consumption of spices in the East, which was always considerable. Between 1560 and 1564 a copy of consular documents from Cairo gives an annual figure of 12,000 quintals for Venetian purchases alone, a figure as high as in the old days before Vasco da Gama, and which tallies with the estimates of the Portuguese ambassador at Rome, who guessed that the total volume of the Alexandrian spice trade was 40,000 quintals. In October 1564, a spy in the pay of Portugal estimated this traffic at 30,000 quintals of which 25,000 (2,800,000 lb Eng.) were pepper, and the Venetian consul at Cairo, in May 1565 refers to 20,000 quintals of pepper unloaded at Jiddah; and this was before the arrival of the convoys from Gujarat, Calicut, and elsewhere (which usually docked in winter). In the previous August twenty-three ships were unloading spices at Jiddah. So once again, we find a figure of approximately 30,000 to 40,000 quintals for the Egyptian trade alone, that is not counting what came through Syria.

 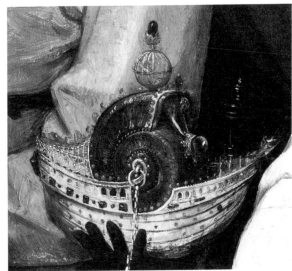

183, 184. Two details from *The Adoration of the Magi* by Pieter Breughel the Elder, showing offerings of a spice dish and a model of a ship made out of shell mounted in gold. *National Gallery, London*

In short, enormous quantities of spices were reaching the Mediterranean. They represented 'millions in gold', as contemporaries said. And along with the pepper and spices came medicinal drugs such as opium, balm of mithridate, Lemnian earth, silk, perfumes, decorative objects, the *pierres de besouard*, bezoar stones or antelope's tears mentioned by Belon, previous stones, pearls. This was of course a luxury trade – but have not luxuries always been what instinctively 'seems the most necessary to man'? Spices still dominated world trade in the seventeenth if not the eighteenth century. In the autumn of 1559 a Ragusan ship, one from Chios, and two Venetian, all laden with spices, were seized by the 'captain' of Alexandria. One of them, the *Contarina*, returned to Venice in January laden with spices and pepper. We know more or less what these vessels carried from the cargo of the *Crose*, a Venetian sailing ship of 540 tons, which in 1561 transported to the Levant copper in the form of ore, bars and beaten sheets, woollen cloth, silk cloth, kerseys, caps, coral, amber, various trinkets, paper, and coin (*contadi*). On the return journey, she brought back pepper, ginger of various origins, cinnamon, nutmeg, cloves, frankincense, gum Arabic, sugar, sandalwood, and a host of other exotic goods.

There was by now a real shortage of pepper in the countries served by the Portuguese spice trade. An extreme case perhaps was the English attempt to push forward from Moscow to the Caspian Sea and on to Persia. Jenkinson's first voyage took place in 1561. As for France, seeing the impossibility of forcing entry to the Portuguese 'magazine', which remained firmly closed to them, Nicot advised his countrymen to go to the coast of Guinea in search of malaguetta, the pepper substitute that continued to find buyers for some time, particularly in Antwerp. The Fuggers after 1559 dispatched a factor to Alexandria and organized a trade route via Fiume and Ragusa. In Spain, the price of spices rose sharply. After remaining fairly stable between 1520 and 1545, then rising regularly with other prices between 1545 and 1558, it suddenly shot up between 1558 and 1565, much faster than any other commodity, tripling in New Castile. This abnormal price increase was first observed by Earl J. Hamilton who pointed out the possible connection between the high price of pepper and the motives behind Legazpi's expedition to the Philippines in 1564. As early as 1558, complaints were being voiced in Genoa about the excessive price of 'drugs' from Portugal.

The revival of the Portuguese pepper trade. In 1568 it was reported from Venice that twenty Turkish galleys were preparing to launch an attack on the Portuguese from Basra and to capture the island of Bahrein and its pearl fisheries. But in the same year, 1568, Arabia rose up in arms. A long series of disturbances began, particularly in the Yemen. Apart from some unlikely political gossip there is little to tell us what became of Aden, the gateway to the Red Sea. Order was restored only in 1573 by the Sinān Pasha who later became Grand Vizier.

Portugal no doubt took advantage of Turkish difficulties although she had her own as well (Goa was besieged for fourteen months from 1570; the fortress of Ternate was to fall in 1575). The threat from the sultan's galleys was receding. And the far-reaching reorganization of the Portuguese spice trade in 1570 was an improvement. By the *regimento* of 1st March, 1570, the king, Dom Sebastian, in effect abandoned the Crown monopoly to his vassals, a reform which some people, Pires in particular, had been advocating for some time. In the same year the viceroy, Dom Luis de Ataide, boasted of having patrolled the sea so effectively that only two ships, instead of sixteen or eighteen as in previous years, had been able to sail from Calicut to Mecca.

A fresh swing of the pendulum can perhaps be dated from 25th November, 1570, when Venice removed the obligation on foreign shippers to bring spices to Venice exclusively in Venetian ships, although several meanings can be attached to this measure, which was in any case a fairly mild one. But the situation was soon to turn against Venice. The war with Turkey (1570–1573) was extremely damaging. All her rivals, Ragusa, Ancona, and above all Marseilles, took advantage of it. Bills of lading from July to September, 1573, show that the French (Mannlich the Elder on at least one occasion) were carrying off from Alexandria in Egypt, entire cargoes of 'zimbre' and pepper 'of Assy'. It is not so much the drop in imports of bales of silk to Aleppo (because of the war or rather the threat of war with Persia) that is disquieting, says a Venetian consul in April, 1574, as the ruinous competition from French merchants who have flocked here since the war. There were no complaints on the other hand about spices, which now seemed to be taking the route through Syria once more. In October, 1574, a rich vessel, the *Ludovica*, left Venice with 150,000 ducats' worth of merchandise aboard. A storm obliged her to put in to Ancona, where the governors of the town found her to be laden with copper and declared her legitimate spoil since she was carrying contraband merchandise. They seized the ship and her cargo and imprisoned master and mariners. From chance references in some commercial correspondence in 1574 and little else to go on, it appears that there were either leaving or lying in Syrian ports some French ships (30th January, 1574), a French barque (3rd April), a Venetian *nave*, the *Moceniga*, which was at Tripoli in March and again in November, the *saëtte Altana*, probably from Venice. And they piled on board mace, *chotoni*, arsenic, spun cotton, spices, ginger, a chest of *mirobolani*; on 12th May, 1575, the merchant-man *Girada* carried away cotton, *peladi*, silks, drugs, and spices.

So the flow of goods from the Levant was not interrupted either on the Syrian or the Egyptian route. Meanwhile Portuguese pepper was making headway once more in the Mediterranean. A deliberation of the Council of the Pregadi, on 13th September, 1577, makes this clear. From a report by the *Cinque Savii alla Mercanzia* the Council learned that at Lisbon four ships had taken on board for Venice *una buona suma di pevere*, but that their owners changed their minds when they heard that they would have to pay a duty of 3 per cent at Venice, according to an old ruling of 1519 (the date is significant), which imposed the duty on spices coming from the western Mediterranean only, not from the Levant. It was decided to postpone the shipment in the hope of obtaining the suppression of this duty, a request duly granted for a period of two years, 'seeing that this merchandise [the Portuguese pepper]' said the experts, 'might be sent to other places, to the loss of this city and export duties'. It would be better then *'since only a little pepper is arriving from Alexandria*, to grant free entry to pepper from the West'. Two years later, Christobal de Salazar was writing to Philip II, 'At Alexandria, trade and traffic are quite destroyed, especially in spices, for the route is abandoned,' *porque se ha dexado el camino.*

Portuguese pepper: deals and projects. This helps to explain three attempts to capture the profits of the pepper trade in the Mediterranean.

The first attempt was Portuguese. It is outlined in a letter written to Philip II on 10th November, 1575, by Friar Mariano Azaro, a Discalced Carmelite and former student at Padua, who was a great expert in these matters. He proposed introducing Portuguese pepper to the Spanish dominions in Italy, Milan, Naples, Sicily, and Sardinia, ousting Venetian pepper, which was commonly sold there; he also proposed enlisting the support of the Pope and other Italian rulers and establishing either at Puerto de Santa Maria or Cartagena or some other peninsula port a distribution centre for Italy, another Antwerp so to speak. The pepper would be transported in the royal galleys. That this project should incidentally suggest that Portuguese pepper had conquered the Spanish markets by 1516 does not increase its credibility. Who knows with what fantastic information we should be inundated if all the pamphlets of the *arbitristas* of Spain had survived! But behind this barefoot friar were two, possibly three, important people: first, Ruy Gómez da Silva, a Portuguese as we know, and who 'shortly before his death had taken it upon him to propose to Your Majesty a certain suggestion I had made to him concerning the spiceries of the Levant'; the secretary Antonio Graciano, to whom the friar had written in the first place; and, finally, the king, who was by now preoccupied with the pepper trade and the Portuguese monopoly, and who, when informed by his secretary of the suggestion, asked for a second report, which is what we have here. So it was a serious project, an attack upon Venice in the grand manner. Since Venice was dependent upon the Turk for her spices and wheat and had therefore out of vile self-interest betrayed Christendom, why should she not be punished, in the name of morality and respectable Portuguese pepper! Besides, as everyone knew (and this is a counterblast to disparaging remarks about the quality of the pepper from Lisbon), the Turks first steeped their spices in infusions to manufacture their beverages and hydromel, and then unscrupulously sold them in the Syrian markets.

The second attempt came from Tuscany, or rather the Medici. Grand Duke Francesco made great efforts between 1576 and 1578, to obtain the *appalto* of the spices that came from the Indies to Portugal. To this effect he dangled the prospect of money in front of that strange descendant of the kings of Lisbon, the last of the crusaders, Dom Sebastian, who, fired with dreams of fighting the Infidel in Morocco, was preoccupied with raising the necessary funds for an adventure that was to prove suicidal to himself, his nobility, and his kingdom. The Grand Duke was extremely ambitious: he was negotiating simultaneously with the sultan and his aim was nothing less than the world monopoly of pepper, according to the Venetians, whose judgment could be as shrewd as their gossip was malicious. These grandiose schemes were finally limited to the negotiation of a loan of 200,000 crowns from the merchants of Florence, the Medici, and the Portuguese ambassador, Antonio Pinto, which was undoubtedly the pretext for a massive shipment of Portuguese pepper to Leghorn in return. By a narrow margin certainly, the Grand Duke nevertheless failed to capture the monopoly in 1587. But after these discussions, closer links were maintained between Florence and Lisbon.

The third and last attempt was made by Philip II himself. His aims were at once to increase his hold over the neighbouring kingdom, to blockade the rebels in the Netherlands (plans to deprive them of salt, grain or spices had been suggested at various times) and finally to establish an active Hispano-Portuguese salt and spice trade. In this he was ceding to pressure from influential businessmen eager to capture the rich Asian trades, a Roth or a Nathaniel Jung, both Germans, who by 1575, were thinking of applying for the Portuguese spice contract.

What had only been a project became a reality when Philip II annexed Portugal. 1580 marked for him, as 1547 had for Charles V, the high point of his reign. If Portugal surrendered to him, as she did, it was in order to receive the threefold protection of Philip II's money, armies, and fleets, and with this three-pronged weapon to strengthen her hold on the Indian Ocean. After 1580 it was natural that the king should want to block the channels through which the Levant trade was supplied, thus destroying with a single blow the fortunes of the Turks and of Venice in the interests of his own empire. But in his determination to organize Asia and the New World and to link them together, Philip II encountered far less resistance in the Indian Ocean than he did around the shores of the Atlantic, particularly the North Atlantic. So it was against the Protestants, the rebels in the Netherlands and England, that he took action rather than against the Turk, with whom he remained unofficially at peace. Here then lies the explanation of the strange policy pursued by the Prudent King who now that he was master of Portugal did his best to promote and place in Mediterranean markets the pepper he had just acquired.

The Welser and Fugger contract: 1586–1591. The Portuguese pepper trade consisted of one minor and two major contracts. The minor one was for Portuguese domestic sales. The two major ones were the Asian contract for buying spices and pepper in the Indies and transporting them to Lisbon, and the European contract for handling sales in Europe. The monarchy, with its enormous warehouses at the *Casa da India*, was the hinge on which everything turned: it received pepper from the farmers of the Asian concession at a certain price; to the farmers of the European concession it sold the pepper at clear double the price.

It was the European contract that Philip II was hawking around Italy, hoping thus to deprive the Dutch and the English of their pepper and spices, which they had been in the habit of buying at Lisbon. As for the Asian contract, a draft project was presented to Philip II by a German, Giraldo Paris, at Monzon on 29th November, 1585. It was signed by the king at Valencia on 15th February, 1586 and delivered to a consortium of capitalists, among whom were the Welsers and Fuggers. The details of the agreement are unimportant. The net result was that the pepper, transported from the east at the risk of the farmers, was sold to the king at 16 *cruzados* and resold by him at 37.

Matthaus Welser, who is found negotiating at Madrid in 1587, was deeply implicated in this affair; he had also accepted the European contract and tried to involve the Fuggers as well. At first they, like the Italians, dragged their feet. 'It is no business for us,' they wrote in November, 1587. 'What should we do in such a labyrinth?' But in 1591, in the somewhat forlorn hope of bringing some order into their difficult agreements with Spain, they allowed themselves to be drawn into the European contract. This was at the time in the hands of a vast international consortium, the Welsers and Fuggers for Germany, Rovalesca

185. Spanish merchants. Engraving,
Antwerp, sixteenth century.

and Giraldo Paris for Italy, Francisco and Pedro Malvenda for Spain, and Andrès and Thomas Ximenez for Portugal. The association was divided into thirty-two shares, of which the Fuggers held seven, the Welsers five, the Rovalesca four, the Malvenda four, and the Ximenez and their associates eleven. It was represented at Antwerp, Middleburg, Zeeland, Hamburg, Lübeck, and Venice, where the Welsers had opened a thriving new branch in 1588. By 1591 it was handling enormous quantities of pepper: 14,000 quintals were sent to Lübeck for instance. Huge cargoes travelled to Venice, the Signoria having agreed to protect all merchandise addressed there and to obtain safe-conducts from the English. But this massive mobilization of capital and capitalists produced disappointing results. Only the king of Spain made anything out of it. In 1591, the same year that it was formed, the Fuggers prudently withdrew, selling their shares on 7th July, to the firms of Evora, Portuguese *marranos* associated with the Ximenez, and Caldeira.

The reason for this failure was that shipping routes in the Atlantic after the defeat of the Spanish Armada were more dangerous than ever. The defeat of Spain meant the rout of her allies and in more than one way a drop in the Atlantic pepper trade. With the rise in selling prices, the consortium's pepper came to be dearer in Venice than pepper shipped from the Levant, an astonishing fact which is made plain in a letter from the Fuggers to their agent in Lisbon, dated 9th November and 7th December, 1587. Many customers were turning back to the Venetian market. Even the Atlantic pepper trade was now being drawn towards the Mediterranean.

The survival of the Levantine spice routes. From the 1580s to the end of the century the Levant remained open to the spice trade, until the total capture of the Indian Ocean by the Dutch. They appeared there for the first time in 1596 with Cornelius Houtmann's voyage; by 1625 they had imposed their rule throughout the ocean and were now looking to America for fresh worlds to conquer. It is somewhere about this time, either just before or just after 1625, that we must date the irremediable decline of the Levant trade. The first warning had been the Twelve Years Truce of 1609, which officially opened the Indian Ocean to the trading ventures of these new arrivals. And in 1614 the appearance of the first large Dutch vessel in the Red Sea had been another hint of what was to come. This capture from the rear, partly by land, partly by sea, of the traffic of the East (including Persian silk), the spread throughout the area of Dutch textiles, the belligerent arrival of the English and the French, marked the beginning of a second European age in the Indian Ocean that was to be more catastrophic to the Levant than the imperfect domination of the Portuguese.

A letter from Aleppo in December 1582 says that trade is scarce and what

186. *Surprise Attack by a Dutch Squadron on Three Portuguese Galleons in the Bay of Goa, 1639*, by Hendrick van Anthonissen. *Rijksmuseum, Amsterdam*

little there is is disastrous. Only the silk trade maintained its position. In July, 1583 business was so bad that instead of making a profit, capital was returning with a loss of 8 per cent and according to the latest information from Egypt, the same was true in Alexandria. Was this why the Englishman Newberie wrote from Baghdad in July 1583: 'I think cloth, kersies and tinne have never been here at so low prices as they are now'?

But after 1583 it was a different story. A wholesale merchant of Marseilles writes on 10th April that pepper prices are rising fast, 'although from Aleppo there come many spices'. It is beyond all understanding, he complains, 'and I assure you that there is no merchant in the district however experienced, but does not have his plans thrown into confusion'. For himself, by the following year he was thinking of leaving for the Indies, together with a Venetian whole-saler, to risk 2000 crowns 'of our own'. John Eldred, in 1583, describes Tripoli in Syria as the port most frequented by Christian merchants and Aleppo as very populous. He refers to a large volume of traffic between Baghdad and Aleppo. At Basra, where he notes the presence of twenty-five fine Turkish galleys, there put in every month he says, several ships of 40 to 60 tons from Hormuz, 'laden with all sorts of Indian merchandise, as spices, drugs, Indico, and Calicut cloth'. He does not give precise details. But during the summer of 1584 when John Eldred returned to Aleppo, he joined a caravan of 4000 camels, 'laden with spices and other rich merchandises'. And at Alexandria in 1584, one could buy 'all sorts of spices'.

In 1587, according to another source, ships were leaving Sumatra every year for Mecca. And we are told that in about 1586 the customs duties at Mecca brought in 150,000 ducats (half to the sultan, half to the Sharif of the city), and that every year about forty or fifty great ships landed there laden with spices. More was to come. In the face of Portuguese interference in the Indian Ocean, there occurred after the 1590s a corresponding expansion of the trading centres outside Portuguese control. The port of Chaul for instance, expanded at the expense of Diu and Goa. Since all the merchants who had dealings with Mecca and Hormuz were settled there, it cost the king of Portugal up to 150,000 *fardaos* in customs duties every year. Further evidence comes from an Augustinian friar, Frey Augustinho d'Azevedo, himself Portuguese, who had returned overland from the Indies, and made his report to Philip II, between 1584 and 1587, according to the historians who discovered this precious document, but in my guess about 1593. In any case, it clearly dates from the last decades of the century. Thanks to this report we have an unforgettable picture of Hormuz, a port open to every kind of immigrant, every kind of commerce, and every kind of smuggling, whether by Venetians, Armenians, the Turks themselves, or Portuguese renegades who left in astonishing numbers for Turkey, where their knowledge of the Indies was a valuable asset in the clandestine trade in spices, pearls, rhubarb, benjamin, and sandalwood in one direction, and contraband goods, munitions, and modern armaments in the other. Thus it was that 'o melhor da India', the best of India, reached Venice, which in return sent a varied assortment of shoddy goods, glass trinkets, mirrors, false pearls, and wallpaper. And it was for Venice, always ready to compromise with the heretical Turks or English, that the pious Augustinian saw up to six thousand camels laden with treasures travelling through the desert, and with his own eyes watched five big

187. *The Venetian Lady*, dressed in silk, by G. G. Savoldo. *Gemäldegalerie, Berlin*

Venetian ships leave Alexandretta. Does this mean that after the visible difficulties of the 1580s in Venetian affairs, there was a revival in trade?

In the Levant, towards the end of the century, the Aleppo route was restored
to favour, because it was shorter, because it was an overland route (piracy was
rife in the Indian Ocean after the 1590s), and above all because of silk and its
increasingly important position in the European economy. Every single letter
from Venetian or Marseilles merchants in Aleppo, Tripoli, or Alexandretta,
carries a major reference to silk, local silk from the region surrounding Tripoli,
or fine silks of Persia brought to Aleppo by the usual merchants, Armenians, or
Tartars. For several years Aleppo was handicapped by the Turco-Persian war
(which ended in 1590). Most of the fighting was of course in the north, round
Tabriz, and along the routes that led from both sides of the Caucasus down to
the Caspian Sea. But the war was sometimes carried suddenly south as far as
Baghdad. And in any case it led to a series of monetary crises in both Turkey and
Persia, which naturally had repercussions in Aleppo where it grew increasingly
difficult to find money, so that in June, 1586 it became necessary to raise the
customs duties on merchandise arriving in Venice from Syria from 1 per cent to
1·5 per cent, to the benefit of the *cottimo*. In spite of these problems trade
survived, as we have already seen. Venice in 1593 admitted to trade worth a
million ducats in Syria, and in 1596 announced that it was worth two million.
The principal commodities were silks and spices. The figure of two million refers
to Venetian exports – the cloth, silk-stuffs, trinkets, and glass left in the *souks*
at Aleppo; but the cargoes that were loaded in exchange on board four or five
big ships increased miraculously in price as they approached Venice.

After 1593 the Levant traffic no longer left from Tripoli but from Alexandretta, which the Venetians now made their shipping headquarters and where
they were followed by other Christian shippers. The new port was free from the
vexations of the old one; although certainly unhealthier, it was nearer Aleppo.
But the lack of buildings to house the stocks of merchandise was an inconvenience for the Venetians (who retained their policy of commerce *a baratto*
and were therefore encumbered with bundles of goods) far more than for the
merchants of Marseilles who arrived with money in their pockets. The increase
in trade probably resulted less from the change of port than from the end of the
war between Turkey and Persia.

It also owed something to the end of hostilities between Turkey and Portugal,
which between 1584 and 1589 had been a quarrel not so much over the pepper
as over the gold of the East African coast. The defeat of the fleet of 'Ali Beg in
1589 brought the war to an end and comparative peace reigned as far as the
East Indies, troubled only by local princes and corsairs.

An entire intelligence network, with direct links between Spain – or rather
the Portuguese government – and the Indies, operated through the Spanish
embassy at Venice, what a document calls 'las nuevas de India por tierra'. The
intermediaries were Jews, agents for trading houses, the factors of the Welsers

for example or the Bontempelli brothers, Antonio and Hieronymo, who were in the service of a wealthy Venetian merchant, Augustino Da Ponte. After 1589 these sources reported all quiet in the Indies, in spite of the appearance of Malabar pirates in the centre and on the borders of the ocean. The peace was to be rudely shattered a few years later by the invasion of the Dutch after 1596.

Another determining factor was the threat to Atlantic shipping. There were English privateers working round all the key islands, the Cape Verde Islands, the Canaries, the Azores, and sometimes they sailed down as far as St Helena, where the ships returning from the Indies put in for fresh water and their crews hunted mountain goats to enliven their diet. There was a shipping crisis in the ocean. And to the vessels captured by pirates must be added the many shipwrecks. The huge ships used on the Indies run became, with the general rise in prices, luxury objects, so their owners economized on timber and on the quality of the crews. In these enormous hulls the weight of the cargoes became dangerous. They put to sea without enough sail, with worm-eaten rudders; as in the Mediterranean, ships were careened in the Italian manner, without bringing the monsters into dry dock. Hence in the course of their long and eventful voyages a series of 'tragico-maritime' disasters, the long catalogue of which, drawn up by Gomez de Brito, marks the line followed after the 1580s by the Portuguese decline which soon became inexorable. Between 1592 and 1602 there foundered, sometimes in fine weather, as a result of leaks or other technical accidents, thirty-eight ships on the Indies run. Reckoning them at the same price as the Venetian ships, 20 million ducats and maybe more must have gone to the bottom.

These huge losses, the repeated blockades of Lisbon (during the winter 1597–1598 for instance) as well as captures by the pirates of Algiers, were all blows to the Portuguese pepper trade. In New Castile between 1595 and 1599, the price of pepper doubled. These blows and price increases opened the door wider to the old firm of the Mediterranean. A letter from some German merchants on 17th February, 1593, announces that the *muda de Suez* has arrived with 30,000 cantars 'which means', writes one historian, 'that the Alexandrian market was providing as much pepper as Lisbon'.

So the Levant trade was still very much alive. We have mentioned the progress made by the Venetians. This was clearly revealed in 1596, when the rates of the *cottimo* of Aleppo were reduced from 5 per cent to 2 per cent. Three years later, in 1599, there was a drop in turnover, but Venetian trade was still reaching the respectable figure of a million and a half ducats, the total figure for the whole of Christendom being in the region of 3 million, of which half a million was handled by the French, or by merchants trading under the French flag. In 1603 Venetian trade in the city was still worth a million and a half ducats. In 1599 further evidence comes from Marseilles bills of lading at Alexandretta, which refer to cargoes of indigo, nutmeg, and cloves.

So in 1600 as far as pepper and spices are concerned the predominance of the ocean route was far from established. With ups and downs, the rivalry between the two routes lasted over a century and, on both sides, crisis alternated with prosperity. The end of the story falls outside the period of our survey which stops in about 1600. The dates and the circumstances of the ultimate eclipse of the Mediterranean have yet to be ascertained. It cannot have been very far off as the seventeenth century began, but it was by no means yet accomplished – a hundred years after the date usually suggested as that of the death of the old queen of the world, the Mediterranean, dethroned by the new king, the Atlantic.

Possible explanations. The preceding account, incomplete and like all chronological accounts prone to mistake appearance for reality, cannot be said to have resolved all the problems. Recent scholarship has made it easier to see what was happening at the other end of the interminable passage to India, in the Far East. The rapacity and lack of foresight of the Portuguese in the East Indies, in the 'drug islands', diverted the flow of luxury spices that had previously been drawn towards Malacca. An independent current became established with the Javanese junks, the drugs of the East Indies and the high quality pepper of the islands of Java and Sumatra. During the last twenty years of the century, these currents, freed from Portuguese control, centred around Atjeh, in Sumatra, the rendezvous of Moslem ships which sailed from there to the Persian Gulf or the Red Sea. Even the fine cinnamon of Ceylon was transported to Atjeh, to be loaded on board ships bound for the Mediterranean. The fortune of Atjeh, where a thriving Turkish trading-station existed by the beginning of the seventeenth century, is the more significant in that during the same period sales of spices to China, Indochina and (apart from the Malabar coast) India were increasing by leaps and bounds, thus reducing the amount available for the Portuguese to ship around the Cape. That is not to say that Portuguese exports were not substantial, even during the early years of the seventeenth century. But it is here that we shall at last find an explanation for the continued prosperity of the Mediterranean route.

It does not by any means provide the whole answer though. For in fact all these explanations we have so patiently assembled: the naïveté of the Portuguese; the sagacity of the Turks; the great expansion eastward to the Malay Archipelago of Islam and of the spice and pepper trade dependent on it; the brutal sorties by the Portuguese squadrons at the beginning of the century; or the war between Turkey and Venice (1570–1573) which both promoted Marseilles and stimulated the secondary route between Tabriz and Poland, Lwow and Danzig – all these explanations which are in fact so many *events* in the pepper and spice war, tend to obscure the problem in its entirety, a problem that is best appreciated

188. *Opposite:* Chart of Western Java showing the Sunda Strait, by G. le Testa, 1556. Nutmeg and spices are ready for export. *Bibliothèque Nationale, Paris*

when viewed in a world context – from the American silver mines to the Moluccas or the western tip of Sumantra. Viewed in this context, how does the problem emerge? Above all as a steady flow of gold and silver coins of every description, travelling from west to east, following the rotation of the earth, carrying along with them a wide range of commodities as a kind of supplementary currency and loosing in the opposite direction a rich and varied stream of different commodities and precious goods from east to west.

Within this circulatory system sweeping through the Mediterranean in both directions, every change had repercussions. If, between the roughly fixed limits of 1550 and 1620, pepper and spices were passing through the Mediterranean, was this not because the Mediterranean was for many years the destination of American silver? This was the cycle that set trade in motion. A Venetian, Piero Zen, pointed out to the Turks at Constantinople in 1530 that 'l'arzento va dove e il piper', silver goes where the pepper is. But the reverse was equally true. Details can be important here. Historians are still debating for example the date of the initial revival of the Levant trade. Kellenbenz has suggested 1540; I prefer 1550 and Godinho agrees. But this is merely guesswork; none of us can claim to know for certain. It is my impression that the precise date would become evident if we ever discovered exactly when the chronic shortage of specie in the Mediterranean of the early sixteenth century was transformed into the relative abundance of the latter half (with occasions, like 1583–1584 for instance, when money was so plentiful as to exceed the usual avenues of investment). From Venice's point of view I think the turning-point must have occurred somewhere between 1545 and 1560. On 9th June, 1545, the workers of the Zecca were unemployed because so little gold and silver was arriving in the city. To relieve their *grandissima povertà* and give them work, a thousand ducats was minted in very small coin. In 1551, incentives were offered to encourage people to bring gold to the Zecca. They would not have to pay the usual 3.5 per cent charge for coining. By 1554 those who wanted *cechini per navegar* were so numerous that the 3 per cent duty was reimposed. In 1561 so much silver (not gold) was brought to the Zecca that it could not all be minted in the small existing coins – that would have taken over a year. It was therefore decided to take the unprecedented step of minting large silver coins, *ducati d'argento*. Finally in 1566 anyone who wanted to have gold minted in the Zecca had to fulfil a whole set of conditions! In short, we need to locate the moment at which American silver, which was flooding into Antwerp for example from 1550 on, arrived in the Italian zone of the Mediterranean in sufficient quantities to restore trade with the Levant. Importance can be attached to coincidences: the crisis of the 1580s in the Levant seems to me to correspond to a short-term fluctuation in the economic *conjoncture*, which went into a clear recession throughout the Mediterranean when Spanish silver flowed back towards the Atlantic at the time of the annexation of Portugal and the great cereal crisis of the Peninsula.

2 Equilibrium and crisis in the Mediterranean grain trade

The Mediterranean has never had a superabundance of grain: the scarcity of home-grown cereals and the constant search for substitutes has bred a kind of ingenuity. The study of the grain problem takes us to one of the most vulnerable areas of Mediterranean life and at the same time to a greater understanding of that life in all its complexity. The pepper and spice trade was one of luxury foodstuffs, and the names most readily associated with it are those of the great merchant families of the sixteenth century: the Affaitati, the Ximenez, the Malvenda, the Welsers, and the Fuggers. The grain trade, although less spectacular, represented an enormous volume of business. As well as the several main supply routes, it fed a network of secondary arteries and capillaries which it would be most unwise to dismiss lightly.

The cereals. Traffic in grain, whether over large or small distances, was not confined merely to wheat or the grains of high commercial quality which in

189. Demeter and Persephone with corn, the gift of the gods to mankind. Attic red-figure skyphos, c.490–480 BC. *British Museum*

Sicily went by the name of *grani forti* or *grani di Rocella*. In Florence three categories were distinguished: *cima delle cime, mezzano, debole*. Grain described as *cima* had had all impurities removed, and weighed 52 pounds to the *staio* or 72·5 kilograms to the hectolitre. The prices of the different categories were respectively 7, 6, and 5 *lire* per *staio* at the 1590 tariff. *Deboli* referred to small grain, from the Levant (usually of rather poor quality); from the Abruzzi or the Duchy of Urbino (scarcely better although Venice was not above eating it); or the grain produced in Spain and elsewhere from irrigated land exhausted by overcultivation.

Besides wheat other cereals appeared every day on Mediterranean tables, especially barley and millet. In 1550 ten ships carrying barley and wheat arrived at Naples from Apulia. Verona in 1559 complained of a disastrous millet crop and was proposing to sell her reserve stocks at one ducat per Venetian *staro*. In 1562, following a catastrophic drought, there was another bad harvest. The entire millet crop was lost – 'and that is what the poor people eat', wrote the Spanish ambassador. In the villages of Zante only black barley-bread was eaten. Near Troy in Asia Minor, Philippe de Canaye observed that for lack of wheat the Turkish villagers ate bread made from oatmeal, which in view of the rarity of oats in the Mediterranean was in its way a luxury. In Corsica the usual substitute was chestnut bread, known as tree-bread. Rice, much eaten in the East of course, as well as in the Po valley and in Valencia, occasionally replaced bread elsewhere. Pulses, chick peas from Spanish overseas territories, or beans, especially Egyptian, were also considered as bread substitutes. Alonso de Pimentel, the new captain of La Goletta, on receiving a large quantity of wheat and barley writes, 'What a misfortune that we have been sent no chick peas!'

Some rules of the grain trade. It is only through small clues (a particular deal, the supplying of a particular city, an isolated speculation or account) that as historians we can glimpse something of the complicated life of the grain merchant. And everything conspired to make that life an anxious one: the unreliability of the harvests, the vigilant watch kept by states and above all cities, speculation by other merchants down to the humblest shopkeeper, the huge outlay involved and the risk of seeing an entire cargo lost through the actions of unscrupulous sailors. And there was no shortage of middlemen. To complicate matters even further, the profession of grain merchant was often exercised alongside other activities.

From the registers of Jacopo and Bardo Corsi, for example, we can see that these wealthy Florentine merchants were at one moment advancing money to Galileo and selling silk and long pepper on credit, the next handling massive wheat purchases at Palermo on behalf of the Grand Duke of Tuscany. The

190. The author weighing grain. From Tommasino de' Bianchi, *Stadera del Formento,* Modena, 1544. *Houghton Library, Harvard University*

STADERA DEL
FORMENTO

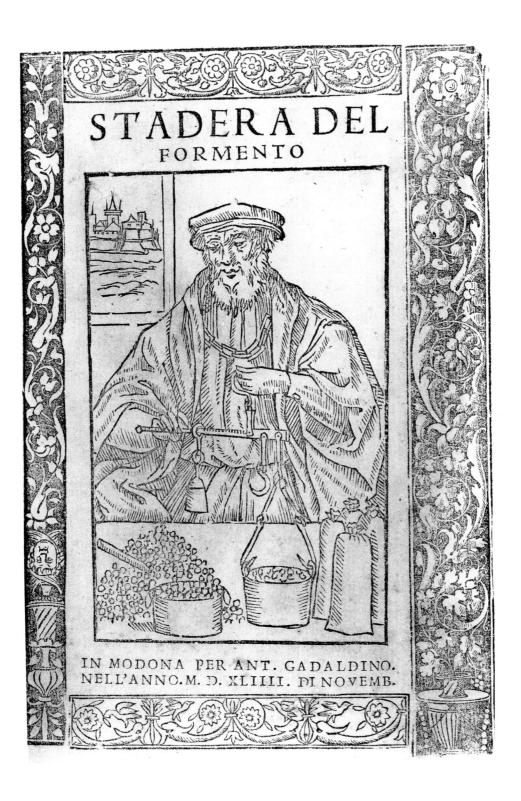

IN MODONA PER ANT. GADALDINO.
NELL'ANNO. M. D. XLIIII. DI NOVEMB.

registers contain a record of all the transactions, completed or still under negotiation, of one of the Corsis' agents, Bartolomeo Corsini. After a series of purchases in 1595 the Florentines owed 11,766 ducats. Further transactions in 1596 concerned 3500 *salme* of wheat bought at Palermo which was to be embarked in two Ragusan ships at the *caricatore* of Girgenti, at a total cost of 10,085 ducats, or just under 3 ducats per *salma*, to be paid at Leghorn. There follows a series of accounts referring to 2000, 7000, and 6000 *salme* of grain standing in various *caricatori* awaiting shipment. Then come financial details of various settlements and transactions, followed by statements of assets and liabilities. The mechanics of grain speculation would be more comprehensible if we knew more about the kind of operation described by the same agent for the Corsi in 1598. For unspecified reasons, a *nave* carrying wheat belonging to the Corsi unloaded at Messina 3700 *salme*, quite a large quantity that had somehow to be disposed of. For this wheat was left over from purchases made in 1595 and it was likely to be in no condition to use for bread or even for biscuit, and scarcely fit to be thrown to the chickens. Some of this grain was then sold on credit, the rest turned into biscuit, which seems to have been difficult to sell. Of 2500 cantars, 564 were sold in June; in August 620 were delivered to the Tuscan galleys; 1316 were left in the warehouse. As time went on the price fell from 37 *tarl* to 30 then to 16. And the agent complains of the bad faith of the buyers and the bakers who undertook to make the biscuit. That was one side of the story. The Neapolitans who in the time of Osuna assassinated a grain hoarder, or so-called, Starace, must have had their own opinion of wholesale grain merchants.

Many jealous eyes kept a careful watch over the grain trade, not least those of governments. Every state was concerned, even the very smallest, even the Duchy of Savoy or Transylvania. Grain was responsible for more espionage, writes the nineteenth-century historian Bianchini, than the affairs of the Inquisition itself. That grain export licences should be a source of income and a means of payment for governments constitutes yet another link between governments and the grain trade, making the latter no easier to follow either in Turkey or in Christendom. And the watchfulness of the states was insignificant compared to the morbid vigilance of the towns.

Grain was a preoccupation simply because it was always scarce: Mediterranean harvests usually verged on the inadequate. Richer kinds of farming, vines, and livestock were in constant competition with cereal growing – an important factor but not the only one. Wheat in the Mediterranean took up a great deal of room, requiring large areas for not very high yields, particularly since the same land could not be sown every year. In Sicily the two-field system (one year crops, one year fallow) usually operated and the same system was also used in the Apulian Tavoliere. In Spain triennial rotation (three *hojas*) was the ideal, since the land was too quickly exhausted under the two-field system. The practice of dry-farming required ploughing the same land at different times, first with a

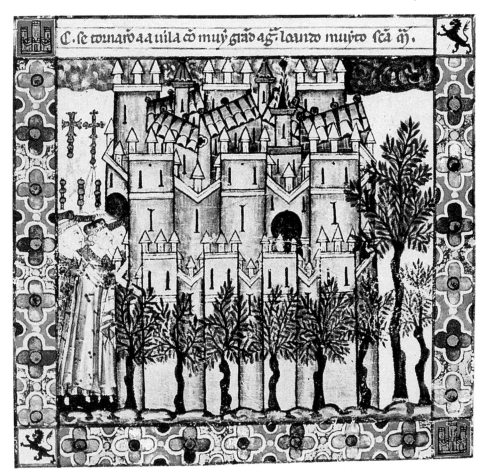

191. Rogation procession praying for rain. Miniature from Alfonso X's *Cantigas de Santa Maria*, thirteenth century. *Escorial, Madrid*

deep then a shallow furrow, to compensate for the lack of rainfall. And all government measures – taxes on grain, the regulation of sales – were so many blows on the back of a peasantry that could only groan under the burden, or, in Spain, allow itself to be tempted by the life of the muleteers or the American colonists.

And then there were the recurrent tragedies of winter floods and summer droughts which devotional processions were powerless to avert. The final result was extreme instability of price levels which fluctuated with the slightest news. It was not until the eighteenth century that a serious attempt was made to discover the cause of these fluctuations, and few books are as enlightening on this subject as one published anonymously (possibly by Sestrini) at Florence in 1793. It abounds with intelligent reflections on the disparity of wheat prices in the various regions of the Mediterranean. In the eighteenth as in the sixteenth century, there was a visible difference between the east, where bread was cheap, and the west where bread was expensive. It also explains how a poor harvest in any one region can create a zone of dear grain with prices even higher on the periphery of this zone than at the centre. The same was already true in the sixteenth century. As soon as scarcity became apparent in a particular area, merchants flocked towards it, dispatched their boats, and cleared their stocks. Prices over an area sometimes extending well beyond the original zone were affected by this movement. But as more ships raced to the zone of shortage, the influx of grain brought prices down again – a perfect lesson in political economy.

This was precisely what happened at Constantinople in 1561, a bad year throughout the Mediterranean, in Portugal where the spring had been 'unusually dry', in Spain where the harvest had been disastrous, in Sicily where the price of the *salma* after the harvest rose to 2½ ducats, and in the east, where the gap between the two harvests was difficult to bridge and there was anxiety as early as spring. A Venetian *nave*, the *Colomba*, was diverted to Nicomedia to load wheat for the capital. Four other *navi*, also Venetian, which were loading grain at Vólos, were captured by the galleys on guard at Salonica and taken to Constantinople. Here at the centre of the crisis the massive arrival of ships soon met the deficit and prices came tumbling down; the *chilo* (equivalent to one ninth of a *salma*,) fell to 17½ aspers, less than three ducats per *salma*. In the following year, the price of wheat went down, in the Greek ports, to 12 aspers a *chilo* or less than two ducats a *salma*.

Take another example: when a terrible famine struck Spain in 1578, the viceroy of Sicily, Marcantonio Colonna, wanted to send ships to the rescue. The merchants loaded 24,000 *salme* and undertook to transport 6000 to Spain. As for the rest, they were unwilling to commit themselves in advance, 'for it may happen', they explained, 'that everyone hastens to the place where he thinks there is most profit and then there is an over-abundance of grain' and of course commercial disaster. This was the situation envisaged in 1584 by the writer of the report quoted above. He warned the government, which was willing to handle the transport, of the risk they might run if the merchants rushed to Spain attracted by the smell of profit, 'el olor de la ganancia'.

The ultimate catastrophe for a merchant was to have one of his ships on her way to some region in difficulties seized by a town, which would always pay in its own time and at far below the expected price. It is easy to understand the rage of the Genoese merchants whose ship, laden with wheat from Apulia, was sailing in 1578 towards the *altissimi* prices of Spain when it was requisitioned – by the Republic of Genoa herself!

In theory, the merchant's aim was a simple one: to carry over from a good year to a bad one, or more often, since grain did not keep well and could not be stored for long, from a region where there was a good harvest to a region where there was a poor harvest, the surplus grain he had bought. Then, depending on the fortunes of the harvest, the currents of exchange might flow back in the opposite direction. In the grain trade anything was possible. There was not a cereal-growing region, on or near a coast, not a port that did not at one time or another have a surplus to offer. We need only go back to the fifteenth century to find that Corfu was then exporting *formento grosso*, and to the first half of the sixteenth century to find Cyprus sending wheat and in particular barley to Venice. In 1570 Spalato found Turkish wheat from the surrounding regions flowing into her warehouses, and allowed it to be exported to Venice, until she became aware of the Turkish preparations for war and, in sudden panic, forbade export of all the grain still within her walls. In some years there were extraordinary anomalies: in 1555, Spanish grain was sent to Rome; in 1564 Andalusia sent grain to Genoa with formal authorization from the Catholic King; Castile opened up her granaries in 1571; in 1587 the viceroy of Sardinia congratulated himself on his achievements: 4000 *salme* of grain had been sent to Genoa under his administration. Anything could happen: even Oran could become an export centre for African grain, as Diego Suárez explains: around the *presidio* local grain was only a quarter or a fifth the price of Spanish grain. The difference was appreciable when, that is, this grain existed – certainly not every year. Algiers too might find herself either very rich or extremely poor, from year to year.

But even the merchants' well-stocked granaries were not always able, unfortunately, to meet the needs of the population during the frequent, violent, and deadly famines. In 1554 there was one *horribilissima in tutta Italia*. And relief cannot have come quickly from abroad, since tens of thousands of people died and in Florence the price of grain rose to 8 *lire* the *stagio*.

The grain trade and the shipping routes. Grain was a transportable but bulky commodity. However precious it might be, it could not support heavy transport costs. On the overland routes, except of course in cases of famine or very high prices, grain was only sent very short distances.

A plan to send grain from Italy to Spain is recorded in 1584. Embarcation was to take place at the *presidios* on the Tuscan coast: Orbetello, Talamona, or 'Puerto Hercules'. The grain (70,000 *fanegas*, Castile measure) was actually to be purchased from Corneto and Toscanella, on papal territory; from Grosseto and the Sienese Maremma, which came under the jurisdiction of the Grand Duke of Tuscany; and from Castro and Montalto, possessions of the Duke of Parma. Some of these places were fifteen, twenty-five, or thirty miles inland. As a result, to the purchasing price of 10 Spanish reals per *fanega*, cost of transport overland to the sea-port had to be added: 3 crowns per *moggio* or 3 reals per *fanega*. This grain had increased in price by 30 per cent in the course of a fairly short journey. So it is easy to understand the scepticism of the viceroy of Naples about the proposed improvement of the road from Apulia to Naples (29th July, 1562). 'As for the preparation of carriageable roads to bring supplies to the city

192, 193. Emblems of the literary Accademia della Crusca, where each member had to invent a personal device relating to the cultivation and provision of cereals. Shown here are wheat and a grain ship. Sixteenth century. *Accademia della Crusca, Florence*

of Naples, it is being carried forward as quickly as possible. But I dare say that seeing the enormous sum of money it will cost to bring grain by cart from Apulia, few people will care to take the risk.' Wheat could not cross Italy by road. Grain sometimes travelled across the Kingdom of Naples but there is no indication that it went all the way from the Adriatic to the Tyrrhenian coast. It hardly seems likely, since in Tuscany transport over a radius of only four to thirteen miles around Florence was sufficient to increase the cost of grain by 4·24 per cent in 1570 and 3·35 per cent in 1600 (which apparently indicates that the price of the commodity itself increased more than the cost of overland transport, but it would be imprudent to generalize from this example, since other percentages, also in Florence, indicate the contrary). In January, 1559 it was decided not to send barley from the villages of Santa Ella and La Rambla to Málaga, since the cost of wagon transport was as much as the barley itself.

We may feel some sympathy then for the Venetian secretary, Marco Ottobon, who travelled to Poland during the winter of 1590–1591 and enquired on the way, both at Innsbruck and Vienna, about the likely price of grain in Cracow and Hungary, then calculated for the *Provveditori alle Biave* how much a *staio* would cost by the time it reached Venice. He had to convert currencies and measures, take into account all duties and commissions, and was almost always forced to conclude that the operation was impossible. The equivalent of a Venetian *staio* could be bought at Cracow for the equivalent of 8 Venetian *lire*. Transport between Cracow and Vienna would cost 7 *lire* 12 *soldi*; from Vienna to Villach, 7 *lire* 10; from Villach to Venzone, 3 *lire*; from Venzone to Porto Gruaro, 1 *lira* 4; from Porto Gruaro (by boat) to Venice 3 *soldi*. On top of this there were duties and commissions to pay, not to mention the cost of sacks or barrels. The total cost would be 30 *lire* 19 *soldi*, almost 31 *lire*: in the course of its travels the merchandise would have quadrupled in price. Transport costs were the greatest single factor in variations in the price of commercialized grain.

So it is easy to understand why grain was more readily sent by waterway. The expansion southwards of Burgundian grain would have been impossible without the boats travelling down the Rhône. When foreign cereals, naturally expensive, were sent to Florence, they were ferried up the Arno as far as possible, to Signa, the river port of the capital. The wealth of the territory of Lentini (Leontinoi) in Sicily was the result both of its agricultural resources and of its fortunate situation: it was not far from the coast, and its *fiume grande*, the San Leonardo was navigable to within a few leagues of the town; at least it was in 1483.

Transport by sea was comparatively cheap. To return to our earlier example of Italian grain travelling to Spain, the buying price per *fanega* was 10 Castilian reals, transport to the coast 3 reals, export duty 5 reals, transport (in a good Ragusan *nave*) only 3½ reals. There was a fairly heavy insurance premium to pay, since the season was late (9 per cent *ad valorem*) which added another 30 *maravedis* per *fanega*. So the cost of shipping amounted to only about 4 reals per *fanega*, whereas the price of a *fanega* at Alicante or Cartagena was 22 reals, 3 *maravedis* (the real is here reckoned at 54 *maravedis*). In the export of grain then, transport by sea was the cheapest operation involved, proportionately cheaper than carriage overland, transport by pack animal, or export licence. And shipping costs did not increase automatically with the distance travelled; it cost the same to ship from Italy to Barcelona or Valencia, whether one left from Sicily or Tuscany. Seacaptains even considered it more advantageous to sail to Spain across the 'Gulf' from Sicily, than to cross further to the north, from the *presidios* in Tuscany: from Sicily, they said, they could 'tener el golfo mas lançado', be better placed for a direct crossing.

So it was the inner region of the Mediterranean, with easy access to shipping routes, which could best afford the luxury of a grain trade. This in itself would suffice to explain why only those cities with direct sea links (apart from certain privileged towns like Milan) grew and developed. If the Mediterranean islands were often able to devote their energies to a rich and pervasive monoculture, it was because they had the sea and the grainships on their doorstep. Although constantly on the verge of food shortage, they were always able to rescue themselves from the brink, a gymnastic feat that the sea alone made possible or inspired. Grain covered extraordinary distances by water – Egyptian or Aegean grain was eaten in Valencia, in Spain, in Genoa and Rome. The bishop of Dax wrote from Ragusa to Charles IX in January, 1572: 'In this city not a single grain of wheat is eaten which does not have to be fetched from five hundred miles away,' a situation dating from well before the sixteenth century. This was how grain travelled in antiquity, in boats sometimes without decks. In the eleventh century, wheat from Aragon went down the Ebro then from Tortosa travelled the long diagonal route across the sea to relieve extreme hardship in Syria.

Ports and countries that exported grain. All the chief markets used by the grain trade were situated on the coast or on a waterway, like the little ports whose boats converged on Leghorn, Grosseto, Montalto, Corneto or the harbours in the Abruzzi which a surviving insurance policy shows to have engaged in a lively traffic with Venice: Grottamare, Sinagaglia. It was even more true of the larger markets: the towns of the Danube plains, linked by the great river with the Black Sea (a report from the Levant in December, 1575 indicates that the tribute of grain from Wallachia and Bogdiana was, on Turkish orders, to be made into biscuit and deposited on the banks of the Danube, where it would be collected); the Aegean markets which served the wheat-growing coastal regions; Gallipoli serving Thrace, Patmos near the Asia coast, Salonica at the entrance to Macédonia and Vólos, the great resource for western buyers, which exported the wheat from the plains of Thessaly. In Egypt, the Nile, like the Danube, carried huge quantities of wheat as well as rice, beans, and chick peas down to the sea. In the West, the great grain exporters were Apulia and Sicily – the latter a sort of sixteenth-century Canada or Argentina.

For this reason alone the case of Sicily would repay study. It also has the advantage of being clearer than any other. The administration and government of Sicily by the viceroys was first and foremost a question of handling grain. Their letters abound in references to harvests, prices, export licences, deals to be made with foreign merchants at Palermo where the Sicilian nobles, enriched by the island's great cereal production, also had their residences. Sicily had played the vital role of grain-supplier for many centuries, since antiquity in fact, with varying degrees of prominence but without interruption. The contract signed between Genoa and Manfred, king of Sicily in 1261, for the export of 10,000 *salme* a year (20,000 quintals) could with a little exaggeration (for Genoa had grown in the meantime) be mistaken for a sixteenth-century contract. The entire West, and the neighbouring Barbary coast most of all, dreamed of Sicilian grain. Leo Africanus relates that the Arabs handed over their children as pledges to obtain Sicilian wheat. When Tripoli was recaptured by the Christian troops, there was immediate concern in Sicily about the duties to be levied on wheat sent to Africa. Only the 2500 *salme* reserved for the fortress itself were to be exempted.

194, 195. *Above:* Baker's shop. Wall
painting from Pompeii. *Museo Nazionale,
Naples. Right:* Bread from Pompeii.

196. *Overleaf:* Grain market in the Yemen.

By the time of Ferdinand the Catholic, the list of *caricatori*, the Sicilian grain wharves, was already established: Solunto, Termini, Roccella, Catania, Bruca, Terranova, Licata, Girgenti, Siculiana, Mazzara, and Castellammare. The record of exports for 1532 reveals the leading position of the south with its hills. The official total of exports for that year (1532) was almost 260,000 *salme* or 520,000 quintals of grain, four times the requirement of Genoa according to an estimate of 1577. Genoa annually imported 60,000 to 70,000 *salme* of Sicilian wheat. But there was hardly a city in the west that had not been eating the island's excellent grain for centuries.

Eastern grain. But the West could not survive on internal exchange alone. During the middle years of the century, in particular, western stocks were replenished by shipments from the Levant, which with its smaller population had more grain available for export, usually at lower prices. The three principal sources of grain in the East were: Egypt; the plains of Thessaly, Macedonia, Thrace, and Bulgaria; and the Romanian lowlands. Romanian wheat soon disappeared from the Mediterranean circuits and was appropriated for the insatiable appetite of Constantinople. There remained the Greek and Bulgarian export markets and the granaries of Egypt. From the latter, the consul Lorenzo Tiepolo estimated in 1554 that the sultan was obtaining 600,000 *ribebe* of wheat, barley, and beans (curiously there is no mention of rice). These 600,000 *ribebe* (at 100 Sicilian *salme* to 165 *ribebe*) correspond to 363,636 *salme* or 720,000 quintals: a gigantic supply, much more than Sicily could provide. While a large part of this grain was destined for Constantinople, some was left in Egypt for the rations of Turkish soldiers and some was sent to Mecca. Besides, the sultan's 'wheat' was not necessarily all the wheat in Egypt. Tiepolo's figures (including the 1,200,000 ducats which this trade was worth to the sultan) are only estimates. In fact, as he himself adds, everything varies according to the height of flooding along the Nile, the incidence of epidemics and the price situation. The report gives two prices for a *ribeba* of beans and three for grain.

Moreover, at Alexandria as well as at Vólos, Salonica, Valona, La Prevesa, or Santa Maura, Turkish grain was loaded on to westbound ships, legally, with the consent of the Grand Turk, as is reported frequently in Ragusan or Venetian commercial papers. In Constantinople there was a constant refrain of requests from western countries: from Tuscany as early as 1528; from Genoa in 1563; in 1580, all such requests were refused, even those of the French, but a flourishing black market nevertheless continued to export Turkish grain westwards even during the prohibition. The headquarters of this black market was the Aegean.

Equilibrium, crisis, and vicissitudes in the grain trade. After this rather long introduction we are now in a better position to tackle the problem of the vicissitudes of the grain trade in the sixteenth century. There is always a risk of overdramatizing in an area where contemporary judgments were rarely dispassionate. On the whole, however, it would be true to say that the food problem grew steadily worse towards the end of the century and the 'peasant situation' became increasingly alarming. Famines increased, not in number – they had always been frequent – but in gravity. Their effects were felt more deeply. Six *carestie* hit Naples between 1560 and 1600; in 1560, 1565, 1570, 1584, 1585, 1591; the last three were more serious than the first three. It is not that 'the harvests are worse than in the past', writes an experienced observer of Neapolitan affairs in 1608, 'but the number of people has increased, as the population counts show: 95,641 more hearths in 1545, 53,739 in 1561; the count now in progress will, it is thought, reveal an increase of 100,000. When grain is in short supply or scarcely sufficient to go round, every one seeks to conceal it.' The shortage was unfortunately not confined to the Kingdom or city of Naples. Throughout the Mediterranean man's resources were failing to keep pace with his numbers. The extreme step of importing grain, from far or very far away, was a measure of men's hunger, a measure too of the wealth of the buyers.

This is demonstrated by the arrival of northern grain in Portugal and Andalusia. Portugal began importing very early, at the beginning of the sixteenth century; Andalusia, still rich in her own wheat, was not affected until much later, in the 1550s or even 1570–1580. There were two separate crises, in fact, the Portuguese and the Spanish, following similar courses and foreshadowing later developments in Italy.

In Portugal maritime expansion had created a curiously modern state. With a little exaggeration it could be described as an earlier version of England, centred like England, on its capital; Lisbon, standing head and shoulders above the multitude of small towns and villages active in its service, especially after the accession of the House of Aviz in 1386. A patriarchal, underpopulated Portugal, producing its own cereals and even exporting some to England, drinking its own wine, was giving way to a Portugal increasingly uncertain of its daily bread. Orchards, olives, and vines were taking up more and more room. Considerable efforts to increase cereal production can be detected in the south in Alemtejo for example, where different varieties of grain were acclimatized. The need for grain, grain 'imperialism', drove the Portuguese to seize control of the markets of the wide Moroccan plains, to introduce cereals briefly to Madeira and later to implant them successfully in the Azores. But the most satisfactory solution was to buy grain from outside, to abandon what was basically an unprofitable domestic activity.

Lisbon was very soon eating foreign grain, imported for many years from Andalusia and Castile and dispatched (though not always) from Sicily. In 1546, the ambassador of the king of Portugal at Rome, Simão de Veiga, made a hasty, but fruitless journey to Palermo. The Portuguese, who had long-standing connections first with Bruges, then with Antwerp, also turned to Flanders, possibly as early as the fifteenth century; in 1508 at any rate they were buying very good grain there, *o muito bom* at 10 *pataques*, and the best, *o melhor* for 11.

These purchases continued throughout the century. Usually northern grain, whether from the Baltic or elsewhere, was carried in the tiny Breton boats which arrived at Lisbon hundreds at a time. Poorest of the poor, how could the Breton sailors resist the temptation of payment in gold which they received in Portugal and were legally allowed to carry away? They 'arrive here every day', writes the French ambassador Jean Nicot, from Lisbon on 4th September, 1559, 'carrying great quantities of corn and without any permission [from the King of France]. I follow after to try to restore order.' But he was not very successful. For Portugal was, according to his own description, 'a country ... marvellously lacking in every kind of cereal'. And almost a century later, in 1633, a hundred of the same little boats are recorded at Lisbon, being first sequestered then released by the Portuguese authorities. In order to survive, these sailors would sell sails, rudder, the boat itself and still die of hunger in the end. It was the merchants of Bilbao and Burgos, or Simón Ruiz at Medina del Campo, who in 1558 were making these movements possible.

By this date the grain carried in these Breton *barques* had already reached Castile, to whose economy it was 'harto dañoso', extremely harmful. By Castile, let us understand, although it is not quite accurate, the ports of Biscay and Galicia. We do not know exactly when it first appeared in Andalusia. In any case, voyages by Breton ships became more frequent about now, giving them an opportunity to bring back, depending on their port of call, either the 'red gold' of Portugal or the silver of Spain.

In Cadiz, Seville, Andalusia, and the south of Spain as far as Málaga and Alicante, a pattern of development similar to that in Portugal began to emerge as the wealth of the New World reached Seville. This newly acquired wealth encouraged the planting of vines and olive trees. But the region was so rich in wheat that this development was slow. Seville was short of grain while neighbouring towns – Puerto de Santa Maria, the rich Jerez de la Frontera, and above all Málaga – had no difficulty in obtaining food supplies. At Málaga the *proveedores* of the armadas found their task an easy one for a long time. By paying one or two extra reals for a *fanega* they could obtain a ready supply of grain. Prices were much lower than in Catalonia, almost down to the level of Naples or Sicily. There was no lack of grain then, but there was a lack of pack animals to transport it. The government had only to requisition the animals for the price of wheat to be at the mercy of its officials. All was well then until mid-century.

In fact, the situation did not deteriorate until about the 1560s. In 1561, Seville protested loudly against the Genoese who controlled her customs and were pressing for payment on the grain (both wheat and barley) that the city had imported in large quantities from France, Flanders and the Canaries. Did they want the poor to die of hunger? These were by no means the first shipments of foreign grain to Seville, but the turning-point had not yet been reached: in 1564, for instance, there were plans to export Andalusian wheat to Genoa (although never carried out, the plans reached a fairly advanced stage). Some time between 1561 and 1569, a lean year, this transformation must have taken place. Andalusia, with more oil, wine, and silver than she needed, was from now on habitually importing foreign wheat. By 1560 at the latest the evolution was complete. Flour from Andalusia was no longer sufficient to make the biscuit for the fleets, and the Spanish Crown had to go in search every year, good or bad, of 100,000 *fanegas* of grain from the North (55,000 quintals) which was at once a little and a great deal. In 1583 the shortage spread to the whole of Spain, disrupting the entire economy.

There can be no doubt that the Spanish economy as a whole took a turn for the worse about the years 1580–1590 and that agriculture was the first sector to show signs of trouble although we do not know how, or why or exactly when it became clear that recession was on the way. The participants and the elements of the problem are clear enough: migrant flocks, settled flocks, the regular cultivation of the *regadios*, the irrigated gardens with their orange, mulberry, and other fruit trees; the *secanos*, dry lands on which vines and olive trees grew; sown fields (one year in two or three, they were sown half with wheat, half with barley) the fallow land, the *barbechos*, growing beans. But often on the *montes* peasants risked growing anything. By the end of the sixteenth century it was becoming a losing battle.

Foreign grain cannot be blamed for this state of affairs. At most it was a warning sign of approaching trouble. In Portugal, where the trouble had deep roots, unusual consequences were noted by contemporaries. The Spanish ambassador at Lisbon noted on 1st October, 1556 that 'the country is sick and in numerous regions many people are dying, it is said, from illnesses provoked by the bad food they have eaten and are still eating. The present year has provided even less bread than in the past and all are terrified at the thought of the future, unless God sends a remedy. Here in Lisbon, there is at present a little bread made from the grain which came by sea from France, but it all disappears quickly . . .'

It was a country rotten at the core, an enormous deadweight of which Philip was to find himself master in 1580, upon the conquest of Portugal. Let us remember in particular the connection between undernourishment and illness, for it was no coincidence. The epidemics that were to strike Spain at the end of the century – before the recession hit any other part of Europe – find an explanation here. This crisis disturbed a previous underlying equilibrium.

The Turkish wheat boom: 1548–1564. With the middle of the century crisis loomed in Italian agricultural production. There began a period of bad harvests, of obvious food shortages, and high prices throughout the peninsula. The causes of these hardships are not clear: over-population, poor meteorological conditions, a decline in agricultural investment, foreign wars – all these are possible or rather contributory causes and the situation deteriorated even further

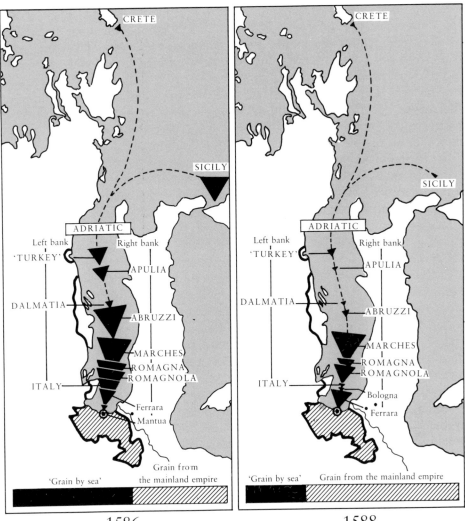

CRETE	CRETE
SICILY	SICILY
ADRIATIC	ADRIATIC
Left bank	Right bank	Left bank	Right bank
'TURKEY'	APULIA	'TURKEY'	APULIA
DALMATIA	ABRUZZI	DALMATIA	ABRUZZI
	MARCHES		MARCHES
	ROMAGNA		ROMAGNA
	ROMAGNOLA		ROMAGNOLA
ITALY		ITALY	Bologna
	Ferrara		Ferrara
	Mantua		

| Grain from |
| 'Grain by sea' | the mainland empire |

| 'Grain by sea' | Grain from the mainland empire |

1586   1588

Venice: imported grain and mainland grain

From Museo Correr 217. Venice had always eaten both home-grown grain and grain brought in by sea. At the end of the sixteenth century, the latter was no longer the chief source of supply (in 1588, for instance). There can be no doubt that increased cereal production in the Venetian mainland empire, which was to continue during the sixteenth century, was one of the major features of the Venetian economy. Note the importance among the sources of imported grain of northern Italy, north of the Abruzzi. The role played by wheat from Naples and Sicily progressively diminished. By these dates no more grain was being shipped from the Levant and none from the western Mediterranean. (The Romagnola is north of the Romagna, more precisely the *Romagna estense*, the territory of Lugo and Bagnacavallo.)

following 'una carestia di formento et altri grani' that did not spare even such a well-protected city as Venice. In any case, Italy quickly discovered a remedy for her often serious difficulties: a few payments in silver and her capacious grain ships, or those of Ragusa, were on their way to the ports of the Levant and the Turkish market.

This departure was sufficiently marked to bring about an increase in average tonnages to about 600 tons and before long even more. Among these big ships, it was typical to find certain Turkish roundships specializing in the long voyage from Constantinople to Alexandria in Egypt. One of these, owned by the Grand Vizier Rustem Pasha, arrived in Venice in December, 1551 with a cargo charged to the account of Zuan Priuli, and the Signoria exempted it from anchorage duty. There was, indeed, during these years active complicity from important Turkish dignitaries who possessed land and crops and were eager for money. Turkey, especially at first, found herself in a begging position, as if she did not know what to do with her surpluses. 'The more reserved our merchants are,' wrote the Venetian *bailo* on 4th September, 1551, 'the better terms they will find, for there is plenty of grain, belonging both to the nobles and to the people and, because of the war with the Emperor, there are no possible buyers except the Venetians and the Ragusans.'

In this year 1551, which saw the victorious expedition of Sinān Pasha against Tripoli, Venice imported from these grain ports between 300,000 and 400,000 *staia* (240,000 to 320,000 hectolitres or 180,000 to 240,000 quintals). If other cargoes are added, in particular those of the Genoese ships, about which unfortunately no details are available, perhaps 500,000 quintals of grain were imported from Turkey that year. At this rate all the ports in the Ottoman Empire must have been involved, not so much the Egyptian but certainly the Greek ports and fairly often the ports of the Sea of Marmara, sometimes even Varna on the Black Sea. Ragusan merchantmen, ostensibly sailing to Rodosto to load hides or wool, would make clandestine calls at Vólos to pick up grain. It meant very good business especially for a few Venetian merchants settled in Constantinople, foremost among whom was Antonio Priuli. The difference was so great, between the buying price in the Levant and the selling price in Italy – which could be twice, two and a half, or three times as much – that the merchants 'could not lose'.

If Italy was eventually obliged to look elsewhere for her daily bread, it was because Turkey was in turn entering an age of scarcity. One historian has classified certain periods as catastrophic – from 1564 to 1568, 1572 to 1581, and 1585 to 1590 – which is not to say that the intervening years were by any means prosperous. Constantinople, the swollen city, suffered every kind of evil: poverty, high prices, spectacular famines and finally plague. 'Between 1561 and 1598', according to the dispatches of the Venetian *bailo*, 'there were reckoned to be 94 months of plague (almost eight years in all) and this figure is probably an underestimate'. Such reports have their value but can sometimes conceal the true situation. Through its military victories, which brought it into contact with the rest of the world (Syria, 1516; Egypt, 1517; Rhodes, 1522; Belgrade, 1540; Hungary, 1541), and through the grain boom which lasted several years, a previously backward country, whose social structures were almost 'Carolingian' based on life-tenure of property ('beneficia' as it were) was drawn into the orbit of a powerful monetary economy already sufficiently strong to disrupt old patterns but not yet strong enough to create new and truly modern structures. This monetary economy with its devaluations, price increases, arbitrary accumulation, and the spread of imported luxury was superimposed onto an archaic economy, creating within the latter aberrant islands and pockets.

The last crisis: imports from the north after 1590. All the problems of the Mediterranean food supply had long prepared the way for the massive importation of grain from the north, carried in Dutch, Hanseatic, and English sailing ships from the Baltic to the Mediterranean after the 1590s. This was by no means the first grain to arrive from the north. Besides the Iberian peninsula, Genoa was already importing grain by the middle of the fifteenth century. In 1527 Venice had grain brought from Flanders or England. The Strozzi apparently did

197. Grain ships on the Mottlau River, Danzig. Eighteenth-century German print by J. F. Schuster.

the same in 1530 for Rome. In October 1539, a correspondent of the Gonzaga in Antwerp referred to the departure for Italy (Genoa, Florence, and Lucca) of 16 *nave grosse* laden with wheat, which he predicted would not keep well. Cosimo de' Medici probably imported Flemish grain as early as the 1540s and in 1575 Tuscany at least tried to buy Breton grain. For every one of these little-known cargoes ten or twelve others probably went unrecorded.

But the movement became widespread only after a series of bad harvests which befell Italy after 1586, producing a cumulative effect. By 1590 the situation was desperate: the Grand Duke of Tuscany was the first Italian ruler to dispatch agents to Danzig, and Venice followed suit when winter came. In 1590 and 1591 ships *probably* arrived at Leghorn and Genoa. In 1591, the Venetian secretary Ottobon sent five from Danzig. In June of the same year, 'it has rained so much', wrote a merchant from Florence, 'that it is feared the harvest will be as bad as last year's; the wheat, at least in the plains, is lying on the ground, and it is so wet that, instead of drying, it is rotting away'. Here we may once again note that the climate was partly responsible. In September the same merchant wrote categorically: 'We are having a difficult year because of the lack of grain; the best and surest remedy is awaited from Hamburg and Danzig.'

Thus began the voyages of the northern grain ships. Really large cargoes were not received before the winter of 1592–1593. Harbour records at Leghorn indicate that in 1593 nearly 16,000 tons of northern wheat and rye were imported, of which almost half had been ordered by the Grand Duke and the rest by merchants, the Buonvisi of Lucca, the Lucchini of Bologna, and the Vernagalli, Buonacorsi, Biachorali, Biachinelli, Capponi, Lanfranchi, Berzighelli, Orlandini, Mendes, Ximenez, Ricasoli, Melinchi, Bardi, Guardi, Taddi, and Massei . . . of Florence. If proof were needed this list of names from the harbour records (subject to errors in transcription) would confirm the dispersion of the grain trade. Between 1590 and 1594 the demand from Leghorn was so great that it led to payments to England, Danzig, and the Dutch of over two million crowns. In 1596 there was still an active demand, the Grand Duke was sending another representative to Poland and Danzig, and was attempting to gain control of all purchases in the North. Thus there was becoming established a massive grain trade of which the Grand Duke gradually became master thanks to his huge capital resources. Leghorn profited greatly from this boom in grain; it had many advantages over the other Italian ports. It was only a week's distance from Gibraltar, said the Danzig mariners, and lay on the same course as the wind that took them through the straits; they could load alum there for the return journey and pick up salt a week or two later in Spain. Going to Venice was quite a different kettle of fish.

But the voyage to Leghorn undertaken by entire fleets was not altogether free from dangers, obstacles and even temptations. Sailing down the Channel or around the British Isles by Scotland could mean an encounter with the English who might or might not allow the ships to pass – and with bad weather; in

KOORN-BEURS.

198. The Corn Exchange at Amsterdam. Dutch print, 1663.

Spanish ports there was always the risk of an embargo; Barbary pirates prowled the Mediterranean. So at Lisbon, Cadiz, or Seville if the grain showed signs of perishing, and if the competent consular authorities were willing, there was a great temptation to unload and sell the grain and return home with all speed. In the end it was with silver, half of it paid in advance, that Leghorn and other Italian towns could force the hand of the poorest towns of the North. Of course, Tuscany and its surrounding regions were not the only places in need of the new cereal supply. The whole of Italy was soon accustomed to it and depending on local ports and needs, the entire western Mediterranean, including North Africa.

Consequently the trade born of necessity before long revealed itself to be quite profitable. Simón Ruiz, the merchant of Medina del Campo was very sceptical at first. 'I am much grieved,' he wrote on 24th April, 1591 to his correspondent in Florence, 'by the lack of bread in Italy. May it please God to bring a remedy! The grain which is carried from Flanders and Danzig cannot in my opinion arrive in good condition since it is already spoilt when it reaches Seville. What must it be like by the time it gets to Italy! Shipping grain is not usually worth the risk. I know what I am talking about, and it has cost me dear in the past. If anyone at all gains any benefit from it, it is the mariners who sail in the grain ships. I have seen men lose much money in that venture.' Simón Ruiz was speaking from experience, since as a young man he had been concerned in shipping grain to Lisbon. But in this case he was wrong. Of the five boats sent to Venice by Ottobon, only three finally reached Venice, one had to unload at Lisbon and the fifth was lost. But even so, from a commercial point of view, the operation was still worthwhile. In large contracts, the Ximenez – in particular Fernando Ximenez of Antwerp who made sure that his associates, the Veiga and the Andrade, were restricted to the contracts negotiated by the Grand Duke of Tuscany – could in the early stages make profits of up to 300 per cent. For the transport of grain from the north was not merely a matter of ships, freighting, and grain purchases, it meant enormous transfers of funds to Antwerp (at first) and other northern cities, as we have seen in connection with Marco Ottobon's journey, and as is testified by the copies of bills of exchange drawn by the *Abbondanza* of Genoa. There were always profits to be made from these operations.

Sicily: still the grain store of the Mediterranean. Let us now consider not simply the grainships of the North, but the Mediterranean itself, its structure and its vital centre – Italy – instead of an episode in its history, a temporary *conjoncture*. In the first edition of this book, I was persuaded both by documentary evidence

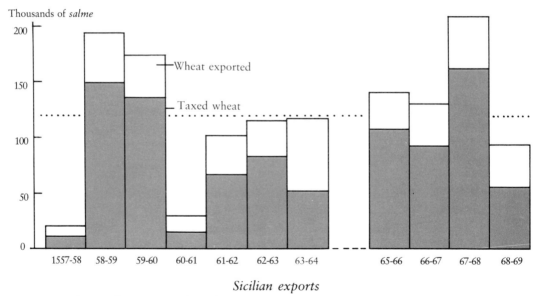

Sicilian exports

According to documents in the archives at Simancas. The shaded area represents the exported grain on which the *tratte* had been paid, the white area that on which the *tratte* had not been paid. The average figure (dotted line) is about 120,000 *salme*. Variations were more a function of differences in the harvest than of varying demand. Every three or four years Sicily had a poor harvest. Exports were maintained at the same level during the seventeenth century and with the same periodic fluctuations.

and the statements of historians to magnify this episode into a symptom of the decline of the Mediterranean. This decline now seems to me, especially in Italy, to have become apparent only very much later. I would now consider that the great economic turning-point did not occur before 1620–1621 and the great biological turning-point – the wave of epidemics – not before 1630.

When I was writing the first edition, the decisive argument in my eyes was what I called the failure of Sicily and Sicily's wheat. I had every reason to be convinced of it at the time. But Sicilian wheat did not fail the Mediterranean. Sicily as a whole, both in the sixteenth century and late into the following century, had a healthy balance of trade, in spite of the hazards inherent to all material existence under the *ancien régime*. In the seventeenth century silk exports did not decline until after 1619; wheat continued to be a principal commodity; an active shipping fleet frequented the coast of Sicily sailing to the Levant and even more to nearby Tunisia, leaving in the Sicilian ports, at least until 1664, some part of the considerable sums of silver it was carrying; the silk industry was flourishing, or rather reviving in Messina and Catania. In Sicily, the decline of the Mediterranean cannot on any reckoning be said to have occurred prematurely.

On grain crises. To sum up, all the wheat crises present similar features. They would be even more similar if there was more documentary evidence of the course they took in Islam, where they are for the most part concealed from the historian. They clearly correspond to patterns of population growth, whose effects were on the whole benign until about 1550 or 1560. The more people there were the more grain was produced. Thereafter, the law of diminishing returns began to operate. The fairly untroubled abundance of the fifteenth and 'first' sixteenth century gave way sooner or later to increasingly serious difficulties of supply. In the west, this was partly the result of the ousting of cereal-growing by more profitable and more reliable crops – vines and olives. These in turn were prompted by large-scale trade, a taste for wine, differential price increases, and sometimes social factors.

I am thinking in particular of the preference of the rich for white bread. To meet such problems 'never before encountered', as a document says with reference to Syria, the solutions envisaged varied according to the amount of wealth available. The purchase of grain from distant sources was, I need hardly point out, an obvious indication of general prosperity – despite the fact that it was at the same time, catastrophic for the poor.

3 Trade and transport: the sailing ships of the Atlantic

A unique gauge of Mediterranean trade as a whole is provided by the successive waves of Atlantic shipping that entered the sea. For there were two massive invasions (with some differences, some similarities), the first roughly between 1450 and 1552, the second after 1570 or rather 1572–1573: with the second invasion, consisting exclusively of northern ships, the route to the Mediterranean with all its advantages was permanently opened up to the North.

I have already suggested an explanation for these major developments in Mediterranean history: that the arrival of foreign ships corresponded to the creation of new opportunities resulting from an economic revival, quite as much as to commercial competition from the North (although this obviously existed); in short the newcomers bore witness to a certain level of prosperity. In a period of economic expansion, the Mediterranean had better things to do than transport commodities, particularly bulky ones. If this really was the case, with the arrival of foreign transport ships, narrative history provides the statistician with a magnificent yardstick. For the stream of ocean vessels was interrupted for a period of about twenty years. Does this mean that Mediterranean prosperity was also interrupted during the middle years of the century?

1. Before 1550: the first arrivals

It is not easy to discover the routes taken by the first Atlantic vessels to enter the Mediterranean, partly because they were often poor wretches who left few traces of their passage, partly because in the early days Iberians and northerners came in side by side, making it hard for us to distinguish one from the other or to establish the exact date of each voyage.

Basque, Biscayan, and even Galician ships. The mariners of the Atlantic Iberian coast entered Mediterranean waters possibly as early as the end of the thirteenth century. When their numbers increased, after 1450, they were already well known in the Mediterranean for their services to both Barcelona and Genoa and were frequent visitors to both the south and north coasts of the western basin. They acted simply as carriers, nothing more. The few Basque merchants recorded at Genoa handled only small transactions (for the most part in wool); their principal function was to answer for the masters of ships, whose reputation was never very good, and to borrow on their behalf the sums of money necessary for fitting out their ships.

And then, one day, these sturdy sailing vessels left their usual haunts and, in the service of various western cities, reached the waters of the eastern Mediterranean. By about 1495 they were sailing straight from Genoa, Málaga and above all Cadiz, to Chios, carrying Atlantic sugar to the island. They continued to do

199. Santander, one of the great Biscayan ports. From *Civitates Orbis Terrarum*.

so for many years. We must also remember their voyages to England and in particular to Flanders. In 1532, a Venetian says that Biscay (in the widest sense) is a jewel in Charles V's crown, the secret of his maritime power, 'from Biscay he can have all the ships he desires'. In fact these ships were to monopolize the Flanders route until 1569 and before this date their galleons were sailing on the long *Carrera de Indias*. For many years these 'vagabonds' were active in every kind of Mediterranean trade, and between 1480 and 1515 they were as likely to be carrying 'wine from Marseilles to London as Irish hides to Marseilles'.

The first to arrive from beyond the Straits of Gibraltar, they remained a long time in the Mediterranean concentrating round Genoa, Marseilles, and Barcelona and along the long Spanish coast. They crop up in sixteenth-century documents when one expects them to be rare or to have already left. There is a record of a Biscay captain anchoring his vessel at Marseilles in February, 1507 preparing to carry wine to Flanders and England; and of another, in 1510, sailing from Bari to Antwerp for Hans Paumgartner; in 1511, a Biscayan ship brought kerseys to Ragusa; in 1521, during the acute grain shortage in Spain, Neapolitan documents refer to Biscay merchants and mariners among those supplying the Peninsula with grain from Apulia; we meet them again in 1526, or January 1527 on the way to Messina with a cargo of sardines and tunny from Portugal; in 1530, two Biscay ships laden with salt were sunk by Barbarossa; in 1532, one of their sailing ships reached Alicante after rough treatment from the Barbary corsairs. On the routes from Spain to Italy, in 1531, 1535 and 1537, when one would have thought their role in the Mediterranean was finished, a port register contains mention of no less than twelve Biscay ships; and they were not the last. Perhaps it was not until the middle of the sixteenth century and the end of the first wave of Atlantic shipping that they entirely disappeared from the active routes of the Mediterranean.

The Portuguese. After the capture of Ceuta which opened wide the door of the Mediterranean, Portuguese ships were soon both as numerous and as active as the Biscayans in these waters. Even before the arrival of their armadas, Portuguese merchant vessels were offering their services and Portuguese pirates imposing theirs: they seized a Venetian merchantman carrying Cretan wine in November 1498; in October, 1501 they captured a Genoese ship off the Barbary coast; any Moorish passengers they captured had to leave rich booty in their hands in order to buy their freedom. They naturally entered the service of the great commercial cities. They are found around Valencia and the Balearics, at Marseilles, employed more often by Florence than by Genoa, although the latter did not reject their offers. Throughout the western basin of the Mediterranean, Portuguese sailing ships were soon carrying hides loaded at Lisbon – a sign of the still backward Portuguese economy – Andalusian wheat, salt from Ibiza, alum from Spain and Italy, sugar from Madeira and other Atlantic islands after 1480 or 1490, above all after the ordinance issued by Dom Manuel (on 21st August, 1498) forbidding any but Portuguese subjects to engage in the sugar trade. Every year by the end of the fifteenth century there were exported according to the official concessions 40,000 *arrobe* of Portuguese sugar to Flanders, 7000 to England, 6000 to Leghorn, 13,000 to Genoa, 2000 to Rome, 15,000 to Venice, 25,000 to Constantinople and Chios. Sugar arrived in Venice in *caravelle grosse*. Gradually, it seems, Portuguese ships were built bigger in order to handle trade over the whole sea, since they were from very early on sailing to Chios, Constantinople, the Levant, and Egypt. Sugar and the light ships used by the Portuguese together account for their success in the Mediterranean, long before Vasco da Gama's voyage around the cape.

As in the case of the Biscayans, we do not know exactly when the Portuguese disappeared from the Mediterranean. The Portuguese episode was undoubtedly almost over by the middle of the sixteenth century. Other ships and seamen had

200. Portuguese Carracks off a Rocky Coast, ascribed to Cornelis Anthoniszoon.
National Maritime Museum, Greenwich

arrived to offer their services and I imagine Portuguese shipping must have become a more lucrative business to the west of the Pillars of Hercules than to the east. Unless, that is, there were now fewer opportunities in the Mediterranean.

Normans and Bretons. The succession did not immediately fall upon the Normans and Bretons, who were latecomers to the Mediterranean although both had appeared quite early off the Atlantic coasts of Spain and Portugal: from 1466 on there may have been a Breton quarter in San Lucar de Barrameda; it is quite possible, although the word *berton* in Spanish, like *bertone* in Italian, was applied throughout the sixteenth century to all northerners indiscriminately. But if piracy is a sign of recent arrival, there can be no doubt that the Italian wars brought these ships in their wake, in 1496–1497 for example or 1502. In January 1497, certain *navi bertone* were engaged in active piracy off Majorca. But apparently trade did not follow them, especially in the case of the Bretons who, when questioned about Venice, in 1500 replied that 'they have hardly navigated in those waters'. It is another forty years before there is a reference to two of their ships at Gibraltar in 1540. A puff of wind would have taken them into the Mediterranean, but they did not enter the sea until just before the second wave of Atlantic invaders, and, as far as we know, even then they only reached the ports on the east coast of Spain. In 1567 a Breton ship was at Alicante; in November, 1570 or 1571, another was at Málaga, the *Baron* with on board her the master, Guillaume Potier, and the merchants Étienne Chaton and François Pin, plus a cargo of canvas and a few thousand quintals of fish. When they had sold it all, they bought 4000 crowns' worth of raisins and other goods and were preparing to return to Brittany when the *proveedor* of Málaga laid an embargo on the vessel, threw one of the merchants into jail, and was intending to send the ship on the king's business either to Oran or Peñon de Velez. This flagrantly contravenes the treaty between the two countries, writes the French ambassador, and 'it is not the first time a French ship like this has been requisitioned at Málaga'. But it was not until 1571 that the first ship from St Malo arrived at Civitavecchia.

Among these humble and discreet visitors, the Normans are mentioned more frequently. In 1499, one of their big ships, the *Magdeleine*, was captured by a Portuguese corsair at Almeria. Ten years later Norman sailing ships were regularly fetching alum from the Mediterranean for the Rouen weaving trade; this mineral came either from Spain, in which case it was picked up at Mazarron, or from the Papal States, loaded at Civitavecchia. In 1522, 1523, 1527, 1531, 1532, 1534, 1535, 1536, 1539, their visits to the Mediterranean can easily be checked: dozens of these little sailing boats figure in the registers of Norman tabellions [clerks] and in the harbour records of Civitavecchia. There was no lack of incidents at the ports. On 3rd February, 1535 at Cartagena, three little Norman ships carrying herring, salt fish and 'otras muchas mercaderias' were requisitioned before they could leave for Leghorn and Civitavecchia. Two of them were called *Maria*, one from Dieppe and the other from St-Valéry-en-Caux, and the third ship also from Dieppe was *La Louve*. The usual route was that taken by the *Fleur de Lys* of Dieppe (80 tons, 22nd May, 1536), sailing to 'Ligorne et Civitegie' and unloading alum at Le Havre de Grâce, London, Antwerp, or Rouen; or that followed by the *Françoise* of Rouen (2nd October, 1535) which put in to Marseilles, Villefranche, Leghorn, Naples, Messina, and Palermo.

Inevitably, in the long run, Norman ships were drawn by contract or by accident, on to other routes, to North Africa for instance, where they loaded coral near Cape Negro and, finally, though not before 1535 or 1536, they reached the eastern Mediterranean, as all the incoming vessels did sooner or later. In 1539, the *Grande Martine* of Dieppe made the trip to Marseilles, Cyprus, Constantinople, and Salonica.

Comparatively late arrivals, the Normans prolonged their stay in the Mediterranean. Civitavecchia could always provide them with cargoes between 1545 and 1552. And longer voyages called them east and south. In 1560, a ship from Dieppe, captured by Euldj 'Ali, turned up in the Black Sea, where she was eventually lost in the service of the Turk. In 1561 another fell prey to the Spanish off the Balearics. It was learned that the said vessel had left Dieppe for the

Barbary coast, that she had taken a pilot at Toulon and that the said pilot – this is the French version – had, unknown to everyone else, brought on board oars, which were contraband goods for ships travelling to the countries of Islam; that lead and shot were also found on board, but these, according to the Admiral of France, were intended for Dieppe, not for Africa, an explanation considered highly improbable by the sceptical Chantonnay who was perhaps right for once. More fortunate were the voyages made by other vessels from Dieppe, the *Coq*, master Le Prieur, for instance which entered Leghorn on 4th January, 1574, carrying lead, barrels of herring, hides, tin, a few kerseys and, a reminder of Dieppe's days of glory, 20,880 logs of brazil-wood; or the *St-Paul*, master Gérard, which sailed into Leghorn on 22nd February, 1578, bringing for the merchants of Lucca barrels of herring, peas, salmon, flax, hemp, linen cloth, and, again, brazil-wood (4700 logs). But these were late appearances and very much an exception. They would not withstand the 'second' English invasion, which cannot of course be adequately dealt with until we have considered the earlier impressive entry of the English to the Mediterranean.

Flemish ships. A few words will suffice for the 'Flemish' (in fact, nine times out of ten, Dutch) vessels, which arrived in fairly large numbers in the Mediterranean in the armadas sent by Charles V against Tunis in 1535 and Algiers in 1541. One of their ships is mentioned at Barcelona in 1535. After 1550 they became rare. In 1571 on the one occasion we can actually trace a Dutch ship, with her master, Joan Giles, *natural de Holanda*, leaving Antwerp for Cadiz and Leghorn, carrying Italian merchandise and Italian merchants (mostly if not all Florentine), the said master sailed into La Rochelle, and pillaging his own ship, sold the entire cargo.

The first English sailing ships. Following Richard Hakluyt, the date of English entry to the Mediterranean has usually been given as 1511. In fact this year saw the beginning of a series of prosperous voyages to the Levant, preceded by a long and not always brilliant apprenticeship. Nor does the English ship mentioned in the port of Genoa by two notarial documents (30th August and 6–7th October, 1412) necessarily signify the beginning of an enterprise that was spread over a period of centuries, any more than the two ventures launched by Robert Sturmy, merchant of Bristol, in 1446 and 1456, at ten years' interval from each other. On the first occasion the cog *Ann*, chartered by him, carried 160 pilgrims to the Holy Land as well as a cargo of wool, woollen cloth and sheets of tin. She reached Jaffa, where the pilgrims disembarked, to make their return journey either overland or in another ship. On 23rd December, the cog *Ann*, surprised by a storm, was wrecked off Modon and her crew of thirty-seven perished with her. Ten years later, Sturmy himself journeyed to the Levant in the *Katharine Sturmy*. His voyage was to last over a year. In 1457 after having stayed in 'divers parts of the Levant' (we have no further details), he apparently procured 'some green pepper and other spices to have set and sown in England, (as the fame went)'. But the expedition ended tragically, not in ship-wreck this time, but as a result of Genoese jealousy. They were waiting for the Englishman off Malta and pillaged his ship. Sturmy himself disappeared in the incident.

In 1461 the English opened a joint consulate at Naples together with the French and Germans; in the same year they also opened one on their own in Marseilles. Twenty years later they were setting up their vital consulate at Pisa, clear proof that they hoped, by using Pisa, Florence, and Tuscany as a base, to challenge the dual monopoly in the Levant of Genoa and Venice. It may be noted in retrospect that Sturmy had also used Pisa as a stopping place.

Nevertheless the progress of the English was slow; and had no doubt to be paid for, like that of all the newcomers, by entering the employ of other states. The precious records of the *Caratorum Maris* of Genoa seem to suggest this. But there is little evidence that there was a long period during which they served other powers, transporting bulky, low-priced merchandise over long distances. It is possible that the English won their way more quickly and at less expense than other newcomers, to the Levant, with its spices, and Crete with her precious wines. But it certainly did not happen overnight: they did not appear at Barcelona, for example until 1535 and it was not until the beginning of the sixteenth century that English commodities – lead, tin, salted fish, peasant cloth – really penetrated the Mediterranean, and in greater quantities than has hitherto been thought.

The period of prosperity (1511–1534). The names and histories of the ships, and the incidents of the voyages to the Levant between 1511 and 1534 are well known to us. The *Christopher Campion*, the *Mary George*, the *Mary Grace*, the *Trinity*, the *Matthew* of London, and several other ships from Bristol and Southampton, sailed regularly to Sicily, Crete, Chios, sometimes to Cyprus, as well as Tripoli in Syria and Beirut. They carried to the Mediterranean woollen cloth and 'kersies of divers colours'; they brought back pepper, spices, silks, camlets, malmseys, muscatels, sweet oils, cotton wool, and carpets. They were frequent visitors: fortunately, write the masters of the *Mahonna* at Chios to Genoa, in January and February, 1531 we have received some merchandise from an English vessel coming from Egypt and Syria (the goods were not, incidentally, in very good condition). The English did not only use their own ships, but often entrusted their merchandise to Venetian 'galleasses' or to Ragusan, Cretan, Spanish, and even Portuguese roundships.

On Chios, their rallying point at the far end of the sea, the English had a 'factor' until 1552. In 1592, Hakluyt, the collector of relations of voyages and discoveries, was to hear from John Williamson, who went as cooper aboard the *Matthew Gonson* of London, in 1534, the story of the voyage he made in that far-off year to Crete and Chios. The ship (300 tons burden and a hundred men on board), a large vessel for the time, sailed with the *Holy Cross*, a 'short shippe'

201. English ships in Dover harbour at the time of Henry VIII.
British Library

of 160 tons burden. After a full year at sea, they returned from this long voyage with a cargo of oil and wine in casks that were found to be so weak on arrival that they had to be drawn as they lay and the wine and oil transferred into new vessels. But the cargo was nevertheless of excellent quality, particularly the muscatels and red malmsey, 'the like whereof were seldom seen before in England', as the old man put it. Also on board were Turkish carpets, spices, and cotton. The *Holy Cross* had been so badly shaken by the voyage however that she was laid up in dock and never sailed again.

The large number of papers and letters collected by Hakluyt and the usually precise character of his accounts are proof enough of the frequency of English shipping, in the age of the Renaissance, to the Mediterranean and as far as the gateways to the east. It prospered during the years 1511 to 1534 and continued until 1552, 'and somewhat longer', then was suddenly interrupted, 'given over'. The last voyage recorded in Hakluyt's collection is that of the 'great Barke *Aucher*' (1550), as told by her captain, Roger Bodenham, and an eventful voyage it was too. She left England in January and in spring arrived in the ports of

Crete, where she met many Turkish boats laden with grain. Accompanied by a number of small boats carrying their goods to Chios, the English ship sailed forward to this island, which was still one of the most active commercial centres of the East, with its Genoese merchants, its mastic plantations, its production of silk bedcovers, and its many ships. She had to leave the island in haste, to avoid the Turkish galleys preceding the victorious fleet on its way back from Tripoli in Barbary. The *Aucher* then went on to Crete, where there were 'many banished men' in the mountains, ready to come down to fight in the island's defence, wild men, booted to the thigh, each with his bow and arrow, sword, and dagger, and drinking wine 'out of all measure'. Then on to Zante, Messina, Cadiz, and England. An interesting detail: on this voyage sailed the same Richard Chamberlain who was two years later to lead the expeditions to the mouth of the Dvina in northern Russia. But one looks in vain in this account for any valid reason why voyages by English ships should have stopped. We have few details concerning the *Jesus* of Lübeck and the *Mary Gonson*, which were chartered in 1552 for a voyage to the Levant.

Perhaps by studying the conditions of trade in English commercial centres one might be able to discover why voyages to the Mediterranean ceased to be worthwhile for London merchants, for this was clearly why they were discontinued. To blame the Turks does not seem very logical. The English were more likely discouraged by competition from Mediterranean shipping as well as from the overland routes across Europe and by the generally unfavourable economic conditions of these difficult years.

II. From 1550 to 1573: the Mediterranean left to Mediterranean ships

Along with the English, all the other intruders from beyond the straits vanished as if swept from the Mediterranean, and if a few laggards were left behind, a ship from Dieppe, a Breton fishing-smack or the odd boat from Saint-Malo, there can be no doubt that the sea was suddenly empty of northerners. The Mediterranean once again took over all the duties of internal transport, for a good twenty years, from 1553 to 1573. All the bulky commodities – salt, grain, wool, cumbersome hides – were carried in Ragusan ships, whose importance was increasing – in 1535 and 1541 for instance, in the fleets that Charles V led against Tunis and Algiers; in Venetian merchantmen whose numbers undoubtedly rose (total tonnage in 1498 was 26,800 *botti*; in 1560 it was 29,000 and, by 1567, 54,400), figures that tell their own story. Venice filled the gap left by the departure of the Atlantic ships. The same was true of Ragusa: the merchant fleet in 1540 totalled 20,000 *carri*; it had risen to 35,000 between 1560 and 1570, the decade that marked its apogee. All these new roundships appeared when the times called for them. They also explain why large Mediterranean ships were once again seen on the distant Atlantic and even North Sea routes.

But this revival in Mediterranean shipping was born of the changing economic climate. Between roughly 1550 and 1570, or rather 1575, there was an obvious recession. Business was bad for everybody. But every state had to see to its own needs. And the richer states, because they rode out the storm while others sank, appeared prosperous. In spite of the usual disastrous accidents which befell the great ships of the Mediterranean, they continued to hold their own, maintaining both internal and external communications. And then fine economic weather returned. If we resist the temptation of the over-simple solution, it was the return of prosperity that brought an end to the Mediterranean voyages to the north, or at any rate made them a rare occurrence. During the extraordinary boom at the end of the century, the rich could once again afford the luxury of delegating certain tasks to others. First English and then Dutch ships once more entered the Mediterranean, this time in larger numbers than they had during the early years of the century.

The return of the English in 1572–1573. The English ships reappeared at least as soon as 1573. It is in this year that we find what seems to be their first appearance at Leghorn. Perhaps they returned even earlier. An English Newfoundland fishing boat may have arrived at Civitavecchia in 1572. A ship certainly arrived at Leghorn on 25th June, 1573: *La Rondine* (the *Swallow*), master *Giovanni Scotto, inglese*, loaded at London and Southampton and carrying three bales of *carisee* (kerseys), two barrels of wrought tin, a few cotton fabrics, thirty-seven casks of broken bells, five whole bells, 380 pigs of lead and a keg of salt tongue – in all a modest cargo. The *St Mary of Grief*, master Sterlich, arrived on 20th July, carrying goods taken on board at Cadiz. The *Kite*, which sailed into Leghorn on 16th December, 1573, brought lead, soda, woollen cloth, and tin from London, all of which, a detail worth noting, had been ordered by merchants of Genoa. These three ships alone point the way to what was to be the chief commodity traffic with England: woollen cloth, lead, and tin. Later additions were to be the countless barrels of pickled herring, cod, and salmon. Once re-established the link was never broken again. In 1573 our Leghorn registers mention three English ships, in 1574, nine; two only (but the evidence is incomplete for this year) in 1575; three in 1576; five in 1578; nine in 1579; two in 1580; thirteen in 1581; ten in 1582; four in 1583; six in 1584; eight in 1585; six in 1590–1591; three in 1591–1592; sixteen in 1592–1593. The English had found their way back to the Mediterranean.

Nothing at the gateway to the Mediterranean, in Spain, seems to offer any explanation for this return and very little in the sea itself. Can it be attributed to the improvements in the sail and rigging of roundships which occurred towards mid-sixteenth century and made these ships easier to handle in a sea of varying moods? Or if one takes the evidence of the Leghorn *portate* (the unloading of barrels of white herring, lead, and tin) was there an increased demand in the Mediterranean for English commodities that satisfied two kinds of hunger, the

202. Detail from *Dock Scene at a British Port* by Jacob Knyff, c.1670. *National Maritime Museum, Greenwich*

hunger of fast days and Lent and the hunger for armaments? It was at about this time of course that bronze artillery was beginning to replace cast iron. There can be no doubt at any rate that the demand for tin and lead was general throughout the Mediterranean, in Moslem countries, and in Russia as well as in the Christian West. By 1580 the English ships that called at Sicily were suspected of being on their way to Constantinople with tin for the casting of artillery. They also supplied Naples and were welcomed at Malta, after the initial, rather cold reception met in 1581 by the *Roe*, an English bark, master Peter Baker, carrying iron, steel, bronze, and tin and in 1582 by the bark *Reynolds*. The Knights of Malta, in July of that year granted a safe-conduct to the English, provided they did not carry contraband, to trade freely with the island and pass on to the Levant. This favour was naturally an opportunity to place several specific orders, powder for cannon and arquebus, saltpetre, tin, steel, iron, copper, common white kerseys, coarse canvas, balls of iron for shot, fine millstones, and trees and masts for galleys; and also the *carboni di petra rosetta*, which the English called 'cole of Newcastle' – a detail in the history of English coal.

Further evidence of the English arrival is provided by a decree of the Venetian Senate dated 26th January, 1580, and blaming once again the post-Lepanto crisis. 'Before the last war,' say the Senators, 'our merchants of Venice were in the habit of engaging in trade and traffic to the western waters [that is England] chartering our ships for the islands of Cephalonia, Zante, and Candia [Crete] where they would take on raisins and wines to be shipped to the west, and on their return they would bring to this city *carisee*, woollen cloth, tin, and other goods.' In this way five or six ships had regularly been sailing to the North Sea every year. But since the war (in other words since 1571–1573) the said voyage had been completely abandoned. 'Foreign' ships now went directly to the Venetian islands and took on board raisins and new wines, with the complicity of certain Venetian subjects resident in these islands, having brought in exchange the *carisee*, cloth, tin, and silver of the north.

So we are brought back yet again to the Venetian crisis of 1571–1573, which was apparently responsible not only for the visible but short-lived fortune of Marseilles, in the Levant, but also for the return of English shipping to the Mediterranean. Here, as in the Levant, Venice could quickly have recovered her position. If she did not so do, it was because the economic situation was once more becoming favourable by 1575, with the result that responsibilities were more readily delegated, as we have already suggested. Certainly, there were still Venetian ships to be seen in the north, up to the end of the century. In 1582, for instance, in the trivial incident of the repatriation of a hundred poor Portuguese 'who had come quite naked' from Terceira to England, mention is made of two Venetian *navi*. In October, 1589 the *Santa Maria di Gracia* (either Venetian or Ragusan) was loading wine for England at Candia and Rethimnon. Or so her freight contract tells us. But on the whole, as we have already explained, Venice, like the other great Mediterranean cities, was increasingly ready to offer employment to 'foreign' ships and mariners. This employment provides the most acceptable explanation for the return of the northern ships to the Mediterranean.

Anglo-Turkish negotiations: 1578–1583. The English had yet to conquer the markets of the Levant. Richard Hakluyt claims that this was the work of two merchants of London, Sir Edward Osborne and Richard Staper who decided to embark upon this course in 1575. At their own expense they sent to Constantinople two agents, John Wight and Joseph Clements, who travelled through Poland and at Lwow, in September, 1578 joined the party of the Turkish ambassador Ahmad Chā'ūsh who brought them safely to their destination on 28th October. They obtained a letter from the sultan for the queen of England, dated 15th March, 1579. Bernardino de Mendoza, who from London followed the operation more closely than the Spanish agent in Constantinople, Giovanni Margliani, noted in November, 1579 that the queen had received by way of France, a letter full of promises from the sultan, enjoining her, in order to preserve and make even closer her ties with the king of France, to marry (no doubt the French had something to do with the insertion of this advice) the Duke of Anjou. The letter adds that English merchants whether coming by land or sea would receive a cordial welcome. The truth is, writes Mendoza, that the Turks could not care less about the marriage; what interests them is the tin, 'which the English began a few years ago to transport to the Levant', the tin without which they cannot 'cast their cannon'. And five ships with over 20,000 crowns' worth of this metal were on the point of leaving London for the Levant. The queen's reply, dated 25th September, 1579, was entrusted to Richard Stanley aboard the *Prudence*. The time was ripe. With the Portuguese succession open, Philip II had embarked upon massive preparations, which gave Elizabeth in particular cause for alarm. The only course open to her was an alliance with the Turk. She even asked during the negotiations that.the Ottoman armada should be sent out.

The final outcome was that England obtained in June, 1580, the thirty-five articles of her original capitulation, including unrestricted trading facilities for her subjects under her own flag, all of which was obtained in the teeth of the French (whose prestige and influence were diminishing in the Levant, according to the English), and by bribing 'the defunct Mehemet Pasha' according to the French, who were deceived by certain promises made by the Turk into thinking that the newcomers were to sail under the French flag. Once the English merchant had obtained his privileges he would not surrender them. In November 1580, a turkish ambassador, probably an Italian renegade, arrived in England. On 11th September, 1581, the Levant Company was set up by Elizabeth, to the greater gain of Sir Edward Osborne, Richard Staper, Thomas Smith, William Garret, and a few others. Its constitution caused some friction with the English merchants who had been trading more or less on their private account in the Levant, and with those who were informally associated in the Venice trade. But the advantages of the new trading facilities, with a large-scale organization, came at a timely moment, just as affairs in Moscow were becoming complicated and risky and the Danish ships in 1582 were beginning to use force to prevent ships trading with St Nicholas Bay. In November, 1582, the *Susan* of London sailed for Constantinople, with presents and a letter for the sultan from the queen. The letter was carried by the new ambassador appointed to Turkey by Elizabeth, William Hareborne, the 'Guillaume Harbron' who appears in French dispatches and who was to be a sturdy pioneer of the English cause. Sicily only learned of the passage of the ship on 15th March, 1583, by which time she had already reached the Aegean.

On 3rd May, William Hareborne was kissing the sultan's hands 'and he has been done as much honour', writes De Maisse, 'as any other king's ambassador

203. Seventeenth-century Moghul drawing of East India Company merchantmen and the port of Surat, India. The artist clearly understood the working of a sailing ship, whether European or Oriental. *Victoria and Albert Museum*

who has ever been there before'. Against him and the consuls he appointed in the East, both the French and the Venetians, those 'malicious and dissembling peoples' with whom, according to Hareborne, one had to 'walk warily', were finally powerless.

The success of English shipping. The Levant Company prospered from the start. In its original form, that of the charter granted on 11th September, 1581, it realized profits of up to 300 per cent. Its progress was even more dazzling after 1592 in its second incarnation after the merger in January with the so-called Venice Company founded in 1583. By 1595 the Levant Company had fifteen ships and 790 seamen at its disposal. It was trading with Alexandretta, Cyprus, Chios, Zante, and to a lesser extent with Venice and Algiers. In 1599 it had twenty ships in Italian waters alone. In 1600 it increased its fleet by sixteen extra ships. This success did not prevent the company from pleading great difficulty, as if by coincidence on the eve of the renewal of its charter on 31st December,

1600, that is in Elizabeth's lifetime, and again on 14th December, 1605, at the beginning of the reign of her successor James I. There were indeed problems: the length of the voyages; the hostility of Spain until 1604; the threat from the Barbary corsairs; the violent rearguard action fought by Marseilles and Venice, who did not yield their positions willingly, not to mention trouble with the Turks and the burden that the maintenance of an embassy at Constantinople and a series of consulates in Barbary and the Levant placed upon the Company. But the perseverance of the English merchants, the excellence of their ships, the low price of their cloth, and the quality of their organization were rewarded by success. A few dozen of their ships could accomplish more in the Levant and the Mediterranean than the hundreds of cockleshells sent out by Marseilles. Marseilles was still considered to have about a thousand ships working in 1610. Among the reasons for their success were the ingenious convoy system insisted upon by the English after 1591; the money they obtained through the favourable

204. The author in Turkish dress. From William Lithgow, *Rare Adventures*, 1632.

balance of trade in Constantinople; and the greater honesty of their merchants (compared to the Venetians and French who were always ready to cheat over the quantity or quality of fabrics).

All these arguments which were first advanced by Hakluyt and repeated by later historians have a certain force. But there was more to it than this. The English were helped on their way by the revival of trade with the Levant, mentioned earlier in connection with the spice trade. The old firm of the Mediterranean gained once more from the terrible battles of the Atlantic. Between 1583 and 1591 it was no coincidence that English agents should have made their way along the roads through Syria to the Indian Ocean, Persia, the Indies, and Sumatra. These wanderers have left us their fantastic travellers' tales of the routes in the Near and Far East. In Egypt, a hot country, the English whose stock-in-trade was thick cloth were obliged to pay cash for their purchases. So here they were outmanoeuvred by skilful and persistent competition from the French. The English therefore turned their attention to Syria and the roads through it; in this area they were able to organize the exchange of commodities for other commodities, a trade that the second circumnavigation of the Cape (by the Dutch) did not immediately disrupt. After all, the East India Company, founded in 1600, was an offshoot of the Levant Company.

In the central Mediterranean, at Leghorn, the figures testify to the increasing success of the northerners, for example the register of *portate* of ships from the 'western waters' (the text gives no further details and lumps Dutch and English ships together): for the period from October to December, 1598, there arrived 5000 casks of lead, 5613 casks of smoked herring, 268,645 *pesci merluzzi*, and 513 *fardi* of *pesci stockfiss*.

The situation at the end of the century. By the end of the century the English were everywhere in the Mediterranean, in Moslem or Christian countries, and travelling along all the overland routes that led to it or away from it to Europe or the Indian Ocean. In 1588 they were attracted to Moldavia and Wallachia. For several years London had been formulating grand designs. In 1583 there was a symbolic success when the *Hercules* (which had already made at least one previous voyage) brought back from Tripoli the richest cargo any English merchant had yet shipped to an English port. Spanish, Greek, and Marseilles pilots helped the newcomers to accomplish the conquest of the sea, port by port, but it is not always possible to date these successive victories, particularly since entry to a port for the first time was usually discreet and cautious. Marseilles, for instance, decided on 26th November, 1590 to allow two English vessels to enter the port. 'It has been . . . resolved and ordered that since the town has need of lead and tin, in the calamitous times in which we find ourselves, the merchandise carried aboard the two vessels will enter the city together with the masters and clerks, in order to sell them, trade and negotiate freely with the inhabitants of the said city and to buy other goods if they so desire, to be laden into the said vessels, except they be prohibited or forbidden goods.' This was certainly not the first time that English ships had put into Marseilles, for connections had existed since 1574, but now they were legally and officially granted entry.

They had come a long way in a few years. As early as 1589, a Genoese note refers to the key points in an English intelligence network covering every sector of the sea: via Constantinople, William Hareborne (who was in fact at this date in London); in Algiers, John Tipton; in Malta, John Lucas; and in Genoa, Richard Hunto. The last mentioned, whose surname has been Italianized, gives the Genoese the impression of being an enemy to all Catholics, 'a most malicious and perverse enemy', and is reputed to be a spy (*inteligencero* says the document, which is written in Spanish) in the pay of Horatio Pallavicino – whom we have already met. In January, 1590, the English were congratulating themselves on having prevented a new Spanish agent, Juan Estefano Ferrari, from concluding a deal. They were now sufficiently integrated into Mediterranean trade to have

205. The port of Danzig, showing the Customs House. Seventeenth-century German print.

Northern grain at Leghorn in 1593
Record of transport ships (from Mediceo 2079, f°s 150 v° to 169 v°)

	Amsterdam and Zeeland	England	Lübeck	Hanseatic Ports			Antwerp and Flanders	Norway	Riga	Unknown origin
				Emden	Hamburg	Danzig				
Ships whose port of origin was ...	12	7	4	5	16	9	4	2	1	13
				34						
Ships loaded at ...	28*	7	3	3	12	11	0	0	1	8
				29						

* Of which only one in Zeeland.

The seventy-three ships arrived at Leghorn as follows: 6th January (2), 9th January (1), 12th January (5), 13th January (37), 14th January (4), 16th January (1), 20th January (8), 26th January (3), 31st January (1), 11th March (1), 14th March (2), 1st April (1), 29th April (1), 3rd May (1), 5th May (1), 6th May (2), 12th May (1), 15th May (1). As for the length of voyage, there is no record for the year 1593, but in 1609–1611 (Mediceo 2097) real lengths of voyage in weeks are as follows: A. Amsterdam–Leghorn (12, 6, 5, 5, 8, 5, 32 days, 16) B. Danzig–Leghorn (14). C. London–Leghorn (4, 8). D. Bristol–Leghorn (12). E. Plymouth–Leghorn 28 days.

The conclusions to be drawn from this table are self-evident (variable length of voyage, predominance of winter voyages, clear indication that Amsterdam acted as a centre for the redistribution of grain), and the reader will be able to work them out for himself. It is however worth noting that 1. In this year 1593, six English ships brought their usual cargoes of lead, tin, and herring, but that there had slipped into their convoy one Dutch ship (loaded in England) and a ship from Emdem, the *Black Eagle*, loaded at Lisbon. 2. That in all, counting both wheat and rye, the northerners landed over 15,000 tons of grain at Leghorn that year, which gives an average tonnage per ship of about 200 tons. 3. That the list of names of ships shows the heavy predominance of non-religious names.

their own policy. It was certainly not based on power and force: the English approach was usually one of subtlety not to say guile (but they were by no means alone in this). They had two strings to their bow, Islam and Christendom, and sometimes fell back on a third – piracy.

The English had been pirates from the very beginning and of the worst kind. In 1581 one of their sailing ships was making raids upon Turkish vessels. Twenty years later, in 1601, a report from London mentions complaints by Genoa, Venice, and others that English ships had been robbing their merchantmen and disposing of their booty in the towns of Barbary. Leghorn became, after the Anglo-Spanish peace of 1604, the favourite haunt of retired English pirates. It is true that piracy can be a sign of weakness. English piracy, during these last years of the century, shows that their place was far from assured in this sea of rich cities and rich ships. It was not until later that that paradox, an English-dominated Mediterranean came to pass. It was not until 1620 that English warships first sailed into the Mediterranean and not until 1630 or 1640 that branches of English trading houses opened at Genoa.

The arrival of the Hansards and the Dutch. The return of the English was connected with the tin trade. The first massive entry of Hanseatic and Dutch shipping was the result of grain purchases by Mediterranean states – grain,

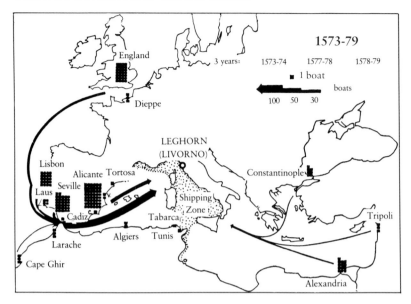

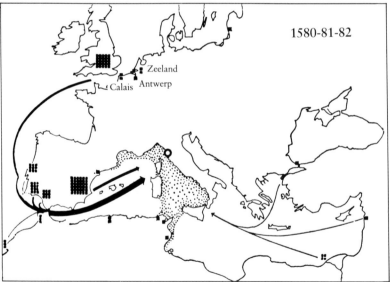

rather than the clumsy and ineffectual policies of the Spanish, who in theory controlled the gateway to the Mediterranean, although these too were partly responsible.

It was the bad Italian harvests of the years 1586 to 1590 that first alerted the Dutch and Hanseatic merchants, with possible assistance from Jewish wholesalers and middlemen. Nothing could be more natural than that these towns – Danzig, Lübeck and Hamburg – standing at the gateway to the great prairies

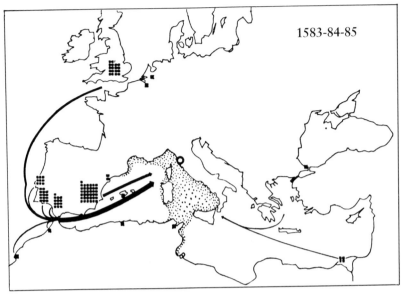

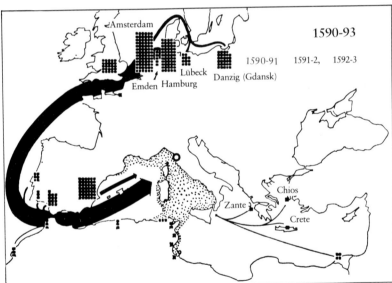

The increasing numbers of northern boats at Leghorn 1573—93

From F. Braudel and R. Romano, *Navires et marchandises à l'entrée du port de Livourne*. The four maps show the rapid increase of traffic entering Leghorn (each map shows the combined shipping of three years).

The importance of the Levant, which was never very great, was to decrease even further, despite the great value of some cargoes.

The numerically more important western shipping at first came mostly from Spain and Portugal, with a few boats arriving from the English Channel and the North Sea. This pattern was disrupted by the massive arrival of the northern grain ships in 1590–1593.

and experienced specialists in the bulk transport of grain, should have heard the appeal of the Mediterranean. It was to Danzig in fact that the Grand Duke of Tuscany sent his agent Ricardo in 1590, along with his aides, with instructions to send 'granajo della Polonia' to Lübeck and then on to Holland, France and England. There is no doubt that the enormous order placed with the North by the Grand Duke that year – worth a million ducats it was rumoured – was reason in itself for the original appearance of the northern fleets. Thereafter this traffic needed no external impetus. Some historians have claimed that in 1591 thirteen sailing ships were placed under embargo in Spain on their way through, in spite of the passports granted them by the Catholic King. Forty arrived at Leghorn. So many appeals were made that it is hardly surprising to find all the northern countries rallying to the call. Dutch, Hansard, and English ships combined to form the grain fleets, as can be seen from the list of *portate* at Leghorn in 1593.

From grain to spices: the Dutch conquer the Mediterranean. Although the Hansards and the Dutch arrived together in the Mediterranean, only the latter found themselves a permanent place. By the beginning of the seventeenth century, the Hansards had been eliminated and their ships hardly ever went any further than Málaga.

What were the causes of this defeat? Probably the Hansards, who had remained profitably neutral during the wars between Iberians and other northern nations, found that this advantage was automatically cancelled out after the peace treaties of 1604 and 1609. In the eighteenth century they were again, thanks to European wars, to extend their trade links with the Mediterranean. But at the end of the sixteenth century there could have been many other reasons. Was it because the Hansards had Spanish connections, therefore found employment in the Atlantic, and did not need the spices and pepper that might have drawn them to the Levant? Or was it because behind these maritime cities there was no thriving industry, if only because of the preferential links between southern Germany and Genoa and Venice? Or was it lack of money? By some paradox which must have an explanation, it was the Dutch who in 1615 and no doubt earlier, transported to Syria certain German commodities: amber, mercury, cinnabar, copper wire, and iron. I do not believe the blame can be laid on the outdated organization of the Hanse. The plethora of shipowners and insurers to be found there was paralleled throughout the Mediterranean. Was it a question of ships? But the Hansards had vessels of every tonnage.

For whatever reason, then, the Dutch were successful and in about 1597 reached the eastern end of the sea. In that year, Balthasar Moucheron, enemy of Spain, sent a ship to Tripoli in Syria under the French flag. In the following year all Dutch shipping obtained permission from Henry IV to trade under the French flag in the Turkish ports (they received their first capitulations only in 1612). In 1599 the Venetian consul reported that that year 'there had again come' a 'Flemish' ship, with over 100,000 crowns in ready money, which had done no little damage to Venetian trade. He was anxious to know whether the merchants of the Netherlands would remain in Syria, since the Dutch 'consul' had declared they would leave if their compatriots continued to make progress in the Indian Ocean. The Venetians would gladly have wished them godspeed. But the Dutch remained, in spite of Houtmann's circumnavigation of the Cape in 1595, the occupation of Java in 1597, the reconnaissance of the Comores, the capture of Mauritius in 1598 and the return of the second fleet in 1598. For it was to take years for the conquest of the Indian Ocean and the diversion of its currents of trade to become effective and for the Company of Distant Territories (*Van Verne*) to be converted into the triumphant Company of the East Indies in 1602. And besides, even if they had been able to intercept the precious drug trade, they would still have been attracted to the Levant by the silk trade (which they were soon, without immediate success to try to divert towards the Persian Gulf) and by spun cotton.

Dutch history on the small Mediterranean stage and elsewhere is far from entirely intelligible. Holland did not become a world power until the end of the century. So why was the victory of Elizabeth's ships over Philip II's clumsy armadas not followed by the English supremacy that would have seemed logical? England won the war and Holland immediately sent her citizens, trade, and ships to the far corners of the earth, to the East Indies and China and continued to do so until the middle of the seventeenth century. There is only one plausible explanation: Holland, by her proximity to the Catholic provinces of the Netherlands and by her persistence in forcing the coffers of Spain, had better access than England to the Peninsula and the American treasure upon which her commerce depended. For without the pieces of eight patiently extracted from Spain, Dutch shipping could not have sailed the seven seas. In England at the beginning of the seventeenth century, the affairs of the Levant Company were considered more advantageous since they were balanced by large exports of commodities to Turkey, than those of the East India Company which required the export of considerable sums of money. Between Spain and Holland there was the link of silver, reinforced by peace between 1609 and 1621, a link that was to be broken, along with Spain's entire fortunes in the middle of the seventeenth century just as – by coincidence? – the wheel of fate turned against Holland.

How the Dutch took Seville after 1570 without firing a shot. The brilliant victory in the seventeenth century of the English and Dutch can only adequately be explained on a world scale. In the first place it was the result of a series of technical improvements in the design and handling of ships, as we have already noted. The appearance of the northern sailing vessel of 100 to 200 tons, well armed and easily manoeuvred, marks a turning-point in maritime history. More progress was made in shipping in the northern seas between 1500 and 1600 than was achieved between the year of the Spanish Armada and Trafalgar. The northerners gave their ships stronger defences, increased the size of their crews and added to their artillery, clearing the upper decks for better manoeuvrability, as Ralph Davis has pointed out, to my mind quite conclusively. Wherever figures are available, the average size of the crew in relation to the ship's tonnage is superior in the north to that in the Mediterranean. The disadvantage of carrying smaller cargoes was balanced by greater security and therefore less expensive insurance rates. The costly Mediterranean galleys could sometimes of course, even in the seventeenth century, make startling comebacks: a sailing vessel was only the stronger when there was enough wind to fill her sails. In a dead calm the agile galley could move to the blind spots of the immobolized fortress and carry off the victory.

But such occasions were exceptional. The military and commercial superiority of the North cannot seriously be questioned. And the English and Dutch were well aware of this before 1588. It was in 1586 that the Spanish, who were now rulers of Lisbon as well as Seville, multiplied their embargoes and prohibitions of northern ships. But these measures did not prevent an active Iberian trade with the enemy: as a 'continental blockade' it was ineffective. Everything continued much the same as before. And then the chronology should make us suspicious. The English returned to the Mediterranean in 1572–1573, that is ten years before the Spanish embargoes, and the Dutch in 1590–1593, that is several years after them . . . Clearly, the major explanation for an economic reversal of this magnitude must lie in or be deduced from the general economic situation.

The north and south had been enemies well before the end of the century. The Netherlands rebelled in 1566, the English severed Spanish shipping routes after 1569. But these 'complementary enemies' could not live without each other. They fought, then made it up or compromised, depending on whether agreement was reached openly or unofficially. As a result the war in the Atlantic would flare up, die down, and break out again, and was for ever being tempered by informal solutions. Then, between 1566 and 1570 came an important turning-point. Until then Atlantic trade had been three-fold: the northerners (the Dutch in the front line, the Bretons soon in second position, the English, later the Hansards and Scandinavian fishing boats, all maintaining links between the north and the Peninsula, supplying grain, timber, dried or salted fish, lead, tin, copper, canvas, woollen cloth, ironware); the Iberians, with the *Carrera de Indias* based on Spain, and the ocean link with the East Indies based on Portugal; and lastly the Italians, chief among whom were the Genoese at Seville who financed this commodity trading, the gap in the trade balance being made good, though always with some delay, by American silver.

Then the system suffered two heavy blows: after 1566, the Genoese merchants, who were now obtaining *sacas de plata* from the king, lost interest in exporting the commodities which had until then been facilitating their payments to the North. And after 1569 the flow of silver from Laredo to Antwerp was interrupted. But the Atlantic trade did not suffer from these setbacks, indeed it prospered and this astonishing fact is a key explanation.

There can be no question of totally interrupting the Atlantic trade, said Spanish economic experts to the king's advisers; that would be the ruin of shipping and the Indies trade and would drain the resources of the treasury. Their arguments appear in a long report issued in 1575. Abandoned by Genoese capitalism, the export trade from Seville found other sponsors. Firms in the Netherlands, enriched by previous years, were to advance their own goods and to wait for payment until the Indies fleets returned with silver. In other words, the merchants of Seville now became merely commission agents: they saw goods pass through and took their percentage, but practically never risked their own property. From now on, their capital was to go into buying land and villages, *juros*, or settling entails. From this passive role, it was only a step to total inactivity, a prospect they viewed with equanimity. In this way Seville was conquered, eaten away from the inside by the obscure gnawing of termites, and all to the advantage of Holland. Antwerp, in the running war that began in 1572, remained the capital of political money: like Saigon before 1953 during the traffic in piastres. But Amsterdam attracted the merchants of Antwerp and, through Seville, drew the huge prize of Spanish America into her net. It was a victory that would never have been achieved without years of patient work, alliances, covered deals, the slow corruption of the Seville market, the cooperation for instance of the Duke of Medina Sidonia if only for the transmission of silver from San Lucar de Barrameda, of which he was the overlord.

Towards the end of the century this infiltration of the trade of Seville became known and during the summer of 1595 the king decided to strike a blow at such clandestine traffic which had by now gone too far to escape a full official enquiry. The orders were executed by the licenciate Diego de Armenteros, assisted by Luis Gaytan de Ayala. They visited sixty-three trading houses in Seville, owned by Castilians, Portuguese, Flemings, Frenchmen, Germans, all suspect because of their relations with Holland, Zeeland, and England. Needless to say not a single Englishman, Dutchman or Zeelander was found on the scene. 'It is well known,' wrote Armenteros, 'that they only trade in Spain through trusted intermediaries.'

The situation is made even clearer in a letter from the same Armenteros written a month later, probably to one of Philip II's secretaries, his friend or protector, at any rate an important political figure. In the confiscated papers, Armenteros had found any number of entries proving that the incriminated merchants were trading quite calmly with the rebels in the Netherlands or with the English, corresponding with them and sending them sums of money. Six ships had arrived at San Lucar carrying merchandise belonging to a Dutch firm

206. *Overleaf:* Capture of Spanish galleons by Dutch West India Company squadron. Seventeenth-century engraving. *National Maritime Museum, Greenwich*

Havana

P

and the Duke of Medina Sidonia had allowed them to land. It is true, added Armenteros, that this was worth 12,000 ducats to him ... 'There is not a foreigner entering San Lucar,' he says, 'who is not fêted and favoured, even helped to export silver.' When he had a reliable person at hand, he would send on the papers concerning the affair. Meanwhile he urged secrecy, 'that I may not add to the number of enemies I have already made by serving His Majesty' ...

There is evidence even more cruelly revealing. In the following year, 1596, sixty ships lying in Cadiz harbour laden for the 'Indies' were surprised by the English fleet which sacked the town. They contained a total of 11 million ducats' worth of merchandise. The English offered not to burn them for a payment of 2 million. The Duke of Medina Sidonia refused the deal and the ships went up in flames – but it was not the Spanish who suffered this enormous loss, for the merchandise did not belong to them. A whole book could be written on Seville, the city of corruption, of vicious denunciation, of prevaricating officials, a city in which silver had wrought havoc.

These harsh facts help us, if not to reach a conclusion, at least to glimpse something of the true explanations. The balance of world history was tipped not by the incompetence of Philip II's agents, nor by the obvious inadequacy of the guard on the Straits of Gibraltar, but quite clearly by the bankruptcy of the Spanish state, a self-evident fact by 1596 and which even before it was finally established had raised once more the problems of silver circulation and the division of world wealth. Holland, now in a period of sudden expansion, towards the Mediterranean on one hand with the grain and other trades, and towards the spice islands on the other, was looking for and finding compensation.

One curious detail: the advance of the Dutch, especially in the Mediterranean but towards the Indies and America too, was preceded by the arrival of Portuguese merchants, for the most part new Christians, coming either from Lisbon or from the cities of the North where they had taken refuge. Was there a 'Lisbon takeover' parallel to the 'Seville takeover'?

New Christians in the Mediterranean. This immense infiltration by northern, Atlantic, international capitalism, based on Amsterdam, could hardly ignore the rich Mediterranean. Like Spain, which was shamelessly looted, it was a tempting prize for a young, sharp-toothed capitalism that soon discovered how to find accomplices on the spot. Preparing and easing the way for the Dutch, sometimes involuntarily, the rich Portuguese *marranos* came on to the scene, the Ximenez of Lisbon and Antwerp, for example, and their associates the Andrade and the Veiga, who arranged deliveries of northern grain for the Grand Duke of Tuscany after the 1590s, making considerable profits for themselves out of it, and who also had a hand in the spice trade with Italy.

Other Portuguese merchants arrived in Italy close on their heels. In February, 1591 two of them, Fernández and Jorge Francisco are about to settle at Pisa. If

207. Detail from *The Dam in Amsterdam* by J. Lingelboch, showing Oriental merchants.
Historisches Museum, Amsterdam

they do 'there is no doubt that they will draw all the trade of Portugal towards them'. In August of the same year, 'if what I hear is true', writes Baltasar Suárez, 'the Ximenez are sending someone to open up a business in their name and are even sending to Pisa Sebastian Ximenez Penetiques, who is at present their agent in Cadiz. A son of Rui Nuñez is coming from Antwerp and, since these are all rich people, the Grand Duke wants to attract them and is preparing to grant them many privileges.'

These details betray a certain change in the economic configuration: since pepper had become difficult to sell by the Atlantic routes, it was naturally diffused towards Italy and from there to Germany, and it was therefore to Italy that for a while Portuguese emigrants flocked. In Venice Philip II's ambassador refers to these Portuguese Jews whom he has seen arriving dressed in the Christian fashion, then declaring themselves *por judios* and 'putting on the red hat which is the distinctive sign they wear in this state'. Venice became once more tolerant towards them, welcomed, supported, and protected them and benefited from their competition. There then seems to have been set up, whether discreetly or openly, effectively or apparently, a prosperous chain of Jewish, Levantine, and western merchants working together from Constantinople to Salonica, Valona, Venice, and west as far as Seville, Lisbon and Amsterdam. It was not for nothing that Spanish, Tuscan, or Maltese pirates were during these years so attentive to 'scouring' merchant vessels and seizing any merchandise belonging to Jews, the *ropa de judios* mentioned in Spanish texts. These cargoes were often worth having.

4

Empires

W E   M U S T   G O far back in time, to the beginning of a long process of evolution, before we can achieve a valid political perspective on the sixteenth century.

At the end of the fourteenth century, the Mediterranean belonged to its towns, to the city-states scattered around its shores. There were of course already, here and there, a few territorial states, fairly homogeneous in character and comparatively large, bordering the sea itself: the Kingdom of Naples – 'il Reame' – the outstanding example; the Byzantine Empire; or the possessions united under the Crown of Aragon. But in many cases, these states were merely the extensions of powerful cities: Aragon in the broad sense was a by-product of the dynamic rise of Barcelona; the Byzantine Empire consisted almost entirely of the extended suburbs of two cities, Constantinople and Salonica.

By the fifteenth century, the city-state was already failing to hold its own; first signs of the crisis could be detected in Italy during the early years of the century. In fifty years, the map of the Peninsula was entirely redrawn, to the advantage of some cities and the detriment of others. It was only a partial eclipse. The upheaval failed to achieve what may have been at issue – though I doubt it – the unification of the Italian Peninsula. Naples, Venice and Milan in turn proved unequal to the task. The attempt would in any case have been premature: too many particular interests were at stake, too many cities eager for an individual existence stood in the way of this difficult birth. So it is only partly true that there was a decline in the power of the city-state. The Peace of Lodi, in 1454, confirmed both a balance of power and a deadlock: the political map of Italy, although simplified, was still a patchwork.

Meanwhile, a similar crisis was becoming apparent throughout the rest of the Mediterranean. Everywhere the city-state, precarious and narrow-based, stood revealed inadequate to perform the political and financial tasks now facing it. It presented a fragile form of government, doomed to extinction, as was strikingly demonstrated by the capture of Constantinople in 1453, the fall of Barcelona in 1472 and the collapse of Granada in 1492.

It was becoming clear that only the rival of the city-state, the territorial state (I have deliberately avoided the term nation-state), rich in land and manpower, would in future be able to meet the huge expense of modern warfare; it could maintain paid armies and afford costly artillery; it was soon to indulge in the added extravagance of full-scale naval wars. And its advance was long to be irreversible. Examples of the new pattern emerging at the end of the fifteenth century are Aragon under John II; Louis XI's expansion beyond the Pyrenees; Turkey under Muhammad II, the conqueror of Constantinople; later France under Charles VIII with his Italian ambitions and Spain in the age of the Catholic Kings. Without exception, these states all had their beginnings far inland, many miles from the Mediterranean coast, usually in poor regions where there were fewer cities to pose obstacles. In Italy by contrast, the wealth and very density of the cities maintained weaknesses and divisions as modern structures emerged only with difficulty from the grip of the past, particularly when that past had been a glorious one and much of its brilliance remained. Past glory could mean present weakness, as was revealed by the first Turco-Venetian war, from 1463 to 1479, in the course of which the Signoria, inadequately protected by her small territory, was eventually obliged, despite her technical superiority, to abandon the struggle; it was demonstrated once more during the tragic occupation of Otranto by the Turks in 1480 and appeared even more strikingly in the beginnings of the storm unleashed by Charles VIII's invasion of Italy in 1494. Was there ever a more extraordinary military display than that swift march on Naples, when, according to Machiavelli, the invader had merely to send his billeting officers ahead to mark with chalk the houses selected for his troops' lodgings? Once the alarm was over, it was easy to make light of it, even to taunt the French ambassador Philippe de Commynes, as Filippo Tron, a Venetian patrician, did at the end of July, 1495. He added that he was not deceived by the intentions attributed to the king of France, 'desiring to go to the Holy Land when he really wanted to become no less than *signore di tutta l'Italia*'.

Such bravado was all very well, but the event marked the beginning of a train of disasters for the Peninsula, the logical penalty for its wealth, its position at the epicentre of European politics and, undoubtedly the key factor, the fragility of its sophisticated political structures, of the intricate mechanisms which went to make up the 'Italian equilibrium'. It was no accident if from now on Italian thinkers, schooled by disaster and the daily lesson of events, were to meditate above all upon politics and the destiny of the state, from Machiavelli and Guicciardini in the early part of the century to Paruta, Giovanni Botero or Ammirato at the end.

Italy: that extraordinary laboratory for statesmen. The entire nation was preoccupied with politics, every man to his own passion, from the porter in the market-place to the barber in his shop or the artisans in the taverns; for *raggione di stato, raison d'état*, an Italian rediscovery, was the result not of isolated reflection but of collective experience. Similarly, the frequent cruelty in political affairs, the betrayals and renewed flames of personal vendettas are so many symptoms of an age when the old governmental structures were breaking up

208. *Opposite:* Ferdinand and Isabella entering Granada. Bas relief from the retable in the Royal Chapel, Cathedral of Granada.

and a series of new ones appearing in rapid succession, according to circumstances beyond man's control. These were days when justice was frequently an absent figure and governments were too new and too insecure to dispense with force and emergency measures. Terror was a means of government. *The Prince* taught the art of day-to-day survival.

But even in the fifteenth century and certainly by the sixteenth, a formidable newcomer confronted the mere territorial or nation-state. Larger, monster states were now appearing, through accumulation, inheritance, federation or coalition of existing states: what by a convenient though anachronistic term one could call empires in the modern sense – for how else is one to describe these giants? In 1494, the threat to Italy from beyond the Alps came not merely from the kingdom of France but from a French empire, as yet hypothetical it is true. Its first objective was to capture Naples; then, without becoming immobilized at the centre of the Mediterranean, to speed to the East, there to defend the Christian cause in reply to the repeated appeals of the Knights of Rhodes, and to deliver the Holy Land. Such was the complex policy of Charles VIII, whatever Filippo Tron may have thought: it was a crusading policy, designed to span the Mediterranean in one grand sweep. For no empire could exist without some mystique and in western Europe, this mystique was provided by the crusade, part spiritual, part temporal, as the example of Charles V was soon to prove.

And indeed Spain under Ferdinand and Isabella was no 'mere nation-state': it was already an association of kingdoms, states and peoples united in the persons of the sovereigns. The sultans too ruled over a combination of conquered peoples and loyal subjects, populations which had either been subjugated or associated with their fortunes. Meanwhile, maritime exploration was creating, for the greater benefit of Portugal and Castile, the first modern colonial empires, the importance of which was not fully grasped at first by even the most perspicacious observers. Machiavelli himself stood too close to the troubled politics of Italy to see beyond them – a major weakness in a commentator otherwise so lucid.

The story of the Mediterranean in the sixteenth century is in the first place a story of dramatic political growth, with the leviathans taking up their positions. France's imperial career, as we know, misfired almost immediately, for several reasons: external circumstances in part, a still backward economy and perhaps also temperamental factors, prudence, a characteristic preference for safe investments and a distaste for the grandiose. What had failed to occur was by no means an impossibility. It is not entirely fanciful to imagine a French empire supported by Florence in the same way that the Spanish Empire (though not at first it is true) was supported by Genoa. And the imperial career of Portugal, a Mediterranean country only by courtesy in any case, developed (apart from a few Moroccan possessions) outside the Mediterranean region.

So the rise of empires in the Mediterranean means essentially that of the Ottoman Empire in the East and that of the Habsburg Empire in the West. As

209. Charles V as conqueror of Africa. The Emperor at the siege of Tunis. Brussels tapestry, mid-sixteenth century. *Musée de Besançon*

Leopold von Ranke long ago remarked, the emergence of these twin powers constitutes a single chapter in history and before going any further let us stress that accident and circumstance did not preside alone at the birth of these simultaneous additions to the great powers of history. I cannot accept that Sulaimān the Magnificent and Charles V were merely 'accidents' (as even Henri Pirenne has argued) – their persons, by all means, but not their empires. Nor do I believe in the preponderant influence of Wolsey, the inventor of the English policy of the Balance of Power who, by supporting Charles V in 1521 (against his own principles) when the latter was already ruler of the Netherlands and Germany, that is by supporting the stronger power instead of François I, the weaker, is said to have been responsible for Charles' rapid victory at Pavia and the subsequent surrender of Italy to Spanish domination for two hundred years.

For without wishing to belittle the role played by individuals and circumstances, I am convinced that the period of economic growth during the fifteenth and sixteenth centuries created a situation consistently favourable to the large and very large state, to the 'super-states' which today are once again seen as the pattern of the future they seemed to be briefly at the beginning of the eighteenth century, when Russia was expanding under Peter the Great and when a dynastic union at least was projected between Louis XIV's France and Spain under Philip V. *Mutatis mutandis*, the same pattern was repeated in the East. In 1516, the sultan of Egypt laid siege to the free city of Aden and captured it, in accordance with the laws of logical expansion. Whereupon in obedience to the very same laws, the Turkish sultan in 1517 seized the whole of Egypt. Small states could always expect to be snapped up by a larger predator.

The course of history is by turns favourable or unfavourable to vast political hegemonies. It prepares their birth and prosperity and ultimately their decline and fall. It is wrong to suppose that their political evolution is fixed once for all, that some states are irremediably doomed to extinction and others destined to achieve greatness come what may, as if marked by fate 'to devour territory and prey upon their neighbours'.

Two empires in the sixteenth century gave evidence of their formidable might. But between 1550 and 1600, advance signs can already be glimpsed of what was in the seventeenth century to be their equally inexorable decline.

1 The origin of empires

A word of warning: when discussing the rise and fall of empires, it is as well to mark closely their rate of growth, avoiding the temptation to telescope time and discover too early signs of greatness in a state which we know will one day be great, or to predict too early the collapse of an empire which we know will one day cease to be. The life-span of empires cannot be plotted by events, only by

careful diagnosis and auscultation – and as in medicine there is always room
for error.

Turkish ascendancy: from Asia Minor to the Balkans. Behind the rise of Turkey
to greatness lay three centuries of repeated effort, of prolonged conflict and of
miracles. It was on the 'miraculous' aspect of the Ottoman Empire that western
historians of the sixteenth, seventeenth and eighteenth centuries tended to dwell.
It is after all an extraordinary story, the emergence of the Ottoman dynasty
from the fortunes of war on the troubled frontiers of Asia Minor, a rendezvous
for adventurers and fanatics. For Asia Minor was a region of unparalleled
mystical enthusiasm: here war and religion marched hand in hand, militant
confraternities abounded and the janissaries were of course attached to such
powerful sects as the Ahīs and later the Bektāshīs. These beginnings gave the
Ottoman state its style, its foundations among the people and its original exal-
tation. The miracle is that such a tiny state should have survived the accidents
and disturbances inherent in its geographical position.

But survive it did, and put to advantage the slow transformation of the

210. Portrait of Sulaimān. Sixteenth-century miniature. *Topkapi Museum, Istanbul*

211. *Overleaf: Venetian Embassy at the Ottoman Court,* attributed to Giovanni Bellini.
Louvre, Paris

Anatolian countryside. The Ottoman success was intimately connected with the waves of invasion, often silent invasion, which drove the peoples of Turkestan westwards. It was brought about by the internal transformation of Asia Minor from Greek and Orthodox in the thirteenth century to Turkish and Moslem, following successive waves of infiltration and indeed of total social disruption; and also by the extraordinary propaganda of the Moslem orders, some of which were revolutionary, 'communist, like the Bābāīs, Ahīs and Abdālān; others more mystical and pacifist, for example the Mawlawīs of Konya'. Their poetry – their propaganda – marked the dawn of western Turkish literature.

Beyond the straits, the Turkish conquest was largely favoured by circumstances. The Balkan Peninsula was far from poor, indeed in the fourteenth and fifteenth centuries it was comparatively wealthy. But it was divided: Byzantines, Serbs, Bulgars, Albanians, Venetians, and Genoese fought amongst themselves. There was religious conflict between the Orthodox and the Roman Churches; and socially the Balkan world was extremely fragile – a mere house of cards. So it should not be forgotten that the Turkish conquest of the Balkans was assisted by an extraordinary social revolution. A seignorial society, exploiting the peasants, was surprised by the impact and collapsed of its own accord. The conquest, which meant the end of the great landowners, absolute rulers on their own estates, was in its way 'a liberation of the oppressed'. Asia Minor had been conquered patiently and slowly after centuries of effort; the Balkan Peninsula *seems* not to have offered any resistance to the invader. In Bulgaria, where the Turks made such rapid progress, the countryside had already been unsettled, well before their arrival, by violent rural disturbances. Even in Greece there had been a social revolution. In Serbia, the native aristocracy was wiped out and some of the Serbian villages were incorporated into the *wakf* (possessions of the mosques) or distributed to the *sipāhis*. And the *sipāhis*, soldiers whose titles were held only for life, at first asked for rents in money, not in kind. It was some time before the condition of the peasants once again became intolerable. And in Bosnia, around Sarajevo, there were mass conversions, due in part to the flourishing Bogomilian heresy. The situation was even more complicated in Albania. Here the landowners were able to take refuge in the Venetian *presidios*: Durazzo for example, which remained in Venetian possession until 1501. When these fortresses fell, the Albanian nobility fled to Italy, where some of their descendants remain to the present day. The Musachi family did not survive: its last member died in Naples in 1600. It left behind however the *Historia della Casa Musachi*, published in 1510 by Giovanni Musachi, a valuable record of the family fortunes which tells us much about the country and its ruling caste. The name of this ancient family is preserved in the Muzekie region of Albania where it once had immense holdings. The story of these exiles and their wanderings is an astonishing one. The same path was not trodden by all nobles and landowners in the Balkans. But whatever their fate, even when they succeeded in maintaining themselves for a while, by abjuring or otherwise, the general pattern was the same: before the Turkish advance an entire society fell into ruins, partly of its own accord, seeming to confirm yet again Albert Grenier's opinion that 'to be conquered, a people must have acquiesced in its own defeat.'

Social conditions in the Balkans help to explain the invader's success and the ravages it brought. The Turkish cavalry, ranging rapidly far and wide, blocking roads, ruining crops and disrupting economic life, went ahead of the main army and prepared the ground for an easy victory. Only the mountainous regions were for a while protected from the relentless invasion. Bowing to the geography of the Balkans, the Turks took control first of the principal highways, along the river valleys leading down to the Danube: the Maritsa, the Vardar, the Drin and the Morava. In 1371, they triumphed at Chernomen on the Maritsa; in 1389 they won the battle of Kossovo Polje, 'the Field of Blackbirds', from which flow the Vardar, Maritsa and Morava. In 1459, this time north of the Iron Gates, the Turk was victorious at Smederevo 'at the very point where the Morava meets the Danube and which as much as Belgrade commands the approaches to the Hungarian plains'.

Conquest was rapid too in the wide spaces of the eastern plains. In 1365, the Turk settled his capital at Adrianople; by 1386 all Bulgaria had been subdued, to be followed by Thessaly. Victory came more slowly in the mountainous west and was often more apparent than real. In Greece, Athens was occupied in 1456, the Morea in 1460, Bosnia in 1462–1466, Herzegovina in 1481, despite the resistance of some 'mountain kings'. Venice herself was unable for long to prevent the Turk from reaching the Adriatic: Scutari was captured in 1479 and Durazzo in 1501. Military victory was followed by another, more leisurely conquest: the construction of roads and fortified posts, the organization of camel trains, the setting in motion of all the supply and transport convoys (often handled by Bulgarian carriers) and finally, most important of all, that conquest which operated through those towns which the Turks had subdued, fortified or built. These now became major centres of diffusion of Turkish civilization: they calmed, domesticated and tamed at least the conquered regions, where it must not be imagined that an atmosphere of constant violence reigned.

In the early days, the Turkish conquest took a heavy toll of the subjugated peoples: after the battle of Kossovo, thousands upon thousands of Serbs were sold as slaves as far away as the markets of Christendom or recruited as mercenaries; but the conqueror was not deficient in political wisdom, as can be seen from Muhammad II's concessions to the Greeks summoned to Constantinople after 1453. Eventually Turkey created, throughout the Balkans, structures within which the peoples of the Peninsula gradually found a place, collaborating with the conqueror and here and there curiously re-creating the patterns of the Byzantine Empire. This conquest brought a new order, a *pax turcica*. Let us take the word of the anonymous Frenchman who wrote in 1528: 'the country is safe and there are no reports of brigands or highwaymen ... The Emperor does not tolerate highwaymen or robbers.' Could as much have been said of Catalonia or

Calabria at the same period? There must have been some truth in this optimistic picture, since for many years the Turkish Empire remained to Christian eyes an extraordinary, incomprehensible and disconcerting example of orderliness; its army astonished westerners by its discipline and silence as much as by its courage, abundant munitions and the high quality and sobriety of its soldiers. Not that their astonishment prevented the Christians from hating these Infidels, 'far worse than dogs in all their works' as one writer put it in 1526.

Gradually however, westerners came to take a more balanced view of the Turks. They were of course a scourge sent by the Lord: Pierre Viret, the Protestant reformer of French Switzerland, wrote of them in 1560: 'we must not be amazed if God is now punishing the Christians through the Turks as he once punished the Jews when they forsook their faith . . . for the Turks are today the Assyrians and Babylonians of the Christians and the rod and scourge and fury of God'. But from mid-century on, others like Pierre Belon were to recognize the virtues of the Turks; and in later years this strange and contrary land was to exercise great fascination over Europeans, for whom it was a convenient place to escape to in imagination from the restrictions of western society.

It was at least an advance to recognize that Turkish actions could be explained by the faults and weaknesses of Europe. A Ragusan citizen said as much to Maximilian I: while the western nations are divided, 'all supreme authority in the Turkish Empire rests in a single man, all obey the sultan, he alone rules; he receives all revenues, in a word he is master and all other men are his slaves'. In substance, this was what was explained to Ferdinand's ambassadors in 1533 by Aloysius Gritti, a singular character, the son of a Venetian and a slave-girl, and for many years the favourite of the Grand Vizier, Ibrāhīm Pasha. Charles V should not risk his strength against that of Sulaimān.

It is certainly true that Turkish strength was drawn, as if by a mechanical process, into the complex of European weaknesses. The bitter internal dissensions of Europe permitted and even encouraged the Turkish invasion of Hungary. 'It was the capture of Belgrade [29th August, 1521],' Busbecq quite rightly says, 'which loosed that multitude of evils under whose weight we continue to groan. This threw open the flood-gates through which the barbarians entered to devastate Hungary, it brought about the death of King Louis, the loss of Buda and the enslavement of Transylvania. If the Turks had not captured Belgrade, they would never have entered Hungary, once one of the most flourishing kingdoms of Europe and now a desolate and ravaged land.'

In fact 1521, the year of Belgrade, also saw the beginning of the long struggle between François I and Charles V. One consequence was the battle of Mohács in 1526; another the siege of Vienna in 1529. Bandello, who wrote his *Novelle* not long after this event, paints a picture of Christendom preparing for the worst, 'reduced to a canton of Europe, as a result of the discords which appear every day more profound between the Christian Princes'. Unless, that is, Europe was less concerned with barring the way to the Turk than with other, brighter prospects in the Atlantic and elsewhere in the world, as some historians have suggested. The time has surely come to turn on its head that hoary and misleading explanation, still sometimes encountered, that it was the Turkish conquest which stimulated the great discoveries, whereas the reverse in fact occurred, for the great discoveries robbed the Levant of much of its appeal, enabling the Turks to extend their influence and settle there without too much difficulty. After all, the Turkish occupation of Egypt in January, 1517 did not occur until twenty years after Vasco da Gama had sailed round the Cape of Good Hope.

The Turks in Syria and Egypt. And surely the major event in the rise of the Ottoman Empire, more significant even than the capture of Constantinople (a mere 'episode' as Richard Busch-Zanter rather deflatingly calls it) was indeed the conquest first of Syria in 1516, then of Egypt in 1517, both achieved in a single thrust. This was the first glimpse of the future greatness of the Ottoman state. In itself, the conquest was not particularly remarkable and posed few difficulties. The disputed frontiers of northern Syria and in particular an attempt by the Mamlūk sultan to act as mediator between Turks and Persians served as a pretext when the right moment came. The Mamlūks, who considered artillery a dishonourable weapon, could not withstand the fire of Selīm's cannon on 24th August, 1516, outside Aleppo. Syria fell overnight into the hands of the conqueror who entered Damascus on 26th September. When the new Mamlūk ruler refused to recognize Turkish sovereignty, Selīm's army advanced into Egypt. The Mamlūk forces were again shattered by Turkish cannon in January, 1517 outside Cairo. Artillery had once more created a major political power, as it had already done in France, in Muscovy and at Granada in 1492.

Egypt succumbed with hardly a struggle, and with a minimal disturbance of the established order. The Mamlūks, who retained their vast estates, very quickly regained effective power: Bonaparte, arriving in Egypt three centuries later, found them there still.

All the same, it was a landmark in Ottoman history. From the Egyptians, Selīm gained much of value. In the first place, the annual tribute, originally modest, grew steadily. Through Egypt, the Ottoman Empire was able to participate in the traffic in African gold which passed through Ethiopia and the Sudan and in the spice trade with Christian countries. Mention has already been made of the gold traffic and of the revived importance of the Red Sea route in Levantine trade while at the same time a link was established between the hungry metropolis of Constantinople and an extensive wheat, bean and rice-producing region. On many subsequent occasions, Egypt was to be a crucial factor in the fortunes of the Turkish Empire and one might even say a source of corruption. It has been claimed with some plausibility that it was from Egypt that there spread to the far corners of the Ottoman Empire that venality of office which has so frequently undermined a political order.

But Selīm derived from his victory something else quite as precious as gold.

Even before becoming ruler of the Nile, he had had prayers said in his name and fulfilled the role of Caliph, Commander of the Faithful. Now Egypt provided consecration for this role. Legend had it – that it was no more than a legend seemed not to matter – that the last of the Abbāsids, having taken refuge in Egypt with the Mamlūks, ceded to Selīm the caliphate over all true Moslem believers. Legend or not, the sultan returned from Egypt radiating an aura of immense prestige. In August, 1517, he received from the son of the Shaikh of Mecca the key to the Ka'ab itself. It was from this date that the élite corps of horseguards was granted the privilege of carrying the green banner of the Prophet. There can be no doubt that throughout Islam, the elevation of Selīm to the dignity of Commander of the Faithful in 1517 was as resounding an event as the famous election, two years later, of Charles of Spain as Emperor was in Christendom. This date at the dawn of the sixteenth century marked the arrival of the Ottomans as a world power and, perhaps inevitably, of a wave of religious intolerance.

Selīm died shortly after his victories, in 1520, on the road to Adrianople. His son Sulaimān succeeded him unchallenged. To Sulaimān was to fall the honour of consolidating the might of the Ottoman Empire, despite the pessimistic forecasts voiced concerning his person. In the event the man proved equal to the task. He arrived at an opportune moment, it is true. In 1521, he seized Belgrade, the gateway to Hungary; in July, 1522, he laid siege to Rhodes, which fell in December of the same year: once the formidable and influential fortress of the Knights of St John had fallen, the entire eastern Mediterranean lay open to his youthful ambition. There was now no reason why the master of so many Mediterranean shores should not build a fleet. His subjects and the Greeks, including those who inhabited Venetian islands, were to provide him with the indispensable manpower. Would the reign of Sulaimān, ushered in by these brilliant victories, have been so illustrious had it not been for his father's conquest of Egypt and Syria?

Spanish unity: the Catholic Kings. In the East the Ottomans; in the West the Habsburgs. Before the rise of the latter, the Catholic Kings, the original authors of Spanish unity, played as vital a part in imperial history as the sultans of Bursa and Adrianople had in the genesis of the Ottoman Empire – if not more. Their achievement was furthered and assisted by the general temper of the fifteenth century after the Hundred Years' War.

Some historians have even suggested that the union between Castile and Aragon, which became a powerful reality through the marriage of 1469, could well have been replaced by a union between Castile and Portugal. Isabella had the choice between a Portuguese husband and an Aragonese, between the

212. *Opposite:* The Ka'ab in the centre of Mecca. Seventeenth-century Ottoman tiled panel. *Topkapi Palace, Istanbul*

213, 214. Polychrome statues of Ferdinand and Isabella from the main altar, Cathedral of Granada.

Atlantic and the Mediterranean. In fact the unification of the Iberian Peninsula was already in the air, a logical development of the times. It was a question of choosing a Portuguese or an Aragonese formula, neither being necessarily superior to the other and both within easy reach. The decision finally reached in 1469 signalled the re-orientation of Castile towards the Mediterranean, an undertaking full of challenge and not without risk, in view of the traditional policies and interests of the kingdom, but which was nevertheless accomplished in the space of a generation. Ferdinand and Isabella were married in 1469; Isabella succeeded to the Crown of Castile in 1474 and Ferdinand to that of Aragon in 1479; the Portuguese threat was finally eliminated in 1483; the conquest of Granada was accomplished in 1492; the acquisition of Spanish Navarre in 1512. It is not possible even for a moment to compare this rapid unification with the slow and painful creation of France from its cradle in the region between the Loire and the Seine. The difference was not one of country but of century.

It would be surprising if this rapid unification of Spain had *not* created the necessity for a mystique of empire. Ximénez' Spain, at the height of the religious revival at the end of the fifteenth century, was still living in the age of crusades; hence the unquestionable importance of the conquest of Granada and the first steps, taken a few years later, towards expansion in North Africa. Not only did the occupation of southern Spain complete the reconquest of Iberian soil; not only did it present the Catholic Kings with a rich agricultural region, a region of rich farming land and industrious and populous towns: it also liberated for foreign adventures the energies of Castile, so long engaged in an endless combat with the remnants of Spanish Islam which refused to die – and these were youthful energies.

Almost immediately however, Spain was distracted from African conquest. In 1492, Christopher Columbus discovered America. Three years later, Ferdinand was engrossed in the complicated affairs of Italy. In the circumstances, nothing could have been more natural than Aragonese policy, with the weight of tradition behind it. Aragon was drawn towards the Mediterranean by her past and by her experience, intimately acquainted with its waters through her seaboard, her shipping and her possessions (the Balearics, Sardinia and Sicily)

215. Conversion of the Moors in Granada. Bas relief from the retable in the Royal Chapel, Granada.

and not unnaturally attracted, like the rest of Europe and the Mediterranean, by the rich lands of Italy. When his commander Gonzalvo de Córdoba captured Naples in 1503, Ferdinand the Catholic became master of a vital position and a wealthy kingdom, his victory marking a triumph for the Aragonese fleet and, under the Great Captain, the creation, no less, of the Spanish *tercio*, an event which can rank in world history on a level with the creation of the Macedonian phalanx or the Roman legion. To understand the attraction of the Mediterranean for Spain we must not let our image of Naples at the beginning of the sixteenth century be coloured by what it had become by the end – a country struggling to survive, hopelessly in debt. By then the possession of Naples had become a burden. But in 1503, in 1530 even, the *Reame* of Naples afforded both a valuable strategic position and a substantial source of revenue.

The final point to note about the Aragonese policy to which Spain became committed is its opposition to the advance of Islam: the Spaniards preceded the Turks in North Africa; in Sicily and Naples, Spain stood on one of the foremost ramparts of Christendom. Louis XII might boast: 'I am the Moor against whom the Catholic King is taking up arms', but that did not prevent the Catholic King, by the mere location of the territories he possessed, from coming more and more to fulfil the role of Crusader and defender of the faith with all the duties as well as the privileges that implied. Under Ferdinand, the crusading ardour of Spain moved out of the Peninsula, not to plunge into the barren continent of Africa on the opposite shore, nor to lose itself in the New World, but to take up a position in the sight of the whole world, at the very heart of what was then Christendom, the threatened citadel of Italy: a traditional policy, but a glorious one.

Charles V. Charles V succeeded Ferdinand in Spain. As Charles of Ghent, he became Charles I in 1516. With his coming, western politics took on new and more complicated dimensions, a development comparable to what was happening at the other end of the sea under Sulaimān the Magnificent. Spain now found herself little more than a background for the spectacular reign of the Emperor. Charles of Ghent became Charles V in 1519; he hardly had time to be Charles of Spain. Or, rather curiously, not until much later, at the end of his life, for reasons of sentiment and health. Spain was not prominent in the career of Charles V, though she contributed handsomely to his greatness.

Nor was it possible in the nature of things for Charles to make Spain his headquarters. Too far from the centre of Europe, Spain did not yet offer the compensating advantage of riches from the New World: not until 1535 was this to be a major consideration. In his struggle against France, the chief occupation of his life after 1521, Charles V was obliged to rely upon Italy and the Nether-lands. Along this central axis of Europe, the Emperor concentrated his effort. After his election in 1519, his policy took flight and was carried away in dreams of Universal Monarchy. 'Sire', wrote Gattinara to the Emperor shortly after his election, 'now that God in His prodigious grace has elevated Your Majesty above all Kings and Princes of Christendom, to a pinnacle of power occupied before by none except your mighty predecessor Charlemagne, you are on the road towards Universal Monarchy and on the point of uniting Christendom under a single shepherd.' This notion of Universal Monarchy was the continuous inspiration of Charles' policy, which also had affinities with the great humanist movement of the age. A German writer, Georg Sauermann, who happened to be in Spain in 1520, dedicated to the Emperor's secretary, Pedro Ruiz de la Mota, his *Hispaniae Consolatio*, in which he tried to convert Spain herself to the idea of a pacific Universal Monarchy, uniting all Christendom against the Turk. Marcel Bataillon has shown how dear this notion of Christian unity was to Erasmus and his friends and disciples. In 1527, after the sack of Rome, Vives wrote to Erasmus in extremely revealing terms: 'Christ has granted an extraordinary opportunity to the men of our age to realize this ideal, thanks to the great victory of the Emperor and the captivity of the Pope,' – a sentence which illuminates the true colours of the ideological mist, the vision in which the policy of the emperor was surrounded and the frequent source of motives for his actions. This is by no means the least fascinating aspect of what was the major political drama of the century.

Philip II's Empire. Emerging from the heritage of the great emperor during the crucial years 1558–1559, this later empire was even more vast, coherent and solid than that of Charles V, less committed to Europe, more exclusively concentrated on Spain and thus drawn towards the Atlantic. It had the substance, the extent, the disparate resources and the wealth of an empire, but its sovereign ruler lacked the coveted title of Emperor which would have united and, as it were, crowned the other countless titles he held. Charles V's son had been excluded, after much hesitation, from the imperial succession which had in theory, but in theory only, been reserved for him at Augsburg in 1551. And he sorely missed the prestige this title would have conferred on him, if only in the minor but irritating war of precedence with the French ambassadors at Rome. So in 1562, the Prudent King thought of seeking an Imperial crown. In January, 1563 it was rumoured that he would be declared Emperor of the Indies. About twenty years later, in 1583, it was whispered at Venice that Philip II once more aspired to the highest title. 'Sire', wrote the French ambassador to Henri III, 'I have learnt from these Lords that Cardinal Granvelle is coming to Rome in September this year to have the title of emperor conferred upon his master.'

Perhaps this was no more than Venetian gossip. Even so it is interesting. The same causes were to produce the same effects when Philip III in his turn was a candidate for the empire. It was not merely a question of vanity. In a century preoccupied with prestige, governed by appearances, a merciless war of precedence was waged between the ambassadors of the Most Christian King of France and His Catholic Majesty of Spain.

216. *Left:* Portrait of Philip II by
Titian. *Gallerie Nazionali di
Capodimonte, Naples*
217. *Right:* The Escorial.

The fundamental characteristic of Philip II's empire was its Spanishness – or rather Castilianism – a fact which did not escape the contemporaries of the Prudent King, whether friend or foe: they saw him as a spider sitting motionless at the centre of his web. But if Philip, after returning from Flanders in September, 1559, never again left the Peninsula, was it simply from inclination, from a pronounced personal preference for things Spanish? Or might it not also have been largely dictated by necessity? We have seen how the states of Charles V, one after another, silently refused to support the expense of his campaigns. Their deficits made Sicily, Naples, Milan and later the Netherlands, burdens on the empire, dependent places where it was no longer possible for the emperor to reside. Philip II had had personal experience of this in the Netherlands where, during his stay between 1555 and 1559, he had relied exclusively on money

imported from Spain or on the hope of its arrival. And it was now becoming difficult for the ruler to obtain such assistance without being in person close to its original source. Philip II's withdrawal to Spain was a tactical withdrawal towards American silver. His mistake, if anything, was not to go as far as possible to meet the flow of silver, to the Atlantic coast, to Seville or even later to Lisbon. Was it the attraction of Europe, the need to be better and more

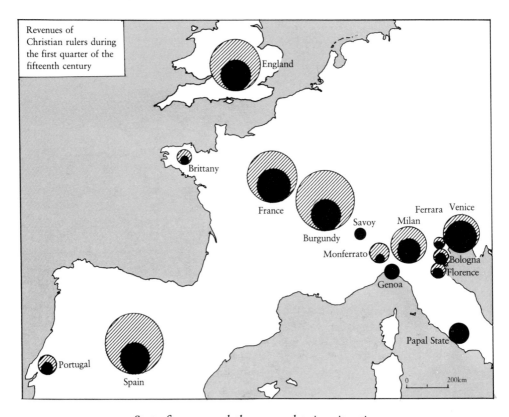

Revenues of Christian rulers during the first quarter of the fifteenth century

State finance and the general price situation

These rather curious Venetian estimates (*Bilanci generali*, Vol. 1, Bk. 1, Venice, 1912, pp. 98–99) are certainly not strictly accurate, but they give an idea of the universal decrease in the financial resources of the European states between 1410 and 1423 (1410 level represented by shaded circle, 1423 level by black circle). English revenues fell from 2 million ducats to 700,000; French from 2 million to 1 million; Spanish from 3 million to 800,000; Venetian from 1,100,000 to 800,000, etc. Even if these figures were accurate one would still have to calculate real income as one does real wages. In general, the state seems always to have lagged a little behind changes in the economic situation, both during upward and downward trends, that is to say its resources declined less quickly than others during a depression – and this was an advantage – and rose less quickly during periods of growth. Unfortunately such a theory cannot be verified either from the document in question here, or from others cited below. One thing is certain: the resources of the state fluctuated according to the prevailing economic conditions.

quickly informed of what was happening in that buzzing hive, which kept the king at the geometrical centre of the Peninsula, in his Castilian retreat, to which personal inclination in any case drew him?

That the centre of the web lay in Spain bred many consequences; in the first place the growing, blind affection of the mass of Spanish people for the king who had chosen to live among them. A further consequence was the logical predominance of Peninsular appointments, interests and prejudices during Philip's reign; of those harsh haughty men, the intransigent nobles of Castile whom Philip employed on foreign missions, while for the conduct of everyday affairs and bureaucratic routine he showed a marked preference for commoners. Charles V was forced to be a homeless traveller in his scattered empire. Philip II's refusal to move encouraged the growth of a sedentary administration whose bags need no longer be kept light for travelling. The weight of paper became greater than ever. The other parts of the empire slipped imperceptibly into the role of satellites and Castile into that of the metropolitan power: a process clear to see in the Italian provinces. Hatred of the Spaniard began to smoulder everywhere, a sign of the times and a warning of storms ahead.

That Philip II was not fully aware of these changes, that he considered himself to be continuing the policy initiated by Charles V, his father's disciple as well as successor, is certainly true. But circumstances were to dictate radical changes. Only the trappings of empire survived. The grandiose ambitions of Charles V were doomed by the beginning of Philip's reign, even before the treaty of 1559, and brutally liquidated by the financial disaster of 1557. The machinery of empire had to be overhauled and repaired before it could be started again. Charles V had never in his headlong career been forced to brake so sharply: the drastic return to peace in the early years of Philip's reign was the sign of latter-day weakness. Grand designs were not revived until later and then less as the result of the personal desires of the sovereign than through force of circumstance. Little by little, the powerful movement towards Catholic reform, misleadingly known as the Counter-Reformation, was gathering strength and becoming established. Born of a lengthy series of efforts and preparations, already by 1560 a force strong enough to sway the policy of the Prudent King, it exploded violently in opposition to the Protestant North in the 1580s. It was this movement which pushed Spain into the great struggles of the end of Philip's reign and turned the Spanish king into the champion of Catholicism, the defender of the faith. Religious passions ran higher in this struggle than in the crusade against the Turks, a war entered upon almost unwillingly and in which Lepanto seems to have been an episode without sequel.

And there was another compelling factor: after the 1580s, shipments of bullion from the New World reached an unprecedented volume. The great war which began in the 1580s was fundamentally a struggle for control of the Atlantic Ocean, the new centre of gravity of the world. Its outcome would decide whether the Atlantic was in future to be ruled by Catholics or Protestants,

218. The siege of Tunis. Tapestry after Vermeyen. In the distance, La Goletta and its channel, the lagoon of Tunis and the town. In the foreground, the galleys.
Kunsthistorisches Museum, Vienna

northerners or Iberians, for the Atlantic was now the prize coveted by all. The mighty Spanish Empire with its silver, its armaments, ships, cargoes and political conceptions, now turned towards that immense battlefield. At the same moment in time, the Ottomans turned their backs firmly on the Mediterranean to plunge into conflict on the Asian border.

2 The state: resources and weaknesses

Of that rise of state and 'empire' witnessed by the sixteenth century, the effects are a great deal more visible than the causes. The modern state had a difficult birth. One of the more obvious of the new phenomena which accompanied it was the multiplication of the instruments and agents of state power: one problem among many.

The 'civil servant'. The corridors of political history are suddenly thronged with the long procession of those men whom we may conveniently, if anachronistically, call 'civil servants'. Their arrival marks a political revolution coupled with a social revolution.

Once summoned to power, the government official quickly appropriated for himself a share in public authority. In the sixteenth century at least, he was invariably of humble origin. In Turkey he often had the additional handicap of being born a Christian, a member of a conquered race, or no less often a Jew. According to H. Gelzer, of the forty-eight grand viziers between 1453 and 1623, five were of 'Turkish' birth, including one Circassian; ten were of unknown origin; and thirty-three were renegades, including six Greeks, eleven Albanians or Yugoslavs, one Italian, one Armenian and one Georgian. The number of Christians who thus succeeded in reaching the peak of the Turkish hierarchy indicates the scale on which they had penetrated the ranks of the servants of the Ottoman Empire. And if ultimately the latter was to resemble the Byzantine Empire, rather than say a Mongol empire, it was because of this large-scale recruiting of civil servants.

In Spain, where we are better acquainted with the government employee, he would typically come from the urban lower classes, or even of peasant stock, which did not prevent him (far from it) from claiming descent from a *hidalgo* family (as who did not in Spain?). At any rate the social advancement of such men escaped no one's attention, least of all that of one of their declared enemies, the diplomat and soldier Diego Hurtado de Mendoza, representative of the high military aristocracy, who notes in his history of the War of Granada: 'The Catholic Kings put the management of justice and public affairs in the hands of the *letrados*, men of middling condition, neither high nor very low born, offending neither the one nor the other and whose profession was the study of the law.'

The *letrados* were brothers beneath the skin of the *dottori in legge* mentioned in Italian documents and the sixteenth century French lawyers, graduates of the University of Toulouse or elsewhere, whose notions of Roman law contributed so much to the absolutism of the Valois. With clear-sighted hatred, Hurtado de Mendoza enumerates the entire tribe. According to these men their competence extends to all matters. Jealous of other men's offices, they are always ready to encroach on the competence of the military authorities (in other words the great aristocratic families). And this scourge is not confined to Spain: 'this manner of governing has spread throughout Christendom and stands today at the pinnacle of its power and authority'. In this respect, Hurtado de Mendoza was not mistaken. As well as those *letrados* who had already reached positions of authority, we must also imagine the army of those preparing to embark upon a government career who flocked in ever-growing numbers to the universities of Spain (and before long to those of the New World): 70,000 students at least, as is calculated at the beginning of the next century by an irritated Rodrigo Vivero, Marquis del Valle, another nobleman and a Creole from New Spain; among these men are the sons of shoemakers and ploughmen! And who is responsible for this state of affairs if not the Church and state, which by offering offices and livings draws more students to the universities than ever did the thirst for knowledge. For the most part these *letrados* had graduated from Alcalà de Henares or Salamanca. Be that as it may and even if one remembers that the figure of 70,000, which seemed so enormous to Rodrigo Vivero, was modest in relation to the total population of Spain, there can be no doubt of the immense political significance of the rise of a new social category beginning in the age of construction under Ferdinand and Isabella. Even then there were appearing those 'royal clerks' of extremely modest origin, such as Palacios Rubios, the lawyer who drafted the *Leyes de Indias* and was not even the son of a *hidalgo*! Or later, under Charles V, the secretary Gonzalo Pérez, a commoner whispered to have been of Jewish origin. Or again, in the reign of Philip II, there was Cardinal Espinosa, who when he died of apoplexy in 1572, combined in his person a wealth of titles, honours and functions, and left his house piled high with dossiers and papers which he had never had time to examine and which had lain there sometimes for years. Gonzalo Pérez was a cleric, like Espinosa and like Don Diego de Covarrubias de Leyva, details of whose career we know from the fairly long memoir written by a relative, Sebastián de Covarrubias de Leyva, in 1594: we are told that Don Diego was born at Toledo of noble parents, originally from Viscaya, that he studied first at Salamanca, went on to become a professor at the College of Oviedo, was later magistrate at the *Audiencia* of Granada, next bishop of Ciudad Rodrigo, then archbishop of Santo Domingo 'en las Indias' and finally President of the Court of Castile and presented with the bishopric of Cuenca (in fact he died at Madrid on 27th September, 1577, at the age of sixty-seven, before he could take possession of it). If proof were needed, his story proves that it was possible to combine a career in the Church

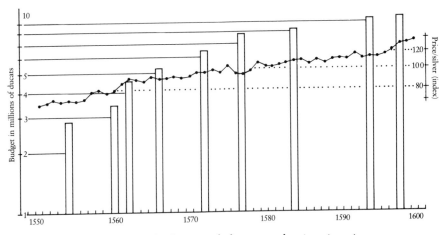

Spanish state budgets and the general price situation

The index of prices in silver is taken from Earl J. Hamilton. The budgets are expressed in millions of Castilian *ducados*, the money of account which did not alter during the period in question. Budget estimates from unpublished research by Alvaro Castillo Pintado. Despite the imperfect calculation of receipts, the coincidence between the price situation and the trend in fiscal revenues is clear. It will be noted that I use the term 'budget' although it is not strictly speaking applicable. Our knowledge of expenditure is always inadequate. To my knowledge, only the archives of Simancas and possibly archives in England contain sufficient material to construct a true budget. Tentative graphs similar to that given here could be calculated for Venice, France, Sicily and the Kingdom of Naples and even for the Ottoman Empire, a project already begun by Ömer Lutfi Barkan and his research group.

with a career in state service. And the Church, particularly in Spain, offered many openings to the sons of poor men.

The more one thinks about it, the more convinced one becomes of the striking similarities, transcending words, terminology and political appearances, between East and West, worlds very different it is true, but not always divergent. Even in America, where civil servants from Spain or Portugal often abused their office, the services rendered by these humble men devoted to the prince cannot be gainsaid. Turkey, now becoming partly against her own will a modern state, appointed to the conquered eastern provinces of Asia increasing numbers of half-pay tax-farmers, who lived off the revenues they collected but transmitted the bulk of it to Istanbul; she also appointed increasing numbers of paid civil servants who, in exchange for specific service, preferably in the towns easiest to administer, would receive a salary from the imperial treasury. More and more of these officials tended to be renegade Christians, who thus gradually infiltrated the ruling class of the Ottoman Empire. They were recruited through the *dew-shirme*, a sort of 'tribute which consisted of taking away from their homes in the Balkans a certain number of Christian children, usually under the age of five'. And the word *dewshirme* designated both a political and a social category. These new agents of the Ottoman state were to reduce almost to ruin the *timarli*

CORE GI MIENTO
COREG.º DEPROVIN
cias deste reyno y sues cunano primer historiadellas

438

219. A royal Spanish official with his scribe in
Peru. Peruvian *mestizo* manuscript, c.1600.
Royal Library, Copenhagen

of the Balkans (the holders of *tīmārs* or fiefs) and for many years to sustain the renewed might of the empire.

Without always explicitly seeking to do so, sixteenth century states moved their 'civil servants' about, uprooting them to suit their convenience. The greater the state, the more likely was this to be the case. One rootless wanderer was Cardinal Granvelle, a son of the Franche-Comté who claimed to have no homeland. And there were others. From Nantes where, at the end of the century, he was an efficient servant of the Crown, the Spanish envoy Don Diego Mendo de Ledesma sent to Philip II, in support of his request for 'assistance' in his financial difficulties, a long record of his loyal service to the king. Of undoubtedly noble birth, he was admitted as a child, along with his brother, to the ranks of pages to Queen Elizabeth, the 'Queen of Peace' (Catherine de Medici's daughter and Philip II's third wife). When still a boy he had served during the War of Granada, then had followed Don John of Austria to Italy. With his two brothers, on the conquest of Portugal in 1580, he had persuaded the town of Zamora to rally to His Catholic Majesty, adding his own vassals to the militia. Later when the same town was reluctant to accept the increase in its fixed payment for the *alcabala*, thus setting a bad example to other cities, the government dispatched Don Diego to bring the citizens to see reason. 'As soon as I entered the *Ayuntamiento*,' he writes, 'I smoothed the way and released all minds from perplexity . . .' There could hardly be a better way to gain favour. Soon afterwards he was *corregidor* at Málaga. It was through the *corregidores*, figures of authority in the cities and powerful individuals, that the state then controlled its subjects. They were the equivalent of the *intendants* in France. In his new capacity, Don Diego supervised, amongst other things, the construction of the harbour mole. When called upon, he went to the immediate assistance of Tangiers and Ceuta which were under threat from Drake – and, he takes pains to point out, this help cost the king not a single *real*! Don Diego himself however was ruined financially by the incident. For in his official capacity, he had been obliged, during the relief of the *presidios*, to keep table for over sixty horsemen and other persons of quality. Next, he became governor of Ceuta and as such was required to investigate the administration of his predecessor. He flatters himself that he exercised such fair judgement on this occasion that the former incumbent was reinstated. Although satisfied that he had done the right thing, Don Diego was once more without a post and back home near Zamora, where he was greeted by the justified clamour of his wife and children, who were living in poverty. At this point he had agreed to leave for six months in Brittany. But the six months have now lasted five long years, in the course of which both his elder brother and his elder brother's wife have died without his being able to claim the least part of their estate for himself. And since judgement always goes against an absentee, he has already lost two cases at law. It is true that since his posting to Brittany, the king has allowed him a commandery of 1500 ducats income, with four years' back pay, but, he says, what is that set against the enormous expense he shoulders, his personal poverty and the poverty of his family?

The Spanish archives contain thousands of similar complaints and records. The historian is not obliged to take literally all the grievances thus voiced, but there can be no doubt at all that the civil servants of modern Spain were poorly and irregularly paid and constantly dispatched to all corners of the Spanish Empire, uprooted and cut off from home ties. That they often underwent hardship there can be little doubt. At Madrid there lived a large unemployed population, in search of posts, pensions, and back pay, and an army of wounded military men waiting to be granted an audience. Meanwhile, wives and daughters prostituted themselves to pay the rent. These were the casualties of history, the unemployed servants of the state, whiling away their hours of waiting on the Calle Mayor, the street of wealthy merchants, seeking the summer shade or the winter sunshine on the Prado San Hierónymo or mingling aimlessly with the throng of evening strollers.

Reversion and sale of office. All these servants were attached to their offices by ties of loyalty, honour or self-interest. They gradually conceived the desire to hold them in perpetuity for their descendants. As the years passed this tendency was to become more marked. Sale of office was a widespread evil. France, notorious for the practice, was by no means an exception. If sixteenth and seventeenth century states everywhere permitted the abuse to thrive, is the true explanation the dwindling of real income? In Spain at any rate, the *Recopilación de las Leyes* enables us to follow the progressive dispossession of the state for private gain and the consequent rise of a new privileged caste. For full details of how this actually took place, one has to search among the enormous body of documents at Simancas relating to the *renuncias* or 'reversions'. *Renunciar*, to resign, meant to dispose of one's office to another person – one example among hundreds is the *alguazil* of the Barcelona Inquisition, who requested permission in June, 1558, to pass his office on to his son. Another example in the same year is the government's compliance with the demands made by the *regidores* or magistrates, who henceforth had the right of reversion in favour of anyone they pleased, even if the beneficiary were under eighteen years of age, with permission to exercise this right of nomination in their lifetime, on their deathbed or in their will. The reversion was to be valid even if they died before the statutory interval of twenty days had elapsed.

These details, so reminiscent of France during the same period, give a notion of the problem without in any way resolving it. I have no doubt that a systematic study of the phenomenon in Spain will one day reveal a situation not unlike that revealed by French historians about their own country during the same

220. The Prado San Hierónymo. Anonymous painting. *Galleria Pallavicini, Rome*

period. The most curious aspect of this development in the Iberian Peninsula, in my view, is its extremely precocious appearance. The first signs can be glimpsed even before Ferdinand and Isabella, during the troubled reigns of John II and Henry IV and probably as early as the beginning of the fifteenth century, at least in the sphere of municipal offices, many of which were already *renunciables*. The numerous prohibitions on reversions unless from father to son or on the sale of judicial or other office testify in their way to the spread of the practice. At what point did office become a saleable commodity? This question preoccupied Georges Pagès and we still do not know the precise answer. Mention is made however in the Pragmatic of Madrid, 1494 of those who have made reversion of their (municipal) offices for money, '. . . los que renuncian por dineros'. The king himself was guilty in so far as he created or sold offices. Antonio Pérez is often accused of encouraging this massive venality; but in such a century, the individual secretary is not wholly to blame. Even the offices of municipal *alcaldes* and the *escrivanias* of the Chancelleries and the Royal Council became *renunciables*. As in France, this growing venality developed in an almost feudal atmosphere, or rather, as Georg Friederici has pointed out, bureaucracy and paternalism now went hand in hand. Clearly the monarchy was the loser as offices continued to be sold and corruption increased. Such abuses created fresh obstacles to the authority of the Crown, which was very far, in the time of Philip II, from the absolute power of a Louis XIV.

Venality, detrimental to the state, was likewise embedded in Turkish institutions. I have already quoted the opinion that the farming of revenues throughout Turkey may have originated in Egypt. The need to *corteggiare* one's superiors, to offer them substantial gifts, obliged every state servant to reimburse himself regularly, at the expense of his inferiors and of the localities he administered, and so on down the scale. The organized misappropriation of public funds operated throughout the hierarchy. The Ottoman Empire was the victim of these insatiable office-holders, obliged by the very tyranny of usage to be insatiable. The individual who drew most benefit from this daylight robbery was the grand vizier, as the Venetians never tired of pointing out and as Gerlach noted in his *Tagebuch* with reference to Muhammad Sokolli, an obscure youth living near Ragusa when he was carried off at the age of eighteen by the sultan's recruiting officers and who, many years later, in June, 1565, became grand vizier, a post he held until his assassination in 1579. He derived a huge income from gifts offered to him by candidates for public office. 'In the average year', writes the Venetian Garzoni, 'it amounts to a million gold ducats, as has been sworn to me by persons worthy of trust.' Gerlach himself notes: 'Muhammad Pasha has an incredible treasure store of gold and precious stones . . . Any man wishing to obtain a post must first bring him a gift of several hundred or several thousand ducats, or else bring him horses or children . . .' The memory of Muhammad Sokolli cannot be defended against these charges, great man though he undoubtedly was.

221. Ottoman miniature from the *Book of Feasts of Murād III. Istanbul University Library*

In the Turkish Empire however, the enormous fortune of a vizier was always at the disposal of the sultan, who could seize it upon the death, whether natural or otherwise, of his minister. In this way, the Turkish state participated in the habitual peculation of its officers. Not everything could be recovered by such straightforward means: religious foundations, of which much architectural evidence survives, provided ministers with a safe keeping-place for their wealth. It was one way of preserving some of the misappropriated gold for the future or the security of a family. Let us recognize that the western system was on the whole less thorough-going than eastern custom, but in both East and West, venality of office was one area where the power of the state was curiously undermined. As for dating this revealing disorganization, what we have in the sixteenth century is no more than a series of warning signs of things to come.

Developments similar to those in Spain had begun to work upon Turkey even before they were felt in the far-off Iberian Peninsula. For it was not until after the ascetic reign of Philip II that Spain could unrestrainedly indulge in a display of luxury and good living. In the East, the change occurred immediately after the death of Sulaimān in 1566. Silken garments, woven with cloth of silver and gold, forbidden under the reign of the old emperor who always wore cotton, made a sudden reappearance. As the century drew to a close, feast succeeded sumptuous feast in Constantinople, their flickering lights casting a lurid glow through even the arid pages of Hammer's history. The luxury of the Seray was unbelievable: the couches were upholstered in cloth of gold; in summer the habit was adopted of sleeping between sheets of the finest silk. Exaggerating only a little, contemporary observers declared that the slipper of a Turkish woman cost more than the entire costume of a Christian princess. In winter, silken sheets were replaced by precious furs. The luxury of even the tables of Italy was surpassed. We must believe the evidence of the touchingly naïve comment made by the first Dutch envoy to Constantinople, Cornelius Haga, who declared after his reception in May, 1612, 'it seemed that this was a day of public celebration'. What is one to say of the great feasts in the time of Murād IV, while the country itself was bled white by the twin perils of war and famine? How strange it is that Turkey at almost exactly the same time as Spain, should have abandoned herself to the delights and revels of a 'Golden Age' at the very moment when this lavish display was in flagrant contradiction to all rules of good management and the relentless realities of the nation's budget.

Local autonomy: some examples. The spectacle of these gigantic political machines can be misleading. Alongside the typical fifteenth century state, the dimensions of sixteenth century powers are easily exaggerated. But it is merely a matter of degree: by comparison with the present day and the size of modern bureaucracies, the number of office-holders in the sixteenth century is insignificant. And indeed, for want of sufficient personnel, the mighty state with its 'absolute' power had a good deal less than total control. In everyday matters the state's authority was imperfect and often ineffective. It was confronted with innumerable bastions of local autonomy against which it was powerless. In the great Spanish Empire, many cities retained their freedom of movement. By contracting for payment of fixed sums to the state, they were able to control indirect taxation. Seville and Burgos, something of whose institutions we know, had considerable liberties. Or again, outside the Peninsula but still within the Spanish Empire, Messina remained until 1675 a republic, a thorn in the flesh of all the viceroys who, like Marcantonio Colonna in 1577, administered Sicily. 'Your Majesty knows', writes Colonna in June of that year, 'how great are the privileges of Messina, and how many outlaws and *matadores* (assassins) are harboured in the city, partly for the ease with which they can pass into Calabria . . . The city is today so surrounded by thieves, that even inside its walls, people are kidnapped and then held to ransom.'

Both in the Peninsula and outside it then, whole districts, towns, sometimes regions with their own *fueros*, or privileges, escaped the jurisdiction of the

222. Ferdinand the Catholic pledging the codes of law of Viscaya at Bilbao. Painting at the Diputation Foral, Viscaya.

Spanish state. This was true of all distant and peripheral zones: the Kingdom of Granada for example until 1570; after 1580 and for many years until the final rupture of 1640 it was true of Portugal, in every sense a 'dominion' with its own liberties and rights which the invader dared not touch. It was always to be true of the tiny Basque provinces and of the possessions of the Crown of Aragon, with whose privileges, even after the rising and troubles of 1591, Philip II dared not interfere. Merely on crossing the Aragonese border, the most unobservant traveller could not fail to remark that as he left Castile he was entering a completely different society. Here he found semi-independent lords, exercising many rights over their long-suffering subjects and entrenched in castles fortified with artillery, only a stone's throw from their neighbour Castile, now humbled and disarmed. Socially privileged, politically privileged and fiscally privileged, the Aragonese bloc governed itself and paid only a fraction of its royal taxes. But the real reason for such impunity was the proximity of the French border and the knowledge that the first signs of unrest would be exploited by her hostile neighbour to force open the imperfectly closed gates of Spain.

Resistance to the state could take the most diverse forms. In the Kingdom of Naples for instance, alongside the still unsubdued Calabria, both the sheep-farmers' associations and the city of Naples itself were prominent in this respect.

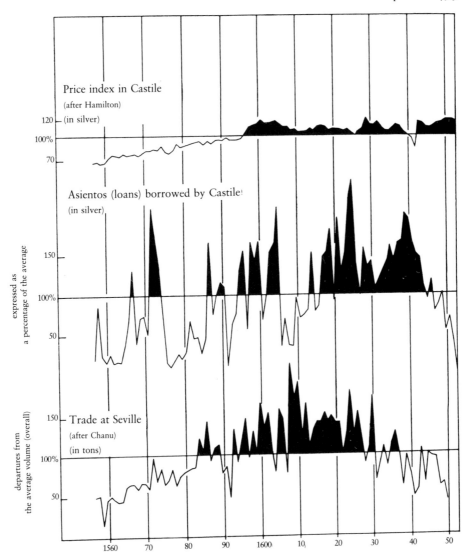

expressed as
a percentage of the average

departures from
the average volume (overall)

Price index in Castile
(after Hamilton)
(in silver)

Asientos (loans) borrowed by Castile
(in silver)

Trade at Seville
(after Chanu)
(in tons)

120
100%
70

150
100%
50

150
100%
50

1560   70   80   90   1600   10   20   30   40   50

The 'asientos' and economic life in Castile

Compared on one hand with the variations in the price index, according to Earl J. Hamilton, which as can be seen were quite modest, and on the other hand with the pattern of Sevilian trade, an enormous boom followed by a substantial recession, the graph representing the *asientos*, that is the short term national debt, has the frantic appearance of a seismograph. It does however present certain analogies with the price curve, particularly at Seville, naturally enough, since it was upon the import of silver from America that the whole system of the advance and repayment of *asientos* depended. By and large the curve rises above the 100 per cent mark in time of war and falls below it during periods of peace or withdrawal (except for the conquest of Portugal). Note the large scale borrowing during the so-called Thirty Years' War. Graph showing *asientos* constructed by Alvaro Castillo Pintado.

Through the sheepfarmers' associations, the peasant could escape both his over-lord and his king. Or if he settled in Naples, the 'city air' made him a free man. Further south, in Sicily, the power of the secular authorities could be escaped by allegiance to the Sicilian Inquisition, whose influence was thus singularly extended. Possibly the monstrous growth of the capital in Turkey was a similar type of response. In the provinces, nothing stood between the individual and the rapaciousness of the local *beglerbegi, sandjak-begi* and *su-bashis* and, most hated and feared of all, their agents the *voivodes*. At least in Constantinople one was assured of a minimum of justice and of relative tranquillity.

There can be no doubt that corruption among state officials was widespread in the sixteenth century, in Islam as in Christendom, in southern as in northern Europe. 'There is no case before a court, whether civil or criminal', wrote the Duke of Alva from Flanders in 1573, 'which is not sold like meat in the butcher's shop . . . most of the councillors sell themselves daily to anyone who will pay the money.' 'The laws of Spain', wrote the ageing Rodrigo Vivero in about 1632, 'are like spiders' webs, catching only flies and gnats.' The rich and power-ful escaped their toils and the only ones who became entangled were the unprivi-leged and the poor, a state of affairs not confined to the sixteenth and seventeenth centuries.

Finance and credit in the service of the state. With the exception of the Italian examples mentioned earlier, the Mediterranean states at the very end of the sixteenth century possessed neither a treasury nor a state bank. In 1583 there was some talk in Philip II's entourage of setting up a state bank but the project was never realized. From the metropolitan centre of the great Spanish Empire, appeals went out to the moneylenders whom we call by the rather too modern name of bankers. The king could not do without them. After his return to Spain in September, 1559, Philip II's major preoccupation for the next ten years was to be the restoring of order to the finances of his realm. Advice poured in from every side, always in the last analysis recommending that he apply to the Affaitati or the Fuggers, or the Genoese, or even, during Eraso's outbursts of nationalism, to homegrown Spanish bankers like the Malvenda of Burgos.

The scattered nature of Philip's possessions and those of his father before him, meant inevitably that revenues had to be collected and payments made over a wide area, thus encouraging the use of international merchant firms. Their assistance was required merely to transfer money from place to place. But they could do more than this: they could advance money, thus mobilizing the resources of the state before they were due. In this capacity, they were frequently concerned in the direct collection of state taxes as reimbursement, which brought them into contact with the taxpayers. The Spanish fiscal system then was organ-ized by the money-lenders to suit themselves. In 1564, Philip II assigned to the Genoese the monopoly of sales of playing cards. On a subsequent occasion, he handed over certain of the Andalusian salt-pans. Another time he might follow

223–5. Greek, Arab and Ragusan merchants in Constantinople. From N. de Nicolay, *Peregrinationes*, 1572.

his father's example and delegate to the Fugger family the exploitation of the mines at Almadén or the administration of the estates belonging to the Military Orders – a step which in this case meant placing extensive arable and pasture land, tolls and peasant dues in foreign hands. The Fuggers' Germans factors and agents were everywhere in Spain, conscientious, methodical and zealous. Even when tax-gathering did not devolve upon a foreign firm it was just as likely to be carried out by the intermediary powers, the towns or the Cortes. Financially then, state control was, to say the least, incomplete.

In France, although the transfer of coin was not the vital necessity it had become for Spain, bankers and moneylenders nevertheless had a part to play, as they did in Turkey, where businessmen made free with state funds. Gerlach notes in his *Tagebuch*: 'there are in Constantinople, many Greeks who have grown rich through trade or other means of making money, but who go about clad in mean clothes so that the Turks shall not know of their riches and steal them . . .' The richest among them was one Michael Cantacuzenus: the devil's son according to the Turks, this pseudo-Greek was rumoured, unconvincingly, to be of English origin. Whatever his beginnings, his fortune was immense and was curiously connected with the services he rendered the Turkish state. For Cantacuzenus had the monopoly of all the saltworks in the empire, farmed innumerable customs duties, trafficked in offices and, like a vizier, could depose Greek patriarchs or metropolitans at his pleasure. In addition to this, he controlled the revenues of entire provinces, Moldavia for instance or Wallachia, and held enough feudal villages to be able to provide crews for twenty or thirty galleys. His palace at Anchioli rivalled the Seray in splendour. This successful adventurer is not to be confused with his humbler Greek compatriots in Galata or elsewhere; he flaunted his wealth before them and, lacking their prudence, was arrested in July, 1576; obliged to forfeit his possessions, he escaped with his life through the intercession of Muhammad Sokolli. On his release, he began once again, this time dealing not in salt but in furs, and as in the past had a personal arrangement in Moldavia and Wallachia. Finally the inevitable happened: on 13th March, 1578, on the orders of the sultan and without any form of trial, he was hanged from the gates of his own palace at Anchioli and his wealth was confiscated.

A comparable, but even more extraordinary story is that of a figure mysterious in many ways, the Portuguese Jew Joseph (or Juan) Nasi, known variously as Migues or Micas and who at the end of his life bore the lofty title of Duke of Naxos. After spending much of his early life wandering aimlessly about Europe, to the Netherlands, Besançon, and for a while Venice, he arrived in Constantinople in about 1550. Already a rich man, he celebrated his marriage with a great display of wealth and reverted to Judaism. The friend and confidant of Sultan Selīm before his accession – discreetly providing him with choice wines – he farmed the customs duty on the wines of the islands. It was he who urged the sultan to attack Cyprus in 1570. Most astonishing of all perhaps is the fact that he died of natural causes in 1579, still in possession of a large fortune. There has been an injudicious effort to rehabilitate the memory of this striking individual, but even after hearing the evidence we are little wiser about this Fugger of the East. Spanish documents describe him as favourably disposed towards Spain, even slightly in league with His Catholic Majesty, but he was not the kind of man who could be classed once and for all as either pro-Spanish or anti-French. To do so would be to ignore the constantly shifting political loyalties in Constantinople. It would be interesting above all to know, as in the case of Cantacuzenus, exactly how he fitted into Turkish state finances. And our knowledge of these finances themselves is very scanty and likely to remain so for some time.

Conspicuously absent from Turkish finances as compared with those of Christian powers was the recourse to public credit, whether long or short term – the government loan, a polite and fairly painless way of appropriating the money of private citizens, of investors both large and small. It was a method univerally practised in the West, where every state created some formula to attract its citizens' money. In France it was the famous *rentes sur l'Hôtel de Ville*. In Spain, as we have seen, it was the *juros*, which by the end of Philip II's reign represented no less than 80 million ducats. Such paper depreciated quickly and occasioned frantic speculation. At prices then current, the state might end up paying as much as seventy per cent interest. One character in Cervantes' short story *La Gitanilla* talks revealingly of saving money and holding on to it, 'como quien tiene un juro sobre las yerbas de Extremadura', like a man who holds a bond on the pasture lands of Extremadura (presumably a good investment, for they could vary). In Italy, the appeal to the public was usually made through the *Monti di Pietà*. As Guicciardini had already noted, 'either Florence will be the undoing of the *Monte di Pietà*, or the *Monte di Pietà* will be the undoing of Florence', a forecast which was to be even more true of the seventeenth century than of the sixteenth. In his economic history of Italy, Alfred Doren maintains that these massive investments in state bonds were both symptom and cause of the decline of Italy at the beginning of the sixteenth century. Investors were reluctant to take risks.

Perhaps nowhere was the appeal for credit more frequently reiterated than in Rome, capital of that singular dominion, both dwarf and giant, the Papal States. In the fifteenth century, after the Council of Constance, the Papacy, finding itself the victim of the growing particularism of other states and reduced to the immediate resources of the Papal States, set about extending and recovering the latter. It was no accident that during the last years of the fifteenth century and the first years of the sixteenth, the Supreme Pontiffs resembled temporal rulers rather than spiritual leaders: papal finances obliged them to it. Towards the middle of the sixteenth century, the situation remained much the same: almost eighty per cent of papal revenues came from the Patrimony or Papal States. Hence the relentless struggle against financial immunity. Victory in this struggle led to the absorption by the Papal States of the urban finances of, for instance, Viterbo, Perugia, Orvieto or the medium-sized towns of Umbria. Only Bologna was able to preserve her autonomy. But these victories left unaltered the old and often archaic systems of tax collection: the sources of revenue were unblocked as it were, 'but only exceptionally did the Papal States come into contact with its taxpayers'.

No less important than this fiscal war was the appeal to public credit. Clemens Bauer rightly says that from now on the history of the papal finances is a 'history of debt', the short-term debt which took the familiar form of borrowing from bankers and the long-term debt, repayment of which was effected through the *Camera Apostolica*. Its origin is the more noteworthy in that it testifies to the venality of offices reserved for laymen. There was from the start confusion between office-holders and creditors of the Apostolic Chamber. The officer-shareholders formed colleges: the purchase price of office was invested capital but as interest they received fixed salaries. In the College of the *Presidentes annonae* for example, founded in 1509 and comprising 141 offices, sold for the total sum of 91,000 ducats, interest-salaries of 10,000 ducats were payable from the revenues of the *Salara di Roma*. Later on, through the creation of the *Societates officiorum*, the papacy succeeded in sharing out these bonds among small investors and the title of officer conferred on shareholders became purely honorary. This was already the case with the series of Colleges of Cavalieri begun in 1520 with the foundation of the *Cavalieri di San Pietro*; later came the *Cavalieri di San Paolo* and the *Cavalieri di San Giorgio*. Finally a conventional system of government bonds was instituted, with *Monti* probably on the model of Florence, by Clement VII, a Medici Pope. The principle was identical with that of the *rentes sur l'Hôtel de Ville*, the granting of a fixed and guaranteed income in return for the payment of a capital sum. Shares in the loan were called *luoghi di monti*, negotiable bonds often in fact negotiated both in Rome and elsewhere, usually above par. Thus were created, through the accident of circumstance or necessity, the *Monte Allumiere*, guaranteed by the alum mines at Tolfa, the *Monte S. Buonaventura*, the *Monte della Carne*, the *Monte della fede* and others. Over thirty are recorded.

Usually these were repayable loans; the *Monte novennale* for instance, set up in 1555, was in theory repayable after nine years. But there were also permanent loans, which could be passed on by inheritance. In fact one way for the papal finances to make a short-term profit, was to convert life-holdings into perpetual holdings, '*vacabili*' into '*non vacabali*', since it meant the rate of interest was lowered. Through these and other details it can be seen that the Roman *Monti* were by no means behind the times; they could stand comparison with those of Venice or Florence, with the Casa di San Giorgio and *a fortiori* with the *juros* of Castile. Any calculation in this sector is nevertheless difficult: between 1526 and 1601, the papacy seems to have borrowed for its own purposes (and sometimes on behalf of representatives of the Roman nobility) 13

x. Charles V at the Battle of Mühlberg, by Titian. The wealth and stability of the Habsburg Empire that supplied the sinews of war are more powerfully suggested than the actual clash of arms. *Prado, Madrid*

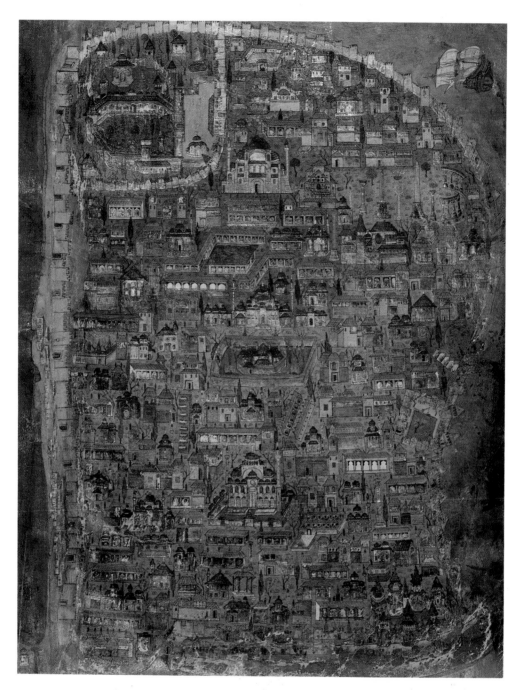

xi. View of Constantinople from the description of Sulaimān's 1534–36 campaign, c.1537. The earliest known Ottoman view of the city. The Topkapi Palace appears at the top left; near it is the Aya Sofya, to the right the Hippodrome. Below are the covered bazaar, the Aqueduct of Valens, the Old Palace and the Mosque of Muhammad II.
Istanbul University Library

xii. Sulaimān's Hungarian Campaign. The Battle of Mohács, 1526. Ottoman miniature from the *Huner-name*, 1588. *Topkapi Museum, Istanbul*

xiii. The Battle of Lepanto. Painting attributed to H. Letter, Venice, seventeenth century.
National Maritime Museum, Greenwich

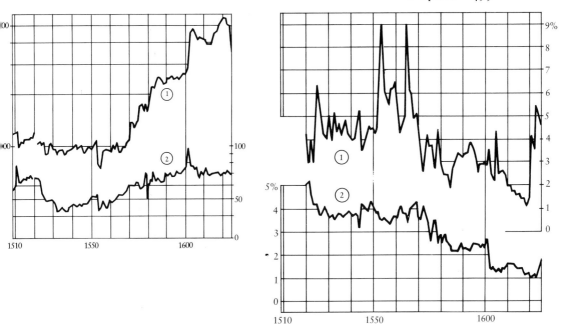

The 'Luoghi' of the Casa di San Giorgio, 1509–1625

These graphs summarize the findings of the important article by Carlo M. Cipolla, 'Note sulla storia del saggio d'interesse, corso e sconto dei dividendi del banco di San Giorgio nel secolo XVI' (1952). The *luoghi* were shares in the public debt of the Republic of Genoa, issued at 100 *lire* (2000 *soldi*) nominal value. These were perpetual annuities with varying interest rates (in Venice by contrast, interest rates were fixed): they depended on the profits made by the *Casa di San Giorgio* which held as security the taxes it collected on behalf of the Signoria. The number of *luoghi* increased a great deal between 1509 (193,185) and 1544 (477,112) hence the drop in prices; the number later settled down (437,708 in 1597 and 476,706 in 1681). The first curve represents the price of negotiable *luoghi* on the market (left-hand axis = 1000 to 5000 *soldi*). The second curve represents the interest, *reddito*, of the *luoghi* (right-hand axis = 40 to 100 *soldi*). There is a clear rise during the second half of the sixteenth century and a falling off in the following century. Now interest on the *luoghi* was never paid immediately; half was paid four years later and the other half after a further year's interval. If a shareholder wanted to be paid straight away he had to have his dividend discounted, so the *sentio* varied on the market (top curve, second graph). It is therefore possible, taking into account both the delay and the *sentio*, to calculate the real interest on the *luoghi*: this is shown in the last curve which reveals a clear decline after 1570 becoming more marked still after 1600. 'So for one reason or another', concludes the author, 'capital was invested at Genoa at the beginning of the seventeenth century, at 1·2 per cent.' What we do not know is whether this abnormal situation is an indication of the healthy condition or otherwise of the financial centre.

million crowns. This figure may not impress a twentieth century reader; let me add however that out of these sums so persistently extracted from private citizens, Sixtus V was able to put by 26 tons of silver and three tons of gold to be locked up in his treasury in the Castel Sant'Angelo, thus gratifying a peasant's urge to hoard by extremely modern means. Since the *Monti* were meant for an international clientele, it is not surprising that the public debt at Genoa stopped growing 'just as it was reaching impressive proportions at Rome'. Was Leopold von Ranke right to call Rome 'perhaps the principal money-market in Europe', at least of investors' money? Although possible, this is by no means certain. The crucial point however is not the scale of government borrowing in Rome, but the enormous expansion of the credit market on which every state drew, prudent and reckless alike, and on which innumerable stockholders did very satisfying business. This infatuation cannot be explained simply by the economic situation, at least as we understand it. Is it to be explained in terms of collective psychology, of a mass urge for security? In Genoa for example, where between 1570 and 1620 inflation 'reached such a point', writes Carlo M. Cipolla, 'that historians have described it as a price revolution, by some paradox there was a visible decrease in interest rates', which had varied between 4 and 6 per cent since 1522 but now dropped to 2 and even to 1·2 per cent, at least during their lowest ebb, between 1575 and 1588. This drop corresponded with the influx into Genoa of bullion, both gold and silver, which it was at this time difficult to invest. 'This was the first time in the history of Europe since the fall of the Roman Empire that capital was made available at such low rates and this was indeed an extraordinary revolution.'

By the beginning of the seventeenth century the heyday of empires was over: the only vigorous states were those of moderate size: France under Henri IV, a reign of sudden glory; or Elizabethan England, combining adventure with literary brilliance; Holland centred on Amsterdam; or Germany which experienced an age of material prosperity from 1555 until the first shots of the Thirty Years' War when it fell into the abyss. In the Mediterranean, there was Morocco, now once more rich in gold, or the Regency of Algiers, a city on the way to becoming a territorial state. And then there was Venice, radiant and resplendent with luxury, beauty and intelligence; or Tuscany under the Grand Duke Ferdinand. It is as if everything conspired in the new century to help these smaller states, of a size to keep their own houses in order. Many minor Colberts rose to eminence in these modest states, men skilled in diagnosing their country's economy, capable of raising tariffs or encouraging the enterprises of their subjects and at the same time keeping a close guard over them. It is this series of small fortunes rather than the complex and sometimes obscure story of the empires which tells us that the wheel of history had indeed turned.

5

Societies

1 Noble reaction

IN CHRISTENDOM AS IN ISLAM, the nobility occupied the first rank and intended to keep it. It was the most conspicuous social group in France, in Spain and elsewhere. Everywhere the aristocracy monopolized symbols of prestige: precedence, lavish costumes, silks woven with thread of gold or silver, satins and velvets, Flemish tapestries, thoroughbred horses, luxurious residences, huge households and, by the end of the century, carriages. These were, it is true, so many roads to ruin. It was said that in the time of Henri II, the French nobility was importing four million *livres'* worth of clothes from Italy a year. But appearances are not always deceptive: they may indicate a solid foundation of power and wealth. Over wide areas, these aristocracies still thrived and drew sustenance from their strong feudal roots. An ancient order had placed these privileged families at the summit of society and maintained them there still. The only exceptions were in and around large cities, the corrupters of traditional hierarchies, in commercial centres (though less than one would expect), in regions which had grown rich early, like the Netherlands and above all Italy – though not all Italy, as one might guess.

Landlords and peasants. If we are to believe many much-quoted accounts, the sixteenth century reduced the aristocracy to poverty. These accounts are often true. But by no means all nobles were in such a plight, nor were they without exception victims either of the king or of war, of the lack of employment in peace time or of overweening luxury.

At any rate in the essential confrontation between landlord and peasant, while the latter may occasionally have got the upper hand, as in Languedoc between 1480 and 1500, and perhaps in Catalonia in the fifteenth century (at least certain well-to-do peasants may have), this was very much the exception. Usually the nobleman had the last word, either in the long or short run, and in some places (Aragon, Sicily) he always had it. The price revolution, too often invoked, was not a worker of democratic miracles. It lightened the burden of

peasant dues payable in money and assessed well before the discovery of America. In fact feudal dues from peasant holdings were often light, sometimes next to nothing. But not always. And above all, the landlord also collected payment in kind which kept pace with current prices. A register of the revenues of the Cardinal Duke of Lerma, in March, 1622, mentions his poultry, wheat, wine, the wheat at fixed rates, the wine at four reals, 'el pan a la tasa, el vino a quatro reales'. Moreover, in the Mediterranean as in Europe, land division was never fixed once and for all. Peasant cunning might be met by aristocratic cunning and, on occasion, brutality. The landlord dispensed justice, held supreme rights over peasant holdings and the lands separating or surrounding them. The end of the fifteenth century and the early years of the sixteenth are remarkable for the construction or reconstruction of whole villages, always according to the landlord's desires. This was true of the Gâtine in Poitou, of the Jura where *granges* were founded; in Haut-Poitou, where a noble family in difficulties might restore its finances by letting off vast tracts of heath previously unoccupied and where peasants were settled. In Spain, villages were founded by charter, the *cartas pueblas*, and often even land occupied for many years by peasants would pass into the landlord's hands.

226. *Opposite*: Conspicuous consumption: *A Member of the Albani Family* wearing a robe of Oriental silk. Painting by Cariani. *National Gallery, London*

227. *Above:* Employer and employee: *The Treasurer Martino Malpaga Paying Two Workmen*. Wall painting in the Castle of Trento, 1531.

A landlord then, whether old or new to the job, was likely to take full advantage of his rights and dues, his mills, hunting grounds and all the many areas in which he opposed the peasant, who was himself aware of the commercial possibilities of grain, wool and livestock. Bernardino de Mendoza, Philip II's ambassador in Paris – and for that reason alone beset with financial problems – made sure, from his distant post, of selling the wheat of the preceding harvest on his Spanish estate. For the ambassador was a grain-farmer and even stockpiler. To take another example, cattle-raising was often introduced by large landowners, in the Roman Campagna and elsewhere. Julius Klein has described the role played by certain nobles (and grandees) in the sheep-farming of the *Mesta*. In Andalusia in the seventeenth century, the nobility and the Church were to appropriate vast areas of land and, by their extensive agriculture, to depopulate the lowlands. Plentiful documents concerning the farming of these estates await the historian's attention and several valuable studies have already shown what wealth they conceal. The remarkable series of the *Sommaria* in Naples alone reveals the activities and speculation carried on by these great landowners, producing and marketing their grain, wool, oil and wood. To cultivate one's land and sell its produce did not signify derogation, quite the contrary.

The price rise warns us in advance what was to be the general tenor of disputes between lord and peasant. During the summer of 1558, the subjects of the marquisate of Finale, near Genoa, rebelled against the excessive demands made by their overlord, Alphonso de Carreto. What were his demands? Was it not, as Carreto himself says, the fact that he had instigated a reassessment of the possessions of his vassals and proposed raising their rents? Since the Finale question was soon taken out of the hands of the marquis (Genoa and Spain were both far too interested in this vital territory not to turn the occasion to profit) the practical origin of the affair is usually forgotten.

Many in the end were the noblemen who succeeded in maintaining their direct contact with the land and income from land, who thus survived, although not always unscathed, the tempest of the price revolution. Nor was this protection their only resource.

In Castile: Grandes *and* Títulos *versus the king*. It has been said quite rightly that the modern state was the enemy of the nobility and of feudal powers. But that is not the whole story: the state was both enemy and protector, even associate. To bring the aristocracy to heel was its first objective, and one never completely attained; the next was to use it as an instrument of government, over it and through it to control the *peuple vulgaire* as they said in Burgundy. It relied on the nobles for the maintenance of peace and public order, for the defence of the regions in which they owned estates or castles, for levying and commanding the *ban* and the *arrière-ban*, still something of importance in Spain: in 1542 for the siege of Perpignan; in 1569 for the war of Granada; in 1580 for the invasion of Portugal. More often, the king merely alerted his vassals when danger threatened, as in 1562 or 1567. In 1580, the lords on the Portuguese border raised small armies at their own expense, a total of 30,000 men who were hardly used at all. These were almost always levies from frontier areas, but they cut deep and were undoubtedly a heavy burden.

In addition, the king would keep prominent nobles constantly informed of his intentions, orders and important news; he would ask their advice and oblige them to lend him large sums of money. But the advantages granted in return by the monarchy were by no means negligible. When we think of the Spanish state, we must think above all of the *Grandes* and *Títulos*, the king's principal interlocutors, that tiny minority of privileged persons through whom the monarchy from time to time indirectly governed, to avoid losing control of potential outbreaks of regional dissidence, for behind each of these great noblemen lay a huge clientele, as there did behind the Guises or the Montmorency family in France. When a royal judge (in 1664 it is true) was about to arrest the *corregidor* of Jeréz, the Duke of Arcos, intervening, did not even trouble to see the judge himself, but had a word with his secretary: 'Tell him that the *corregidor* of Jeréz is of my house, that will suffice.' The nobility paled like the stars of the morning before the rising sun of the monarchy, as the imagery of the day described it. But the stars continued to shine in the firmament.

Castile provides the outstanding example. Here the unconcealed conflict took on a multitude of forms, not the least effective of which was the permanent hostility of the officers of royal justice to the pretensions of baronial justice and to the persons of the nobles themselves. Nothing was easier for example than to divide the nobles amongst themselves on the occasion of inheritance and property disputes. It was an opportunity to score off them. In 1572, Ruy Gómez was overjoyed at the news that the Duke of Medina Sidonia had won his suit against the Count of Alba, a nephew of the Prior Don Antonio, over the county of Niebla, a property, according to the Tuscan ambassadors, worth 60,000 ducats' income. After winning his case – was it purely coincidence? – the Duke of Medina Sidonia married Ruy Gómez' daughter. And, infrequently it is true, but occasionally, the king's justice would uphold the claims of vassals against their lords.

As for the justice meted out by the feudal nobles, it was strictly supervised from above, never allowed to escape observation. Their sentences, notes a Venetian in 1558, are referred to the *Chancillerías*. Paolo Tiepolo confirms this in 1563: 'The nobles of Castile own huge estates and fairly good land, but their jurisdiction and power is much limited; in fact they do not dispense justice; they cannot levy any tribute from their people and have neither fortresses nor soldiers nor many weapons . . . unlike the lords of Aragon who, although of less consequence, yet usurp greater authority.'

These minor victories of the monarchy – or even such a major success as the king's recovery in 1559 of the *diezmos de la mar*, the customs posts along the Cantabrian coast, on the death of the Almirante of Castile who had held them as a hereditary concession – should not create any illusions. The power of the nobility had lost little of its vigour. In 1538, all the might of Charles V had been unable, in the face of resistance from the representatives of the nobility, to obtain from the Cortes the establishment of a general tax on consumption. 'When Charles V tried to destroy their privileges', Michele Suriano later wrote, 'he was opposed by all the grandees and most of all by the Grand Constable of Castile, although he was greatly devoted to His Majesty.'

However as years went by, royal authority gained in effectiveness and certainly in severity, revealed in many signs: the arrest by the king's agents of the son of Hernán Cortés, Marquis del Valle, on a charge of seeking to make himself independent ruler in New Spain; or that of the Grand Master of Montesa, in Valencia through the intermediary of the Inquisition in 1572, on a charge of either heresy or sodomy – public opinion being a little uncertain on that point; the banishment of the Duke of Alva himself to his estates in 1579; or the disgrace and punishment in 1580 of the influential widow of Ruy Gómez, the Princess of Eboli, though only it is true after much royal heart-searching; then there was the arrest of the Almirante of Castile, Count of Modica, in his father's house in April, 1582; the accused was, it is true, guilty of murdering his rival in love ('and this execution', noted a Venetian correspondent, 'has much saddened all the nobility and in particular the grandees of Spain, for they see that they are now no more respected than common mortals'); or again, the Prudent King in September, 1586 brought to heel the extravagant *jeunesse dorée* of Madrid without any form of trial. In the time of Philip III and later of Philip IV, such acts of authority were frequently repeated. In December, 1608, the Duke of Maqueda and his brother Don Jaime were condemned to death for striking a notary and alcalde of the Royal Council. The furore eventually died down, but at the time feelings ran high, as they did in April, 1621 at the abrupt disgrace of the Dukes of Osuna, Lerma and Uceda, which astonished even the French ambassador.

The nobility then was brought to heel, sometimes with its own consent. Great families had in fact already begun to live at court during the reign of Philip II; they settled at Madrid, not without hesitation and a little repugnance at first, camping out in houses 'che sono infelici rispetto a quelle d'Italia', as Cardinal Borghese noted in 1597. Sumptuous tapestries and silver did not prevent them from living 'porcamente senza una minima pollitia, che entrare nelle case loro par proprio d'entrare in tante stalle'. There is little point in defending them against these scornful Italian judgments: they really did live like the peasants they were, often violent and uncouth, although there were brilliant exceptions. And then of course, these houses in Madrid were only temporary residences, the pied-à-terre in the capital. It was on their country estates that all important festivities and ceremonies were held. The outstandingly rich Dukes of Infantado had a magnificent palace at Guadalajara, the finest in Spain declared Navagero in 1525, and it was here that the marriage of Philip II to Elizabeth of

228. Façade of the palace of the Duke of Infantado, reputedly the richest nobleman in Spain, Guadalajara.

France was celebrated. Most of the noble palaces were set in the heart of the countryside. It was at Lagartera, a village in the Sierra de Gredos, not far from Oropesa, a village where, not so very long ago, 'the peasant women . . . still wore their traditional costumes, stockings in the form of gaiters and heavy embroidered skirts', that the Dukes of Frías had their country seat, with its Renaissance windows cut in the thick walls, its spacious courtyard, broad staircases, moulded ceilings, exposed beams and huge fireplaces.

Gradually the lords yielded to the lure of the city. The Duke of Infantado was already at Guadalajara. In Seville, urban palaces sprang up in the sixteenth century. In Burgos, some of these houses are still standing today, with their

229. *Philip III Enters Madrid*, seen here on the *Plaza Mayor*. Anonymous
seventeenth-century painting. *Museo Municipal, Madrid*

Renaissance doors and porticoes and large armorial bearings supported by
sculpted figures. In 1545, Pedro de Medina was admiring the number and the
distinction of the noble mansions in Valladolid.

When Philip II's reign ended, the aristocracy flocked first to Madrid then to
Valladolid, once more for a short period capital of Spain, towards the life of
display of the *Corte*, the *fiestas* and the bullfights on the *Plaza Mayor*. The
nobility built up round the monarch that ever-thickening screen which was to
divide him from his people. Taking advantage of the weakness of Philip III, this
class filled all the chief posts of government with its own men, bringing its own
factions and passions to the capital. This was the age of favourites, of *válidos*,
the heyday of the courtier. They began to enjoy the luxury and relaxed atmosphere of Madrid, the long walks through the streets and the nocturnal life of
the city: theatres, merry widows, courtesans who began to dress in silks for the
fine company, scandalizing the virtuous. Intoxicated by this new style of life,
the nobility took a certain perverse pleasure in slumming, mingling with the
sophisticated crowd of the big city. The Duke of Medina Sidonia, the unfortunate leader of the Spanish Armada, is traditionally supposed to have founded
the Cabaret of the Seven Devils. At any rate, Madrid was not only the home of
the king, the theatre and the underworld, it was also the city of the nobles, the
scene of their extravagance, their eventful lives and their quarrels, whether

settled in person or by their henchmen at street corners: murders occurred, according to observers, at the rate of more than one a day.

But the nobility also thronged to Madrid to watch over the royal government and to take advantage of it. Having been kept so long at a distance during the interminable reign of the Prudent King, it took its revenge by imposing its own rule on his successor. Commoners continued to occupy pen-pushing jobs in the councils and to advance slowly along the road to honours. *Grandes* and *Titulos* went in search of royal favours, substantial gifts, profitable appointments, *ayudas de costa* (royal expense accounts), concessions of the *encomiendas* (commanderies) of the different Military Orders. They solicited on their own behalf or on that of their families. An appointment to a viceroyalty in Italy or America meant an assured fortune. Nominally, the income of the higher nobility did not cease to grow as inheritances and property regularly tended to be concentrated within a few hands. It kept pace unfailingly with the economic cycle. Between them all, *Grandes* and *Titulos* totalled an income of 1,100,000 ducats in 1525, according to the Venetians, the Duke of Medina Sidonia alone being in receipt annually of 50,000 ducats. In 1558, the duke's income reached 80,000; in 1581, twenty-two dukes, forty-seven counts and thirty-six marquises between them disposed of 3 million ducats and the Duke of Medina Sidonia alone of 150,000.

Or so it appeared and was popularly believed. Actually these brilliant fortunes were mortgaged to the hilt; even in Philip II's day, families were regularly running up catastrophic debts and noble revenues were often assigned, like those of the crown, to pay off past debts. In the following century, when we have more information about these princely yet bankrupt treasuries, the same difficulties continued. A royal favour, a timely inheritance, a substantial dowry or a loan authorized by the king on an entailed estate might restore a precarious budget. But the balancing act soon began again. In the end this made the monarch's task easier. Cut off from active economic life, the nobility was doomed to resort to moneylenders: it did so to excess.

And the king had yet another means of pressure at his command. It was in about 1520 that there first emerged the distinct category of a select higher nobility, that of the *Grandes* and *Titulos*, 20 *Grandes* and 35 *Titulos*. They numbered about 60 in 1525; 99 at the end of Philip II's reign (18 dukes, 38 marquises, 43 counts); Philip III created 67 new marquises and 25 counts. So there was a promotion ladder. In 1533 and 1539, for instance, the Navas and Olivares families, both recently ennobled, were moved up in rank. Later came the division of the high nobility into three classes. By such means the king could govern and remain master.

230. *Overleaf:* Detail from *Philip IV Hunting Wild Boar* by Velázquez. An eloquent social contrast. *National Gallery, London*

Hidalgos and regidores *in Castile*. The high nobility of Castile consisted, at the end of Philip II's reign, of 100 persons, with their wives and children 400, or 500 at most. Any estimate of the total number of nobles in Castile must be very tentative, possibly 130,000, that is a quarter of a million people out of a total population of six or seven million, a category which by its very size must have included a large proportion of poor and poverty-stricken aristocrats. In their thousands of sometimes tumbledown houses, often bearing 'gigantic scutcheons carved in stone', dwelt a race that sought to live 'nobly', not soiling its hands with dishonourable work, serving king and Church, sacrificing everything, even its life, to this ideal. If there was noble folly, it was at its worst in Castile, despite the misery it could bring and the popular ridicule which expressed itself in so many sayings: 'to catch what a *hidalgo* owes you, send out your greyhound'; 'on the *hidalgo*'s table is much linen but little food'; 'God save you from the poor *hidalgo* and the rich peasant.'

Such ridicule was to be expected: there was a contradiction in wishing but being unable to live like a noble, for lack of that money which justified almost anything. Certain towns even went so far as to refuse entry to the *hidalgos* who did not pay their share of the common fiscal burden. Written in letters of gold, it is said, in the *Ayuntamiento* of Gascueña, a village in the province of Cuenca, were the words: 'No consienten nuestras leyes hidalgos, frailes, ni bueyes.' The oxen (dullards?) must be there for the rhyme: 'Our laws do not allow for *hidalgos*, monks or oxen.' A great many other towns and villages refused to allow a distinction to be made between *hidalgos*, minor nobles, and *pecheros* or ordinary taxpayers. Yet most of the time, the two 'peoples' shared equally between them municipal offices and duties, which put the smaller group at an advantage. And in many large cities, the vital port of Seville for instance, the nobility had taken over all the posts of command. We have already noted the prevalence of venality which brought profit to families already holding positions, controlling the offices of *regidores* sold by the crown and resold by the incumbents. It was never, we may be sure, a question of mere vanity, but one of vital and often sordid necessity. Unable to plunder the whole of Castile as the grandees did, local nobles plundered urban and village revenues within their reach and depended on them for a living. Disputes, tension, class struggles were rarely absent from these troubled microcosms; incidents within them might be tragic or ridiculous but they were never meaningless.

Other nobilities. Mutatis mutandis, the Castilian pattern is repeated elsewhere, in France, even in Catalonia and Valencia. In these two distinctive provinces of Spain, the king's authority was weak, and the nobles took such advantage of the fact that foreign observers credited them with intentions even more subversive than they actually had. At Valencia in April, 1616, the viceroy, the Duke of Feria, to punish a nobleman for some practical joke, had him paraded on a mule through the streets of the city. All the nobles immediately closed their houses, went into mourning and some even travelled to Madrid to protest to the king.

In Naples, the violent invasions of Charles VIII and Louis XII had brought a whole series of tragedies to noble families. Great magnates like the Princes of Salerno and Taranto, or the Duke of Bari disappeared. Their 'states' were divided up. But in the process, lesser nobles enlarged their properties and fairly large states survived, the counties of Albi and Tagliacozzo, Matera and Cellano for instance. In 1558, a Venetian report lists in the Kingdom of Naples 24 dukes, 25 marquises, 90 counts, about 800 barons and of these, 13 noblemen had incomes of between 16,000 and 45,000 crowns. These figures later rose. In 1580 there were 11 princes, 25 dukes, 37 marquises; in 1597, 213 'titolati', consisting of 25 princes, 41 dukes, 75 marquises, 72 counts and 600 or more barons. Later one loses count altogether of this small fry. In 1594, some noblemen had incomes of between 50,000 and 100,000 ducats. How could the state, which sold patents of nobility through the intermediary of the *Sommaria*, lead the fight against its own clients?

Oppose them it did however, but never wholeheartedly. In 1538 and again later, Charles V made it known that he would not permit his feudatories in Naples to exercise the *mero* and *misto impero* unless this right was duly specified in their privileges or established by a legitimate prescription; any feudatory infringing this ruling would be charged with usurping the right of jurisdiction. The emperor also tried to rescue land owned by the community and the freedom of vassals from the goodwill and pleasure of the lords: he attempted to restrict the number of 'services' to those fixed by custom. His efforts were in vain. To the baronage everything was fair game: forests, common grazing lands, the labour of their subjects (over whom they claimed total rights: Bianchini even talks of chairs covered with human skin), the rights of the sovereign and some-times even the money due in royal taxes. Short perhaps of coining money, they were free to do as they pleased. Only their extravagance, their preference, in Naples, for living near the viceroy and in the atmosphere of the big city, their vanity and their dependence on Spain in the struggle against the Turk and the 'popular', prevented them from giving too much trouble. Add to this perhaps the fact that among them were several foreigners, Spanish or Genoese, who had acquired fiefs by paying for them.

As a class, the baronage continued to grow. The last, disastrous years of the century undoubtedly ruined more than one nobleman, particularly in the city. Pressing debts led to the sale and sequestration of property by the *Sommaria*. But these were everyday occurrences in the life of the aristocracy; in Naples and elsewhere, certain risks were attendant upon gentle birth. The nobles survived. The individual might lose everything but the nobility as a class grew and pro-spered. Looking right ahead to the dramatic years of the mid-seventeenth cen-tury, we can see, behind the picturesque images and personalities of the revolution of Naples in Masaniello's time (1647), the completion of an unequivocal social revolution, from which the reactionary class of seigneurs emerged triumphant.

The nobility had won for many years to come, and not only in Naples. It had won the battle in Milan and in Tuscany, in Genoa, Venice and Rome. There is an abundance of dossiers to choose from and each tells the same story.

The successive aristocracies of Turkey. By far the most astonishing is the dossier on the Turkish Empire. Too many western historians are inclined, when talking of Turkey, to confuse landscapes which emerged only over a period of centuries; while societies rarely progress with giant's strides, major transformations can nevertheless be accomplished with the passing of time. There were three if not four successive ruling classes in Turkey, and the last, which boldly seized power towards the end of the sixteenth century, was, so to speak, the least legitimate; it overran the totalitarian Ottoman state, weakening its fabric if it did not altogether cause its ultimate collapse.

The earliest Turkish nobility can be found by exploring the darkness of the fourteenth century; it settled in Anatolia either just before or just after the first Ottoman victories (from the capture of Bursa, 1326, to that of Adrianople, 1360). As described by historians, this ruling caste was oppressive, presenting a menacing united front, at the same time slave-owning, feudal and seignorial and yet free, too free in fact, vis-à-vis the sultan who was no more than *primus inter pares.*

The second Turkish nobility was not exclusive to the Ottoman possessions in Europe during the fifteenth century, but it is here that we have the clearest picture of it as it takes root and flourishes.

Far in advance of the rapid Turkish conquest of the Balkans, a whole society had already been brought to the point of collapse by a series of peasant revolts. Before the final assault, from the capture of Belgrade in 1521 to the invasion of Hungary (Mohács, 1526), the Hungarian peasants rose up; the Christian ruling class suppressed them but the effort proved fatal. A series of ancient feudal regimes crumbled away almost of its own accord, all long-standing regimes composed of mixed elements (Greeks, Slavs, even westerners). On the eve of conquest, the Balkans were socially comparable to the West by reason of their wealth and even in such details as the movement of nobles into towns close to their estates (an *inurbamento* as in Italy). The Musachi, a great Albanian family, settled in Durazzo, in fortified palaces similar to those of Bologna and Florence. And more than one inland city had its street of rich noblemen's dwellings, Tirnovo its *bojarska mahala*, Vidin its *bojarska ulica*, all this luxury founded on the *latifundia* and a harshly exploited peasantry. It was this system which tumbled like cardboard scenery before the Turkish advance.

In the wake of conquest came devastation, the retreat of the native populations to the forbidding mountains, but also to some extent the liberation of the peasants. They remained grouped in their communities, masters of their land, not entirely free certainly, for they were subject to taxation, from which no one was exempt, and reorganized into new seignorial estates modelled on the old, fiefs or rather benefices, the *timārs* into which the conquered territory and population were divided. The peasant still paid rent in money and rent in kind, the latter far less substantial than the former, but was now liberated from the traditional unpaid labour. The suspicions of the central government towards its feudal barons were never allayed, hence the abundance of prudent safeguard measures. From the start, the favours granted to the Christian nobility of the Balkans, who were generously provided with *timārs*, had basically no other motive.

These *timārs* were no ordinary fiefs, despite their resemblances to western feudal estates; like the latter, they consisted of villages, land both farmed and uncultivated, waterways, tolls and sometimes rights on the market of a neighbouring town, as at Kostur, a small Bulgarian town. But these domains served to maintain soldiers, horsemen, the *sipāhis* (indeed the *timārs* were often known as *sipāhiliks*). In fact they were conditional fiefs, a kind of salary, in return for which the holder was obliged to report when requisitioned, with a band of cavalry proportionate to the size of the *timār*, to the *sandjak-beg* of the province. Failure to obey the summons would mean forfeiting the *timār*. These revocable domains, granted only for life tenure, were benefices in the Carolingian sense rather than true fiefs. But from a very early time, the *timārs* began to pass from father to son, a move towards the hereditary fief rather than the benefice. From 1375, a legal provision recognized the right of succession of sons of timariots.

The third age of the Turkish nobility, after 1550–1570 approximately, was characterized by the development of the large estate though this dates from before the middle of the sixteenth century. The new element was the halting of the profitable age of Turkish conquest, and the consequent obligation felt by all nobles, of whatever standing or origin, to turn back to the peasantry and relentlessly and shamelessly to grind the faces of the poor, as money rents became worthless with the repeated devaluations of the asper. The Seray had become the source of distribution of *timārs* and it reserved them for the courtiers and servants surrounding the sultan and his ministers. This handout of fiefs went far beyond anything of the kind in the West. Letters of nobility distributed in France were nothing compared to the *fermāns* given out often twice over and shamelessly granting noble privileges even to *ecnebi*, 'outsiders' (that is those who did not belong to the ruling Ottoman class). 'Vagabonds, brigands, gypsies, Jews, Lazis, Russians and townsfolk' was how an Ottoman chronicler described what in the West would have been known as the new nobility. The days of 'ignominy' had come, and they were to be prolonged as traditional values were trampled underfoot. The money economy propelling all before it, vast estates grew up, poisonous plants against which there was no remedy. Under false names, a timariot could amass twenty or thirty domains. Lesser estates were swallowed up by larger ones and nobles demoted or threatened with demotion

231. A Greek peasant in the Ottoman
Empire. Sixteenth-century German
woodcut. *British Museum*

from their rank soon became prominent figures in the peasant uprisings of the
end of the century and the next century.

As well as the heyday of parvenu nobles, this third age ushered in the era of
usurers, of 'financiers' exploiting simultaneously state, nobility and peasants.
After 1550, the Ottoman state was in fact to resort to the old practice of selling
fiscal revenues, the system of tax-farming operated earlier by the Seldjuk Turks
and by Byzantium. It was a system already extensively practised in the West,
alike in Naples, Venice, Paris or Spain. Military service was evaded and the
checks ordered by the central government became a mockery.

On this count, the evidence of 'Ain-i 'Alī, financial Intendant of the Sultan
Ahmad, is explicit: 'Most of the feudal lords today', he wrote, 'release themselves
from their military obligations, so that on campaign, when military service is
required, from ten *tīmārs* not a man will turn up.' The warrior mentality from
which the institution had drawn its solidity was no more. Koči Beg, a native of
Korytsa in southern Albania, says as much in his writings published in 1630.
But even before this, an obscure Bosnian, Mallah Hassan Elkjadi, had sounded
a similar warning in 1596. The decadence was visible even to foreigners. In the
seventeenth century, the *sipāhis* were to leave their country residences and move

into the towns. The migration to the towns was one sign among many of the formation of an aristocracy with strong local roots, confident of its future.

The čiftliks. It seems probable that the *čiftlik* represents a new and important phenomenon. The word appears originally to have designated the acreage of land that could be ploughed in a day (a counterpart of the Byzantine *zeugarion*, the German *Morgen* or *Joch* and the *jour* or *journal* of some regions of France). It later seems to have come to mean privately owned property, whether that of the peasants or of great noblemen and finally the large estate of modern times, a sort of colonial plantation or *Gutsherrschaft*. We cannot adequately explain this evolution, but the word is certainly used in this sense after about 1609–1610.

These estates are reminiscent of the highly productive colonial plantation, or the impressive estates of the *Ostelbien* or Poland. In the centre stood the lord's manor, stone-built as in the south Albanian plain of Korytsa, and, with its tower-like appearance, typical of the *kula* or fortress-dwelling, always several storeys high, dwarfing the pitiful clay huts of the peasants. As a rule, the *čiftlik* converted the low-lying lands of the plains, the marshes between Lárisa and Volos for example, along the muddy banks of Lake Jezero or the wet river-valleys. It was a conqueror's type of farming. The *čiftliks* produced cereals, first and foremost. And cereal-growing, in Turkey as in the Danube provinces or in Poland, when linked to a huge export trade, created from the first the conditions leading to the 'new serfdom' observable in Turkey. These large estates everywhere debased the peasantry and took advantage of its debasement. At the same time, they were economically efficient, producing first wheat, then rice, before long maize, later cotton, and were from the start characterized by the use of sophisticated irrigation techniques and the spread of yoked buffalo teams. The conversion of the Balkan plains closely resembles what was taking place in the West, in the Venetias for example. These were unquestionably massive and far-reaching land improvement schemes. As in the West, large proprietors put to use the depopulated land whose possibilities had never been fully explored by previous generations of nobles and peasants. The price of progress, here as elsewhere, was clearly social oppression. Only the poor gained nothing, could hope for nothing from this progress.

2 The defection of the bourgeoisie

The bourgeoisie in the sixteenth century, committed to trade and the service of the crown, was always on the verge of disappearing. Financial ruin was not the only cause. If it grew too rich and tired of the risks inherent in commercial life, the bourgeoisie would buy offices, government bonds, titles or fiefs, succumb to the temptations, the prestige and carefree indolence of the aristocratic life. The king's service was a short cut to nobility; this course, which did not exclude

232–4. Professions and trades: *Left:* Bust of the physician Gabriele Fonseca by Bernini, in S. Lorenzo in Lucina, Rome. *Centre: The Physician Giovanni Agostino della Torre and his Son Niccolò* by Lorenzo Lotto. *National Gallery, London. Right: The Tailor* by G. B. Moroni. *National Gallery, London*

others, was one way of thinning the ranks of the bourgeoisie. The bourgeois turned class traitor the more readily since the money which distinguished rich from poor was in the sixteenth century already appearing to be an attribute of nobility. Moreover, at the turn of the century trade slumped, sending wise men back to the land as a safe investment. And land ownership was almost by definition a characteristic of the aristocracy.

'Among the principal Florentine merchants dispersed in the trading cities of Europe', writes the historian Galluzzi, 'many were those who [at the end of the sixteenth century] repatriated their fortunes to Tuscany to invest them in agriculture, such as the Corsini and the Gerini who returned from London, the Torrigiani who left Nuremberg and the Ximenez, Portuguese merchants who became Florentines' – a revealing picture of the move back to the land by wealthy merchants barely a century after Lorenzo the Magnificent. Turn the pages and in 1637, on the occasion of a new reign there emerges a different

Tuscany, one of stiff, unbending court nobles, Stendhal's Italy, foreseeable for a long time, yet still somehow shocking in the city where once beat the brave heart of the Renaissance. An old order had fallen away.

Bourgeoisies of the Mediterranean. In Spain what was vanishing had hardly existed in the first place. Insufficiently urbanized, the Peninsula was obliged to entrust essential commercial functions to intermediary groups unable to identify with the true interests of the country yet playing a vital part in the economy, as has been the case in certain South American countries, for instance in 1939. In the Middle Ages these functions had been carried out by the Jewish communities which provided merchants, moneylenders and tax-collectors. After their expulsion (1492), the gaps were filled somehow. In the towns and villages in the sixteenth century, retail trade was often handled by Moriscos, new Christians, who were frequently accused of conspiring against public safety, of trafficking in arms and of hoarding. The wholesale trade, in Burgos in particular, was often represented by converted Jews.

Such complaints, prejudices and suspicions, for lack of better evidence, would suggest that there did exist here and there a native Spanish bourgeoisie, in Seville, Burgos, Barcelona (awakened at the end of the century from its long sleep). We know of certain wealthy Spanish merchants such as the Malvenda of Burgos or Simón Ruiz of Medina del Campo.

On the other hand one cannot properly term 'bourgeois' the host of civil servants, the *letrados* in the king's service, habitually prefixing their names with a *Don*, lesser nobles or aspirant nobles far more than true bourgeois. It is remarkable in that most remarkable of countries, Spain, to find even the illegitimate sons of the clergy acquiring the title of *hidalgo*. Not so remarkable after all perhaps, if one remembers the dishonour attached in Spain to manual work

235. An Armenian merchant of Constantinople.
Sixteenth-century French woodcut.

and trade, and the innumerable violations of the fragile borderline between the very minor nobility and commoners: of the seven hundred *hidalgos* in a modest town near the Portuguese frontier, perhaps three hundred are genuine, says a remonstrance of 1651, not to mention the *hidalgos de gotera* (gutter aristocracy) and the fathers of twelve children, who were granted fiscal exemption without being noble and were vulgarly known as *hidalgos de bragueta* (codpiece aristocracy). In Spain, the bourgeoisie was hemmed in on all sides by a fast-multiplying and fast-encroaching nobility.

In Turkey the urban bourgeoisie – essentially a merchant class – was foreign to Islam: Ragusan, Armenian, Jewish, Greek and western. In Galata and on the islands there still survived pockets of Latin culture. Symptomatic of change here is the rapid decline of those who had once been the great merchants of the empire – the Venetians, Genoese and Ragusans. Two foreign businessmen were prominent in the sultan's entourage: one, Michael Cantacuzenus, was a Greek, the other, Micas, a Jew. Iberian Jews, both Spanish and Portuguese, immigrants at the end of the fifteenth century, gradually came to occupy leading positions in trade (especially the Portuguese), in Cairo, Alexandria, Aleppo, Tripoli in Syria, Salonica, Constantinople. They were prominent among the tax-farmers (and even the bureaucrats) of the empire. How many times does one find the Venetians complaining of the bad faith of the Jews who retailed Venetian merchandise! Soon, no longer content with the role of retailers, they were to enter into direct competition with the Ragusans and Venetians. Already in the sixteenth century, they were handling a large seaborne trade with Messina, Ragusa, Ancona, and Venice. One of the most profitable ventures of Christian pirates in the Levant became the search of Venetian, Ragusan or Marseillais vessels, for Jewish merchandise, the *ropa de judios* as the Spanish called it, likening it to contraband, a convenient pretext for the arbitrary confiscation of goods. And the Jews themselves soon met competition from the Armenians who, in the seventeenth century, began to freight ships for the West, travelled there themselves and became the agents of the commercial expansion of the Shah 'Abbās. These men were the successors, in the Levant, of that rich Italian merchant bourgeoisie which once controlled the entire Mediterranean.

In Italy itself, the situation was complex. Once more the heart of the problem lies here, where once had flourished the vital bourgeoisies and their cities. The splendour of Florence in the days of Lorenzo the Magnificent coincided with the heyday of an opulent and cultivated higher bourgeoisie, lending confirmation to Hermann Hefele's theory of the Renaissance, as a coincidence of an intellectual and artistic explosion and a powerful movement towards social change from which Florence emerged an altered and more open society. The Florentine Renaissance represents the achievement of a bourgeois order: that of the *Arti Maggiori* which both controlled the avenues of power, disdaining none of the necessary tasks of commerce, industry and banking, and also paid homage to the refinements of luxury, intelligence and art. As a class it lives again before

236, 237. A triumphant bourgeois dynasty: *Left: Portrait of Lorenzo the Magnificent* by Giorgio Vasari. *Uffizi, Florence. Below: Portrait of Cosimo de' Medici* by Bronzino. *Galleria Borghese, Rome*

our eyes, through the work of the painters it befriended, in that series of portraits in Florence which is sufficient witness in itself to a bourgeoisie at the height of its power. But a few steps in the Uffizi take the visitor to Bronzino's portrait of Cosimo de' Medici in his long red robe: another age with its princes and court nobles. However a Spanish merchant living in Florence could still write in March, 1572: 'in this city, by an ancient tradition, merchants are held in high regard.' It is true that he was speaking of the highest category of merchants, the *hombres de negocios*, many of whom were in fact nobles. To make the transformation complete, these men had only to abandon their commercial activities and live, as was perfectly possible, off their land and revenues.

Elsewhere too the scene was changing. In 1528, Genoa received the aristocratic constitution which was to last until the troubles of 1575–1576. In Venice, the merchant aristocracy at the end of the century resolutely turned its back on trade. In central and southern Italy the trend was very similar. In Rome the bourgeoisie received its chastening in 1527. In Naples the only refuge left for it was the practice of law: chicanery was now to be its bread and butter. Everywhere its role was being curtailed. In Lentini in Sicily, the town magistrates were recruited exclusively from the nobility. So we need not imagine that there was a fight to the death between the lords and the domanial towns in Sicily. Even when the towns were still controlled by their bourgeoisie, and this was rare, the latter were only too ready to compromise with the nobles and their clientele.

The defection of the bourgeoisie. If the social order seems to have been modified, the change was sometimes more apparent than real. The bourgeoisie was not always pushed out, brutally liquidated. It turned class traitor.

Everywhere, rich bourgeois of every origin were irresistibly drawn towards the aristocracy as if towards the sun. One can see from their correspondence the curious attitudes of Simón Ruiz and Baltasar Suárez towards those who lived like gentlemen and sponged on occasions off these prudent and thrifty merchants. The chief ambition of these pseudo-bourgeois was to reach the ranks of the aristocracy, to be absorbed into it, or at the very least to marry their richly-dowered daughters to a nobleman.

From the beginning of the century at Milan, *mésalliances*, although always giving rise to scandal, were no less frequent for that. And our informant, Bandello, for all his liberal opinions, expresses his indigation. He writes for instance of a noblewoman, who having married a merchant of undistinguished ancestry, on her husband's death makes her son withdraw from his father's business and tries, by removing him from the world of commerce, to have him reinstated to noble rank. Such conduct did not invite ridicule; at the time it was considered perfectly acceptable behaviour. On the other hand much spiteful fun was poked at a whole series of unequal matches, shameful blots on illustrious escutcheons which were nevertheless restored to their former financial glory by them. A relative of Azzo Vesconte marries the daughter of a butcher, with a dowry of

12,000 ducats. The narrator does not wish to attend the marriage: 'I have seen the bride's father', he writes, 'in his white smock, as is the habit of our butchers, bleeding a calf, his arms red with blood up to the elbow . . . For myself if I were to take such a woman to wife, it would seem to me ever afterwards that I stank of the butcher's shop. I do not think I would ever be able to hold up my head again.' And alas, it is not an isolated case: a Marescotto has taken to wife the daughter of a gardener (at least he has the excuse of being in love with her); and Count Lodovico, one of the Borromeo counts, a great feudal family of the empire, has married the daughter of a baker; the Marquis of Saluzzo has wed a simple peasant girl. Love perhaps, money certainly, multiplied such unequal matches. 'I have heard it several times said', continues the narrator, 'by Count Andrea Mandello di Caorsi, that if a woman had but a dowry of over 4000 ducats, one might marry her without hesitation, even if she were one of the women who sell their bodies behind the cathedral in Milan. Believe me, the man who has money and plenty of it is noble; the man who is poor is not.'

In Spain, dramatic situations could always result from tragic preoccupations with honour and dishonour. Crimes against *limpieza de la sangre* (purity of the blood) committed in the very highest society, marriages to the daughters of rich *marranos* (converted Jews), the everyday drama of a match across class barriers, took on a tragic aspect in this rank-conscious country. But they existed none the less.

Nobility for sale. Hardly a state in the sixteenth century, hardly a prince, did not trade patents of nobility for cash. In Sicily after 1600, marquisates, counties and principalities were put up for sale, at low prices and to all comers, whereas until then only rarely had titles been conceded. The age of false money was also the age of false titles. In Naples, according to a long Spanish report written in about 1600, the number of title-holders, *titolati*, had increased out of all measure. And like all goods in plentiful supply, the titles had depreciated, if not those of counts at least those of marquises. There had even been 'created several dukes and princes who could have been done without'. So nobility was on the market everywhere, in Rome, Milan, in the empire, in the Franche-Comté, in France, in Poland, even in Transylvania, where there were any number of 'parchment gentlemen'. In Portugal, concessions had begun in the fifteenth century in imitation of the English. The first dukes appeared in 1415, the first marquis in 1451, the first baron in 1475. Even in Spain, the crown, which soon began increasing the number of grandees, was quite undiscriminating at lower levels.

It has been said that the fashion – soon to become a mania – for titles originated in Spain, that she exported it along with tight-fitting clothes for men, *bigotes*, perfumed gloves and the themes of her comedies. But the new fashion was more than mere vanity. The bourgeoisie knew what it was doing and no small measure of calculation entered into its purchases. It turned to land as a prime safe investment, thus reinforcing a social order based on aristocratic

238. The *noblesse de l'épée*. A Spaniard and his servant
at the harbour in Seville. Early seventeenth-century
French print.

privilege. In short, as with states so with men, quarrels of precedence often
masked extremely precise and down-to-earth claims. But at first sight, vanity
alone struck the observer.

'It is at present impossible,' writes Montchrestien of his native France in
1615, 'to distinguish men by their appearance. The shopkeeper dresses like a
gentleman. Moreover who can fail to see that this conformity of apparel intro-
duces corruption to our old discipline? . . . Insolence will increase in the cities
and tyranny in the fields. Men will grow effeminate with too many luxuries,
and women, in their desire to parade themselves, will neglect both their chastity
and their households,' an outburst worthy of a preacher, but it testifies to an
age, in France at least, of discontent with the existing social order.

Hostility to the new nobles. As several quotations have already indicated, no
one applauded the fortune of the new nobles. Any pretext would do to pick a
quarrel with them; no opportunity to humiliate them was passed by. An incident
at Naples illustrates it well: a financier of the city, extremely rich but of humble
birth, Bartolomeo d'Aquino, sought in 1640, with the approval of the viceroy

himself, to marry Anna Acquaviva, sister of the Duke of Conversano. The bride-to-be was carried off by a band of armed horsemen belonging to the nobility, determined to prevent by force that 'a mano di vile uomo la gentil giovina pervenisse'. She was taken to a convent at Benevento where she was doubly safe since Benevento was a papal possession. Similar incidents abound in chroniclers' accounts but they had no effect on a growing trend. With the exception of the Venetian aristocracy, which barricaded itself behind locked doors, all the aristocracies of Europe could be penetrated by outsiders, all received an infusion of new blood. In Rome, seat of the Church (and undoubtedly the most liberal of all western societies), the Roman nobility advanced along this path even more quickly than any other, through the regular promotion to the nobility and indeed to the high nobility, of the relations of each new Pope, who was not necessarily himself of illustrious extraction. All aristocracies were moving with the times, shedding a certain amount of dead wood and accepting the new rich, who brought solid wealth to prop up the social edifice. It put the nobility at a great advantage. Instead of having to struggle against the Third Estate, it found the latter only too eager to join it, and to part with its wealth in order to do so.

This continuing trend could of course be hastened. In Rome, the papacy contributed to the rejuvenation of the nobility. In France, two series of wars, the first terminated by the treaty of Cateau-Cambrésis (1st–3rd April, 1559) and the second by the peace of Vervins (2nd May, 1598), hastened the collapse of the old nobility and cleared the way towards social power for the new rich.

3 Poverty and banditry

Of the life of the poor, history gives us few glimpses, but the little that is recorded had its own way of compelling the attention of the powers of the day, and through them reaches us. Uprisings, riots and disturbances, the alarming spread of 'vagabonds and vagrants', increasing attacks by bandits, the sounds of violence, although frequently muffled, all tell us something about the extraordinary rise of poverty towards the end of the sixteenth century, which was to become even more marked in the next.

The lowest point in this collective distress can probably be located in about 1650. So at any rate it appears from the unpublished journal of G. Baldinucci to which I have already referred more than once. Poverty was such in Florence in April, 1650 that it was impossible to hear Mass *in pace*, so much was one importuned during the service by wretched people, 'naked and covered with sores', 'ignudi et pieni di scabbia'. Prices in the city were terrifyingly high and 'the looms stand idle'; on the Monday of Carnival week, to crown the misfortunes of the townsfolk, a storm destroyed the olive trees as well as mulberry and other fruit-trees.

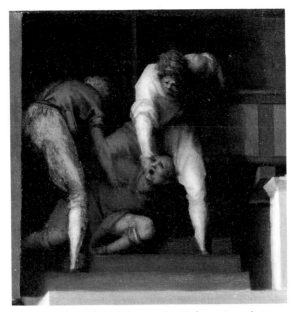

239. Everyday violence: detail from *Joseph in Egypt* by Pontormo. *National Gallery, London*

Unfinished revolutions. Pauperization and oppression by the rich and powerful went hand in hand. The result was not far to seek. And the underlying cause is also clear to see: the correlation between over-population and economic depression, an unrelieved double burden which dictated social conditions.

By contrast with the north of Europe, where so-called wars of religion masked a series of social revolutions, the Mediterranean in the sixteenth century, although hot-blooded enough, for some reason never managed to bring off a successful revolution. It was not for want of trying. But the Mediterranean seems to have been the victim of some spell. Was it because the cities were overthrown so early that the strong state was irresistibly led to assume the function of keeper of the peace? The result in any case is plain to see. It is possible to imagine a huge book recording the succession of riots, disturbances, assassinations, reprisals and revolts in the Mediterranean, the story of a perpetual and multiple social tension. But there is no final cataclysm. A history of revolution in the Mediterranean might run to many pages, but the chapters would be disconnected and the basic conception of the book is after all questionable – the very title is misleading.

For these disturbances broke out regularly, annually, daily even, like mere traffic accidents which no one any longer thought worth attention, neither principals nor victims, witnesses nor chroniclers, not even the states themselves. It is as if everyone had resigned himself to these endemic troubles, whether the banditry occurred in Catalonia or in Calabria or the Abruzzi. And for every recorded incident, ten or a hundred are unknown to us and some of them will never be known. Even the most important are so minor, so obscure and so difficult to interpret. What exactly was the revolt of Terranova in Sicily in 1516? What was the real significance of the so-called Protestant rebellion in Naples in 1561–1562, the occasion of a punitive expedition sent out by the Spanish authorities against the Vaudois of the Calabrian mountains, when several hundred men were left with their throats cut like animals? Or even of the war of Corsica (1564–1569) from start to finish, and the war of Granada towards the end, both of them disintegrating into indecisive episodes, wars of poverty rather than of foreign or religious significance? And how much is known about the troubles in Palermo in 1560, or the 'Protestant' conspiracies of Mantua in 1569? In 1571, the subjects of the Duke of Urbino rose up against the oppressive demands of their overlord, Francesco Maria, but this little-known episode remains hard to explain: the Duchy of Urbino was a land of mercenary soldiers, so whose was the hidden hand? The internal crisis of Genoa in 1575–1576 is hardly clearer. In Provence in 1579, the *jacquerie* of insurgent peasants – the *Razas* – their capture of the chateau of Villeneuve and massacre of the local landlord, Claude de Villeneuve, is swallowed up in the confused history of the Wars of Religion, like so many other social disorders, like the *jacquerie* of 1580 in the Dauphiné, Protestant but democratic too, inspired by the example of the Swiss Cantons and directed against the nobility. It is comparable to the revolutionary and destructive outbursts of the Protestants in Gascony, a few years earlier in the time of Monluc, or the troubles, many years later far away in the Cotentin (1587). So too is the revolt in 1590 of the Aragonese peasants of the county of Ribagorza, as a result of which they were eventually incorporated into the crown domains. The previous year, the subjects of the Duke of Piombino, on the Tuscan coast, had also rebelled. The Calabrian insurrection, the occasion of Campanella's arrest in 1599, was no more than a trivial incident magnified. Equally numerous were the revolts throughout the Turkish Empire during the years 1590–1600, not to mention the endemic unrest among the Arabs and nomads of North Africa and Egypt, the disturbing uprisings of the 'Black Scribe' and his followers in Asia Minor, on which Christendom was to pin such wild hopes; the rioting among the Serbian peasants in 1594 in the Banat district of what is today Hungary, in 1595 in Bosnia and Herzegovina and again in 1597 in Herzegovina. If to this very incomplete list we add the fantastic wealth of incidents relating to brigandage, what we shall have is not so much a book as a huge collection of reports.

So it seems at first sight certainly: but are these incidents and accidents, a mere scatter of events, the surface signs of a valid social history which, lacking any other means of expression, is forced to communicate in this confusing, clumsy, sometimes misleading language? Is this evidence meaningful at some deeper level? That is the historian's problem. To answer yes, as I intend to do, means being willing to see correlations, regular patterns and general trends where at first sight there appears only incoherence, anarchy, a series of unrelated happenings. It means accepting for instance that Naples, 'where there are rob-beries and crossed swords [every day] as soon as darkness falls', was the theatre of a perpetual social war, something going far beyond the limits of ordinary crime. It was a social war and was therefore waged both cruelly and cheaply, using pre-existent conflicts and passions.

Cruelty: all the incidents mentioned above also bear the marks of relentless cruelty on both sides. The rural crimes which began around Venice with the coming of the century, were as pitiless as was the repression which followed. Inevitably the chroniclers, or those who inscribed these events on public records, were opposed to the trouble-makers who are regularly painted in the blackest colours. In the Crema region, during the winter of 1506–1507, a band broke into the house of a certain Caterina de Revoglara and 'per vim ingressi, fractibus foribus, ipsam violaverunt et cum ea rem contra naturam habuere', relates the scribe of the Senate. In all these reports, the imperfectly identified enemy is guilty before being tried. These men are *ladri*, of a 'malignity and an iniquity ever increasing', they are blackguards, especially the peasants who, one day in winter 1507 failed to kill the patrician Leonardo Mauroceno in his country residence but took their revenge on his orchards. As the years go by, the tone of the documents hardly alters at all. An *avviso* dated the end of September, 1585 impassively reports: 'This year in Rome, we have seen more heads [of bandits] on the Ponte Sant'Angelo than melons on the market place.' This sets the tone of a kind of journalism still in its infancy. When a celebrated brigand chief, the Sienese Alfonso Piccolomini, was betrayed and captured by the agents of the Grand Duke of Tuscany on 5th January, 1591, then on 16th March hanged 'al faro solito del palagio del Podesta', every opportunity was taken to demean his miserable end, by insinuating that the bandit 'si lasció vilmente far prigione', without offering resistance. Such venom in the written word, such cruelty, both in the acts committed and the reprisals they drew, place the seal of authenticity on these scattered happenings, make them meaningful episodes in the endless subterranean revolution which marked the whole of the sixteenth century and then the whole of the seventeenth.

Class struggle? Can we call it a class struggle? After all, we historians are forever using terms we have invented ourselves, *feudalism, bourgeoisie, capitalism,* with-out always keeping an exact record of the disparate realities such terms may cover in different centuries. If by *class struggle* we simply mean the fratricidal vengeance, the lies, and one-sided justice which appear from this record, why not use it? But if the term implies, as I think it must, some degree of conscious-ness, while a class struggle may be apparent to the historian, he must remember that he is looking at this bygone age with twentieth century eyes: it did not seem nearly so obvious to the men of the sixteenth century who were certainly far from lucid on this point.

The examples noted by a single historian in the course of his personal

240. Everyday poverty: *A Crowd of Peasants.* Drawing
by Guercino. *Royal Library, Windsor Castle*

research necessarily constitute an inadequate sample: I have found a few glim-
merings of class-consciousness only during the first half of the sixteenth century.
There are for instance the astonishing words of Bayard (or of the Loyal Serviteur)
before besieged Padua in 1509. Bayard did not agree with the Emperor Maximilian's request that the French *gendarmerie* be dismounted and put alongside the
Landsknechte to force the breach: 'Does the Emperor think it a reasonable thing
to put so many nobles in peril and danger along with foot-soldiers, one of whom
may be a shoemaker, another a smith, another a baker, and rough mechanicals
who do not hold their honour as dear as does a gentleman?' Or the report of
nobeli taking up arms *contra li villani* in October, 1525 in Friuli, which had
been infected by the German peasants' revolt; or, in December, 1528, the peasants near Aquila in the Abruzzi, who, dying of starvation and anger, tried to
rise up against the 'traitors' and 'tyrants' to the cry of *Viva la povertà!* without
apparently being sure (according to the suspect account of the chronicler) who
exactly were the tyrants to be punished; or in Lucca in 1531–1532, the insurrec-

tion known as that of the *Straccioni* (the ragged men) which is described as a 'battaglia di popolo contro la nobiltà'. After that, there is nothing, at least as far as I know. So if this extremely scanty survey proves anything, it is that between the first and the second half of the century there was a decline in lucidity or if we are prepared to use the term, in revolutionary consciousness, without which there can be no significant revolution with a serious chance of success.

And indeed the earlier part of the century, the spring whose flowering was brought to a close by the harsh years 1540–1560, seems to have been particularly restless: the *Comuneros* in 1521, the *Germanias* of Valencia in 1525–1526; the uprisings in Florence, the crisis in Genoa in 1528; the peasant rebellion in Guyenne in 1548. Much, much later, in the seventeenth century, were to come the internal revolts of the Ottoman Empire, the French disturbances studied by Porchnev, the secession of Catalonia and Portugal, the great rebellion of Naples in 1647, the Messina uprising of 1674. Between these two series of conspicuous social disturbances, the long half-century from 1550 to 1600 (or even to 1620

241. The Naples revolt of 1647: *The Killing of Don G. Carafa* by M. Spadaro. Carafa was killed on the orders of Masaniello. *Museo di Capodimonte, Naples*

or 1630) comes off rather poorly for revolutions, which hardly ever seem to reach boiling point and have to be divined like underground streams. In fact, and this makes the historian's task more difficult, these revolts and revolutions were not directed exclusively against the privileged orders but also against the state, the protector of the rich and pitiless collector of taxes, the state which was itself both social reality and social edifice. The keeper of the peace held his own, although often beaten, often derided and inefficient – and more often still an accomplice in crime.

Against vagrants and vagabonds. In the cities there now began to appear that silent and persistent expression of poverty, the 'vagrants and vagabonds' as they were called by the Consuls and Magistrates of Marseilles, who decided in a council meeting of 2nd January, 1566, to proceed to all quarters of the city and expel these undesirables. It would not have seemed an inhuman decision to the spirit of the times. Towns were obliged to act as their own watchmen and for their own good periodically to drive out the poor: beggars, madmen, genuine or simulated cripples, men without occupation who gathered in public squares, taverns and round the doors of convents where soup was distributed. Expelled, they would return, or others would arrive in their place. The expulsions, gestures of rage, are a measure of the impotence of the respectable towns in the face of this constant invasion.

In Spain, vagrants cluttered the roads, stopping at every town: students breaking bounds and forsaking their tutors to join the swelling ranks of *picardia*, adventurers of every hue, beggars and cutpurses. They had their favourite towns and within them their headquarters: San Lucar de Barrameda, near Seville; the Slaughterhouse in Seville itself; the Puerta del Sol in Madrid. The *mendigos* formed a brotherhood, a state with its own *ferias*, and sometimes met together in huge gatherings. Along the roads to Madrid moved a steady procession of poor travellers, civil servants without posts, captains without companies, humble folk in search of work, trudging behind a donkey with empty saddle bags, all faint with hunger and hoping that someone, in the capital, would settle their fate. Into Seville streamed the hungry crowd of emigrants to America, impoverished gentlemen hoping to restore their family fortunes, soldiers seeking adventure, young men of no property hoping to make good, and along with them the dregs of Spanish society, branded thieves, bandits, tramps, all hoping to find some lucrative activity overseas, debtors fleeing pressing creditors and husbands fleeing nagging wives. To all of them, the Indies represented the promised land, 'the refuge and protection of all the *desperados* of Spain, the church of rebels and sanctuary of murderers': so says Cervantes at the beginning of one of his most delightful tales, *El celoso extremeño*, the story of one of these returned travellers from the Indies, now rich, who invests his money, buys a house, settles down to a respectable living and, alas, takes a wife.

Habitual wayfarers too were the soldiers, old timers and new recruits,

242–5. Four beggars by Jacques Callot.
Paris, 1629.

picaresque characters whose life of wandering and chance encounters might lead them to ruin in the fleshpots, the *casas de carne*, perhaps accompanied on the road by some submissive camp follower. One fine day they might follow the recruiter's drum and find themselves embarking, at Málaga or some other port, in a crowd where raw youths rubbed shoulders with old soldiers, deserters, murderers, priests and prostitutes, setting sail on the orders of the administration, for the fair land of Italy or the living prison of the African *presidios*. Among the crowds passing up the gangway were a few honest men, such as Diego Suárez, who as a young man had travelled from master to master across the whole of Spain, from Oviedo to Cartagena, where he embarked for Oran in 1575: he was to stay there a third of a century, proof that it was a great deal easier to get into the African barracks than it was to get out of them.

A universal danger, vagrancy in Spain was a threat to both town and countryside. Vagrants and bandits were brothers in hardship and might change places. To expel the poor from one place was merely to drive them to another. Unless, that is, one followed the example of Seville. In October, 1581, all vagabonds rounded up in a police raid were forcibly embarked on Sotomayor's ships, bound for the Strait of Magellan. It was intended that on arrival they should work as labourers, *guastatori*, but four vessels foundered and one thousand men were drowned.

All these incidents raise the question of the urban underworld: every town had its *Cour des Miracles*. From *Rinconete y Cortadillo*, that hardly 'exemplary' novel, we can, with the aid of scholarly commentaries, discover a great deal about the Sevilian underworld: the prostitutes, merry widows, double-crossing alguazils, genuine wanders, the true *pícaros* of literature, the *peruleros*, comic dupes – they are all there. And it was just the same elsewhere, in Madrid or Paris. Italy was completely overrun with delinquents, vagabonds and beggars, all characters destined for literary fame. Forever being expelled, they always came back. Only the statutory authorities ever believed in the efficacy of official measures – which always took the same unvarying course.

At Palermo, in February, 1590, energetic measures were taken against the 'vagabonds, drunkards and spies of this kingdom'. Two incorruptible proctors, with a salary of 200 crowns, were to divide the town between them. Their task was to pursue this lazy, good-for-nothing fraternity which spent workdays gambling, wallowing in all the vices, 'destroying their goods and what is more their souls'. Gamble they certainly did – but then so did everyone else. Anything served as a pretext for a wager and not only card-games: at Palermo there were wagers on the price of wheat, the sex of unborn children and, as everywhere else, on the number of cardinals to be named by the Holy Father. In a packet of commercial correspondence at Venice, I once found a lottery ticket left behind by accident. In their battle against the alliance of wine, gaming and idleness, the Palermo authorities ordered police raids on inns, *fonduks*, taverns and furnished rooms and inquiries into the suspicious persons who frequented them. Their place of origin, nationality and source of income were all to be investigated.

This game of cops and robbers, of respectable township versus vagrant, had no beginning and no end: it was a continuous spectacle, a 'structure' of the times. After a raid, things would be quiet for a while, then thefts, attacks on passers-by and murders would begin to increase once more.

It would be interesting to tabulate all these expulsion orders to see whether they are interconnected like the dates of the trade fairs; where did they come from, the vagabonds whom the towns hurriedly set back on the road, and where did they go? They arrived in Venice from as far away as Piedmont. In March, 1545, over 6000 'di molte natione' beleaguered the city. Some returned to their native villages, others took boat; the rest were expelled since they were wastrels and idlers from Piedmont and other foreign cities and places. Five years earlier, in 1540, a year of great hunger, the city had been invaded by a throng of unfortunate family men, who arrived by boat with their wives and children and took up residence under the bridges, along the banks of the canals.

Soon the problem of the poor had progressed beyond the narrow confines of the unsympathetic towns, reaching nation-wide and European dimensions. By the beginning of the seventeenth century, men like Montchrestien were aghast at the swelling of the ranks of the needy; if he and others in France like him were 'colonialist', it was in order to find a way to be rid of this silent and terrifying army of proletarians. Throughout Europe, too densely populated for its resources and no longer riding a wave of economic growth, indeed even in Turkey, the trend was towards the pauperization of considerable masses of people in desperate need of daily bread. This was the humanity which was about to plunge into the horrors of the Thirty Years' War, pitilessly drawn by Callot and only too accurately chronicled by Grimmelshausen.

Brigands everywhere. But police records of city life pale beside the blood-stained history of banditry in the Mediterranean, banditry on land that is, the counter-part of piracy on sea, with which it had many affinities. Like piracy and just as much as piracy, it was a long established pattern of behaviour in the Mediter-ranean. Its origins are lost in the mists of time. From the time when the sea first harboured coherent societies, banditry appeared, never to be eliminated. Even today it is very much alive. In different ages, brigandage might change its name or the form it took, but *malandrini, masnadieri, ladri, fuorusciti, banditi (masna-dieri* were originally mercenary soldiers, *fuorusciti* and *banditi* outlaws) – they were all brigands, or as we should call them, misfits, rebels against society.

No region of the Mediterranean was free from the scourge. Catalonia, Cal-abria and Albania, all notorious regions in this respect, by no means had a monopoly of brigandage. When the sultan's army marched along the Stambul road to Adrianople, Niš, Belgrade and on into Hungary, it left behind along the roadside scores of hanged brigands whom it had disturbed in their lairs. There were brigands and brigands of course. Their presence on the main highway of the Turkish Empire, famed for its security, is sober evidence of the quality of public safety in the sixteenth century.

At the other end of the Mediterranean, in Spain, the scene is the same. It is quite unthinkable, writes a Florentine in 1567, to take the post between Barcelona and Saragossa. Beyond Saragossa yes, but not between these two cities. His solution was to join a caravan of armed noblemen. And yet through Barcelona ran one of the major routes of imperial Spain, her main line of communication with the Mediterranean and Europe. It frequently happened that official couriers were robbed or even failed to get through, as was the case in June, 1565, the very year that the route from Madrid to Burgos, Spain's other main artery towards Europe and the Ocean, was closed as a result of plague. Here stands revealed one of the thousand weak points in the unwieldy Spanish Empire. But there were as many *bandouliers* in Languedoc as there were *bandoleros* in Catalonia. All the farms in the Lower Rhône valley were fortified houses like the peasant fortresses of Catalonia we have already mentioned. In Portugal, Valencia, even in Venice, throughout Italy and in every corner of the Ottoman Empire, robber bands, states in miniature with the great advantage of mobility, could pass unobtrusively from the Catalan Pyrenees to Granada, or from Albania to the Black Sea: these tiny forces irritated established states and in the end wore them down. Like the guerrilla forces of modern popular wars, they invariably had the people on their side.

Between 1550 and 1600, then, the Mediterranean was consumed by this agile, cruel, everyday war, a war hardly noticed by traditional historians.

Banditry and the state. Banditry was in the first place a revenge upon established states, the defenders of a political and even social order. 'These brigands were the opposition to the vile governments which in Italy took the place of the medieval Republics.' Thus Stendhal. As it happened, his judgement was based on the evidence before his own eyes, for banditry was still flourishing in Italy in his lifetime. 'Even in our own day,' he writes, 'everyone certainly dreads an encounter with brigands; but when they are caught and punished, everyone is sorry for them. The fact is that this people, so shrewd, so cynical, which laughs at everything published under the official censorship of its masters, finds its favourite reading in the little poems which narrate with ardour the lives of the most renowned brigands. The heroic element that it finds in these stories thrills the artistic vein that still survives in the masses . . . in their heart of hearts, the people were for them, and the village girls preferred to all the rest the boy who once in his life had been obliged *andare alla macchia*, to flee to the woods.' Spain, particularly Andalusia, notes Théophile Gautier, 'has remained Arab on this count and bandits are easily elevated into heroes'. Yugoslav and Romanian folklore too is full of stories of *haiduks* and outlaws. A form of vengeance upon the ruling class and its lopsided justice, banditry has been at all times, more or less everywhere, a righter of wrongs. Within living memory, a Calabrian brigand

246. The author beset by six murderers in Moldavia. Print from William Lithgow,
Rare Adventures, 1623.

'defended himself before the Court of Assizes by claiming to be a Robin Hood,
robbing the rich to pay the poor. He told his rosary every day and village priests
used to give him their blessing. In order to accomplish his private social justice,
he had by the age of thirty already killed about thirty people.'

Bandits and nobles. Sea-pirates were aided and abetted by powerful towns and
cities. Pirates on land, bandits, received regular backing from nobles. Robber
bands were often led, or more or less closely directed, by some genuine nobleman: Count Ottavio Avogadro for instance, whom a French correspondent in

Venice reported as operating with his band against the Venetians in June, 1583. 'Count Ottavio, Sire, continues to trouble the lords of Sanguene, to which place, since I last wrote to Your Majesty, he has twice returned and burned several houses in the Veronese.' The Venetians pursued him and arranged that Ferrara and Mantua, where he usually took refuge, close their gates to him. But they never caught him: two years later he reappeared at the Court of Ferdinand of Tyrol. Among the bands roaming the Papal States, the rendezvous of thieves and murderers from both northern and southern Italy, not to mention indigenous bandits who were legion, another noble brigand and one of the most desperate in the time of Gregory XIII, was the Duke of Montemarciano, Alfonso Piccolomini, whom we have already met. His life was saved *in extremis* by the Grand Duke of Tuscany, who had for some time been the unseen hand manipulating this curious character. Alfonso, escaping with his life, fled to France – where he found regular war very different from guerrilla war and not at all to the taste of a leader of *masnadieri*, so he was soon lending an ear to invitations and promises and before long he was back in Italy, in Tuscany this time, operating, imprudently and ungratefully, against the grand duke. From his lair in the mountains of Pistoia, far from the fortresses and garrisons, he was in a position to 'sollevare i popoli' to carry out 'delle scorrerie', all the more so since where he was that year, 1590, a very poor year for the wheat harvest, 'la miseria potea più facilmente indurre gli uomini a tentare di variar condizone', extraordinarily clairvoyant words. With the arrival in the heart of Tuscany of this trouble-maker, the worst might be feared, particularly since he was in touch with the Spanish *presidios* and all the enemies of the *Casa Medici*. If he moved into Siena and its Maremma, there could be real trouble. However, his bands of men, who were unskilled at strategic warfare, failed to capture any key-positions, fell back before the guards of Tuscany or Rome and the prince had the last word. On 16th March, 1591, Piccolomini was executed at Florence. Thus ended a curious domestic war, watched with attention by the outside world, for the threads of the plot led back to some very distant hands, some to the Escorial, others to Lesdiguières in the Dauphiné.

These are famous cases where international politics intrude. Humbler examples would suit our purpose better, but they are the least easy to discover. There were undoubtedly however connections between the Catalan nobility and brigandage in the Pyrenees, between the Neapolitan or Sicilian nobility and banditry in southern Italy, between the *signori* and *signorotti* of the Papal States and the brigands round Rome. The nobility played its part everywhere, whether politically or socially. Money was the key: the aristocracy was often economically unsound. Impoverished gentlemen, some ruined, others the younger sons of families of small fortune, were very often the leaders of this disguised social war, a never-ending, 'hydra-headed' conflict. They were driven to make a living from adventure and rapine, driven (as La Noue said of France where the spectacle was the same) 'à la désespérade', to desperate means. The same social

247. Votive picture of Stefan Praun, a Nuremberg merchant, escaping from an attack by Venetian mercenaries on Lake Garda. Workshop of Paul Lautensack, Bamberg, 1511.
Germanisches Nationalmuseum, Nuremberg

mechanism can frequently be seen at work, in much later times. In the eighteenth century, Turkey had a problem with a nobility too numerous to be rich, the *Krjalis* of Bulgaria. In Brazil at the beginning of the nineteenth century, bandits were the henchmen, the *cabras*, of wealthy landowners, all threatened to some extent by modern development and obliged to defend themselves.

But we should beware of making the picture too simple. A many-sided and complex affair, brigandage, while serving the interests of certain nobles, might be directed against others: as is illustrated by the exploits in Lombardy of Alexio Bertholoti, 'a notorious bandit and rebel against the Marquis of Castellon'. On 17th August, 1597, with over 200 men, he scaled the walls of the castle of Solferino, and seized the marquis' mother and his son, a boy of thirteen. He took the prisoners to Castellon where he tried to make the old marquessa open the doors, in the hope of capturing the marquis himself, but in vain. When she refused he savagely wounded her, killed the child then went on a rampage of looting and 'barbaric cruelty' according to the report made by the governor of Milan.

Banditry had other origins besides the crisis in noble fortunes: it issued from peasantry and people alike. This was a groundswell, 'a flood tide' as an eighteenth-century historian called it, which stirred up a variety of waters. As a political and social (though not religious) reaction, it had both aristocratic and popular components (the 'mountain kings' in the Roman Campagna and around Naples were more often than not peasants and humble folk). We hear in a Florentine diary of 1591 of a Pope elected by the *banditti* of the Forli region, one Giacomo Galli: they obeyed him as if he were the Holy Father himself. He was later hanged wearing a golden hat. The anecdote is as much political as religious. There are no other recorded details of the kind. The partisans of order certainly accused bandits of violating both divine and human laws, but that was no more than a manner of speaking. It was a latent form of the *jacquerie*, or peasant revolt, the product of poverty and overpopulation; a revival of old traditions, often of brigandage in its 'pure' state of savage conflict between man and man. But we should beware of reducing it merely to this last aspect, the one most stressed by the rich and powerful who trembled for their possessions, their positions and their lives.

All the same, even allowing for exaggeration, can so much brutality be entirely passed over? It is true that human life was not valued highly in the sixteenth century. The career of Alonso de Contreras, as narrated by himself, one of the finest picaresque novels ever written, because it is true, contains at least ten murders. Benvenuto Cellini's escapades would have taken him to prison or to the scaffold in modern times. From these models, we may imagine the scruples of men whose profession was to kill. And then there are the remarks attributed to Charles V on the occasion of the siege of Metz, by Ambroise Paré, physician to the besieged. 'The Emperor asked what manner of people were dying, whether they were gentlemen and men of note; he was told that they were all poor soldiers. Then he said it was no harm if they died, comparing them to caterpillars, insects and grubs which eat buds and other fruits of the earth and that if they were men of property they would not be in his camp for six *livres* a month.'

The increase in banditry. By the end of the sixteenth century at any rate, banditry was on the increase. Italy, a mosaic of states, was a brigands' paradise: driven out of one place, they would take refuge somewhere else, reappear further away, aided by the mutual support of these underground networks in crime if sometimes weakened by the bitter feuds between them. Their ranks were swelled by a bizarre collection of adventurers, professional assassins, peasants, nobles, priests breaking their ban, monks no longer willing to submit to the Holy See. Their origins can be deduced from the processions of galley slaves whom the Papal States delivered up, for instance, to Gian Andrea Doria, records of whom have sometimes survived. In Sardinia and Corsica, there were considerable numbers of bandits. Tuscany's difficulties during the reign of Francesco (1574–1587) were their doing. In 1592–1593, Italy was considering ridding the country of these unwelcome persons by a general amnesty on condition they left for Dalmatia to serve Venice.

No country better illustrates the rise of brigandage during the latter years of the sixteenth century and the early part of the seventeenth than Spain, which, after the death of the old king in the Escorial, was to experience that extraordinary flowering of art and intelligence, luxury and *fiestas* known as the Golden Age, in that new and rapidly growing city, the Madrid of Velázquez and Lope de Vega, the divided city, where the rich were extravagantly rich and the poor miserably poor: beggars sleeping at street corners, rolled up in their cloaks, bodies over whom the nobles had to step to reach their palaces, *serenos* guarding the doors of the rich, the disquieting underworld of ruffians, soldiers, hungry valets, gamblers fingering their greasy cards, cunning prostitutes, guitar-playing students forgetting to return to their universities, a city of many colours fed by the rest of Spain and invaded every morning by the peasants of the nearby countryside, coming to town to sell their bread. During the last years of the reign, banditry increased all over the Peninsula.

Slaves. One final feature characterizes these Mediterranean societies. In spite of their pretensions to modernity, they all retained slavery, in the West as in the East. It was the sign of a curious attachment to the past and also perhaps of a certain degree of wealth, for slaves were expensive, entailed responsibilities and competed with the poor and destitute, even at Istanbul. It was shortage of labour, combined with the high yield of the mines and sugar-plantations, which was to allow the slavery of antiquity to be revived in the New World, that huge and traumatic step backwards. At all events, slavery, which had been virtually wiped out in northern Europe and France, survived in the Mediterranean west,

248. Sketch of a slave market by Jacques Callot. *Uffizi, Florence*

in Italy and in Spain, in the fairly persistent form of domestic slavery. The ordinances of the Consulate of Burgos in 1572 regulated the conditions for the insurance of black slaves for transportation to the New World, but also to Portugal and 'a estos Reynos', that is to Spain. At Valladolid, which towards 1555 was still capital of Castile, slaves waited at table in great houses, 'were well fed on kitchen leftovers', and often given their liberty in their masters' wills. In Italy, a series of acts indicates the survival of domestic slavery, in the Mezzogiorno in particular but elsewhere as well. In Naples, notarial documents announce slave sales (at 35 ducats 'apiece' as a rule during the first half of the sixteenth century); similar references are found in the minute books of Venetian lawyers and also in the correspondence of the Gonzaga, who bought little black boys presumably for the amusement of their court. At Leghorn, the *portate* from time to time mention the arrival aboard ship of a few black slaves.

This uninterrupted traffic fully reveals itself only on exceptional occasions. The capture of Tripoli in 1510 for instance, put so many slaves on the Sicilian market that they had to be sold off cheaply, 3 to 25 ducats each, and the galleys of the western powers soon had a full complement of oarsmen. In 1549 the Grand Duke of Tuscany (and he was not the only one) sent an agent to Segna to buy Turkish slaves or *morlachi*. Slavery was a structural feature of Mediterranean society, where life was so harsh for the poor, in spite of the widespread movement towards piety and religious charity gathering strength at the end of the century. Slavery was by no means exclusive to the Atlantic and the New World.

Possible conclusions. There can be no doubt that society was tending to polarize into, on the one hand, a rich and vigorous nobility reconstituted into powerful dynasties owning vast properties and, on the other, the great and growing mass of the poor and disinherited, 'caterpillars and grubs', human insects, alas too many. A deep fissure split open traditional society, opening up gulfs which nothing would ever bridge, not even, as I have already remarked, the astonishing move towards charity in the Catholic world at the end of the sixteenth century.

249. Religious charity: *St. Lucia Distributing Alms* by Aniello Falcone. *Museo di Capodimonte, Naples*

In England, France, Italy, Spain, and Islam, society was undermined by this dramatic upheaval, the full horror of which was to be revealed in the seventeenth century. The creeping evil reached states as well as societies, societies as well as civilizations. This crisis coloured the lives of men. If the rich stooped to debauchery, mingling with the crowd they despised, it was because society stood on two banks facing each other: on one side the houses of nobles, over-populated with servants; on the other *picardia*, the world of the black market, theft, debauchery, adventure, but above all poverty, just as the purest, the most exalted religious passion coexisted with the most incredible baseness and brutality. Here, some will say, are the astonishing and marvellous contradictions of the Baroque. Not so: these were the contradictions, not of the Baroque but of the society which produced it and which it only imperfectly conceals. And at the heart of that society lay bitter despair.

6

Civilizations

OF ALL the complex and contradictory faces of the Mediterranean world, its
civilizations are the most perplexing. No sooner does the historian think he has
isolated the particular quality of a civilization than it gives proof of the exact
opposite. Civilizations may be fraternal and liberal, yet at the same time exclusive and unwelcoming; they receive visits and return them; they can be pacific
yet militant; in many ways astonishingly stable, they are nevertheless constantly
shifting and straying, their surface disturbed by a thousand eddies and whirl-
pools, the tiny particles of their daily life subject to random 'Brownian movements'. Civilizations, like sand dunes, are firmly anchored to the hidden contours
of the earth; grains of sand may come and go, blown into drifts or carried far
away by the wind, but the dunes, the unmoving sum of innumerable movements,
remain standing.

1 Mobility and stability of civilizations

Movement and immobility complement and explain one another. We may
choose without risk either approach to the civilizations of the Mediterranean,
even if we take what is at first sight their least significant aspect, that miscellany
of trivia and daily happenings which rises like a cloud of dust from any living
civilization.

The significance of anecdote. These apparently trivial details tell us more than
any formal description about the life of Mediterranean man – a wandering life,
tossed in every direction by the winds of fortune. A Ragusan sea-captain, on
board ship somewhere in the Mediterranean in 1598, is taken into the confidence
of a Genoese traveller from Santa Margherita, the legal executor of another
Ragusan who has died rich at Potosí and entrusted him with the task of finding
his heirs in Mezzo, the small island off Ragusa which was the nursery of all her
sailors and ocean-going captains. And the impossible happens: inquiries are
made and the rightful heirs are found. We know less about another Ragusan,
Blas Francisco Conich, who had also settled in Peru and in whom Venice was
interested because he owned half-shares, towards the end of the year 1611, in

a boat, the *Santa Maria del Rosario e quatr'occhi* which the Signoria had seized in reprisals. Another incident concerns the proceedings for certification of death, again in Ragusa. The man presumed dead, a ship's captain, had been lost with the armada sent against England by Philip II in 1596. The court heard a letter written by the missing captain to his wife before setting sail, dated 15th October at Lisbon; it reads like a last farewell. 'We leave today for Ireland. God knows who will return.' He was one who did not. At Genoa, on 8th June, 1601, the captain *Pompeus Vassalus quodnam Jacobi*, as he is described in the Latin text, is giving evidence before the grand *Magistrato del Riscatto dei Schiavi* about the presumed death of Matteo Forte of Portofino. 'Being in Egypt last year', he says, 'from the month of May to 11th September, I enquired there of several persons, if Matteo Forte, formerly a slave in the galleys of the *bailo* of Alexandria, were still living, for the said Matteo owns a house near my own which I wished to buy.' But 'all those who knew him told me that he had died several months before, and there were there some slaves from Rapallo who had known him'.

A commonplace story too was that of a Genoese from Bogliasco, Gieronimo Campodimeglio, a captive in Algiers. He was about fifty years old in 1598 and no record appears of the date of his capture or of the name of his former master in Algiers who on his death, left his shop to his slave. Meanwhile he has been seen in the street 'vestito de Turcho'; someone testifies that he has married a Moslem woman. 'I think he has abjured his faith and will not want to come back': a more frequent conclusion than one might expect. In fact Christians went over to the Turks and Islam by the thousand, as even a contemporary writer testifies. Great civilizations – or strong governments – might resist and struggle, buying back their lost sheep; individuals were usually more accommodating. As time went by, statutes were drawn up against them. In the sixteenth century, they did not even forfeit their civil status. A renegade living in Tunis was able to dispose of his estate to his brother in Syracuse. In 1568, Fray Luis de Sandoval even proposed a massive programme of redemption by the Christian princes of the Mediterranean: a pardon would be offered to these lost souls and an end thus be put to the measureless harm they were inflicting on Christianity. In the meantime it was possible for any renegade to return without danger, as did the Venetian Gabriel Zucato, captured and enslaved by the conquerors of Cyprus in 1572, who on his return to Venice and 'la sanctissima fede', thirty-five years later, in 1607, applied for a post as *sansaro* or broker, a petition favourably received by the *Cinque Savii* in view of his poverty and his knowledge of Greek, Arabic and Turkish, 'which he can even write'; and yet 'si feci turco', he had abjured his faith.

In any case, the two great Mediterranean civilizations, warring neighbours, were frequently drawn, by circumstances and chance encounters, into fraternization. During the unsuccessful attack on Gibraltar by the Algerines in 1540, eighty Christians fell into the hands of the corsairs. After the alarm was over, there were as usual negotiations. A sort of armistice was agreed and bargaining began. The Algerine ships entered the port, their sailors went ashore and met old acquaintances, their former captives or masters, before going off to eat in the *bodegones*. Meanwhile the civilian population helped to transport casks of fresh water for the supply of the enemy fleet. There was an exchange of goodwill and a familiarity comparable perhaps to fraternization between soldiers in the trenches. Between the two enemy religions, it would be unrealistic to imagine a watertight barrier. Men passed to and fro, indifferent to frontiers, states and creeds. They were more aware of the necessities of shipping and trade, the hazards of war and piracy, the opportunities for complicity or betrayal provided by circumstances. Hence many an adventurous life story, like that of Melek Jasa, a Ragusan converted to Islam, whom we find in India at the beginning of the sixteenth century, and in charge of the defence of Diu against the Portuguese – a post he was to hold for many years. Then there were the three Spaniards who were picked up in 1581 at Derbent, on the Caspian Sea, by the little English ship freighted every two or three years by the Muscovy Company, on its way back from Astrakhan. The Spaniards were no doubt renegades, deserters from the Turkish army, who had been taken prisoner at La Goletta seven years earlier. Their remarkable story has a no less remarkable parallel. In 1586, the English ship *Hercules* brought back to Turkey twenty Turks whom Drake had liberated in the West Indies, a detail mentioned briefly in the account of the voyage of this sailing ship to the Levant.

Similar adventures occur at the beginning of the seventeenth century. In 1608 there was still imprisoned in the Castle of S. Julião da Barra at Lisbon, a certain Francisco Julião who had received baptism and who had been in command of the Turkish galleys off Malindi when he was captured. Then in 1611, the Persians captured from the ranks of the Turkish army led by the Grand Vizier Murād Pasha, three Frenchmen and a German (how they got there is anyone's guess – through Constantinople in any case) and a Greek from Cyprus; their lives were spared by their captors and they were eventually taken in by the Capuchin friars of Ispahan.

One last example: towards the end of the seventeenth century, we hear of the travels of a Greek adventurer, Constantine Phaulkon, originally from Cephalonia, who described himself as the son of a Venetian noble and became a favourite of the king of Siam: 'everything passed through his hands'.

How cultural exports travelled. Men travelled; so did cultural possessions, both the everyday and the unexpected, following expatriates round the world. Arriving with a group of travellers one year they might be carried further by others a year or a century later, ferried from place to place, left behind or taken up again, often by ignorant hands. The first printing-presses in the Danube plains, which were to produce Orthodox devotional works, were brought in at the beginning of the sixteenth century by Montenegrin pedlars from Venice or from Venetian possessions. The Jews expelled from Spain in 1492 organized in

Salonica and Constantinople markets for everything they found lacking there: they opened ironmongery shops, introduced the first printing-presses with Latin, Greek or Hebrew characters (not until the eighteenth century did the first presses with Arabic characters appear); they began producing woollen cloth and brocade and, it is said, built the first wheeled gun-carriages, thus providing the army of Sulaimān the Magnificent with its field artillery, one of the secrets of its success. And it seems that they took as their model the gun-carriages of Charles VIII's artillery in Italy in 1494.

But most cultural transfers were the work of anonymous carriers. So many were they, some moving quickly, others slowly, that it is almost impossible to find one's way through this immense baggage hall in perpetual confusion. For every piece of cultural baggage recognized, a thousand are untraceable: identification labels are missing and sometimes the contents or their wrappings have vanished too. In the case of works of art, the corner-stones of Bayeux cathedral, for instance, a Catalan painting found at Sinai, iron work of Barcelona manufacture identified in Egypt, or the curious paintings of Italian or German inspiration which were executed in the sixteenth century in the monasteries of Mount Athos, the origin may be discovered without too much trouble. It is still possible when we are dealing with tangible entities like words, whether geographical names or everyday vocabulary: we may be reasonably if not absolutely sure of their provenance. But when it comes to ideas, attitudes, techniques, the margin of error is very wide. Is it possible to say that Spanish mysticism in the sixteenth century can be traced back to Moslem Sufism through such intermediaries as the eclectic genius of Ramón Lull? Is it true that the use of rhyme in the West owed its origin to the Moslem poets of Spain? That the *chansons de geste* (as is quite probable) borrowed from Islam? We should be equally wary of those who are too positive in their identification of cultural phenomena (for example the borrowings from Arabic by French troubadours) and of those who by reaction deny all borrowings between civilization and civilization, when in the Mediterranean to live was to exchange – men, ideas, ways of life, beliefs – or habits of courtship.

Lucien Febvre in an entertaining article, imagined how astonished Herodotus would be if he were to repeat his itinerary today, at the flora which we think of as typically Mediterranean: orange, lemon and mandarin trees imported from the Far East by the Arabs; cactus from America; eucalyptus trees from Australia (they have invaded the whole region from Portugal to Syria and airline pilots say they can recognize Crete by its eucalyptus forests); cypresses from Persia; the tomato, an immigrant perhaps from Peru; peppers from Guyana; maize from Mexico; rice, 'the blessing brought by the Arabs'; the peach-tree, 'a Chinese mountain-dweller who came to Iran', the bean, the potato, the Barbary fig-tree, tobacco – the list is neither complete nor closed. A veritable saga could be written about the migrations of the cotton-plant, native to Egypt from which it emerged to sail the seas. It would be interesting too to have a study of the arrival

250–2. Coffee reaches Europe:
Above: Venetian coffee house. German
print, 1698. *Above right:* Turkish coffee house.
Detail from sixteenth-century miniature.
Chester Beatty Library, Dublin. Right: Coffee
tree with travellers drinking coffee. Print from
O. Dappert, *Beschryving van Asië . . .*,
Amsterdam, 1680.

in the sixteenth century of maize, an American plant which Ignacio de Asso
wrongly supposed, in the eighteenth century, to have come from two sources,
the New World and the East Indies, brought from the latter by Arabs in the
twelfth century. The coffee-shrub was growing in Egypt by 1550: coffee had

arrived in the East towards the middle of the fifteenth century; certain African tribes ate grilled coffee beans. As a beverage it was known in Egypt and Syria from that time on. In Arabia in 1556, it was forbidden at Mecca, as being a drink of dervishes. It reached Constantinople in about 1550. The Venetians imported it to Italy in 1580; it appeared in England between 1640 and 1660: in France it was first seen at Marseilles in 1646, then at court in 1670. As for tobacco, it arrived in Spain from Santo Domingo and through Portugal 'the exquisite herb nicotiana' reached France in 1559, or possibly even in 1556, with Thevet. In 1561, Nicot sent some powdered tobacco from Lisbon to Catherine de' Medici as a remedy for migraine. The precious plant had soon crossed the Mediterranean; by 1605 it had reached India; it was quite often forbidden in Moslem countries but in 1664, Tavernier saw the Sophy himself smoking a pipe.

It is tempting to prolong the list: the plane tree of Asia Minor appeared in Italy in the sixteenth century; rice cultivation spread, again in the sixteenth century, around Nice and along the Provençal coast; the kind of lettuce known as 'roman' or cos was brought to France by a traveller called Rabelais; and it was Busbecq, whose Turkish letters I have frequently quoted, who brought back to Vienna from Adrianople the first lilacs which, with the aid of the wind, soon covered the Viennese countryside. But further identification can add nothing to what is already plain: the extent and immensity of the intermingling of Mediterranean cultures, all the more rich in consequences since in this zone of exchanges cultural groups were so numerous from the start. In one region they might remain distinctive, exchanging and borrowing from other groups from time to time. Elsewhere they merged to produce the extraordinary charivari suggestive of eastern ports as described by romantic poets: a rendezvous for every race, every religion, every kind of man, for everything in the way of hairstyles, fashions, foods and manners to be found in the Mediterranean.

Cultural diffusion and resistance. There had of course always been a gulf between the North and the Mediterranean, two worlds bound together but quite distinct, each with its own horizons, its own heart and, religiously speaking, its own soul. For in the Mediterranean religious sentiment is expressed in a way which even today still shocks the northerner as it once shocked Montaigne in Italy, or the ambassador Saint-Gouard in Spain, and as at first it shocked the whole of western Europe when it was introduced by the Jesuits and the Capuchins, the poor man's Jesuits. Even in a region as profoundly Catholic as the Franche-Comté, the processions of penitents, the new devotional practices, the sensual, dramatic and, to the French mind, excessive element in southern piety, scandalized many serious, reflective and reasonable men.

Protestantism did succeed in pushing into the Austrian Alps, the Massif Central, the French Alps and the Pyrenees of Béarn. But in the end it failed, universally, to cross the frontiers of the Mediterranean states. Was the lack of success of the Reformation south of the Pyrenees and the Alps a question of

253, 254. The flamboyance of Southern piety: *Left:* Procession of penitents, Seville.
Right: Child Christ carrying the Cross. *Cofradia de Navarros, Madrid*

government, as has been frequently suggested, the results of well-managed repression? No one will underestimate the efficacy of systematic persecution carried out over a long period. The example of the Netherlands, very largely won back to Catholicism by the ruthlessness of the Duke of Alva and his successors, is sufficient in itself to guard us from such an error. But neither should one overestimate the impact of 'heresies' whether Spanish or Italian; they cannot seriously be compared to the powerful movements in the North. To mention only one difference, Protestantism in the Mediterranean hardly touched the masses at all. It was a movement confined to an élite and frequently, in Spain, this was a Reformation accomplished within the Church. Neither the disciples of Erasmus in Spain, nor the little group of Valdesians in Naples sought a rupture with the Church, any more than the circle around Marguerite de Navarre in France.

If the Italian Reformation, as Emmanuel Rodocanachi has said, 'was not a true religious revolt'; if it remained 'humble, meditative, in no way aggressive towards the Papacy'; if it was opposed to violence, it is because much more than a 'Reformation', it was a Christian revival. The word Reformation is inappropriate. Danger, or the semblance of danger, loomed only in Piedmont, with the Vaudois (but how Italian was Piedmont?); in Ferrara, at the court of Renée of France; in Lucca, where the opulent aristocracy of silk-manufacturers welcomed the Reformation in 1525; in Cremona, where a few assemblies gathered at about the same period; in Venice, which welcomed northerners and where in about 1529 Franciscan or Augustinian friars founded small groups where artisans were fairly well represented. Elsewhere in Italy, the Reformation was a matter of individuals; its history one of scandals such as that of the 'senoys' Ochino, formerly a celebrated Catholic preacher in Italy and now, writes de Selve who saw him arrive in England in 1547, converted 'to the new opinions of the Germans'. Frequently it was carried by travelling preachers who passed through, sowing the seed as they went, but the harvest was disappointing. These were solitaries, thinkers, men marked for unusual destinies, whether an obscure figure like the Umbrian Bartolomeo Bartoccio, settled in Geneva as a merchant, who was arrested on one of his trips to Genoa, handed over to the Roman inquisition and burned on 25th May, 1569, or an illustrious victim like Giordano Bruno, who was burned on the Campo dei Fiori in 1600.

Finally, let us beware of judging the Protestant threat in Italy by Catholic, Papal or Spanish anxiety, ever ready to magnify it. Such anxiety was so acute that during the summer of 1568, it was even feared that the French Huguenots were preparing to invade Italy where, it was said, they would find the whole Peninsula dangerously corrupted from within.

The Reformation in Spain (if Reformation there was at all) was concentrated in two cities: Seville and Valladolid. After the repression of 1557–1558 there were only isolated instances. Sometimes they were merely madmen like Hernández Díaz to whom the shepherds of the Sierra Morena spoke of the Protestants of Seville; he retained enough of what they said to be arrested by the Toledo Inquisition in 1563 – a contented madman as it happened, who cheerfully boasted that in prison he ate more meat than at home. A few genuine Spanish Protestants travelled through Europe, hunted from refuge to refuge, like the famous Michael Servetus, or the dozen or so exiles who in 1578 'were studying the sect' in Geneva and who were denounced to the ambassador, Juan de Vargas Mexia, because they were said to be preparing either to go and preach in Spain or to send works of propaganda to the Indies.

The Spanish authorities were indeed deeply disturbed by these erring souls and pursued them relentlessly. The Inquisition received popular support in its persecution of them. The trial *in absentia* of Michael Servetus was followed with passionate attention, for the honour of the nation was concerned. The same sentiments inspired Alonso Díaz when, at Neuberg on the Danube, in 1546, he had a servant execute his own brother, Juan, a disgrace not only to the family but to all Spain. It is as unrealistic therefore to talk of the Reformation in Spain as it is to generalize about the Reformation in Ragusa on the strength of the heretic of the city of St Blaise, Francisco Zacco, who in 1540 refused to believe in either heaven or hell, or of the 'Protestant tendencies' which, according to the writer of the latter part of Razzi's history of Ragusa, apparently manifested themselves in 1570. Such injections of Protestantism apparently served chiefly as vaccinations.

What became known as the Counter-Reformation was, if you like, the Italian

255. Head of the Virgin, Seville.

Reformation. It has been remarked that the southern countries were less drawn than those of the North to the reading of the Old Testament and thus escaped being submerged by that incredible wave of witchcraft which unfurled from Germany to the Alps and northern Spain towards the end of the sixteenth century. Possibly because of an ancient substratum of polytheism, Mediterranean Christendom remained, even in its superstitions, attached to the cult of the saints. Is it pure coincidence that devotion to the saints and the Virgin increased in intensity just as outside assaults became more vigorous? To view it as some manœuvre by Rome or the Jesuits is idle. In Spain it was the Carmelites who propagated the cult of Saint Joseph. Everywhere the popular associations

256. Statue of St. James of Compostela.

of the Rosary fostered and exalted the passionate cult of the Mother of Jesus: witness the Neapolitan heretic, Giovanni Micro, who in 1564 declared that he had lost his faith in many articles of religion including the saints and holy relics, but clung to his belief in the Virgin; this at the very moment when Spain was bringing to perfection her own resplendent and militant saints, Saint George and Saint James.

The refusal then was deliberate and categorical. It has been said of the Reformation that it 'burst upon the Platonic and Aristotelian theology of the Middle Ages as the barbarian Germans burst upon Greco-Roman civilization'. All one can say is that what remained of the Roman Empire on the shores of the Latin sea put up more resistance in the sixteenth century than it had in the fifth.

Survivals and cultural frontiers. To man as an individual, no feat of exploration, no odyssey is impossible. Nothing can stop him or the belongings, both material and spiritual, which he carries, as long as he travels alone and on his own account. Mass removal, by a group or a society, is more difficult. A civilization cannot simply transplant itself, bag and baggage.

For at bottom, a civilization is attached to a distinct geographical area and this is itself one of the indispensable elements of its composition. Before it acquires the identity expressed in its art which Nietzsche saw as its major truth (possibly because, with others of his generation, he made the word a synonym for quality) a civilization exists fundamentally in a geographical area which has been structured by men and history. That is why there are cultural frontiers and cultural zones of amazing permanence: all the cross-fertilization in the world will not alter them.

So the Mediterranean is criss-crossed with cultural frontiers, both major and minor, scars which are never completely healed and each with a role to play. J. Cvijić has identified three cultural zones in the Balkans. And who can fail to be aware, in Spain, of the sharp contrast between the parts north and south of the parallel running through Toledo, the divided city which is the true heart of Spain? To the north lies the barren landscape peopled by small, semi-independent peasants and noblemen exiled in their small provincial towns; to the south the exploited colony, the Spain of history, where reconquering Christians found not only a sophisticated agricultural system and huge organized estates but a mass of hard-working *fellahin*, an extraordinary legacy which they did not destroy.

But there are even greater divisions both within the Mediterranean region and on its borders. One vital frontier for the Mediterranean world remains the ancient border of the Roman Empire, the line running along the Rhine and the Danube which was to be the advance line of the Catholic revival of the sixteenth century: the new *limes* along which there soon appeared the cupolas and accolades of the Jesuit churches and colleges. The split between Rome and

Reformation occurred exactly along this ancient divide. It was this, rather than enmity between states, which conferred its 'solemn' (Madame de Staël's expression) character upon the frontier of the Rhine. France in the sixteenth century, caught between this Roman front line and the line of the Pyrenees, the latter broken into at the very edge by the Protestant advance – France, torn in two directions, was once more to suffer the consequences of her geographical position.

But the most extraordinary scar line in the Mediterranean was one which, like the maritime frontiers we have already mentioned, separated East from West: that immutable barrier which runs between Zagreb and Belgrade, rebounds from the Adriatic at Lesh (Alessio) at the mouth of the Drin and the angle of the Dalmatian and Albanian coastline, then passes through the ancient cities of Naissus, Remesiana and Ratiara to the Danube.

The slow pace of change and transfer. The force of resistance of civilizations anchored to the soil explains the exceptional slowness of certain movements. Civilizations are transformed only over very long periods of time, by imperceptible processes, for all their apparent changeability. Light travels to them as it were from distant stars, relayed with sometimes unbelievable delays on the way: from China to the Mediterranean, from the Mediterranean to China, or from India and Persia to the inland sea.

Who knows how long it took for Indian numerals – the so-called Arabic numerals – to travel from their native land to the western Mediterranean through Syria and the outposts of the Arab world, North Africa or Spain? Who knows how long it took, even after their arrival, for them to displace Roman numerals, which were considered more difficult to falsify? In 1299, the *Arte di Calimala* forbade their use in Florence; even in 1520, the 'new figures' were forbidden in Fribourg; they only came into use in Antwerp towards the end of the sixteenth century. The apologue travelled far from its home in India or Persia, before it was first taken up by the Greek and Latin fabulists who were La Fontaine's sources, and then went on to enjoy perennial popularity in Atlantic Mauritania. Who can tell how many centuries passed before bells, originally from China, became the voice of Christian music and were placed on top of churches? Some sources say it cannot have been before bell-towers were built in the West, in imitation of Asia Minor. The journey of paper took almost as long. Invented in China in 105 AD, where it was made from vegetable matter, the secret of its manufacture is said to have been disclosed at Samarkand in 751 by Chinese prisoners of war. The Arabs replaced the vegetable matter by rags, and cloth paper seems to have begun its career in Baghdad in 794. From there it slowly travelled to the rest of the Moslem world. In the eleventh century its presence is recorded in Arabia and Spain, but the first paperworks at Xativa (now San Felipe in Valencia) do not date from earlier than the twelfth century. In the eleventh it was used in Greece and by about 1350 it was replacing parchment in the West.

I have already remarked that according to G. I. Bratianu, the sudden changes in men's costume in France towards 1340, the substitution for the flowing robes of the crusaders of the short, tight-fitting doublet, worn with clinging hose and pointed shoes, a new fashion introduced from Catalonia along with the goatee beard and moustache of the Trecento, in fact came from much further away; the Catalans had imported these styles from the eastern Mediterranean which in turn had received them from Bulgaria or even Siberia; while women's costumes, notably the pointed headdress whose immediate source was the Lusignan court in Cyprus, actually dated far back in space and time to the China of the T'ang dynasty.

Time: unimaginable ages passed before these journeys were safely completed and before the innovations could take root in their new environment. The old tree-trunks of civilization by contrast remained astonishingly sturdy and resistant. The teachings of the religious centres of early Christianity, Alexandria and Antioch, survived in the sixteenth century in the Christianity of Abyssinia and the Nestorians. At Gafsa in North Africa, Latin was still spoken in the twelfth century according to al-Idrīsī. It was only in 1159, under the persecution of 'Abd al-Mu'min, that the last indigenous Christian communities disappeared from North Africa. In 1159: that is four or five centuries after the Moslem conquest.

2 Overlapping civilizations

If we now wish to turn from such vast perspectives to the history of civilization in the shorter term, a history of rapid but significant change, of more human and less universal proportions, we can do no better than consider the violent conflicts between neighbouring civilizations, one triumphant (or believing itself to be), the other subjugated (and dreaming of liberation). There is no lack of such conflicts in the Mediterranean in the sixteenth century. Islam, through its agents the Turks, captured the Christian strongholds of the Balkans. In the West, Spain under the Catholic Kings captured, with Granada, the last outpost of Islam on the Peninsula. What did either of the conquerors make of their victories?

In the East, the Turks were often to hold the Balkans with only a handful of men, much as the English used to hold India. In the West, the Spaniards mercilessly crushed their Moslem subjects. In so doing both powers were obeying the imperatives of their separate civilizations more than one might think: Christendom was over-populated, Islam short of men.

The Turks in the eastern Balkan plains. The breath of Asia which is so manifest throughout the Balkans is a legacy of Turkish Islam. It disseminated the gifts it had itself received from the distant East. Through it, town and countryside alike were permeated with oriental culture. A significant detail is that at Ragusa, that

257. St. Demetrius. Bulgarian folk print, c.1870.

island of Catholicism (and a particularly ardent form of Catholicism), women were still veiled and sequestered in the sixteenth century, and a husband did not see his wife before the marriage ceremony. Western voyagers who came ashore on this narrow promontory were immediately aware that here began another world. But the Turks who set foot in the Balkans must have had exactly the same impression.

Asia seems to have left no corner of Bulgaria untouched, to have invaded the whole country with the heavy tramp of her soldiers and camels, submerging (with the aid of a few collaborators, especially the usurers, the *corbazi* of sinister repute who might inform upon their compatriots) a people which by its blood, its origins and the nature of its territory was less well protected than most.

To this day, there are still traces in Bulgaria of its impregnation by an exotic, perfumed civilization of the East. To this day, its cities are steeped in memories of it: oriental cities, with long narrow streets closed in by blank walls, the inevitable bazaar and its close-packed shops behind wooden shutters; the shopkeeper puts down the shutter and crouches on it waiting for his customers, beside his *mangal*, the brazier of hot coals indispensable in these lands scoured by the snow-bearing winds from the north and the east. In the sixteenth century, a whole population of artisans worked in these shops for the caravan trade, blacksmiths, carpenters, pack and saddle-makers. Before their doors, in the shade of the poplar trees by the fountains, camels and horses would stop on market days amid the bustle of costumes, merchandise and people: Turks, lords of the *čiftliks*, returning briefly to their lands, Greeks from the Phanar travelling to the Danube provinces, spice-merchants or Aromani caravaneers, gypsy horse-dealers trusted by nobody.

For the Bulgarian people life was a succession of invasions. And yet the Bulgarian retained what was essential, for he remained himself. Whatever his borrowings during the long cohabitation, he did not allow himself to be swallowed up by the invading Turk, but safeguarded what was to preserve him from total assimilation: his religion and his language, guarantees of future resurrection. Firmly attached to the soil, he clung to it doggedly, always keeping the best regions of his dark earth. When the Turkish peasant from Asia Minor settled alongside the Bulgarian, he had to be content with the wooded slopes or marshy plots bordered with willows, down in the hollows, the only land left unoccupied by the *raia*. When the Turks finally departed, the Bulgarian found himself a Bulgarian still, the same peasant who five centuries before had spoken his own language, prayed in his own churches and farmed the same land under the same Bulgarian sky.

Islam in Spain: the Moriscos. At the other end of the Mediterranean, the Spaniards too were at odds with an inassimilable population and the conflict ended in tragedy. Few other problems have so profoundly disturbed the Peninsula.

As the very name suggests, the problem of the Moriscos arose from a conflict between religions, in other words a conflict in the very strongest sense between civilizations, difficult to resolve and destined to last many years. The name Moriscos was given to the descendants of the Moslems of Spain who had been converted to Christianity, in 1501 in Castile and in 1526 in Aragon. By turns bullied, indoctrinated, courted, but always feared, they were in the end driven out of Spain during the great expulsions of the years 1609–1614.

But the most difficult question to answer is not whether Spain paid a high price for the expulsion and the policy of violence it implied, or whether or not she was *right* to take such action. We are not here concerned with judging Spain in the light of present-day attitudes: all historians are of course on the side of the Moriscos. Whether Spain was morally right or wrong to rid herself of the hardworking and prolific Morisco population is beside the point. Why did she do it?

Above all it was because the Morisco had remained inassimilable. Spain's actions were not inspired by racial hatred (which seems to have been almost

258. *Expulsion of the Moriscos.* Drawing by Vicente Carducci. *Prado, Madrid*

totally absent from the conflict) but by religious and cultural enmity. And the explosion of this hatred, the expulsion, was a confession of impotence, proof that the Morisco after one, two or even three centuries, remained still the Moor of old, with his Moorish dress, tongue, cloistered houses and Moorish baths. He had retained them all. He had refused to accept western civilization and this was his fundamental crime. A few spectacular exceptions in the religious sphere, and the undeniable fact that the Moriscos who lived in the cities tended increasingly to adopt the dress of their conquerors, could not alter this. The Morisco was still tied deep in his heart to that immense world, which as Spain was well aware, stretched as far as distant Persia, a world of similar domestic patterns, similar customs and identical beliefs.

Of all the possible solutions, Spain chose the most radical: deportation, the uprooting of a civilization from its native soil.

But had Spain really seen the last of her Morisco population? Of course not. In the first place, it was not easy in some instances to distinguish between a Morisco and a non-Morisco. Mixed marriages were frequent enough to be taken

259. Moorish woman of Granada. Print from
Hans Weigel, *Trachtenbuch*, Nuremberg, 1577.

into account in the expulsion edict. And there were certain interested parties who undoubtedly intervened on behalf of some who would otherwise have been deported. The Moriscos in the towns were expelled almost to a man; rather less were expelled of those who inhabited the *realengos* and there were even greater exceptions among the Morisco tenants of seignorial estates, mountain dwellers and isolated peasants.

For the Morisco often stayed on, now only a face lost in the crowd, but leaving his own indelible mark upon the rest. The Christian population of Spain, and indeed the aristocracy, already bore the traces of its Moorish ancestry. Historians of America too have described in a variety of ways how the Morisco played a part in the settlement of the Americas. One thing is certain: Moslem civilization, supported by the remnants of the Morisco population as well as by those elements of Islam which Spain had absorbed over the centuries, did not cease to contribute to the complex civilization of the Peninsula, even after the drastic amputation of 1609–1614.

That surge of hatred was unable to wipe out everything which had taken root in Iberian soil: the black eyes of the Andalusians, the hundreds of Arabic place-names, or the thousands of words embedded in the vocabulary of the former conquered race who had become the rulers of Spain. A dead heritage, some will say, unimpressed by the fact that culinary habits, certain trades and structures of hierarchy still convey the voice of Islam in the everyday life of Spain and Portugal. And yet in the eighteenth century, when French influence

was at its height, an artistic tradition survived, in the art of the *mudejares*, with its stuccoes, ceramics and the tender colours of its *azulejos*.

The supremacy of the West. But the Morisco question was only an episode in a wider conflict. In the Mediterranean the essential struggle was between East and West — for the latter there was always an 'eastern question' — fundamentally a cultural conflict, revived whenever fortune favoured one or other protagonist. With their alternating rise and fall, major cultural currents were established running from the richer to the poorer civilization, either from west to east or east to west.

The first round was won by the West under Alexander the Great: Hellenism represents the first 'Europeanization' of the Middle East and Egypt, one which was to last until the age of Byzantium. With the fall of the Roman Empire and the great invasions of the fifth century, the West and its ancient heritage collapsed: now it was the Byzantine and Moslem East which preserved or received the riches, transmitting them for centuries back to the barbaric West. Our Middle Ages were saturated, shot through with the light of the East, before, during and after the Crusades. 'Civilizations had mingled through their armies; a host of stories and narratives telling of these distant lands entered circulation: the Golden Legend teems with these tales; the story of St Eustace, of St Christopher, of Thaïs, of the Seven Sleepers of Ephesus, of Barlaam and Josaphat are eastern fables. The legend of the Holy Grail was grafted on to the memory of Joseph of Arimathea; the Romance of Huon of Bordeaux is a fantasmagoria sparkling with the spells of Oberon, spirit of dawn and morning; Saint Brendan's voyage is an Irish version of the adventures of Sindbad the Sailor.' And these borrowings are only a fraction of the substantial volume of cultural exchange. 'A work composed in Morocco or Cairo', says Renan, 'was known to readers in Paris or Cologne in less time than it takes, in our own day, for an important German book to cross the Rhine. The history of the Middle Ages will not be complete until someone has compiled statistics on the Arabic works familiar to scholars of the thirteenth and fourteenth centuries.' Is it surprising then that Moslem literature should have provided some of the sources of the Divine Comedy; that to Dante the Arabs were shining examples to be imitated, or that St John of the Cross had notable Moslem precursors, one of whom, Ibn 'Abbād, the poet of Ronda, had developed well before him the theme of the 'Dark Night'?

From the time of the Crusades onwards, a movement in the opposite direction was beginning. The Christian became ruler of the waves. His now was the superiority and wealth brought by control of routes and trade. 'From the middle of the seventeenth to the end of the eighteenth century, European travellers' tales appeared in great numbers and in every European language'. For now travel in the East 'was open to permanent embassies, consuls, merchant colonies,

260. *Opposite: Mudejar* architecture: the Casa de Pilate, Seville.

261. *View of Smyrna* with the reception of the Dutch Consul. Turkish school.
Rijksmuseum, Amsterdam

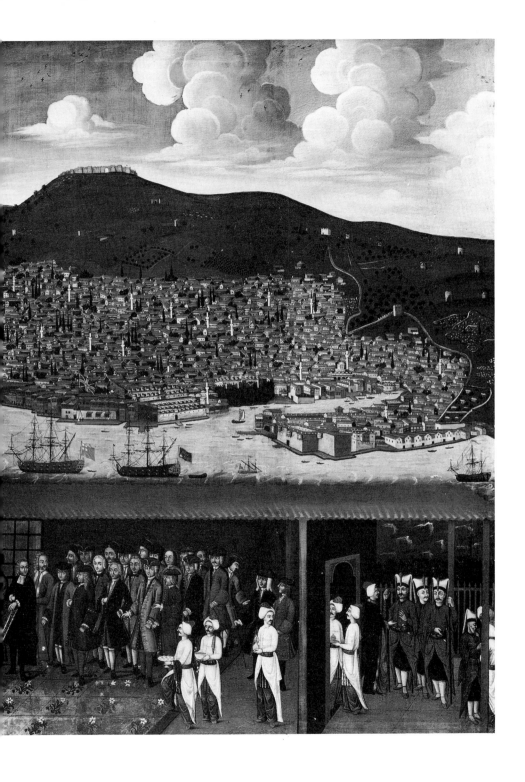

missions of economic enquiry, scientific missions, Catholic missions ... to adventurers entering the service of the Grand Turk'. There was suddenly an invasion of the East by the West: an invasion which contained elements of domination.

But to return to the West in the sixteenth century: at this period it was far ahead of the East. To say so does not imply any value judgement on either civilization: it is merely to record that in the sixteenth century, the pendulum had swung the other way, western civilization now being the more forceful and holding the Islamic world in its dependence.

Human migration alone is sufficient indication of the change. Men flocked from Christendom to Islam, which tempted them with visions of adventure and profit – and paid them to stay. The Grand Turk needed artisans, weavers, skilled shipbuilders, experienced seamen, cannon-founders, the 'iron-workers' (in fact handling all metals) who constituted the chief strength of any state; 'as the Turks and several other peoples very well know', writes Montchrestien, 'and keep them whenever they can catch them'. The curious correspondence between a

262. *The Reception of an Imperial Ambassador by a Turkish Pasha*, attributed to Pietro Longhi. *L. A. Mayer Memorial Institute for Islamic Art, Jerusalem*

Jewish merchant in Constantinople and Murād Agha in Tripoli shows that the former was looking for Christian slaves able to weave velvet and damask. For prisoners too supplied the East with labour.

Was it because it was over-populated and not yet fully committed to trans-Atlantic colonization, that Christendom did not attempt to reduce the flow of emigrants to the East? On coming into contact with Islamic countries, Christians were often seized with the urge to turn Moslem. In the *presidios* on the African coast, Spanish garrisons were decimated by epidemics of desertion. On Djerba in 1560, before the fort surrendered to the Turks, a number of Spaniards had already joined the enemy, 'abandoning their faith and their comrades'. Not long afterwards at La Goletta, a plot to surrender the position to the Infidel was uncovered. Small boats frequently left Sicily with cargoes of candidates for apostasy. At Goa the same phenomenon was observable among the Portuguese. The call was so strong that it even reached the clergy. The 'Turk' who accompanied one of His Christian Majesty's ambassadors back to France, and whom the Spanish authorities were advised to capture en route, was a former Hungarian priest. It cannot have been such a very rare occurrence: in 1630, Père Joseph was asked to recall the Capuchins living in the Levant, 'lest they turn Turk'. From Corsica, Sardinia, Sicily, Calabria, Genoa, Venice, Spain, from every point in the Mediterranean world, renegades converged on Islam. There was no comparable flow in the other direction.

263, 264. Christian subjects of the Grand Turk: Greek (*left*) and Armenian women of Constantinople. Early seventeenth-century engravings.

Perhaps unconsciously, the Turks were opening doors just as Christendom was shutting them. Christian intolerance, the consequence of large numbers, did not welcome strangers, it repelled them. And all those expelled from its lands – the Jews of 1492, the Moriscos of the sixteenth century and 1609–1614 – joined the ranks of the voluntary exiles, all moving towards Islam where there was work and money to be had. The surest sign of this is the wave of Jewish emigration, particularly during the second half of the sixteenth century, from Italy and the Netherlands towards the Levant: a wave which was strong enough to alert the Spanish agents in Venice, for it was through that city that this curious migration was channelled.

Through these immigrants, sixteenth-century Turkey completed its western education. 'The Turks', wrote Philippe de Canaye in 1573, 'have acquired, through the renegades, all the Christian superiorities.' 'All' is an exaggeration. For hardly had the Turk acquired one kind than he became aware of another still outside his grasp.

It was a strange war, this cultural rivalry, fought with any means, large or small. One day the enemy needed a doctor, another time a bombardier from the experienced artillery schools of the West; another time perhaps a cartographer or a painter. He might be in search of precious goods: gunpowder, yew wood, which it is true grew round the Black Sea (since in the past the Venetians had fetched it from there to sell to the English) but no longer in sufficient quantities for the long bows needed by the sixteenth-century Turkish army which now imported this wood from southern Germany. In 1570, Ragusa was accused, by Venice ironically enough, of providing the Turks with gunpowder and oars, and what was more a Jewish surgeon – Ragusa so often herself in search of Italian doctors. Towards the end of the century some of the most important English exports to the East were lead, tin and copper.

Pieces of artillery cast in Nuremberg may have been delivered to the Turks. Constantinople also received imports from her frontier zones, through Ragusa or the Saxon towns of Transylvania, whether of arms, men, or as a letter from a Vlach prince to the people of Kronstadt suggests, of doctors and medical supplies. The Barbary states too performed a similar service for the capital, for poor and literally 'barbaric' as they were, they stood – among Moslem states that is – closest to new developments of western progress: through their immigrants, voluntary or otherwise, their position in the western half of the sea and before long their connections with the Dutch, they were the first to be informed of technical innovations. They had their workers: the abundant crop of prisoners harvested every year by the corsairs of Algiers, as well as the Andalusians, skilful craftsmen some of whom could manufacture and all of whom could handle the carbine. Was it purely coincidence that the reconstruction of the Turkish war fleet after 1571, armed in the western style (with arquebuses instead of bows and arrows and considerably reinforced artillery aboard the galleys), was the feat of a Neapolitan, Euldj ('Ulūj) 'Alī, a renegade schooled by the corsairs of Algiers?

But cultural grafts did not always take. In 1548, the Turks had tried, during their campaign against Persia, to revolutionize the equipment of the *sipāhis*, providing them with pistols; the attempt was a hopeless failure and the *sipāhis*, at Lepanto and even later, were still armed with bows and arrows. This minor example shows how difficult it could be for the Turks to imitate their enemies. Had it not been for the divisions among the latter, their quarrels and betrayals, the Turks, for all their discipline and fanaticism and the excellence of their cavalry, would never have been able to hold their own against the West.

All these gifts from the other side were still insufficient to keep the Turkish bark afloat: it was showing signs of sinking from the end of the sixteenth century. Until then, war had been a powerful means of obtaining the necessary goods, men, techniques or products of technical advance, of picking up crumbs from the affluent Christian table, on land, on sea or from the zone bounded by Russia, Poland and Hungary. Gassot, when visiting the Arsenal at Constantinople, saw artillery pieces lying in heaps, most of them acquired as spoils of war rather than by informed purchases or local manufacture. War is perhaps, who knows, the great equalizer of civilizations. The war in question had ended in deadlock in the Mediterranean by 1574 and in 1606, on the battlefields of Hungary, in an inescapable stalemate. At this point there first appeared that inferiority which was to become plainer still in later years.

Many Christians were mistaken, it is true, about the Ottoman future, in the early years of the seventeenth century, years which saw the revival of the idea of crusade. But was it not perhaps division in Europe and the beginning of the Thirty Years' War which fostered illusions of Ottoman strength and, for the time being, saved the mighty eastern empire?

3 One civilization against the rest: the destiny of the Jews

All the conflicts discussed so far have been confined to a dialogue between two civilizations. In the case of the Jews, every civilization was implicated and invariably found itself in a position of overwhelming superiority. Against such strength and numbers the Jews were but a tiny band of adversaries.

But these adversaries had unusual opportunities: one prince might persecute them, another protect them; one economy might ruin them, another make their fortunes; one civilization might reject them and another welcome them with open arms. Spain expelled them in 1492 and Turkey received them, glad perhaps of the opportunity to use them as counters against the Greeks. It was also possible to exert pressure, to be the indirect source of action, as the Jews of Portugal amply demonstrated. They were able to obtain the tolerance which money can buy and at Rome they had an ambassador generally sympathetic to their cause. So it was comparatively simple to see to it that the measures enacted against them by the Lisbon government remained a dead letter: they were unfailingly either repealed or rendered ineffective, as Luis Sarmiento explained to Charles V in December, 1535. The *conversos*, converted Jews, had obtained from the Pope a bull pardoning them for their previous errors, which would impede government action against them, the more so since the *conversos* had lent money to the king of Portugal who was hopelessly in debt: 500,000 ducats, not counting the rest in Flanders 'and on the exchanges'.

The Christians were not mistaken when they complained that the rich *marranos* (the pejorative name for converted Jews) secretly persisted in practising Judaism. There was quite undoubtedly a Jewish civilization, so individual that it is not always recognized as an authentic civilization. And yet it exerted its influence, transmitted certain cultural values, resisted others, sometimes accepting, sometimes refusing: it possessed all the qualities by which we have defined civilization. True it was not or was only notionally rooted to any one place; it did not obey any stable and unvarying geographical imperatives. This was one of its most original features, but not the only one.

An unquestionable civilization. The matter of this civilization was dispersed, scattered, like tiny drops of oil, over the deep waters of other civilizations, never truly blending with them yet always dependent on them. But even when numbers did not favour or exaggerate the Jewish presence, these small communities, primary cells, were linked by education, beliefs, the regular travels of merchants, rabbis and beggars (who were legion); by the uninterrupted flow of letters of business, friendship or family matters; and by printed books. And yet the Jews are not a race: all scientific studies prove the contrary. Their colonies are biologically dependent on the host-nations with which they have lived for centuries. German Jews or *Ashkenazim*, Spanish Jews or *Sephardim* are biologically at least half German or Spanish, for there was frequent intermarriage and Jewish communities often originated in local conversions to Judaism; they never cloistered themselves from the outside world to which, on the contrary, they were often wide open. It would in any case be surprising if the accumulation of sometimes very many centuries had not led to such intermingling of different populations. The Jews who left Sicily in 1492 had been there after all for over 1500 years.

Moreover the Jews did not always live apart, nor wear any distinctive dress or sign, such as the yellow cap or the *rotella*, a yellow badge. They did not always inhabit a separate quarter of the city, the *ghetto* (from the name of the quarter which was assigned to them in Venice and whose name is derived from its formerly being the foundry where iron was cast – *ghettare* for *getare* – into moulds to make cannon). In August, 1540, the Jews of Naples for example, in their battle against that deep-rooted hostility towards them which finally triumphed a year later, were still protesting against orders obliging them to 'live together and wear a special badge', which was contrary to their privileges.

And even when there was official segregation, it was very often infringed and disobeyed. In Venice, Jews passing through the city and others, says a senatorial debate of March, 1556, 'have recently been spreading throughout the city, staying in Christian houses, going wherever they please, by day and night'. It is essential that this scandal cease: they must be ordered to live in the ghetto 'and not to keep an inn in any other part of the city but that one'. At about the same period, Jews from Turkey were arriving in Italy wearing white turbans (the privilege of the Turks) when they should have been wearing yellow. In 1566, though this was not the first alarm, the Jews of Milan were obliged to wear a yellow cap.

Frequently segregation was enforced at a late date and was only partially effective. At Verona in 1599 (although it had been mooted since at least 1593) the Jews, who 'lived scattered, one here, another there', had to take up residence 'near the main square of the city', 'where they sell wine', along the street running to the church of San Sebastiano, thereafter popularly known as the *via delli Hebrei*. It was not until 1602 that a similar measure was enacted at Padua, where until then, the 'Israelites had for the most part lived scattered in all four corners of the town'. In August, 1602, there were incidents at Mantua arising from the fact that Jews were walking about in black caps like anybody else.

In Spain and Portugal, coexistence had been the rule for centuries. In fact, in Portugal, the Jews had intermarried with the aristocracy even more than with the common people. In Turkey, the Jews had Christian slaves, both men and women, and 'use Christian slave-women with no more qualms over mixing with them than if they were Jewish women'. The isolation of the Jewish communities was the result not of racial incompatibility, as is often suggested, but of the hostility of others towards them and their own feelings of repugnance towards others. The root of it all was religion: isolation was the consequence of a whole complex of inherited habits, beliefs, even methods of preparing food. Of converted Jews, Bernaldez, the historiographer of the Catholic Kings, says: 'they never lost the habit of eating in the Jewish manner, preparing their meat dishes with onions and garlic and frying them in oil, which they use instead of bacon fat' – to a modern reader a description of Spanish cooking today. But the use of pork fat in cooking was of course the way of the Old Christians and, as Salvador de Madariaga says, its eventual displacement by oil was a legacy of the Jews, a cultural transfer. The converted Jew or *marrano* also gave himself away by carefully forgetting to light a fire in his house on Saturdays.

But all Jewish communities were obliged to engage in a dialogue, sometimes in dramatic circumstances when around them the entire nature of the dominant civilization changed. The Moslems replaced the Christians in Spain, then the Christians returned after the belated victories of the Reconquest. Jews who had spoken Arabic now had to learn Spanish. They were in the same unhappy position in Hungary when, with the imperial advance of 1593–1606, the Jews of Buda were caught between the twin perils of the Imperials and the Turks.

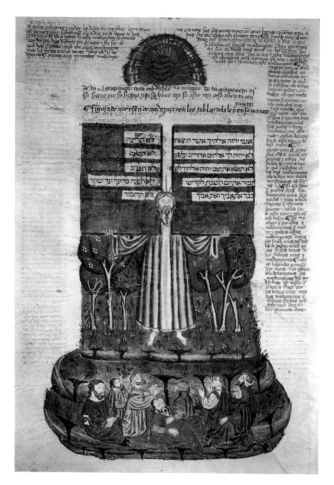

265. A famous example of cooperation between
Christians and Jews: translation of the Old Testament
into Castilian commissioned in 1422 by the Grand
Master of the Order of Calatrava from the Rabbi Moses
Arragel of Guadalajara. *Statens Konstmuseers, Stockholm*

Changing circumstances made them the involuntary heirs of once-powerful civilizations, whose gifts they were to pass on in one direction or another. Unintentionally, they were until the thirteenth century and even later, the intermediaries through whom the West received Arab thought and science, as philosophers, mathematicians, doctors and cosmographers. In the fifteenth century they rapidly developed an enthusiasm for printing: the first book to be printed in Portugal was the Pentateuch (at Faro, in 1487, by Samuel Gacon). Not until about ten years later did German printers appear in Portugal. When one remembers that printing was not introduced to Spain by the Germans until 1475, the haste with which the Jews set about printing sacred texts is the more striking. Expelled from Spain in 1492, the Jews took the art of printing with them to Turkey.

In 1573, Venice was preparing to drive out her Jews in accordance with the decision of 14th December, 1571. But things had changed since Lepanto, and at this point Soranzo arrived from Constantinople, where he had held the office of *bailo*. According to a Jewish chronicler, he addressed the Council of Ten in the following terms: 'What pernicious act is this, to expel the Jews? Do you not know what it may cost you in years to come? Who gave the Turk his strength and where else would he have found the skilled craftsmen to make the cannon, bows, shot, swords, shields and bucklers which enable him to measure himself against other powers, if not among the Jews who were expelled by the Kings of Spain?'

They had a further advantage: the Jews were, in the East, born interpreters of all speech and without their help much business would have been impossible or difficult. Linguistically, it is curious that the Jews expelled from Germany in the fourteenth, fifteenth and even sixteenth centuries, who were to contribute to the fortunes of Polish Jewry, should have introduced their own language, Yiddish, a form of German, just as the Spanish Jews who after 1492 formed the large colonies in Istanbul and above all Salonica, brought with them their own language, *ladino*, Renaissance Spanish, and preserved a genuine feeling for Spain, of which there is abundant evidence, proof that the soil of a man's native land may cling to his shoes.

Several Jewish nations could be distinguished and there was sometimes conflict between them. Venice for instance set up one after another, between 1516 and 1633, three ghettoes, the *vecchio*, the *nuovo* and the *nuovissimo*, linked islands where the houses stood sometimes as much as seven storeys high – for space was scarce and the density of the population here was the highest in the city. The *ghetto vecchio*, reserved for Jews from the Levant (*levantini*), had been under the control of the *Cinque Savii alla Mercanzia* since 1541; the *nuovo*, under the control of the *Cattaveri*, harboured German Jews (*Todeschi*), some of whom, since there was not room for all, went to live in the old ghetto. These *Todeschi*, who had been accepted in the city at the time of the League of Cambrai, were poor Jews dealing in second-hand clothes and pawnbroking and they were to run the *Monte di Pietà* in Venice – 'li banchi della povertà'. Meanwhile certain Jews specializing in large-scale trade, Portuguese and Levantine, by turns detested and wooed by the Signoria, obtained a special status, probably after 1581. But in 1633, all the Jews, including the *Ponentini*, were confined to the same ghettos – hence the many social, religious and cultural conflicts within this artificial near-concentration-camp world.

The ghetto may have been the prison within which the Jews were confined but it was also the citadel into which they withdrew to defend their faith and the continuity of the Talmud. A historian as sympathetic towards the Jewish cause as the great Lucio de Azevedo maintained that Jewish intolerance, at the beginning of the sixteenth century, was 'certainly greater than that of the Christians', which is probably an exaggeration. But clearly intolerance there was.

It was even rumoured – absurd though it seems – in about 1532, that the Jews had tried to convert Charles V to the Mosaic faith during his stay at Mantua!

The ubiquity of Jewish communities. Willingly or unwillingly, the Jews were forced into the role of agents of cultural exchange. It could hardly have been otherwise. They were, or had been, everywhere; despite expulsion orders they did not always leave the forbidden land, and they might return. Officially, they were absent from England between 1290 and 1655, the date of their so-called 're-entry' under Cromwell; in fact London had its Jewish merchants from the beginning of the seventeenth century and perhaps earlier. France too in theory expelled all Jews in 1394 but they very soon reappeared (as *marranos* and outwardly Christian it is true) in Rouen, Nantes, Bordeaux, Bayonne, the natural stopping places for Portuguese *marranos* travelling to Antwerp and Amsterdam.

In the south of France, the Jews were few in number. Towards 1568–1570, they were driven out of the cities of Provence and were received amicably in Savoy. In Marseilles, where municipal policy varied, there were only a few Jews at the beginning of the seventeenth century. Jews expelled from Spain in 1492 settled in Languedoc, remained there and 'accustomed [the French] to trade with Barbary'. As New Christians they became apothecaries and doctors at Montpellier: Felix Platter lodged in the house of one of them. In Avignon at the end of the century, when his brother Thomas was there, they numbered about 500, protected by the Pope, but did not have the right 'to buy either house, garden, field or meadow, within or without the town', and were reduced to the trades of tailor or old clothes dealer.

Germany and Italy were of course too divided to be able to expel the Jews simultaneously from every region, and yet heaven knows they were harassed enough. One city would close its gates to them, another open them up. When Milan, after much hesitation, finally ordered the few 'Hebrews' in the city to leave in 1597, the latter went, as far as we can see, to Vercelli, Mantua, Modena, Verona, Padua 'and the surrounding localities'. Their trek from door to door, even when unsuccessful, had farcical overtones: in Genoa for instance, from which city the Jews were solemnly expelled in 1516 – only to return in 1517. The same kind of thing happened at Venice and Ragusa because they were always allowed back in the end: in May, 1515, Ragusa was stirred up by a Franciscan monk and drove out its Jews; the latter immediately organized a grain blockage in Apulia and Morea against the Republic of St Blaise (proving that they controlled the grain trade) and the city had to take them back. In 1550, it was the turn of Venice to think of expelling the Jews, but she immediately realized that they controlled and handled the bulk of her trade: wool, silk, sugar, spice – and that the Venetians themselves were often content merely to

266. *Opposite:* The Levantine synagogue in Venice, constructed by Jews who came to Venice from the eastern Mediterranean between 1538 and 1561.

retail the merchandise of Jews, earning only the usual commission. In fact Italy had taken in large numbers of Jews, following the mass expulsions from France, Spain and Portugal, a frequent destination being the Papal States, where more Jews settled for preference than elsewhere. They became remarkably prosperous at Ancona: before their violent persecution at the hands of Paul IV in 1555 and 1556, they numbered 1770 heads of household and bought as much property as they wished, houses, vineyards, 'and bore no sign to distinguish them from Christians'. In 1492, the expulsion of the Jews from Sicily affected over 40,000 persons, we are told, the vast bulk of whom were the humble artisans whose departure the island could not well afford.

It would be incongruous to compare these fugitive Jews with the vigilant bands of outlaws, but after all both Jews and brigands were able to take advantage of a complicated political map, whether in Italy or Germany. Germany had the convenient nearby refuge of Poland, towards which the wagons piled with the possessions of refugees could make their way; Italy offered convenient means of escape by sea and to the Levant. When, in 1571, there was talk of expelling the Jews from Venice, some were already aboard departing ships when the order

267. Unnamed cemetery markers in the Jewish cemetery in Fez, Morocco.

was revoked. Escape by sea was not without its risks of course. The master of a vessel might be tempted to sell his passengers and seize their belongings. In 1540, the captain of a Ragusan ship robbed his passengers, Jews fleeing from Naples, and abandoned them at Marseilles, where the king of France, François I, took pity on them and sent them in his own ships to the Levant. In 1558, Jews escaping from Pesaro made their way to Ragusa then took ship for the Levant. The ship's crew, possibly Ragusan, seized them and sold them as slaves in Apulia. In 1583, a Greek crew massacred 52 of their 53 Jewish passengers.

If one wished to pursue the dispersion of the Jews throughout the Greater Mediterranean and indeed the world, one could easily find them in Goa, Aden, in Persia. They had also managed to enter Marseilles, where 'imperceptibly they had possessed themselves of a major part of the Levant trade, which obliged the late M. de Seignelay to expel them from Marseilles by royal ordinance'. But they were soon handling the other end of the line, in the Levant. There were Jews in Madeira and so numerous were they on the island of São Tomé, that (these were obviously New Christians) they 'openly' practised Judaism; they were among the earliest arrivals in America and the earliest martyrs (in 1515 in Cuba), of the Spanish Inquisition, which did not stop there; in 1543, Philip as regent of the kingdoms of Spain had expelled them – a purely theoretical gesture – from the Castilian Indies. Jews were also numerous in North Africa as far south as the Sahara.

Judaism and capitalism. The Jew, originally, like the Armenian, a peasant, had many centuries earlier turned away from life on the land. Now he was invariably financier, supply-master, merchant, usurer, pawnbroker, doctor, artisan, tailor, weaver, even blacksmith. He was often very poor: sometimes an extremely modest pawnbroker. Pawnbrokers, even the very humblest, constituted as it were the bourgeoisie of these often impoverished communities. In Italy the number of such small moneylenders was high and their services were much appreciated in the countryside and small market towns. In September, 1573, the *podestà* of Capodistria asked for a Jewish banker to be sent to the town, otherwise the inhabitants, victims of continually rising prices, would be obliged to go (as they were already) to usurers in Trieste who lent money at 30 and 40 per cent; this would never happen with a local Jewish moneylender.

But as well as small-time moneylenders and usurers, there were the great Jewish merchant families, sometimes expelled only to be recalled, always in demand. We find them at Lisbon masquerading as New Christians, or, if they were rich, as perfect Christians, the Ximenez, Caldeira and Evora. They might be innovators: for example Michael Rodríguez or Rodrigua, the Levantine Jew of Venice who conceived the idea of the port of Spalato; they might be powerful like the rich Abravanel family. Samuel Abravanel and his relations for years controlled the fate of the Jews of Naples, lending money to the king, holding interests in the Madeira sugar trade, the Lanciano fairs and the grain trade.

268, 269. Jewish doctor (*left*) and merchant at Constantinople.
Sixteenth-century French prints.

Success on a colossal scale can be glimpsed in the unparalleled career of the
Portuguese Mendes family, in particular of a nephew, Juan Mínguez or Miques,
the Joseph Micas of Spanish *avisos* from the Levant. A *marrano*, he reverted to
Judaism at Constantinople, where he became a sort of eastern Fugger, powerful
almost until his death (1579), dreaming of becoming a 'King of the Jews' and
founding a state in the Holy Land (he had surveyed the ruins of Tiberias), or
'King of Cyprus', finally contenting himself with the title conferred on him by
the sultan, of Duke of Naxos, the name by which he is known to those historians,
usually willing hagiographers, who have concerned themselves with him.

Jewish merchants went towards regions of growth and took advantage of
their advance as much as they contributed to it. The services rendered were
mutual. Capitalism can mean many things. It implies amongst others a system
of calculation, an acquaintance with certain techniques relating to money and
credit: even before the fall of Jerusalem to the Crusaders in 1099, the Jews were
already familiar with the *suftaya* (bill of exchange) and the *sakh* (cheque), which
were in common use in the Moslem world. This acquisition was maintained
through all the forced migrations of Jewish communities.

But beyond this, capitalism, to be successful, presupposes a network, the organization of mutual confidence and cooperation throughout the world. This had been true for centuries of the Jewish merchants. They formed the leading commercial network in the world, for they had representatives everywhere: in backward or under-developed regions where they were artisans, shopkeepers and pawnbrokers and in key cities where they participated in economic growth and booming trade, although their numbers might be very small: there were only 1424 Jews in Venice in 1586; barely a hundred in Hamburg at the beginning

270. Jewish marriage certificate from Sana'a, Yemen, 1794. *Israel Museum, Jerusalem*

of the seventeenth century; 2000 at most in Amsterdam, 400 in Antwerp in 1570.

In the thirteenth century, the Fairs of Champagne were the centre of western commerce. Into the fairs and out of them flowed every kind of merchandise. The Jews were there too, in the towns and villages of Champagne, some of them concerned in the agricultural or artisanal life of the region, owning fields, vines, real estate or houses which they bought and sold, but for the most part they were already merchants and moneylenders, 'lending, it appears, being more popular with them than trade', their loans being made to noblemen, particularly the Counts of Champagne, and to monasteries. Though attracted by the Champagne fairs and the prosperity surrounding them, the Jews (with a few exceptions) did not participate directly and certainly did not dominate them, but they did control certain of the approaches to them.

With the general recession of the sixteenth century, the only region not economically threatened in the West was Italy: Jewish merchants spread all over the country and a recent study shows that they were colonizing the lower levels of usury, ousting their rivals from this elementary plane of commercial life.

In the fifteenth and sixteenth centuries, the major Mediterranean trade currents led to North Africa and the Levant. In North Africa, according to Leo Africanus, the Jewish colonies were thriving, still defiant at the beginning of the sixteenth century, and capable of resistance, thus managing to survive in the inhospitable Spanish *presidio* of Oran until 1668, with a finger in every pie. An enquiry conducted in the Oran *presidio* in 1626 mentions the arrival of camel trains from the Sahara, one of them, coming from Tafilalet and Figuig, accompanied by 'Jews of war' – 'judíos de guerra' – in fact simple merchants, for in Spain as in the Islamic countries, a distinction was made between the *Moros de paz*, subjects who lived near the citadel, and the still unsubdued *Moros de guerra*: in the same way there were Jews *de paz* and *de guerra*. But the presence of Jewish merchants on this ancient trade axis is in itself worth noting.

In the Levant, contemporary accounts all agree on the major role played by the Jewish merchants; they controlled the markets at Aleppo and (particularly Portuguese Jews) in Cairo, as moneylenders to whom the Christians often had recourse and in whose hands the entire caravan trade was clearly concentrated.

What else is there to say? In Venice, the Jewish presence was maintained in spite of tensions and quarrels followed by pacts or reconciliation. One expulsion certainly took place, that of the rich *marranos* in 1497, following their speculation in the Sicilian wheat upon which Venice depended, but they were only a small fraction of the Jewish population and recent arrivals at that (who seem to have returned, since there was once more talk of expelling them in 1550 and we find them mentioned by name in Venice until the end of the century and even later).

One would like above all to know what their situation was in Genoa, capital of world finance, but on this subject there is very little information. One thing

271. Fifteenth-century painting of Mantuan Jews wearing the yellow badge
which singled them out.

is certain: there was hostility towards them. In Genoa, the jealousy felt by local
artisans and doctors towards their Jewish rivals led to the expulsion of the
community on 2nd April, 1550, the decree being 'proclaimed to the sound of
trumpets, as it was', writes a witness, 'in the time of my father, Rabbi Jehoshua
ha-Cohen' in 1516. The same witness, the physician Joseph Ha Cohen, went to
live not far away, still in the territory of the *Dominante*, at Voltaggio, where he
continued to practise medicine. In June, 1567, the Genoese expelled them from
the *Dominio* where they had been tolerated after the edict forbidding them to
live within the city itself.

One last point to bear in mind is the spread of the *marranos* throughout the
Mediterranean, preparing the way for the Dutch and marking the beginning of
the age of Amsterdam in world history. In 1627, the Count Duke of Olivares
introduced the Portuguese *marranos* to the vital business of the *asientos*, giving
formal recognition to a new financial era which had in fact begun well before
this date.

Jews and the economic cycle. If a chronological table were drawn up of the
persecutions, massacres, expulsions and forced conversions which make up the
martyrology of Jewish history, a correlation would be discernible between
changes in the immediate economic climate and the savagery of anti-Jewish
measures. Persecution was always determined by, and accompanied, a worsening
in the economic climate. On this point it seems to me that no argument is
possible. Similarly, to take the single example of the expulsion of the Jews from
Spain (1492), this event 'of world-wide import', according to Werner Sombart

occurred late on in a long period of economic depression, which had begun with the reign of the Catholic Kings and lasted until at least 1509 and possibly 1520.

Just as the secular recession of 1350–1450 sent the Jews to Italy and its sheltered economy, so the crisis of 1600–1650 found them in the equally sheltered economic sector of the North Sea. The Protestant world saved them and showed them kindness and in return they saved and showed kindness to the Protestant world. After all, as Werner Sombart has remarked, Genoa was just as well placed as Hamburg or Amsterdam for access to the maritime routes to America, the Indies or China.

But when the long-term trend re-asserted itself between 1575 and 1595 and the sky lightened, an improvement appeared in the economic activity of the whole Mediterranean and in particular in that of the Jewish colonies, wherever they had taken root. In Rome, Sixtus V himself protected them (1585–1590). Thereafter it looks as if the part played by Jewish capitalism in maritime exchange grew unhindered.

Understanding Spain. The destiny of the Jewish people both reflects and is reflected in the many-faceted mirror of Spanish history. One major difficulty will be to prevent the emotions, vocabulary and polemic of our own age from intruding into this highly-charged debate; to refuse to be drawn by the simple language of moralists into the rigid separation of black and white, good and evil. I cannot consider Spain guilty of the murder of Israel. Has there been any civilization at any time in the past which has sacrificed its own existence to that of another? Certainly not Islam or Israel any more than anyone else. I say this in no partisan spirit, for I am a child of my time: my sympathy invariably lies with all those who are oppressed in their liberty, their persons, their possessions and their convictions. In the Spanish situation I am therefore naturally on the side of the Jews, the *conversos*, the Protestants, the *alumbrados* and the Moriscos. But such feelings, which I cannot avoid, are irrelevant to the basic problem. To call sixteenth century Spain a 'totalitarian' or racist country strikes me as unreasonable. It has some harrowing scenes to offer, but then so do France, Germany, England, or Venice (from a reading of the judicial archives) at the same period.

When they expelled the Jews in 1492, Ferdinand and Isabella were not acting as individuals, in the aftermath of the fall of Granada, victory as always being a bad counsellor: their action was encouraged by the poor economic climate and the reluctance of certain wounds to heal. Civilizations, like economies, have their long-term history: they are prone to mass movements, carried as it were imperceptibly forward by the weight of history, sliding down a hidden slope so gradual that their movement is unaided and unheeded by man. And it is the fate of civilizations to 'divide' themselves, to prune their excess growth, shedding part of their heritage as they move forward. Every civilization is the heir to its own past and must choose between the possessions bequeathed by another

272. A Jew wearing the badge.
Fourteenth-century mural from Tarragona
Cathedral.

generation. Some things must be left behind. During the 'extended' sixteenth century, the Peninsula, in order to reintegrate itself with Europe, turned itself into the Church Militant; it shed its two unwanted religions, the Moslem and the Hebrew. It refused to become either African or Oriental in a process which in some ways resembles that of modern de-colonization. The great discoveries later did the rest: they placed the Peninsula at the centre of the modern world, that is at the centre of European world conquest.

Before the nationalism of the nineteenth century, peoples felt truly united only by the bonds of religious belief; in other words by civilization. The massive cohesion of Spain in the fifteenth century was that of a people which had for centuries been in relation to another civilization, the underdog the weaker, the less intelligent, the less brilliant and the less rich, and was now suddenly liberated.

In the context of this cultural conflict, a Christian Spain was struggling to be born. The glacier displaced by its emergence crushed the trees and houses in its path. And I prefer not to divert the debate to a moralizing level by saying that Spain was amply punished for her crimes, for the expulsion of 1492, the persecution inflicted on so many *conversos* and the angry measures taken against the Moriscos in 1609–1614. Some have said that these crimes and passions cost her her glory. But the most glorious age of Spain began precisely in 1492 and lasted undimmed until Rocroi (1643) or even 1650. The punishment, depending on which date one chooses, came at least forty years if not a century late. Nor can I accept that the expulsion of the Jews deprived Spain of a vigorous bourgeoisie. The truth is that a commercial bourgeoisie had never developed in Spain in the first place. Another argument frequently heard is that the tragedy of *limpieza de sangre*, purity of blood, was to be the trial and scourge of Spain. No one would deny the trials it brought and their fearful sequels, but all western societies erected barriers in the seventeenth century and consecrated social privileges.

If the train in which I am sitting moves off, the passenger in a train alongside has the sensation of moving in the opposite direction. Civilizations too may be carried past one another. Do they understand each other? I am not at all sure that they do. Spain was moving towards political unity, which could not be conceived, in the sixteenth century, as anything other than religious unity. Israel meanwhile was being carried towards the destiny of the *diaspora*, a single destiny in its way, but its theatre was the whole world, it spanned oceans and seas, new nations and ancient civilizations. The one thing of which we can be certain is that the destiny of Israel, its strength, its survival and its misfortunes are all the consequence of its remaining irreducible, refusing to be diluted, that is of being a civilization faithful to itself. Every civilization is its own heaven and hell.

4 Civilizations and their zones of influence

He who gives, dominates. The theory of the donor works not only at the level of individuals and societies but also for civilizations. That such giving may in the long run cause impoverishment is possible. But while it lasts it is a sign of superiority and this observation completes the central thesis of Part Two of this book: the Mediterranean remained, for a hundred years after Christopher Columbus and Vasco da Gama, the centre of the world, a strong and brilliant universe. How do we know? Because it was educating others, teaching them its own ways of life. And I would stress that it was the *whole* Mediterranean world, Moslem and Christian, which projected its light beyond its own shores. Even North African Islam, often treated by historians as a poor relation, spread its influence southwards towards the Saharan borders and through the desert as far as the *Bled es Sudan*. As for Turkish Islam, it illuminated a cultural area which it owned in part, from the Balkans to the lands of Araby, into the depths of Asia and as far as the Indian Ocean. The art of the Turkish Empire, of which the Sulaimānīye mosque is the crowning achievement, spread far afield, affirming its supremacy, and architecture was only one element in this vast cultural expansion.

273. The Lepanto Monstrance, made by the Augsburg goldsmith Johann Zeckl.
Church of S. Maria Victoria, Ingolstadt.

Even more distinctive, to our eyes, is the penetrating influence of western
Mediterranean civilization. It spread in fact against the current of world history,
reaching out to northern Europe which was soon to become the centre of world
power: Mediterranean, Latin culture was to Protestant Europe what Greece was

to Rome. It rapidly crossed the Atlantic both in the sixteenth and seventeenth centuries, and with this geographical extension over the ocean, the Mediterranean sphere of influence was finally complete, embracing Hispano-Portuguese America, the most brilliant America of the time. To make identification even easier, a word given general currency by Burckhardt, the Baroque, conveniently designates the civilization of the Christian Mediterranean: wherever we find the Baroque we can recognize the mark of Mediterranean culture. The influence of the Renaissance – putting value judgements aside – cannot compare, for sheer mass and volume, with the enormous explosion of the Baroque. The Renaissance was the child of the Italian cities. The Baroque drew its strength both from the huge spiritual force of the Holy Roman Empire and from the huge temporal force of the Spanish Empire. With the Baroque a new light began to shine; since 1527 and 1530 and the tragic end of the great cities of the Renaissance, Florence and Rome, the tone had changed: new and more lurid colours now bathed the landscapes of western Europe.

Having said this, I hope the reader will appreciate my problem. This is a book about the Mediterranean: if I attempted to describe this enormous transgressive metamorphosis in all its aspects, I should be writing a book about the world. I therefore decided that a single demonstration would satisfy both the glory of the Mediterranean and the equilibrium of this book. Regretfully then, I have had to leave aside Islam, regretfully too Hispano-Portuguese America and the late but rare splendour of Ouro Preto in the mining heart of Brazil. The Baroque, the sprawling and extravagant Baroque, will be more than enough to occupy us, in the single sector, itself enormous, of western Europe.

The different stages of the Baroque. Its origins are usually discerned in the *Pietà* sculpted by Michelangelo for St Peter's between 1497 and 1499, and also in the *Stanze* of Raphael, the tumultuous movements of the *Fire in the Borgo* and *The Expulsion of Heliodorus from the Temple*, the St Cecilia frescoes at Bologna which, according to Émile Mâle, already foreshadow the genius of the new age and, it has been said, the 'language of gesture the Baroque was to make its own'. One could also look for its origins in Leonardo's cartoon of the *Battle of Anghiari* or (outside Italy this time) in some of Dürer's engravings: a strange gathering at the christening. One of the unquestionable fathers of the Baroque is said to be Correggio, the Correggio of the *Assumption of the Virgin* at Parma. To be fully acceptable as a Baroque artist, he need only have manifested a little more disdain or indifference to the joys of the earth and the beauty of the Nude, that Nude on which Michelangelo expended such labour and love. On the other hand Michelangelo's taste for the grandiose, his pathos and *terribilità*, were, along with the *grazia* of Raphael and the movement and play of light in Correggio, the first gifts laid before the cradle of the infant Baroque. Thus endowed, the child grew quickly and had almost reached maturity when Correggio died in 1534, certainly by the time that Michelangelo, after seven years of exhausting

274, 275. *Above: The Expulsion of Heliodorus from the Temple* by Raphael. Stanza di Eliodoro, Vatican, Rome. *Right:* Detail from the *Last Judgment* by Michelangelo. Sistine Chapel, Vatican, Rome.

labour had in 1541, finished the *Last Judgment* in which 'the terrors of the Middle Ages' were revived.

The curtain fell suddenly on the splendours of the Renaissance after the Sack of Rome in 1527 and the capture of Florence in 1530. 'The fearful Sack of Rome' appeared to contemporaries a divine punishment. It abruptly recalled the city to its Christian mission. While Clement VII held out in the Castel Sant'Angelo, the city was for months at the mercy of the soldiery and looting peasants. Nothing was spared. Raphael's pupils had scattered far and wide, Penni to Naples, Pierino del Vaga to Genoa, Giulio Romano to Mantua from which he would never want to return. 'So the pupils of Raphael had no pupils' concludes Stendhal rather hastily. Thus the fragility of all artistic life, all life of the intellect, was once more revealed. The siege and capture of Florence, 'a second judgment of God', the violent effect of which on economic life has been demonstrated by G. Parenti, repeated in 1530 the disaster of 1527. With this, 'something died, and died quickly'. A new generation, of which Giuliano de' Medici predicted that it would be more Spartan than Athenian, was moving into position, new fashions were triumphing. What had died was the Renaissance, perhaps Italy herself. What was triumphing was *la maniera*, imitation, emphasis,

276. *Opposite:* Detail from *Paradiso* by Tintoretto. *Palazzo Ducale, Venice*
277. *Above: The Madonna del Popolo* by Federico Barocci. *Uffizi, Florence*

exaggeration: it inflated the work of those of Raphael's pupils who were still working and their academicism had its followers.

The wind of change was felt first in painting. This was the beginning of Mannerism, the definition and aims of which were outlined in 1557 by Lodovico Dolce in a formal apologia for *la maniera*. All Italy was intoxicated with it from about 1530–1540, except for Venice, where there were a few *manieristi*, but where there was also for many years the indomitable Titian.

Mannerism was re-christened by the twentieth century as the Pre-Baroque, a long period typified by Tintoretto and ending with his death in 1590. The last masterpiece of Mannerism was the great *Paradiso*, painted between 1589 and 1590 in the *Sala del Maggior Consiglio*, Venice. Almost immediately began the first phase of the Baroque, inaugurated, according to G. Schnürer, by Federico

Barocci of Urbino, whose celebrated *Madonna del Popolo* is now in the Uffizi. It was to be the reigning manner until 1630; but this was far from its end, for from the 'Italian Baroque' there immediately derived a vigorous art which was to flourish in Switzerland, southern Germany, Austria and Bohemia until the eighteenth and even nineteenth centuries, nourished by a fertile popular imagination which gave it the life it never possessed in its Italian period. It was here indeed, in the countries of central Europe, that the word Baroque (whatever its origins) began to be applied in the eighteenth century to an art which was in fact already in decline. Hence, so German scholars have said, the equation Baroque = German; a false equation if one looks at the sources.

Begging the question. There is endless possibility for debate about this chronology and the assumptions behind it. But such problems are rather different from the point we are at present considering, which is that whatever the precise nature of this civilization, it originated in the Mediterranean. The Mediterranean was the donor, the transmitter and therefore a superior force, whose teachings, ways of life and tastes were adopted in lands far from its shores. It is this evidence of the vigour of that civilization, its resources and the reasons behind it, which must occupy us here.

Rome: centre for the diffusion of Mediterranean culture. Rome was a great centre of cultural diffusion, by no means the only one, but certainly the most important. At the beginning of the sixteenth century it was still undistinguished, as Rabelais saw it on his first voyage in 1532 and as it is described in Marliani's *Topography* and various other guides. It was a small city, in the centre of a pastoral economy; strewn and ringed round with ancient monuments often half-destroyed, atrociously disfigured, more often still buried to their foundations under earth and rubble. The inhabited part of the city was characterized by brick houses, sordid narrow streets and vast vacant lots.

During the sixteenth century, the city was transformed, new life was breathed into it as palaces and churches rose from the ground. Its population grew, maintaining its level even in the seventeenth century, an age generally unfavourable to Mediterranean cities. Rome became a gigantic building site. Any artist could find work there, an army of architect-masons to begin with: Baldassare Peruzzi of Sienna (d. 1536), Sammicheli of Verona (d. 1549), Sansovino of Florence (d. 1570), Vignola (d. 1573) from northern Italy (the cradle of almost all the great Italian architects), Ligorio of Naples (d. 1580), Pellegrini of Bologna (d. 1592). Olivieri (d. 1599), an exception, was a native of Rome. On the heels of these artisans, architects and stone-cutters, pressed the army of painters necessary in an age of art when decorative painting reached its apogee. Domes and ceilings offered unlimited space to painters, while imposing upon them

278. *Opposite:* The cupola of St. Peter's, Rome.

sometimes strictly defined themes. The sacred painting of the Baroque was the logical consequence of its architecture.

It was at this time that the basilica of St Peter's was completed, and the Gesù built, between 1568 and 1575, by Giacomo Vignola, who died in 1573 without seeing his work completed. The first Jesuit church had now appeared; it was to serve many times as a model throughout Christendom. Every order would now wish to possess its own churches, in Rome and outside Rome, decorated in an individual style with the images of its particular patterns of worship. So there now sprang up, in the Eternal City and then all over the Christian world, the first churches with accolades and cupolas of sober geometry, of which the Val-de-Grâce is a later but still typical example in France.

The prodigious growth of Rome entailed vast expenditure. This brings us back to the history of the papal finances; it is now beyond dispute that the Popes drew enormous revenues from the Papal States and also appealed successfully to public credit. The churches of France and Spain were meanwhile abandoned to the covetousness and financial needs of His Most Christian Majesty and His Catholic Majesty respectively. The Papal States, during the fifty years which concern us, only rarely (in 1557 and during the three years of the Holy League) incurred heavy military expenses. So the papacy was able to allot a large budget to the fine arts. The invasion of the Mediterranean by American silver was to facilitate these luxurious investments. It was in the years after 1560–1570 that all the dreams of Leo X and Julius II were realized. Not only that but the religious orders, whose numbers were increased by the wave of Catholic piety, added their efforts to those of the Popes. Rome being also the capital of these little states within the state, their shop window so to speak, Jesuits, Dominicans, Carmelites and Franciscans all contributed their share of financial effort and artistic emulation and copied, outside Rome, the achievements of the capital. If there was an artistic and religious expansion of the Baroque, it was the work of these orders, above all that of St Ignatius. It is for this reason that the adjective Jesuit seems to me in a way far more appropriate than that of Baroque to describe this expansion, notwithstanding the reservations which have been expressed concerning this claim.

I do not think it is necessary to retrace here the history of the widespread move towards monasticism, which preceded by many years the success of the Council of Trent, that first victory of the new generation. As early as 1517, the Oratory of Divine Love, founded in Genoa in the preceding century by Bernardino da Feltre, established itself at Rome. In the same year, Leo X agreed to the separation of the Observants from the Conventuals in the Franciscan order. From the ranks of the Reformed Franciscans were to emerge, amongst others, the Capuchins in 1528. But it was not until 1540, the year of the founding of the Society of Jesus, that the movement gained impetus and could finally be said to be under way.

Three years earlier, in 1537, the Commission of Cardinals convoked by Paul

III, had been pessimistic; it had even considered allowing corrupt congregations to die out in order to repopulate them later with new monks. Then in the decade of the 1540s the whole picture changed: the first round was played and won: the creation and reformation of monastic orders continued and the movement towards monastic renovation gathered pace. It moved even more quickly after the Council of Trent: the Oratorians were founded by St Philip Neri in 1564; the Oblati of St Charles Borromeo in 1578; the Congregation of Minor Clerks Regular was founded by the Genoese Giovanni Agostino Adorno and St Francesco Caracciolo in 1588 (the first establishment at Naples dates from 1589) and three years later, in 1592, the Fathers of the Christian Doctrine settled in Avignon.

Who can say what support the religious orders, often released, in order to do battle, from the old restrictions of choral life and monastic observance, 'vrais clers réguliers', brought to the papacy? Thanks to them the Church was saved; it was able, from Rome, to coordinate one of the most extraordinary revolutions from above in history. The battle it fought was waged with intelligence. The civilization it carried forward – whatever name we choose to give it – was a militant civilization; and its art was merely one more means to an end.

Baroque art then, often smacks of propaganda. In some respects it is an art done to order, with all the advantages and disadvantages that implies. Shrewd theologians and friars demanded of Rubens, Caracciolo, Domenichino, Ribera, Zurbaran or Murillo, the physical execution of pictures spiritually composed by themselves, turning them down if the execution appeared in any way deficient. In the fight against Protestantism, the enemy of decorated churches and images, the Church set out to build the most beautiful houses of God on earth, images of Paradise, portions of heaven. Art was a powerful means of combat and instruction; a means of stating, through the power of the image, the Immaculate Holiness of the Mother of God, the efficacious intervention of the saints, the reality and power of the Eucharistic sacrifice, the eminence of St Peter, a means of arguing from the visions and ecstasies of the saints. Patiently compiled and transmitted, identical iconographical themes crossed and re-crossed Europe. If the Baroque exaggerates, if it is attracted by death and suffering, by martyrs depicted with unsparing realism, if it seems to have abandoned itself to a pessimistic view, to the Spanish *desengaño* of the seventeenth century, it is because this is an art which is preoccupied with convincing, because it desperately seeks the dramatic detail which will strike and hold the beholder's attention. It was intended for the use of the faithful, who were to be persuaded and gripped by it, who were to be taught by active demonstration, by an early version of *verismo*, the truth of certain contested notions, whether of Purgatory or of the Immaculate Conception. It was a theatrical art and one conscious of its theatricality: had not the theatre itself provided the Jesuits with arms, notably in their conquest of Germany, in an age moreover when the theatre was establishing its rights everywhere, with strolling players and before long fixed stages?

So it was both a way of life and a way of belief which travelled northwards from the shores of the Mediterranean, towards the Rhine and the Danube as well as to Paris, the heart of France, where in the early years of the seventeenth century so many churches and convents were being built. It was a way of life and belief specifically Mediterranean: witness Jacob Burckhardt's description of Pius II processing through Viterbo 'surrounded by live tableaux representing the Last Supper, St Michael battling with the Devil, the Resurrection of the Lord and the Virgin carried in triumph to heaven by Angels'. One immediately thinks of Spanish processions with the *tratos* representing scenes from the Passion; no more than in Italy does this exclude *autos sacramentales*. This then was a dramatic form of Christianity which northerners found astonishing. The manner of devotion and the flagellation practised by Spaniards shocked and scandalized the people of Flanders. Baroque art, nourished on this southern religiosity, carried something of it to the North. A whole book could be written on the devotional practices imported to all parts of Europe, on the part played by men of the Mediterranean in the violent reclamation of the contested lands of the North which returned to the fold of the Roman Church. Remembering this, one can no longer talk of the decadence of the Mediterranean; unless decadence and the disintegration it implies can be credited with a powerful capacity for diffusing a dying civilization.

Another centre of cultural diffusion: Spain. Moving westwards from Vienna to Lyons then to Toulouse or Bayonne, one begins to feel the pull of another civilization – that of Spain. In Vienna and Munich, Roman and Italian (every kind of Italian) influence predominated. In France too, travellers, fashions and ideas from Rome and Italy were to be found, but stronger than either was the influence of Spain.

One of the problems of the Pyrenees was that they never allowed simultaneous two-way traffic. Either France was the predominant cultural influence and everything travelled from north to south – as was the case from the eleventh and twelfth centuries until the fifteenth – or else Spain suddenly rose to eminence and reversed the flow from south to north, as happened in the sixteenth and seventeenth centuries. The traditional dialogue between France and Spain abruptly took a new turn and it was to change again in the eighteenth century. In the time of Cervantes, France hankered after the fashions and ideas of her neighbour beyond the Pyrenees, a country at once mocked, reviled, feared and admired. Spain on the contrary broke off all contact, kept a watch over her frontiers, forbade her subjects in the Netherlands to study in France and recalled her medical students from Montpellier.

It was a strange dialogue and as usual one without affection. Where, if not in the Netherlands, was the Spaniard so mocked as in France? A French translation appeared in 1608 of a satirical fantasy published in Middelburg by Simon Molard: *Emblèmes sur les actions, perfections et mœurs du Segnor espagnol.*

279. *The Ecstasy of St. Teresa* by Bernini. Cornaro Chapel, S. Maria della Vittoria, Rome.

Poor *Segnor*! He is compared to every kind of beast, a devil in the house, a wolf at table, a swine in his bed-chamber, a peacock in the street, a fox with women and more besides. 'So beware of the *Segnor* in all places' warns the pamphlet in conclusion. But the *Segnor* though ridiculed was envied and imitated as well. The influence of Spain was that of a strong nation, of an immense empire 'on which the sun never set', of a civilization more refined than that of France. Any man of culture in France was obliged to know Spanish and did. Translations abounded. Cervantes was much read. In 1617, his long book, *Los Trabajos de Persiles y Sigismunda*, was reprinted in Paris in Spanish, then translated into French. And the picaresque novel had an even more devoted following. Soon would come the adaptations of Spanish comedies for the French stage. In England too, Italian and Spanish works were translated and incorporated into the country's intellectual heritage.

Alongside such literary influences came a host of minor cultural borrowings. The court of Louis XIII, said to be as Spanish as it was French, set the tone. Anything Spanish was in fashion. Women daubed their faces with 'Spanish white' and 'Spanish vermilion' – which did not necessarily come all the way from Spain. They doused themselves – and so did men – in perfumes, some of which came from Nice and Provence, but most of which, especially the more costly ones – forbidden to 'peasants' – were imported from Spain and Italy. If Brantôme is to be believed, the women of those two countries 'have always been more excitingly and exquisitely perfumed than our great ladies in France'. There was competition for the secrets of rare essences and beauty preparations at least as complicated as those of Molière's *précieuses*. A gallant would promise to buy his mistress gloves of 'Spanish leather' and indeed, although fine goods were already being produced in France and the reputation of French fashions and elegance was beginning to appear, Spanish gloves made from fine supple hides, the famous toiletwater of Córdoba, *guadameciles*, the gilded leather used for wall hangings, enjoyed the kind of prestige that the twentieth century was to give to the *article de Paris*. And they were just as expensive. When the wife of Simón Ruiz took it into her head to 'do business' and sent 'perfumed gloves' from Spain to Florence, to be exchanged for Italian merchandise, her husband's partner, Baltasar Suárez, claimed that in this city of grave bourgeois, nobody would buy such a costly and frivolous article (three crowns a pair). But this was in 1584. One wonders what the Florentines would have thought a couple of decades later.

It is at least clear that yet again, the marginal regions of the Mediterranean, rather than its tumultuous centre, are the best place to view and possibly to decipher its destiny. Those Mediterranean influences which spill over its borders are sign enough of its forceful presence in the turmoil of exchange and conflict which makes up the life of the world. These influences underline, as the seventeenth century begins, the eminent position of the Mediterranean, the cradle of ancient civilization, in the building of the modern world on which it left so large a mark.

7

The Forms of War

WAR IS NOT SIMPLY the antithesis of civilization.

Historians refer constantly to war without really knowing or seeking to know its true nature – or natures. We are as ignorant about war as the physicist is of the true nature of matter. We talk about it because we have to: it has never ceased to trouble the lives of men. Chroniclers give it first place in their narratives; contemporary observers are addicted to discussion of the responsibilities for and consequences of the wars they have witnessed.

While I am determined not to exaggerate the importance of battle history, I cannot allow myself to neglect the history of warfare, a powerful and persistent undercurrent of human life. During the fifty years with which we are concerned, war punctuated the year with its rhythms, opening and closing the gates of time. Even when the fighting was over, it exerted a hidden pressure, surviving underground.

I shall not however claim to draw any philosophical conclusions about the 'nature' of war from an excursion into this dramatic field. Polemology, if indeed it is a science at all, is still in its infancy. It must learn to identify the long-term patterns, regular rhythms and relationships underlying the history of events: a stage we have not yet reached.

1 Formal war: naval squadrons and fortified frontiers

War in the Mediterranean: one thinks at once of the slim and powerful silhouettes of galleys, racing along the coast in summer, laid up in port during the winter. The documents abound with information about their voyages, their maintenance and their costly splendour. We have scores of expert estimates of what they cost in repairs, supplies, crews and money. Experience quickly showed how difficult it was to marshal them for major engagements, since they had to be accompanied, when sailing in large formation, by roundships carrying their bulky supplies. After a lengthy period of preparation, departure was sudden and the voyage usually rapid. Any point on the coast could be reached. But one should not exaggerate the harm a squadron of galleys could do. Any troops they disembarked were unlikely to go far inland. In 1535, Charles V captured the

city of Tunis but went no further; in 1541, he made an unsuccessful attack on Algiers: his campaign took him only from Cape Matifou to the heights overlooking the town. The Turks fared no better: in 1565 their fleet arrived to besiege Malta and became immobilized there. In 1572, the aged García de Toledo advised Don John of Austria, after Lepanto, that if the victorious powers should launch an expedition to the Levant, it would be better to attack an island than the mainland.

One thinks too of the many armies which by the sixteenth century are remarkable for their greatly increased size. Moving them from place to place, even mustering them beforehand, presented enormous problems. It took months for the king of France to assemble mercenaries and cannon at Lyons in order to 'make a sudden sally over the mountains'. In 1567, the Duke of Alva successfully moved his troops from Genoa to Brussels, but this was a peaceful manœuvre, not a series of encounters. It required all the vast resources of the Turkish Empire to transfer the sultan's armies from Istanbul to the Danube or to Armenia and then to wage a war so far from home. These were extraordinary and expensive feats of organization. When there was enemy opposition, any long march was ordinarily out of the question.

281. *Above: The Siege of Malta* by Perez d'Aleccio, showing the town's fortifications. *National Maritime Museum, Greenwich*

280. *Opposite:* The Procurator of Venice, Girolamo Zarne, with his commander's baton, about to embark onto a war galley as captain of the fleet against the Turks in the Cyprus war, 1570. *British Library*

One remembers lastly the series of fortified positions, already looming large in the sixteenth century and soon, in the seventeenth, to become all-important. To the Turks and corsairs, Christendom presented a frontier bristling with defences, the product of the skill of its engineers and the strong arms of its labourers. These fortifications testify to the mentality of a whole civilization. *Limes* or Great Wall of China, a barrier invariably expresses a state of mind. That Christendom – and not Islam – should have surrounded itself with a string of forts is of some significance; indeed it is a major distinction to which we shall be returning.

But these images, familiar and essential though they are, cannot tell us everything about war in the Mediterranean. The scenes they present are those of official war. But no sooner was regular war suspended than a subterranean, unofficial conflict took its place – privateering on sea and brigandage on land – forms of war which had existed all along but which now increased to fill the gap like second growth and brushwood replacing a fallen forest. There are different 'levels' of warfare then, and it is only by studying the contrasts between them that sociologists and historians will make progress towards explaining them. The dialectic is essential.

War and technology. War has always been a matter of arms and techniques. Improved technology can radically alter the course of events. Artillery, for instance, transformed the conditions of war in the Mediterranean as it did everywhere else. The appearance, widespread adoption and modification – for it was always being modified – of artillery, constitute a series of technical revolutions. The problem is dating them. When and how did artillery reach the narrow decks of the galleys? When did it become the distinctive and formidable arm first of the galleasses or large galleys and later of the galleons and tall ships? When was it installed on the ramparts and gun-placements of fortresses and how did it keep up with armies on the move? Well before the victories of Sulaimān, Charles VIII's Italian expedition in September, 1494, brought immediate and world-wide fame to field artillery. Several ages of gun manufacture succeeded each other – the age of bronze guns, iron guns, reinforced guns – and there were ages of *geographical* preponderance too, depending on the location of the munitions industry. The policies of Ferdinand the Catholic depended on the foundries of Málaga and Medina del Campo, the latter created in 1495, the former in 1499. Both were to decline quickly: the material they produced was to be worn out in Italy, immobilized in Africa or along the frontiers facing France. A longer reign was that of the foundries of Milan and Ferrara. Then the lead was taken by German and French foundries and, more important than either for supplying Spain and Portugal, the gunfounders of Flanders. From the first decades of the sixteenth century, the superiority of northern guns (and possibly of northern gunpowder too) was becoming evident. These were all matters of consequence. When a hundred or so pieces of ordnance arrived at

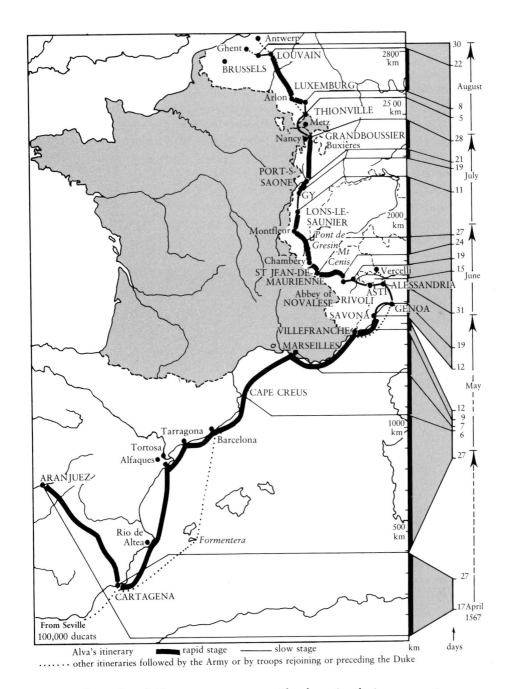

The Duke of Alva moves troops to Flanders, April–August, 1567

To move an army almost 3000 km, without opposition it is true, was a feat in itself. Note the fast sea passages and the time taken to cross the Alps. Unwelcome on French territory, the army had to take the long way round. Measurements, research by J. J. Hémardinquer.

Málaga from Flanders, the event was immediately noted in diplomatic corre-spondence. Similarly, the dispatch of forty pieces from Málaga to Messina was read by the Tuscan ambassador as a sign that an expedition was to be launched against Algiers, Tripoli or Barbary. In 1567, Fourquevaux declared that 15,000 cannon balls would be sufficient to take Algiers. This does not seem excessive if one is prepared to accept – as not all historians are – that Malta was saved in 1565 because the Duke of Florence had supplied it, the previous year, with 200 barrels of powder. Such at least was the opinion of a Spanish informant and for us it is an opportunity to note the importance of Tuscany for the manufacture of gunpowder, cannon balls and match for arquebuses.

It remains difficult to say precisely when these transformations occurred and had their effect. Occasional glimpses of developments are all we have. Similarly, while we can with confidence date from 1550 the appearance in the Venetian fleet of the great galleys or galleasses carrying artillery (they were undoubtedly technically responsible for the victory at Lepanto), we know next to nothing about the development in the Mediterranean of the armed galleons which we suddenly find being used by the Turks themselves towards the end of the century, on the route from Constantinople to Alexandria. For although Christendom had a head start, technical advances passed from one shore of the sea to another, similar materials came to be used and the political impact of innovation was diminished. Artillery played as great a part in the Christian attack on Granada and North Africa as it did in the victories of the Turks in the Balkans, at the vital battle of Mohács for instance or in Persia or again in North Africa.

War and states. War is a waste of money. 'Les nerfs des batailles sont les pécunes', 'coine, is the sinews of war', as Rabelais was certainly not the first to say.

To make war or peace at the time of one's own choosing, never to *undergo* one or the other, was theoretically the privilege of the strong; but surprises were always possible. Opinions round every prince were divided and his own feelings might be precariously in the balance. The conflict was often incarnated in the eternal protagonists, the war party and the peace party, of which the court of Philip II, up to 1580, provides the classic example. For years the vital question was who would sway the Prudent King – the circle surrounding the spokesman of peace, Ruy Gómez (who remained a faction even after their leader's death), or the supporters of the Duke of Alva, the warmonger always prompt to favour aggression. Indeed what prince or political leader has not been constantly con-fronted with these two alternatives embodied in opposing factions? Richelieu

282. *Opposite above:* Detail from *The Spanish Artillery Deployed at the Battle of Mühlberg.* Mural in the Palace at Oriz, Navarre. *Museo de Navarra, Pamplona*
283. *Below: The Siege of Malta* by Perez d'Aleccio, showing the Knights of Malta fighting the Turkish artillery. *National Maritime Museum, Greenwich*

himself, at the end of the dramatic year 1629, encountered opposition from his peace-loving Garde des Sceaux, Marillac. The choice between the parties was often imposed by events and some 'man of the moment' was propelled to the forefront.

The expenses of war crippled states and many wars were unproductive. The inglorious and costly Irish wars ruined Elizabeth's finances towards the end of her brilliant reign and, more than any other single factor, prepared the way for the truce of 1604. The cost of war in the Mediterranean was so great that bankruptcy often followed, both in Spain and in Turkey. Philip II's expenditure was phenomenal. In 1571, it was estimated at Madrid that the maintenance of the allied fleet (belonging to Venice, the Pope and Spain) comprising 200 galleys, 100 roundships and 50,000 soldiers, would cost over four million ducats a year. Floating cities, such war fleets devoured money and supplies. The annual upkeep of a galley equalled the cost of its original construction, about 6000 ducats in 1560, and this figure later rose. Between 1534 and 1573, naval armaments tripled, even by conservative estimates. At the time of Lepanto, there were active in the Mediterranean between 500 and 600 galleys, both Christian and Moslem, that is (according to the figures given in notes) between 150,000 and 200,000 men – oarsmen, soldiers and sailors, all flung into the hazards of shipboard life, or as García de Toledo said, to the mercy of the elements – earth, air, fire and water – for all four threatened the precarious existence of men at sea. One bill for provisions supplied to the fleet in Sicily (biscuit, wine, salt meat, rice, oil, salt, barley) comes to some 500,000 ducats.

On another occasion the bill for 15 galleys was 95,000 *escudos* to the nearest round number, not counting the arms distributed to the men. This price is presented as very reasonable in the report. We learn that the hull of the galleys accounts for less than half the cost price, the rest is represented by sails, oars, yards, masts, rigging, chains, irons, receptacles, spades and other implements, casks, thread to sew the sails, tallow for the ship's bottom. Of the total cost of 95,000 crowns then, the hulls of the 15 galleys represent 37,500, the rigging 9000, the sails almost 20,000, yards and masts 3000, oars 2900, artillery 22,500. These figures omit the price of convicts and slaves which, along with the indispensable supplies of biscuit, constituted the major item of maintenance expense. On the 22 Sicilian galleys there were in May, 1576, 1102 convicts, 1517 slaves and 1205 volunteer oarsmen; in May, 1577 these figures had dropped to respectively 1207, 1440 and 661 which works out at a total of 173 oarsmen to a galley in the first case and 143 in the second. Galleys were sometimes reinforced with extra oarsmen: the galley belonging to a grandson of Barbarossa had 220 slaves at the oars. Besides oarsmen there were officers, crews and infantrymen. In August, 1570, total numbers on board the 20 Neapolitan galleys were 2940 men, or roughly 150 men to a galley. So including convicts, seamen and soldiers, each galley represented about 300 men.

Regular fleet warfare then depended on the mobilization of large quantities

284. *San Marco and Three Venetian Magistrates Recruiting Naval Infantry* by
G. B. Angelo, called 'Il Moro'. *Museo Navale, Genoa*

of both money and men: ragged soldiers levied in Spain and given clothes on
the march if at all; *Landsknechte* who had made their way to Italy on foot by
way of Bolzano then queued up in La Spezia waiting for galleys, Italians, adventurers recruited or accepted to fill the gaps caused by desertion and epidemics,
and above all the long files of convicts trudging towards the ports. There were
never enough of them to ply the red oars of the galleys – hence the constant
need to press poor men, capture slaves and recruit volunteers; Venice sought
them as far afield as Bohemia. In Turkey and Egypt, forced levies exhausted the
resources of the population. Willingly or unwillingly, massive numbers of men
flocked to the coast.

When one remembers that land armies too were expensive – a Spanish *tercio*
(about 5000 combatants) cost per campaign, in pay, provision and transport,
1,200,000 ducats, according to an estimate at the end of the century – one readily
understands the close connection between war with its prodigious expense and
the revenues of a ruler. Through these revenues, war ultimately touched every
human activity. But the rapid development and modernization of war made it
too much for the old structures to handle; eventually it brought its own end.
Peace was the result of chronic inadequacy, prolonged delays in paying the
troops, insufficient armaments, of all the misfortunes which governments
dreaded but could not escape.

War and civilizations. Every nation experienced these conflicts. But there are
wars and wars. If we think in terms of civilizations, major participants in Mediterranean conflicts, we should make a distinction between 'internal' wars, within
any one civilization, and 'external' wars, between two mutually hostile worlds,
distinguishing in other words between on one hand the Crusades or *Jihāds* and
on the other the intestinal conflicts of Christendom and Islam, for these great
civilizations consumed themselves in an endless series of civil wars, fratricidal
struggles between Protestant and Catholic, Sunnite and Shiite.

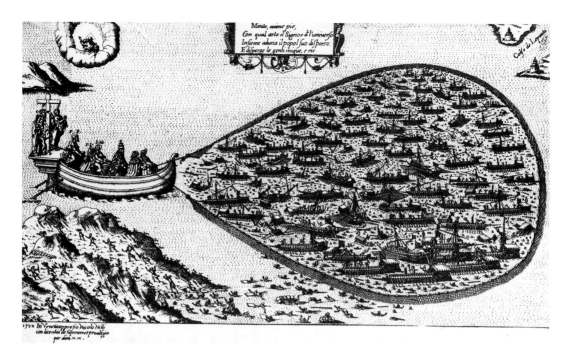

285. Symbolic image of the Battle of Lepanto. Venetian engraving, 1572.
Museo Navale, Venice

It is a distinction of major importance. In the first place, it provides a regular geographical delimitation: Christendom and Islam correspond to given areas with known frontiers, whether on land or sea. So much is obvious. But it also suggests an interesting chronology. As time passes, an age of 'external' wars is succeeded by an age of 'internal' wars. There is no clear dividing line, yet the transition is plain to see: it offers a new perspective on a confused period of history, illuminating it in a way which is neither artificial nor illusory. It is impossible to avoid the conviction that contrasting ideological patterns were first established and then replaced. In Christendom, where the documentary evidence is more plentiful, the Crusade, that is external war, was the dominant force until about 1570–1575. It might be supported with greater or smaller enthusiasm, and already there was a growing tendency towards evasion, excuses, luke-warmness or downright refusal – by taxpayers on one hand and sceptics on the other. But the Crusade had always had its fervent apologists and its critics. Dissident voices cannot conceal the fact that a wave of militant religion was flowing through Europe in the sixteenth century.

But Lepanto was the end of an era. The waning of the crusades had long been foreseeable. The brilliant victory of 1571 was an illusion: Don John of Austria, a crusader when the age of crusades was past, was as isolated from his contemporaries as his nephew, Dom Sebastian, the hero of Alcázarquivir. Their vision dated from other times. Part of the explanation at least is the strength of the Catholic reaction to the Reformation, at least after 1550, bringing an ideological change of front. Mediterranean Christendom abandoned one war to fight another, as its religious fervour carried it in a new direction.

The change of heart became evident in Rome with the accession of Pope Gregory XIII (1573–1585), which was marked by an outbreak of renewed hostility towards Protestant Germany. This was now the major concern of the Supreme Pontiff, eclipsing the moribund Holy League which he had inherited and which collapsed in 1573 with the defection of the Venetians. Papal policy now looked northwards (conveniently for the success of Turco-Spanish negotiations). It is scarcely surprising then, that with the volte-face of the last third of the sixteenth century, the notion of the crusade against Islam should have lost much of its force. In 1581, we find the Spanish Church protesting – not against the abandonment of the Turkish wars, but against paying taxes to no purpose.

After 1600 however, as the Protestant wars declined in ferocity and peace slowly returned to the Christian countries of Europe, the idea of the crusade regained force and vigour on the shores of the Mediterranean, in France for instance on the occasion of the Turco-Imperial war of 1593–1606. 'After 1610', notes one historian, 'the Turcophobia which reigned in public opinion, degenerated into a veritable mania.' An explosive mixture of plans and hopes now came together: until once again, a Protestant, 'internal' war put an end to them in 1618.

This overall interpretation seems virtually irrefutable, even though there is insufficient chronological evidence to tell us whether popular feeling followed or preceded – or as I prefer to think both followed and preceded – these volte-faces, provoking them, adding fuel to them and finally being consumed in the resulting explosion. But any explanation which takes account of only one belligerent is extremely unlikely to be satisfactory. We tend always to view the world through naïve western eyes. The other half of the Mediterranean had its own life to live, its own history to make. A recent study suggests that there were comparable phases, coincident *conjonctures* on the Turkish side too. The Christians abandoned the fight, tiring suddenly of the Mediterranean, but the Turks did precisely the same, at the same moment; they were still interested, it is true, in the Hungarian frontier and in naval war in the Mediterranean, but they were equally committed in the Red Sea, on the Indus and the Volga. It is as if in this continuous history of violence, reaching from the Straits of Gibraltar and the canals of Holland to Syria and Turkestan, everything was inter-related. This was a history operating so to speak at the same voltage everywhere; its variations were electrically identical. At a certain point in time, Christian and Moslems clashed in the *Jihād* and Crusade, then turned their backs on one another, discovering internal conflicts. But this equation of confluent passions was also, as I shall try to show at the end of this book, the consequence of the slow rhythms of the economic *conjoncture*, identical throughout the known world which in the sixteenth century saw the beginning of its existence as a unit.

Defensive frontiers in the Balkans. To meet the Turkish threat, Mediterranean Christendom erected a chain of fortresses, now to be one of the characteristic marks of its approach to war. As well as fighting, it was constantly extending its defensive and protective lines, encasing itself within a shell of armour. It was a policy both instinctive and unilateral: the Turks built neither very many nor very effective fortifications. Does this indicate a difference in levels of technology or in attitude: on one side confidence in the strength of the Janissaries, the *sipāhis* and the galleys, on the other a desire for security and even, in the major wars, a tendency to economize both strength and resources? Similarly, if the Christian powers maintained a large intelligence service in the Levant, it was not merely out of fear, but in order to obtain the most accurate estimate of the possibility of attack, so that the defence effort could be proportionate to it. The Turks will not come this year: so all extra troops are demobilized and all recruiting is cancelled.

Mediterranean Christendom thus erected between itself and Islam a series of fortified fronts, military 'curtains', the defence lines behind which, conscious of its technical superiority, it felt secure. These lines stretched from Hungary to the Mediterranean coast, a series of fortified zones separating one civilization from another.

The Venetian 'limes'. On the edge of the western sea, Venice had long been keeping vigil. To meet the Turkish threat, a string of Venetian outposts and coastal watch-towers ran along the shores of Istria, Dalmatia and Albania, as far as the Ionian islands and beyond, to Crete and Cyprus: this last base, acquired by the Signoria in 1479, was to be hers until 1571. But Venice's straggling maritime empire, a parasite plant on eastern shores, had been broken through several times by Turkish attacks. To go no further back, the peace of 12th October, 1540 had deprived it of two precious positions on the Dalmatian coast, Nadino and Laurana (Vrana), of some *isolette* in the Aegean, Chios, Pátmos, Cesina, of some 'feudal' islands, Nios (Ios), the fief of the Pisani family, Stampalia (Astipália), the fief of the Quirini and Paros, which belonged to the Venier family. Venice had also been forced to give up the important stations of Monemvasia and Napoli di Romania in Greece. Thirty-three years later, in the separate peace of 1573, completed by the difficult agreements of 1575, she ceded more positions in Dalmatia, paid a war indemnity and renounced her claim to Cyprus, which had been a *de facto* Turkish possession since 1571. The Venetian Empire has often been compared to the British; Venice's possessions at the end of the sixteenth century then would be the equivalent of the British Empire stripped of its holdings east of Suez. But the comparison is misleading: the frontier possessions of Venice were merely a string of tiny settlements in often archaic forts. The populations of the towns and the islands rarely exceeded a few thousand: in 1576, Zara had just over 7000 inhabitants, Spalato just under 4000, Cattaro only about a thousand after the epidemic of 1572, Cephalonia scarcely

286. The Lion of St. Mark hovering over a map of Crete.
Venetian print, c.1651.

20,000, Zante 15,000, Corfu 17,517. Only Crete with its 200,000 inhabitants carried a certain weight and was indeed the major link in the revised chain. But the Greek island was known to be unreliable, as it was to prove in 1571 and again in 1669. The empire was insignificant, in demographic terms, compared with Venice and the Terraferma, the population of which was estimated about the same time as one and a half million.

It was little short of a miracle then that the barrier held back the swirling tide of Turkish invasion. In 1539 after all, the Spanish had been unable to hold the bridgehead of Castelnuovo on the Balkan coast. The remarkable solidity of the Venetian defences was a triumph of improvisation, the result of endlessly revised calculations: of the scrupulous maintenance of the fortresses, of the vigilance of the Arsenal, that mighty factory, of incessant patrols by roundships and galleys and, it should be added, of the loyalty of the frontier population, the high quality of the men who commanded in the name of the Signoria, and the courage of the deportees who were serving their sentence there, not to mention the efficiency of the artillery schools and the possibility of recruiting soldiers from the Albanian, Dalmatian and Greek populations of these troubled zones.

287. The sea battle fought between the Turks and the Venetians off Modon.
Sixteenth-century miniature. *Topkapi Museum, Istanbul*

But at either extremity of the chain of defences, Venice encountered problems. The furthest point east was Cyprus, hard to defend and with an unreliable population. This island, like Rhodes, had the disadvantage of being close to Asia Minor and therefore vulnerable to Turkish attack; the defeat of 1571 forced the Venetians to withdraw to Crete, which had a narrow escape in 1572 and which the Signoria felt thereafter to be under constant threat from the ambitions of the conqueror. At the other end of the front, in the north, on the borders of Istria and Friuli, Venice's possessions were adjacent to Habsburg and almost to Turkish territory – a double menace, the more serious in that it threatened the Terraferma, Venice's very flesh and blood. Already between 1463 and 1479, the Turks had launched raids as far as Piave and on the Habsburg side, the frontier, although established *de facto* in 1518, had not yet been accorded formal recognition. It was to meet all these perils that Venice was to build the massive and costly fortress of Palma at the end of the century.

The Venetian Empire, no more than a line of frontier posts, while it did not hold the Turkish Empire in a stranglehold was nevertheless something of an impediment. Venetians were fully aware of the extreme vulnerability of these outposts.

Perhaps after all the Venetian line held because of its very weakness, because the Turks had already made breaches in it, doors and windows through which they could reach the West: Modon, which although poorly fortified, held out during the dramatic siege of 1572, and which Pierre Belon had, as early as 1550, described as 'the key to Turkey'; further north Navarino, which was fortified after 1573; and lastly Valona in Albania, which although unfortunately surrounded by a perennially restless region, was nevertheless an excellent base for expeditions to the western sea and Christendom. Can it be true that the gaps in the Venetian *limes*, by decreasing its effectiveness as a barrier, enabled it to survive longer?

On the Danube. North of the Balkans, the Turkish Empire extended to and crossed the Danube, a vital but fragile frontier. It partly controlled the Danube provinces, although it was never to be unchallenged master of the wooded mountains of Transylvania. To the west, it advanced along the longitudinal valleys of Croatia, beyond Zagreb to the strategic gorges of the Kulpa (Kupa), the upper Sava and the Drava, overlooked by those poor, mountainous, inaccessible regions, inhabited by few men, where the Dinaric bloc meets the towering mass of the Alps. So the Turkish frontier north of the Balkans became fixed fairly early both in the extreme west and the east: on both sides it was confined by geographical obstacles. There were human obstacles too: in the eastern lands of Moldavia and Wallachia, Tartar hordes periodically launched devastating and irresistible invasions. In the west, a German frontier was militarized, at least in the *Windischland*, between the middle reaches of the Sava and those of the Drava, under the command of the *Generalkapitän* of Laibach. The imperial order for its fortification was issued at Linz in 1538. In the Windisch March and later in Croatia, these military frontier installations were to grow up of their own accord under Charles V and Ferdinand. A ruling of 1542 laid down the administration of the whole area. As Nicholas Zrinyi was soon to write, in 1555, this was the breastplate, the *Vormauer*, of Styria and therefore of the entire hereditary Austrian state. Was it not in fact this need for a common defence system, financed locally, which gradually cemented into a fairly recognizable unit the Austrian *Erbland*, previously a miscellaneous collection of small states and nations? In 1578, the solid fortress of Karlstadt (Karlovac) rose up over the Kulpa; at about the same time, Hans Lenkovitch was given command over the Croatian and Slavonic frontier, the administration of which was redefined in the Bruck Edict (1578). Its most original feature was the settlement along the frontier of numerous Serbian peasants fleeing Turkish rule and territory. These peasants received land and privileges. They were grouped in large families, patriarchal and democratic communities, in which military and economic tasks were distributed by an Elder.

With the passing of time then, the organization of these military zones was strengthened; one might suppose that, as Busbecq remarks in a note, if a frontier of this kind hardened along more or less stable lines, it was because for many years and at least until 1566, it was relatively untroubled. But peace and stability were only partial. For if resistance was possible at the edges, it was more risky in the central region of the frontier, on the vast bare Hungarian plains. After the Turkish advance on Vienna in 1529, it was necessary, in order to defend what had become the chief rampart of the Germanic world, to multiply the artificial barriers along the roads and rivers; to create and maintain a Danube fleet, about a hundred boats as estimated in 1532 by the *Generaloberst* of the Vienna Arsenal, Jeronimo de Zara. The *Salzamt* of Gmunden received orders to build these boats along with the barges it regularly provided for the transport of salt. They came to be called *Tscheiken*, from the Turkish *caïque*. Right up to the nineteenth century there were *Tscheiken* on the Danube, with *Tscheikisten* on board. In 1930, *Tscheiken* from the time of Prince Eugene were displayed at a retrospective exhibition at Klosterneuberg.

Towards the end of the sixteenth century, the location of the long Hungarian frontier became more permanent. It was never completely pacified. But despite constant border incidents, raids after captives or tribute, the line was more or less fixed.

The central Mediterranean: along the coasts of Naples and Sicily. The coast of Naples and Sicily, along with Malta which provided a link with the Maghreb, was a military zone of a very different kind. Its strategic position derived from its position on the central axis of the sea. Its function was at the same time to provide a naval base for the Spanish fleets, to offer resistance to Turkish armadas and to defend its own territory against pirate attacks.

Brindisi, Taranto, Augusta, Messina, Palermo and Naples were all possible rallying points for the Christian galleys. Brindisi and Taranto were possibly too far east, Palermo and Augusta looked more towards Africa than the Levant, and Naples was too far north. That left Messina. In times of danger, Messina was the crucial naval base of the western powers. Its commanding position on a narrow channel of water, its easy access to supplies of both Sicilian and foreign wheat, its proximity to Naples, all contributed to its suitability.

It was in about 1538 that major defence works began throughout the Mezzogiorno, on the initiative in Naples of Pietro de Toledo, in Sicily of Ferrante Gonzaga. For 1538 was the year of Prevesa and the year that Turkish fleets, invincible on sea, began to pound the coasts of Naples and Sicily. The anonymous *Vita di Pietro de Toledo* indicates that it was at this time that the viceroy had work begun on the fortifications of Reggio, Castro, Otranto, Leuca,

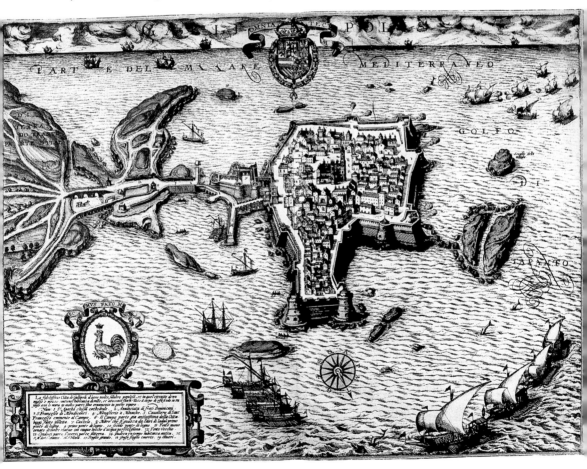

288. The fortified city and harbour of Gallipoli in the gulf of Taranto. Sixteenth-century Italian print.

Gallipoli, Brindisi, Monopoli, Trani, Barletta, Manfredonia and Vieste and also took steps to fortify Naples. From then on, it seems, watch-towers were being built along the Neapolitan coast. In 1567, 313 were built throughout the kingdom. Pietro de Toledo's efforts in Naples were paralleled in Sicily between 1535 and 1543, by those of Ferrante Gonzaga. He had 137 towers built along the southern and eastern coasts, the former protected to some extent by the lie of the land, the latter exposed to Turkish attacks and soon to become a 'mere military frontier facing the Ottoman Empire'. On this sensitive front, defence works had begun in 1532 at Syracuse. This, as Ferrante Gonzaga himself said, in a report to the king, was the only exposed coast of the island. The north coast was mountainous, the south, 'le più cattiva e più fluttuosa spiaggia di quei mari', offered no harbour for an enemy fleet. But the east, with its low, fertile and easily accessible shores, was a different matter. In Sicily in 1573, since it was impossible to defend the whole island, it was decided to protect only Messina, Augusta, Syracuse, Trapani and Milazzo, abandoning for the time being, since they were too vulnerable, Taormina, Catania, Terranova, Licata, Girgenti, Sciacca, Mazzara, Castellammare, Termini, Cefalu and Patti.

Such were the preoccupations of summer (at the approach of winter, the whole system was dismantled) of the viceroys of Naples and Sicily, until the 1580s and even later. If 1538 roughly marks the beginning of this adaptable defence system, it was working to full capacity only after about 1558. Its efficiency was recognized by the Venetians. The labours of the Spanish viceroys were not in the end to be despised.

The defence of the coasts of Italy and Spain. The Naples–Sicily line, prolonged by the formidable Christian base at Malta to the Barbary coast, where the *presidio* of La Goletta was a Spanish possession until 1574, was not usually crossed by the Turkish fleets. Not that it was capable of stopping them; but once they had captured their prey, the Turks were rarely concerned to go farther afield. There was nothing to prevent them doing so however, any more than there was to prevent ships from moving between Turkey and Barbary. Meanwhile the pirates of Algiers were always active. So the Christian powers had to take serious steps to defend all coasts, equipping them with towers and fortresses.

Like the Sicilian defence works, these walls did not rise overnight: they would be started, then the site would be moved or modernization be called for. When and how? It is hard to say. In 1563, it was realized that the old towers of Valencia would have to be replaced by new works allowing room for artillery placements. The immediate question at Barcelona was, who would pay, the king, the city or the *Lonja*? In August, 1536, in Majorca, watchers sighted enemy sails from the top of the *atalayas*. So there must have been towers on the island by this date. How long had they been there? In 1543, fortifications were begun at Alcudia, but what kind of fortifications were they? And when were the round watch-towers of Corsica built, as distinct from the square towers of village fortifications? Was it in 1519–1520 that the coastguard patrols were set up in Valencia on the model of the Holy *Hermandad* with 'musters' and alarm systems? They cannot have amounted to much, since in 1559, Philip II in Brussels is expressing surprise that the fort at Alicante is held by only six men. In 1576, plans were still being made for the fortification of Cartagena. In Granada by contrast, in 1579, there was a coastal defence service, under the command of Sancho Davila, *Capitan general de la costa*, perhaps because there were more specific reasons for taking precautions in this region. Similarly Sardinia was obliged to consider defence (detailed plans drawn up for the fortification of the island in 1574 still exist) and built watch-towers under the administration of the viceroy Don Miguel de Moncada, in about 1587. Fishermen off the island's coral reefs would take refuge under these towers and use artillery in their defence.

Needless to say, these works were never completed. There was always more to be done to assure the protection of the *poveri naviganti* and the inhabitants of the coasts. On the whole, these were defences on a much smaller scale than those described earlier. The Spanish coasts were often raided by corsairs, particularly the Barbary pirates, but had little to fear from the Constantinople fleet. There was quite a difference.

The coasts of North Africa. The North African defence network presents fewer problems to the historian than the others – not that it is less complicated, but it is better documented. Although no more than a string of forts, the line of *presidios* was implicated in the histories of the regions it contained: along this frontier two civilizations met, hence the evidence from many sources which illuminates both the general and the particular history of the Spanish positions in North Africa. Established in the time of Ferdinand the Catholic, chiefly between 1509 and 1511, the *fronteras* had been deployed along the borders of an ancient but fragmented land, incapable of defending itself. Perhaps only the Aragonese preoccupation with the riches of Italy prevented Spain from moving in to capture the inland Maghreb. But the lost opportunity never presented itself again. In 1516, the Barbarossas settled in Algiers; in 1518, they placed themselves under the protection of the sultan; in 1529, their city liberated the small but troublesome fortress on the Peñon, which had been held by the Spaniards since 1510. Even before this date, Algiers had been the urban centre of the barren regions of the central Maghreb, sending out its swift marching columns, settling garrisons, drawing to the city all the trade of this vast intermediary zone. From now on a land held from within was to oppose and threaten the Spanish in North Africa. Charles V's two major expeditions, against Tunis in 1535 and against Mostaganem in 1558, did not alter the situation. And indeed after the

289. *Overleaf: The Battle of Tripoli.* One of the greatest disasters suffered by the Christians. Venetian print, 1569.

TRIPOLI

failure at Mostaganem, which brought the collapse of grandiose projects of alliance with Morocco, a new age, the age of the *presidios*, had already begun.

Inaugurated in the reign of Philip II, it was an age marked by prudence and calculation rather than adventure. Grand schemes for African expeditions did not altogether vanish it is true. But there was much deliberation and little action now, except at points known – or thought – to be particularly weak. Such was the case of the expedition against Tripoli which ended in disaster at Djerba in 1560. Even this was undertaken less on the king's initiative than on that of the viceroy of Sicily, the Duke of Medina Celi, and of the Grand Master of Malta. The great expedition against the Peñon de Velez, mounted with over 100 galleys in 1564, was something of an anticlimax. The recapture of Tunis in 1573 by Don John of Austria and his obstinacy in clinging to his trophy in the face of opposition from his brother and his advisers, who desired only to see the position evacuated and destroyed, was merely a sudden outburst of megalomania, a brief revival of the spirit of Charles V's reign, of which there were several during the reign of the Prudent King.

Meanwhile the steady, discreet but in the long run effective labour of reinforcing and extending the *presidios* themselves was undertaken during the years 1560–1570. Mortar, lime, bricks, beams, planks, stones, baskets for earthworks, picks and shovels become the subject matter of all the letters from the *presidios*. Parallel to the authority of the captain of the position, the role and authority of that other figure, the *veedor* or quartermaster, was gradually increasing, as was that of the engineer-architect, a civilian, which did not always make for good relations. Giovanni Battista Antonelli for instance was in charge of the defence works here at Mers-el-Kebir and another Italian, Il Fratino (whom Philip II was also to use in Navarre), moved the entire old *presidio* of Melilla, brick by brick, to the edge of the lagoon. Two of his drawings, preserved at Simancas, show the little settlement in its new site, a tiny cluster of houses round the church, with either side of it stretching the steep and endless coastline. Il Fratino also worked at La Goletta, where his relations with the governor, Alonso Pimentel, were stormy: their antagonism was that of men isolated from society, driven to almost murderous lengths and sending home mutual accusations. The *presidio* grew nevertheless; around the original rectangle with its bastions of 'old Goletta', engravings of 1573 and 1574 show a string of new fortifications, completed in summer 1573. There were also a windmill, powder magazines, cisterns and 'cavaliers' on which the powerful bronze artillery was mounted. For artillery was the strength and the *raison d'être* of the fortresses in Africa.

In the time of Philip II, the *presidios* expanded, forever building new fortifications, devouring constructional materials often carried over great distances (lime from Naples for Mers-el-Kebir for instance) and continually calling for more 'pioneers' – *gastadores*. Oran and its annex Mers-el-Kebir – which after 1580 was a model of its kind – hummed with activity. By the end of the century this was no mere fortress but a fortified zone, created at huge expense and with heroic effort. The soldier, like the humble *gastador*, had to handle pick and shovel. Diego Suárez, the soldier-chronicler of Oran, who had worked on the Escorial in his youth, could not find words to express the achievement. It was as good as the Escorial, he had to say in the end. But this exceptional masterpiece was only built in the final years of Philip II's reign, and in 1574 oddly enough it had been threatened with total destruction. The Spanish government was then on the verge of the second bankruptcy of the reign (1575). In Tunisia, Don John of Austria, who had just captured Tunis, was hanging on against instructions, and his obstinacy led to the disaster of August–September, 1574, when the Turks succeeded in taking both La Goletta and Tunis. This double tragedy showed that the two fortresses, which had had to share supplies sent out from Spain, had finally been harmful to each other. In the light of this, it was logical to suppose that the double *presidio* of Oran–Mers-el-Kebir, linked only by a poor road of about a league, unsuitable for artillery, was also a mistake. The enquiry conducted on the spot by Prince Vespasiano Gonzaga, in December, 1574, concluded that Oran should be evacuated, the fort dismantled and razed to the ground, in order to concentrate the entire strength of the garrison at Mers-el-Kebir, which was better situated and had a good harbour. 'La Goletta', writes the author of the report, 'was lost the day we took Tunis.' As for fortifying Oran, all the engineers in the world would never be able to do it, short of building a great city there. But when the emergency was over, it was this 'great city' which the Spaniards did in fact patiently hollow out of the rock, providing the stable environment in which there later flourished the 'Corte chica', or little Madrid, as it was called with some exaggeration in the eighteenth century.

The fall of the Tunisian bases in 1574 did not have the feared result. No subsequent disaster befell Sicily or Naples. It is true that the latter used the one arm left to them, the galley-fleets. Mobile squadrons had their advantages. The Spaniards now seem to have realized this and to have seen that the best way to defend the threatened coastline was to send out the galleys, instead of leaving them, as they had too often before the 1570s, lined up defensively at Messina, waiting for Turkish aggression. Many schemes of reconquest were advanced after the fall of Tunis. One of them, dating from 1581, stated as a general principle that naval strength was a prerequisite – at least someone had seen the light.

The new method of defence – by aggression – was likely to be even more profitable than in the past as a result of the economic revival of the Maghreb. There were now, as never before, many rich prizes to be had. Besides, was not this method more economical than the maintenance of the *presidios*? A financial report, dating from some time between 1564 and 1568, sets out the expenses incurred by the *presidios*, from the Peñon de Velez, recovered in the West in 1564, to La Goletta (Tripoli had been lost in 1551 and Bougie captured by the Algerines in 1555, so they are not included). Total wages for the garrisons were as follows: the Peñon 12,000 ducats, Melilla 19,000, Oran and Mers-el-Kebir

290. *The Siege of a Fort in Africa* by Vicente Carducho.
Possibly the Peñon de Velez, 1564. *Accademia di S. Fernando,
Madrid*

90,000, La Goletta 88,000 – a grand total of 209,000 ducats. Note the relatively
high bill at La Goletta: the garrison of a thousand regular troops plus a thousand
extraordinary troops, cost almost as much as the double *presidio* of Oran,
manned at that time by 2700 soldiers and 90 light horse. This was because
infantrymen at Oran were paid less (1000 maravedís a month) 'por ser la tierra
muy barata', since the cost of living there was low. In the west, only the garrison
on the Peñon received the high wages of Italy.

The figure of 200,000 ducats refers only to expenditure on personnel: there
was much more besides, for instance the maintenance and construction of fortifications. Philip II sent 50,000 ducats for the building of the new Goletta in
1566 and another 50,000 two years later. These may not have been the only
two payments. Then there was the heavy burden of supplying ammunition. A

consignment for La Goletta alone in 1565 consisted of 200 quintals of lead, 150 of match for arquebuses, 100 of fine gunpowder at 20 ducats a quintal, 1000 baskets for earth, 1000 shovels with handles, the total bill amounting to 4665 ducats, not including transportation. A similar cargo in 1560 had required eight galleys to transport it. Each *presidio* had its own building fund, from which the authorities might borrow if necessary and repay later. These accounts merit detailed study. They would enable us to calculate (quite apart from the original expense involved in capturing the positions, 500,000 ducats for the capture of the Peñon in 1564 for instance, not including the expenses of the fleet) the enormous sum required to maintain these tiny fortresses, always in need of repair, strengthening or extension, with their constant demand for food and supplies.

By way of comparison, at the same period, the guard on the Balearic islands (although they were seriously threatened) cost a mere 36,000 ducats, as did the guard on the coast from Cartagena to Cadiz. As for the annual maintenance of a galley, it was at this time about 7000 ducats. The guard of the *presidios* immobilized, between 1564 and 1568, approximately 2500 regular troops (2850) and 2700 summer reinforcements (men transported there in spring and repatriated at the approach of winter, in theory that is, for delays in arrival and more frequently in departure, were common). 5000 men – more than His Catholic Majesty had in the whole Kingdom of Naples. Without entering upon calculations and considerations worthy of the *speculativi* referred to by a Genoese agent, can one suggest that it might have been better to keep thirty galleys at sea than to hold on to the African *presidios*? What these figures unquestionably demonstrate is the magnitude of the sacrifice made by Spain for the Barbary coast.

The presidios: *only a second best.* Robert Ricard too has questioned whether this solution, 'only second best', was not prolonged beyond the point of usefulness. Cortés on arriving in Mexico burnt his boats: he had to triumph or die. In North Africa, there was always the supply ship with its fresh water, fish, cloth or *garbanzos*. The administration was looking after you. Did the technical superiority of the Christian, which allowed him to establish and then maintain *presidios* 'defended by cannon-fire', dispense him from more direct and perhaps more profitable effort? To some extent it must have. But the country was also defended by its immensity and its aridity. Here it was impossible to live like the *conquistadores* of America, who drove herds of cattle and pigs before them. As for sending settlers, it had been considered: in the time of Ferdinand the Catholic, there was a proposal to populate the towns with Castilian Moriscos; in 1543 to colonize Cape Bon. But how were these deportees to live? In a Spain dazzled by the lure both of the New World and the good fare of Italy, where were the men to be found? There were also plans to make these strongholds economically viable, to create some kind of link with the vast interior, off which they would live. In the time of Ferdinand and later Charles V, there was actually some attempt at an economic policy aiming at the development of these African positions in hopes of making them a centre for Catalan shipping, and of obliging the Venetian galleys to put in there. But all in vain. The doubling of the customs duties in 1516 in all the Spanish ports in the Mediterranean did not have the effect of forcing the Venetian galleys to concentrate their African trade in Oran. The commercial currents of the Maghreb of themselves by-passed the Spanish *presidios* and preferred to use as export outlets Tajura, La Misurata, Algiers and Bône, none of which was in Christian hands. The volume of traffic in these free ports gives some idea of the lack of success of the Spanish *fronteras*, just as in Morocco, at the end of the sixteenth century, the fortune of the Moroccan ports of Larache, Salé, Cabo da Guer (now Agadir) underlines the collapse of the Portuguese strongholds, which had long been prosperous trading-posts. Similarly, the trade even of Spain with North Africa – which seems in any case to have concentrated more on Atlantic Morocco than on the Barbary coast – for all that it revived in the 1580s, bringing to the African coast cloth (woollens, silks, velvets, taffetas and peasant weaves), cochineal, salt, perfumes, lacquer, coral, saffron, thousands of caps, lined and unlined, from Córdoba and Toledo, cow and goat hides and even gold – all this trade (apart from a few crossings to Ceuta and Tangier) was transacted outside the *presidios*. They were virtually excluded from commercial routes. Under such conditions, the *presidios*, condemned to deal only with sutlers and camp-followers, neither prospered nor put out shoots. As grafts they had barely taken and the best they could hope for was to stay alive.

Life in the *presidios* must have been miserable. So near the water, rations rotted and men died of fever. The soldiers were hungry all year round. For a long time, the only supplies came by sea. Later, but only at Oran, the surrounding countryside provided meat and grain, which had become a regular supplement by the very end of the century. Garrison life was in many ways similar to shipboard life, not without its hazards.

The supply station of Málaga, with its *proveedores*, occasionally helped by the services of Cartagena, was responsible for supplying the western sector, Oran, Mers-el-Kebir, Melilla. On more than one occasion, the boat was seized by galliots from Tetouan or Algiers, and the Spanish would be lucky if they could buy it back from the corsairs when they anchored, as was their habit, off Cape Falcon. So pirates, quite as much as negligence by the administration, were responsible for the recurrent famines in the western *presidios*.

The fate of La Goletta was no different, despite its apparently fortunate location near the inexhaustible supplies of bread, wine, cheese and chick peas of Naples and Sicily. But those who succeeded in making the short crossing from Sicily could not always do so at their convenience. When Pimentel took command of La Goletta in 1569, the garrison was living off its reserves of cheese – without either bread or wine. The administration on the Italian side was partly to blame of course. Was it from here or from Spain that the garrison received 2000 pairs of shoes, of good Spanish leather, but in little girls' sizes?

Furthermore, the internal organization of the *presidios* did not contribute to their smooth running, as can be seen from the administration in 1564 of Mers-el-Kebir. Soldiers were supplied with rations by the storekeepers at the price fixed on the shipping labels and often on credit: this was the dangerous practice of allowing advances on their pay, by which soldiers could amass frightening debts, since they were always buying on credit from passing merchants. Sometimes, in times of difficulty, or through the complicity of the local authorities, prices would rise beyond all measure. To escape their intolerable burden of debts, the soldiers would desert and go over to Islam. The problem was aggravated by the fact that pay was lower in the *presidios* than in Italy – one more reason, when troops were being embarked for the *presidios*, not to tell them in advance the name of their destination and once they were there, never to repatriate them. Diego Suárez spent twenty-seven years in Oran, in spite of several attempts to escape as a stowaway in the galleys. Only the sick, and then not always, could come back from the hated coast to the hospitals of Sicily or Spain. The *presidios* then were virtually places of deportation. Nobles and rich men might be sent there as a punishment. The grandson of Columbus, Luis, arrested at Valladolid for trigamy, was condemned to ten years' exile: he arrived in Oran in 1563 and was to die there on 3rd February, 1573.

For and against raids. Let us imagine the atmosphere in these garrisons. Each was the fief of its captain general, Melilla for many years that of the Medina Sidonia family, Oran that of the Alcaudete family; Tripoli was ceded in 1513 to Hugo de Moncada for life. The governor reigned with his family and the lords who surrounded him. The favourite pastime of the rulers was the *razzia*, the planned sortie combining sport with work and, it must be admitted, strict necessity: it was the duty of the garrison to police the surrounding districts, protecting their inhabitants and dispersing intruders, collecting pledges, gathering information and requisitioning supplies. Necessity apart however, there was a certain temptation to play soldiers, to lay ambushes in the gardens of Tunis and kidnap unsuspecting farmers arriving to pick fruit or harvest a field of barley; or beyond the *sebka* at Oran, by turns glistening with salt or covered with water, to surprise a douar, the presence of which had been betrayed by hired spies. This was a more exciting, more dangerous and more profitable sport than hunting wild animals. Everyone had his share of the booty and the Captain General sometimes took the 'Quint' or royal fifth, whether in grain, beasts or humans. Sometimes the soldiers themselves, tiring of their everyday fare, would go off in search of adventure, from a desire for fresh food, or money, or simply out of boredom. In many cases, such raids naturally prevented the establishment of vital good relations between the fortress and its hinterland, if, as they were intended to, they spread wide the terror of the name of Spain. Contemporary judgments are far from unanimous on this point. We must strike hard, says Diego Suárez, and at the same time be accommodating, increase the number of *Moros de paz*, the subdued populations who took shelter near the fortress and in turn protected it. 'Cuantos más moros más ganancias', writes the soldier-chronicler, repeating the old proverb that the greater the number of Moors, the greater the profit – in grain, everyday foods and livestock. But was it possible to refrain from striking, terrorizing and therefore driving away the precious sources of supplies, without destroying what was by now the traditional way of life and pattern of defence of the *presidios*, the development, by persuasion or by force, of a zone of influence and protection as indispensable to the Spanish *presidio* as it was to the Portuguese *presidio* in Morocco? Without it, the fort would have suffocated.

Defensive psychology. That a mighty civilization – Christendom – should have surrounded itself with defences against Islam, is both important and instructive. Islam, preferring wars of aggression, flinging masses of cavalry into the field, took no such precautions. It was because it wanted to continue the dialogue, or force it to continue. It needed access to the superior techniques of the enemy. Without them, it would be impossible for Islam to fulfil towards Asia the same role that Christendom fulfilled towards Islam itself. In this respect it is revealing to see the Turks, after experiencing western gunfire on the Carniola frontier, attempting, unsuccessfully as it happened, to train the *sipāhis* in the use of pistols against the Persians. Even more conclusive is the evident connection between the nautical vocabulary of the Turks and that of the Christians: *kadrigha* (galley), *kalliotta* (galliot), *kalium* (galleon). The easterners borrowed more than the word: by the end of the century, they were building mahonnas for the Black Sea on the model of western galleasses and, what was more, imitating the Christian galleons. The Turks possessed about twenty of them, large cargo vessels, with a tonnage of about 1500 *botte*; in the last quarter of the century, they carried pilgrims, rice and sugar on the Egypt–Constantinople route – and sometimes gold, although this was also transported overland.

The Turks did however build one *limes*: between themselves and the Persians, who were one degree poorer still.

2 Piracy: a substitute for declared war

By 1574, the age of war by armada, expeditionary force and heavy siege was practically over. It was revived to some extent after 1593, but effectively only on the Hungarian frontier, outside the Mediterranean. Did the end of official war mean peace? Not entirely, for by some apparently general law, warfare simply took on new forms, reappearing and spreading in this guise.

In France, the massive demobilization of armies which followed the peace

291, 292. *Above: The Horrors of War*
by Paolo di Franchesci.
Fugger-Glött'sche Kunstsammlung,
Kirchheim. Right: A soldier-beggar by
Jacques Callot. Paris, 1629.

of Cateau-Cambrésis contributed in no small measure to the outbreak of the
Wars of Religion, disturbances far more serious in the long run than foreign
wars. If Germany by contrast was quiet between 1555 and 1618, it was because
her surplus of adventure-seeking troops had been sent abroad to Hungary, Italy
and in particular to the Netherlands and France. The reward of making trouble
for others was peace at home.

The suspension of major hostilities in the Mediterranean after 1574 was
undoubtedly one cause of the subsequent series of political and social disturbances, including the increase in brigandage. On the water, the end of conflict
between the great states brought to the forefront of the sea's history that secondary form of war, piracy. Already a force to be reckoned with between 1550 and
1574, it expanded to fill any gaps left by the slackening of official war. From
1574–1580, it increased its activities even further, soon coming to dominate the
now less spectacular history of the Mediterranean. The new capitals of warfare
were not Constantinople, Madrid and Messina, but Algiers, Malta, Leghorn and
Pisa. Upstarts had replaced the tired giants and international conflicts degenerated into a free-for-all.

293. View of Algiers. *Spanish State Archives, Simancas*

294. Pirate ships from Algiers. Seventeenth-century Dutch print.

Piracy: an ancient and widespread industry. Piracy in the Mediterranean is as old as history. There are pirates in Boccaccio and Cervantes just as there are in Homer. But in the Mediterranean, the words *piracy* and *pirates* were hardly in current usage before the beginning of the seventeenth century: *privateering* and *privateers* or *corsairs* were the expressions commonly used and the distinction, which is perfectly clear in the legal sense, while it does not fundamentally change the elements of the problem, has its importance. Privateering is legitimate war, authorized either by a formal declaration of war or by letters of marque, passports, commissions or instructions. Strange though it now appears to us, privateering had 'its own laws, rules, living customs and traditions'. Drake's departure for the New World without any form of commission was considered illegal by many of his fellow countrymen. In fact it would be wrong to suppose that there was not already in the sixteenth century a form of international law with its own conventions and some binding force. Islam and Christendom exchanged ambassadors, signed treaties and often respected their clauses. Insofar as the entire Mediterranean was an arena of constant conflict between two adjacent and warring civilizations, war was a permanent reality, excusing and justifying piracy; to justify it was to assimilate it to the neighbouring and in its way respectable category of privateering. The Spaniards in the sixteenth century use both terms: they speak of Barbary 'corsairs' in the Mediterranean and of French, English and Dutch 'pirates' in the Atlantic. If the word piracy was extended in the seventeenth century to activities in the Mediterranean, it was because Spain now wished to stigmatize as dishonourable all robbery on the inland sea, recognizing that the privateering of the old days had degenerated into nothing more or less than an underhand and disguised war waged by all the Christian powers against her trade, dominion and wealth. The word piracy was applied to the Algerine corsairs, according to one historian, only after the capture of the

Marmora by the Spanish (1614) when the corsairs of the town were driven to take refuge in Algiers. The word may have sailed in through the Straits of Gibraltar with the Atlantic ships; but this is only conjecture.

Privateering and piracy, the reader may think, came to much the same thing: similar cruelties, similar pressures determined the conduct of operations and the disposal of slaves or seized goods. All the same there was a difference: privateering was an ancient form of piracy native to the Mediterranean, with its own familiar customs, agreements and negotiations. While robbers and robbed were not actually accomplices before the event, like the popular figures of the *Commedia dell' Arte*, they were well used to methods of bargaining and reaching terms, hence the many networks of intermediaries (without the complicity of Leghorn and its open port, stolen goods would have rotted in the ports of Barbary). Hence too the many pitfalls and oversimplifications in wait for the unwary historian. Privateering in the sixteenth century was not the exclusive domain of any single group or sea-port; there was no single culprit. It was endemic. All, from the most wretched to the most powerful, rich and poor alike, cities, lords and states, were caught up in a web of operations cast over the whole sea. In the past, western historians have encouraged us to see only the pirates of Islam, in particular the Barbary corsairs. The notorious fortune of Algiers tends to blind one to the rest. But this fortune was not unique; Malta and Leghorn were Christendom's Algiers, they too had their bagnios, their slave-markets and their sordid transactions. The fortune of Algiers itself calls for some serious reservations: who or what was behind its increased activity, particularly in the seventeenth century? We are indebted to Godfrey Fisher's excellent book *Barbary Legend* for opening our eyes. For it was not merely in Algiers that men hunted each other, threw their enemies into prison, sold or tortured them and became familiar with the miseries, horrors and gleams of sainthood of the 'concentration camp world': it was all over the Mediterranean.

Privateering often had little to do with either country or faith, but was merely a means of making a living. If the corsairs came home empty-handed there would be famine in Algiers. Privateers in these circumstances took no heed of persons, nationalities or creeds, but became mere sea-robbers. The Uskoks of Segna and Fiume robbed Turks and Christians alike; the galleys and galleons of the *ponentini* (as western corsairs were called in the waters of the Levant) did just the same: they seized anything that came their way, including Venetian or Marseilles vessels, under the pretext of confiscating any goods on board belonging to Jews or Turks. In vain both the Signoria and the Pope, protector of Ancona, protested, demanding that a flag should guarantee immunity to the cargo. The right of search, whether abused or not, was retained by Christian privateers. Turkish galleys invoked similar rights in order to seize Sicilian or Neapolitan cargoes. A legal fiction on both sides, the practice continued despite the severe blows which the Venetian galleys sometimes inflicted on corsairs of any nation.

When Ibiza was plundered in August, 1536, were the attackers French or Turkish? How can one tell? In this case they were probably French since they carried off several sides of salt pork. Even amongst themselves, Christians and Moslems fought and looted. From Agde, during the summer of 1588, Montmorency's soldiers (who had not been paid, or so they said) began making pirate raids with a brigantine, capturing anything that sailed out of the gulf. In 1590, corsairs from Cassis robbed two Provençal boats. In 1593, a French ship, the *Jehan Baptiste*, probably from Brittany, carrying all the necessary certificates and passes issued by the Duke of Mercoeur and by the Spanish representative at Nantes, Don Juan de Aguila, was nevertheless seized by Prince Doria, her cargo sold and her crew clapped in irons. In 1596, French and above all Provençal *tartanes* were raiding the coasts of Naples and Sicily. About twenty years earlier, during the summer of 1572, a Marseilles freighter, the *Sainte-Marie et Saint-Jean*, master Antoine Banduf, returning from Alexandria with a rich cargo, became separated from the flotilla of other French ships by bad weather and met a Ragusan merchantman coming from Crete to fetch wheat from Sicily and take it to Valencia. The big ship captured the Marseilles boat and 'sent it to the bottom, drowning the said captain, his officers and mariners, having first looted and stolen the cargo'. Such were the hazards of life at sea. In 1566, the captain of a French vessel found himself in difficulties at Alicante – and to judge from the countless complaints of French sailors, the Spaniards could create powerful difficulties when they wanted to. But the captain was a bold man: he seized the men who boarded his ships and what was more scaled the walls of the town. Anything was allowed – provided it succeeded. In 1575, a French ship took on board in Tripoli in Barbary a cargo of Moorish and Jewish passengers bound for Alexandria, 'people of all ages and both sexes'. Without hesitation, the captain sailed straight to Naples where he sold his passengers, and all their baggage. Such mishaps were not infrequent: in 1592 for example, a certain Courture of Martigues, having accepted some Turkish passengers at Rhodes, took them to Messina, instead of to their destination in Egypt. And there was pure brigandage: during the summer of 1597, bandits armed several *leuti* and prowled the Genoese coast in search of prey. What kind of history have we been taught, that these acts, familiar to seamen of all nationalities, should nevertheless seem so astonishing?

Privateering sponsored by cities. Like Monsieur Jourdain who had been speaking prose all his life, there must have been many seamen who sailed *more piratico* and would have been scandalized to hear themselves described as privateers, let alone pirates.

Privateering – perhaps one should say 'true' privateering – was usually instigated by a city acting on its own authority or at any rate only marginally attached to a large state. This was as true in the age of Louis XIV as it was in the sixteenth century. When the Sun King could no longer maintain a regular battle fleet against England, he encouraged or allowed war by piracy; Saint-Malo and Dunkirk became belligerents in place of France.

Already in the sixteenth century, Dieppe and in particular La Rochelle, were centres of privateering, the latter operating virtually as a city-republic. The list of privateering centres in the Mediterranean is a roll-call of strategic cities: in Christendom, Valetta, Leghorn and Pisa, Naples, Messina, Palermo and Trapani, Malta, Palma de Majorca, Almeria, Valencia, Segna and Fiume; on the Moslem side, Valona, Durazzo, Tripoli in Barbary, Tunis-La Goletta, Bizerta, Algiers, Tetouan, Larache, Salé (Sallee). From this list, three new towns stand out: Valetta, founded by the Knights of Malta in 1566; Leghorn, re-founded in a sense by Cosimo de' Medici; finally and above all the astonishing city of Algiers, the apotheosis of them all.

This was no longer the Berber town of the beginning of the century but a new city, sprung up American-fashion almost overnight, complete with its harbour mole, its lighthouse, its archaic but solid ramparts and beyond them the mighty defence works which completed its protection. Privateers found shelter and supplies here, as well as a fund of skilled labour, caulkers, gun-founders, carpenters, sails and oars, a busy market on which stolen goods could quickly be disposed of, men willing to sign up for adventures at sea, galley-slaves, not to mention the pleasures of a port of call without which the life of the corsair with its violent contrasts would have been incomplete. Alonso de Contreras, on his return from a pirate raid to Valetta, which was famous for other things besides duels and prayers, lost no time in spending all his gold with the child *quiracas* in the brothels of the city. The *re'īs* of Algiers, on returning from an expedition, would hold open house, either in their city residences or in their villas on the Sahel where the gardens were the most beautiful in the world.

Privateering required above all things a market for its spoils. Algiers could not become a pirate stronghold without also becoming an active commercial centre. By the time Haëdo turned his observant eye on the city, in 1580, the transformation had been accomplished. In order to have food and equipment and to sell the prizes of war, the city had to be open to foreign caravans and ships, to the boats bringing ransom for captives, and to Christian vessels – Marseillais and Catalan, Valencian, Corsican, Italian (from every corner of Italy), English or Dutch. It was necessary too to attract by the prospect of affluence *re'īs* of every nation – Moslems or half-Moslems, sometimes northerners, in their galleys or nimble sailing ships.

In the sixteenth century, all states, despite their disagreements, were deeply committed to the law of nations and supposed to respect it. But the cities of the corsairs were worlds on the margins of society. Algiers, at the height of its prosperity, between 1580 and 1620, might or might not, depending on its own convenience, obey the orders of the sultan, and Istanbul was a long way off. On the Christian side, Malta was a rendezvous for adventurers with pretensions to autonomy. A revealing detail is the effort made in 1577–1578 by the Grand

295. Christians being tortured in Algiers.
From P. Dam, *Historie van Barbaryen*, Amsterdam, 1639–84.

Duke of Tuscany, master of the Knights of St Stephen, to distinguish, when negotiating with the Turks, his own cause from that of the Knights: here was a prince at once exercising very real authority, yet at the same time protesting his powerlessness.

But the corsairs who operated from urban bases were not the only ones. There were lower levels of piracy, often little more than petty thieving. It was pirates of this sort whom Pierre Belon saw at work in the Aegean, 'three or four men, accustomed to the sea, boldly pursuing the life of adventure, poor men, with only a small barque or frigate or perhaps some ill-equipped brigantine: but they have their *bussolo* or mariner's compass to navigate by and also the means to wage war, that is a few small arms for firing at a little distance. Their rations are a sack of flour, some biscuit, a skin of oil, honey, a few bunches of garlic

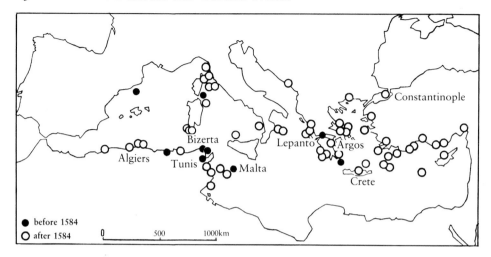

The privateers of Tuscany

From G. G. Guarnieri, pp. 36–37. The map represents the major exploits of the Florentine galleys of the Order of San Stefano between 1563 and 1688. Without wishing to read too much into this evidence, let us note in passing that before 1584, Tuscan attacks occurred in the western rather than the eastern part of the sea; after this date, they become general throughout the Mediterranean.

and onions and a little salt and on these they support themselves for a month. Thus armed they set out in search of prey. And if the winds keep them in port, they will drag their boat ashore and cover it with branches, chop wood with their axes, light a fire with their guns . . . and make a round loaf with their flour, which they cook in the same way as the Roman soldiers of antiquity on campaign.' From such humble beginnings too came the Caribbean buccaneers of the seventeenth century.

Such minor carnivores did not always inflict the least damage, nor amass the smallest fortunes in the end. Privateering, like America, was the land of opportunity and the wind of prosperity was unpredictable. A humble shepherd boy could become 'king' of Algiers and many were the careers that began in rags to end in riches. When the Spaniards were trying in 1569 to bribe Euldj 'Alī, the Calabrian fisher-boy who had become 'king' of the Berber city and was soon to astonish the world by rebuilding the sultan's navy, they dangled a marquisate in front of him – the kind of offer they assumed would be irresistible to one of such humble birth.

The prizes. Without prizes, privateering would have died out. During the years 1560–1565, the very success of piracy was reducing the numbers of prizes and pirates could not live without booty, even among friends, unfortunately for the subjects of the French king. Algiers was still expanding at the beginning of the seventeenth century, but why? Her corsairs were now to be found venturing into the Levant (though perhaps less than has been claimed), moving into the Adriatic, chasing the little boats of Marseilles and then, with the help of their northern recruits, passing through the Straits of Gibraltar, sailing out into the Atlantic, reaching English shores in 1631, attacking the clumsy Portuguese carracks and appearing as far off as Iceland, Newfoundland and the Baltic. Does this mean that their regular prey in the Mediterranean was growing scarce? Piracy in short, by its shifts and alterations, reacted in a characteristically direct and rapid fashion to the broader currents of Mediterranean life. The hunter had to follow the game. Its value as an indicator is unfortunately vitiated by the lack of statistical evidence. The descriptions, complaints, rumours and false reports we have are a slender basis for serious calculation.

The chronology of privateering. Certain key dates punctuate the history of privateering: 1508, 1522, 1538, 1571, 1580, 1600. In about 1500 (except in Venice), captives and convicts replaced the voluntary oarsmen who had until then almost exclusively manned the galleys. 1522: the fall of Rhodes removed the last remaining barrier in the East to large-scale Moslem privateering. 1538: Prevesa gave Islam that control of the sea of which the Christian victory at Lepanto was to deprive it in 1571. It is between these two dates (1538–1571) that the first great age of the Barbary corsairs can be situated, in particular during the decade from 1560 (after Djerba) to 1570, in those years when, apart from the siege of Malta, there were comparatively few major naval engagements. After 1580, both Christian and Moslem piracy, as the great armadas lay idle, increased at about the same rate. And finally after 1600, the Algerine corsairs, adopting completely new techniques, sailed out into the Atlantic.

Christian privateers. There had always been Christian pirates in the Mediterranean, even in the darkest hours. This piracy has not been fully recorded by historians, partly for psychological reasons, partly because it was carried out in very small ships, brigantines, frigates, *fregatillas*, barques, sometimes the tiniest fishing-smacks. The short distance separating Sicily or Spain from North Africa made it possible to proceed in such modest vessels; the meagreness of the booty made it necessary. Game was scarce and the scavengers were correspondingly few, only occasionally receiving a mention in the documents of the time. One of these rare glimpses is Haëdo's account of the exploits of the Valencian Juan Canete, master of a brigantine with fourteen oar-benches based at Majorca, an assiduous hunter off the coasts of Barbary who had been known to steal by night up to the very gates of Algiers and capture the people sleeping under the city walls. In the spring of 1550, he ventured inside the port at night with the intention of setting light to the poorly guarded foists and galliots. The attempt was a failure. Nine years later, he was to be executed by his gaolers in the bagnio. In 1567, his plan was revived by another Valencian, Juan Gascon, who was employed with his brigantine in the Oran supply fleet and did a little privateering on his own account. More successful than his predecessor, he entered the port and set fire to a few ships, but was later captured on the high seas by the *re'īs*.

Such occasional mentions tell us very little about the sailors of southern Spain. One has the impression that they must have become more active in 1580, since from then on they figure more frequently in the documents. They were probably never completely idle. When they emerge from the years of obscurity, we find them still using the same light vessels with their tall sails and still as audacious as ever. Take for example the account of the third voyage of one Juan Phelipe Romano, a sort of Scarlet Pimpernel for refugees from Algiers. On 23rd May, 1595, he left the Grao of Valencia, probably aboard a Barbary brigantine captured the year before. On 7th June, he lowered anchor near Algiers in a bay at the edge of a garden which was his rendezvous. The first night no one came, so he remained ashore and sent his companion back to the ship with orders to put back to sea and wait for a signal before returning. On the following night, the owner of the garden and his wife, with whom Romano had long ago made an agreement, arrived at the rendezvous. The refugee was a certain Juan Amador of Madrid, taken prisoner at Mostaganem in 1558 (that is about forty years before). In the interval he had embraced the Moslem faith, but now wished to return with his wife and a grand-daughter aged seven months. With him there embarked on the frigate the same night a 'princess', the *soldina*, daughter of Mustafā, ten Christian captives and two black slaves belonging to her, as well as a young Morisco girl of twenty-two; one of the wives of Mami Re'īs, the daughter of a lieutenant in Majorca, who was also accompanied by slaves, four men and a woman, all Christians; a Portuguese master locksmith of Algiers, his wife and two children and finally some Christian slaves who were on the spot and took advantage of the chance to escape: a total of thirty-two passengers, whom Romano carried without incident to Valencia. It makes a good story – but such *tours de force* were rare. On the whole these pirates operated in a very small way.

The Levant was easily the most rewarding hunting-ground for Christian privateers. And to the Levant sailed a steady stream of well-manned galleys, brigantines, galleons, frigates and swift sailing-ships well able to batter their way through the rough seas of the end of winter and the spring months. The reason was always the same: for the privateers the eastern Mediterranean meant rich prizes, to be found in the Aegean and even more on the Rhodes–Alexandria route, the route taken by pilgrims and by cargoes of spices, silks, wood, rice, wheat and sugar. The game was certainly plentiful, but the gamekeeper was vigilant: every year at the approach of spring, the Turks sent out their galley patrols, employed far more for the defence of ships than to guard the coast.

In the middle years of the century there were active in the Levant only the Maltese galleys, a few Tuscan galleys and the occasional sailing vessel like the galleon of the Genoese captain Cigala, put out of action in 1561; with here and

296. *Encounter at Sea Between Algerian Pirates and Spaniards*. Detail from anonymous seventeenth-century Spanish painting. *Prado, Madrid*

there a Sicilian ship, the galleon fitted in 1559 by the viceroy himself for example or the galliot fitted out the year before by the captain Joseph Santo. The said captain, having captured off Alessio a Turkish vessel worth over 15,000 ducats, was obliged by bad weather to take refuge with the Venetians, who promptly confiscated the ship. It is only through this incident that we know of the boat's existence at all. In 1559, a Tuscan galley, the *Lupa*, and a galliot belonging to Andrea Doria both set off on a privateering expedition; the first was seized by the guard off Rhodes and the second, after many adventures, limped exhausted into Cyprus and the clutches of the Venetians. Irritation in the West at this quasi-Turkish behaviour on the part of the Signoria can easily be imagined. Why should the Venetians have the right, argued the Duke of Florence, to prevent a Christian ship from putting out against the Infidel, if the said Christian vessel did not enter one of their ports? 'Does not the sea belong to everybody?' Poor Venetians: at the same time the Turks were reproaching them with failing to control the *ponentini*, and Turkish reprisals, usually after due warning and usually effective, were a threat to all peaceful Christian travellers and merchants in the East.

In these middle years of the century, the boldest western corsairs were the Knights of Malta, led by La Valette, in the years 1554–1555 and by Romegas in about 1560. In 1561, the latter captured 300 slaves and several rich cargoes at the mouth of the Nile; in 1563, having set out with two galleys, he was seen sailing back to Cape Passaro with over 500 slaves, black and white and, heaped on to two ships (the rest had been sunk) the cargoes of eight ships he had captured. These prizes, the letters add, 'must have been very rich since they came from Alexandria'. In 1564, Romegas brought home three *corchapins* laden with oars, tow and munitions for Tripoli in Barbary, and a Turkish roundship of 1300 *salme* which had left Tripoli for Constantinople with a cargo of 113 black slaves. The ship was taken to Syracuse, the *corchapins* to Naples.

Second place in those days went to the Florentines, who were presently to challenge the supremacy of the Knights of St John. In 1562, Baccio Martelli sailed to Rhodes, scoured the sea between Syria and the Barbary coast and captured a boat-load of Turks and Ethiopian Moors, the latter carrying gifts for the sultan: precious stones, a gold cross, conquered Christian standards and a *filza* of ritually amputated Christian noses. In 1564, the Knights of St Stephen made their first sortie *in forma di religione*, sailing to the Levant where they seized two rich Turkish vessels.

These were by no means the only prizes. But at this stage the Levant was not yet being plundered without mercy. A Venetian *avviso*, dating from early spring 1564, refers to twelve western galleys in the Aegean. This was by no means negligible, but during the same period the Moslem foists and galliots shamelessly plundering the riches of the West could be counted in multiples of twenty or thirty. At this point honours were far from equal.

Christian piracy in the Levant. From about 1574 onwards however, the Levant was invaded by pirates from the West. The Knights of Malta now virtually abandoned the nearby Barbary coast to make expeditions into the eastern seas. There was a visible increase in the activity of the Florentine galleys. They always worked in teams of four or five fast and powerful ships. In 1574, a voyage from Italy to Rhodes and Cyprus and back took them only twenty-nine days (leaving Messina on 7th August and arriving back at Catania on 5th September). They

297. Uskoks off the Dalmatian coast being fired on by a Venetian galley.
Venetian print, 1598.

occasionally made a foray into western waters too. From time to time a galleon
belonging to the Grand Duke would try its luck. Guarnieri's picturesque book
celebrating these bloodthirsty feats does not tell the complete story of the restless
voyages of the Knights of St Stephen, from which there is so much to be learnt
about the traffic in the Turkish seas, with its *gerbe, caramusali, passa cavalli,*
barques, brigantines and heavy western ships. The extremely precise accounts
of privateering expeditions in the Florentine Archives are full of lively detail.
Here we can read how the Venetians come swooping down in their galleys like
watchdogs between Cerigo and Cerigotto and force the galleys sailing under the
red cross to turn about and head for Italy and the protection of darkness.
Elsewhere a series of long direct voyages made without incident is dismissed in
a single line: the ships sail out under a fair wind and their destination soon
appears on the horizon, a cape, a cluster of lights winking in the darkness or a
flurry of sails, usually a sign that land is near. Other voyages are taken slowly,
following the coast from one watering-place to the next, calling at coves or
anchoring off sandbanks. The prizes themselves are described briefly and without emotion: item a *caramusali*, the number of cannon shots fired by the *capitana*
to shatter its yards or dismast it, casualties on our side, casualties among the
enemy; then on to the cargo: Greeks, Turks, dried fish, sacks of rice, spices,
carpets . . . and on to the next. A brief note explains the classic tricks of the
trade: if one is bold enough to enter the Aegean 'alla turchesca, costeggiando la
terra firma', it is sometimes possible to capture without a struggle passengers
coming down to the quayside mistaking the Christian pirates for the galleys of
the Grand Turk. We learn what is, among pirates, normal practice: any
unwanted vessels are sunk after their cargo has been taken; the Genoese captain
of a Venetian ship is tortured, with a heavy weight tied on his foot, until he
admits to having on board some *robbe*, the property of Jews or Turks; a ransom
is fixed, say 1000 crowns payable in 250 lb bales of silk at a crown a pound;
or a captured ship is loaded to the brim with stolen rice or wheat, manned with
a Greek crew and sent off to Sicily, with prayers to God and all his saints to

bring it safe to port. The Greek crew of the previous victim (now at the bottom of the sea) is transferred to a plundered Turkish vessel – and if some Greek pope protests overmuch he is dumped at Malta without ceremony.

In order to discover the whole truth about these ruthless expeditions the historian will have to unearth accurate accounts of battles and captures, calculate the profits and losses of this unique commercial enterprise and look closely at the equally specialized markets created by privateering, in particular the market in human beings which was the speciality of Malta, Messina and Leghorn. A register of captives intending to pay ransom (their birthplaces range from Fez to Persia and the Black Sea) or a list of galley-slaves with their ages and place of origin gives an idea of the probable benefits of the operation to the pirate-knights of St Stephen and their shrewd master. They can also be detected from the innumerable letters addressed to the Grand Duke by his rivals in Tripoli and Algiers: would his highness be willing to release so-and-so in exchange for a person of his choice? Would he consent to hear the respectful petition addressed by the wife of Mami Arnaut to the Grand Duchess herself? And would he in any case deign to accept this horse as a gift?

In this respect too, times were changing. In 1599, the five galleys flying the red cross seized the citadel of Chios which they were to hold temporarily. And in 1608, excelling themselves, the galleys of the Knights of St Stephen captured all the Turkish ships off Rhodes carrying pilgrims to Mecca. The reprisals envisaged at Constantinople were those of a waning power. In 1609, there was some talk in the Divan of forbidding the pilgrimage to Jerusalem, in the hope of arousing indignation in the Christian world against the pirates of Tuscany – times had certainly changed by now. And the Knights of St Stephen and St John,

298. Slave market in Algiers. From *Historie van Barbaryen*.

the invaders of the Aegean as a document of 1591 calls them, were not the only people to realize it. Other corsairs were forcing their way into the Levant: Sicilians, Neapolitans, even Barbary pirates, not to mention the minuscule but not negligible scavengers of the Levant itself, often in league with the patrols to fleece what was left in the devastated Aegean. The Neapolitans (apart from a brief episode between 1575–1578) did not appear in large numbers before the end of the century, if information given in Venice is correct. It was only then that the viceroys allowed ships to conduct privateering raids for public or private gain. It is not altogether surprising perhaps to find among these adventurers Alonso de Contreras, whose description of the plundering of the islands is particularly brutal, as well as two Provençal sea-captains who were credited in Paris with sinister intentions.

From Sicily, on the other hand, a whole fleet of privateers was, even before 1574, beginning to launch raids on the Levant. The names of some are famous: Filippo Corona, Giovanni di Orta, Jacopo Calvo, Giulio Battista Corvaja and Pietro Corvaja, who were present at Lepanto, along with several others, notably the amazing Cesare Rizzo, an expert at reconnaissance in the Levant: from the great battle, in which he participated in his light *fregatina* decked in all her canvas, he was to bring home as a trophy to the Chapel of Santa Maria della Gracia in the parish of S. Nicolò Kalsa at Messina, a bell which the Turks 'havianu priso a l'isola di Cipro', in the previous year. There were other names too: Pedro Lanza, a Greek from Corfu and a well-known chaser of frigates and galliots, Venetian ships and Venetian subjects, employed in 1576–1577 by Ribera, the governor of Bari and Otranto; or Philip Cañadas, the notorious corsair who in 1588 commanded one of the privateering galliots of Pedro de Leyva, general of the Sicilian galleys, another threat to Venetian shipping.

For the entire piratical world was, by the end of the century, eager to settle scores with the Republic of St Mark. The galleys of the *Serenissima* patrolled in vain. There were many ways – if only by taxing her merchants in Taranto – of making Venice loosen her hold. Diplomatic protests in Florence or Madrid were rarely heeded. Venice did succeed in obtaining from Philip II a ban on privateering by Naples and Sicily. Naples obeyed, more or less; in Sicily, both private individuals and the viceroy himself continued their profitable trade. In any case, Philip's orders dating from 1578, were taken to refer far more to the Turk, with whom negotiations were under way, than to Venice. The Venetians argued, to little or no avail, that seizing 'ropas de judios y de turcos' carried in Venetian ships harmed the trade of Venice and therefore in the long run that of Spain, with whom she had commercial ties, and furthermore that by such actions the pirates were molesting poor 'stateless' Jews who, although expelled from Spain, nevertheless considered themselves subjects of the Catholic King, as well as humble and peaceloving Turkish merchants. Madrid usually viewed with equanimity the difficulties of Venice, whom she knew to be unkindly disposed towards Spain and whom she suspected of having made an illicit fortune out of the peace which Venetians were prepared to go to any lengths to preserve. In the Levant, even the Turks plundered Venetian ships, so much so that the all-round increase in piracy deserves careful consideration in relation to both Venice and Ragusa (Ragusan ships did not escape the right of search). The historian should ask himself whether the success of the western privateers does not explain in part why both Ragusa and Venice withdrew to the safer routes of the Adriatic, far from the seas and islands 'harassed' and 'starved' by the insolence of the 'vasselli christiani'. In Venice, insurance rates tell their own story: for the Syria route, they went up to 20 per cent in 1611 and to 25 per cent in 1612.

The first brilliant age of Algiers. In the western waters of the sea, Moslem privateering was equally prosperous and had been so for many years. It had several headquarters, but its fortunes are epitomized in the extraordinary career of Algiers.

Between 1560 and 1570, the western Mediterranean was infested with Barbary pirates, mostly from Algiers; some made their way to the Adriatic or to the coasts of Crete. The characteristic method of attack during these years was the regular assault in large groups if not in actual battle formation. In July, 1559, fourteen pirate vessels were sighted off Niebla in Andulasia; two years later, fourteen galleys and galliots again appeared near Santi Pietri, off Seville. In August, Jean Nicot reported '17 galères turcquesques' on the Portuguese Algarve. At the same period, Dragut was operating off Sicily and in a single raid captured eight Sicilian galleys off Naples. With a fleet of thirty-five sail, he blockaded Naples in midsummer. Two years later, in September, 1563 (that is after the harvest) he was prowling off the coast of Sicily and was twice sighted at the Fossa di San Giovanni near Messina with twenty-eight ships. In May 1563, twelve ships, four of them galleys, were reported off Gaeta. In August, nine Algerine ships were sighted between Genoa and Savona; in September there were thirteen of them off the Corsican coast. Thirty-two appeared at the beginning of September on the Calabrian coast, probably the same ships which were reported as a fleet of about thirty sail arriving off Naples one night and taking shelter near the island of Ponza. Still in September, eight ships sailed past Pozzuoli, making for Gaeta and twenty-five sails were sighted *sopra Santo Angelo in Ischia*. In May, 1564, a fleet of forty-two sail appeared off Elba (forty-five according to a French report). Forty sails, this time off the coast of Languedoc on the track of the galleys bound for Italy, were reported by Fourquevaux in April, 1569. A month later, twenty-five corsairs were seen sailing past the shores of Sicily, which they hardly bothered to trouble, being utterly engrossed in the pursuit of ships and boats.

Such numbers explain the severe blows dealt by the corsairs, who on one occasion seized eight galleys and another time, off Málaga, captured twenty-eight Biscay ships (June, 1566). In a single season they accounted for fifty ships in the Straits of Gibraltar and on the Atlantic coasts of Andalusia and the Algarve; a raid into the kingdom of Granada furnished them with 4000 prisoners. During this period, according to the Christians, the audacity of the corsairs knew no bounds. Where once they had operated only by night, they now showed themselves in broad daylight. Their raids reached as far as the *Percheles*, the criminal quarter of Málaga. The Cortes of Castile refer, in 1560, to the desolation and emptiness of the Peninsula coasts. In 1563, when Philip II was at Valencia, 'all the talk', writes Saint-Sulpice, 'is of tournaments, jousting, balls and other noble pastimes, while the Moors waste no time and even dare to capture vessels within a league of the city, stealing as much as they can carry'.

Valencia threatened, Naples under a blockade (in July, 1561, 500 men were unable to cross from Naples to Salerno because of corsairs), Sicily and the Balearics surrounded – all these can be explained by geography, given the proximity of North Africa. But the corsairs were active as far north as the coasts of Languedoc, Provence and Liguria, which had until then seen little disturbance. Near Villefranche, in June, 1560, the Duke of Savoy himself barely escaped falling into their hands. In the same month, June, 1560, Genoa's stocks of grain and wine ran low and prices rose; the boats which usually brought wines from Provence and Corsica dared not put to sea, for fear of the twenty-three pirate ships prowling the coast. Nor were these isolated incidents: every summer the Genoese coast was plundered. In August, 1563, it was the turn of Celle and Albissola on the western riviera. All 'this trouble', wrote the Republic of Sauli, its ambassador in Spain, 'comes from the sea's being empty of galleys, there is not a single Christian ship to be seen'. As a result, no shipping dared put out. In May of the following year, a memorandum from Marseilles, annotated by Philip II himself, reports that fifty corsairs have put out from Algiers, thirty from Tripoli, sixteen from Bône and four from Velez (the Peñon which blocked the entry to this port was not captured by the Spanish until September, 1564). If this is to be taken literally, a hundred ships, galleys, galliots and foists were at large in the Mediterranean. The same source adds: 'It is raining Christians in Algiers.'

The second brilliant age of Algiers. Between 1580 and 1620, Algiers entered upon a second age of prosperity, as spectacular as the first and certainly more far-reaching. The corsair capital benefited both from the concentration of piracy and also from a technical revolution of decisive importance.

As it had towards the middle of the century, privateering was once again replacing fleet warfare. 'The corsairs do much harm in this island', writes Marcantonio Colonna, viceroy of Sicily, in June, 1578, 'in the many coastal regions which are without towers.' Not even far-away Catalonia (indeed it was particularly harassed), Provence or Marseilles was spared. On 11th February, 1584,

299. *Overleaf:* Algiers and its surroundings. From *Civitates Orbis Terrarum.*

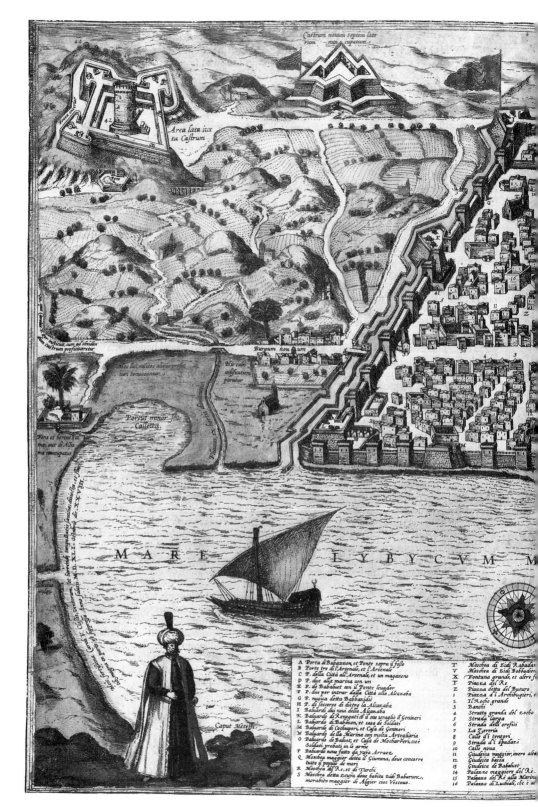

Castrum nouum Septem late
rium nuncupatum

Area lata iux
ta Castrum

Burgum nouum

Hoc loci,milites aliquo profe
turi tumaerentur

Hic et ædificationi
parantur

Portus minor siue
Calletta

Fons et hortus Pal
mæ, aut di Alba
ma nuncupatus

M A R E   L Y B Y C V M   M

Caput Meteiss.

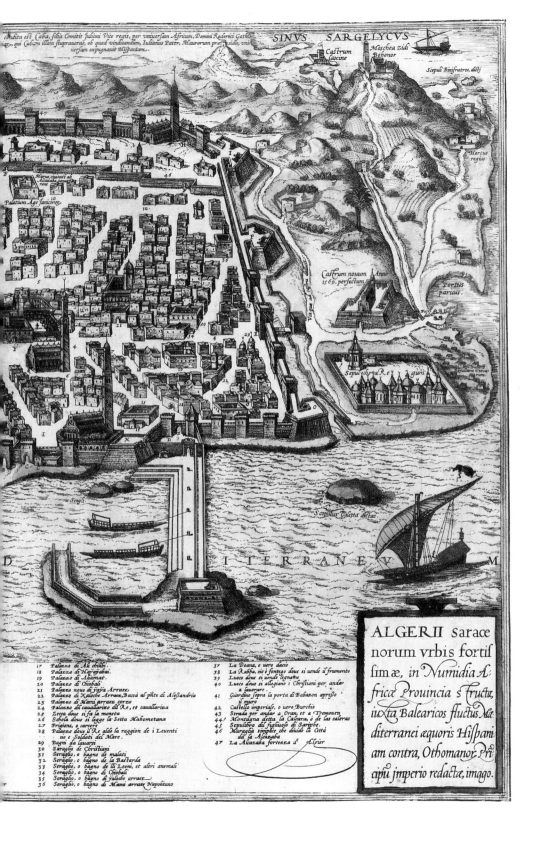

the municipal council is found discussing the ransoming of citizens of Marseilles who were prisoners in Algiers; on 17th March, 1585, the council decided to 'inquire into the speediest means of ending the ravages wrought by the Barbary pirates on the Provençal coast'. Years went by without bringing any relief. During the winter of 1590, Marseilles decided to send an envoy to the king of Algiers to negotiate ransoms. In Venice, which one would have expected to be protected by its position, the *procuratori sopra i capitoli*, on 3rd June, 1588, elected a consul for Algiers with particular responsibility for the interests of Venetian slaves.

There is no shortage of explanations for this revival of prosperity in Algiers: in the first place it was a natural consequence of the general prosperity in the Mediterranean. As has already been remarked, when there were no merchant vessels, there were no pirates. Above all, the dynamism of Algiers proved to be that of a new and rapidly growing city. With Leghorn, Smyrna and Marseilles it was one of the young powers of the sea. In Algiers, all life depended, needless to say, on the volume and success of pirate shipping, down to the pittance of the poorest muleteer in the city or the cleanliness of the streets which was maintained by an army of slaves, even more of course the buildings under construction, costly mosques, rich men's villas, and aqueducts, the work apparently of Andalusian refugees.

Algiers in 1516–1538 was a city of Berbers and Andalusians, of renegade Greeks and of Turks, thrown together pell-mell. This was the period that saw the rise of the Barbarossas. Between 1560 and 1587, Algiers under Euldj 'Alī was becoming increasingly more Italian. After 1580–1590 and towards 1600 came the northerners, Englishmen and Dutchmen, one of whom was Simon Danser (Dansa in the French and Italian documents), that is *der Tantzer*, the dancer – his real name was Simon Simonsen and he was a native of Dordrecht. The English consul in Algiers saw him arrive in 1609 aboard a ship 'of great force' built in Lübeck and manned by a mixed crew of Turkish, English and Dutch sailors, with about thirty prizes already to her credit that year. Little is known with any certainty about his eventful life, his return to Christendom and Marseilles where he had a wife and children, his entry into the service of that city, his capture and probable execution years later in Tunis, on the orders of the Dey in February, 1616. The fair-skinned invaders did not come empty-handed. They brought with them cargoes of sails, timber, pitch, gunpowder and cannon – and best of all their sailing ships, the same ships which had for many years been sailing the Atlantic, running rings round the unwieldy galleons and carracks of the Iberians. Unbeatable galley-crews had been the main strength of the *re'is*. But now Algiers adopted the light sailing ships, which were also capable of speed and surprise.

In 1580, the Algiers fleet amounted to perhaps thirty-five galleys, twenty-five frigates and a certain number of brigantines and barques. Towards 1618, she probably possessed about a hundred sailing vessels of which the smallest had

300, 301. *Left:* Portrait of Ariadeno Barbarossa, after Capriolo. From *Ritratti di cento capitani illustri*, Rome, 1596. *Below:* Caricature portraits of the Barbarossas. Seventeenth-century Dutch print.

ARUCH En CHERIDYN BARBAROSSA
Koningen van Algiers

18 to 20 guns. In 1623 (a rather more reliable figure furnished by Sir Thomas Roe, English commercial representative at the Golden Horn) the fleet consisted of seventy-five sail and several hundred small boats. From now on the Barbary pirates were concentrated almost exclusively at Algiers; once-fearsome Tripoli (in Italy in about 1580, the usual parting words to those putting out to sea had been 'May God preserve you from the galleys of Tripoli') by 1612 possessed only a couple of sailing ships; Tunis seven in 1625. Was the same true of the ports in the West where, in 1610 and 1614, the Spaniards had taken Larache and the Marmora without a struggle? Algiers in any case was soon overflowing with wealth. A Portuguese prisoner tells us that between 1621 and 1627 there were some twenty thousand captives in Algiers, a good half of whom were people 'of pure Christian stock', Portuguese, Flemish, Scottish, Hungarian, Danish, Irish, Slav, French, Spanish and Italian; the other half were heretics and idolaters – Syrians, Egyptians, even Japanese and Chinese, inhabitants of New Spain, Ethiopians. And every nation of course provided its crop of renegades: even allowing for the lack of precision in the account, it seems clear that the fabric of Algiers was now of many colours. Meanwhile the corsairs swarmed all

over the sea, their city now of a size to dominate the entire Mediterranean. In 1624, the Algerines plundered Alexandretta, capturing two ships, a Frenchman and a Dutchman. Even more significant, they sailed out of the Straits of Gibraltar, plundering Madeira in 1617, Iceland in 1627, reaching England, as we have already seen in 1631 and becoming, particularly in the 1630s, pirates of the Atlantic. Moslem piracy had concluded an alliance with Atlantic piracy. According to some sources it was none other than the notorious Simon Danser (alias Simon Re'īs) who taught the mariners of Algiers, perhaps as early as 1601, how to slip through the difficult Straits of Gibraltar.

Ransoming prisoners. All over Christendom, institutions were being introduced to handle the ransoming of prisoners: rich men, as we know, arranged their own ransoms. In 1581, the papacy led the way: Gregory XIII created the *Opera Pia dellà Redenzione de' Schiavi* and attached it to the ancient and active *Arciconfraternità del Gonfalone* of Rome. The first ransoms were negotiated in 1583, the first mission arrived in Algiers in 1585. In 1586, there was set up in Sicily the *Arciconfraternità della Redenzione dei Cattivi* with as headquarters the church of Santa Maria Nuova at Palermo. In fact this was merely a revival of a former institution which had already functioned in the fifteenth century. On 29th October, 1597, Genoa set up the diligent *Magistrato del Riscatto degli Schiavi* which was also the second incarnation of an organization dating back to 1403, the *Magistrato di Misericordia*. There was a need for administration and for tribunals on behalf of these prisoners, temporarily without rights of citizenship, who returned, when they did return at all, to incredibly complicated situations at home. After being absent too long, or having become renegades, they had left unresolved business behind them: their families had had to take steps to have the disappearance legally certified while the 'ministry of prisoners' for its part was intervening to protect the interests and effects of former captives. The long series of papers in Genoa is a magnificent mine of information for the researcher who is interested in the true history of these imprisonments rather than the picturesque narrative.

Saving prisoners was all very well, but even more important was the salvation of their souls. The religious orders devoted themselves seriously to this task. It meant slipping into Barbary under the plausible cover of arranging ransoms, reaching an agreement with the charitable organizations, obtaining a passage and the relevant funds from Rome, Spain, Genoa or elsewhere.

The traffic in ransoms and the exchange of men and goods led to the establishment of new commercial circuits. The voyages of redemptionists increased in number and they carried aboard their ships either money or goods, all duly insured. After 1579, it was all registered at the French Consulate at Algiers, as it had been in Tunis since 1574. Tabarka was, towards 1600, another active headquarters for ransom, dealing with Tunis and Bizerta. The return of the liberated prisoners would be marked by grand ceremonies, processions and

302. *The Sack of Tunis and the Liberation of the Christian Captives*. Detail from a cartoon for the series of tapestries on Charles V's Tunis campaign by J. G. Vermeyen. *Kunsthistorisches Museum, Vienna*

thanksgivings. As early as 1559 a convoy of released captives marched through the streets of Lisbon carrying on the end of sticks pieces of brown bread – the only food in the bagnios. Inevitably a network of communications was created by the capture, negotiation and release of prisoners. With piracy on both sides, complicated bargaining situations could arise. A document from the French consulate at Tunis mentions a Sardinian priest, the slave of the wife of Mami Arnaut who was himself a slave of the king of Spain. Such predicaments made exchanges possible, if not rapid.

And with overpopulation in the bagnios, escapes became more frequent. We have already noted the exploits of the frigate of Felipe Romano, the Valencian who operated a quasi-official escape route for prisoners from the bagnios of Algiers. Prisoners also arranged their own getaways and mass escapes were commonplace. One day they would steal a foist, another time a galley and sail out trusting to luck – one of the more cheering incidents in these unfortunate lives. The ease with which escapes were effected came largely from the growing numbers of that hybrid race, half-Christian, half-Moslem, living on the borders of the two worlds in a fraternal alliance which would have been even more evident if the states had not required appearances to be preserved. Fraternization could be the result of changing one's faith (not the noblest, but undoubtedly the most common cause) or of trade, whether in ransoms or in merchandise. In Constantinople, this was the special province of Italian renegades; in Algiers that of the seamen of Cape Corse, familiar both to the *re'īs* and to the bagnios, who fished for coral and sometimes transported wax, wool and hides; in Tunis it was virtually the monopoly of the French consuls, who were accused of securing the release of those they chose, even making sure, on payment of a bribe, that certain prisoners never returned. And everywhere Jews acted as intermediaries.

These operations were all remunerative. Trading in Algiers brings a sure profit of 30 per cent, said a Genoese merchant under interrogation. And in Spain, several reminders had to be issued that it was unlawful to ship to Algiers certain prohibited goods, to buy stolen merchandise or indeed any goods sold by corsairs. But the latter could always find buyers by looking to Italy and in particular to Leghorn. These links still existed in the seventeenth century. The capture of a Portuguese vessel in 1621 left in the hands of the *re'īs* of Algiers a collection of diamonds 'with which all Italy became rich' says the source. The Turks, who did not know a great deal about precious stones, had sold them at low prices. But we have only brief glimpses of these daily, unspectacular transactions. Tunis, as much as, possibly more than Algiers, was a centre for clandestine trade: the Shanghai of the sixteenth century as a Sicilian historian has called it, probably with some justification.

One war replaces another. So when we say that war in the Mediterranean came to an end in 1574, we should make it clear which kind of war we mean. Regular war, maintained at great expense by the authoritarian expansion of major states, yes, that certainly came to an end. But the living materials of that war, the men who could no longer be kept in the war fleets by what had become inadequate rewards and wages (as a perceptive Venetian, the Captain of the Gulf, Filippo Pasqualigo, noted in 1588) were driven to a life of roving by the liquidation of international war. Sailors from the galleys, even sometimes the galleys themselves, deserting from the fleet, soldiers, or those who would normally have been soldiers, adventurers of large or small ambitions were all absorbed into the undeclared war which now raged on land and sea. One form of war was replacing another. Official war, sophisticated, modern and costly, now moved into northern Europe and the Mediterranean was left with its secondary, minor forms. Its societies, economies and civilizations had to adapt as best they could to what was on land guerrilla warfare, on sea warfare by piracy. And this war was to absorb much of their energy, regrets, bad consciences, vengeance and reprisals. Brigandage subsumed as it were the energies of a social war which never surfaced. Piracy consumed the passions that would in other times have gone into a crusade or *Jihād*; no one apart from madmen and saints was now interested in either of these.

With the general return of peace (1598, 1604, 1609) regular war died out

303. Pirate ships captured by the Dutch at Algiers – the pirates are hanging from the yard-arms. From *Historie van Barbaryen*.

in the North and the Atlantic; its spectre returned to haunt the Mediterranean with plans, threats and dreams. Was it to break out again? No: the abortive war launched by Osuna and Spain against Venice (1618–1619) provides a convenient test. It failed to spark off a wide conflict, proof perhaps that the Mediterranean was no longer able to support the burden, pay the terrible price; and yet its waters were still haunted by bloodshed.

Having come thus far, we are forced to a pessimistic conclusion. If the history of human aggression in the Mediterranean in the sixteenth century is neither fictitious nor illusory, war in its metamorphoses, revivals, Protean disguises and degenerate forms, reasserts its perennial nature: its red lines did not all break at once. *Bellum omnium pater*, the old adage was familiar to the men of the sixteenth century. War, the begetter of all things, the creature of all things, the river with a thousand sources, the sea without a shore: begetter of all things except peace, so ardently longed for, so rarely attained. Every age constructs its own war, its own types of war. In the Mediterranean, official hostilities were over after Lepanto. Major war had now moved north and west to the Atlantic coasts – and was to stay there for centuries to come, where its true place was, where the heart of the world now beat. This shift, better than any argument, indicates and underlines the withdrawal of the Mediterranean from the centre of the stage. When in 1618, the first shots of the Thirty Years' War rang out, and nations went to battle once more, it was far from Mediterranean shores: the inland sea was no longer the troubled centre of the world.

8

By Way of Conclusion:
Conjoncture and *Conjonctures*

IF, AFTER A SERIES OF CHAPTERS discussing the economics, politics, civilizations and wars of the Mediterranean, I now introduce the term *conjoncture*,
(short-to-medium-term economic change) my intention is not to bring together
under a single heading all that has gone before, but to suggest possible new
directions for research and some tentative explanatory hypotheses.

In the preceding pages, the reader has been constantly reminded of the
inter-relationship between change and the near-permanent in history. If we now
narrow our range to focus exclusively on the element of change, of movement,
the picture alters dramatically: a mathematical parallel might be the transition,
by eliminating one dimension, from solid geometry to the necessarily simpler
field of plane geometry. In this case we are now faced with a narrative view of
history, the episodic content of which – periods, crises, phases and turning-points
– may tempt the historian to dramatize or to jump to convenient if sometimes
fallacious explanations. For the economic *conjoncture*, the most obvious and
familiar of those we have to deal with, very rapidly comes to tower above all
the others, imposing upon them its own terminology and categories. Neo-
materialism is an inviting path. How valid is it as an approach?

A word of warning. Our problem now is to imagine and locate the correlations
between the rhythms of material life and the other diverse fluctuations of human
existence. For there is no single *conjoncture*: we must visualize a series of overlapping histories, developing simultaneously. It would be too simple, too perfect,
if this complex truth could be reduced to the rhythms of one dominant pattern.
How clear, in any case, is that pattern itself? It is impossible to define even the
economic *conjoncture* as a single movement given once and for all, complete
with laws and consequences. In the web of vibrations which makes up the
economic world, the expert can without difficulty isolate tens, dozens of movements, distinguished by their length in time: the secular trend, 'longest of the
long-term movements'; medium-term trends – the fifty-year Kondratieff cycle,

304. *Opposite:* The port of Ravenna. Mosaic, c. AD 520.

the double or hypercycle, the intercycle; and short-term fluctuations – inter-decennial movements and seasonal shifts. So, in the undifferentiated flow of economic life, several languages can be distinguished by the somewhat artificial process of analysis.

If then we propose to use the economy in order to locate the chain of causality stretching back into the past, we may be obliged to handle ten or twenty possible languages – and as many causal chains. History becomes many-stranded once more, bewilderingly complex and, who knows, in seeking to grasp all the different vibrations, waves of past time which ought ideally to accumulate like the divisions in the mechanism of a watch, the seconds, minutes, hours and days – perhaps we shall find the whole fabric slipping away between our fingers.

But rather than prolong a theoretical discussion, let us give it practical application. Here before us, we have the whole of the Mediterranean during the period I have sometimes described as the 'long' or extended sixteenth century, as this book has tried to reconstruct it. Putting aside for the moment our doubts and reservations, let us try to effect some measurements in terms of the secular trend and the medium-term economic *conjoncture*, omitting for the time being short-term and seasonal fluctuations.

The secular trend. An upward secular trend, beginning in about 1470, reached a peak, or slowed down for a while, during the years of record high prices 1590–1600, then continued after a fashion until 1650. These dates, 1470 (or 1450), 1590, 1595 or 1600, 1650, are only very approximate landmarks. The long upward movement is confirmed essentially by variations in grain prices which give us a clear and unequivocal series of figures. If the wage curve, say, or the production curve had been used as a basis for calculation one would no doubt find somewhat different chronologies, but they would ultimately have to be checked against the all-powerful grain curve.

It seems clear then that during the 'long' sixteenth century, a slow but powerful upsurge favoured the advance of the material economy and of everything dependent on it. It was the secret of the fundamental healthiness of the economy. 'In the sixteenth century,' Earl J. Hamilton once told me, 'every wound heals over.' There were always compensations: in industry, production might soar in one sector if it was declining in another; in the world of commerce, as soon as one type of capitalism was on the wane, it was succeeded by another.

This hidden resilience did not vanish overnight at the end of the sixteenth century – indeed the recession was slow to appear: not before the short but structural (in other words deeply felt) crisis of 1619–1623, according to Ruggiero Romano, whose opinion is almost that of Carlo M. Cipolla; possibly not even until the 1650s, as Emmanuel Le Roy Ladurie, René Baehrel, Aldo de Maddalena and Felipe Ruiz Martín suggest, and as I am more and more inclined to think myself, within the limits of my observation. For on the downward path there were pauses, recoveries even in agriculture, which one would expect to have been the first affected. Felipe Ruiz Martín tells me: 'the decline of Spanish agriculture after the crisis of 1582 was not as precipitous as is usually thought: within the general downward trend, there was a cyclical [i.e. short-term] recovery, between 1610 and 1615 and another in the 1630s. Disaster did not really strike until after the 1650s.'

There is clearly no simply solution to this much-debated question which is further complicated by the possible time-lag between economic cycles in different parts of Europe; although on this last point too, I think it is an over-simplification merely to distinguish between northern Europe and the Mediterranean, the latter succumbing more quickly to the general decline of the seventeenth century. The debate is still open. As far as historians of the Mediterranean are concerned, we must once again rid ourselves of the persistent but false notion of its early decline.

This having been said, it is interesting to note that the general estimates calculated long ago by professional economists also suggest as the terminal date of the long upward trend, the middle years of the seventeenth century, including within it that is the first fifty years of the century, although a certain deceleration of the growth rate was already visible.

On the point of take-off however, they are by no means agreed. We have the choice between Marie Kerhuel's estimate, to which I personally incline (1470 or even 1450) and Jenny Griziotti Kretschmann's (1510). Either date can be defended. The earlier, 1470, is deduced from the nominal price curves, the later from silver prices. Speaking for myself, I, like René Baehrel, prefer nominal price indexes as a basis for calculation – but that dispute need not concern us here.

Further light will no doubt be shed on the question by future historians using evidence of a rather different order. In Venice, which I have personally studied in some detail, I am impressed, for example, by the scale of public building and decoration in the city after 1450: the replacement of the wooden bridges over the canals by stone bridges, the digging of the great well near the church of Santa Maria di Brolio in August, 1445, the construction in May, 1459 of a new loggia *in loco Rivoalti*, where the weavers' shops were demolished to make way for the extension to the Doges' Palace. 'The city increases in beauty every day,' notes a document of 1494, 'let us hope people will respect its beauties.' In March, 1504, indeed, order went out to remove from St Mark's Square (which had boasted its magnificent clock tower since 1495) the huts erected by the stone-masons, who had planted trees and vines alongside – 'et quod pejus est: è facta una latrina che ogniuno licensiosamente va lì a far spurtitie . . .'. Needless to say, this evidence does not prove anything one way or the other, either in Venice (where construction may have been carried out because or in spite of the economic climate) or in the Mediterranean as a whole. But it inclines me to classify the whole vigorous period from 1450 to 1650 as a unit, the 'long'

sixteenth century, and therefore to agree with Jean Fourastié and his pupils that
the first wave of prosperity was independent of American bullion. To take a
single city, in this case Venice, as an index, can be a fruitful exercise; it may
even reveal a truer picture of economic change than we have from price curves.

That these two hundred years, 1450–1650, should form a coherent unit, at
least in some respects, clearly demands some explanation. Whether cause or
effect, we know for certain that these two centuries show a steady increase in
population, varying somewhat from region to region and year to year, but never,
as far as one can see, interrupted. It should be noted however, that the upward
trend did not, as we have already pointed out, betoken a rise in living standards.
During every period, until at least the eighteenth century, economic progress
was inevitably at the expense of the ever-increasing masses, the victims of 'social
massacres', to borrow a phrase of Ernest Labrouste.

The constant pressure of the mounting secular trend clearly appears to have
encouraged the growth first of territorial states and then of empires. Its reversal
was to create obvious difficulties for them. Economic growth, with all its vicissitudes, had favoured a comparatively open society. The aristocracy was, as we
have seen, reinforced by the 'bourgeois' invasion, itself encouraged by a run of
prosperity. The repeated evidence of such prosperity presupposes an upward
turn in economic life. With the reversal of the secular trend, society presumably
closed its doors, though here we have too little evidence to construct an acceptable chronology.

War at home and abroad. Wars fit even more obligingly into our attempt at
classification. We have already identified two types of war, the internal (within
Christendom or Islam) and the external (between two hostile civilizations). It is
possible to claim that the *Jihād* or Crusade was almost invariably encouraged
by an unfavourable economic situation. Civil wars, in which Christian fought
Christian and Moslem Moslem, were on the contrary usually preceded by a
'boom'; they come speedily to a halt when the economy takes a downward turn.
In Christendom therefore, the major diplomatic treaties, the 'Ladies' Peace' (Paix
des Dames) (1529), Cateau-Cambrésis (1559), Vervins (1598) occur either at
the very peak of an upward curve or close to one; the great battles between
Turk and Christian on the other hand (Prevesa, 1538, Lepanto, 1571) occur
where one would logically expect to find them, in periods of recession. I would
not claim that this correlation is either perfect or inevitable. The capture of
Belgrade by the Turks for instance, took place in 1521, Mohács in 1526, when
according to our model, such confrontations should not have occurred. To cite
another discrepancy, Charles VIII crossed the Alps in 1494, while the foregoing
analysis suggests that the Italian wars should not have begun until 1509 (the
year, I cannot resist pointing out, of Agnadello!). But if the timetable does not
exactly fit the actions of France under Charles VIII and Louis XII, it seems to
apply very well to Spain under Ferdinand and Isabella. The period 1483–1509

saw the conquest of Granada and the expeditions against North Africa. The latter were accelerated between 1509 and 1511 and came to a halt with the renewal of the so-called Italian wars.

I would not wish to overstate my case, nor do I seek to suppress inconvenient evidence. It is a fact nevertheless that the Italian wars, although they did indeed break out in 1494, got off to a slow start. Similarly, while the years 1521–1526 undoubtedly opened up Hungary to the Turkish invasion, it has been suggested by some historians that Hungary was not truly overcome until later, that the lengthy conquest dragged out until 1541.

One might note, by contrast, that it was at the end of the sixteenth century, after 1595 – that is, exactly when we should expect it – that anti-Turkish feeling came to a head: a crusade was planned, though never, it is true, put into execution. However war by privateer was waged throughout the Mediterranean with exceptional savagery, for reasons which must go beyond those of techonology, economics or individual enterprise; passions played a part; in Spain, the expulsion of 300,000 Moriscos took place between 1609 and 1614, the outcome of one of the most brutal wars of the period; lastly, in about 1621, a critical year, the war which had first flared up in Bohemia in 1618 was to find fresh fuel and ravage the heart of central Europe. The Thirty Years' War began right on cue.

These coincidences teach us something. In fair weather, family quarrels came to the fore; when times were bad, war was declared against the Infidel. The rule seems to apply equally well to Islam. From Lepanto until the revival of the war against Germany in 1593, Turkey, turning towards Asia, flung herself into a fanatical war against Persia. From such observations, we can perhaps glimpse something of the psychological origins of major wars.

Within Christendom, outbreaks of anti-Semitism appear to coincide with foreign wars. It was in times of economic depression that the Jews were persecuted throughout the Christian world.

Conjoncture *and history.* I make no claims for the infallibility of the foregoing analysis, any more than I would for any attempt to classify the known data of history by the use of explanatory grids derived from our notions of the many possible *conjonctures.* Conjunctural analysis, even when it is pursued on several levels, cannot provide the total undisputed truth. It is however *one* of the necessary means of historical explanation and as such a useful formulation of the problem.

We have the problem of classifying on the one hand the economic *conjonctures* and on the other the non-economic *conjonctures.* The latter can be measured and situated according to their length in time: comparable, let us say, to the secular trend are long-term demographic movements, the changing dimensions of states and empires (the geographical *conjoncture* as it might be called), the presence or absence of social mobility in a given society, the intensity of industrial growth; parallel to the medium-term economic trend are rates of industrialization, the fluctuations of state finances and wars. A conjunctural scaffolding helps to construct a better house of history. But further research is essential and at this stage much prudence is called for. Classification will be no simple matter and should be approached with caution. The long-term trends of civilizations, their flowering in the traditional sense of the word, can still surprise and disconcert us. The Renaissance for instance, between 1480 and 1509, falls in a period of clear *cyclical* depression; the age of Lorenzo the Magnificent was one of economic stagnation. The Golden Age in Spain and the splendours of the sixteenth century, even in Istanbul, all blossomed after the first great reversal of the secular trend. I have offered a possible explanation – but who shall say how valid it is? My suggestion would be that any economic recession leaves a certain amount of money lying idle in the coffers of the rich: the prodigal spending of this capital, for lack of investment openings, might produce a brilliant civilization lasting years or even decades.

This tentative answer may formulate the problem, but it does not resolve it – any more than the familiar observations we have all heard about the unexpected flowering of the Renaissance and Baroque and the troubled societies which give birth to them, of which they are, one might almost say, the morbid product. The Renaissance spelt the end of the city-state; with the Baroque, the great empires of the sixteenth century began to feel the cold wind at their back. Perhaps the extravagance of a civilization is a sign of its economic failure. Such problems take us well outside the narrow confines of the *conjoncture*, whether medium or short term. But once more, it is a useful path by which to approach them.

Conclusion to the First English Edition

THIS BOOK has been in circulation now for almost twenty years: it has been quoted, challenged, criticized (too seldom) and praised (too often). In that time I have frequently had occasion to elaborate its explanations, to defend its arguments, to reflect upon the attitudes it embodies, and to correct its mistakes. I have now re-read it thoroughly in order to prepare the second edition and have made very extensive alterations. But inevitably a book has its own career, its own existence, independent of its author. One can improve it here and there, embellish it with a whole apparatus of footnotes and details, maps and illustrations, but never radically change its outline. Not uncommonly in the sixteenth century, a ship purchased elsewhere would be brought to Venice, where it was overhauled from stem to stern and refitted by skilful carpenters; underneath it was still the same ship, built in the yards of Dalmatia or Holland, and recognizable at a glance.

So in spite of the lengthy process of revision, readers of the first edition of this book will have little difficulty in recognizing it here. Conclusion, message and meaning have remained the same. It is the result of research into a very considerable number of previously unpublished documents from every corner of the broad Mediterranean stage during these ambiguous years at the threshold of modern times. But it also represents an attempt to write a new kind of history, *total history*, written in three different registers, on three different levels, perhaps best described as three different conceptions of time, the writer's aim being to bring together in all their multiplicity the different measures of time past, to acquaint the reader with their coexistence, their conflicts and contradictions, and the richness of experience they hold. My favourite vision of history is as a song for many voices – but it has the obvious disadvantage that they may drown each other out: reality will not always adapt conveniently into a harmonized setting for solo and chorus. How then can we consider even one single moment in time and perceive simultaneously, as though in transparent layers, all the different histories that coexist in reality? I have tried to meet this problem by using certain words and explanations as key themes, motifs which reappear in all three sections of the book. But the worst of it is that there are not merely two or three measures of time, there are dozens, each of them attached to a particular history. Only the sum of these measures, brought together by the human sciences (turned retrospectively to account on the historian's behalf) can give us that total history whose image it is so difficult to reconstitute in its rich entirety.

I

None of my critics has reproached me for including in this historical work the very extended geographical section which opens it, my homage to those timeless realities whose images recur throughout the whole book, from the first page to the last. The Mediterranean as a unit, with its creative space, the amazing freedom of its sea-routes (its automatic free trade as Ernest Labrousse called it), with its many regions, so different yet so alike, its cities born of movement, its complementary populations, its congenital enmities, is the unceasing work of human hands; but those hands have had to build with unpromising material, a natural environment far from fertile and often cruel, one that has imposed its own longlasting limitations and obstacles. All civilization can be defined as a struggle, a creative battle against the odds: the civilizations of the Mediterranean basin have wrestled with many often visible obstacles, using sometimes inadequate human resources, they have fought endlessly and blindly against the continental masses which hold the inland sea in their grip, and have even had to contend with the vast expanses of the Indian and Atlantic Oceans.

I have therefore sought out, within the framework of a geographical study, those local, permanent, unchanging and much repeated features which are the 'constants' of Mediterranean history; the reader will not find here all the unspectacular structures and recurrent patterns of life in the past, but the most important of them and those which most affect everyday existence. These provide the reference grid as it were, the most easily recognizable part of the book as well as its most haunting images – and one has not far to search for more of the same. They are to be found unchanged in Mediterranean life today: one may stumble across them in a journey, or in the books of Gabriel Audisio, Jean Giono, Carlo Levi, Lawrence Durrell or André Chamson. All western writers who have at some time in their lives encountered the Mediterranean, have been struck with its historical or rather timeless character, its *longue durée*. Like Audisio and Durrell, I believe that antiquity lives on round today's Mediterranean shores. In Rhodes or Cyprus, 'Ulysses can only be ratified as an historical figure with the help of the fishermen who today sit in the smoky tavern of *The Dragon* playing cards and waiting for the wind to change.' I also believe, with Carlo Levi, that the wild countryside which is the true subject of his evocative book *Christ Stopped at Eboli*, takes us back into the mists of time. Eboli (from which Ruy Gómez took his princely title) is on the coast near Salerno, at the point where the road turns inland towards the mountains. Christ (in other words civilization, the rule of law, the gentle arts of living) never reached the highlands of Lucania, and the village of Gagliano, crouching among the barren treeless slopes 'above the cliffs of white clay'. Here the poor *cafoni* are ruled now as in the past by the privileged men of the time: today these are the pharmacist, the doctor, the schoolteacher, people whom the peasant avoids, fears and shies away from. Here vendettas, brigandage, a primitive economy and tools are still the rule. An emigrant may return to his almost deserted village from America laden with the strange new gadgets of the outside world: but he will never change the way of life in this isolated, archaic little universe. This is the deep bone-structure of the Mediterranean and only with the eye of the geographer (or the traveller or novelist) can one truly discern its rugged contours and oppressive reality.

II

The second undertaking of this book – to discover the collective destiny of the Mediterranean in the sixteenth century, its 'social' history in the fullest sense of the word – immediately and continuously brings us face to face with the insidious and still unsolved problem of the decline of material existence, of the decadence one after another of Turkey, the whole of Islam, Italy and the Iberian supremacy, as older historians would say or, as today's economists would put it, of the malfunctioning and collapse of its vital sectors (public finance, investment, industry, shipping). There have always been historians who have argued that in any unit there is an inbuilt process of decline, of which the destiny of the Roman Empire provides the perfect example. Amongst other laws, all decline is compensated for by some simultaneous advance elsewhere; in the life of mankind, it would seem, nothing is ever created or destroyed. Similar categorical theories have been advanced by Toynbee and Spengler. I have made it my business to challenge these to my mind over-simple theories and the sweeping explanations they imply. How could the course of Mediterranean destiny easily fit into any of these classifications? There is surely no such thing as a model of decadence. A new model has to be built from the basic structures of every particular case.

Whatever meaning one attributes to the very imprecise term decadence, I cannot accept the view that the Mediterranean fell an easy and resigned victim to a vast, irreversible and above all early process of decline. In 1949 I said that I could not detect any visible decline before 1620. Today (1965) I would be inclined to say, though without any guarantee of certainty, that 1650 is a likelier date. At any rate three highly significant books on the fortunes of the Mediterranean regions – René Baehrel on Provence, E. Le Roy Ladurie on Languedoc and Pierre Vilar on Catalonia – do not contradict my original thesis. To my mind, if one were to reconstruct the new panorama of the Mediterranean after the great divide marking the end of its prosperous youth, one would have to choose a date as late as 1650 or even 1680.

One would also, as local research permits more precision, have to proceed further with the calculations, estimates and pursuit of orders of magnitude to be found in this book, which have brought me nearer than my very imperfect essays in this direction might appear to suggest to the thought of economists whose chief concerns are the problems of growth and national accounting. As we advance along this path, one thing will become strikingly evident: the Mediterranean in the sixteenth century was overwhelmingly a world of peasants, of tenant farmers and landowners; crops and harvest were the vital matters of this world and anything else was superstructure, the result of accumulation and of unnatural diversion towards the towns. Peasants and crops, in other words food supplies and the size of the population, silently determined the destiny of the age. In both the long and the short term, agricultural life was all-important. Could it support the burden of increasing population and the luxury of an urban civilization so dazzling that it has blinded us to other things? For each succeeding generation this was the pressing problem of every day. Beside it, the rest seems to dwindle into insignificance.

In short, even in the investigation of short-term crises, we are often obliged to look to structural history for an answer. This is the sea-level by which we must measure everything else, the achievement of progressive cities for example (in 1949 I was perhaps over-impressed by them – civilization can be a blinding spectacle) but also the short-term historical *conjoncture* which is sometimes too ready with its explanations, as if its shallow eddies were responsible for the deeper currents of history instead of the other way about. The fact is that economic history has to be rethought step by step, starting from these slow, sometimes motionless currents. Still waters run deep and we should not be misled by surface flurries.

At all events, neither the reversal of the secular trend in the 1590s, nor the sharp shock of the brief crisis of 1619–1621, marked the end of Mediterranean splendour. Nor can I accept, without further evidence, that there was a catastrophic discrepancy between the 'classic' *conjonctures* obtaining in northern and southern Europe, a discrepancy which if it really existed would have sounded both the death knell of Mediterranean prosperity and the summons to supremacy of the Northerners. This solution conveniently kills two birds with one stone, but I see no corpses.

The division of history into the slow- and fast-moving levels, structure and conjuncture, remains at the centre of a still unresolved debate. We have to classify these movements in relation to each other, without knowing before we start whether one type has governed the other or vice versa. Identification, classification and comparison must be our first concern then. Unfortunately, it is not yet possible to trace the general fluctuations of 'national incomes' in the sixteenth and seventeenth centuries and this is a grave drawback. But we are at least in a position now to study the changing fortunes of the cities, thanks to the work of Gilles Caster on Toulouse, and of Carlo Cipolla and Giuseppe Aleati on Pavia. The complex economic life of the cities provides us with an indicator of economic change at least as reliable as the familiar wage and price curves.

305. A peasant world: grape harvest. Wall painting, Trento Castle, 1390–1407.

Finally we have the problem of reconciling contradictory chronologies. How for instance did short-term changes in the economic climate affect states or whole civilizations, prominent actors on the historical stage with a will of their own? It appears from our study of the states that difficult times tended to favour their relative expansion. Was the same true of civilizations? Their brightest flowerings often seem to thrive under lowering skies. It was during the autumn of the city-state or even (in Venice and Bologna) its winter, that there flourished the last blossoms of an Italian Renaissance. And it was in the waning years of the great maritime empires, whether of Istanbul, Rome or Madrid, that the mighty imperial civilizations set out on their conquering path. As the sixteenth century ended and the seventeenth began, these brilliant shadows floated where great bodies politic had stood fifty years before.

III

Alongside such problems, the role of the individual and the event necessarily dwindles; it is a mere matter of perspective – but are we right to take so Olympian a view? 'Under the formal pageant of events which we have dignified by our interest, the land changes very little, and the structure of the basic self of man hardly at all,' to quote a twentieth-century novelist, Durrell, who is, like me, passionately attached to the Mediterranean. Well yes, but the question is frequently put to me, both by historians and philosophers, if we view history from such a distance, what becomes of man, his role in history, his freedom of action? And indeed, as the philosopher François Bastide once objected to me, since history is always a matter of development, of progression, could we not say that a secular trend is an 'event' too? I grant the point, but my definition of the 'event' is closer to that of Paul Lacombe and François Simiand: the pieces of flotsam I have combed from the historical ocean and chosen to call 'events' are those essentially *ephemeral* yet moving occurrences, the 'headlines' of the past.

That is not to say that this brilliant scatter of surface dust is of no value to the historian, or that historical reconstruction cannot perfectly well take this micro-history as its starting-point. Micro-sociology, which it calls to mind (wrongly, I believe) is after all not generally frowned upon in the world of scholarship. Micro-sociology, it is true, consists of constant repetition, while the micro-history of events consists of the unusual, the outstanding, and atypical; a series in fact of 'socio-dramas'. But Benedetto Croce has argued, not without reason, that any single event – let us say the assassination of Henri IV in 1610, or to take an example outside our period the arrival in power in 1883 of the Jules Ferry government – contains in embryo the entire history of mankind. To put it another way, history is the keyboard on which these individual notes are sounded.

That having been said, I confess that, not being a philosopher, I am reluctant to dwell for long on questions concerning the importance of events and of individual freedom, which have been put to me so many times in the past and no doubt will be in the future. How are we to interpret the very word freedom, which has meant so many different things, never signifying the same from one century to another? We should at least distinguish between the freedom of groups, that is of economic and social units, and that of individuals. What exactly is the freedom today of the unit we call France? What was Spain's 'freedom' in 1571, in the sense of the courses open to her? What degree of

306. *Venice, Queen of the Adriatic* by Tintoretto. *National Gallery of Ireland, Dublin*

freedom was possessed by Philip II, or by Don John of Austria as he rode at anchor among his ships, allies and troops? Each of these so-called freedoms seems to me to resemble a tiny island, almost a prison.

By stating the narrowness of the limits of action, is one denying the role of the individual in history? I think not. One may only have the choice between striking two or three blows: the question still arises: will one be able to strike them at all? To strike them effectively? To do so in the knowledge that only this range of choices is open to one? I would conclude with the paradox that the true man of action is he who can measure most nearly the constraints upon him, who chooses to remain within them and even to take advantage of the weight of the inevitable, exerting his own pressure in the same direction. All efforts against the prevailing tide of history – which is not always obvious – are doomed to failure.

So when I think of the individual, I am always inclined to see him imprisoned within a destiny in which he himself has little hand, fixed in a landscape in which the infinite perspectives of the long term, *la longue durée*, stretch into the distance both behind him and before. In historical analysis as I see it, rightly or wrongly, the long run always wins in the end. Annihilating innumerable events – all those which cannot be accommodated in the main ongoing current and which are therefore ruthlessly swept to one side – it indubitably limits both the freedom of the individual and even the role of chance. I am by temperament a 'structuralist', little tempted by the event, or even by the short-term *conjoncture* which is after all merely a grouping of events in the same area. But the historian's 'structuralism' has nothing to do with the approach which under the same name is at present causing some confusion in the other human sciences. It does not tend towards the mathematical abstraction of relations expressed as functions, but instead towards the very sources of life in its most concrete, everyday, indestructible and anonymously human expression.

26th June, 1965

Illustrations

258. *Expulsion of the Moriscos.* Drawing by Vicente Carducci. *Prado, Madrid.*

259. Moorish woman of Granada. Print from Hans Weigel, *Trachtenbuch,* Nuremberg, 1577.

260. The Casa de Pilate, Seville. (YAN, Toulouse/Jean Dieuzaide)

261. *View of Smyrna,* Turkish school. *Rijksmuseum, Amsterdam.*

262. *The Reception of an Imperial Ambassador by a Turkish Pasha,* attributed to Pietro Longhi. *L. A. Mayer Memorial Institute for Islamic Art.*

263, 264. Greek and Armenian women of Constantinople. Early seventeenth-century engravings.

265. Translation of the Old Testament into Castilian commissioned in 1422 by the Grand Master of the Order of Calatrava from the Rabbi Moses Arragel of Guadalajara. *Statens Konstmuseers, Stockholm.*

266. The Levantine synagogue in Venice. (Cameraphoto, Venice)

267. Unnamed cemetery markers in the Jewish cemetery in Fez, Morocco. (Camera Press/Bernard G. Silberstein)

268, 269. Jewish doctor and merchant at Constantinople. Sixteenth-century French prints.

270. Jewish marriage certificate from Sana'a, Yemen, 1794. *Israel Museum, Jerusalem.*

271. Fifteenth-century painting of Mantuan Jews.

272. A Jew wearing the badge. Fourteenth-century mural from Tarragona Cathedral.

273. The Lepanto Monstrance. Church of S. Maria Victoria, Ingolstadt. (Wim Swaan)

274. *The Expulsion of Heliodorus from the Temple* by Raphael. *Stanza di Eliodoro, Vatican, Rome.* (Mansell Collection/Anderson)

275. Detail from the *Last Judgment* by Michelangelo. *Sistine Chapel, Vatican, Rome.* (Mansell Collection/Alinari)

276. Detail from *Paradiso* by Tintoretto. *Palazzo Ducale, Venice.* (Mansell Collection/Anderson)

277. The *Madonna del Popolo* by Federico Barocci. *Uffizi, Florence.* (Alinari)

278. The cupola of St. Peter's, Rome. (Mansell Collection/Alinari)

279. *The Ecstasy of St. Teresa* by Bernini. *Cornaro Chapel, S. Maria della Vittoria, Rome.* (Mansell Collection/Anderson)

280. The Procurator of Venice about to embark onto a war galley, 1570. *British Library.*

281, 283. *The Siege of Malta* by Perez d'Aleccio. *National Maritime Museum, Greenwich.*

282. Detail from *The Spanish Artillery Deployed at the Battle of Mühlberg.* Mural in the Palace at Oriz, Navarra. *Museo de Navarra, Pamplona.*

284. *San Marco and Three Venetian Magistrates Recruiting Naval Infantry* by G. B. Angelo ('Il Moro'). *Museo Navale, Genoa.*

285. Symbolic image of the Battle of Lepanto. Venetian engraving, 1572. *Museo Navale, Venice.*

286. The Lion of St. Mark hovering over a map of Crete. Venetian print, c.1651.

287. The sea battle off Modon. Sixteenth-century miniature. *Topkapi Museum, Istanbul.*

288. The fortified city and harbour of Gallipoli in the gulf of Taranto. Sixteenth-century Italian print.

289. *The Battle of Tripoli.* Venetian print, 1569.

290. *The Siege of a Fort in Africa* by Vicente Carducho. *Accademia di S. Fernando, Madrid.*

291. *The Horrors of War* by Paolo di Franchesci. *Fugger-Glött'sche Kunstsammlung, Kirchheim.*

292. A soldier-beggar by Jacques Callot. Paris, 1629.

293. View of Algiers. *Spanish State Archives, Simancas.*

294. Pirate ships from Algiers. Seventeenth-century Dutch print.

295. Christians being tortured in Algiers. From P. Dam, *Historie van Barbaryen,* Amsterdam, 1639–84.

296. *Encounter at Sea Between Algerian Pirates and Spaniards.* Detail from anonymous seventeenth-century Spanish painting. *Prado, Madrid.*

297. Uskoks off the Dalmatian coast being fired on by a Venetian galley. Venetian print, 1598.

298. Slave market in Algiers. From *Historie van Barbaryen.*

299. Algiers and its surroundings. From *Civitates Orbis Terrarum.*

300. Portrait of Ariadeno Barbarossa, after Capriolo. From *Ritratti di cento capitani illustri,* Rome, 1596.

301. Caricature portraits of the Barbarossas. Seventeenth-century Dutch print.

302. *The Sack of Tunis and the Liberation of the Christian Captives.* Detail from a cartoon by J. G. Vermeyen. *Kunsthistorisches Museum, Vienna.*

303. Pirate ships captured by the Dutch at Algiers. From *Historie van Barbaryen.*

304. The port of Ravenna. Mosaic, c. A.D. 520. (Josephine Powell)

305. Grape harvest. Wall painting, Trento Castle, 1390–1407.

306. *Venice, Queen of the Adriatic* by Tintoretto. *National Gallery of Ireland, Dublin.*

Colour plates

i. The Bay of Kotor on the Adriatic coast. (F. Quilici)

ii. *St. Blaize Presenting a Maquette of the City of Ragusa,* by Nicola Bozidareviz. Detail from the altarpiece in the Dominican church, Dubrovnik. (André Held)

iii. Cultivated fields on the lagoon of Venice. (F. Quilici)

iv. The personification of autumn, carrying hoe and spade together with the newly harvested grapes. Ferrarese painting, c.1450. *Gemäldegalerie, Berlin.*

v. *Good Government* by Ambrogio Lorenzetti, Sala delle Pace, Palazzo Pubblico, Siena. (Scala)

vi. Lateen-rigged Turkish ship. Mid-seventeenth century, probably Nicaean. *Benaki Museum, Athens.*

vii. Detail from the Fra Angelico altarpiece of St. Nicholas of Bari. *Pinacoteca, Vatican, Rome.* (Scala)

viii. *The Market in Genoa* by Alessandro Magnasco. *Museo Civico d'Arte Antica, Milan.* (Scala)

ix. The export of bullion from Venice, the Doge in the foreground directing operations. The majolica dish is itself probably Venetian, c.1495. *Fitzwilliam Museum, Cambridge.*

x. Charles V at the Battle of Mühlberg, by Titian. *Prado, Madrid.* (Giraudon)

xi. View of Constantinople from the description of Sulaimān's 1534–36 campaign, c.1537. *Istanbul University Library.* (Sonia Halliday)

xii. Sulaimān's Hungarian Campaign. The Battle of Mohács, 1526. Ottoman miniature from the *Huner-name,* 1588. *Topkapi Museum, Istanbul.* (Sonia Halliday)

xiii. The Battle of Lepanto. Painting attributed to H. Letter, Venice, seventeenth century. *National Maritime Museum, Greenwich.*

Index of Proper Names

678 Index of Proper Names

Netherlands (Dutch) – cont'd.
342; spice trade 383; textile industry
349; trade balance 354; war 157,
338, 351, 374, 396, 453
Neuberg 552
Neusohl 331
Newberie, English traveller 379, 400
New Castile 394, 403
Newcastle 441
Newfoundland 103, 163, 165, 439, 633
New Spain 178, 298, 376, 481, 506
Nicaea 36
Nice 85, 263
Nicomedia 412; gulf of 109
Nicosia 117, 267
Nicot, Jean 421, 550, 640
Niebla 505, 640
Nietzsche, Friedrich 555
Niger: river 123, 124, 333; Upper 333
Nile: river 204, 388, 416, 419; delta
36, 204; land routes 204; Upper 124
Nino, Rodrigo 310
Niolo 119
Nios (Ios) 608
Niš 535
Nobili, Tuscan ambassador 345–6
Nola 44
Normandy, Normans 77, 84, 178;
shipping 434–5
North Sea: fishing 103; German ports
154; pilotage 168; shipping 220;
trade 167
Norway 143
Novalesa 149
Novi-Pazar 208
Nuñez, Rui 458
Nuremberg: arms trade 568; banking
141, 156; communications 272;
Italian merchants 154, 156, 157, 168,
291; spice trade 384; Swedish capture
(1633) 157; trade links 143, 151,
278
Nurra, La 18

Ochino, Bernardino 552
Oder, river 145
Oglio, river 204
Oisans 53
Olbright, Konrad 293
Olivares family 509
Olivares, Count, Viceroy of Naples 324
Olivares, Gaspar de Guzmán, Conde
Dugne de 121, 352, 366, 581
Olivieri, architect 590
Or, Iles d' see Hyères
Oran: Cartagena crossing 263;
chronicles 23; fortifications 618, 619;
foundation 27, 80, 333; governor
623; grain trade 413; Jews 580;
nomads 129; presidio life 622, 623;
shipping 434, 633; silos 192; slave
trade 124; snow supplies 6; Spanish
occupation 80, 124; supplying 80,
622
Orange 160
Orbetello 68, 413
Orgosolo 16
Orlandini, merchants 426
Orléans 158
Oropesa 507
Orosei 287
Orta, Giovanni di 639
Orvieto 498
Osborne, Sir Edward 441, 442
Osorio, G. F. 25
Ostia 39
Osuna, Duke of 410, 506
Otranto 88–9, 268, 322, 460, 613, 639

Otranto, Cape 88
Ottobon, Marco 135, 145, 156, 222,
414, 426, 428
Ottoman Empire: Asian border conflict
480; banditry 536; civil servants 480,
482; immigrants 243; revolts 528,
531; rise 462, 465–70; road network
206; see also Turkey
Oudegherste, Peter van 317
Oued El Harrach 37
Oued Mazafran 37
Ouled Abdala 128–9
Ouled Sidi Cheikh 128
Ouro Preto 586
Oviedo 23

Pacific Ocean 166, 274
Padua: grain 303; Jews 571, 575;
population 293; siege (1509) 530;
University 96, 152, 235, 323;
Venetian capture (1406) 245
Paduano region 57
Pagès, Georges 489
Palamos 263
Palermo: banking 371–2; capture
(1071) 77; communications 267;
decline 78; drainage 44; privateering
630; ransom administration 646; sea
route 84; shipping 434, 613; troubles
(1560) 528; vagrants 534–5; wheat
trade 408, 410, 416
Palestine 176, 295
Pallavicino, Horatio 446
Palma, Venetian fortress 611
Palma de Majorca 630
Pamphylia 55
Panama 166
Panormos see Palermo
Pantelleria 110
Papal: fleet 604; government 317;
States 17, 92, 237, 497, 576
Paré, Ambroise 540
Parenti, G. 528
Paris: cloth trade 160; communications
267, 271, 274; financial centre 350;
inns 158, 159, 161; merchants 354;
routes 158, 159, 161; Spanish coins 345;
status 203; taxation 516
Paris, Giraldo 397, 398
Pariset, George 297
Parma 98
Parma, Duke of see Farnese, Alexander
Paros 608
Paruta, Paolo 460
Passaro, Cape 636
Patmos 416, 608
Patti 614
Paul, St 186
Paul III, Pope 592
Paul IV, Pope 244, 576
Paumgartner, Hans 432
Pavia 312; battle of 464
Pavia, Bishop of 370
Pedraça see Bermúdez de Pedraça
Pegolotti see Balducci-Pegolotti
Pelion 110
Peloponnese 8, 206
Penni, pupil of Raphael 588
Peñon de Velez: Barbarossas capture
(1529) 615; corsairs 641; Spanish
capture (1564) 187–8, 618, 619, 621,
641; Spanish occupation 82, 434,
615, 620
Pera (Constantinople) 77, 88, 256, 391
Perasto 106
Perejil, island of 84
Pereti, Giovan Battista 313

Pereyra, Carlos 52, 338
Pérez, Antonio 486
Pérez, Gonzalo 484
Peri, Giovanni Domenico 314, 359, 360
Perpignan 298; siege of 504
Persia, Persians (Iran, Iranians), caravan
traffic 124; cloth trade 313;
cypresses 548; devaluation 379;
English trade 138; Jews 577;
landscape 124–5; merchants 25,
137; Russian trade 137–8; silk trade
400, 402; trade routes 210; Turkish
relations 402, 569, 624, 655; war
threat 394; wine 176
Persian Gulf 123, 133, 390, 404, 451
Peru 51, 165, 166, 178, 338, 545, 548
Perugia 238, 498
Peruzzi, Baldassare 590
Pesaro 88, 577
Pescara 312
Pescara, Marquis of, Viceroy of Sicily
312
Peschici 106
Pestalozzi family 154
Peter the Great, Tsar 113, 464
Peter Martyr 128
Petrarch, Francesco 39
Pézenas 161
Phaulkon, Constantine 547
Philip I (the Fair), King of Castile 135
Philip II, King of Spain: bankruptcy
362–3; bureaucracy 479; capital city
257, 355, 476–7; communications
263, 271; court removal 206; empire
275, 475–80; English relations 338,
442; entourage 355; finances 492–4;
financial barons 250; hunting 295;
marriage 162; money transport
342–8; moneylenders 339; noblemen
245, 506; North African policy
618; Portuguese annexation 397;
Prado extension 43; privateering ban
639; recruitment of English sailors
105; revenues 373; sea battles 101;
sea journeys 164; shipbuilding 109,
113; shipping regulations 220; silver
transport 342; Spanish nationalism
121, 355; spice trade 395–7; summer
residence 194; war expenses 604;
weather information 183; winter
campaigns 187
Philip III, King of Spain 245, 297, 362,
475, 508, 509
Philip IV, King of Spain 121
Philip V, King of Spain 464
Philippines 26, 166, 394
Philippson, Alfred 27, 180
Phocaea 217
Phoenicians 100, 178
Piacenza 227, 232, 281, 292, 354–60
Piave 611
Piccolomini, Alfonso, Duke of
Montemarciano 529, 539
Piedmont 145, 160, 293, 535, 551
Pillars of Hercules 164, 433
Pimentel, Alonso de 408, 618, 622
Pin, François 434
Pinaruolo 195
Pindus mountains 10
Pinto, Antonio 396
Piombino 188
Piombino, Duke of 528
Pirenne, Henri 464
Pires, Portuguese ambassador 394
Piri Re'is 389
Pisa: English base 436; Genoese
competition 84; journey times 277;
Leghorn port 85; piracy 626, 630;

General Index